THE CONSTITUTION
AND
CHIEF JUSTICE MARSHALL

The Constitution
AND
Chief Justice Marshall

WILLIAM F. SWINDLER

Introduction by WARREN E. BURGER,
Chief Justice of the United States

ILLUSTRATED WITH PHOTOGRAPHS

DODD, MEAD & COMPANY
NEW YORK

1   2   3   4   5   6   7   8   9   10

Picture Acknowledgments

Grateful acknowledgment is made to the following for the use of illustrations: *Supreme Court Historical Society*: Supreme Court Chamber in United States Capitol, sketch of Dartmouth College campus, photograph of statue of John Marshall, and portraits of William Cushing, William Paterson, Samuel Chase, Bushrod Washington, Alfred Moore, William Johnson, Brockholst Livingston, Thomas Todd, Joseph Story, Gabriel Duvall, Smith Thompson, John McLean, Henry Baldwin, James Wayne, Philip Pendleton Barbour, and Roger B. Taney. *Library of Congress*: portraits of Thomas Jefferson, James Madison, Andrew Jackson, John Quincy Adams, and Robert Trimble. *Maryland Historical Society*, Baltimore: portrait of William Marbury. *New Jersey Historical Society*: portrait of Aaron Burr. *New-York Historical Society*: portrait of Aaron Ogden. *Virginia State Library*: portrait of Spencer Roane. *Georgia Historical Society*: portrait of Thomas Gibbons.

Library of Congress Cataloging in Publication Data

Swindler, William Finley.
  The Constitution and Chief Justice Marshall.
  Includes index.
  1. United States—Constitutional law—Cases.
  2. Marshall, John, 1755-1835. I. Title.
KF4549.S94   342'.73'002643   77-25895
ISBN 0-396-07500-2

To the memory of my wife
BENETTA
until we meet again

Contents

PART THREE

OPINIONS IN THE MAJOR CASES AND
RELATED DOCUMENTS

Illustrations (following page 82)

The Antagonists and the Arenas
The Great Chief Justice and His Court

Introduction

WARREN E. BURGER

Chief Justice of the United States

The Judicial Branch of the United States government, during the course of the nation's bicentennial year, was authorized to initiate projects to commemorate the development of the federal court system. The Bicentennial Committee of the Judicial Conference selected a number of projects, the chief one being a series of documentary films designed to better acquaint the American public with the role of the judiciary in our constitutional system. The series, primarily for use by the public television network, schools and colleges, bar associations and civic groups, was commissioned accordingly by the Judicial Conference and produced by WQED of Pittsburgh.

Throughout the production of the series, there were frequent consultations between the Bicentennial Committee and the film producers, the Public Broadcasting Service and WQED. Synopses for the five films were submitted as guides to the script writers and directors following almost two years of editorial preparation. A subcommittee of judges assumed responsibility for making sure the scripts faithfully reflected the cases selected for dramatization, and WQED and Dr. Mathias Von Brauchitsch, director of the films, designated a panel of six historians to assure that the background and setting of each film was historically accurate.

The cases selected for dramatization illustrate five of the fundamental constitutional principles that evolved during the first fifty years under the Constitution—major principles in the American credo of constitutional freedom. Chief Justice John Marshall dominated those years of the Court's history, as his words gave life to the great concepts found in the Declaration and underscored the need to guard closely the basic freedoms for which the Revolution had been fought.

The film series captures the human drama and accurately portrays the constitutional principles which underlay each case. First, as might be expected from those familiar with our constitutional history, is the well-known case of *Marbury* v. *Madison* and its pronouncement of the doctrine of judicial review. This opinion is the bedrock upon which the constitutional structure in the United States rests.

Four years after the Marbury case, Marshall, being the Circuit Justice of the Circuit including Richmond, Virginia, presided in the celebrated treason trial of Aaron Burr. The Chief Justice found himself confronted with three fundamental, emotionally-laden problems: first, how to assure a fair trial to a highly unpopular, nationally known political leader; second, how to secure from the Executive Branch material evidence sought by the defendant but within the exclusive control of the Executive; and third, how to apply the unique, American constitutional standards for proof of treason. Two thirty-minute films were produced to dramatize these great constitutional issues.

Although there were a number of other major constitutional decisions in the thirty-four-year tenure of John Marshall, there were two that completed particularly well the message which these films sought to convey. Each had direct bearing on the process of nation-building: the welding of thirteen once-independent, sovereign states into one nation. One case was concerned with the nature of the national authority created by the Constitution, and the means necessary and proper for carrying out that authority. The so-called "Bank case" of *McCulloch* v. *Maryland* in 1819 was a key to the fiscal aspects of our national unity and growth. The second, in 1824, explained how the Constitution provided the means to implement cohesive national power through the commerce clause—*Gibbons* v. *Ogden* or the Hudson River "steamboat case." This case is critical to our history since it gave America a common market nearly a century and a half before that term had the meaning now so familiar to the world.

It is widely acknowledged that the Supreme Court is the least understood of the three branches of government; the role of the other federal courts is similarly clouded. It is hoped that this film series may make it easier for laymen to understand the judicial process and its importance to the rights and liberties guaranteed by the Constitution. The present volume is an effort, through the printed word, to supplement what the films portray. Clearly, many important details in the complete story of the Supreme Court and the District Courts and their shaping of our constitutional principles had to be omitted. In the short time allotted—approximately half an hour each—for the telling of these momentous narratives, and within the context of a dramatization of basic issues, only so much can be covered.

The Bicentennial Committee of the Judicial Conference concluded that it should not itself undertake responsibility for a book to supplement the film series. The present volume, therefore, is an independent undertaking, related to the film project by the fortuitous fact that the author, Dr. William F. Swindler, has served as consultant to the Bicentennial Committee. Dr. Swindler is also Chairman of the Publications Committee of the Supreme Court Historical Society and an Advisory Editor to the Papers of John Marshall being published under the auspices of the College of William and Mary and its Institute of Early American History and Culture. His credentials for this task are obvious.

The book, while providing the background details for the film subjects already mentioned, undertakes to round out the story of Marshall's Supreme Court in the American constitutional process. That is to say, other cases—the famous Dartmouth College case, for example—have been added in the story as told by the book. The other landmark constitutional opinions of the Court under Chief Justice Marshall have been introduced where relevant to the main theme of constitutional development. Illustrations of the members of the bench and bar during the years of the Marshall Court, and carefully edited documents essential to the principal cases, complete the story as told in the printed medium. Thus, film and volume, while complementary of each other, also remain independent devices for making "the least understood branch" better understood by Americans as we celebrate 200 years of independence and approach the Bicentennial of the Constitution itself.

The cornerstone of our constitutional history and system remains the firm adherence of the Supreme Court to the Marbury principle of judicial review that "someone must decide" what the Constitution means. It explains John Marshall better, perhaps, than any of his other renowned opinions, and may make clearer to our own time the essential role of the judiciary in our governmental system.

It seems appropriate, therefore, to complement this Introduction by reproducing a substantial part of the Bentham Lecture on the subject delivered at London University College several years ago (see Appendix). It may provide a kind of counterpoint to the treatment of the same subject in Chapter II of the present volume, and in the opening film in the series previously described. The subject certainly cannot be explained to the American people too often, or in too many variations, because a complete understanding of its nature and significance is the key to a final understanding of our constitutional character.

PART ONE

THE SHAPING
OF JUDICIAL
FEDERALISM

I

John Marshall, His Court and His Times

> Your expositions of constitutional law . . . constitute a monu-
> ment of fame far beyond the ordinary memorials of political or
> military glory. They are destined to enlighten, instruct and con-
> vince future generations; and can scarcely perish but with the
> memory of the constitution itself.
>
> Dedication to John Marshall in Joseph Story,
> 1 *Commentaries on the Constitution* (1833), iii.

i

In the late spring of 1788, at a convention gathered in Richmond, Virginia, to debate the ratification of the proposed new Constitution for the
United States, a youthful thirty-three-year-old lawyer addressed himself
to the question of the practical limits to the powers of the government to
be created by this new instrument. If the new Federal Congress, being
vested with far wider authority than the discredited Confederation Congress, should "make a law not warranted" by the provisions in the Constitution, John Marshall declared, such a law "would be considered by the
judges as an infringement of the Constitution which they are to guard,"
and they would accordingly "declare it void." [1]

The argument, made fifteen years before Marshall as Chief Justice
would apply it in the landmark opinion in *Marbury* v. *Madison*,[2] was no
demonstration of clairvoyance but of matter-of-fact conclusion from the
logic of the system of written frames of government being implemented in
Virginia and other erstwhile colonies and now being proposed for the
"more perfect Union" of these states. Nor was there clairvoyance in the
argument which Marshall would make, as counsel for the College of
William and Mary in 1790,[3] that a charter between a sovereign and a
grantee was analogous to a contract, the obligations of which were not to
be impaired by action of one party without the acquiescence of the other.

3

Nearly thirty years later, in the *Dartmouth College* case,[4] his opinion would follow the same reasoning. The fact that there was no indication in 1819 that the Chief Justice even recalled his argument on the 1790 brief only served to demonstrate that Marshall had settled on the principle itself before either date.

In both law and politics, the man who would come to the Supreme Court at the age of forty-six would bring well-matured convictions of what was needed to make operable the system of federalism which the Constitution projected. In the law, where the new Commonwealth of Virginia had elected to "receive" only certain portions of the English common law, Marshall spent nearly twenty years in practice which relied on logic rather than precedent, on the pragmatic relationships between basic legal principles and contemporary facts. He was not, as occasionally critics would allege, ignorant of the orthodox authorities; [5] rather, he understood that such authorities were only relevant if the conditions from which they themselves had developed, over centuries of English history, were materially similar in a society which itself was without precedent in history.

Marshall's preeminence at the bar of this new society grew from this ability to muster a succession of related premises and then construct a persuasive argument drawn from them.[6] Not that he won every case—his record seems to have been no better than the typical lawyer's—but a client could be assured that his suit would be presented with the strongest possible advocacy by this gangling, carelessly dressed, often awkwardly spoken attorney. William Wirt, one of the most brilliant lawyers of the period, succinctly stated: "Marshall's maxim seems always to have been, 'aim exclusively *at Strength*' "; and he admonished his son-in-law, Francis Gilmer, zealously to imitate "Marshall's simple process of reasoning." [7]

Marshall, in fact, lost his only constitutional case before the Supreme Court, in 1796 [8]—a case which, as one biographer observes, required him to advance a theory "which he had opposed throughout his public career thus far," and compelled him to press a suit which, if won for his clients, "would have wrecked the only considerable business transaction in which he ever engaged." [9] Yet his argument, that the act of Revolutionary Virginia sequestering debts owed to British nationals, left the national government without jurisdiction of subject matter under the postwar settlement treaty, was so eloquent that Wirt would remember it throughout his professional life, and moved Rufus King of Massachusetts to declare that "his head was one of the best organized of anyone that I have known." [10]

Marshall was persuaded, long before he came to the bench, of the imperative necessity of a strong national government, adequately invested with powers to discharge national obligations. His prescient-seeming comment on judicial review at the 1788 ratifying convention was, in context, virtually a dictum in an extended, carefully reasoned speech in favor of the new Constitution. Replying to arguments against ratification offered by Patrick Henry and George Mason, Marshall struck off a succession of propositions which would echo in opinions written over three and a half decades in the next century.

I conceive that the object of the discussion now before us, is, whether Democracy, or Despotism, be most eligible. I am sure that those who framed the system submitted to our investigation, and those who now support it, intend the establishment and security of the former. . . . What are the favorite maxims of Democracy? A strict observance of justice and public faith, and a steady adherence to virtue. These, sir, are the principles of a good Government. No mischief—no misfortune ought to deter us from a strict observance of justice and public faith. Would to Heaven that these principles had been observed under the present Government! Had this been the case, the friends of liberty would not be so willing now to part with it.[11]

. . . The prosperity and happiness of the people depend on the performance of these great and important duties of the General Government. Can these duties be performed by one State? Can one State protect us, and promote our happiness? . . . How then can they be done? By the national Government only. Shall we refuse to give it power to do them? We are answered, that the powers may be abused. That though the Congress may promote our happiness, yet they may prostitute their powers to destroy our liberties. This goes to the destruction of all confidence in agents. Would you believe that men who had merited your highest confidence would deceive you? Would you trust them again after one deception? Why then hesitate to trust the General Government? The object of our inquiry is, —*Is the power necessary—and is it guarded?* [12]

By the time of his Supreme Court appearance in Philadelphia, Marshall had already begun attracting (and frequently declining) offers of national service—a Cabinet post (Attorney General) in 1795, a diplomatic assignment (minister to France) in 1796, membership on the X.Y.Z. commission [13] in 1797, election to Congress in 1799, nomination first as Secretary of War and then as Secretary of State in 1800. He first accepted the membership on the commission to France, and then the election to the House of Representatives, where fate brought his path across that of John Adams and created for the new President two debts of gratitude.

Adams's administration was whipsawed between the ambitions of Alexander Hamilton, which were breaking up the Federalist coalition, and the growing aggressiveness of Thomas Jefferson, whose followers chose the radical name of Republican to flaunt their sympathy for the French revolutionaries. When Marshall reached Congress, the unhappy President was badly in need of the best advocate he could obtain; the Alien and Sedition Acts had already given the Jeffersonians a cause which they were exploiting with full fury, and now came the Jonathan Robins affair. Robins, alias Thomas Nash, allegedly a British subject wanted for mutiny and murder, had been apprehended in South Carolina and, on Adams's request, examined by a federal court and turned over to British authorities despite his insistence that he was a native-born American.

Because Adams had referred the extradition matter to the courts, the Jeffersonians chose to charge the Executive with improper interference with the judicial process and arbitrary application of treaty power. Marshall's fortuitous arrival in the House of Representatives at the opening of debate on the anti-Federalist resolution embodying this charge, propelled him onto the national stage to speak on a basic constitutional principle. In demolishing the Jeffersonian argument, the new Congressman laid down, as definitively as he would ever do on the bench, the essence of the executive power and duty in discharge of international law. The treaty obligation was unequivocal; the nationality of the fugitive was established beyond reasonable doubt; the extraditing of the fugitive under the treaty was an executive function and hence not an interference with the judiciary.[14]

ii

Marshall's exposition on the "necessary and proper" powers of the executive branch, which he had to delimit in the *Burr* case (cf. Part Two, Chapter I, pages 100–101, and Part Three, Chapter II-4), but which he sought to preserve in its largest possible dimensions, makes interesting reading in advance of his great constitutional opinions on the Court. In the course of his speech, Marshall said:

The well considered opinion, then, of the American Government on this subject is, that the jurisdiction of a nation at sea is "personal," reaching its "own citizens only"; and that this is the "appropriate part of each nation" on that element.

This is precisely the opinion maintained by the opposers of the resolutions. If the jurisdiction of America at sea be personal, reaching its own citizens only; if this be its appropriate part, then the jurisdiction of the nation cannot extend to a murder committed by a British sailor, on board a British frigate navigating the high seas under a commission from His Britannic Majesty.

As a further illustration of the principle contended for, suppose a contract made at sea, and a suit instituted for the recovery of money which might be due thereon. By the laws of what nation would the contract be governed? The principle is general that a personal contract follows the person, but is governed by the law of the place where it is formed. By what law then would such a contract be governed? If all nations had jurisdiction over the place, then the laws of all nations would equally influence the contract; but certainly no man will hesitate to admit that such a contract ought to be decided according to the laws of that nation to which the vessel or contracting parties might belong. . . .

It has already been shown that the legislative jurisdiction of a nation extends only to its own territory, and to its own citizens, wherever they may be. Any general expression in a legislative act must, necessarily, be restrained to objects within the jurisdiction of the Legislature passing the act. Of consequence an act of Congress can only be construed to apply to the territory of the United States, comprehending every person within it, and to the citizens of the United States.

But, independent of this undeniable truth, the act itself affords complete testimony of its intention and extent. The title is: "An act for the punishment of certain crimes against the United States." Not against Britain, France, or the world, but singly "against the United States." . . .

Gentlemen have cited and relied on that clause in the Constitution, which enables Congress to define and punish piracies and felonies committed on the high seas, and offences against the law of nations; together with an act of Congress, declaring the punishment of those offences; as transferring the whole subject to the courts. But that clause can never be construed to make to the Government a grant of power, which the people making it do not themselves possess. It has already been shown that the people of the United States have no jurisdiction over offences committed on board a foreign ship against a foreign nation.

Of consequence, in framing a Government for themselves, they cannot have passed this jurisdiction to that Government. The law, therefore, cannot act upon the case. But this clause of the Constitution cannot be considered, and need not be considered, as affecting acts which are piracy under the law of nations. As the judicial power of the United States extends to all cases of admiralty and maritime jurisdiction, and piracy under the law of nations is of admiralty and maritime jurisdiction, punishable by every nation, the judicial power of the United States of course extends to it. On this principle the Courts of Admiralty under the Confederation took cognizance of piracy, although there was no express power in Congress to define and punish the offence.

But the extension of judicial power of the United States to all cases of admiralty and maritime jurisdiction must necessarily be understood with some limitation. All cases of admiralty and maritime jurisdiction which, from their nature, are triable in the United States, are submitted to the jurisdiction of the courts of the United States. . . .

The clause in the Constitution which declares that "the trial of all crimes, except in cases of impeachment, shall be by jury," has also been relied on as operating on the case, and transferring the decision on a demand for the delivery of an individual from the Executive to the Judicial department.

But certainly this clause in the Constitution of the United States cannot be thought obligatory on, and for the benefit of, the whole world. It is not designed to secure the rights of the people of Europe and Asia, or to direct and control proceedings against criminals throughout the universe. It can then be designed only to guide the proceedings of our own courts, and to prescribe the mode of punishing offences committed against the Government of the United States, and to which the jurisdiction of the nation may rightfully extend.

It has already been shown that the courts of the United States were incapable of trying the crime for which Thomas Nash was delivered up to justice. The question to be determined was, not how his crime should be tried and punished, but whether he should be delivered up to a foreign tribunal, which was alone capable of trying and punishing him. A provision for the trial of crimes in the courts of the United States is clearly not a provision for the performance of a national compact for the surrender to a foreign Government of an offender against that government.

The clause of the Constitution declaring that the trial of all crimes shall be by jury, has never even been construed to extend to the trial of crimes committed in the land and naval forces of the United States. Had such a construction prevailed, it would most probably have prostrated the Constitution itself, with the liberties and the independence of the nation, before the first disciplined invader who should approach our shores. Necessity would have imperiously demanded the review and amendment of so unwise a provision. If, then, this clause does not extend to offences committed in the fleets and armies of the United States, how can it be construed to extend to offences committed in the fleets and armies of Britain or of France, or of the Ottoman or Russian Empires?

The same argument applies to the observations on the seventh article of the amendments to the Constitution. That article relates only to trials in the courts of the United States, and not to the performance of a contract for the delivery of a murderer not triable in those courts. . . .

The case was in its nature a national demand made upon the nation. The parties were the two nations. They cannot come into court to litigate their claims, nor can a court decide on them. Of consequence, the demand is not a case for judicial cognizance.

The President is the sole organ of the nation in its external relations, and its sole representative with foreign nations. Of consequence, the demand of a foreign nation can only be made on him.

He possesses the whole Executive power. He holds and directs the force of the nation. Of consequence, any act to be performed by the force of the nation is to be performed through him.

He is charged to execute the laws. A treaty is declared to be a law. He must then execute a treaty, where he, and he alone, possesses the means of executing it.

The treaty, which is a law, enjoins the performance of a particular object. The person who is to perform this object is marked out by the Constitution, since the person is named who conducts the foreign intercourse, and is to take care that the laws be faithfully executed. The means by which it is to be performed, the force of the nation, are in the hands of this person. Ought not this person to perform the object, although the particular mode of using the means has not been prescribed? Congress, unquestionably, may prescribe the mode, and Congress may devolve on others the whole execution of the contract; but, till this be done, it seems the duty of the Executive department to execute the contract by any means it possesses. . . .

The Executive is not only the Constitutional department, but seems to be the proper department to which the power in question may most wisely and most safely be confided.

The department which is entrusted with the whole foreign intercourse of the nation, with the negotiation of all its treaties, with the power of demanding a reciprocal performance of the article, which is accountable to the nation for the violation of its engagements with foreign nations, and for the consequences resulting from such violation, seems the proper department to be entrusted with the execution of a national contract like that under consideration.

If, at any time, policy may temper the strict execution of the contract, where may that political discretion be placed so safely as in the department whose duty it is to understand precisely the state of the political intercourse and connexion between the United States and foreign nations, to understand the manner in which the particular stipulation is explained and performed by foreign nations, and to understand completely the state of the Union?

This department, too, independent of judicial aid, which may, perhaps, in some instances, be called in, is furnished with a great law officer, whose duty it is to understand and to advise when the *casus fœderis* occurs. And if the President should cause to be arrested under the treaty an individual who was so circumstanced as not to be properly the object of such an arrest, he may perhaps bring the question of the legality of his arrest before a judge, by a writ of habeas corpus.

It is then demonstrated, that, according to the principles of the American Government, the question whether the nation has or has not bound itself to deliver up any individual, charged with having committed murder or forgery within the jurisdiction of Britain, is a question the power to decide which rests alone with the Executive department.

It remains to inquire whether, in exercising this power, and in performing the duty it enjoins, the President has committed an unauthorized and dangerous interference with judicial decisions.

That Thomas Nash was committed originally at the instance of the British Consul at Charleston, not for trial in the American courts, but for the purpose of being delivered up to justice in conformity with the treaty between the two nations, has been already so ably argued . . . that nothing further can be added to that point. . . .[15]

With this maiden speech on the Robins affair, John Marshall was carried by the force of events into the political maelstrom of 1800. It was obvious that the Federalist domination of government was disintegrating; Adams had won the Presidency in 1797 by a majority of only three electoral votes, and his party was now so violently torn by Hamiltonian intrigues that its defeat in the fall elections was all but certain. As nominal captain of the ship of state, Adams wryly recalled in later years, he had "all the officers and half the crew always ready to throw me overboard." [16]

Disloyalty among his own Cabinet members was an open scandal, so flagrant that the President was forced to dismiss the Secretaries of War and State that spring, thus irreparably broadening the chasm between Federalist factions.

With so few friends, Adams discerned one in the new Congressman from Virginia and offered him the War Department position. Marshall refused; he felt no particular qualifications for the office, and it was obviously a dead end. His own political instincts followed those of Hamilton, whom Virginia Federalists regarded as the protégé of the heroic Washington; on the other hand, Marshall sympathized with Adams personally, and shared the President's concern at the future of the national government. When, on the heels of his rejection of the Secretaryship of War, Adams offered him the chief Cabinet position, of the State Department, Marshall felt compelled to accept.

The rapid decline of the Federalists was evident all around, and could only give consternation to one who, like Marshall, was convinced that strong central government was the only hope for survival of the constitutional system. But his own vacant seat in Congress had promptly been filled by a strong Jefferson supporter (Littleton Waller Tazewell), "one of the most decided democrats [i.e., radicals] in the union," as Marshall described him in a letter to Harrison Gray Otis. He added: "There is a tide in the affairs of nations, of parties, and of individuals. I feel that of real Americanism is on the wane." [17]

The Jeffersonians were campaigning aggressively against the dissension-rent administration, excoriating the Alien and Sedition Acts, the substantial rise in federal taxes to meet the rising costs of preparedness in the face of a bellicose Revolutionary France, and the attendant drop in trade with that country. Geographically, the Federalists were also badly divided; their main centers of strength were with Adams in New England and with the other Presidential contender, Charles Cotesworth Pinckney, in South Carolina. Republican strength, for the test in the fall elections, was at least centralized between Jefferson in Virginia and Aaron Burr in New York.

The Republicans won the elections, but with Jefferson and Burr tied in the electoral vote. Hamilton, who had engineered Adams's defeat by a vitriolic attack upon him in October 1800, had thus opened the doors to both White House and Congress to one or another of his greatest enemies—Jefferson, with whom he had fought ideological duels for a quarter of a century, or Burr, who now emerged as the major threat to Hamilton's own New York power base.[18] To protect his own interest, Hamilton now sought to divert votes in the Federalist-controlled House of Representatives to break the electoral tie in favor of Jefferson; but House Federalists, for whom Jefferson was the main enemy, began to lean toward Burr as the prospective leader of a new, anti-Jeffersonian coalition.

Hamilton appealed to the Secretary of State to announce a preference for Jefferson, hoping that such a move would pull Adams support away from Burr. Marshall replied that he could never find it possible to support Jefferson, and since he took at face value Hamilton's reasons for finding Burr unacceptable, he had no choice but to remain uncommitted. Meantime, the confusion in national government was being compounded; Chief Justice Oliver Ellsworth had tendered his resignation. On this one point, all Federalists could find themselves in agreement—the judiciary alone of the branches of government could and must be preserved from the debacle that was bringing in the Republicans. On December 19, 1800, President Adams signed and Secretary of State Marshall sealed the commission to John Jay, the first Chief Justice, to return to service as the fourth, the Senate having confirmed him the previous day.[19] But on January 7, 1801, Jay declined the commission; there were too many defects in the judicial system, he wrote the President, to persuade him to resume an office he had given up more than five years earlier.

There was general agreement, among Federalists and even Republicans, that the national court system needed overhauling. At the opening of Congress in December, Adams's message (written by Marshall) had reiterated a proposal made a year before, that the Judiciary Act of 1789 be revised, and a bill to that effect was introduced on the same day that Jay's commission had been issued. As finally enacted on February 27, the new statute met many of the objections to the old system; it created a number of new circuit judgeships and relieved the Supreme Court of the onerous task of riding circuit, while it expanded the judicial personnel to serve the new system. The Act of 1801, however, overreached itself politically; it proposed to reduce the Supreme Court from six to five Justices, by leaving unfilled the first vacancy to occur after it took effect, an obvious effort to minimize Republican chances of placing one of their men on that bench. In addition, Adams was hastening to fill all new judicial positions with "steady men" who would keep the judiciary Federalist for years to come.[20]

Meantime, John Marshall had been nominated, confirmed, and commissioned as Chief Justice of the United States. John Adams had discharged two debts of gratitude—one incurred by Marshall's masterful defense of the administration in the Robins affair, the other by Marshall's acceptance of the State Department position in the declining days of the Adams Presidency—although these were merely incidental to Adams's overriding concern to keep the highest judicial position safe from the Jeffersonians. Justice William Paterson had been recommended by Marshall himself, before the nomination of Jay, but Adams disliked Paterson's close association with Hamilton. With time running out, the President reasoned, he had to take whoever was at hand—and this was to be his Secretary of State.[21]

In the final weeks of the Adams Presidency (and for almost a fortnight into the Jefferson administration), Marshall would remain as Secretary of State—as Jay had done for six months at the beginning of the government. While modern commentators would find a number of objections to such a practice, the Jeffersonians contented themselves with charging—falsely—that Marshall was enriching himself with the salaries of both offices during this period. What was more remarkable was that Marshall was assisting Adams in finding persons to fill the numerous positions created by the legislation of the expiring Federalist Congress. By 9:00 P.M. on March 3, the final commissions had been signed by the President and sealed by the Department of State. But as the term ended, there were a fateful few which, though signed and sealed, remained undelivered (see Part One, Chapter II).

iii

Of the five men whom John Marshall formally joined on the Court on February 4, 1801, William Cushing of Massachussetts was the only remaining original appointee of 1789. The second Justice from the Washington years was William Paterson of New Jersey, appointed in 1793. The others were Adams choices—Samuel Chase of Maryland (1796), Bushrod Washington of Pennsylvania (1798), and Alfred Moore of North Carolina (1799). They represented the current incumbents from among a total of a dozen appointments in the first uncertain decade—all of them having come from Federalist ranks.

Between 1801 and 1835, fifteen Associates would serve with the incoming Chief Justice—although James Wayne of Georgia, appointed in the same year as Marshall's death, could hardly be counted among the lawgivers who were destined, in three and a half decades of intimate and generally cordial association with the great Chief Justice, to shape the Constitution and the Supreme Court into two of the most remarkable institutions in the history of Western law. Five Presidents would select these Associates, with at least Thomas Jefferson and Andrew Jackson hoping in the process to change the judicial course which Marshall was charting; until the final years, there could be few claims that they had enjoyed any success.

William Howard Taft, as Chief Justice, frequently spoke of the

Chief's responsibility to "marshal the Court"—an act of leadershp that sought to develop a consistent institutional position on points of ruling case law. It was John Marshall's ability to define positions and by force of logic to convert them into common ground for himself and his colleagues that Taft took as his ideal. Because, then as now, the Court was made up of strong-minded individuals, there were obviously factors more fundamental than Marshall's own personality that accounted for the shaping of an institutional posture. But the ultimate fact was that in eighteen major constitutional cases over thirty-five years, ten were recorded as without dissent. (See Part Two, Chapter III, pp. 121–122.)

In part, the consistent unanimity may have been encouraged by the intimacy of the Justices during each term, living and dining together at a single boardinghouse as they often did. The comparative leisure in which cases could be discussed—less than fifty opinions were written in an average term between 1810 and 1820, as compared with 359 written opinions in the 1975 term (ended June 1976) [22]—also provided opportunity to find common ground for the final opinion delivered by the Court, and customarily signed by the Chief Justice in the name of the Court.

But Marshall as leader of the Court applied the same techniques which had made him such a solid lawyer at the bar, proceeding from one logical position to the next, testing with his colleagues each step of the progression toward a conclusion based solidly upon consensus. "It is a Constitution we are interpreting," he said on several occasions [23]—a written fundamental law whose apparently explicit powers in reality had to be construed and applied without benefit of precedent and with only the most general analogies from British constitutional tradition. If Marshall provided one irreducible proposition from which the Justices' constitutional dialogues began, it was the essential need for strength in government—state and national—sufficient for the carrying out of the functions assigned to it. The Chief subscribed fully to Hamilton's insistence that vigor and energy in government equated with effective government (see the commentary in Part II, Chapter I, under the legislative, executive, and judicial articles). For this "Constitution, and the Laws of the United States . . . in Pursuance thereof" to be in truth "the supreme Law of the Land," as Article VI proclaimed, it was incumbent on the Court to find adequate power vested in each of the branches.

Among Marshall's Associates, four played major roles in shaping constitutional doctrine in the climactic decade from 1816 to 1827: Bushrod Washington, who was on the bench when Marshall came to it and would serve from 1798 to 1829; William Johnson, 1804–1834; Henry Brockholst Livingston, 1806–1823; and the greatest of this company, Joseph Story, 1811–1845. The length of their service with the Chief obviously was a factor in the common approach which they came to make to issues brought before them; the mutual respect and, in the instances of Washington and Story, warm personal affection which marked their relationship was another. But the greatest good fortune was the intellectual and professional competence upon which these five men could draw to articulate the first principles of American constitutional law for the course of national history.

Bushrod Washington, the nephew of the first President who was Marshall's lifelong hero, would have naturally been a beneficiary of the Chief Justice's affection. Their own paths had continually crossed and recrossed, beginning in 1780 when both were students in George Wythe's pioneer law course at the College of William and Mary. Later that year, Marshall returned to his home in Fauquier County and presented himself for admission to the bar, while Washington went to Philadelphia for two more years of reading law under James Wilson, one of the first Justices, whose seat Washington himself would ultimately occupy. But in 1788 Washington and Marshall were working together again, in the Virginia ratifying convention, and shortly thereafter Washington moved to Richmond, joining the brilliant and close-knit circle of lawyers of whom Marshall was an acknowledged head. Washington went to the House of Representatives a few months ahead of Marshall, in the Adams administration. Finally, there was the biography of the Father of His Country which the Chief Justice would undertake to write at the request of the nephew.

Story regarded Washington as "a profound scholar" in the law, but because he generally shared the basic Hamiltonian persuasions of his more scintillating colleagues, Washington's own prescience in constitutional matters was self-effacing. Two opinions, however, document the contributions he himself made to constitutional fundamentals. In the first, a concurring opinion in the *Dartmouth College* case in 1819 (see Part One, Chapter V), he admonished the majority that its opinion on the contract clause (Article I, Section 10) would ultimately have to be modified. The modification was stated in the second case, the opinion of the Court (from which Marshall made a rare dissent) in *Ogden* v. *Saunders* in 1827 (12 Wheaton 213) holding that a contract made in the knowledge of existing legal limits to its terms could not be impaired by a subsequent invoking of the limits.[24]

The second of the quadrumvirate, William Johnson, represented a "great white hope" of the Jeffersonians—the first chance to place an anti-Federalist on the Marshall Court, the year following the *Marbury* case. Johnson had read law under one of the leading southern Federalists, Charles Cotesworth Pinckney, but when he ran for his first state office, it was as a Republican. His philosophy seemed to be a compromise between the opposing political creeds, and during four years on the bench of common pleas his opinions continued to reflect this compromise; but when Jefferson picked him for the first opening on the Marshall Court, it was in consideration of his "Republican connections, and . . . good nerves in his political principles." [25]

Johnson indeed would prove to be a frequent dissenter on a bench encouraged by its Chief to take Hamiltonian principles as a starting point for preparing the ultimate draft of constitutional opinions. Yet, as Circuit Justice in 1808, Johnson himself strongly reiterated the principle Marshall had insisted upon in the Burr trial of the year before, on the obligation of the judiciary to protect the individual from the arbitrary use of executive power (*Gilchrist* v. *Collector of Charleston* [10 Fed. Cas. 355, No. 5420]). While Johnson, on the Supreme Court, later had to confess error in the jurisdictional basis for his circuit opinion (*McIntire* v. *Wood*, 7 Cranch 504 [1813]), his *Gilchrist* holding served notice on the executive and legislative branches that executive actions affecting private rights were least suspect when they followed Congressional guidelines—a principle that the Court reiterated in 1952 in the Steel Seizure Case (*Youngstown Sheet & Tube Co.* v. *Sawyer* [343 U.S. 579]).

In major constitutional cases, Johnson often appeared to be searching for the compromise between nationalism and states' rights that had been evident in his years on the South Carolina court. In his concurring opinion in *Martin* v. *Hunter's Lessee* in 1816 (1 Wheaton 304), he joined Story (Marshall had disqualified himself) in the judgment but differed with Story on the reason for upholding the federal jurisdiction. In words that sounded strikingly like Justice Felix Frankfurter's doctrine of judicial restraint a century and a half later he spoke of the initiative which Congress, rather than the judiciary, should exercise in extending jurisdiction under Article III of the Constitution. Five years later, in the climactic decision in *Cohens* v. *Virginia* (6 Wheaton 264), his concurrence stressed a similar theme.

Johnson concurred with the majority, but for separately stated reasons, in the basic contract clause restraints upon the states expressed by Marshall in *Fletcher* v. *Peck* in 1810 (6 Cranch 87), *Dartmouth College* v. *Woodward* (4 Wheaton 518), and *Sturges* v. *Crowninshield* (4 Wheaton 122), both in 1819.

Thus Johnson's judicial positions left the Jeffersonians only half satisfied; the reasoning in his concurring opinions spoke the language of limited government, but his vote was with the nationalistic majority. In the great opinions establishing the power of the federal government as the supreme law of the land—*McCulloch* v. *Maryland* in 1819 (4 Wheaton 316) and *Gibbons* v. *Ogden* in 1824 (9 Wheaton 1)—he followed the same practice. Like Frankfurter, and the second Justice John Marshall Harlan,* Johnson accepted the necessity of strength in national government, but consistently argued that it should be invoked by a representative branch (Congress) more directly accountable to the people of the states.[26]

Thus Johnson consistently supported the Marshall Court in the basic principles of constitutional federalism while insisting upon the need for keeping the federal system itself in balance. The legislatures, and particularly the state legislatures, he considered the proper guardians of personal and property rights; but the courts, and the right of appellate review in the Supreme Court, in his view in turn were the best safeguard against legislative and executive abuse. In the long struggle between Marshall and Jefferson themselves, William Johnson offered the best chance for an amalgam of viewpoints.

In 1806, two years after the Johnson appointment, Jefferson chose an even more pronounced anti-Federalist for another Court vacancy—Henry Brockholst Livingston of New York. Like Johnson, Livingston and the several branches of his powerful family gradually moved from the Hamiltonian to the Jeffersonian end of the political spectrum. Still, as close analysis of the situation in New York would reveal, Brockholst Livingston's political transition was more personal than philosophical, bred of a prolonged antipathy for his brother-in-law, John Jay. There was a significant political debt owed by Jefferson to Livingston as a result of this family rivalry, in any case; Livingston's work in the 1800 campaign had swung New York behind Aaron Burr and the Republicans and thus, whatever the outcome of the electoral deadlock thrown into the House of Representatives, away from the Federalists.

If John Marshall ever captured the support of any one Associate by the force of his own personality, it may well have been Livingston. Both men were of congenial nature and apparently quickly attracted to each other. In consideration of the fact that Livingston's anti-Federalism was, in the apt phrase of one biographer, essentially opportunistic,[27] his viewpoint on the bench was affected in proportion to his removal from the parochial considerations of New York State politics. Moreover, Livingston's area of expertise was not in public but commercial law, and he felt called upon to write few opinions, even in concurrence, in the great constitutional cases. Even when, as his out-of-Court correspondence with Justice Story revealed, he had disagreed with the majority in the contract and bankruptcy issues in *Sturges* v. *Crowninshield,* he abstained from setting forth his own view in detail for the record.

How completely Livingston accepted Marshall's leadership, and that

* The first Justice Harlan (grandfather of the second) served on the Court from 1877 to 1911.

of his colleagues Washington and Story, on the main principles of constitutional federalism was evident in the *Dartmouth College* case, where Livingston specifically concurred in the Chief's opinion and in the concurrences of the two Associates (see Part One, Chapter V). For the most part, Livingston's contributions to the jurisprudence of the Court in the course of his long tenure were in nonconstitutional areas, and thus he was a loss to the Jeffersonians in their efforts to offset the Marshall majority. On the other hand, his very passivity in following Marshall's lead in constitutional matters contributed to the solidifying of the base for an institutional position on these matters.

The greatest triumph for the Marshall doctrine resulted from the appointment of Joseph Story in 1811. The appointment itself had been somewhat fortuitous; it was the fourth of the nominations which James Madison sent to the Senate in his efforts to fill the vacancy created by Cushing's death. Jefferson's former Attorney General, Levi Lincoln of Massachusetts, declined his confirmation because of ill health; Oliver Wolcott of Connecticut was rejected by the Senate, partly in retribution for his rigid enforcement of the embargo laws which were to lead to the War of 1812; and John Quincy Adams declined his appointment after confirmation, stating that he preferred the diplomatic and political life to the law. Still searching for a strong New England anti-Federalist, Madison then turned to Story, although Jefferson, in retirement at Monticello, warned his fellow Virginian that Story was not a totally committed Republican. Madison, whose own constitutional position tended to vacillate over the years, made his own judgment; he had first met the prospective Justice at Princeton, where he and Joseph's uncle, Isaac Story, had been classmates, and he had been impressed with the nephew as lawyer and Congressman in more recent years.[28]

Jefferson's misgivings were to prove warranted from the outset. In 1813, in his second year on the Court, Justice Story wrote the opinion in *Fairfax's Devisee* v. *Hunter's Lessee* (7 Cranch 603) affirming the Court's appellate jurisdiction over state tribunals on constitutional questions. When the same case reappeared three years later, under the title of *Martin* v. *Hunter's Lessee* (1 Wheaton 304), the Virginia high court having denied the federal tribunal's doctrine on appellate jurisdiction, Story emphatically reiterated the doctrine: the Supreme Court had final authority to review acts of all branches of government, state and federal, which involved federal questions. In 1819 the onetime Republican politician unequivocally asserted his support of nationalism in concurring opinions in the great trilogy of constitutional decisions in that term—*McCulloch* v. *Maryland,* with its comprehensive definition of the "necessary and proper" clause (see Part One, Chapter VI); the Dartmouth College case, establishing the contract clause as a restraint upon state action (see Part One, Chapter V); and *Sturges* v. *Crowninshield* (4 Wheaton 122), voiding a state insolvency statute which conflicted with the contract and bankruptcy clauses (Article I, Section 8, Clause 4; Section 10).

Thus, by the end of the second decade of the Marshall Court, Joseph Story had emerged as one of the most articulate advocates of judicial federalism as the Chief Justice himself envisioned it. In the single dissent recorded by Marshall on a constitutional case—*Ogden* v. *Saunders* in 1827 (12 Wheaton 213)—Story joined (with Justice Gabriel Duvall) in the dissent, insisting that the contract clause protected all contracts, future as well as past, from state action unless a specific right of action was reserved by the state. Two years later, Story advanced to a position from which, for the oncoming generations, he would be able to perpetuate Marshall's constitutional jurisprudence in a definitive treatise—the Dane professorship of law at Harvard University. The chair had been endowed by Nathan Dane from the royalties received from his own considerable work, *An Abridgement of American Law,* and was expressly reserved for Story as the first occupant. A further stipulation was that the occupant be given opportunity to prepare a succession of treatises or commentaries on various fields of law.

When, in 1833, the three volumes of the *Commentaries on the Constitution* were completed, the doctrine of judicial federalism of the Marshall years was engraved upon the records of the nation as the enduring, primary tenet of the American system. Two powerful minds, remarkably in harmony over a quarter of a century, had refined and enlarged upon this doctrine, and for a decade after Marshall's death in 1835 Story would continue, both on the bench and in the classroom, strengthening the structure which had been the result of their great collaboration. (See excerpts from the first edition of the treatise throughout the annotations in Part Two, Chapter I.) The *Commentaries* would go through a succession of new editions over the coming century, succeeding editors bringing them up to date and continuing their paramount authority in constitutional interpretation. If the *Commentaries* in the last half of the twentieth century do not have the unchallenged influence they had in earlier generations, they nevertheless provide the frame of reference for all interpretative writing which followed.

While Washington, Livingston, Johnson, and Story were Marshall's best known Associates, three others who served during his Chief Justiceship had tenure of sufficient length to have had a measurable impact upon the evolution of judicial doctrine. Thomas Todd, chief justice of Kentucky, came onto the tribunal in 1807, when a seventh circuit was created for the new western states of Kentucky, Tennessee, and Ohio. Todd remained on

the Court until 1826. Gabriel Duvall of Maryland succeeded Justice
Samuel Chase in 1811, coming onto the bench at the same time as Story,
and served until 1835. Smith Thompson, related by marriage to the
Livingston dynasty in New York, succeeded Livingston himself in 1823
and served for twenty years.

The ordeal of Samuel Chase—impeached by the House of Representatives in 1805 and saved from removal by failure of the Senate to muster
the required majority—was the result of another effort of the Jeffersonians
to purge the judiciary of Federalist influence. With judges under the Constitution granted life tenure (the actual language was "during good Behaviour"), removal by impeachment was the only alternative, albeit
a heavy-handed one. Chase's behavior on circuit, where he harangued
grand juries with intemperate Federalist argument, made him a prime
target for some form of censure, whether or not it amounted to improper
conduct for an incumbent Justice. But the Jeffersonians let it be known
that Chase was only the initial target, with the remainder of the Supreme
Court likely to follow if his removal could be effected. When the Senate
failed to muster the two-thirds majority required by the Constitution (Article I, Section 3, Clause 6), the Jeffersonians abandoned the strategy.

Todd, who seized the opportunity offered by Kentucky's separation
from Virginia to become a specialist in land law and secretary to the new
state's legislature, in 1801 became a judge of the state court of appeals
and its chief justice five years later. His service on the Supreme Court was
sporadic, as ill health and the difficulties of reaching the new national
capital from the western country caused him to miss terms of Court in five
years out of the eighteen he served. He wrote no opinions on constitutional
subjects, and tended to join with the Chief Justice in these cases, thus virtually assuring Marshall of an automatic second vote.

Duvall, who recorded a dissent without opinion in the Dartmouth
College case, was to be found for the most part in Marshall's camp. He
joined Marshall and Story in their dissent in *Ogden* v. *Saunders* in 1827,
and in the other great constitutional cases of the decisive decade from
1816 to 1827 he voted consistently with the majority.

Smith Thompson, coming to the bench toward the end of this decade,
was the harbinger of a gradual diminution of the solid nationalistic consensus of the earlier years. As early as 1812, when on the New York
judiciary, Thompson had demonstrated his basic difference in approach to
constitutional doctrine—his opinion in *Livingston* v. *Van Ingen* (9 Johns.
Rep. 507) upheld the New York steamboat monopoly which would eventually be overturned in *Gibbons* v. *Ogden* (see Part III, Chapter V, pages
332–352). Thompson was ambitious for high political office at the time of
his nomination to the Court; his mentor, Martin Van Buren, was a rising

star in Andrew Jackson's party and Thompson even entertained ideas of his own nomination for the Presidency. It was only when these hopes were dispelled that he came onto the bench, and he came as a proponent of a changing political order. His vote in 1827 in *Ogden* v. *Saunders* put Marshall and Story into a rare dissenting posture on a constitutional case.

By this date, the major work of the Marshall Court had been accomplished. The aging Chief Justice seemed less equal to the task of confronting an aggressive Executive in the days of Andrew Jackson than he had been in the days of Thomas Jefferson. Jackson's legendary aphorism— "John Marshall has made his decision; now let him enforce it"—was symptomatic of the changing times, and of a faltering leadership on the bench. In 1831, in *Cherokee Nation* v. *United States* (5 Peters 1), Marshall had clearly temporized, holding the Cherokees had no standing in the Court to contest Georgia's blatantly unconstitutional expropriating of their lands. To his old friend, Justice Story, the failing Chief wrote that he saw no way out of this dilemma and was on the verge of resigning. The following year, with some of the old spirit returning, he held unconstitutional Georgia's imprisoning of a missionary who had sought to counsel the Cherokees on their rights (*Worcester* v. *Georgia* [6 Peters 515]); it was to this opinion that Jackson made his defiant comment.[29]

iv

If the Marshall leadership of the Court during the last years of his Chief Justiceship lacked the bold initiatives of the preceding three decades, what had been accomplished by then would be sufficient to confirm the epochal nature of his tenure. Beginning with the historic confrontation between the judiciary and the political branches of government in *Marbury* and *Burr,* the Court by the end of the Jeffersonian dynasty had established judicial federalism—which is to say, the rationale of government functions in a federal system as reviewed by the judiciary—for all subsequent American political history.

Marshall delivered, either under his own pen or under his name as the institutional representative of the Court. more than thirty-five opinions touching upon significant constitutional matters, extending over a thirty-year period from *Marbury* in 1803 to *Barron* v. *Baltimore* (7 Peters 243) in 1833. The *Marbury* opinion settled the principle that Congressional actions were to be tested against the Constitution by the judiciary (see Part One, Chapter II) and *Burr,* among other things, extended this principle to executive actions (see Part One, Chapter III). The next extension, to the states, came in 1810 with the invoking of the contract clause as a restraint in *Fletcher* v. *Peck.* In 1813 Marshall's loyal lieutenant, Joseph

Story, further broadened the Court's appellate jurisdiction with reference
to state action in *Fairfax's Devisee* v. *Hunter's Lessee* and reiterated it
emphatically in 1816 in *Martin* v. *Hunter's Lessee*. Marshall was thereupon in strong position to carry the doctrine to its full force in 1819 in
the *Dartmouth College* case (see Part One, Chapter V).

The 1819 term saw the completion of the judicial dogma of reviewability of state action in the companion cases of *McCulloch* v. *Maryland*
(see Part One, Chapter VI) and *Sturges* v. *Crowninshield*. In 1821
Cohens v. *Virginia* completed the supremacy clause rationale introduced
by Story in *Fairfax's Devisee,* and two years later *Green* v. *Biddle* completed the contract clause rationale. The construction of Marshall's constitutionalism was then rounded out in 1824 with the commerce clause
interpretation in *Gibbons* v. *Ogden* (see Part One, Chapter VII). Of the
leading constitutional cases which arose in the following decade, the
McCulloch rule was refined by *Osborn* v. *Bank of the United States* (9
Wheaton 738) in 1824 and by *Providence Bank* v. *Billings* (4 Peters 514)
in 1830, while the *Gibbons* doctrine was extended in 1827 in *Brown* v.
Maryland (12 Wheaton 419).

Signs of the ending of the Marshall Court's activism, either through
the aggressiveness of the Jacksonian administration as in the Cherokee
cases or the breaking up of the old judicial consensus with Justice Thompson, were clear to see in the 1830s. *Ogden* v. *Saunders,* a 4-to-3 division
in a contract clause issue, was only partly offset in 1830 by *Craig* v.
Missouri, another contract clause issue with a 4-to-3 division in Marshall's
favor. Most significant of all was the last constitutional opinion in 1833—
Barron v. *Baltimore*—which found the Chief Justice declining to take an
initiative eloquently offered by counsel, to extend the Bill of Rights provisions to the states.

The Marshall Court was able to dominate the constitutional process
for as long as it did (1803–1824) because of a unique combination of
circumstances. There was, first of all, the malleable nature of the young
republic; Jefferson, as clearly as Marshall, understood that this first generation of the nineteenth century, successor to the Revolutionary generation, would be the one to shape that nature, and he strove mightily to
control the shaping. In addition—and in particular before the westward
movement began to gather momentum after the War of 1812 and thus
diversify the social economy—this first post-Revolutionary generation was
still remarkably homogeneous and intimate, sharing a general interest in
political events over which they were still able to exert a direct control.
This "era of good feeling," which later historians ascribed to the administrations of Madison and Monroe, to the extent that it actually existed,
derived from the fact that most of the national leaders knew each other

personally and placed similar degrees of value on their heritage under the new Constitution.

The long tenure of the Chief Justice himself, and the relative stability of the Court under him—William Johnson was associated with Marshall for thirty years, Washington for twenty-eight, Story and Duvall for twenty-four, Todd for nineteen, Livingston for eighteen—combined with the mutual respect which, with rare exceptions, manifested itself between the Justices, was another unique factor affecting the times. Given the generally nationalistic leanings of such Associates as Washington, Livingston, and Story, and the disposition of Johnson to express his philosophical differences by concurrences more often than by dissent, Marshall could consistently anticipate a majority on most constitutional cases. The attitudes of Justices Duvall and Todd were sufficiently conformist to make it possible to extend this majority on many occasions to an appearance of institutional unanimity.

But most fundamental in importance was the fact that the questions presented to the Marshall Court, particularly during the first twenty-five years, growing out of the burgeoning society of the period, offered the chance to mold the future. Jeffersonianism made its own contributions, demonstrating the interaction of Republican thesis and judicial federalism's antithesis which so impressed Alexis de Tocqueville (who published his *Democracy in America* in the year of Marshall's death) with the inherent tolerance of the system: "as the minority may shortly rally the majority to its principles, it is interested in professing that respect for the decrees of the legislature which it may soon have occasion to claim for its own." [30]

In the very years that he was locked in intellectual combat with the Chief Justice, Thomas Jefferson was making his own contribution to cataclysmic forces in American life, particularly in his support of the Louisiana Purchase. In the very process of questioning his constitutional power to do so, Jefferson converted the United States from a small seaboard-oriented power to a continental power, in the very time of the struggle with the judiciary. When Marshall and Jefferson each took office in 1801, there were already sixteen states in the Union, and in 1807 the states of the new West—Kentucky, Tennessee, and Ohio—would require extension of the federal judicial system by formation of a new circuit of their own. By the time Marshall died in 1835, there were twenty-four states, all of the territory held at the time of the Revolution had been converted into equal members of the Union, and a succession of trans-Mississippi states were coming into being.

The unchallenged position of the Supreme Court in this steadily widening national geography—the product of Marshall's great works in his earlier years—meant that as the national economic character changed (the Industrial Revolution was already gathering momentum by the time of Marshall's death), there would be an assured dimension of governmental power when the time came to seek to regulate this economic character. That time would come long after Marshall's day, near the close of his century and the beginning of the twentieth. By then, the Fourteenth Amendment would have prepared the ground for a fundamental reorientation of the federal system with which the Marshall Court had dealt. Marshall's Constitution was the Constitution of the post-Revolutionary age (see Part Two, Chapter I); after 1868, it would be the Constitution of the post-Civil War era; and a third era would shape the Constitution of the post-Depression and New Deal years. Nevertheless, it was the Supreme Court as Marshall and his Associates had shaped it in the formative decades that was the ultimate counterbalance in each period.

De Tocqueville expressed it aptly when he wrote:

> In all the civilized countries of Europe the government has always shown the greatest reluctance to allow the cases in which it was itself interested to be decided by the ordinary course of justice. This repugnance is naturally greater as the government is more absolute; and, on the other hand, the privileges of the courts of justice are extended with the increasing liberties of the people; but no European nation has yet held that all judicial controversies, without regard to their origin, can be left to the judges of the common law.
>
> In America this theory has been actually put in practice; and the Supreme Court of the United States is the sole tribunal of the nation. Its power extends to all cases arising under laws and treaties made by the national authorities, to all cases of admiralty and maritime jurisdiction, and, in general, to all points that effect the law of nations. It may even be affirmed that, although its constitution is essentially judicial, its prerogatives are almost entirely political. Its sole object is to enforce the execution of the laws of the Union. . . .
>
> A second and still greater cause of the preponderance of this court may be adduced. In the nations of Europe the courts of justice are called upon to try only the controversies of private individuals; but the Supreme Court of the United States summons sovereign powers to its bar. . . . Without [the Justices] the Constitution would be a dead letter; the executive appeals to them for assistance against the encroachments of the legislative power; the legislature demands their protection against the assaults of the executive; they defend the Union from the disobedience of the states, the states from the exaggerated claims of the Union, the public interest against private interests, and the conservative spirit of stability against the fickleness of democracy. Their power is enormous, but it is the power of public opinion. They are all-powerful as long as the people respect the law; they would be impotent against popular neglect or contempt of the law.[31]

II

The Supreme Court and Congress

Marbury v. *Madison*

As John Marshall assumed his duties as Chief Justice, and Thomas Jefferson his duties as Chief Executive—the one on February 4, the other on March 4, 1801 [1]—it was quite clear that the judiciary was to become a battleground, an Armageddon and (as it turned out) a Waterloo as well. The struggle was first joined in the legislative arena; in his opening message to Congress that December, Jefferson sounded the signal to his followers:

> The judiciary system of the United States, and especially that portion of it recently erected, will of course present itself to the contemplation of Congress, and, that they may be able to judge of the proportion which the institution bears to the business it has to perform, I have caused to be procured from the several States and now lay before Congress an exact statement of all the causes decided since the first establishment of the courts, and of those which were depending when additional courts and judges were brought to their aid. [2]
>
> And while on the judiciary organization it will be worthy your consideration whether the protection of the inestimable institution of juries has been extended to all the cases involving the security of our persons and property. Their impartial selection also being essential to their value, we ought further to consider whether that is sufficiently secured in those States where they are named by a marshal depending on Executive will or designated by the court or by officers dependent on them. [3]

Both Federalists and anti-Federalists had to share the blame for the ensuing legislative melee. The Circuit Court Act of the preceding February had dealt realistically and effectively with a number of problems which a decade of experience with the Judiciary Act of 1789 had turned up. That first legislation, establishing the federal court system, had followed the organization common in most of the states, with a two-tiered structure of trial courts and the Supreme Court as the tribunal of last resort. Judges had been provided for the District Courts and for the Supreme Court; the Circuit Courts were to be staffed by two Justices from the high bench and one District Court judge.[4]

The circuit arrangement had been objectionable from the outset. Supreme Court Justices had to travel the circuits under the execrable transportation conditions of the early republic, and to do this twice a year was an arduous assignment. Hardship aside, the plan was more objectionable from the standpoint of administration of justice, since any case appealed from the circuits to the Supreme Court would find one-third of the Justices—the two assigned to that circuit [5]—sitting in review of the case they had already tried.

The Circuit Court Act of 1801 sought to deal with both of these problems by abolishing circuit riding by the Justices and replacing the original three circuits with six, served by sixteen newly created circuit judges. The number was probably too much of a swing of the pendulum; John Crittenden of Kentucky decried the sudden size of the federal judiciary: "The time never will arrive when America will stand in need of thirty-eight Federal judges," he declared in the Senate now under Republican control.[6] What was left unsaid was that the sixteen new circuit judges were all Federalists, occupants of seats created by the outgoing Federalist Congress and filled by the outgoing Federalist President. As if that were not enough, the expiring Sixth Congress had also created a number of lesser judicial positions in the new District of Columbia, for which organizing legislation had also been passed in February 1801.

The Republicans proceeded forthwith to repeal the Circuit Court Act, in the process abolishing the sixteen new circuit judgeships. A fine constitutional question might thus have been presented to the new Chief Justice, in consideration of the constitutional prohibition of legislative acts affecting the tenure of lifetime judicial appointments (Article III, Section 1).[7] As fate would have it, however, the major constitutional issue was joined, between the Jeffersonians and the Federalist Court, on the much less momentous question of the delivery or nondelivery of certain commissions for justice of the peace, issued under the District of Columbia act for fixed terms of years (see Part Three, Chapter I-2).[8] Marbury's petition for a justice of the peace commission directed against Secretary of State Madison, therefore, became the basis for the great confrontation between Marshall and Jefferson, while the more substantial question of the extinguished circuit judgeships would be answered ambivalently in the wake of the case of the missing commissions.[9]

After the repeal of the Circuit Court Act, the Jeffersonian Congress retained the provision for six circuits, but required the Supreme Court Justices to return to the task of sitting in these circuits. The repeal also had the effect of restoring the number of Supreme Court Justices to six; for in overreaching themselves in 1801 the Federalists had sought to frustrate early efforts of the Jeffersonians to get representation on the Court by providing that the first vacancy to occur should remain unfilled, thus reducing the size of the tribunal to five.[10] The combination of Federalist machinations, in creating a host of new judicial positions to pack with their followers and in seeking to deny the incoming administration an opportunity to appoint one of their men to the high bench, provoked the new Congress to wipe out the 1801 legislation, its good features as well as the bad.

This statutory nullification was only part of the Jeffersonian program for reducing the Federalist control of the judiciary. If judges were to be in office, as the Constitution phrased it, "during good Behaviour," a series of challenges to behavior—impeachment—would be the only practical means of clearing out the bench. What constituted good or bad behavior, and whether it was a matter of personal behavior or behavior in an official capacity, was never to be persuasively dealt with in most of the judicial impeachments treated by Congress.[11] But it was a strategy of intimidation, if nothing else; three weeks before the Marshall Court was to deliver the opinion on Marbury's case, the President sent to the House of Representatives a collection of documents aimed at the impeachment of District Judge John Pickering of New Hampshire (see Part Two, Chapter II).

Thus, by the time it eventually reached the high bench, the question of Marbury's commission had been magnified by other events, more political than legal. Jefferson, outraged at finding forty-two District judicial appointments filled by Federalists in the very last hours of the Adams administration, ordered a review of the entire lot (although he eventually reappointed twenty-five of the Adams men). Strictly put, this review did not affect Marbury, or three other claimants to commissions—Dennis Ramsay, William Harper, and Robert Townsend Hooe. Their commissions had simply never been delivered, and when they requested them the new administration in the State Department professed to know nothing of their whereabouts, although the senior clerk, Jacob Wagner, was a holdover from Marshall's Secretaryship.

It was fairly evident that these four commissions, at least, had simply not been delivered by Marshall late on the night of March 3. As Marshall himself explained, Wagner had been pressed into service at the last minute as secretary to President Adams and thus Marshall's own office had been understaffed as the Secretary affixed the great seal of the United States to the appointments and piled the documents on his desk for delivery. James Marshall, brother of the Chief Justice, would submit an affidavit that he had in fact picked up certain commissions to deliver, signing a receipt for the same, and that when he returned several because it was impractical to take them all, he recalled that these included the commissions for Hooe and Harper.[12]

The affront offered by the Court, as the Jeffersonians viewed it, was in requesting Secretary of State Madison to show cause why Marbury's petition for mandamus should not be granted. This was, according to the Republican argument, an attempt to subject the executive branch of government to the jurisdiction of the judicial. The show-cause order to Madison in December 1801 undoubtedly accelerated the Congressional plan to repeal the Circuit Court Act. Thereafter, the administration was concerned less with Marbury's nuisance petition than with the prospect that the Court would entertain another suit—an appeal from several actions already under way in the federal trial courts—challenging the constitutionality of the repeal and its abolition of the circuit judgeships. Thus Congress in March 1802 passed an amendment to the Judiciary Act of 1789, abolishing the August and December terms of the Court; by February 1803, it was hoped, the resumption of circuit riding by the Justices would render the question moot.

The Chief Justice himself considered the constitutionality of the repeal statute, affecting lifetime judicial positions, as the soundest issue on which to confront the Jeffersonians. During the spring following the statute restoring circuit riding, he wrote to the other Justices soliciting their opinions on the matter and even questioning whether they ought to refuse to sit in their circuits; but Justice Washington and others replied negatively, and that August Marshall himself tacitly acknowledged the validity of the Congressional action by sitting as Circuit Justice in Richmond and Raleigh.[13]

The power to declare an act of Congress unconstitutional was, in its own context, sound Jeffersonian doctrine. Essentially this was what Jefferson himself and Senator John Breckenridge, shortly to become the President's new Attorney General, had sought to do in the Virginia and Kentucky Resolutions condemning the Alien and Sedition Acts.[14] In another generation a still more militant states' rightist, John Calhoun, would invoke the principle in South Carolina's ordinance purporting to nullify the Congressional tariff of 1833.[15] The Jefferson/Calhoun thesis, of course, was that the finding of unconstitutionality was the prerogative of the states as the ultimate sovereigns. While a preponderance of the states in 1798 had declined to join in the Virginia and Kentucky Resolutions or support the rationale, that had been before the great "revolution of 1800." Jeffersonian doctrine now was ascendant in the executive and legislative branches of the national government, and for the Federalist judiciary to appear prepared to assert the power of declaring acts of these branches to be unconstitutional now flew in the face of that doctrine.

In any event, the question would be tested through William Marbury's petition for his justice of the peace commission. The Jefferson administration made clear what its course of action would be: Madison was instructed not to respond to the show-cause order, and it was quite apparent that if mandamus did in fact issue, the Secretary of State would continue to ignore the Court. By now the anti-Federalists were quite satisfied to let the test proceed, confident that the judiciary was in an untenable position. It would either be compelled to deny the writ because it would confess that the actions of the executive were not within its cognizance, or it would be compelled to issue the writ and let the world see that it was unable to enforce its own orders.[16]

Marbury's counsel—former Attorney General Charles Lee—was in an equally difficult position, trying to establish the very facts upon which his whole case rested. On all sides the Jeffersonians were cutting off access to essential evidence. An application to the Senate for a copy of the record of confirmations (which would have established that Marbury and the other petitioners in fact had been named to the positions they were claiming) was rejected on the ground that it was part of the executive journal not open to any other parties. The State Department, on the other hand, repeatedly advised that it had no knowledge of the missing commissions, although at length there was a statement that all documents found in the office after March 4 had gone into the hands of the Attorney General, Levi Lincoln.

Lincoln, indeed, was the one person most logically to look to for information on the commissions, since he had held the office of Secretary of State as well as that of Attorney General for a number of weeks until Madison had finally arrived to assume his duties. Lincoln, obviously, had taken over all the papers from Marshall when the latter finally left office in mid-March (see Part Two, Chapter II, p. 114) following Lincoln's own confirmation.[17] But Lincoln was anything but forthcoming; upon being summoned before the Court as a witness, he asked that any questions be put to him in writing so that he could have time to determine whether, as a member of the executive branch, he ought to answer. The Chief Justice advised that if the Attorney General "wished time to consider what answers he should make, they would give him time, but they had no doubt he ought to answer." The ranking legal officer of the government was also an officer of the Court.[18]

When Lincoln returned to the stand after studying the written questions, he conceded that he had indeed seen some commissions, but could not remember whether Marbury's was among them. The obvious next question—what had become of those commissions—the Court did not demand to be answered. Marshall's political instinct warned him that he had pushed the confrontation with the executive branch far enough, and in any case he had established the essentials of Lee's case. The evidence tended to show the existence of undelivered commissions, and the Court could now proceed to the ultimate questions: did Marbury have a right to his commission; did the law afford him a means to secure this right; and was the writ of mandamus directed to an officer of the executive department the proper means? (See Part Three, Chapter I-3.)

These, at least, were the questions which Marbury's counsel submitted to the Court in his final argument on February 11 and 12. In less than two weeks, the Chief Justice would deliver the opinion—rather clearly suggesting that he had been giving thought to the underlying constitutional principle for a substantial period of time before that. For the constitutional issue immediately presented by the Marbury case—whether an officer of the executive branch could be legally compelled to deliver a valid document to the party entitled to it—was essentially secondary to the principle of the paramount right of the Supreme Court to determine the constitutionality of any government action at all. Fifteen years before, John Marshall had enunciated this principle in the Virginia ratifying convention (see Part One, Chapter I, page 1); if it was not unequivocally established now as a first principle of government, it never could be.

The Chief Justice alone, apparently, understood the momentousness of the question. Some of his Associates, seeing only the manifest fact that any mandate in favor of Marbury would be unenforceable, suggested that the impasse be avoided by dismissing the case for want of jurisdiction. Marshall now pointed out to them the real means for dealing with the case: it was not *want* of jurisdiction but the unconstitutionality of Congress's *vesting* jurisdiction in this Court in this type of action that was to be the basis of decision. In effect, the Chief Justice converted his colleagues from a confession of limited power to an assertion of exclusive power in the judicial branch to make the final determination of the constitutional validity of acts of the other branches.[19]

Argument on Marbury's petition began on February 11 and continued for three days. Although it was reported that "most of the gentlemen of the Bar" attended, public attention in general was caught up in a greater crisis in the Jefferson administration—the Republican efforts to negotiate a purchase of a small piece of the Louisiana Territory held by France, to convert New Orleans into an American port, and the Federalist demands that it be taken outright by military action. The partisan assault on administration policies abroad may have heightened the Jeffersonians' reaction to the apparent judicial threat on the domestic front; in any case, the executive department had made it clear that it would defy any mandamus issued in favor of Marbury. As an administration newspaper declared: "The Court must be defeated and retreat from the attack; or march on, until they incur an impeachment and removal from office." [20]

Marshall himself was fully aware of the politics of the situation; after all, he had grown up in Virginia, where it was somewhat self-consciously asserted that politics was a way of life. Moreover, he knew Jefferson, his deep convictions and deep prejudices. It was no mere rhetoric, therefore, that appeared in the opening statement in the Chief Justice's opinion, referring to "the peculiar delicacy of this case, and the real difficulty attending the points which occur in it." [21] Having made this initial acknowledgment, Marshall then announced that he was accepting Lee's statement of the basic questions involved in the case and would take them up in the same order.

Hindsight would show that the Chief Justice had chosen a course from the outset which would logically establish the foundation of his ultimate constitutional decision. The first question phrased by Marbury's counsel— "Has the applicant a right to the commission he demands?"—need never have been answered if Marshall had begun instead with the question of jurisdiction. Since his ultimate conclusion would be that the Court in fact lacked jurisdiction, his addressing this question first (as now is standard in appellate procedure) would have disposed of the entire case.

Later commentators would also argue that Marshall's answer to Lee's opening question—affirming Marbury's right to the commission—had the potential for more difficulties than the practical matter of seeking to compel the commission's delivery. If Marbury's commission for a term of years was valid, what of the circuit judgeships with lifetime appointments which had been eliminated with the repeal of the 1801 act? Had Marshall ever intended to make the current case turn on the enforcing of Marbury's claim, he would have had a serious embarrassment in attempting to decide *Stuart* v. *Laird,* the case of the repealed judgeships. When the *Laird* case did come before the Supreme Court, on appeal from Marshall's ruling as Circuit Justice that it had been improperly brought, the Chief Justice abstained from the Supreme Court opinion on the ground that he had tried the case in the court below.

This raised another issue which subsequent commentators were long to belabor—whether Marshall, who disqualified himself in *Laird,* should not by the same criterion of prior involvement have recused himself in *Marbury,* since everyone conceded that as retiring Secretary of State he had been a fundamental actor in the nondelivery of the commissions. There was also a question of whether the commissions for the justices of the peace were literally analogous to the circuit judge commissions—whether the latter, which were "Article III judicial positions" (i. e., created by the authority vested in Congress by the judicial article), were to be compared with the former, which were "Article I" positions (i. e., legislative courts created as part of Congress's administrative plan for the new District of Columbia).[22]

Jefferson and his followers—equally astute lawyers and politicians—perceived quite clearly that Marshall was "travelling out of his case" in the *Marbury* opinion. They might even have accepted the ultimate holding, that Section 13 of the Judiciary Act of 1789, construed by Marshall as conferring original jurisdiction upon the Supreme Court in cases where the Constitution did not confer it, was reviewable by the Court. What rankled intolerably was the fact that perhaps three-fourths of the *Marbury* opinion was not addressed to that idea and was therefore dictum, a gratuitous criticism of the behavior of the executive branch of government.

For Marshall proceeded to give an affirmative answer to the second question put by Marbury's counsel—that for any wrong the law would afford a remedy. This truism had to be qualified, however, by recognition of the discretion of the Executive to act without hindrance in the discharge of his duties. Some executive actions, the Court conceded, were not judicially, but only politically, cognizable. Marshall, in spite of Jefferson, was seeking to establish the groundwork for a strong executive power, and thus appeared in an almost paradoxical posture of affirming inherent authority in the executive branch of government while proceeding toward a conclusion that in certain circumstances that branch had to be amenable to the law as construed by the judicial (see Part One, Chapter III).

Where the law had clearly established a duty in the officers of government, discretion ended and the law compelled performance of the duty. Marshall spent much of this portion of the opinion—on legal remedies counterbalancing political powers—distinguishing between cases in which the Executive had a "constitutional" discretion and cases in which he had a "political" discretion. Under the "constitutional" heading came such matters as the issuing of pardons and reprieves (Article II, Section 2, Clause 1) or vetoing legislative bills (Article I, Section 7, Clauses 2, 3). "Political" discretion was definable in terms of the "necessary and proper" powers of an Executive (see Part Two, Chapter I, pages 104–105).

The answer to the final question in Marbury's case—whether mandamus was the proper remedy afforded by law—the Jeffersonians were confident would prove Marshall's undoing. If the delivery of a commission was a discretionary act, incumbent on Madison only if Jefferson authorized it, "political" discretion could remove the matter from judicial cognizance. If, on the other hand, delivery of the commission was a "ministerial" act for which no discretion, constitutional or political, was involved, the ancient writ commanding a ministerial officer to perform his legal duty was appropriate. The Judiciary Act of 1789, in fact, stipulated that mandamus should issue "in cases warranted by the principles and usages of law" to any persons "holding office under the authority of the United States."

Subtly approaching his ultimate ruling, however, Marshall had divided the final question into two parts—one, whether mandamus should issue, and the other, whether it could issue from this Court. If it could not, the reason had to be that the Court lacked jurisdiction over the case—something, as already noted, which should have been settled at the outset. But the Chief Justice was now, and only now, ready to take up the jurisdictional—and thus the constitutional—question. Whether (as some have consistently charged since 1803) Marshall had taken elaborate pains to create a false dilemma, or whether he properly anticipated that the 1789 statute *could* be applied in a manner in conflict with the Constitution, the fact remained that the Court had not set down the constitutional question, upon which the rule of decision was now to be based, for argument by counsel, as would be the usual modern procedure.[23] His eyes fixed on the paramount importance of establishing the role of a strong judiciary in a strong national government, Marshall proceeded on his own initiative and inspiration to his epochal conclusion.

Marshall declared:

It is emphatically the province and duty of the judicial department, to say what the law is. Those who apply the rule to particular cases, must of necessity expound and interpret that rule. If two laws conflict with each other, the courts must decide on the operation of each.

So if a law be in opposition to the Constitution: if both the law and the Constitution apply to a particular case, so that the Court must either decide that case conformably to the law, disregarding the Constitution; or conformably to the Constitution, disregarding the law; the Court must determine which of these conflicting rules governs the case. This is of the very essence of judicial duty.

If, then, the courts are to regard the Constitution, and the Constitution is superior to any ordinary act of the legislature, the Constitution, and not such ordinary act, must govern the case to which they both apply.

Those then who controvert the principle that the Constitution is to be considered, in court, as a paramount law, are reduced to the necessity of maintaining that courts must close their eyes on the Constitution, and see only the law.

This doctrine would subvert the very foundation of all written constitutions. It would declare that an act which, according to the principles and theory of our government, is entirely void, is yet, in practice, completely obligatory. . . .

It is also not entirely unworthy of observation, that in declaring what shall be the *supreme* law of the land, the *Constitution* itself is first mentioned; and not the laws of the United States generally, but only those which shall be made in *pursuance* of the Constitution, have that rank.

Thus, the particular phraseology of the Constitution of the United States confirms and strengthens the principle, supposed to be essential to all written constitutions, that a law repugnant to the Constitution is void; and that *courts,* as well as other departments, are bound by that instrument.

Thus, upon what were rather tenuous premises, the concept of judicial review was pronounced as an inherent, or "necessary and proper," power of the judiciary. Contemporary reaction was generally less passionate than the preliminary and collateral attacks on judicial authority might have suggested. Ordinary judicial review, of nonconstitutional matters, was by definition the very essence of the appellate process. Even constitutional judicial review seemed to be accepted by the majority, and Jefferson would only have disputed the narrowness of the doctrine, insisting that other branches of government had equal power to determine constitutional meaning and limits.[24] The principal criticism of the *Marbury* decision, Jeffersonian and otherwise, was that it was itself dictum masquerading as a rule of decision—that the doctrine, in other words, was not essential to the disposition of the case.

The general acceptance of the outcome of the case may also be explained by the fact that a kind of code of chivalry obtained, between the various leaders of government, in this early period of the republic. It was still a small and intimate society of elite, despite the voluble Republican credo of the yeoman. As professional lawyers (and, for that matter, professional politicians), all sides conceded the adroitness of the Court in this intellectual passage of arms. It is notable that the Republican Congress made no serious effort to rewrite the jurisdictional provisions in the judiciary statutes, in the aftermath of *Marbury* and in the heat of the impeachment efforts directed at the courts. The *Laird* decision, dismissing without comment the appeal from Marshall's own Circuit Court opinion denying a challenge to Congressional authority to eliminate judicial positions once created, was a kind of quid pro quo in the circumstances.

The fact remains that more than half a century was to elapse before the Court again would assert its right to hold an act of Congress unconstitutional—in the Dred Scott case in 1857. The Marshall Court was concerned with defining constitutional sources of strength for a national government, Congress particularly included. On the other hand, the process of construing a strong judiciary required that the ultimate authority of the courts to test the constitutional limits to the powers of government must be applied to the executive as well as the legislative branch. In *Marbury,* after making elaborate arguments on the rights and obligations of the executive, Marshall had then based his pivotal holding on the reviewability of acts of the legislature. It remained to apply the reviewability doctrine to the executive branch whenever a proper case arose upon which to base the rule. That opportunity presented itself, four years later, in the celebrated treason trial of Aaron Burr.

III

The Supreme Court and the President

United States v. *Burr*

For the westward-moving Americans in the first generation after the Revolution, and into the early nineteenth century, the wilderness beyond the early seaboard settlements was filled with mystery and opportunity. The opportunity would provide the unique element in the American character for the next hundred years, until the last of the enormous expanse of territory had been converted into states; adventurers eager to explore and exploit the seemingly inexhaustible wealth of the continent poured across the Alleghenies and over the Ohio-Mississippi-Missouri waterways in a growing flood. The Northwest Territory—the "old Northwest" from which came five states and part of a sixth—was organized in 1787 as one of the last acts of the moribund Continental Congress. Before the end of the century, the territory "south-west of the river Ohio" was similarly organized, with three future states to be created therefrom. By 1803, Kentucky, Tennessee, and Ohio had in fact been admitted to the Union.

Mystery and wondrous works also bedazzled the frontier social order. In western New York, various religious revelations were experienced by whole communities, a product of the mingling of many variants of the New England theocracy from which most of the settlers had come. Cut off from the older cultures and resources of their past, many a visionary saw himself as the founder of a new order in a beckoning destiny to the West. One such was Joseph Smith, who founded Mormonism; another was Harman Blennerhasset, who established on an island in the Ohio River a feudal manor complete with Old World art and riches—and dreamed of yet more marvelous achievements. For men like this, all events assumed larger-than-life proportions in this strange New World.[1]

Far to the south, in the French-Spanish city of New Orleans near the mouth of the Mississippi, the dreams of the western leaders seemed to reach their apogee. An exotic culture, the product of nearly a century of evolution, endowed it with glamor. What was of far greater practical importance was the fact that it was the natural port for the marketing of western produce, infinitely more accessible than the old Atlantic seaports. All that was needed was to make it an American possession, and for a decade a variety of schemes had been devised to bring this about. Colonial administrations, either French or Spanish, appeared vulnerable to direct military adventure; an alternative was a recurrent proposal to separate the western territory altogether from the young American republic and join with New Orleans in a vast new empire.[2]

Aaron Burr was therefore only the latest in a line of speculators and empire builders who were caught up in these grand designs when, after his term of office as Vice-President of the United States ended in March 1805, he eventually moved westward to seek to remake his own fortune. There was nowhere else in America for him; his fatal duel with Alexander Hamilton in the summer of 1804 had ended his legal and political career in New York, and Jefferson made it clear that there was no future, after the close of their first administration, for him in Republican national politics. Restless, brilliant, unstable, ambitious—Burr in this period and the dazzling, enigmatic aspects of the new West were made for each other. Only in this area could such a man snatch a new career from the apocalypse of the previous two years.

What Burr ultimately intended to do has remained unclear to this day; in all likelihood, his first impulses in this situation were essentially opportunistic. Whenever the main chance manifested itself, he would seize upon it—whether this meant an imperialistic war against Spanish Mexico, a secession of the West from the Union, or both, or, as he steadfastly maintained, the development of a land scheme on the Louisiana–Texas border known as the Bastrop Grant. From the outset, however, his behavior was enough to arouse suspicion in a national government already concerned with recurrent rumors of separatism in the unknown wilderness. The first stop in Burr's odyssey was Blennerhasset's island, that improbable feudal manor in the Ohio; thence to New Orleans and back into the fastnesses of Kentucky and Tennessee.

Even before he had left office, the Vice-President had spent a number of months, from the summer of 1804 to the spring of 1805, indulging in all manner of discussions. Even when in flight from the scene of the fatal duel with Hamilton, he had taken time in New Jersey to make big talk with a naval officer, Commodore Thomas Truxton, about a seaborne adventure against Spanish Florida or Mexico. Later on that same journey, in Philadelphia, Burr had met the British minister, Anthony Merry, and their conversations subsequently were reported to have dealt with Great Britain's underwriting a plan to separate the trans-Allegheny region from the rest of the United States. In due course, Burr and Wilkinson had even talked with the Spanish minister, Casa Yrujo, who leaked the information back to Washington, where Jefferson added it to the portfolio of intelligence against the enigmatic New Yorker.

By now Burr had come to some sort of understanding with Blenner-hasset, who seemed to be endowed with a powerful Gaelic imagination, and with General James Wilkinson, commander of American military forces in the lower Mississippi. By the fall of 1806 it was rumored that men and arms were being assembled at Blennerhasset's island, and flat-boats constructed to carry them somewhere. Jefferson became alarmed and, on November 27, 1806, issued a public proclamation warning against aiding and abetting the former Vice-President (see Part Three, Chapter II-1). It was a belated warning, whatever Burr was up to; for more than two years—before his term as Vice-President had expired—Burr had been consulting with Wilkinson, who had long since become a secret agent of Spain and who spoke of dazzling opportunities in the Gulf Coast, where Mexico was in virtual insurrection against Madrid and New Orleans leaders were reported discontented with their lot under the new American authorities.

Already, in July 1806, Burr had prepared a coded letter to Wilkinson, confirming his own preparations for a joint venture and advising that his flotilla of riverboats with men and supplies would be starting down the Ohio within a month. He concluded his message with a flourish, declaring, "the gods invite us to glory and fortune." [3] This fateful communication was entrusted to one of his young hero-worshipers, Samuel Swartwout, who, with another emissary, Dr. J. Erich Bollman, set out for New Orleans to alert Wilkinson.

But by now Wilkinson—agent number thirteen in Madrid's secret foreign files—had begun to fear for his own skin. American pressure on Spain had resolved what had until then seemed like an inevitable clash of arms on the Texas frontier, and a torrent of rumors about Burr and his grandiose plans threatened to expose Wilkinson as a co-conspirator. The general began hastily to extricate himself and assume the role of a loyal soldier; when Swartwout and Bollman appeared with their message from Burr, they were arrested and clapped aboard a ship to be taken to Washington—a slow passage which gave Wilkinson time to send by overland courier his own version of the events, which touched off Jefferson's alarm.

Meanwhile Burr, unaware of the betrayal, completed his plans and set off—despite a raid on Blennerhasset's island in his absence, which scattered a number of would-be followers and resulted in the destruction of several of his boats and much of Blennerhasset's once imposing estate. Sometime later, when his remaining flotilla arrived at Natchez, Burr learned for the first time of the trap that Wilkinson had waiting for him in New Orleans. It could not have come as a complete surprise, however; news of Jefferson's proclamation by now had spread throughout the West, and, indeed, Burr's departure from the Ohio had been delayed by two efforts of United States attorneys to secure indictments against him. In personal appearances before the grand juries, Burr had defeated both attempts.

But Wilkinson's treachery made it clear that the game was up; a third attempt at indictment, by a grand jury in Mississippi Territory, was also defeated, but Burr knew what lay ahead in New Orleans, and fled in disguise into the southern wilderness. On March 6, 1807, the former Vice-President was recognized and captured, and three weeks later, having made a prisoner's march overland to Richmond, he was committed to jail. America was about to witness its first major state trial—of a man already pronounced by Jefferson as guilty of treason in a special message to Congress (see Part Three, Chapter II-2). A stream of attorneys, as well as rabid partisans, began to converge on Richmond and the sensational proceedings expected in the United States Circuit Court (which had jurisdiction over Blennerhasset's island).[4]

How firmly Thomas Jefferson believed in Aaron Burr's treason was as difficult to determine as Burr's real objectives in the lower Mississippi. The President had committed an impropriety in declaring Burr's guilt before his trial, to say the least, and some apologists later saw it as part of the frustration bred of the *Chesapeake* outrage, when a British warship in American waters had boarded an American vessel in search of British-born seamen. After seizing crewmen and setting fire to the ship, the British had sailed away without challenge. It was one of many signs of the desperate weakness of the young nation in the vortex of continuing struggles of European colonial powers. Who could say how long the United States would be permitted to continue its independent existence or to hold the vast territories beyond the Mississippi which Napoleon had recently sold to the Americans?

Napoleon was now launched upon his campaigns of conquest, with clear warnings to the New World that he would deal with it at his pleasure. Spain, outraged at the sale of Louisiana to the United States, had rejected American overtures for a reduction of tensions. As for Great Britain, the news of Burr's apparent conspiracy reached Jefferson almost at the same time as the harsh terms of a treaty which Washington had hoped would settle the question of impressment of American sailors. Now Wilkinson's carefully doctored letters, which purported to establish Burr's treason, proved the final straw. Here, at least, was a chance for the harassed republic to show a strong hand.

But fate had decreed that the treason trial of Aaron Burr should be a second meeting place for those foredestined antagonists, Jefferson and Chief Justice Marshall. Under the Jeffersonians' own Judiciary Act of 1802, the chore of riding circuit by Supreme Court members had been reinstituted, after the abortive Federalist legislation which had sought to create separate judgeships for the circuits. And the new Fifth * Circuit, with its principal court in Richmond, was (as it has remained ever since) the Chief Justice's Circuit. Marshall himself, therefore, would preside at the trial of this "crime of the century," sometimes sitting alone in the course of the coming months and sometimes sitting with District Judge Cyrus Griffin. In either case, Burr would have the highest as well as the most experienced judicial officers in the federal system for his trial: Griffin had been a national judge before there had been a Constitution, serving on the old Court of Appeals established by the Continental Congress for almost a decade.[5]

Marshall, as presiding officer of the Circuit Court, was to issue the orders and opinions required in the involved procedural struggles in the course of the trials. On Monday, March 30, Burr was turned over to the court by the military guard which had brought him to Richmond from the depths of the Mississippi wilderness, whereupon the government prosecutors and Burr's lawyers began the first arguments, over probable cause for charging the former Vice-President with unlawful acts and over the admissibility of the accused to bail. Two days later, the Chief Justice gave in an opinion on the elements constituting treason (see Part Three, Chapter II-7), ruled that the government had failed to support the treason charge with its evidence, and thereupon admitted Burr to bail in the amount of $10,000. Burr was directed to appear at the term beginning May 22, some seven weeks later.[6]

In the ensuing time, the President prodded his prosecutor vigorously, assuring him that there was more than enough evidence to support a treason charge. When the new term began, U.S. Attorney George Hay advised Marshall that he intended to move to commit Burr on the basis of further evidence now to be submitted to the grand jury. Marshall agreed to hear the motion, but at the same time read into the record his concern at "any attempt which may be made to prejudice the public judgment, and to try any person, not by the laws of his country and the testimony exhibited against him, but by public feelings which may be and often are artificially excited against the innocent as well as the guilty." [7] After this public notice of the mounting Jeffersonian efforts to whip up public enmity for the defendant, Marshall indicated to Hay that he could proceed with his motion.

* Virginia was placed in the Fifth Circuit by the Jeffersonians' act of 1802, and remained in that Circuit for forty years. Before and since, it has been in the Fourth Circuit.

Again, as in *Marbury* four years before, a major constitutional issue was to be thrashed out by men who knew each other intimately in a social microcosm soon to be broken forever by the accelerating western movement. In this hour, however, a professional elite appeared together: Griffin had admitted Marshall himself to practice years before. The chief prosecutor was George Hay, whom Jefferson had appointed United States Attorney for the Virginia District, who had known Marshall from their younger days in Williamsburg, and who was to marry the eldest daughter of James Monroe, Jefferson's minister in the tough negotiations with Great Britain. William Wirt, who would be Hay's co-counsel, was widely known in Richmond's social circles for his gossipy *Letters of a British Spy,* published there in 1803. And among the several distinguished lawyers summoned to Burr's defense were Edmund Randolph, first Attorney General of the United States, and Luther Martin of Maryland. Martin had been one of the defense counsel for Justice Samuel Chase in his recent impeachment trial and more recently had attracted something of a scandal by his "idolatrous admiration" for Burr's beautiful daughter Theodosia.[8]

John Wickham, another of Burr's lawyers, was yet another example of the closeness of the American bar of these times. A friend and neighbor of Marshall's in Richmond, he had been opposing counsel in the 1793 case of *Ware* v. *Hylton* (3 Dallas 199) with the winning argument in favor of the paramountcy of treaty law made under the authority of the Constitution. While Wickham would inadvertently embarrass the Chief Justice in the course of Burr's freedom on bail, by inviting both men, among many others, to one of the "lawyers' dinners" in which both Marshall and Wickham delighted, he would subsequently provide the constitutional argument for a narrow definition of the law of treason on which the Chief Justice ultimately instructed the jury in the trial in late August.

Many "beautiful people" were coming to Richmond for the trial, in fact: Theodosia and her husband, Governor John Alston of South Carolina, would be on hand; Andrew Jackson of Tennessee, already involved in more than one Burr-like land-grabbing deal in the West as well as several duels of the Burr–Hamilton type; and Washington Irving, onetime law student, peripatetic wit, and now a newspaper commentator at the trial (between periods of being lionized by Richmond society). The town was jammed with legal and political leaders, intellectuals, curiosity seekers, and—as it would prove—mobs of partisans to be mobilized and manipulated by the Jeffersonians as the case proceeded. Except for the vulgar noises of the latter, the scene was to be that of a major social event, exciting conversation in salons and taverns and provoking out-of-court comment on the trial in progress until the chances of avoiding prejudice to a fair hearing on the case became highly conjectural.

In these circumstances, it was all but inevitable that Jefferson and

Marshall should be drawn personally into the churning emotions of a "crime of state." Certainly, from Washington or Monticello, the President avidly followed the progress of the case, consulting regularly with George Hay on the procedural aspects and with his Virginia crony, William B. Giles, on the political aspects. Hay saw the problem as one of paucity of evidence; after all, three grand juries had refused to return indictments of Burr on this same question. Jefferson assured Hay that in his opinion there was ample evidence—the damning "cypher" letter sent by Wilkinson and, if that were not conclusive, the testimony in open court of Wilkinson himself and a fellow officer, William Eaton (see Part Three, Chapter II-3).

The letter might prove to be the key to the prosecution. There were strong indications that Wilkinson had edited and amended the original, and possibly invented his own key for transcribing the message from code. Jefferson may have discerned this when he received either the original or Wilkinson's draft version. Burr certainly suspected that the document was spurious and knew that a reasonable doubt as to the authenticity of the letter itself or the transcription would demolish a major part of the government's case. The obvious defense strategy, therefore, was to compel production of the document or documents in order to examine and challenge them.

But compelling production would be a thorny matter indeed. The documents were in the possession of the President, and Marshall's initial suggestion to Hay that a copy would not be admissible as "best evidence" had been unavailing. Jefferson, for whatever ultimate reasons, reacted violently to Hay's report of the Chief Justice's position. Giles, ever at the President's side, darkly declared that the judiciary was bent upon completing the unfinished business of *Marbury,* to subjugate the executive as it had already subjugated the legislative branch of government. The cipher letter and the affidavits of Wilkinson and others charging Burr with treason were becoming a time bomb in the administration. (See Part Three, Chapter II-4.)

Jefferson had dealt ambivalently with these documents before, in responding to demands for their production by Congress following his remarkable message of January 22 in which he had said of Burr that his "guilt is placed beyond question." When Congress, including many members of his own party, had insisted upon some supporting evidence, the President had sent copies of some documents, but had refrained from pointing out that the notorious coded message from Burr was obviously in response to an inquiry from Wilkinson. Even more astounding had been the executive department's behavior in seeking to block, by special emergency legislation, the efforts to secure habeas corpus for Wilkinson's first victims, Swartwout and Bollman. While Giles had been able to push the legislation through the Senate, a House revolt defeated the maneuver, and the defendants, together with two others sent from New Orleans by Wilkinson, had been granted their releases.[9]

Burr had every reason to believe, therefore, that production of the documents—the cipher letter, the affidavits of Wilkinson and Eaton and others, and the accompanying military orders—would reveal their inconclusive, and indeed insubstantial, nature. He moved boldly, then, to seek issuance of a subpoena *duces tecum* (literally, "under penalty, come and bring with you"), directing the President of the United States to appear at the trial with the evidence upon which the government was basing its prosecution. Now, at length, the drama for which Richmond and the rest of the country had been waiting erupted: must a sitting President obey an order of the judicial branch when the latter determined that the order was essential to the administration of a fair trial for an accused? (See Part Three, Chapter II-5.)

George Hay, the prosecuting attorney, was in an unenviable, and perhaps impossible, position. As an officer of the court he was bound to carry out its orders without qualification; but he was also Jefferson's direct agent in the conduct of the case against the accused. With the issuance of the subpoena by the Chief Justice, he was compelled to advise his commander-in-chief in this politicolegal battle not to seek to defy the court. Marshall had already excoriated Hay in the preliminary hearings for failure to produce acceptable evidence; the subpoena now ordered him to produce it.

The propriety, if not the constitutionality, of the subpoena had been passionately argued—so passionately, indeed, that Marshall had had to admonish the attorneys for both sides. But after the argument, it remained for the Chief Justice to deal with the basic questions—the right of a defendant "before, as well as after indictment, to the process of the court to compel attendance of his witnesses" and the power of the court to issue such process against the highest executive officer in the government.[10]

The threshold question, the Chief Justice stated, concerned the guarantees in the Constitution to a speedy and public trial with every reasonable safeguard for the defendant's right to assemble evidence in his defense. Was this "something more than a dead letter?" Congress had affirmatively intended that it should be, Marshall ruled, because it had provided in the procedural act which accompanied the Judiciary Act of 1789 [11] that "in all capital cases, the accused shall be entitled to process before indictment found." Nothing in the Constitution or the statute exempted anyone from this process, he pointed out, and the logical conclusion to be drawn from this fact was that the character of the document rather than "the character of the person who holds it" determined whether the court had the duty to issue the writ.

Marshall, however, was so keenly aware of the political sensitivities involved in the question that he had made two rhetorical missteps in his opinion. In the first place, he had made a comment that the prosecution "expected" a conviction—a prejudicial statement almost as grave as Jefferson's public declaration of Burr's guilt. Hay and one of his associates, Alexander MacRae, instantly rose to proclaim that the phrase betrayed the court's own bias against the President. In the second instance, Marshall had warned that "the hand of malignity" should not be permitted to bar an accused person from his constitutional rights—another phrase that Jefferson took personally.[12]

The Chief Justice, discomfited, assured Hay that he would expunge the first phrase from the final version of the opinion, but this did nothing to allay the President's fury when his prosecuting attorney duly reported the words to him. What was much more galling to the President, however, was the fact that the issuing of the subpoena was generally greeted with enthusiasm by the overwhelmingly pro-Republican public in Richmond. Even that rabid spokesman for the Jeffersonians, Thomas Ritchie of the Richmond *Enquirer,* had no fault to find with this action. By a singular paradox the Federalist Chief Justice found himself momentarily in the role of champion of one of the most fundamental of democratic principles, the constitutional guarantee of equal justice to all persons against all others. Even Thomas Jefferson, that self-proclaimed defender of such equality, was now in the position of being compelled to demonstrate his adherence to the principle by submitting to a court mandate.

The President's resentment at being placed in this position was now reflected not against Marshall, but against Luther Martin, one of Burr's attorneys. In the excited view of the Executive, Martin was clearly privy to Burr's conspiracy, and therefore was an unindicted co-conspirator (assuming there were to be any indictments), guilty of "misprision of treason at least." For that matter, Jefferson declared, all of the lawyers who defended Burr "are all his accomplices." [13] Having thus vented his frustrations, the President allowed reason and his own legal knowledge to regain control while he wrote to Hay, setting out his case against the issuance of the subpoena. He did, indeed, begin with a criticism of Marshall: "As is usual where an opinion is to be supported, right or wrong, he dwells much on smaller objections, and passes over those which are solid." If the Constitution required the Chief Executive to be continually responsible for the interests of the whole nation ("the concerns of 6. millions of people"), ought any single defendant be able to compel him to set aside these responsibilities and appear personally before a court? What if the sheriff were to summon the Chief Justice from the bench to join a posse or the lower courts were to subpoena the Justices of the Supreme Court? [14]

The argument cogently expressed Jefferson's own concept of the separation of powers; indeed, Marshall himself, in his opinion on the subpoena, had conceded that the duties incumbent on the President might "demand his whole time for national objects." However, once again Marshall permitted personal gibing to compromise his argument, gratuitously observing that such demand "is not unremitting"—a statement which Jefferson took to criticize his habit of retiring to Monticello "during the sickly season" in Washington.

Thus punctuated with the pettiness of both sides, Marshall and the President rested their cases; Hay, of course, remained under court order to see that his client—the President—obeyed the subpoena. Meantime, the sensations in the trial in Richmond were building up. James Wilkinson, commanding general of the armies of the West, had arrived in the city in full uniform, "with ten witnesses, eight of them Burr's select men." Whatever might be said of the eight, two were clearly Wilkinson's creatures— General William Eaton, a dissolute career officer whose claims against the government were suddenly settled when he agreed to be a prosecution witness; and Sergeant Jacob Dunbaugh, who had been demoted from his rank and then restored to it when he also agreed to testify with Wilkinson.[15]

If Jefferson had expected Wilkinson to present such powerful testimony that there would be no practical effect of submitting the subpoenaed documents, he was quickly to be disappointed. The pompous general was subjected to a devastating interrogation which led the grand jury to propose his own indictment, a maneuver that barely failed, 7 to 9, to win a majority of the sixteen jurymen. In court and out, the self-serving general was quickly and universally marked as a scoundrel; hardbitten Andrew Jackson, as Hay reported, unhesitatingly denounced Wilkinson "in the coarsest terms in every company." John Randolph, foreman of the grand jury and a cousin of Edmund Randolph, one of Burr's counsel, expressed his own private regret that a rascal had been allowed to escape justice.[16]

There remained the matter of a return on the subpoena. Jefferson now proposed to Hay that, while as President he would continue to refuse to appear at the bar, the relevant documents be turned over to Hay and the Attorney General of the United States, Caesar A. Rodney (whose father, Thomas Rodney, had been the Mississippi territorial judge at Burr's third grand jury). Hay and Rodney were to scan the documents for any matters vital to the national interest and withhold them from the drafts then to be delivered to Marshall. In due course, Hay made the delivery; and the Chief Justice, recognizing that a confrontation with the Chief Executive had been carried as far as it could be allowed to go, accepted the copies as substantial compliance with the subpoena.

Thus the two branches of government drew back from an attempt to force the ultimate issue of a President's answerability to a judicial mandate. Marshall considered that the principle had been vindicated; Jefferson was satisfied that he had successfully maintained the principle of separation of powers. The question was, by everyone's agreement, one of exceeding delicacy; the Chief Justice, indeed, conceded that "vexatious and unnecessary" subpoenas were not to be countenanced as against the Chief Executive. They only became necessary when Presidential material was "essential to the justice of the case." [17]

Thus the matter of the Supreme Court's ultimate authority over the executive branch, in such circumstances, was to remain unsettled for more than a century and a half. *United States* v. *Burr,* of course, was a series of opinions in a criminal trial.[18] The case was never carried on appeal to the high court because of the ultimate acquittal of the defendant on the treason charge (see Part One, Chapter IV). Treason itself became something of an anomaly as the country matured; the attempt to try Jefferson Davis on such grounds, after the Civil War, came to an indeterminate end, thanks to the strict definition of the constitutional requirements as expressed by Marshall in 1807. After World War II, the Supreme Court eventually upheld two out of three treason convictions, in 1947 and 1952.[19]

As for other issues on which to test the question of Presidential accountability to the judiciary, it was not until 1974—167 years after the Burr case in Richmond—that the Supreme Court at last came to the ultimate disposition of the constitutional issue reflected in the Jefferson subpoena. In the Watergate tapes case (*United States* v. *Nixon*),[20] an 8-to-0 opinion of the Court declared:

> [Two arguments are advanced.] The first contention is a broad claim that the separation of powers doctrine precludes judicial review of a President's claim of privilege. The second contention is that if he does not prevail on the claim of absolute privilege, the court should hold as a matter of constitutional law that the privilege prevails over the subpoena *duces tecum.*

Thus the two propositions expressed respectively by Marshall and Jefferson in 1807 were to be reduced to a balancing test. Indeed, the Nixon administration had substantially compromised its position by insisting upon a self-defined and self-executing concept of executive privilege (a term not mentioned in the executive article of the Constitution) and confusing it with what English constitutional law describes as executive (i. e., Crown) prerogative.[21] In either case, privilege/prerogative was subject to qualification—in English practice by action of Parliament, and now in American practice by action of the courts:

In the performance of assigned constitutional duties each branch of the government must initially interpret the Constitution and the interpretation of its powers by any branch is due great respect from the others.[22]

Jefferson's basic premise was thus accommodated. But the Court then went on to point out that when a serious question of correctness of such interpretation arises, "it is emphatically the province and duty of the judicial department to say what the law is." And it was no novelty, the Court went on, to find that the courts "on occasion interpret the Constitution in a manner at variance with the construction given the document by another branch." The principle which was controlling was the principle established by *Marbury*—neither the executive nor the legislative branches of government could be the final arbiters of their own constitutional powers.[23] Thus Jefferson's premise was to be qualified by Marshall's:

In support of his claim of absolute privilege, the President's counsel urges two grounds, one of which is common to all governments and one of which is peculiar to our system of separation of powers. The first ground is the valid need of protection of communications between high government officials and those who advise and assist them in the performance of their manifold duties; the importance of this confidentiality is too plain to require further discussion. . . . Whatever the nature of the privilege of confidentiality of Presidential communications in the exercise of Article II powers, the privilege can be said to derive from the supremacy of each branch within its own assigned area of constitutional duties. Certain powers and privileges flow from the nature of enumerated powers; the protection of the confidentiality of Presidential communications has similar constitutional underpinnings.[24]

With this statement, the Court vindicated the Marshall thesis that the Constitution provided "necessary and proper" powers for each of the three branches of government (see Part Two, Chapter I, pages 104–105). But acceptance of the first ground, for an executive version of the "privileges and immunities" clause of Article I, did not sustain a claim of unqualified executive prerogative under the separation of powers ground.

However, neither the doctrine of separation of powers, nor the need for confidentiality of high level communications, without more, can sustain an absolute, unqualified Presidential privilege of immunity from judicial process under all circumstances. The President's need for complete candor and objectivity from advisers calls for great deference from the courts. However, when the privilege depends solely on the broad, undifferentiated claim of public interest in the confidentiality of such conversations, a confrontation with other values arises. Absent a claim of need to protect military, diplomatic, or sensitive national security secrets, we find it difficult to accept the argument that even the very important interest of Presidential communications is significantly diminished by production of such material for *in camera* inspection, with all the protection that a district court will be obliged to provide.

The impediment that an absolute, unqualified privilege would place in the way of the primary constitutional duty of the Judicial Branch to do justice in criminal prosecutions would plainly conflict with the function of the courts under Article III. In designing the structure of our government and dividing and allocating the sovereign power among three co-equal branches, the Framers of the Constitution sought to provide a comprehensive system, but the separate powers were not intended to operate with absolute independence.[25]

Thus, at last, the principle for which John Marshall had stood firm in 1807 was upheld by the Supreme Court in 1974. The reviewability of the constitutional powers of Congress, which had been established by *Marbury v. Madison* in 1803, required a logical complement of reviewability of the constitutional powers of the Executive, which was finally established on the eve of the republic's two hundredth anniversary.

IV

The Supreme Court and the Individual

United States v. *Burr*

Aaron Burr, Harman Blennerhasset, and others were formally indicted for treason by the Circuit Court grand jury on June 24, 1807. The great constitutional issue represented in the Jefferson subpoena never aroused sustained public excitement in comparison with the growing fascination with the Burr personality. For Richmond society as well as for substantial numbers of Republicans, the former Vice-President was becoming a popular figure; while there were die-hard Federalists who saw him as the killer of Washington's protégé Hamilton, very few condemned him for the duel itself—the code of honor would be observed punctiliously in the Old Dominion for years yet to come.[1] So far, moreover, Burr had come off victoriously from each judicial test of the past several weeks: he had been able to win his release on bail over the strong opposition of government counsel; his confederates, Swartwout and Bollman, had joined him in Richmond after a successful appeal for their release from detention in Washington, and Swartwout publicly spurned Jefferson's offer of a pardon which he said would have been tantamount to an admission of guilt.

That this should be happening in Jefferson's own commonwealth was also a measure of the rough sailing which the administration had been undergoing ever since the beginning of the President's second term. An intraparty revolt, led by John Randolph of Roanoke, raged enthusiastically from the winter of 1806 to the end of the Jefferson years, with those who opposed the President looking toward James Monroe as their candidate for his successor, as against the heir apparent, James Madison. While the administration forces eventually beat back Randolph's challenge in Congress, a powerful anti-Jefferson force was building up in Virginia itself, ready to rally around a figure with a national following.[2] Burr, with his magnetic mannerisms, offered the best opportunity for the moment: his immense popularity in the new West was attested by the general conviction that he could readily secure election to the Senate from any state in which he might choose to establish residence. Jefferson, who had believed he had witnessed Burr's political demise the previous year, now was nagged by the possibility that a phoenix was about to rise from the ashes of his former career.

Chief Justice Marshall as well was enjoying considerable popularity in his home town of Richmond. Among the brilliant lawyers of that city, professional admiration for Marshall's judicial adroitness would always run high; and as Chief Justice he was continuing his practice of "lawyers' dinners," at which stimulating conversation ranging over the whole field of law and politics was the standard fare. It became common, in the summer of 1807, to see various parties of ladies and gentlemen feting both Burr and Marshall, the chief defendant and the presiding judge in the coming treason trial. The situation was fraught with potential for a compromising incident—indeed, on one occasion, when both men unexpectedly turned up at the same gathering, the Jeffersonians were presented with a providential opportunity to scream prejudicial behavior.

With the mounting concern at Burr's Richmond popularity, the Jeffersonians were eager to mount a countermove. The humiliating affair of the *Chesapeake* had occurred two days before the indictments; and, unable to retaliate for Britain's arrogant behavior, the Jeffersonians quickly turned the national fury against the domestic scapegoat. What was manifestly necessary was to inflame the yeomen—the mobs which in earlier times the President had tended to disdain. Now they were to be organized to shout down the growing sentiment for Burr so that by the time of the actual trial there would be outright terror raging in the streets.

The administration was also unhappy at Burr's relative freedom of movement pending his trial; the fact that he was confined at night in locked and guarded rooms in the house of Luther Martin was hardly reassuring in the light of Jefferson's view of Martin himself. Upon strenuous representations by George Hay, the prosecutor, and a formal offer from the Virginia executive council of a more secure apartment in the state penitentiary, Marshall eventually transferred the prisoner there. However, to the government's chagrin, this did not dampen the ardor of the friends of the defendant; a steady stream of callers came to see him in the new institution, while messengers daily brought "oranges, lemons, pineapples, raspberries, cream, butter, ice and some ordinary articles," as Burr wrote to his daughter.[3] Soon the beautiful Theodosia, with her husband and infant son, arrived in Richmond, creating fresh sensations and sympathies.

Both Jefferson and Marshall, however, realized that this synthetic heroism posed a threat to the country, tempting other attention-seekers to some desperate adventures. The Federalist zeal for secession in New England was mounting, with rumors that the administration was planning a general embargo in retaliation for British outrages—an embargo which would predominantly affect northeastern commerce. To the southeast, the fire-eating Andrew Jackson was ever ready for fresh attempts to take Florida from the Spanish or to begin the task of clearing out the Indian tribes from the beckoning lands of the Mississippi Territory. It was an apocalyptic time, and both the Chief Justice and the Chief Executive perceived that the republic might be torn apart by the zeal of its friends as much as by its enemies. Unfortunately, the old antagonists were bound to come to different, and opposing, solutions to the problem.

For Jefferson, a public example of the prosecution, conviction, and punishment of the former Vice-President would appease the national passions and furnish an example of national will. For Marshall, the increasingly urgent need was to insure that Burr's trial would establish explicit constitutional criteria for such prosecutions in general and for the constitutional rights of accused persons in particular. Marshall turned to his colleagues on the Supreme Court for counsel as he began preparations for the trial itself. There ought to be some common agreement as to the American law of treason, he wrote, not only for guidance of the court in the case now coming on, but as a means of forestalling conflicting definitions in various circuits where other treason trials seemed likely to arise.[4]

The fundamental question was the manner in which treason was to be defined. Under the ancient common law the definition was broad and general, admitting almost any action offensive to the sovereign; but already the English constitution had moved away from that—the Treason Trials Act of 1695[5] had introduced the requirement of testimony of two separate witnesses to the same overt act. John Marshall had no problem, therefore, in concluding that the same language appearing in the Constitution (Article III, Section 3) would require this proof by the prosecution. Moreover, the only overt acts of treason allowed by the Constitution were the actual levying of war against the United States or giving aid and comfort to its enemies. Thus the trial would turn upon the issue of whether the levying of war had to be done in person or whether it could be done constructively, i. e., by judicial attribution.

The only site within the jurisdiction of the Circuit Court where such an overt act could have taken place was Blennerhasset's island. The only incident to be offered in proof of the act was the assembling of men and supplies for an apparent martial purpose in support of Burr's alleged conspiracy. At the time of the raid on the island by government agents, Burr himself was hundreds of miles away. For Hay and Jefferson, the facts uncovered in the raid were sufficient to support the charge of treason, while Burr's constructive liability was thought to be provable by language used by the Chief Justice himself in the habeas corpus appeal of Bollman and Swartwout (see Part Three, Chapter II-6). However, Hay wrote to the

President on August 11, warning that the trial court might now rule that the habeas corpus opinion was not controlling in the current case and that the facts uncovered on Blennerhasset's island did not constitute an act of actual levying of war.[6]

Hay made a strong opening statement to the jury, quoting Marshall's own words in the Bollman–Swartwout case before the Supreme Court. That opinion had said that if there were an actual levying of war, "all those who perform any part, however minute, or however remote from the scene of action, and who are actually leagued in the general conspiracy, are to be considered as traitors." But Burr and his lawyers made a shrewd counterargument: they contended that the overt act itself must first be proved before admitting any collateral testimony. Marshall eventually ruled that the government could introduce its evidence in either order, provided that the evidence went to the actual act of treason.

The testimony of the first prosecution witnesses was virtually a fiasco: no one could confirm that there had been more than twenty-five or thirty men on Blennerhasset's island at the time of the raid or that more than a handful of guns were in their possession. As to Blennerhasset himself, who fled at the approach of government agents, his visible materials for the great adventure consisted of his apparatus for chemical experiments, books of literature, and his violin. As to Burr, the government stipulated that he was nowhere near the scene at the time.

The denouement in the prosecution—handicapped as it was by the reticence or inability of the President to provide prima facie evidence to support the treason charge—came with the testimony and devastating cross-examination of General William Eaton on August 17. With much bombast, to which Burr and his counsel shrewdly made no objection, Eaton delivered from the witness box the standard administration argument: He himself had warned the President, Eaton proclaimed, of a "central general revolution" in the western territories, the purpose of the warning being "to avert a great national calamity which I saw approaching." [7]

Under direct examination, the general further asserted that Burr had offered—and Eaton had rejected—the opportunity to assume a key role in the developing adventure. The court reporter's transcript of the cross-examination, first by Martin and then by Burr himself, preserves the ripostes across the years:

MARTIN: "Do you recollect any particular conduct of yours calculated to put an end to Colonel Burr's importunities?"

EATON: "Yes. At some of our last interviews I laid on his table a paper containing the toast which I had given to the public, with an intention that he should see it . . . 'The United States: Palsy to the brain that should plot to dismember, and leprosy to the hand that will not draw to defend our Union.'"

MARTIN: "Where was that toast drunk?"

EATON: "I cannot say. . . . It was sent, with other toasts I had corrected, to a paper at Springfield. . . . But I had received many hospitalities throughout the Union; many of my toasts were published; and in the hurry of passing and repassing, I have completely forgotten."

MARTIN: "Did you transmit the toast for publication, and to what printer?"

EATON: "I do not recall distinctly."

BURR: "You spoke of accounts with the government. Did you or the government demand money?"

EATON: "They had no demand on me. I demanded money of them."

MARTIN: "What was the balance against you?"

EATON: "That is my concern, sir."

BURR: "What was the balance against you?"

EATON (to the court): "Is that a proper question?"

BURR: "My object is manifest: I wish to show the bias which has existed on the mind of the witness."

The CHIEF JUSTICE saw no objection to the question.

EATON: "I cannot say to a cent or a dollar, but I have received about $10,000."

BURR: "When was the money received?"

EATON: "About March last." [8]

The defense now moved to strike all the testimony introduced, since it failed to establish an overt act beyond all reasonable doubt; and the government counsel, in consternation, took an extraordinary step of requesting two days' recess to prepare arguments against the motion. Marshall granted the request; to have refused to do so, he told a friend afterward, would have been construed by critics as "not being disposed to give the prosecution an opportunity to answer." [9]

The best that the prosecution could do, however, was to indulge in histrionics when arguments resumed. Alexander MacRae, a former lieutenant governor of Virginia, ranted that Burr's repeated threats to do "great harm" to Jefferson and the government were sufficient proof of his intention to levy war. William Wirt, in a florid allegorical speech that created a sensation in the rapt courtroom, pictured Blennerhasset as a simple dupe whom Burr now sought to thrust "between himself and punishment." One of Burr's counsel, in surrebuttal, bluntly strove to expose the government's motives for the whole undertaking; Benjamin Botts, a young anti-Jeffersonian lawyer, charged that it was all a plot to restore the rapidly deteriorating reputation of the administration.

Botts reviewed the mounting pressures applied outside the courtroom, the distorted party press reports, the threats to persons favorable to the defendant or even neutral in their sentiments, the generally accepted fact that several of the jurymen had prejudicial views on the defense simply because it had been impossible to impanel twelve persons who were uncommitted on the subject. He concluded with a significant warning: "If the law of constructive treason were to be adopted in America," trials like this would merely rubber-stamp the orchestrated prejudices of the people. Luther Martin followed with a vigorous condemnation of "bloodthirsty enemies" in high office seeking to cover up their own shortcomings by hounding a convenient victim to his ruin.[10]

The case was now to go to the jury, with such instructions as the Chief Justice was prepared to give, after a long hot summer of part theatrics, part electioneering, and part critical constitutional challenges. The charge to the jury, on August 31, was to be one of Marshall's most elaborate statements on a constitutional subject in his entire career (see Part Three, Chapter II-7); unlike most of his opinions, it was heavily laden with citations of authorities, although most of these simply went to the matter of establishing the exclusive controlling force of the specific constitutional provisions.[11] Although neither Marshall nor Story, in his *Commentaries* a generation later, made a particular effort to link the principles in Burr's case to the Bill of Rights, the standards which Marshall now set forth for the trial jury were essentially those which the Supreme Court in the twentieth century would reiterate in the judicial activating of the great rights in the Fourth, Fifth, and Sixth Amendments.

In the present case, Marshall admonished the jury that the validity of their verdict depended upon two issues: Could the law of constructive treason be applied in the face of the specific definitions in the Constitution? And could treason itself be proved without proof of actual levying of war against the United States? Not altogether persuasively, Marshall advised the trial jury that his words in the Bollman–Swartwout appeal had been misunderstood by the grand jury: while he had said in the appellate opinion that all persons involved in a treasonable act were equally liable, the involvement had to be direct and intentional and the treason had to be proved. This was hardly the description of the men and materials found on Blennerhasset's island by the testimony of the government's own witnesses.

The constitutional requirement was that the accused person's treason had to be established by the testimony of two witnesses to the same overt act. If the overt act was not an actual levying of war, the testimony itself would be immaterial. The fundamental constitutional consideration was that no person offending against the government should be made to answer to any overt act alleged in any part of the country by the device of holding him constructively present. Thus the two basic questions were interdependent, and a defendant's guilt had to be established by showing his direct relationship to a specific wrongful act.

The trial jury, thus circumscribed in its options, returned a verdict the following day that "Aaron Burr is not proved to be guilty by any evidence submitted to us," an indirect protest against not being permitted to vote its prejudices.[12] Defense counsel insisted that such wording was not a verdict according to law; but Marshall allowed it to stand, with an accompanying notice that it was "in effect a verdict of acquittal." It was hardly the epochal ending for which the forensics of the four preceding months had raised such great hopes; Hay entered *nolle prosequi* declarations as to the co-defendants, but upon Jefferson's insistence demanded trial on the accompanying indictments for "high misdemeanor" in plotting war against Spanish Mexico. In due course the jury in this trial returned a verdict of "not guilty"; whereupon the administration doggedly demanded that all parties be bound over for a trial for crimes and misdemeanors in the Ohio venue. Eventually, this maneuver came to naught, and the protracted prosecution died of exhaustion.

It had been a nasty business from the beginning, and none of the principal characters emerged with any trappings of glory. Chief Justice Marshall, after his early defiant independence, seemed increasingly to vacillate and temporize as the successive litigation wore on. Burr, whose skin was saved by Marshall's insistence upon a strict adherence to constitutional requirements for proof of treason, treated the Chief Justice with insolent contempt as the intransigent prosecution continued. Federalists became outraged that their onetime hero turned indecisive in the anticlimax of the later stages of the prosecution. In retrospect, the two great constitutional principles which later generations would trace from the Burr cases were seen as inchoate and indeterminate—the amenability of the executive branch to judicial process, represented in the Jefferson subpoena, would not be definitively settled for a century and a half; and the rights of the defendant to a fair trial and due process, if vindicated at all, were sadly dissipated in the aftermath of the "Scotch verdict" in the main treason trial.

Seeds of bitterness and vengeance were sprouting noxious threats, however. Jefferson, apoplectic at the loss of the cases against Burr, was more determined than ever to bring down Marshall. It was not enough to have mobs fomented by the Republicans hanging the Chief Justice in effigy; the President was determined upon impeachment. A vindictive comment was inserted into the draft of his coming annual message to Congress in which Jefferson declared that "wherever the laws were appealed to in aid of the public safety, their operation was on behalf of those only against whom they were invoked," and complained that the evidence for conviction was illegally kept from the jury.[13] Even the Cabinet members felt that the charges were too extreme, however, and these phrases were deleted from the final draft; nevertheless, what was said was grim enough:

I informed Congress at their last session of the enterprises against the public peace which were believed to be in preparation by Aaron Burr and his associates, of the measures taken to defeat them and to bring the offenders to justice. Their enterprises were happily defeated by the patriotic exertions of the militia whenever called into action, by the fidelity of the Army, and energy of the commander in chief in promptly arranging the difficulties presenting themselves on the Sabine, repairing to meet those arising on the Mississippi, and dissipating before their explosion plots engendering there. *I shall think it my duty to lay before you the proceedings and the evidence publicly exhibited on the arraignment of the principal offenders before the circuit court in Virginia. You will be enabled to judge whether the defect was in the testimony, in the law, or in the administration of the law; and wherever it shall be found, the Legislature alone can apply or originate the remedy.* The framers of our Constitution certainly supposed they had guarded as well their Government against destruction by treason as their citizens against oppression under pretense of it, and if these ends are not attained it is of importance to enquire by what means more effectual they may be secured.[14]

Although Congress took no action on the thinly concealed invitation to institute impeachment proceedings, the campaign against Marshall mounted steadily in the party press. Ritchie's Richmond *Enquirer,* the Jeffersonian organ, published a scathing succession of letters denouncing the opinions in the Burr cases, the Chief Justice's "culpable partiality toward the accused," his efforts to "implicate the government," and the "juggle of a judicial farce." Senator Giles introduced legislation to redefine the law of constructive treason, and the Senate instituted a move to expel John Smith of Ohio, allegedly one of the co-conspirators. In the end, however, Giles himself cast the deciding vote against the expulsion, convinced as he was of Smith's innocence. By the spring of 1808 the Jefferson administration was entering its final year, its full attention demanded by the increasing depredations of all the European powers as the Napoleonic wars spread abroad.[15]

The passion of John Marshall gradually was eased. In such a crucible, as later generations would come to understand, he had forged the shield and buckler for constitutional protection of the individual against the forces of government, compelling the state as well as the person to submit to the rule of law.

The bizarre story of Aaron Burr, however, continued its epic course. In June 1808 he sailed for England under an assumed name, hounded out of Baltimore by Jeffersonian mobs, and out of Philadelphia by creditors, while New York, New Jersey, and possibly Ohio lay in waiting with new indictments for past acts. In London Jefferson's ministers were able to frustrate his proposals for British support of new adventures in North America; and in due time Spain, now allied with Britain, forced his deportation. Burr wandered about Europe for more than a year, and then in

1810 turned up in Napoleon's France to make a final effort to promote his grand design for a Western empire. Whatever evidence of treason may or may not have been lacking in Richmond in 1807, his schemes now smacked of desperation—the inciting of war between Great Britain and the United States, the separation of Louisiana from the Union, even the fomenting of a political revolution in America which only waited for a leader "superior in talent and in energy" who could offer the people "something grand and stable." [16]

Neither Bonaparte, who had his own share of visions, nor the American authorities to whom Burr's proposals eventually filtered back any longer regarded the man seriously. In May 1812, the proceedings stemming from the Hamilton duel having been dropped, Burr returned to New York; but tragedy again overtook him. In July came word of the death of Theodosia's only son; then, in December, Theodosia herself was lost at sea, embarked on a voyage from Charleston to visit her beloved father. For two decades Burr lived on, rebuilding his law practice and, at the age of seventy-seven, marrying a wealthy widow whose estate he proceeded to dissipate. Her petition for divorce was granted in 1836 on the day of Burr's death. His body was placed in an unmarked grave in the city, a final sign of the undying hatreds of many of his countrymen. Two years later, in the dead of night, unknown friends erected a small marker at the grave—a final sign of the ambivalent verdict of history.[17]

V

The Supreme Court and the States

Trustees of Dartmouth College v. *Woodward*

"I do not think the United States would come to an end if we lost our power to declare an act of Congress void," wrote Justice Oliver Wendell Holmes in 1913. But, he added, "I do think the Union would be imperiled if we could not make that declaration as to the laws of the several states." [1] It was in this area—the definition of federal supremacy through judicial review—that the Marshall Court was to express its most pervasive and forceful construction of constitutional powers. The Judiciary Act of 1789 had provided specifically for judicial review of state actions which were charged with being in conflict with the paramount national law (see Part Three, Chapter III-1); but Marshall's concern was that the Supreme Court's right of review in these cases should be based on constitutional mandate rather than depending upon implementing legislation subject to amendment by changing administrative majorities in Congress.

The roots of this mandate were to be found, in Marshall's view, in a composite of specific clauses which added up to a comprehensive confirmation of judicial power. Article I, Section 10 laid a certain number of specific prohibitions on the states, while Article VI, Clause 2 asserted: "This Constitution, and the Laws of the United States which shall be made in Pursuance thereof; and all Treaties made, or which shall be made, under the Authority of the United States, shall be the supreme Law of the Land; and the Judges in every State shall be bound thereby, any Thing in the Constitution or Laws of any State to the Contrary notwithstanding." There was also the provision of Article I, Section 8, Clause 18 that vested Congress with all powers necessary and proper for implementing any other powers vested by the Constitution (see Part One, Chapter VI) and the commerce clause of the same section (Clause 3) which provided the implement for carrying many of these powers into effect (see Part One, Chapter VII).

Just as each of these several provisions required its own definitive interpretation, whenever a case arose which presented the Court with an opportunity to construe the powers therein, so the supremacy of national government over state governments in a federal system was to be established by fitting each of these interpretations into a mosaic, a matrix. When this was finally accomplished, in a series of opinions which began in 1810 and reached a climax in 1824, the Marshall Court's jurisprudence of judicial federalism was virtually complete. Characteristically, as in his individual opinions, the Chief Justice developed this jurisprudential system by moving from one logical position to the next until, at the last, he had built a structure which could withstand the changes and chances of generations to come. By a consensus of colleagues' opinions in one case, upon which a subsequent case would then be based, the major opinions making up the final structure showed remarkably consistent unanimity, or at least absence of strong dissent (see Part Two, Chapter III).

The contract clause (Article I, Section 10)—the provision that "No State shall . . . pass any . . . Law impairing the Obligation of Contracts"—was to become for Marshall the practical implement for asserting judicial surveillance of state actions as the commerce clause in his day would become the implement of national power. In three major cases—one involving corruption and land fraud in Georgia and Mississippi, another a bankruptcy law in New York, and the third a college charter in New Hampshire—the Chief Justice developed the restraints in the contract clause into a firm foundation upon which his colleague, Justice Story, would begin the counterbalancing doctrine of federal power in *Martin* v. *Hunter's Lessee,*[2] complemented by Marshall's own opinion in *McCulloch* v. *Maryland* [3] (see Part One, Chapter VI).

The Yazoo land claims, the outgrowth of more than fifteen years of machinations and litigation, presented the first opportunity to construe the contract clause, in 1810. Although the cession of western lands to the United States by the several original colonies had been a condition for ratification of the old Articles of Confederation in 1781, the state of Georgia—second largest landholder after Virginia—postponed final action on its cession until 1802. The reason was that many a Georgia speculator in the final decade of the eighteenth century saw possibilities for making fortunes from the virgin lands in the far western part of the state's territories. In 1795 the state legislature passed a statute authorizing the sale of an enormous tract of land—more than 35,000,000 acres—to four land companies (the Georgia Company, the Georgia–Mississippi Company, the Tennessee Company, and the Upper Mississippi Company). The state made the sale for a total of $500,000, or slightly less than one and a half cents an acre.

It became obvious almost at the outset that the legislative assembly of 1795 had been bought, almost to a man. Outraged voters turned out the culprits in the fall elections, and the 1796 assembly repealed the enactment of the previous year with the flourish of a public burning of the offending law to show the public indignation. But by now the mischief had been done; in the interim before the repeal in 1796, the Georgia Company had sold its entire land grant to a New England company and a basic contract question was in the making. Could a valid sale of land under the 1795 law, vesting legal title in real estate, be rendered invalid by the 1796 act of the state legislature? After half a dozen years of litigation, Georgia washed its hands of the business by belatedly selling its western lands to the United States in 1802, thus dumping the problem into the laps of Congress.

The issue in the courts was initially a matter of private contract law, although its constitutional ramifications were already manifest in 1803 when Robert Fletcher of Amherst, Massachusetts, filed a suit against John Peck of Boston, a heavy speculator in Georgia lands, demanding recovery of his purchase money for Yazoo lands for which Peck allegedly could not convey a valid deed of title. The case was continued until the fall of 1807 when Justice William Cushing, sitting as a judge of the Circuit Court, gave judgment in favor of Peck.[4] Fletcher then sued out a writ of error to the Supreme Court of the United States, where the case was set down for argument on March 1, 1809. After three days, the Chief Justice recessed court for two hours, while he proceeded to another part of the Capitol to administer the oath of office to incoming President James Madison.[5] Thereafter, because of a defect in the pleadings, the case was set for reargument the following year. (Joseph Story, who would succeed Cushing on the Court in 1811, appeared in 1810 as one of the counsel for Peck, substituting for John Quincy Adams, whom Madison had appointed as minister to Russia.)

On March 10, 1810, the Chief Justice delivered the opinion of the Court finding a valid title which Peck could convey; a contract of sale which had been made and relied on under a valid state law, the opinion held, could not subsequently be rendered void by a second state law repealing the first. That holding, by itself, required no constitutional sanction; English common law might have produced the same result. What was of far greater significance—although for most contemporary observers it was a cloud no larger than a person's hand—was that the Supreme Court for the first time had asserted the right to set aside a state law in conflict with the law of the land. As subsequent history would demonstrate, the rule in *Fletcher* v. *Peck* [6] had closed the ring of national power begun with *Marbury* v. *Madison* in 1803: where the latter had established the right of judicial review of acts of Congress, the former now established the right of judicial review of acts of state legislatures. (See Part Three, Chapter III-2.)

Marshall followed the *Fletcher* case two years later with a still more affirmative statement of the contract clause, in *New Jersey* v. *Wilson*.[7] This case involved a 1758 contract of sale with the Delaware Indians for lands in exchange for certain other tribal claims. A term of the contract provided for perpetual exemption of the lands from taxation. Forty years later the state of New Jersey repealed the 1758 statute authorizing the contract, and subjected the Indian lands to taxation. Purchasers of the lands challenged the constitutionality of the repealing statute, and, after it was upheld by the New Jersey supreme court, the case was taken to the Supreme Court of the United States. In reversing the New Jersey holding, the Chief Justice declared that the contract clause covered "contracts to which a state is a party, as well as . . . contracts between individuals"—an interpretation which the New Hampshire court would challenge again in the *Dartmouth College* case.

The seed planted in 1810 grew steadily under the nurturing of the Chief Justice and his new colleague, Justice Story, who was quickly to reveal himself as a fervent supporter of paramount federal power in all areas where the Constitution vested such power. Story's argument as counsel for Peck had been accepted as the rule of decision; in 1814, sitting as a Circuit Justice, he had held invalid a New Hampshire law which sought to alter the rights of a pre-Revolutionary grantor of land with respect to his tenants' obligations. The following year Story wrote a Supreme Court opinion (*Terrett* v. *Taylor*)[8] striking down a Virginia law purporting to abrogate rights of a charter party, basing his holding "upon the principles of natural justice" and "upon the spirit and letter of the Constitution."

Earlier than this, in 1813, Story had prepared the way for a vast extension of federal power complementing the contract clause restraints upon state power. In an extraordinarily complex case growing out of Revolutionary expropriation of British-held lands, the question of a superior title came before the Court (*Fairfax's Devisee* v. *Hunter's Lessee*)[9] in terms of the rights of pre-Revolutionary grants as against state-created grants. Because the Treaty of Paris in 1783 had tolled any further expropriations, a Virginia trial court had found the British title to be superior (i.e., not having been extinguished by state action before the treaty had taken effect). Some years later, the state court of appeals had reversed the trial court,[10] and the case was taken on appeal to the Supreme Court. Story, in a 3-to-1 opinion (three Justices having disqualified themselves), reversed the Virginia high court.

In 1816 this case returned to the Supreme Court under the name of *Martin* v. *Hunter's Lessee*.[11] Upon remand of the 1813 appeal, the Virginia high court had rejected the Supreme Court's assumption of jurisdiction under Section 25 of the Judiciary Act of 1789. The question was now a wholly constitutional one—the reviewability of state laws and decisions first established in *Peck*—with the state court, in the spirit of the Virginia Resolution against the Alien and Sedition Act (see page 5), insisting that the Congressional legislation of 1789 violated the compact theory (the fundamental doctrine of states' rights advocates) of reserved sovereignty of the states. The argument gave Story the opportunity to extend the Marshall constitutional doctrine from the power of review of state acts under the contract clause to the supremacy principle which Marshall would assert in full dimensions in *McCulloch* v. *Maryland* three years later.

Rejecting the argument of the Virginia court, Story asserted in concise, brilliant fashion the rule upon which the supreme law of the land would be established. The Constitution vested the judicial power of the United States in such courts, and through such judicial process, as Congress chose to create. "If, then, it is the duty of Congress to vest the judicial power of the United States, it is a duty to vest the *whole judicial power*." Wherever the Constitution created a power in the national government, that power was plenary unless limited by the Constitution itself.

Thus, by 1819, the Court had completed the groundwork for a great trilogy of cases in that term which brought judicial federalism to full flower. In the first of these—*Sturges* v. *Crowninshield* [12]—the Court would combine the plenary power of the national government over bankruptcies with the restraints upon the states in the contract clause. In the second, the *Dartmouth College* case, the doctrine begun in *Fletcher* v. *Peck* in 1810 and reiterated in *Terrett* v. *Taylor* in 1815 was brought to its apogee. The third, the famous "bank case," is the subject of Part One, Chapter VI.

In 1817 Josiah Sturges of Massachusetts sued Richard Crowninshield of New York to recover payments on promissory notes which had come due. Crowninshield, who was then insolvent, pleaded his discharge of the debt under a recently passed New York insolvency law. The judges of the Circuit Court were divided in their opinions as to whether the New York law was a bankruptcy law and thus conflicted with the federal Constitution and as to whether any such law conflicted with the contract clause of the Constitution. These questions were therefore certified to the Supreme Court (i.e., the Circuit Court stayed its own decision on the case until the Supreme Court could answer these controlling questions).

On February 17, 1819, Chief Justice Marshall delivered a unanimous opinion for the Supreme Court on the second question, holding that the

New York law violated the contract clause insofar as it had retroactive effect on prior contracts. This disposed of the immediate case, in favor of Sturges; while the opinion then spoke about the states' powers in the field of bankruptcy, it was in such general terms that no rule of decision could be discerned therein. Not until 1827, in *Ogden* v. *Saunders*,[13] did the Court address itself to the concurrent jurisdictions of the states and nation in the area of bankruptcy; Marshall's dissent in this latter case revealed the division of views on the Court in 1819 which confined the authority of *Crowninshield* to the contract clause.

On the contract clause, however, there was no division; and thus *Crowninshield,* coming at this term, added force to the major opinion on the subject which was to come with *Trustees of Dartmouth College* v. *Woodward*.[14]

The *Dartmouth College* case grew out of the characteristic intimacies and enmities arising in a closely knit society. Begun as Moor's Indian Charity School in Lebanon, Connecticut, by the Reverend Eleazar Wheelock, the college was transferred to Hanover, New Hampshire, in 1768 as a result of a fundraising campaign in England and named for one of the contributors, the Earl of Dartmouth. (See Part Three, Chapter III-3.) When Wheelock, the first president of the new institution, died in 1807, he decreed that his son John should be appointed as his successor. John, however, immediately began to bicker with the trustees under the charter, and in 1815 brought matters to a head by writing an anonymous diatribe against the trustees which he sent to Jeffersonian members of the state legislature. The trustees invoked their charter powers and dismissed him as president.[15]

The Jeffersonians swept all state offices the following year, and the legislature proceeded to offer relief and redress to the deposed Wheelock. A statute was drafted amending the Dartmouth charter, increasing the number of trustees from twelve to twenty-one, adding a board of overseers with veto power over trustees' actions, and changing the institution's name to Dartmouth University. (See Part Three, Chapter III-4.) In effect, the College was converted into a state institution by unilateral action altering the character established by its charter. (Two of the new trustees appointed under the legislation were Justice Story and Secretary of the Navy Benjamin Crowninshield, a relative of Richard Story, who clearly foresaw the coming constitutional challenge, declined his appointment.[16])

In fact, eight of the old trustees, who came to be called "the Octagon," were preparing a test case, against the former secretary-treasurer of the College, William H. Woodward, one of the former president's men. The case began in February 1817 in the state courts, where it was admitted that the chances were bleak; in orthodox Jeffersonian fashion, the new state government had made a clean sweep of the judiciary, and all the judges were committed Republicans. Obviously, any victory for the trustees would have to be found in the Supreme Court; and in preparation for carrying the case all that way, the trustees retained among their counsel Jeremiah Smith, the recently ousted chief justice of the state, and Daniel Webster, one of the leaders of the Supreme Court bar.

The argument at the trial level, on the initial pleadings, was based on the contract clause of the federal Constitution and the state constitutional prohibition against deprivation of property without due process. As expected, however, the Jeffersonian philosophy of the high court of the state would admit of no such view. The new chief justice, William M. Richardson, stated categorically: "A corporation, all of whose franchises are exercised for public purposes, is a public corporation." The offices of College trustee were, by this reasoning, to be regarded as public offices subject to state legislative control as were other public offices. The opinion was well reasoned—indeed, it would echo in the "public accommodations" tests of the Supreme Court of the later twentieth century—and Richardson anticipated the appeal on the federal question by emphasizing that the contract clause had to do with private, rather than public, contracts or grants. (See Part Three, Chapter III-5.)

Having disposed of the issue in the pleadings, the New Hampshire court now heard argument on the facts; and here the University counsel made a serious error by including a statement that since reorganization the institution had received "the greater part of its funds and properties" from the state of New Hampshire. This suggested that the support for the *University* was different from the support for the *College,* which by its charter had been endowed entirely with private gifts. However, the Jeffersonian administration of the University considered this a minor point; it was so confident that the Richardson opinion would withstand any challenge in the federal court that it decided to save money by not sending its local attorneys but referring the appeal to resident Washington counsel. Of these William Wirt would have been an able representative, but since he had just become Attorney General of the United States he could give scarcely any attention to the case. The other appellate lawyer was John Holmes of Massachusetts, a Congressman who was not at home in the special environment of the Supreme Court.

On the other hand, the College continued to retain Daniel Webster and authorized him to seek the best co-counsel known to him. He did, selecting Joseph Hopkinson of Philadelphia, who had been one of the defense team in the impeachment trial of Justice Chase. Even so, Webster entertained no great hopes of success in the Supreme Court; he did not at the time perceive that Marshall was building steadily upon the contract clause, which was the only federal question which Webster was entitled to argue on the appeal. Indeed, Webster was so persuaded of the weakness of his case on the contract question he suggested that Judge Smith initiate a second suit on behalf of the College, against a resident in Vermont; this suit would come into the United States Circuit Court under the "diversity of citizenship" provision of Article III of the Constitution, and thus all the evidence introduced there could be carried to the Supreme Court for review.[17]

With this prospect of a second appeal in which he would have a wider choice of issues to argue, Webster then appeared before the Supreme Court in March 1818 to argue the contract clause question. With the craftiness of a veteran advocate, he was able to insinuate a number of his state arguments (which should have been ruled inadmissible) into his oral argument. Ironically enough, the Chief Justice did not admonish Webster in this, since he was, as later indications would show, intent on using the College charter case to project a sweeping restatement of constitutional powers over the states through the contract clause. At the close of argument, the Court was unprepared for its decision, and therefore set the case for reargument in the 1819 term.

When, at length, the Court's ruling in the case was handed down, it was evident that several members had elected to make this a vehicle for their own views on the contract clause. With Justice Todd absent for the term and Justice Duvall filing a dissent without opinion, the remaining five Justices emphasized their unanimity on the powers over the states conferred upon the Court by the clause, but took the opportunity to suggest varying degrees of extension of the contract doctrine. Marshall delivered what was called the opinion of the Court, in which Justice Johnson joined; Justices Washington and Story wrote separate concurring opinions, with Justice Livingston concurring in all three opinions. (See Part Three, Chapter III-6.) Thus, although such a divided majority frequently weakened the authoritative force of such a case, in this instance it emphasized the fact that the clause was at the least an unequivocal limitation upon the states and at the most could be an indefinitely expanding immunity for public and private agreements from all future impairments.

The interim between the 1818 arguments and the opening of the February term in 1819 had been marked by widespread activity on behalf of both parties—and certain Justices as well. Other colleges had become alarmed at what might happen to their own charters if Dartmouth College failed in its present test of the contract clause, and two institutions—Princeton and Harvard—conferred honorary degrees on Justices Johnson and Livingston respectively, while Harvard elected Justice Story to its board of overseers. The prestigious Chancellor James Kent of the New

York judiciary traveled in person to Hanover to familiarize himself on the spot with the facts in the case, and thereafter discussed it with Johnson and Livingston—a dubious act upon which twentieth-century professionals would frown.[18] The University, realizing that it had not been effectively represented by its first appellate counsel, now retained William Pinkney of Baltimore, one of the leading members of the Supreme Court bar, who prepared to introduce in reargument the record of the endowments with public funds which had been made to the College even before the reorganization.

But when the 1819 term opened, the Chief Justice announced that the members of the Court had formed their opinions on the basis of the arguments of the previous term—and promptly began reading his own. It would run, as one observer reports, for "eighteen folio pages," and when it was delivered Marshall proceeded to other business. Pinkney never had an opportunity to speak; the concurring opinions which were filed in due time with the court reporter were not discussed at this session, and the famous litigation was, for all practical purposes, concluded.

Marshall was intent upon reading into the constitutional law his doctrine that a corporate charter was a contract in itself—a final broadening of the *Fletcher* doctrine of 1810—and that the original Dartmouth charter established a private corporation which was all the more firmly within the protection of the *Fletcher* rule. He declared:

A corporation is an artificial being, invisible, intangible, and existing only in contemplation of law. . . .

A corporation is no more a state instrument than a natural person exercising the same powers would be. . . . It is probable that no man ever was, and that no man ever will be, the founder of a college, believing at the time that an act of incorporation constitutes no security for the institution; believing that it is immediately to be deemed a public institution, whose funds are to be governed and applied, not by the will of the donor, but by the will of the legislature. . . .

Marshall candidly conceded that his interpretation of the contract clause "was not particularly in the view of the framers of the Constitution"; but where no qualifying language had been written into the document, the "plain meaning" of the words would guide the judicial construction.[19] Story's concurring opinion, filed for publication but not delivered at the time, pointed out that a grantor such as a legislature could reserve in the grant the right to make subsequent revisions, and Marshall himself, in 1830, denied that the absence of a state reservation of a right of taxation was an implied immunity from taxation (*Providence Bank* v. *Billings*).[20] Two years after Marshall's death his successor, Chief Justice Roger B. Taney, substantially qualified the contract doctrine in the *Dartmouth College* case and extended the *Providence Bank* holding to show the other side

of the coin—absence of charter references to restraints on state action left
the state free to act (*Charles River Bridge Co.* v. *Warren Bridge Co.*).[21]

While much was made of the contract clause doctrine as a device for
encouraging unencumbered economic development (and subsequent economic exploitation), the major and continuing constitutional principle to
emerge from the *Dartmouth College* case—taken with the sweeping
opinion in the "bank case" in this same term—was the paramountcy of the
federal Constitution and acts of the national government under its authority in a state–federal relationship. After the middle of the nineteenth
century, the expanding doctrines of due process—either relating to the
federal government under the Fifth Amendment or to the states under the
Fourteenth Amendment—gradually reduced the judicial reliance on the
contract clause as the means of asserting this paramount authority.

The Marshall Court itself never viewed the contract clause or the commerce clause as categorical bars to state regulatory power in its own
proper sphere. In *Ogden* v. *Saunders* [22] in 1827, the majority in a 4-to-3
opinion (Marshall dissenting) held that any contract was subject to pre-
existing state laws. In 1829 Marshall himself upheld a Delaware court in
holding that a state's police powers were appropriately exercised in areas
where Congress had not preempted the field (*Willson* v. *Black Bird Creek
Marsh Co.*) [23]—a balancing of the supremacy and commerce clause doctrines. The Taney Court in 1837 broadened the constitutional areas in
which states could exercise their powers over commerce (*Mayor of New
York* v. *Miln*),[24] and ten years later Marshall's successor was to declare
that "the mere grant of power to the general government cannot, upon
any just principles of construction, be construed to be an absolute prohibition to the exercise of any power over the same subject by the states"
(*The License Cases*).[25] This comports with the modern view; Marshall's
lasting accomplishment in the cases from *Peck* to *Dartmouth College* was
to establish the basic doctrine that state action, like federal action, is
reviewable by the Supreme Court in all areas with which the federal Constitution deals.

VI

The Supreme Law of the Land

McCulloch v. *Maryland*

The development and management of a national currency system was one of the primary objectives of the new government when it began organizing itself in 1789. For Federalists like Alexander Hamilton, it was an essential part of the overall reforms he found necessary to rehabilitate a political economy which had languished to the point of almost total collapse under the old Articles of Confederation. For Hamilton, also, there was a ready example to be followed in the Bank of England, then almost a century old and the nerve center of the British commercial empire from which the Americans had so recently withdrawn. What the Bank of England had been able to accomplish for a small island kingdom now growing into a worldwide power, a Bank of the United States could do for a young republic on the fringe of a virgin continent.

In 1791, after heated debate, Congress established the first such Bank and pledged to subscribe public funds to the amount of $10,000,000. Of this amount, $2,000,000, or one-fifth of the total capitalization, was immediately advanced to the government as a loan. The Jeffersonians rent the air with objections and dire predictions: a recurrent objection was the claim that the institution was unconstitutional, since there was no specific mention of a bank in the language of the document adopted only two years earlier. Another Jeffersonian complaint was that the immediate indebtedness of the government to the Bank would immediately commit the government to underwriting the institution's program of commercial loans and investments, and hence to a permanent involvement of the United States in a national financial system. The best that the opposition could do at that time, however, was to place a twenty-year limit on the life of the charter (a general provision in state-chartered banks), with the option of reviewing the record and renewing the debate when the question of renewal of the charter should come up.[1]

Acting as fiscal agent for the government, issuing its own bank notes, which amounted to a federal currency, conducting a disconcertingly well managed private investment business, and restraining the tendencies of smaller and local banks to extend credit in all directions, the first Bank of the United States was a conspicuous success. But the steadily growing Jeffersonian commitment to agrarian interests as against urban and commercial, by the expiration date of the charter in 1811, foredoomed the institution to termination. The first Madison administration failed to secure a renewal of the charter, and the nation entered the War of 1812 without any kind of central banking system to cope with the inevitable demands upon the national economy. The result was financial chaos at the end of the conflict and a sufficient political pressure, at the end of the second Madison administration, to secure passage of a charter (see Part Three, Chapter IV-1) for a second Bank of the United States, which began operation in 1816. (It was this second Bank which Andrew Jackson would make the target of his own "war" under the generalship of Treasury Secretary Roger B. Taney, who would succeed John Marshall as Chief Justice in the year the charter of the second, and last, Bank expired.) [2]

The second Bank got off to an inauspicious start under the presidency of William Jones (1816–1819), was reformed and put on a sound basis by the second president, Langdon Cheves (1819–1822), and went on to spectacular financial success under the third president, Nicholas Biddle (1823–1836). It remained throughout its history a *bête noir* of agrarian and small debtor classes of the South and West, where easy credit and perennially optimistic plans for the future were the life and breath of the economy. Nor did the Bank enhance its own image by its early policies, which strove too soon and too strenuously to establish the dominance which the first Bank had enjoyed. Harsh foreclosure policies, bad management, and erratic loan policies—together with violent and unremitting opposition of state banks with their legislative lobbies—made the federal institution a ready target for political attack.[3]

Within two years of its chartering, a number of states had passed laws aimed at penalizing or forbidding outright the conducting of businesses by the Bank within their jurisdictions. The Maryland law of that year (see Part Three, Chapter IV-2) required the Bank to buy stamped paper from the state, on which to print any of its commercial issues, at a cost amounting to 2 percent of the institution's financial operations. James McCulloch, cashier of the Baltimore branch (one of thirty-five branches around the country emanating from the central branch in Philadelphia), ignored the state law and in due course was made the defendant of record in a suit to recover the fines provided by the Maryland law in such case, a total of about $2,500. Thus a major, two-pronged constitutional battle opened—

first, on the question of whether a state could lay a burden upon an agency of the federal government, and second, whether the federal government had the constitutional authority to charter a bank at all.

In finding the authority in the "necessary and proper" clause of Article I, Section 8, the Court would precipitate a furious political attack, prompted more by the local hatreds engendered by the Bank than by the assertion of the "necessary and proper" doctrine itself. For already in 1805 the Court—although by a 3-to-1 majority (see Part Two, Chapter III)—in *United States* v. *Fisher* [4] had rejected the argument "that no law was authorized which was not indispensably necessary to give effect to a specified power." The case involved a relatively unexceptionable question—whether the United States government was entitled to priority in the settlement of a bankrupt's estate—but five years earlier, in an early test of strength between Federalists and anti-Federalists, Congress had been persuaded to reject a proposal to charter certain copper mines in New Jersey in reliance upon this clause. The meaning and scope of the phrase had been bitterly debated again in the legislation to charter the second Bank of the United States in 1816, and by now the strict constructionists had the full force of anti-Bank emotions behind them when they launched their attack on the Court's opinion.

The Baltimore branch of the Bank was hardly apt to mollify the popular animosity by its own record of management: at the time of the suit, it was reporting a loss of $1,700,000 on transactions that verged on the fraudulent and was just short of insolvency.[5] Thus both sides were eager for a test case on the two constitutional questions and moved with alacrity to see that the issue would go to the Supreme Court. On May 8, 1818, the trial was held in the county court for Baltimore County, and upon judgment rendered in favor of the state an appeal was taken the next month to the Maryland high court, where the judgment was affirmed as expected. Writ of error was then immediately taken to the Supreme Court of the United States, where the case was docketed on September 18, 1818—four months and ten days after it had begun in Baltimore. Even in an age of light dockets, the question had been carried to the Marshall Court with dazzling expedition. (One result was an insignificant record of the case as represented in the transcript from the lower courts; see Part Three, Chapter IV-3.)

The importance of the question was also attested by the selection of the leading lawyers of the country by both sides: Maryland was represented by its attorney general, Luther Martin, together with Joseph Hopkinson of Philadelphia (who had just argued the *Dartmouth College* case a month earlier) and William Jones of the District of Columbia. The Bank retained as its counsel the Attorney General of the United States, William Wirt,

along with Daniel Webster of Massachusetts and William Pinkney of
Maryland. The arguments of these titans would consume nine days in
February 1819. The outcome, at least in Webster's view, was never in
doubt, and the assumption that the Maryland courts would be overruled
was so general that a movement was hastily organized in Congress to
repeal the Bank's three-year-old charter and thus render the issue moot.
Opponents of the movement cited the recent *Dartmouth College* opinion
declaring the inviolability of contracts to defeat the effort.[6]

Both Webster and Congress, as it turned out, correctly anticipated the
Court's position on the issues. The unanimous holding (6-to-0, with
Justice Todd absent) came only three days after the close of argument.
On both matters the opinion was emphatic: No state could lay upon the
national government, or its agencies, any burden which potentially could
hamper or preclude the agencies from discharging their authorized functions. The difference between state sovereignty and national sovereignty,
the Chief Justice declared, "is that which always exists, and always must
exist, between the action of the whole on a part . . . between the laws of a
government declared to be supreme, and those of a government which,
when in opposition to those laws, is not supreme." As for the "necessary
and proper" clause, Marshall made it the definitive statement of judicial
federalism: "Let the end be legitimate, let it be within the scope of the
Constitution, and all means which are appropriate, which are plainly
adapted to that end, which are not prohibited, but consist with the letter
and spirit of the Constitution, are constitutional." [7]

On its face, the opinion was essentially a statement of the paramount
power of the federal government; if paramount, no state action could be
allowed to qualify it. A quasi-official bank was "a convenient, a useful and
essential instrument in the prosecution of the government's fiscal operations," the Court had declared, and any determination by Congress that
it was appropriate to act through the medium of such a bank was not to
be interdicted by any state; for "if the right of the states to tax the means
employed by the General Government be conceded, that declaration that
the Constitution and the laws made in pursuance thereof, shall be the
supreme law of the land, is empty and unmeaning declamation." [8]

The first reaction to the Bank opinion was in terms of the degree of
antipathy toward the Bank itself; the effect of the ruling was to make the
Bank a force to be reckoned with in every part of the Union, and in the
South and West, where it was most virulently opposed, the decision provoked paroxysms of outrage. Former President James Madison, somewhat
naïvely if his own words are to be taken at face value, complained that
"the occasion did not call for the general and abstract doctrine interwoven
with the decision of the particular case"—a comment that echoed Thomas

Jefferson's original objection to the doctrine expressed in *Marbury*.[9] Yet Jefferson, in the present juncture, wrote deploring the Court's failure to hold the Bank unconstitutional, and waxed equally illogical in declaring that Congress had "the right to declare for itself what is its duty under the Constitution," which was what Congress had done in debating the chartering of the Bank in 1816.[10]

But it was clear that the Bank itself was a secondary issue, that the substance of the *McCulloch* opinion lay in its unequivocal assertion of the paramountcy of federal power under the Constitution. An editor in Tennessee wrote: "The Court, above the law and beyond the control of public opinion, has lately made a decision that prostrates the state sovereignty entirely." This was the real rub: in *McCulloch,* Chief Justice Marshall had now carried to full force the doctrine which Justice Story had first introduced in *Martin* v. *Hunter's Lessee* in 1816, and with this judicial federalism reached its apogee. In *Martin* Story had declared:

> The government, then, of the United States can claim no powers which are not granted to it by the Constitution, and the powers actually granted, must be such as are expressly given, or given by necessary implication. On the other hand, this instrument, like every other grant, is to have a reasonable construction, according to the import of its terms; and where a power is expressly given in general terms, it is not to be restrained to particular cases, unless that construction grow out of the context expressly, or by necessary implication. The words are to be taken in their natural and obvious sense, and not in a sense unreasonably restricted or enlarged.
>
> The Constitution unavoidably deals in general language. It did not suit the purposes of the people, in framing this great charter of our liberties, to provide for minute specifications of its powers, or to declare the means by which those powers should be carried into execution. It was foreseen that this would be a perilous and difficult, if not an impracticable, task. The instrument was not intended to provide merely for the exigencies of a few years, but was to endure through a long lapse of ages, the events of which were locked up in the inscrutable purposes of Providence. It could not be foreseen what new changes and modifications of power might be indispensable to effectuate the general objects of the charter; and restrictions and specifications, which, at the present, might seem salutary, might, in the end, prove the overthrow of the system itself. Hence its powers are expressed in general terms, leaving to the legislature [Congress], from time to time, to adopt its own means to effectuate legitimate objects, and to mold and model the exercise of its powers, as its own wisdom, and the public interests, should require.[11]

Now Marshall (who had disqualified himself in *Martin*) adopted virtually the language of Story and expanded it in a definition of the Constitution itself, and the government it created, as independent of the states and the people of the states. For the document drawn up at Philadelphia in 1787 was the creation of the people of the United States, acting to accommodate their own needs. This people, "acting as sovereigns for the whole country," were concerned with a document "for their own government, and not for the government of the individual states," and any limitations upon the federal power are to be found in this document— "limitations of power granted in the instrument itself; not of distinct governments, framed by different persons for different purposes." [12]

The Bank case of 1819 settled the question of paramount federal authority in respect of powers created by the Constitution; two years later, the Marshall Court would complete the doctrine of reviewability of state actions which might be in conflict with these powers. The 1821 *Cohens* case presented a clear transition to the final great decision in the steamboat case in 1824 (see Part One, Chapter VII) and confirmed Jefferson's never-ending declaration that "the Federal Judiciary [was] gaining ground step by step, and holding what it gains." [13]

P. J. and M. J. Cohen, two citizens of Norfolk, Virginia, had been convicted of selling lottery tickets in violation of state law, although the lottery was conducted by the District of Columbia under authority of an act of Congress. The Cohens, unable to secure review of their conviction in the state courts, carried the case on writ of error to the Supreme Court, where Virginia counsel reiterated the losing arguments in both *Martin* and *McCulloch*—that the Court had no jurisdiction over a state process, and that Congress had no constitutional power to establish a lottery, particularly where sale of lottery tickets came into conflict with state law.

On instructions from state officers, final argument for Virginia was confined to the first, or jurisdictional, question; and the Court unanimously (6-to-0) affirmed its right of review over state actions, whether arising in civil cases, as in *Martin,* or in criminal cases, as in this instance. (See Part Three, Chapter V-1.) But just as, in *Marbury* in 1803, the Court had allowed Jefferson to claim a victory on the merits while asserting its own power on the constitutional principle, so now in *Cohens* the Court ruled on the merits that Congress, although it had the power to do so, had not intended to extend this power into a state where a contrary local law was in force. With that, the rule of supremacy of national law reached an accommodation with state sovereignty.[14]

The most vehement attacks upon *McCulloch,* therefore, came from the most engrained states' rights advocates in Marshall's own commonwealth of Virginia—and the attacks came with such force that the Chief Justice was moved to conclude that they could not be allowed to go unanswered. This was the final moment of truth: if the concept of the Constitution as a flexible and adaptable charter of a nation, "intended to endure for ages to come," was to be established, it must depend upon all future generations of Americans (and Supreme Court Justices) accepting it as the *McCulloch* opinion had expressed it.

Marshall knew the danger of permitting unanswered attacks from the states' rights intransigents. The attacks were appearing in the Richmond *Enquirer,* Thomas Ritchie's unwavering Jeffersonian organ and the official voice of the Richmond Junto, a powerful political machine which, together with a similar cluster of Democratic Republicans in Albany, New York, could control the direction of national politics in Congress and perhaps the Presidency. Already the Virginia Congressional delegation, one of the largest in Washington, had become solidly Jeffersonian in the course of the postwar elections. In the Senate, they had James Barbour, a vigorous States' Rights Democrat (the more radical name was coming into vogue) and brother of Representative (and future Supreme Court Justice) Philip Pendleton Barbour in the lower chamber. The other senator, John W. Eppes, would resign in December and be replaced by another strong Jeffersonian, James Pleasants. A solid phalanx of Democratic Republicans made up the state delegation in the House.

The Junto was an Old Guard which neither died nor surrendered, and its antipathy toward judicial federalism had been fed by the two Fairfax cases of 1813 and 1816 which had gone against it, and would be exacerbated by *Cohens* v. *Virginia* in 1821. Its power nationally was attested by the twenty-four years of the Virginia dynasty in the White House— although neither Madison nor Monroe was an undeviating Jefferson apostle. Thus the Chief Justice was fully aware of the formidable challenge of revitalized anti-Federalism which appeared in print in the *Enquirer* in late March 1819—within the same month that the *McCulloch* opinion had been delivered.

The first series of essays or letters appeared under the pseudonym of "Amphictyon"—coined from the *amphictyony* or Amphictyonic League of Greek city states which, normally independent sovereignties in their own right, banded together whenever confronted with a common threat. Later evidence [15] would indicate that these letters were written by Judge William Brockenbrough, president of the Virginia State Bank and hence doubly sensitive to the impact of the *McCulloch* case with reference to the Bank of the United States. They were soon followed by an even more vitriolic series of letters signed "Hampden"—for John Hampden, cousin of Oliver Cromwell and one of the leaders of the English Revolution of the seventeenth century against Charles I. These, by all evidence, were written by Spencer Roane, Marshall's lifelong antagonist.

Spencer Roane was yet another in the remarkable group of men who, as students of George Wythe, became shapers of American law in Virginia and the nation. Like Marshall, he had studied originally at the College of William and Mary; like Bushrod Washington, he had continued his studies in Philadelphia. His judicial career began a decade earlier, where in 1793 he had upheld the right of the state high court to declare an act of the legislature unconstitutional (*Kamper* v. *Hawkins,* 1 Va. Cas. 20). But it was judicial review within a sovereign jurisdiction—state or federal—that Roane found valid; in 1815 he would reject Justice Story's ruling in the original Fairfax land title case (4 Munford, 3). He was the ultimate Jeffersonian, son-in-law of Patrick Henry and disciple of George Mason. His ultimate quarrel with Marshall was over "an *unlimited* grant of power and a grant limited in its terms, but accompanied with *unlimited* means of carrying it into execution," which he saw as the result of the *McCulloch* doctrine.[16]

For the Supreme Court, as for most judicial bodies before and since, there has been a time-honored policy of avoiding replying in public to attacks upon any actions by the judiciary. John Marshall, in this juncture, determined that it was imperative that this policy be set aside and a defense in the public press offered to the unremitting and increasingly violent condemnations of the Court and this opinion in the "Amphictyon" and "Hampden" letters. The Chief Justice's first rejoinders appeared under the pen name of "A Friend of the Union," and were placed in the Philadelphia *Union,* probably through the mediation of Justice Bushrod Washington who was in that city at the time. However, the *Union* garbled some of the passages in publication, and Washington, who had meantime returned to Mount Vernon, undertook to have them republished in correct form in the Alexandria *Gazette.*[17]

When the "Hampden" letters in the *Enquirer* continued their vituperative volume, Marshall returned to the task of replying, in the *Gazette,* now under the pen name of "A Friend of the Constitution." Throughout the summer of 1819 the battle of the essayists continued—resulting, in Marshall's case, in the only out-of-court constitutional commentary he ever published. It was an earnest task; not only was the Chief Justice defending the whole concept of judicial federalism which he had been carefully developing since he took his seat, but the convictions that extended back to the Virginia ratifying convention of 1788, and to the bitter memories of the winter of 1777 at Valley Forge, when a ragged, starving, and poorly armed Continental Army looked in vain for a national government capable of giving meaning to their sacrifices.

Thus what Marshall wrote as "A Friend of the Constitution" became a great gloss on the passages he had already set down in *McCulloch,* and would emphasize and extend in *Cohens* v. *Virginia* two years later, and bring to a final climax in *Gibbons* v. *Ogden* in 1824 (see Chapter VI). The Chief Justice wrote:

The zealous and persevering hostility with which the constitution was originally opposed, cannot be forgotten. The deep rooted and vindictive hate, which grew out of unfounded jealousies, and was aggravated by defeat, though suspended for a time, seems never to have been appeased. The desire to strip the government of those effective powers, which enable it to accomplish the objects for which it was created; and, by construction, essentially to reinstate that miserable confederation, whose incompetency to the preservation of our union, the short interval between the treaty of Paris and the meeting of the general convention at Philadelphia, was sufficient to demonstrate, seems to have recovered all its activity. The leaders of this plan, like skilful engineers, batter the weakest part of the citadel, knowing well, that if that can be beaten down, and a breach effected, it will be afterwards found very difficult, if not impracticable, to defend the place. The judicial department, being without power, without patronage, without the legitimate means of ingratiating itself with the people, forms this weakest part; and is, at the same time, necessary to the very existence of the government, and to the effectual execution of its laws. Great constitutional questions are unavoidably brought before this department, and its decisions must sometimes depend on a course of intricate and abstruse reasoning, which it requires no inconsiderable degree of mental exertion to comprehend, and which may, of course, be grossly misrepresented. One of these questions, the case of McCulloch against the state of Maryland, presents the fairest occasion for wounding mortally, the vital powers of the government, thro' its judiciary. Against the decision of the court, on this question, weighty interests & deep rooted prejudices are combined. . . .

I gladly take leave of the bitter invectives which compose the first number of Hampden, and proceed to a less irksome task—the examination of his arguments.

These are introduced by laying down these propositions which he declares to be incontrovertible in themselves, and which he seems to suppose, demonstrate the errors of the opinion he censures.

I do not hazard much when I say that these propositions, if admitted to be true, so far from demonstrating the error of that opinion, do not even draw it into question. They may be all true, and yet every principle laid down in the opinion be perfectly correct.

The first is that the constitution conveyed only a limited grant of powers to the general government, and reserved the residuary powers to the government of the states and to the people.

Instead of controverting this proposition, I beg leave to add to the numerous respectable authorities quoted by Hampden in support of it, one other which, in this controversy at least, is entitled to some consideration, because it is furnished by the opinion he condemns. The supreme court say, "The government [of the nation] is acknowledged by all to be one of enumerated powers. The principle that it can exercise only the powers granted to it, would seem too apparent to have required to be enforced by all those arguments which its enlightened friends, while it was depending before the people, found it necessary to urge. That principle is now universally admitted. But the question respecting the extent of the powers actually granted, is perpetually arising, and will probably continue to arise, as long as our system shall exist."

The supreme court then has affirmed this proposition in terms as positive as those used by Hampden. The judges did not indeed fortify it by authority, nor was the necessity of doing so very apparent; as mathematicians do not demonstrate axioms, neither do judges or lawyers always deem it necessary to prove propositions, the truth of which "is universally admitted."

2d. The second proposition is that the limited grant to congress of certain enumerated powers, only carried with it such additional powers as were *fairly incidental* to them; or in other words, were necessary and proper for their execution.

I will here remark, merely for the sake of perspicuity, that the second branch of this proposition, which seems to be intended as explanatory of the first, introduces I think a distinct idea. The power to do a thing, and the power to carry that thing into execution, are, I humbly conceive, the same power, and the one cannot be termed with propriety "additional" or "incidental" to the other. Under the confederation, congress could do scarcely any thing, that body could only make requisitions on the states. The passage of a resolution requiring the states to furnish certain specified sums of money, was not an "additional" or "incidental" power, but a mode of executing that which was granted. Under the constitution, the powers of government are given in terms which authorise and require congress to execute them.—The execution is of the essence of the power. Thus congress can lay and collect taxes. A law to lay and collect taxes and making all the provisions to bring the money into the treasury, is not the exercise of an "additional power" but the execution of one expressly granted. The laws which punish those who resist the collection of the revenue, or which subject the estates of collection in the first instance to the claim of the United States, or which make other collateral provisions, may be traced to incidental powers. Not to those laws which simply execute the granted power. They are a part of the original grant. . . .

It can scarcely be necessary to say, that no one of the circumstances which might seem to justify rather a strict construction in the particular cases quoted by Hampden, apply to a constitution. It is not a contract between enemies seeking each other's destruction, and anxious to insert every particular, lest a watchful adversary should take advantage of the omission.—Nor is it a case where implications in favor of one man impair the vested rights of another. Nor is it a contract for a single object, every thing relating to which, might be recollected and inserted. It is the act of a people, creating a government, without which they cannot exist as a people. The powers of this government are conferred for their own benefit, are essential to their own prosperity, and are to be exercised for their good, by persons chosen for that purpose by themselves. The object of the instrument is not a single one which can be minutely described, with all its circumstances. The attempt to do so, would totally change its nature, and defeat its purpose. It is intended to be a general system for all future times, to be adapted by those who administer it, to all future occasions that may come within its own view. From its nature, such an instrument can describe only the great objects it is intended to accomplish, and state in general terms, the specific powers which are deemed necessary for those objects. To direct the manner in which these powers are to be exercised, the means by which the objects of the government are to be effected, a legislature is [created]. This would be totally useless, if its office and duty were performed in the constitution. This legislature is an emanation from the people themselves. It is a part chosen to represent the whole, and to mark, according to the judgment of the nation, its course, within those great outlines which are given in the constitution. It is impossible to construe such an instrument rightly, without adverting to its nature, and marking the points of difference which distinguish it from ordinary contracts. . . .

It is the plain dictate of common sense, and the whole political system is founded on the idea, that the departments of government are the agents of the nation, and will perform, within their respective spheres, the duties assigned to them.—The whole owes to its parts the peaceful decision of every controversy which may arise among its members. It is one of the great duties of government, one of the great objects for which it is instituted. Agents for the performance of this duty must be furnished, or the government fails in one of the great ends of its creation.

To whom more safely than to the judges are judicial questions to be referred? They are selected from the great body of the people for the purpose of deciding them. To secure impartiality, they are made perfectly independent. They have no personal interest in aggrandizing the legislative power. Their paramount interest is the public prosperity, in which is involved their own and that of their families.—No tribunal can be less liable to be swayed by unworthy motives from a conscientious performance of duty. It is not then the party sitting in his own cause. It is the application to individuals by one department of the acts of another department of the government. The people are the authors of all; the departments are their agents; and if the judge be personally disinterested, he is as exempt from any political interest that might influence his opinion, as imperfect human institutions can make him.[18]

With this eloquent exposition of his constitutional views, the great Chief Justice felt no need to take up the pen again in 1821 when Roane attacked his opinion in *Cohens* v. *Virginia*. The furor over *McCulloch* had blown itself out in state and congressional bombast the previous year; the national excitement over the Missouri Compromise raised the first questions over the powers of government to regulate, limit—perhaps even abolish—the "peculiar institution" of slavery. In *Cohens* the Court had asserted its final measure of authority over state actions by asserting jurisdiction over criminal matters involving a federal question, as *Martin* five years before had asserted jurisdiction over civil matters. The ring had now been completed; it remained only to identify the principal instrument of national power, in the commerce clause, which would be the achievement of the Court in the steamboat case of 1824 (see Chapter VII, following).

VII

The Implement of National Power

Gibbons v. *Ogden*

Robert Fulton's perfection of the steamboat in 1807 was to prove a lucrative monopoly for the following fifteen years, for himself and the powerful Livingston family of New York, into which he married the year following the successful first voyage of the *Clermont*. Artist, civil engineer, inventor, Fulton had spent the first twenty years of his adult life in England and France, applying his fertile imagination to a number of devices essential to the gradually developing mercantile economy; and it was in France that he met the American minister, Robert R. Livingston, and joined with him on solving the problem of steam-powered navigation. Livingston was the grantee of a monopoly from the New York legislature, to provide steamboat service on the Hudson from New York City to Albany, and while this had been renewed in 1803, it was obviously unlikely to be renewed another time unless there was some tangible accomplishment toward a successful steam-power process.

Within four years Fulton had solved the practical problems, steamboat service was established on a regular basis, and the monopoly agreement was revised in 1808 in favor of a new firm of Livingston and Fulton. Three years later, still another amendment to the law authorized the firm to license other operators who would develop branch lines from the waters of New York to other points (see Part Three, Chapter V-2); and in 1815, the year of Fulton's death, one of these licensees, a former governor of New Jersey named Aaron Ogden, began a regular steam ferry service from New York to New Brunswick.

Ogden himself had challenged the New York monopoly in 1813, when he attempted to operate an unlicensed service from Elizabethtown to New York; but his suit in the state court had been defeated on the authority of another suit two years before (*Livingston* v. *Van Ingen*) [1] in which the New York Court of Appeals had unanimously and emphatically upheld the monopoly grant (see Part Three, Chapter V-3). Caught in the fever of steamboat fortune-making, however, Ogden committed the sizable funds he had built up in law practice to pay the exorbitant fees for a ten-year license, and secured what seemed like a major prize—the monopoly of steam ferry service from New Jersey to New York.

Two years later, in 1817, Ogden made an agreement with Thomas Gibbons, a Georgia-born lawyer and onetime federal judge, who by now was running vessels between New Brunswick and Elizabethtown. By linking the two lines for a continuous steamboat service from Albany to New York City (the Livingston monopoly), thence to New Brunswick (the Ogden monopoly), and on to Elizabethtown (the Gibbons line), the several entrepreneurs seemed to have the best of all commercial worlds. But Gibbons, an aggressive and ambitious competitor, within a year had persuaded himself, first, that he was getting the smallest portion of the business, and, second, that his own license under the federal navigation and coasting act of 1793 (see Part Three, Chapter V-1) was superior to and independent of the New York monopoly licenses. In 1818 Gibbons broke off the arrangement with Ogden and prepared to send his own steamboats on to New York City.

The challenge to the monopoly statute was a calculated risk. In more than a dozen cases in New York and New Jersey, extending over a dozen years, the Livingston and Fulton firm had been able to turn back every challenge, beginning with *Livingston* v. *Van Ingen*,[2] where three judges, including the future commentator on American law James Kent and a future Supreme Court Justice, Smith Thompson (another in-law of the ubiquitous Livingstons), affirmed the right of an inventor to a monopoly for a reasonable term of years, refusing to distinguish the invention from the public need for inexpensive transportation.

In 1819, in four cases, the New York courts held that "all the waters lying between Staten Island and . . . the Jersey shore" were part of the river and bay under New York jurisdiction (*Livingston* v. *Ogden and Gibbons*),[3] that Gibbons could not remove the case to the federal courts after relying on the state court for injunctive relief (*Livingston* v. *Gibbons*),[4] that Gibbons's agent, young Cornelius Vanderbilt, a master of one of the unlicensed steamboats, was personally liable to the monopoly (*In re Vanderbilt*),[5] and that transferring passengers from Elizabethtown, on Gibbons's unlicensed vessel, to another steamboat at Staten Island licensed to carry traffic from there to New York City, infringed upon the monopoly (*Ogden* v. *Gibbons*).[6]

The litigation continued both in New York and New Jersey for another five years. In New York, in 1820 and 1821, Livingston sought to tighten his monopolistic grip (*Livingston* v. *Gibbons*),[7] and Gibbons began the final litigation which would go to the Supreme Court (*Gibbons v. Ogden;* cf. Part Three, Chapter V-4). In New Jersey, in 1822, Gibbons succeeded in getting a trespass judgment against Livingston (*Gibbons v. Livingston*),[8] although it was not practicable to seek to recover on the judgment; and in a similar action against Ogden (*Gibbons v. Ogden*)[9] the court declined to grant relief although it expressed doubts as to the constitutional issue.

Moreover, the principal case now moving toward the Supreme Court had already suffered one rebuff, in 1821, when the decree of the New York courts was found not to be a final decree[10] as required by the Judiciary Act. In addition, the New York court had anticipated much of the constitutional ground and had sought to confine its own decision to the state grounds * asserting the right of the state to grant exclusive rights to its citizens. Chancellor Kent, in denying Gibbons's renewed effort to dissolve the monopoly injunction, declared that "a necessary attribute of every independent government" was the power to make "grants of exclusive privileges for beneficial purposes."[11]

On the other hand, a bitter legal and political reaction to the New York monopoly had already set in. Connecticut, New Jersey, and Ohio had enacted legislation denying use of their own state waters to vessels operating under licenses of the monopoly. The Livingston–Fulton firm had retaliated by granting licenses to operators in Georgia, Massachusetts, New Hampshire, and Vermont, while members of the Livingston family in Louisiana began steamboat service in the lower Mississippi.[12] This situation had brought a number of states, in the words of Attorney General William Wirt, to the brink of "civil war," and pointed up the fundamental issue in the appeal which finally was docketed in January 1822 (although it was not reached for two more years). Wirt, Daniel Webster, and David B. Ogden represented the appellant, Gibbons, while Thomas Addis Emmet and Thomas J. Oakley argued the case for the appellee, Aaron Ogden.

With so much riding on the case—ultimately, the question of whether the United States would be a common market without "balkanizing" state controls over interstate commerce—President Monroe was anxious to learn what position the members of the Supreme Court were likely to take. While the judicial tradition, then as now, was to avoid any discussion of a case pending in the Court, Monroe subtly resorted to his own devices in the spring of 1822. In May of that year, the President had vetoed a bill which would have extended federal authority over turnpikes

---

* The Supreme Court usually declines to grant review of state cases where there are found to be adequate state grounds to sustain the judgment, thus avoiding the constitutional issue.

within the boundaries of the states.[13] Monroe prepared a memorandum expressing his opinion in a pamphlet which was sent, among others, to the Justices of the Supreme Court,* hoping to glean at least some hints as to the Justices' position. Marshall and Story, in acknowledging the President's pamphlet, were ambivalent in their comments; but Justice Johnson, the original Jeffersonian appointee who was intended to press a states' rights viewpoint on the Court, undertook on his own initiative to find out his colleagues' views—and to report them to Monroe. In an undated letter to the President that summer, he wrote:

> Judge Johnson has had the Honour to submit the President's argument on the subject of internal improvement to his Brother Judges, and is instructed [sic] to make the following Report. The Judges are deeply sensible of the mark of confidence bestowed on them in this instance and should be unworthy of that confidence did they attempt to conceal their real opinion. Indeed, to conceal or disavow it would be now impossible as they are all of opinion that the decision on the Bank question [*McCulloch* v. *Maryland*] completely commits them on the subject of internal improvement, as applied to Postroads and Military Roads. On the other points, it is impossible to resist the lucid and conclusive reasoning contained in the argument. The principle assumed in the case of the Bank is that the granting of the principal power carries with it the grant of all necessary and appropriate means of executing it. That the selection of these means must rest with the General Government, and as to that power and those means the Constitution makes the Government of the U.S. supreme.[14]

This letter clearly "telegraphed" the ultimate determination of the "steamboat case" in 1824; if a state tax could not be permitted to hamper the exercise of national power, a state monopoly would not be permitted to do so. And this was no "necessary and proper" power to be subject to different constructions—it was an express power vested in Congress "to regulate commerce . . . among the several states." If the Constitution, and the laws enacted in implementation of the Constitution, was indeed the supreme law of the land, the power of the national government over commerce, the fundamental economic reason for drafting the Constitution, had to be paramount and plenary.[15]

Meanwhile, in 1823, Justice Johnson would go on to write a circuit opinion (see Part Three, Chapter V-5) which would further establish the judicial position on the federal power over interstate commerce. In his native state, this southern Jeffersonian would pronounce, as emphatically as Chief Justice Marshall the following year, the doctrine that no state

---

* Until well into the twentieth century, it was difficult and often impossible for the government to intervene in a private suit, as this one between Gibbons and Ogden, even when a major constitutional issue was involved. Today the executive branch would either petition or be invited to file its own briefs on such a question.

could impede or qualify the authority of the federal government in the interstate area. He would do it, moreover, on the most explosive of all issues, the right of free men (blacks, in this case) to cross state lines without hindrance—explosive not simply for its abstract moral implications but because hardly a year before nearly three dozen blacks had been hanged for their parts in an insurrection fomented by a free black in this very town of Charleston, South Carolina.

Telemaque Vesey—his first name corrupted to "Denmark"—had purchased his own freedom in 1800 and settled in Charleston, having served up to that time as a slave and seaman for nineteen of his thirty-three years. Energetic and well read, Vesey had established himself in trade and sired a large family by several slave women. By 1818, resenting his children's slave heritage, he began a systematic plan for recruiting and arming men to rise up and overthrow the system at a given signal. The plan came so close to success, at least in Charleston, where a last-minute betrayal led to capture of the leaders, that a wave of fear swept the state, and the legislature passed the Negro Seamen Act prohibiting free blacks from entering or residing in the state. In July 1822, Vesey and thirty-four of his confederates were executed.

The constitutionality of the statute was quickly challenged in the federal Circuit Court in Charleston, and Johnson, as Circuit Justice, delivered the opinion in the case in August 1823. A free black seaman, born in Jamaica and a British subject, was arrested when his ship arrived in Charleston harbor from Liverpool. Although the opinion was somewhat ambivalent as to specific procedures and remedies (see Part Three, Chapter V-5), it was unequivocal as to the provisions of the state law: As these bore upon the power to regulate "commerce with foreign nations" they were unconstitutional; those regulations could only be established through the treaty power, which was exclusively vested in the national government. Therefore the commerce power, as to international trade, was totally within the jurisdiction of the United States. It now remained, in the steamboat case, to determine whether the power as to interstate trade was also totally within the jurisdiction of the nation.[16]

It was not the South Carolina seamen's act, however, that offered the major issue in *Gibbons* v. *Ogden* (see Part Three, Chapter V-6) as the case at last came on for argument in February 1824. There was a flurry of activity on the part of counsel when the case was called; as Webster later remarked, "the tapes had not been off the papers [in the case] for more than a year." Yet Webster knew what was expected of him, and he worked all night to prepare his brief. In the intimacy of the bench and bar, there was no need to issue a formal invitation to counsel to argue a particular point; the man who had delivered the great oral argument in the

Dartmouth College case, and had joined with Wirt and Pinckney in the case of *McCulloch* v. *Maryland,* understood that Marshall in this hour was seeking the implement by which the supreme law of the land, defined in the Bank case, could now be administered by the United States, making it a nation economically as well as politically.[17]

In its final opinion, as Webster was to observe afterward, the Marshall Court adopted virtually all of his argument, which, as a later commentator phrased it, "released every creek and river, every lake and harbor in our country from the interference of monopolies." [18] The Massachusetts lawyer was as confident, at the close of arguments, as he had been at the conclusion of oral presentations on the Bank case; "it can go but one way," he wrote his brother a week later.[19] How closely he had understood the mind of the Chief Justice and the entire Court was to be seen in the remarkable parallels of his argument and the opinion. The commerce power, said Webster, is "complete and entire, and, to a certain extent, necessarily exclusive"; the letter and spirit of the power vested by the Constitution was by definition barred to the states. Any concurrent power over commerce held by both states and nation was circumscribed by this principle; for if the Constitution intended Congress to maintain a uniform commercial system among the states, this purpose controlled the degree to which state action could enter the field.

As to New York's insistence on its sovereign authority, Webster said, this went to the question of police power to protect health and safety;[20] a reasonable construction of the responsibilities of both state and national authority could distinguish their respective areas of jurisdiction. But where the intention of the Constitution was to insure free trade within the Union, state action which necessarily prejudiced this purpose had to fall. "It requires no greater power, to grant a monopoly of trade, than a monopoly of navigation." [21]

In Marshall's paraphrase of Webster, the supremacy doctrine in *Mc-Culloch* v. *Maryland* was reaffirmed and made specific; the commerce power, said the Chief Justice, "like all others vested in Congress, is complete in itself, may be exercised to its utmost extent, and acknowledges no limitations other than are prescribed in the Constitution." For under the system of government created by the Constitution, "the sovereignty of Congress, though limited to specific objects, is plenary as to those objects." Only upon such a premise could a Constitution "intended to endure for ages to come" be a viable instrument. In anticipation of the protests of the Spencer Roanes of his own and future generations, Marshall concluded:

Powerful and ingenious minds, taking as postulates, that the powers expressly granted to the government of the Union, are to be contracted by con-

The epochal constitutional battles of the Marshall Court were waged between many parties, from Presidents to ordinary citizens, and over many battlefields in the young republic. Eventually the action moved into the courtrooms over which John Marshall presided—at first, a makeshift meeting place in the raw new capitol building (in which no provision had been made for the Supreme Court of the United States), where the momentous decision in *Marbury* v. *Madison* was handed down in 1803; then, to a chamber in Richmond, Virginia, where the succession of cases involving Aaron Burr were argued and disposed of by the Chief Justice sitting as a Circuit Court judge together with United States District Judge Cyrus Griffin.

Supreme Court chamber in United States Capitol, used 1810–1860

In 1810 Congress finally provided the highest court in the land with a proper courtroom within the capitol. Shown above in its restored form, a project completed in 1975 by the Senate Commission on Arts and Antiquities, this became the final scene for the constitutional arguments and opinions in the *Dartmouth College* case, *McCulloch* v. *Maryland,* and *Gibbons* v. *Ogden,* as well as other great decisions of the Supreme Court in the days of Marshall.

MARBURY V. MADISON

William Marbury, who had moved from Baltimore to the new "federal city" in the District of Columbia, may have been persuaded to seek the delivery of his commission as a justice of the peace by Federalists looking for a test case. In any event, he was typical of many an individual whose name accidentally achieves renown not for the person but for the great issue with which it is associated. The other three parties to the famous litigation — Dennis Ramsay, William Harper, and Robert Townsend Hooe — never attained even that degree of notoriety. Marbury himself slipped back into anonymity after the constitutional contest in which he served virtually as a surrogate for the Chief Justice in a test of strength with Thomas Jefferson. Later in life he became a director of a Georgetown bank.

Jefferson's surrogate — indeed, his official agent — in the contest with John Marshall was James Madison, who succeeded Marshall as Secretary of State. When Madison in due course succeeded Jefferson as President, he would make his own contribution to Supreme Court history by appointing Joseph Story as Associate Justice; Story's authoritative *Commentaries on the Constitution* provided the ultimate rationale for the precedents which he and Marshall established in their years together on the bench. Madison, whose own *Notes* on the Convention of 1787 would earn him the sobriquet of "Father of the Constitution," did not always follow the Jeffersonian line, but in the case of the commissions he did what was required of the Secretary of State upon an instruction from the Chief Executive: he withheld, and perhaps ordered the destruction, of the undelivered commissions.

William Marbury

James Madison

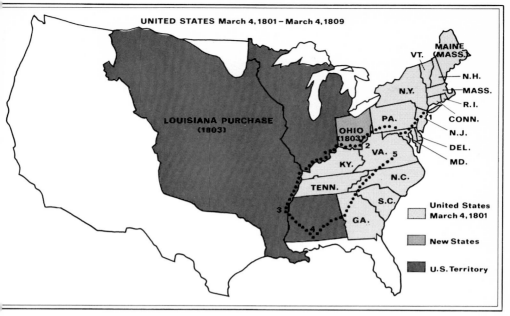

UNITED STATES March 4, 1801 – March 4, 1809

LOUISIANA PURCHASE
(1803)

MAINE
(MASS.)

VT.

N.H.

N.Y.

MASS.

R.I.

PA.

CONN.

OHIO
(1803)

N.J.

DEL.

VA.

MD.

KY.

N.C.

TENN.

S.C.

GA.

United States
March 4, 1801

New States

U.S. Territory

Odyssey of Aaron Burr, from the duel with Alexander Hamilton to the treason trials in Richmond

UNITED STATES V. BURR

The bizarre, cryptic, and often tragic career of Aaron Burr is graphically suggested in the excerpt from the map of the United States in his day tracing his wandering trail from Washington, where he all but won the Presidency in 1801, to New York, where the fatal duel with Alexander Hamilton took place, to Blennerhasset's island in the Ohio River and down the Mississippi to New Orleans, where disaster rather than destiny greeted him. The flight and ignominious capture on the wild frontier, the prisoner's march back to Richmond, the deadly contest with Thomas Jefferson, and the indeterminate judicial test of what his ultimate purposes had been — these also were part of his odyssey, while, somewhere off the coast of the Carolinas, his beloved daughter Theodosia died at sea in 1813.

As in the *Marbury* case four years earlier, the ultimate contest was between Jefferson and Marshall, although in this instance the President fixed his retribution upon Burr as well. It had not always been so between Jefferson and his first-term Vice-President; even with Hamilton's blood on his hands, Burr had been urged to return to Washington to preside over the impeachment trial of Supreme Court Justice Samuel Chase. As in his other attacks upon the Marshall tribunal, Jefferson was to be disappointed in this maneuver to place an anti-Federalist in charge of the impeachment proceedings; Burr was described as presiding over the Chase trial with "ferocious impartiality."

Jefferson may not have felt the great alarm for the safety of the nation that he professed in his increasingly strident allegations of Burr's treason. Frustration at national impotence to deal with powerful European intrigues, exacerbated by

Aaron Burr

Thomas Jefferson

the indication that the national courts intended to insure a fair and dispassionate trial for all accused persons, finally reached an explosive level when Chief Justice Marshall, his perennial adversary, turned up as the Circuit Justice in Burr's case. On the other hand, Jefferson was acutely aware of the chronic pressure for secession in the trans-Appalachian West; the complaints that opportunities for trade were stifled while New Orleans was in the hands of a foreign power had not yet been effectively offset by the purchase of the Louisiana Territory.

But these considerations were quickly swallowed up in the challenge flung down by John Marshall, set off by Burr's motion to subpoena certain documents in the President's possession and alleged to be material to Burr's defense. The nature of treason and the Constitution's requirements for proof of treason became, for the moment, subsidiary questions, while the judicial and executive branches locked in battle over Presidential privilege and discretion.

TRUSTEES OF DARTMOUTH COLLEGE V. WOODWARD

The case of the "small College" and "those who love her," as Daniel Webster put it in his final flourish of oral argument, was in reality the kingpin in the Marshall Court's progressively constructed doctrine of constitutional restraints upon the states reviewable in the federal court of last resort. By treating a sovereign grant of a charter as equivalent to a contract between parties — a premise whose shakiness was offset by analogous precedents established in earlier cases — Marshall was able to read the contract clause of the Constitution (Article I, Section 10, Clause 1) as a general restraint upon state laws tending to limit the advantages which contracting parties might secure for themselves. While the Dartmouth College doctrine was qualified even in Marshall's day by recognition that a state as a contracting party might reserve certain options at the time of a grant, the noninterference with the "obligations of contracts" by the early twentieth century had become a means of exploitation of labor before the age of collective bargaining.

Sketch of Dartmouth College campus by George Ticknor in 1803. Part of the original caption in verse read: "Where late the Savage roam'd in search of prey/ Fair science spreads her all enlightening way."

Andrew Jackson

McCULLOCH V. MARYLAND

Neither the Second Bank of the United States nor the cashier of its Maryland branch could be said to have acted in ways likely to endear themselves to citizens of the state; indeed, the Bank was an unsavory monster in the view of many Americans — including Andrew Jackson when, as President, he launched his historic fight against the institution. (Jackson's field commander in this struggle was Roger B. Taney, who would succeed Marshall as Chief Justice in 1835.)

Nevertheless, the Marshall Court saw the issue in terms of the constitutional provision for supremacy of federal power where it was authorized by the Constitution—and the power to establish a national bank as one of the "necessary and proper" means of carrying into effect any power vested in the United States by the Constitution. Thus John James, attempting to levy the Maryland tax on notes issued by the Bank of the United States, was to be found by the Supreme Court as attempting to burden a legitimate function of federal government in a manner which would make federal power subordinate rather than supreme.

GIBBONS V. OGDEN

The case on judicial review in 1803 and the commerce clause, or "steamboat" case, in 1824 represented the beginning and end of a continuum of constitutional exposition of government power; and, like *Marbury,* the parties named in the "steamboat" litigation were otherwise little known to history. Thomas Gibbons and Aaron Ogden were originally partners enjoying the benefits of a monopolistic franchise offered by the state of New York. When the partnership dissolved, Gibbons then challenged Ogden's rights under the state franchise as against his own license under act of Congress. The question provided the Marshall Court with its patiently defined objective — to assert the paramount authority of Congress over interstate commerce (Article I, Section 8, Clause 3). This commerce clause power in the United States — enlarged over the following generations to cover federal regulation of interstate business, the goods transported in that business, the conditions of labor producing the goods, and ultimately public policy as relating to interstate travel (e.g., the racial integration of "public accommodations") — marks *Gibbons* v. *Ogden* as the climactic decision in the Marshall Court's definition of the powers of federal government.

mas Gibbons   *Aaron Ogden*

Spencer Roane

THE CHALLENGERS: SPENCER ROANE AND ANDREW JACKSON

In the lifetime of the Marshall Court, two Presidents and a state high court judge offered challenges to the constitutional presumptions of the Chief Justice and his Associates. Jefferson's long campaign of resistance continued to the end of his life.

Spencer Roane of Virginia sought to use his own position as judge of the state court of appeals to curb what he considered to be the threats to states' rights in the Marshall Court's decisions. In 1813, when the Court (speaking through Justice Story) reversed the Virginia court in the renowned Fairfax lands dispute, Roane on remand denied the federal tribunal's jurisdiction over the case. On the second review of the question in 1816 (*Martin* v. *Hunter's Lessee*), Story unequivocally affirmed the Supreme Court's jurisdiction. Three years later Roane unleashed a vigorous pamphleteering attack on Marshall's opinion in *McCulloch* v. *Maryland,* prompting the Chief Justice to depart from established practice to reply (under a pseudonym) in defense of his decision.

Neither Jefferson nor Roane — who is generally considered to have been Jefferson's choice for Chief Justice had Adams not foreclosed that option — could claim demonstrable success in their disputes with the Marshall Court. Changing times and issues, the decline in Marshall's own vigor near the end of his Chief Justiceship, and the brawling instincts of a frontier Indian fighter made it possible for Andrew Jackson to defy the Court, at least on one occasion, where Jefferson and Roane failed. "John Marshall has made his decision; now let him enforce it," was Jackson's retort to the decision in *Worcester* v. *Georgia.* Ironically enough, Jackson was as much an advocate of national power as the Chief Justice ever was. His political base in friendly Georgia politics and his belief in manifest destiny where Indian rights were in question led him easily to conclude that Georgia's actions of expropriation of Cherokee titles were convenient implementations of national power. While he refused to enforce the *Worcester* decision, Jackson soon thereafter invoked the principle in the case to justify his attack on South Carolina's attempt at nullification. John Marshall, in the end, was to be vindicated by his last challenger.

THE GREAT CHIEF JUSTICE AND HIS COURT

Following John Marshall's death in 1835, efforts to raise funds for a suitable statue were initiated, but languished over the next half-century. In 1882 Congress approved an appropriation of $20,000 (supplementing a similar private amount) to commission a statue by the sculptor William Wetmore Story, son of Justice Joseph Story. Two years later the statue was delivered from Italy to Washington and dedicated by Chief Justice Morrison R. Waite. A replica of the statue stands in front of the Pennsylvania Museum of Fine Arts in Philadelphia.

Marshall's thirty-five-year tenure is the longest for any Chief Justice, followed by twenty-eight years for his successor, Roger B. Taney. While Taney's judicial federalism was less affirmative than Marshall's the sixty-three-year continuity of the two Chief Justiceships firmly established the Supreme Court's role in American life.

Statue of John Marshall by William Wetmore Story (1884)

William Cushing

William Paterson

When Marshall assumed the Chief Justiceship in 1801, he joined five Associates on what was then a six-man Court. William Cushing of Massachusetts was the senior Justice and the only original appointee of President George Washington in 1789. Cushing's eloquent support of the new Constitution in the Massachusetts ratifying convention, and his service as chief justice of the commonwealth's Supreme Judicial Court, made him a logical appointee for the new federal judiciary. Although President John Adams nominated him to be Chief Justice in 1800, and the Senate confirmed him, Cushing declined the position and remained as Associate until his death in 1810.

William Paterson of New Jersey served from 1793 to 1806. He had been a delegate to the Constitutional Convention in Philadelphia, and as a member of the first Senate had been a strong advocate of the Judiciary Act of 1789 which created the federal court system. He performed a useful pragmatic service to the Marshall Court in his opinion in *Stuart* v. *Laird* (1 Cranch 299) declaring the validity of the anti-Federalist Congress's repeal of the Circuit Court Act of 1801, thus avoiding an impasse with the Jefferson administration over the abolishing of the circuit judgeships created by that Act.

Samuel Chase of Maryland served from 1796 to 1811 and was the target of impeachment proceedings in 1805 — the only member of the Supreme Court ever to incur this fate. Although Chase's intemperate and highly partisan behavior on circuit was hardly to be condoned, the question of whether it was impeachable conduct was distorted by the Jeffersonian plan to seek removal of a number of Federalist judges by this device. The House of Representatives returned eighteen articles of impeachment; and while the Senate found a majority for three articles, it was not the three-fourths majority required by

Samuel Chase

Bushrod Washington

Alfred Moore

the Constitution. As a result of the failure to remove Chase, the Jeffersonians abandoned their strategy.

Bushrod Washington (1798–1829), nephew of the first President, was to serve a long and intimate association with the Chief Justice. A leading practicing attorney, first in Pennsylvania and later in Virginia, he succeeded to the seat of James Wilson, under whom he had studied law in Philadelphia nearly twenty years earlier. His training under Wilson and his personal association with Marshall in practice in the Richmond bar provided the Chief Justice with a consistent supporter in all of the great constitutional issues of the first quarter of the nineteenth century.

Alfred Moore of North Carolina, appointed in 1799, served only three years under Marshall before he resigned in 1804. The most significant feature of his career on the Court was the opening created by his resignation, which was the first opportunity for President Jefferson to place an anti-Federalist on the bench.

William Johnson   *Brockholst Livingston*

THE FIRST JEFFERSONIANS

After Marshall's appointment in 1801, exactly fifty years were to pass before there would be another appointment of a Justice whose political affiliation was close to the old Federalist philosophy. All of the Associates who succeeeded the Federalists on the Court at the time of Marshall's accession were to be Republicans — later identified as Democratic Republicans and finally as Democrats. While party allegiance of Justices has traditionally been muted if not disavowed, the first selections by the Jeffersonians were frankly intended to alter the political philosophy of the Marshall Court.

When Justice Moore resigned in 1804, Jefferson appointed William Johnson of South Carolina, who would serve for thirty years — not so much as a committed dissenter as a "yes, but" exponent of views distinguishable from the often categorical nationalism or centrism of the Marshall majority.

Henry Brockholst Livingston (1806–1823) succeeded Justice Paterson and quickly moved to the Chief Justice's coterie, where for the most part he would remain throughout his tenure. Some critics, then and later, charged him with breaches of the tradition of judicial confidentiality in deciding cases; in some instances, at least, these were leaks that were almost unavoidable in consideration of his continued contacts with his many influential relatives and former

mas Todd   *Joseph Story*

ON THE FEDERALIST COURT

colleagues in the New York bar.

The expanding number of new states required establishment of a seventh circuit in 1807, with a new seventh Justice to represent it. Thomas Todd, chief justice of Kentucky, thus became the seventh member of Marshall's Court and served until 1826, although illness and the difficulty in reaching the nation's capital caused him to miss several complete terms.

When Justice Cushing died in 1811, it took four nominations by President James Madison to fill the vacancy. After two appointees declined commission and a third was rejected by the Senate, Madison finally chose a nominal' Republican lawyer from Massachusetts named Joseph Story. Story quickly joined Marshall's nationalistic nucleus on the Court, writing the official opinions on the two Virginia cases — *Fairfax's Devisee* v. *Hunter's Devisee* in 1813 and *Martin* v. *Hunter's Lessee* in 1816 — which laid the foundation for Marshall's opinion in *McCulloch* v. *Maryland* in 1819, establishing the paramountcy of federal power over the states in areas where the national interest was established. Story's great *Commentaries on the Constitution* in 1833 and his continued service on the Court until 1845 provided continuity and definitive authority to the doctrines of the Marshall years.

Gabriel Duvall of Maryland joined the Court at the same time as Story, following the death of Justice Chase, and served until 1835, the year of Marshall's death, when he resigned. His early record was essentially anti-Federalist — he declined the appointment to serve as delegate to the Philadelphia Convention in 1787, and he was a member of Jefferson's administration as the first comptroller of the currency. With his appointment the Republicans gained the majority on the Court; but Duvall for the most part sided with the Chief Justice, Washington, and Story. His dissent in the *Dartmouth College* case was without opinion. Increasing deafness made him ineffective in his latter years on the bench.

Smith Thompson was appointed by President James Monroe, serving from 1823 to 1843 in the seat previously held by Justice Livingston, his kinsman by marriage. Thompson's appointment marked the beginning of the end of the centrist federalism which the Marshall Court had maintained, usually with unanimity. In 1827 he dissented in *Brown* v. *Maryland* (12 Wheaton 419), where the majority held an unbroken interstate shipment immune from state taxation; and in the same term he put Marshall into a rare dissenting minority by writing the Court's opinion in *Ogden* v. *Saunders* (12 Wheaton 213), a case which began the qualification of the contract clause restraints suggested in 1819 in *Sturges* v. *Crowninshield* (see Chapter III).

Gabriel Duvall   *Smith Thompson*   *John Quincy Adams*

bert Trimble

John McLean

Henry Baldwin

The shortest term on the Marshall Court was served by Robert Trimble of Kentucky (1826–1828), John Quincy Adams's only nomination to the high bench during his Presidency. Trimble, successor to Justice Todd, had had a distinguished professional career in his state, but his unexpected death cut short any chance to establish a record on the federal tribunal.

John McLean was Andrew Jackson's first appointment to the Supreme Court and served from 1829 to 1861. An astute and ambitious Ohio politician, he posed a possible threat to Jackson's own plans for a two-term Presidency, and the judicial appointment was supposed to dispose of this problem. Throughout most of his tenure on the Court, however, McLean continued to take an active interest in political developments of the state and nation. Even his appointment was a consequence of partisanship; the outgoing Adams administration had sought to fill the Trimble seat with John Crittenden of Kentucky.

The last member of the Marshall Court was Henry Baldwin of Pennsylvania, who served from 1830 to 1844. He succeeded Justice Bushrod Washington, and Jackson had expected him to be "his man" on the bench. During Marshall's declining years as Chief Justice, however, Baldwin generally supported the Marshall viewpoint.

James Wayne   *Roger B. Taney*   *Philip Pendleton Barbour*

In the closing period of the Marshall Court, three appointments epitomized the transition to a new era—John M. Wayne of Georgia, who succeeded Justice Johnson in 1834; Roger B. Taney of Maryland, who would become Chief Justice upon Marshall's death; and Philip Pendleton Barbour of Virginia, who filled the position left by Justice Duvall's retirement.

All three men were henchmen of Andrew Jackson — indeed, that was the fundamental criterion for their selection. Congressman Wayne had categorically asserted the right of Georgia to expropriate Cherokee Indian lands and in the House of Representatives had been an administration stalwart in the war on the Bank of the United States — both high on Jackson's list of objectives. Taney, as Attorney General and then as Secretary of the Treasury, had been the field marshal of the "Bank war," and though his earlier nomination as an Associate Justice had been tabled, Jackson pushed him through as the new Chief Justice. Barbour, an ultra-conservative Congressman, was a leading member of the "Albany–Richmond axis" which dominated national Democratic politics. With these three additions to the Court, the age of Marshall — and the giants who worked with him — passed into history.

struction into the narrowest possible compass, and that the original powers of
the states are retained, if any possible construction will retain them, may, by
a course of well digested, but refined and metaphysical reasoning, founded on
these premises, explain away the Constitution of our country, and leave it, a
magnificent structure, indeed, to look at, but totally unfit for use.[22]

With this opinion, the great Chief Justice put the final gloss upon the
doctrine of constitutional supremacy which he had asserted in the Bank
case of 1819. Indeed, with the steamboat case of 1824, the Constitution
as John Marshall construed it had received its final essential definition.
Over a twenty-one-year period, extending from the momentous decision
on judicial review in *Marbury* v. *Madison,* through the stormy passages
of Burr's treason trial, the Yazoo contract issue, the assertion of a review
power over state actions in cases from *Martin* v. *Hunter's Lessee* to
Dartmouth College, the evolution of constitutional jurisprudence had been
consistent. Now the commerce clause—complete in itself and capable of
such application as Congress might choose to make of it—was the practical implement by which this constitutional system would function.

Webster's argument for a reasonable division of activities between
states and the nation in the federal structure was accepted by the Marshall
Court, as was Justice Johnson's insistence upon exclusive federal authority
in areas which were clearly interstate and foreign in subject. In 1827 the
Court struck down state efforts to levy taxes on foreign commerce,[23]
and two years later accepted Webster's dual arguments for concurrent
jurisdiction and the essential application of state police powers in navigable waters.[24] In 1837, two years after Marshall's death, the Taney Court
extended the police power basis for concurrent jurisdiction with reference
to port quarantine regulations [25]—although not without a dissent from
Story. In 1851 a divided Court upheld, again as a reasonable application
of police power, a state requirement that incoming and outgoing vessels
in a harbor take on local pilots familiar with the harbor.[26]

In the last quarter of the nineteenth century the implementing of federal power through the commerce clause, which Marshall had developed
in the first quarter, began to be applied in broadening economic and
social areas. Interstate commerce was defined as transcontinental commerce in the generation following the Civil War, a definition which implied
far more than the relatively simple economic organization of navigable
streams, canals, and post roads of Marshall's day. The railroad age substantially presaged these changing frames of reference even before the
Civil War; and the emergence of an industrial America after that era
permanently altered the structure of American society. The administrative
regulatory agency appeared on the scene—first validated as a police power
extension at the state level in the Granger cases [27] of the seventies, then
given federal cognizance in the form of the Interstate Commerce Com-

mission Act of 1888, its very title indicating its foundation upon the structure Marshall had established.

Where the ideological struggles over national power implemented by the commerce clause in the time of Marshall had been between states' rights advocates and nationalists, the antagonists now assumed the roles of free enterprise, laissez faire advocates, and a slowly growing number of supporters of social controls in the interests of a larger public. The latter were alternately known as populists, trust busters, and progressives, but the essential product of their half-century of struggle, from the eighties to the Great Depression, was a steadily widening use of the commerce clause—countered by laissez faire reliance on the contract clause (e.g., noninterference with labor contracts) and the due process restraints of the Fourteenth Amendment.

The intricate contentions of the rival schools raged in full fury in the nineties, with the Congressional effort in the Sherman Anti-Trust Act offset by the narrow construction of the statute in the Sugar Trust case [28] of 1895, then rehabilitated by the holding company (*Northern Securities*) [29] case of 1904. In turn, this advance was counterbalanced by the opinion outlawing the secondary boycott (Danbury Hatters case) [30] in 1908. But amid this ebb and flow of legal and economic argument, the use of the commerce clause as an implement of a national police power, as in the Lottery Case [31] of 1903, presaged a wider potential. In the climax of the progressive movement on the eve of the first World War, this police power was validated in the enforcement of the Pure Food and Drug Act in 1911, and three years later in the judicial affirmance of a federal right to control *intrastate* railroad rates where this was a "necessary and proper" means of making *interstate* rate controls effective.[32]

But the trend toward broadening national power under the Constitution—commerce clause or whatever—was an uneven one, against the bitter-end resistance of the forces of localism and laissez faire. A long period of judicial reaction to the Progressive Era began in 1918 in the Child Labor Case,[33] in which the Court denied the constitutionality of a police power claim to control the shipment in interstate commerce of goods produced by exploited juvenile labor. The reaction continued through most of the decade of the twenties [34] and through the first New Deal of Franklin D. Roosevelt, when a succession of emergency laws of the Depression years were struck down.[35] A major constitutional crisis, as acute as that of the great Jeffersonian–Supreme Court confrontation of 1803 and 1807, eventually led to a breaking of the intransigent conservatism of the Court and a final triumph of the Marshall doctrine that the commerce clause, as the implement of national power, could be used to its greatest extent.[36]

There remained, after the settling of the economic conflicts, the matter of using the commerce clause for social reform as well, beginning with the Civil Rights Act of 1964 and the definitive judicial opinions upholding this use of the commerce power.[37] In summing up the long evolution of the clause to this point in the twentieth century, Justice Tom Clark observed:

The same interest in protecting interstate commerce which led Congress to deal with segregation in interstate carriers and the white slave traffic has prompted it to extend the exercise of its power to gambling; to criminal enterprises; to deceptive practices in the sale of products; to fraudulent security transactions; to misbranding of drugs; to wages and hours; to members of labor unions; to crop control; to discrimination against shippers; to the protection of small business from injurious price cutting; to resale price maintenance; to professional football; and to racial discrimination by owners and managers of terminal restaurants.

That Congress was legislating against moral wrongs in many of these areas rendered its enactments no less valid. In framing . . . this Act Congress was also dealing with what it considered a moral problem. But that fact does not detract from the overwhelming evidence of the disruptive effect that racial discrimination has had on commercial intercourse. It was this burden which empowered Congress to enact appropriate legislation, and, given this basis for the exercise of its power, Congress was not restricted by the fact that the particular obstruction to interstate commerce with which it was dealing was also deemed a moral and social wrong.[38]

The heritage of John Marshall, which had been completed in the steamboat case of 1824, had reached full flower in the Constitution of the late twentieth century. With this heritage, the Constitution did indeed show promise of being able to endure for ages to come.

PART TWO

JOHN MARSHALL'S CONSTITUTION

I

John Marshall's Constitution
1787-1835

The Constitution as it had developed by the time of the Marshall Court consisted of the original language of 1787 and twelve amendments. In 1804, the third year of Marshall's Chief Justiceship, the Twelfth Amendment, fundamentally revising the procedure for electing President and Vice-President, was ratified by the requisite three-fourths of the states then in the Union (thirteen out of seventeen). Throughout Marshall's career on the bench, this remained the basic framework for the government of the United States; not until 1868, long after his day, would the Fourteenth Amendment be adopted, and, a generation later, the interpretation of that Amendment would create a constitutional frame of reference sharply distinguishable from the federalism designed by the Marshall Court.

The landmark cases treated in this volume, as well as a number of other constitutional comments by the great Chief Justice and his Associates, were—except for a few opinions of the pre-Marshall decade—the first interpretations of a pristine text. They provided both catalyst and counterbalance in a generation which was struggling to define its own national character. The Marshall years extended from the anti-federalism of Thomas Jefferson's administration to the floodtide of western democracy on which Andrew Jackson came to power. In some instances, the Court's response to the changes in American life which occurred between 1801 and 1835 meant the modification of earlier doctrines in later opinions. It was by this means that the Chief Justice viewed the primary function of the judiciary, preserving the flexibility of "a Constitution intended to endure for ages to come, and, consequently, to be adapted to the various crises of human affairs" (*McCulloch* v. *Maryland,* 4 Wheaton 316, 415).

The Marshall Court's construction of particular passages in the Constitution was summarized, from his own viewpoint, by Joseph Story, Marshall's great colleague, in his definitive *Commentaries,* published in 1833, two years before Marshall's death. Much of the annotation of the text which follows is based on Story's treatise, the annotation being kept to the minimum required to illustrate the construction put upon the text by the Marshall Court. The constitutional text preserves the spelling and grammatical usages of the day, and clauses which provided the spring-board for the major decisions (or otherwise figured significantly in the constitutional issues of this period) are printed in boldface type. The annotations are printed in slightly smaller type and indented under the relevant articles of the constitutional text.

The Text of the Constitution, 1787–1835

Preamble

We the People of the United States, in Order to form a more perfect Union, establish Justice, insure domestic Tranquillity, provide for the common defense, promote the general Welfare, and secure the Blessings of Liberty to ourselves and our Posterity, do ordain and establish this Constitution for the United States of America.

> The Constitution was the creation of the people of the United States as a nation—not of the states or the people of the separate states—as Marshall and Story repeatedly stressed; "the American people are one; and the government which is alone capable of controlling and managing their interests in all these respects, is the government of the Union," said the Chief Justice in 1821 (*Cohens* v. *Virginia,* 6 Wheaton 264, 413), a position he had first taken two years before in *McCulloch* v. *Maryland* (see Part Three, Chapter IV, page 319) and would assert again in 1827 in *Brown* v. *Maryland* (12 Wheaton 419, 445, 446). Story added authorities such as the first Chief Justice, John Jay, one of the early Associate Justices, James Wilson, and the authors of the Federalist Papers to conclude that "the uniform doctrine of the highest judicial authority has accordingly been, that it [the Constitution] was the act of the people, and not of the state; and that it bound the latter, as subordinate to the people." (1 *Commentaries on the Constitution,* Section 463, and references cited thereat.)

I. The Legislative Article

Section 1. All legislative Powers herein granted shall be vested in a Congress of the United States, which shall consist of a Senate and House of Representatives.

Section 2. The House of Representatives shall be composed of Members chosen every second Year by the People of the several States, and the Electors in each State shall have the Qualifications requisite for Electors of the most numerous Branch of the State Legislature.

No Person shall be a Representative who shall not have attained to the age of twenty five Years, and been seven Years a Citizen of the United States, and who shall not, when elected, be an Inhabitant of that State in which he shall be chosen.

Representatives and direct Taxes shall be apportioned among the several States which may be included within this Union, according to their respective Numbers, which shall be determined by adding to the whole Number of free Persons, including those bound to Service for a Term of Years, and excluding Indians not taxed, three fifths of all other Persons. The actual Enumeration shall be made within three Years after the first Meeting of the Congress of the United States, and within every subsequent Term of ten Years, in such Manner as they shall by Law direct. The number of Representatives shall not exceed one for every thirty Thousand, but each State shall have at Least one Representative; and until such enumeration shall be made, the State of New Hampshire shall be entitled to chuse three, Massachusetts eight, Rhode-Island and Providence Plantations one, Connecticut five, New-York six, New Jersey four, Pennsylvania eight, Delaware one, Maryland six, Virginia ten, North Carolina five, South Carolina five, and Georgia three.

When vacancies happen in the Representation from any State, the Executive Authority thereof shall issue Writs of Election to fill such Vacancies.

The House of Representatives shall chuse their Speaker and other Officers; and shall have the sole Power of Impeachment.

Section 3. The Senate of the United States shall be composed of two Senators from each State, chosen by the Legislature thereof, for six Years; and each Senator shall have one Vote.

Immediately after they shall be assembled in Consequence of the first Election, they shall be divided as equally as may be into three Classes. The Seats of the Senators of the first Class shall be vacated at the Expiration of the second Year, of the second Class at the Expiration of the fourth Year, and of the third Class at the Expiration of the sixth Year, so that one third may be chosen every second Year; and if Vacancies happen by Resignation, or otherwise, during the Recess of the Legislature of any State, the Executive thereof may make temporary Appointments until the next Meeting of the Legislature, which shall then fill such Vacancies.

No Person shall be a Senator who shall not have attained to the Age of thirty Years, and been nine Years a Citizen of the United States, and who shall not, when elected, be an Inhabitant of that State for which he shall be chosen.

The Vice President of the United States shall be President of the Senate but shall have no Vote, unless they be equally divided.

The Senate shall chuse their other Officers, and also a President pro tempore, in the Absence of the Vice President, or when he shall exercise the Office of President of the United States.

The Senate shall have the sole Power to try all Impeachments. When sitting for that Purpose, they shall be on Oath or Affirmation. When the President of the United States is tried the Chief Justice shall preside: **And no Person shall be convicted without the Concurrence of two thirds of the Members present.**

Judgment in Cases of Impeachment shall not extend further than to removal from Office, and disqualification to hold and enjoy any Office of honor, Trust or Profit under the United States: but the Party convicted shall nevertheless be liable and subject to Indictment, Trial, Judgment and Punishment, according to Law.

Section 4. The Times, Places and Manner of holding Elections for Senators and Representatives, shall be prescribed in each State by the Legislature thereof; but the Congress may at any time by Law make or alter such Regulations, except as to the Places of chusing Senators.

The Congress shall assemble at least once in every Year, and such Meeting shall be on the first Monday in December, unless they shall by Law appoint a different Day.

Section 5. Each House shall be the Judge of the Elections, Returns and Qualifications of its own Members, and a Majority of each shall constitute a Quorum to do Business; but a smaller Number may adjourn from day to day, and may be authorized to compel the Attendance of absent Members, in such Manner, and under such Penalties as each House may provide.

Each House may determine the Rules of its Proceedings, punish its Members for disorderly Behaviour, and, with the Concurrence of two thirds, expel a Member.

Each House shall keep a Journal of its Proceedings, and from time to time publish the same, excepting such Parts as may in their Judgment require Secrecy; and the Yeas and Nays of the Members of either House on any question shall, at the Desire of one fifth of those Present, be entered on the Journal.

Neither House, during the Session of Congress, shall, without the Consent of the other adjourn for more than three days, nor to any other Place than that in which the two Houses shall be sitting.

Section 6. The Senators and Representatives shall receive a Compensation for their Services to be ascertained by Law, and paid out of the Treasury of the United States. They shall in all Cases, except Treason, Felony and Breach of the Peace, be privileged from Arrest during their Attendance at the Session of their respective Houses, and in going to and returning from the same; and for any Speech or Debate in either House, they shall not be questioned in any other Place.

No Senator or Representative shall, during the Time for which he was elected, be appointed to any civil Office under the Authority of the United States, which shall have been created, or the Emoluments whereof shall have been encreased during such time; and no Person holding any Office under the United States, shall be a Member of either House during his Continuance in Office.

Section 7. All Bills for raising Revenue shall originate in the House of Representatives; but the Senate may propose or concur with amendments as on other Bills.

Every Bill which shall have passed the House of Representatives and the Senate, shall, before it becomes a law, be presented to the President of the United States: If he approve he shall sign it, but if not he shall return it, with his Objections to that House in which it shall have originated, who shall enter the Objections at large on their Journal, and proceed to reconsider it. If after such Reconsideration two thirds of that House shall agree to pass the Bill, it shall be sent, together with the Objections, to the other House, by which it shall likewise be reconsidered, and if approved by two thirds of that House, it shall become a Law. But in all such Cases the Votes of both Houses shall be determined by yeas and Nays, and the Names of the Persons voting for and against the Bill shall be entered on the Journal of each House respectively. If any Bill shall not be returned by the President within ten Days (Sunday excepted) after it shall have been presented to him, the Same shall be a Law, in like Manner as if he had signed it, unless the Congress by their Adjournment prevent its Return, in which Case it shall not be a Law.

Every Order, Resolution, or Vote to which the Concurrence of the Senate and House of Representatives may be necessary (except on a question of Adjournment) shall be presented to the President of the United States; and before the Same shall take Effect, shall be approved by him, or being disapproved by him, shall be repassed by two thirds of the Senate and House of Representatives, according to the Rules and Limitations prescribed in the Case of a Bill.

Section 8. **The Congress shall have Power To lay and collect Taxes**, Duties, Imposts and Excises, to pay the Debts and provide for the common Defence and general Welfare of the United States; but all Duties, Imposts and Excises shall be uniform throughout the United States;

To borrow Money on the credit of the United States;

To regulate Commerce with foreign Nations, and **among the several States,** and with the Indian Tribes;

To establish an uniform Rule of Naturalization, and uniform Laws on the subject of Bankruptcies throughout the United States;

To coin Money, regulate the Value thereof, and of foreign Coin, and fix the Standard of Weights and Measures;

To provide for the Punishment of counterfeiting the Securities and current Coin of the United States;

To establish Post Offices and post Roads;

To promote the Progress of Science and useful Arts, by securing for limited Times to Authors and Inventors the exclusive Right to their respective Writings and Discoveries;

To constitute Tribunals inferior to the supreme Court;

To define and punish Piracies and Felonies committed on the high Seas, and Offenses against the Law of Nations;

To declare War, grant Letters of Marque and Reprisal, and make Rules concerning Captures on Land and Water;

To raise and support Armies, but no Appropriation of Money to that Use shall be for a longer Term than two Years;

To provide and maintain a Navy;

To make Rules for the Government and Regulation of the land and naval Forces;

To provide for calling forth the Militia to execute the Laws of the Union, suppress Insurrections and repel Invasions;

To provide for organizing, arming, and disciplining, the Militia, and for governing such Part of them as may be employed in the Service of the United States, reserving to the States respectively, the Appointment of the Officers, and the Authority of training the Militia according to the discipline prescribed by Congress;

To exercise exclusive Legislation in all Cases whatsoever, over such District (not exceeding ten Miles square) as may, by Cession of Particular States, and the Acceptance of Congress, become the Seat of the Government of the United States, and to exercise like Authority over all Places purchased by the Consent of the Legislature of the State in which the Same shall be, for the Erection of Forts, Magazines, Arsenals, dock-Yards and other needful Buildings;—And

To make all Laws which shall be necessary and proper for carrying into Execution the foregoing Powers and all other Powers vested by this Constitution in the Government of the United States, or in any Department or Officer thereof.

Section 9. The Migration or Importation of such Persons as any of the States now existing shall think proper to admit, shall not be prohibited by the Congress prior to the Year one thousand eight hundred and eight, but a Tax or duty may be imposed on such Importation, not exceeding ten dollars for each Person.

The Privilege of the Writ of Habeas Corpus shall not be suspended, unless when in Cases of Rebellion or Invasion the public Safety may require it.

No Bill of Attainder or ex post facto Law shall be passed.

No Capitation, or other direct, Tax shall be laid, unless in Proportion to the Census of Enumeration herein before directed to be taken.

No Tax or Duty shall be laid on Articles exported from any State.

No Preference shall be given by any Regulation of Commerce or Revenue to the Ports of one State over those of another; nor shall Vessels bound to, or from, one State, be obliged to enter, clear or pay Duties in another.

No Money shall be drawn from the Treasury, but in Consequence of Appropriations made by Law; and a regular Statement and Account of the Receipts and Expenditures of all public Money shall be published from time to time.

No Title of Nobility shall be granted by the United States: And no Person holding any Office of Profit or Trust under them, shall, without the Consent of the Congress, accept of any present, Emolument, Office, or Title, of any kind whatever, from any King, Prince or foreign State.

Section 10. **No State shall** enter into any Treaty, Alliance, or Confederation; grant Letters of Marque and Reprisal; coin Money; emit Bills of Credit; make any Thing but gold and silver Coin a Tender in Payment of Debts; **pass any** Bill of Attainder, ex post facto Law, or **Law impairing the Obligation of Contracts**, or grant any Title of Nobility.

No State shall, without the Consent of the Congress, lay any Imposts or Duties on Imports or Exports, except what may be absolutely necessary for executing it's inspection Laws: and the net Produce of all Duties and Imposts, laid by any State on Imports or Exports, shall be for the Use of the Treasury of the United States; and all such Laws shall be subject to the Revision and Controul of the Congress.

No State shall, without the Consent of Congress, lay any Duty of Tonnage, keep Troops, or Ships of War in time of Peace, enter into any Agreement or Compact with another State, or with a foreign Power, or engage in War, unless actually invaded, or in such imminent Danger as will not admit of delay.

Justice Story summarized the general view of the Marshall Court as to the powers of Congress thus: "Whenever . . . a question arises concerning the constitutionality of a particular power, the first question is whether the power be expressed in the Constitution. If it be, the question is decided. If it be not expressed, the next enquiry must be whether it is properly an incident to an express power and necessary to its execution. If it be, then it may be exercised by Congress. If not, Congress cannot exercise it." 2 *Commentaries*, Section 1243.

Generally speaking, the Court's position was one of supporting broad Congressional power where this tended to strengthen the national power and, conversely, of broadly construing restraints upon the states where this would further enhance the national power in areas of national interest.

Thus Marshall began implementing the contract clause (Section 10, Clause 1) as early as 1810 in *Fletcher* v. *Peck* (see pages 58–59) and 1812 in *New Jersey* v. *Wilson* (11 U.S. 164), and brought it to full force in the *Dartmouth College* case (Part One, Chapter V) in 1819, supplemented with a companion opinion (*Sturges* v. *Crowninshield;* see pages 60–61). While the later Court was less categorical, the principle of state surveillance through this clause was now established. In 1820 Marshall conceded that the clause did not control contracts made before the Constitution was adopted (*Owings* v. *Speed,* 18 U.S. 420), nor did it inhibit an action against land claims based on grants to individuals from Indian tribes prior to independence (*Johnson* v. *McIntosh,* 21 U.S. 543 [1823]). But in 1821 Marshall reiterated the *Crowninshield* doctrine, that a state could not, in discharging a bankrupt, discharge his private contract obligations (*Farmers and Mechanics Bank* v. *Smith,* 19 U.S. 131). By 1830 a synthesizing of all of these opinions was attempted in *Providence Bank* v. *Billings* and *Craig* v. *Missouri* (see pages 64–65); but a basic modification of Marshall's *Crowninshield* and *Dartmouth* rationale came two years after his death when his successor, Chief Justice Roger B. Taney, held in *Charles River Bridge Co.* v. *Warren Bridge Co.* (11 Peters 420) that the recipient of a prior grant from a state could not claim an implied immunity from impairment by subsequent state action.

Marshall, with Story and Washington, dissented in 1827 in *Ogden* v. *Saunders* (25 U.S. 214), in which a badly divided majority (4-to-3 with four separate opinions for the majority) held that contracts made after enactment of a state bankruptcy law were not impaired by state action subsequently taken in reliance on the law.

The major instrument of national power in the legislative article, however, was the commerce clause (Section 8, Clause 3). As Part One, Chapter VII seeks to illustrate, the economic first principle of such power, so clearly lacking in the old Articles of Confederation, was exclusive federal jurisdiction over interstate trade. *Gibbons* v. *Ogden,* in 1824, therefore, was a readymade rule of law which had only waited for the right case, and the steamboat monopoly presented the opportunity. The way had been prepared in 1819 by the opinion in *McCulloch* v. *Maryland* (see Part One, Chapter VI), which had been built upon the tax and coinage clauses (Section 8, Clauses 1 and 5), the "necessary and proper" clause (Section 8, Clause 18) and the "supremacy clause" (Article VI, Clause 2). The flexibility made possible by the "necessary and proper" clause had been discerned by Marshall as early as 1805 (*United States* v. *Fisher,* 6 U.S. 396), upholding a statute giving preference to the federal government in a bankruptcy proceeding with the

statement that "it would be incorrect, and would produce endless difficulties, if the opinion should be maintained that no law was authorized
which was not indispensably necessary to give effect to a specified
power."

Again, in 1821, in *Cohens* v. *Virginia* (6 Wheaton 264), the Court
further strengthened the national power by including state criminal as
well as civil judgments within its jurisdiction under the Judiciary Act of
1789. (The jurisdictional issue is annotated under the text of Article III,
at pages 101–105.) Finally, in 1827, the Court again broadened the
McCulloch and *Gibbons* doctrines by invalidating state burdens on foreign commerce as well (*Brown* v. *Maryland,* 12 Wheaton 419). The *Mc-
Culloch* rule had been reiterated in 1824 by rejecting attempts by individual state officers to lay a burden upon federal agencies which the
states had been forbidden to lay (*Osborn* v. *Bank,* 22 U.S. 738; cf. also
Bank v. *Planters Bank,* 22 U.S. 904; and *Weston* v. *Charleston Bank,* 27
U.S. 450 [1829]).

The "necessary and proper" clause was emphatically endorsed by
Justice Story, while he conceded that since its adoption it "has been made
a theme of constant attack, and extravagant jealousy." Relying on the
unequivocal pronouncements in *McCulloch* v. *Maryland,* Story declared
that the clause "is only declaratory of a truth, which would have resulted
by necessary and unavoidable implication from the very act of establishing the national government, and vesting it with certain powers. . . . In
truth, the constitutional operation of the government would be precisely
the same, if the clause were obliterated, as if it were repeated in every
article." (3 *Commentaries,* Section 1232.) It should be noted, in the
boldface type in Section 8 above, that the clause speaks of "the foregoing
Powers and all other Powers"—a sweep of language which enabled
Marshall, in the *Gibbons* case, to define the commerce clause itself, as
Justice Robert Jackson later observed, "with a breadth never exceeded."
(*Wickard* v. *Filburn,* 317 U.S. 111 [1942])

Paradoxically, the Marshall Court's systematic encouragement of
national authority by means of such constructions as *McCulloch* and
Gibbons was met with inaction on the part of Congress for most of the
first three-quarters of the nineteenth century. Until the growth of interstate railroads and interstate corporations, after the disruption of the
Civil War and Reconstruction, the Marshall Court's guidelines were
little used. Indeed, Marshall himself had to keep open the way for ultimate Congressional initiative by holding in 1829 (*Willson* v. *Blackbird
Marsh Co.,* 2 Peters 245) that state action in an interstate area was per-
missible unless and until the national jurisdiction was asserted. The post-
Marshall Court was even more disposed to permit the field to be shared
by the states (e.g., *Cooley* v. *Board of Wardens of the Port of Philadelphia,* 12 Howard 299 [1851]). When, in 1887, Congress finally reentered
the field with passage of the Interstate Commerce Commission Act, the
modern history of constitutional federalism envisioned by Marshall in
commerce clause cases would at last begin.

II. The Executive Article

Section 1. The executive Power shall be vested in a President of the United States of America. He shall hold his Office during the Term of four Years, and, together with the Vice President, chosen for the same Term, be elected, as follows:

Each State shall appoint, in such Manner as the Legislature thereof may direct, a Number of Electors, equal to the whole Number of Senators and Representatives to which the State may be entitled in the Congress: but no Senator or Representative, or Person holding an Office of Trust or Profit under the United States, shall be appointed an Elector.

[The Electors shall meet in their respective States, and vote by Ballot for two Persons, of whom one at least shall not be an Inhabitant of the same State with themselves. And they shall make a List of all the Persons voted for, and of the Number of Votes for each; which List they shall sign and certify, and transmit sealed to the Seat of the Government of the United States, directed to the President of the Senate. The President of the Senate shall, in the Presence of the Senate and House of Representatives, open all the Certificates, and the Votes shall then be counted. The Person having the greatest Number of Votes shall be the President, if such Number be a Majority of the whole Number of Electors appointed; and if there be more than one who have such Majority, and have an equal Number of Votes, then the House of Representatives shall immediately chuse by Ballot one of them for President; and if no Person have a Majority, then from the five highest on the List the said House shall in like Manner chuse the President. But in chusing the President, the Votes shall be taken by States, the Representatives from each State having one Vote; a quorum for this Purpose shall consist of a Member or Members from two thirds of the States, and a Majority of all the States shall be necessary to a Choice. In every Case, after the Choice of the President, the Person having the greatest Number of Votes of the Electors shall be the Vice President. But if there should remain two or more who have equal Votes, the Senate shall chuse from them by Ballot the Vice President.]

The Congress may determine the Time of chusing the Electors, and the Day on which they shall give their Votes; which Day shall be the same throughout the United States.

No person except a natural born Citizen, or a Citizen of the United States, at the time of the Adoption of this Constitution, shall be eligible to the Office of President; neither shall any person be eligible to that Office who shall not have attained to the Age of thirty five Years, and been fourteen Years a Resident within the United States.

In Case of the Removal of the President from Office, or of his Death,

Resignation, or Inability to discharge the Powers and Duties of the said Office, the Same shall devolve on the Vice President, and the Congress may by Law provide for the Case of Removal, Death, Resignation or Inability, both of the President and Vice President, declaring what Officer shall then act as President, and such Officer shall act accordingly, until the Disability be removed, or a President shall be elected.

The President shall, at stated Times, receive for his Services, a Compensation, which shall neither be increased nor diminished during the Period for which he shall have been elected, and he shall not receive within that Period any other Emolument from the United States, or any of them.

Before he enter on the Execution of his Office, he shall take the following Oath or Affirmation:—"I do solemnly swear (or affirm) that I will faithfully execute the Office of President of the United States, and will to the best of my Ability, preserve, protect and defend the Constitution of the United States."

Section 2. The President shall be Commander in Chief of the Army and Navy of the United States, and of the Militia of the several States, when called into the actual Service of the United States; he may require the Opinion, in writing, of the principal Officer in each of the executive Departments, upon any Subject relating to the Duties of their respective Offices, and he shall have Power to grant Reprieves and Pardons for Offenses against the United States, except in Cases of Impeachment.

He shall have Power, by and with the Advice and Consent of the Senate, to make Treaties, provided two thirds of the Senators present concur; and he shall nominate, and by and with the Advice and Consent of the Senate, shall appoint Ambassadors, other public Ministers and Consuls, Judges of the supreme Court, and all other Officers of the United States, whose Appointments are not herein otherwise provided for, and which shall be established by Law: but the Congress may by Law vest the Appointment of such inferior Officers, as they think proper, in the President alone, in the Courts of Law, or in the Heads of Departments.

The President shall have Power to fill up all Vacancies that may happen during the Recess of the Senate, by granting Commissions which shall expire at the End of their next Session.

Section 3. He shall from time to time give to the Congress Information on the State of the Union, and recommend to their Consideration such Measures as he shall judge necessary and expedient; he may, on extraordinary Occasions, convene both Houses, or either of them, and in Case of Disagreement between them, with Respect to the Time of Adjournment, he may adjourn them to such Time as he shall think proper; he shall receive Ambassadors and other public Ministers; **he shall take Care that the Laws be faithfully executed, and shall Commission all the Officers of the United States.**

Section 4. The President, Vice President and all Civil Officers of the United States, shall be removed from Office on Impeachment for, and Conviction of, Treason, Bribery, or other high Crimes and Misdemeanors.

The executive article had already figured in constitutional issues before the time of the Marshall Court: the recess appointment of the second Chief Justice, John Rutledge, had been rejected in 1795 by a hostile Senate, while the third clause of Section 1, on the procedure of the Electoral College, was soon to be modified by the Twelfth Amendment, introduced in Congress in December 1803 and ratified by the majority of the states by September 1804.

In *The Federalist,* No. 70, Alexander Hamilton had written in 1788: "There is an idea, which is not without its advocates, that a vigorous executive is inconsistent with the genius of republican government." He rejected the argument; a feeble executive, Hamilton countered, "implies a feeble execution of the government. A feeble execution is but another phrase for a bad execution. And a government ill executed, whatever it may be in theory, must be in practice a bad government." Nothing more aptly illustrates the Marshall–Story affinity for the Hamiltonian view than a virtual paraphrasing of *The Federalist* in the *Commentaries:* "It may be stated in general terms, that that organization [of government] is best, which will at once secure energy in the executive, and safety to the people. The notion, however, is not uncommon, and occasionally finds ingenious advocates, that a vigorous executive is inconsistent with the genius of a republican government." Story concluded that the lessons of ancient and modern history demonstrated that "energy in the executive is a leading character in the definition of a good government." Citing *Marbury* v. *Madison,* the Justice added: "There are . . . incidental powers, belonging to the executive department, which are necessarily implied from the nature of the functions, which are confided to it. Among these, must necessarily be included the power to perform them, without any obstruction or impediment whatsoever. . . . In the exercise of his political powers he is to use his own discretion, and is accountable only to his country, and to his own conscience. His decision, in relation to these powers, is subject to no control; and his discretion, when exercised, is conclusive." (3 *Commentaries,* Sections 1411, 1563.)

Ironically, it was in the area of implied powers—the unwritten "necessary and proper" clause in Article II—that the Marshall Court came to a confrontation with the Presidency in the treason trial of an ex-Vice-President (see Part One, Chapter III and Part Three, Chapter II). The "faithful execution of the laws" concept invited a construction of executive discretion, or privilege, or prerogative (as English constitutional law would phrase it) which made *United States* v. *Burr* an essential authority for the Court in 1974, in *United States* v. *Nixon* (418 U.S. at 707, 713, 715). The accepted fact of reserved powers in the executive branch still required that some other branch be responsible for pronouncing the limits to the uses of these powers. The basic constitutional theory of checks and balances rested on this; and while Burr's case never forced the issue to an ultimate judicial test, the logic of the requirement led directly from 1807 to the 8-to-0 holding of the Court in 1974.

III. The Judicial Article

Section 1. The judicial Power of the United States, shall be vested in one supreme Court, and in such inferior Courts as the Congress may from time to time ordain and establish. The Judges, both of the supreme and inferior Courts, shall hold their Offices during good Behaviour, and shall, at stated Times, receive for their Services, a Compensation, which shall not be diminished during their Continuance in Office.

Section 2. **The judicial Power shall extend to all Cases**, in Law and Equity, arising under this Constitution, the Laws of the United States, and Treaties made, or which shall be made, under their Authority;—to all Cases affecting Ambassadors, other public ministers and Consuls;—to all Cases of admiralty and maritime Jurisdiction;—to Controversies to which the United States shall be a Party;—to Controversies between two or more States;—between a State and Citizens of another State;—between Citizens of different States;—between Citizens of the same State claiming Lands under Grants of different States, and **between a State, or the Citizens thereof, and foreign States, Citizens or Subjects.**

In all Cases affecting Ambassadors, other public Ministers and Consuls, and those in which a State shall be Party, the supreme Court shall have original Jurisdiction. In all the other Cases before mentioned, the supreme Court shall have appellate Jurisdiction, both as to Law and Fact, with such Exceptions, and under such Regulations as the Congress shall make.

The Trial of all Crimes, except in Cases of Impeachment, shall be by Jury; and such Trial shall be held in the State where the said Crimes shall have been committed; but when not committed within any State, the Trial shall be at such Place or Places as the Congress may by Law have directed.

Section 3. **Treason against the United States, shall consist only in levying War against them, or in adhering to their Enemies, giving them Aid and Comfort. No Person shall be convicted of Treason unless on the Testimony of two Witnesses to the same overt Act, or on Confession in open Court.**

The Congress shall have Power to declare the Punishment of Treason,

but no Attainder of Treason shall work Corruption of Blood, or Forfeiture
except during the Life of the Person attainted.

The broad powers which the Marshall Court found in the legislative
and executive branches under Articles I and II it also found for the
judiciary in Article III. Much of the constitutional function of the judicial system was—and still is—dependent on Congressional action: e.g.,
the only specific tribunal named in Article III is "one supreme Court,"
with the option of creating other national courts left to legislative initiative. The second and third clauses of Section 2 also rest upon Congressional action. There were pragmatic reasons for this semblance of checks
and balances vis-à-vis the court system, effectuating the compromises
necessary in the Constitutional Convention (cf. 3 *Commentaries,* Sections 1568–72).

The federal court system was established by the Judiciary Act of
September 24, 1789—nearly five months after the other two branches
of the new government began functioning. The first and second clauses
of Article III, Section 2—defining judicial powers and jurisdiction—
aroused alarms of states' rights advocates almost immediately, when the
Supreme Court in 1793 heard a suit by a South Carolina resident against
the sovereign state of Georgia (*Chisholm* v. *Georgia,* 2 Dallas 419).
Congress proceeded to draft the Eleventh Amendment, limiting the su-
ability of states, and the states proceeded to adopt it with what Justice
Felix Frankfurter later termed "vehement speed" (dissent, in *Larson* v.
Domestic & Foreign Corp., 337, U.S. 682, 708 [1949]). As for the
judiciary statutes—in 1789, 1801, and 1802—these bred issues of their
own, on which the Marshall Court built the doctrine of its own ultimate
power (cf. Robert H. Jackson, *The Struggle for Judiciary Supremacy,*
[1941]).

The doctrine of judicial review was the cornerstone for Marshall's
constitutional federalism, adroitly established in *Marbury* v. *Madison*
and extended to the states in *Martin* v. *Hunter's Lessee* and *Cohens* v.
Virginia. In these and other cases the Court asserted—not without criticism from lawmakers and legal scholars throughout the national history
—an implied power analogous to the implied powers it ascribed to both
the legislative and executive branches. Under Marshall it was accepted
as "necessary and proper" for the effective implementation of a jurisdictional authority as in *Marbury,* or of a supremacy clause issue (Article VI) as in *Martin* and *Cohens.* Thus by indirection and inference the
right of review became what British constitutional law calls a "convention," or tacitly accepted principle of the constitutional system.

Certainly the concept of judicial review was recognized by Americans from the time of the Constitutional Convention and earlier. The
right of the Privy Council to negate enactments of colonial legislatures,
or to overturn decisions of colonial courts, was quite familiar to the
Founding Fathers, but the debates at Philadelphia in 1787 tended to

accept the idea as a necessary function of the judicial process. James Madison—although he would shift his position in the heat of politics in the Adams administration—unequivocally endorsed the principle at the Philadelphia convention, in his writings in *The Federalist*, and in the Virginia ratifying convention. A circuit opinion of the Justices as early as 1792 ruled a federal pension law unconstitutional (*Hayburn's Case*, 2 Dallas 409), and in 1797 a state law was negated in favor of preemptive federal constitutional power (*Ware* v. *Hylton*, 3 Dallas 199), and the next year the Court construed the ex post facto clause (Article I, Section 10) as applying to state criminal, and not civil, laws (*Calder* v. *Bull*, 3 Dallas 386).

It is a matter of record that the same term that established judicial review found the Court (with Marshall abstaining) declaring that "a contemporary exposition . . . practiced and acquiesced under a period of years, fixed its construction" (*Stuart* v. *Laird*, 5 U.S. 299). The next term, Marshall himself construed the same District of Columbia act which figured in *Marbury*, as not creating citizenship status for residents of the District (*Hepburn* v. *Ellzey*, 6 U.S. 451). On the other hand, Congress was held, in 1820, to have exclusive tax power in the District (*Loughborough* v. *Blake*, 18 U.S. 317).

In addition, in 1809, Marshall established the flexibility of the jurisdictional rules—to be brought to full flower in *Cohens* v. *Virginia* in 1821—by declaring that jurisdiction arose either from the nature of the parties (e.g., citizens of different states) or from the nature of the case (e.g., controversies affecting a federal question); *Hope Ins. Co.* v. *Borden* (9 U.S. 57); *Bank* v. *Deveaux* (9 U.S. 61); and cf. *United States* v. *Peters* (9 U.S. 115). In 1812, however, the Court rejected an argument (with Marshall dissenting) that it had common law criminal jurisdiction, holding instead that its criminal jurisdiction was exclusively statutory, based upon acts of Congress or on its own inherent contempt powers (*United States* v. *Hudson and Goodwin*, 11 U.S. 32; cf. also *New Orleans* v. *Winter*, 14 U.S. 91 [1816] and *United States* v. *Bevan*, 16 U.S. 336 [1818]).

Although the Court, in a confrontation with Andrew Jackson, clearly backed down in its refusal to adjudicate the constitutionality of Georgia's invasion of Indian rights (*Cherokee Nation* v. *Georgia*, 30 U.S. 1) in 1831, it recovered its posture the following year and firmly declared that invasions of individual liberties by states were reviewable in the Court (*Worcester* v. *Georgia*, 31 U.S. 515; cf. also *Fisher* v. *Cockerell*, 30 U.S. 248 [1831]).

Events enabled the Marshall Court in *Marbury* v. *Madison* to place the doctrine of judicial review conspicuously as a first principle of American constitutionalism; cf. Chapter II and the opening group of documents in Part Three. Yet *Marbury* was the only case in Marshall's Chief Justiceship to apply the doctrine to an act of Congress; it was in reference to state enactments, and their review under the paramount authority of the national Constitution, that the doctrine reached its zenith—witness *Fletcher* v. *Peck* in 1806, *Martin* v. *Hunter's Lessee* in 1816, the *Dartmouth College* case in 1819, and the climactic expression of the doctrine in *Cohens* v. *Virginia* in 1821. The first and third of these cases were founded on the controls over state action in the contract clause, the second and third on a combination of the supremacy clause in Article VI and the jurisdictional clause in Article III. Thus Marshall declared in *Cohens:*

> It is most true that this Court will not take jurisdiction if it should not; but it is equally true, that it must take jurisdiction if it should. The judiciary cannot, as the legislatures may, avoid a measure because it approaches the confines of the Constitution. We cannot pass it by because it is doubtful. With whatever doubts, with whatever difficulties, a case may be attended, we must decide it, if it be brought before us. We have no more right to decline the exercise of jurisdiction which is given, than to usurp that which is not given. (6 Wheaton 264, 404.)

Other Chief Justices and their Associates have not always been prepared to assert the jurisdictional imperative as comprehensively as Marshall. The Court has tended in the twentieth century to emphasize its discretionary power to limit the appeals it will hear; Chief Justice William Howard Taft worked vigorously in behalf of the Judiciary Act of 1925, which greatly broadened the discretion to consider petitions for writs of *certiorari* (cf. Frankfurter and Landis, *The Business of the Supreme Court* [1927], Chapter VI). Very early in his own career on the Court, Justice Oliver Wendell Holmes wrote: "I do not think that the United States would come to an end if we lost our power to declare an act of Congress void. I do think the Union would be imperiled if we could not make that declaration as to the laws of the several states." (*Collected Legal Papers* [1920], 295.) Benjamin N. Cardozo, before coming onto the bench, warned that "a jurist is not to innovate at pleasure" (*The Nature of the Judicial Process* [1921], 141). Justice Harlan F. Stone added the admonition that where the Court's power of review was conclusive, the only restraint upon it had to be "our own sense of self-restraint" (297 *United States* v. *Butler*, 1, 79 [1935] in dissenting opinion). Justice Robert Jackson summed up the pragmatic effect of judicial review in 1953 when he observed: "We are not final because we are infallible; we are infallible because we are final" (*Brown* v. *Allen*, 344 U.S. 443, 540 in concurring opinion).

The treason provisions in Article III, Section 3, were strictly construed in Burr's case in 1807. Story approvingly quoted Montesquieu, who "has not scrupled to declare, that if the crime of treason be indeterminate, that alone is sufficient to make any government degenerate into arbitrary power." (3 *Commentaries,* Section 1791.) The Constitutional

Convention "deemed it necessary to erect an impassable barrier against arbitrary constructions" by confining treason to acts of levying war against the United States or giving aid and comfort to its enemies; and the Justice reminisced that "the judges have uniformly adhered to the established doctrine, even when executive influence has exerted itself with no small zeal to procure conviction" (cf. Part One, Chapter II). The Constitution further demands two witnesses to the same overt act, and "declined to suffer the testimony of a single witness, however high, to be sufficient to establish such a crime." (3 *Commentaries,* Sections 1793, 1794, 1796.)

IV. State–Federal Relations

Section 1. Full Faith and Credit shall be given in each State to the public Acts, Records, and judicial Proceedings of every other State. And the Congress may by general Laws prescribe the Manner in which such Acts, Records and Proceedings shall be proved, and the Effect thereof.

Section 2. The Citizens of each State shall be entitled to all Privileges and Immunities of Citizens in the several States.

A Person charged in any State with Treason, Felony, or other Crime, who shall flee from Justice, and be found in another State, shall on Demand of the executive Authority of the State from which he fled, be delivered up, to be removed to the State having Jurisdiction of the Crime.

No Person held to Service or Labour in one State, under the Laws thereof, escaping into another, shall, in Consequence of any Law or Regulation therein, be discharged from such Service or Labour, but shall be delivered up on Claim of the Party to whom such Service or Labour may be due.

Section 3. New States may be admitted by the Congress into this Union; but no new State shall be formed or erected within the Jurisdiction of any other State; nor any State be formed by the Junction of two or more States, or Parts of States, without the Consent of the Legislatures of the States concerned as well as of the Congress.

The Congress shall have Power to dispose of and make all needful Rules and Regulations respecting the Territory or other Property belonging to the United States; and nothing in this Constitution shall be so construed as to Prejudice any Claims of the United States, or of any particular State.

Section 4. The United States shall guarantee to every State in this Union a Republican Form of Government, and shall protect each of them against Invasion; and on Application of the Legislature, or of the Executive (when the Legislature cannot be convened) against domestic Violence.

V. Amending Procedure

The Congress, whenever two thirds of both Houses shall deem it necessary, shall propose Amendments to this Constitution, or, on the Application of the Legislatures of two thirds of the several States, shall call a Convention for proposing Amendments, which, in either Case, shall be valid to all Intents and Purposes, as Part of this Constitution, when ratified by the Legislatures of three fourths of the several States, or by Conventions in three fourths thereof, as the one or the other Mode of Ratification may be proposed by the Congress; Provided that no Amendment which may be made prior to the Year One thousand eight hundred and eight shall in any Manner affect the first and fourth Clauses in the Ninth Section of the first Article; and that no State, without its Consent, shall be deprived of it's equal Suffrage in the Senate.

VI. The Supremacy of the Constitution

All Debts contracted and Engagements entered into, before the Adoption of this Constitution, shall be as valid against the United States under this Constitution, as under the Confederation.

This Constitution, and the Laws of the United States which shall be made in Pursuance thereof; and all Treaties made, or which shall be made, under the Authority of the United States, shall be the supreme Law of the Land; and the Judges in every State shall be bound thereby, any Thing in the Constitution or Laws of any State to the Contrary notwithstanding.

The Senators and Representatives before mentioned, and the Members of the several State Legislatures, and all executive and judicial Officers, both of the United States and of the several States, shall be bound by Oath or Affirmation, to support this Constitution; but no religious Test shall ever be required as a Qualification to any Office or public Trust under the United States.

> The supremacy of the national government, under the express and implied powers vested in it by the Constitution, was recognized as essenital by the Convention of 1787; the manifest need to reverse the situation under the Articles of Confederation had been the overriding reason for calling the Convention itself. The strength of the new federal structure accordingly derived from three sources: the enumeration of particular powers in Congress (Article I, Section 8), the supremacy of these powers (Article VI, Clause 2), and an authoritative construction of specific instances in the nature and use of these powers by a national Supreme Court vested with appropriate jurisdiction (Article III, Section 2, Clauses I and 2).
>
> From *McCulloch* v. *Maryland* in 1819 to *Gibbons* v. *Ogden* in 1824,

the tenor of Marshall's jurisprudence was the establishment of the exercise of this strength beyond challenge of future ages. The Chief Justice recognized that there could be no retreat from the position taken in *McCulloch,* and he proceeded to depart from the judicial tradition of not commenting on opinions once delivered, to mount an eloquent, albeit pseudonymous, defense of the position (see Part One, Chapter VI). The principle declared in that case was that national power was not to be burdened by actions of the state: "the states have no power, by taxation or otherwise, to retard, impede, burden, or in any manner control, the operations of the constitutional laws enacted by Congress to carry into execution the powers vested in the general government." (4 Wheaton 316, 436.)

In *Gibbons* v. *Ogden* the supremacy doctrine—applied to the national power expressed in the commerce clause—was carried to its logical conclusion: rejecting the argument that the states and the federal government could legislate in the same subject area "like equal opposing powers," the Court declared: "But the framers of our Constitution foresaw this state of things, and provided for it, by declaring the supremacy not only of itself but of the laws made in pursuance of it." Acts of state legislatures, "though enacted in the execution of acknowledged state powers, [which] interfere with, or are contrary to the laws of Congress, made in pursuance of the Constitution, . . . must yield to it." (9 Wheaton 1, 210.) This rounded out a line of reasoning begun eight years before, when the Court, speaking through Justice Story, had said: "[State courts] would be called upon to pronounce the law . . . not . . . merely according to the laws or constitution of the state, but according to the laws and treaties of the United States—'the supreme law of the land.' " (*Martin* v. *Hunter's Lessee,* 1 Wheaton 304, 355. Cf. also *Am. Ins. Co.* v. *Canter,* 1 Peters 517 [1828].)

Because the *McCulloch* case dealt with state tax burdens on federal agencies and agents—and was broadened, in 1824, in an opinion invalidating an Ohio attempt to tax the directors of the Bank of the United States rather than the bank itself (*Osborn* v. *Bank,* 9 Wheaton 738)—a rule of tax exemption of the instruments and agents of the one government by the other gained general acceptance in the mid-nineteenth century. In 1842 the immunity from state taxes was extended to federal employees' salaries (*Dobbins* v. *Erie County,* 16 Peters 435), and a reciprocal doctrine exempting state employees' salaries from federal taxes was adopted in 1871 (*Collector* v. *Day,* 11 Wallace 113). These cases were not overturned by the Court until 1938 (*Helvering* v. *Gerhart,* 304 U.S. 405) and 1939 (*Graves* v. *New York ex rel. O'Keefe,* 306 U.S. 466).

Harlan F. Stone, as Associate Justice and later as Chief Justice, strove to balance the tax immunity aspect of the supremacy clause with a "rule of reason"—which was only partly successful, probably because of the intricate relationship between Article VI and the commerce clause which the Marshall Court had established. Cf. *South Carolina Highway Department* v. *Barnwell Bros., Inc.,* 303 U.S. 177 (1938). While immunities today tend to be limited to the actual governmental functions affected by taxation, other subject areas (social security, labor relations, consumer protection, and the like) have come within the supremacy principle as the Congresses of the mid-twentieth century have increasingly implemented the constitutional federalism defined by Marshall (and redefined by the later Courts in terms of the Fourteenth Amendment).

VII. *The Ratifying of the Constitution*

The Ratification of the Conventions of nine States, shall be sufficient for the Establishment of this Constitution between the States so ratifying the Same.

Done in Convention by the Unanimous Consent of the States present the Seventeenth Day of September in the Year of our Lord one thousand seven hundred and Eighty seven and of the Independence of the United States of America the Twelfth In witness whereof We have hereunto subscribed our Names,

GO. WASHINGTON—Presidt.

and deputy from Virginia

Attest WILLIAM JACKSON
            Secretary

New Hampshire
  John Langdon
  Nicholas Gilman
Massachusetts
  Nathaniel Gorham
  Rufus King
Connecticut
  Wm. Saml. Johnson
  Roger Sherman
New York
  Alexander Hamilton
New Jersey
  Wil: Livingston
  David Brearley.
  Wm. Paterson.
  Jona: Dayton
Pennsylvania
  B Franklin
  Thomas Mifflin

  Robt. Morris
  Geo. Clymer
  Thos. FitzSimons
  Jared Ingersoll
  James Wilson
  Gouv Morris
Delaware
  Geo: Read
  Gunning Bedford jun
  John Dickinson
  Richard Bassett
  Jaco: Broom
Maryland
  James McHenry
  Dan of St. Thos. Jenifer
  Danl. Carroll
Virginia
  John Blair
  James Madison Jr.

North Carolina
  Wm. Blount
  Richd. Dobbs Spraight
  Hu Williamson
South Carolina
  J. Rutledge

Charles Cotesworth Pinckney
Charles Pinckney
Pierce Butler
Georgia
  William Few
  Abr Baldwin

Amendments to the Constitution, 1791–1804

The Bill of Rights (I–X)

Amendment I. Freedom of Religion, Expression, Assembly

Congress shall make no law respecting an establishment of religion, or prohibiting the free exercise thereof; or abridging the freedom of speech, or of the press; or the right of the people peaceably to assemble, and to petition the Government for a redress of grievances.

Amendment II. Bearing Arms in Public Service

A well regulated Militia, being necessary to the security of a free State, the right of the people to keep and bear Arms, shall not be infringed.

Amendment III. Quartering Troops on Private Premises

No Soldier shall, in time of peace be quartered in any house, without the consent of the Owner, nor in time of war, but in a manner to be prescribed by law.

Amendment IV. Privacy; Unreasonable Searches and Seizures

The right of the people to be secure in their persons, houses, papers, and effects, against unreasonable searches and seizures, shall not be violated, and no Warrants shall issue, but upon probable cause, supported by Oath or affirmation, and particularly describing the place to be searched, and the persons or things to be seized.

Amendment V. Elements of Due Process of Law

No person shall be held to answer for a capital, or otherwise infamous crime, unless on a presentment or indictment of a Grand Jury, except in cases arising in the land or naval forces, or in the Militia, when in actual service in time of War or public danger; nor shall any person be subject for the same offence to be twice put in jeopardy of life or limb; nor shall be compelled in any criminal case to be a witness against himself; nor be deprived of life, liberty, or property, without due process of law; nor shall private property be taken for public use, without just compensation.

Amendment VI. Rights of Defendants

In all criminal prosecutions, the accused shall enjoy the right to a speedy and public trial, by an impartial jury of the State and district wherein the crime shall have been committed, which district shall have been previously ascertained by law, and to be informed of the nature and cause of the accusation; to be confronted with the witnesses against him; to have compulsory process for obtaining witnesses in his favor, and to have the Assistance of Counsel for his defence.

Amendment VII. Rights in Civil Suits

In Suits at common law, where the value in controversy shall exceed twenty dollars, the right of trial by jury shall be preserved, and no fact tried by a jury, shall be otherwise re-examined in any Court of the United States, than according to the rules of the common law.

Amendment VIII. Excessive Bail, Fines, Punishment

Excessive bail shall not be required, nor excessive fines imposed, nor cruel and unusual punishments inflicted.

Amendment IX. Preservation of Unexpressed Rights

The enumeration in the Constitution, of certain rights, shall not be construed to deny or disparage others retained by the people.

Amendment X. Reservation of Powers in States or People

The powers not delegated to the United States by the Constitution, nor prohibited by it to the States, are reserved to the States respectively, or to the people.

Amendment XI. Sovereign Immunity of States

The Judicial power of the United States shall not be construed to extend to any suit in law or equity, commenced or prosecuted against one of the United States by Citizens of another State, or by Citizens or Subjects of any Foreign State.

Amendment XII. Presidential Electoral Procedure

The Electors shall meet in their respective states and vote by ballot for President and Vice President, one of whom, at least, shall not be an inhabitant of the same state with themselves; they shall name in their ballots the person voted for as President, and in distinct ballots the person voted for as Vice-President, and they shall make distinct lists of all persons voted for as President, and of all persons voted for as Vice-President, and of the number of votes for each, which lists they shall sign and certify, and transmit sealed to the seat of the government of the United States, directed to the President of the Senate;—The President of the Senate shall, in the presence of the Senate and House of Representatives, open all the certificates and the votes shall then be counted;—The person having the greatest number of votes for President, shall be the President, if such member be a majority of the whole number of Electors appointed; and if no person have such majority, then from the persons having the highest numbers not exceeding three on the list of those voted for as President, the House of Representatives shall choose immediately, by ballot, the President. But in choosing the President, the votes shall be taken by states, the representation from each state having one vote; a quorum for this purpose shall consist of a member or members from two-thirds of the states, and a majority of all the states shall be necessary to a choice. And if the House of Representatives shall not choose a President whenever the right of choice shall devolve upon them, before the fourth day of March next following, then the Vice-President shall act as President, as in the case of the death or other constitutional disability of the President—The person having the greatest number of votes as Vice-President, shall be the Vice-President, if such number be a majority of the whole number of Electors appointed, and if no person have a majority, then from the two highest numbers on the list, the Senate shall choose the Vice-President; a quorum for the purpose shall consist of two-thirds of the whole number of Senators, and a majority of the whole number shall be necessary to a choice. But no person constitutionally ineligible to the office of President shall be eligible to that of Vice-President of the United States.

To students of the last quarter of the twentieth century, the most striking feature of John Marshall's Constitution is its paucity of commentary on the Bill of Rights. Essentially, this is explained by the fact that Congress—with the notorious exception of the Alien and Sedition

Acts—scarcely ventured into the subject areas of these amendments. As for jurisdiction over state action in these areas, Marshall in 1833 explicitly rejected an argument that the Bill of Rights be made to extend to the states (*Barron* v. *Baltimore*, 7 Peters 243). Even after the Fourteenth Amendment, with its affirmative restriction on state action abridging the privileges and immunities of citizens and their rights to due process and the equal protection of the laws, fundamentally reoriented the constitutional structure, it would be another century before the Court under Chief Justice Earl Warren substantially "incorporated" the specific provisions of the Bill of Rights into the Fourteenth Amendment and thus applied them to the states.

The lack of a Bill of Rights was one of the principal objections to the new Constitution in state ratifying conventions, even though it was argued that the protection of individual liberties was essentially the responsibility of the states (cf. *The Federalist*, No. 84). Story accepted the amendments, speaking with an unwitting clairvoyance: "a bill of rights may be important, even when it goes beyond powers supposed to be granted. It is not always possible to foresee the extent of the actual reach of certain powers, which are given in general terms. They may be construed to extend (and perhaps fairly) to certain classes of cases, which did not at first appear to be within them. A bill of rights, then, operates as a guard upon any extravagant or undue extension of such powers." (3 *Commentaries*, Section 1859.)

Even in the most celebrated criminal case in Marshall's Chief Justiceship—Burr's treason trial—the rights of a defendant embodied in the Fourth, Fifth, and Sixth Amendments were considered only indirectly.* Marshall placed his main emphasis upon procedural safeguards implicit in the judicial process, and upon a strict construction of the definition of treason in Article III, Clause 3. Federal jurisdiction in criminal causes was limited to Congressional creation of such causes by legislative enactments, as the Court would specifically declare in 1812 (*United States* v. *Hudson and Goodwin*, 7 Cranch 32).

Story was ambivalent on the Sedition Act of 1798, expressing no opinion as to its constitutionality under the First Amendment and suggesting that it was "impolitic" and unlikely to be repeated (3 *Commentaries*, Sections 1288, 1885–86). The experience of twentieth-century America in two World Wars was to prove his hopes ill-founded; cf. Jus-

---

* In the Burr trial, Marshall refers to the *Eighth* Amendment but quotes the language of the Sixth Amendment (see pages 178, 205). To avoid confusion for modern readers, the correct number has been inserted in the text. The discrepancy is explained by the fact that until the Thirteenth Amendment (1865) there was no official numeration for any Amendment. Twelve proposals for Amendments were submitted by the First Congress in 1789, and while the first two failed of the necessary three-fourths majority for ratification, they remained technically open for ultimate ratification by the states. Marshall and his contemporaries could logically still have considered the present Sixth Amendment as ranking eighth among the proposed twelve. See Swindler, *The Modern Interpretation* (1974), 23, 50.

tice Oliver Wendell Holmes's majority opinion in *Schenck* v. *United States* (249 U.S. 647) and his dissent in *Abrams* v. *United States* (250 U.S. 616), both in 1919; and *Dennis* v. *United States* (341 U.S. 494) in 1951. For these, and others of what Edmond Cahn has called "the great rights," the age of Marshall and Story was essentially an age of innocence.

The Eleventh Amendment, overturning a decision of the pre-Marshall Court (*Chisholm* v. *Georgia*, 2 Dallas 419 [1793]), and the Twelfth, seeking to resolve an electoral impasse which occurred on the eve of Marshall's Chief Justiceship, completed the constitutional text of the Marshall era. These amendments, however, were modifications of the original process of government set out in the 1787 text. The Marshall Court undertook, on two occasions, to limit the effect of the Eleventh, which otherwise might have foreclosed much of the constitutional matter over which judicial federalism required jurisdiction. In *Cohens* v. *Virginia* (6 Wheaton 264) in 1821, the "sovereign immunity" principle in the amendment was narrowly construed to give the Court appellate power of review of action against an individual originated by a state; and three years later, in *Osborn* v. *Bank of the United States* (9 Wheaton 846) it denied immunity to a state agent acting under color of authority of an unconstitutional state law.

The Constitution of the Marshall era was viewed by the Court essentially as a charter of national power; as Story summed it up, it was "an attempt to create a national sovereignty, and yet to preserve the state sovereignties." He concluded: "The very elements, out of which it is to be built, are susceptible of infinite modifications; and theory too often deludes us by the attractive simplicity of its plans, and imagination by the visionary perfection of its speculations. . . . Time, and long and steady operation, are indispensable to the perfection of all social institutions. To be of any value they must become cemented with the habits, the feelings and the pursuits of the people." (3 *Commentaries*, Sections 1905, 1906.)

II

A Chronology of Constitutional
Development, 1801-1835

1801   *January 27*. John Marshall confirmed as Chief Justice.

February 4. Marshall presented commission as Chief Justice in Supreme Court and sat with Court for February term.

February 13. Sixth Congress enacted Circuit Court Act, establishing six circuits (instead of original three), abolishing circuit duty for Supreme Court, and creating sixteen new circuit judgeships; also providing that Supreme Court was to be reduced to five Justices (from the original six established in 1789) by leaving first occurring vacancy unfilled.

February 27. District of Columbia Government Act passed, providing among other things for a number of administrative and judicial offices to be filled by retiring President John Adams ("midnight judges").

March 4. Thomas Jefferson sworn in as third President, with Chief Justice Marshall administering oath. Jefferson requested Marshall to continue as Secretary of State until his successor could be confirmed and qualified.

March 16. Marshall was still signing papers as Secretary of State, although the new Attorney General, Levi Lincoln, had assumed the position *ad interim*.

May 2. James Madison finally assumed office of Secretary of State.

August 12. August term of Supreme Court opened August 3, but with no cases docketed for hearing; Court adjourned on this date.

December 8. Marshall attended opening of December term of Court. On this same day, Jefferson delivered opening address to new Seventh Congress (see Part One, Chapter II, page 24), among other things calling attention to need to reconsider existing judiciary legislation.

December 27. Four days before end of this term, William Marbury filed petition in Supreme Court for writ of mandamus directing Secretary of State James Madison to deliver Marbury's commission as justice of peace for District of Columbia.

1802   *March 31.* Seventh Congress repealed Circuit Court Act of 1801.

April 29. Amendment to Judiciary Act of 1789 abolished August and December terms of Supreme Court, thus preventing its meeting until February term 1803. Jeffersonians sought to delay anticipated hearing on constitutionality of abolishing circuit judgeships by repeal act of March 31, until restored system of circuit riding by Justices had become established.

November 2. Chief Justice Marshall tacitly accepted circuit riding provision by sitting in Fifth Circuit in Richmond.

November 21. Marshall apparently spent this enforced Court recess working on manuscript of his life of Washington. On this date he wrote Charles Coatesworth Pinckney seeking data on southern Revolutionary campaign.

1803   *February 3.* Revealing second phase of anti-Federalist campaign against judiciary, Jefferson sent to House of Representatives documents to serve as basis for instituting impeachment proceeding against District Judge John Pickering of New Hampshire.

February 4. With opening of new term of Court, Chief Justice Marshall presided over hearing on Marbury's petition.

February 24. **Marshall, for the Court, delivered opinion in *Marbury* v. *Madison,* dismissing rule for petition because Section 13 of Judiciary Act of 1789 unconstitutionally vested original jurisdiction in Supreme Court in this case.** (See Part One, Chapter II.)

April 25. Justice Paterson delivered the opinion in *Stuart* v. *Laird,* affirming the constitutionality of Congress's abolishing circuit judgeships on ground that issue was moot. Marshall having sat on the case in the Fifth Circuit, disqualified himself.

1804   *March 12.* Judge Pickering, having been impeached by the Senate, was removed from office; on the same day, the House of Representatives approved articles of impeachment against Justice Samuel Chase.

March 22. William Johnson of South Carolina succeeded Justice Alfred Moore as Jefferson's first Supreme Court appointee.

September 25. State Department issued circular letter proclaiming ratification of Twelfth Amendment to Constitution.

1805   *February 5.* Senate impeachment trial of Justice Chase opened.

February 10. In *United States* v. *Fisher* (2 Cranch 358), Marshall cited "necessary and proper" powers in national government, a doctrine finally developed in *McCulloch* v. *Maryland* in 1819.

February 27. Senate having failed to muster required two-thirds majority on any article of impeachment, trial of Justice Chase was terminated, thus ending Jeffersonian plan to remove Federalist judges by this procedure.

March 4. Thomas Jefferson inaugurated for second term, with Chief Justice Marshall administering oath of office.

March 6. On certified question from Fifth Circuit, Court held (*Hepburn & Dundas* v. *Ellzey*) that a resident of District of Columbia was not a citizen of a state entitled to bring action in federal court under "diversity of citizenship" provision of Constitution.

1806 *November 27.* President Jefferson, having received alarming reports of quasi-military activity in Ohio Valley, issued proclamation warning participants to desist and ordering federal officers to arrest any persons in arms participating in activity.

1807 *January 22.* Jefferson denounced Aaron Burr in special message to Congress. The following day Virginia Senator William B. Giles introduced bill suspending habeas corpus for three months; although the measure passed the Senate, it was rejected by House of Representatives. It was aimed at preventing Supreme Court from granting habeas corpus writ to two alleged co-conspirators, J. Erich Bollman and Samuel Swartwout.

February 22. Supreme Court granted habeas corpus to Bollman and Swartwout.

February 24. New Seventh Circuit for federal court system established, and seventh seat on Supreme Court authorized.

March 3. Thomas Todd, chief justice of Kentucky, confirmed as occupant of new seventh seat on Supreme Court.

May 22. Marshall sat as Circuit Justice in Richmond, with District Judge Cyrus Griffin, to begin treason trial of Aaron Burr.

June 10. **Marshall ruled that Chief Executive was constitutionally required to provide original documents in evidence material to Burr's defense.** While Jefferson never fully complied with this ruling, the Chief Justice had made his basic constitutional point on the Executive's liability to do so. (See Part One, Chapter III.)

September 3. **After extended litigation on related issues, treason trial on this date resulted in jury verdict of not guilty on basis of Marshall's narrow definition of treason.** Although Burr remained under indictment for conspiracy to violate American peaceful relations with Mexico, he was later acquitted on this charge. (See Part One, Chapter III.)

1809 *March 4.* James Madison became fourth President.

March 16. In *Bank of United States* v. *Deveaux*, Court held that a corporation could not institute action in federal courts under "diversity of citizenship" clause, although stockholders could sue in corporate name if they were all citizens of same state. In companion case (*Hope Insurance Co.* v. *Borden*) it was ruled that failure to allege "diversity" jurisdiction in federal court barred an action there.

In *United States* v. *Peters*, Court held invalid a Pennsylvania statute barring enforcement of a judgment recovered under Revolutionary court of appeals created by Continental Congress.

1810   *March 11.* Supreme Court in *Fletcher* v. *Peck* held unconstitutional a Georgia law repealing an earlier law granting vast tracts of land for development in Yazoo District of Mississippi, then under Georgia jurisdiction. Marshall held that contract obligations incurred under earlier law were unconstitutionally impaired by second law.

1811   *January 11.* Justice Cushing having died, President Madison nominated Levi Lincoln as his successor, but Lincoln declined because of ill health.

February 13. Madison's second nominee, Oliver Wolcott, was rejected by Senate.

February 22. John Quincy Adams, Madison's third nomination for Cushing's vacant seat, declined commission, stating he preferred diplomacy and politics to legal career.

November 18. Joseph Story of Massachusetts, Madison's fourth nomination for Supreme Court vacancy, was confirmed and accepted commission.

1813   *March 4.* James Madison inaugurated for second term as President.

March 15. Justice Story, for the Court, handed down opinion in *Fairfax's Devisee* v. *Hunter's Lessee* holding unconstitutional a Virginia effort to acquire jurisdiction over lands covered by treaty agreement between United States and Great Britain. Marshall abstained from participation because of his own financial interest in the Fairfax estate.

1816   *March 20.* The Virginia supreme court had refused compliance with the Fairfax decision, holding unconstitutional Section 25 of the Judiciary Act of 1789 providing for appellate review in the Supreme Court of state decisions. Story, again speaking for the Court in *Martin* v. *Hunter's Lessee,* emphatically affirmed the constitutionality of Section 25 as well as the general constitutional right of Supreme Court review of state decisions on federal issues.

March 22. Court ruled that residents of territory were not entitled to sue in federal courts under "diversity" clause (*New Orleans* v. *Winter*).

1817   *March 4.* James Monroe became fifth President.

1818   *February 21.* Court ruled in *United States* v. *Bevans* that Federal
        Crimes Act of 1790, although it created statutory jurisdiction for
        criminal causes, did not vest in federal courts jurisdiction over
        common law crimes cognizable in state courts.

1819   *February 2.* **In the *Dartmouth College* case, Marshall developed
        broad interpretation of contract clause as constitutional restraint
        upon states reviewable in Supreme Court.** (See Part One, Chap-
        ter V.)

        February 17. In another variant on the contract clause, the Court
        in *Sturges* v. *Crowninshield* held unconstitutional a New York
        bankruptcy law which gave relief to debtors for obligations in-
        curred before enactment of the law.

        March 6. **In a third great constitutional case in this term, *McCul-
        loch* v. *Maryland,* Marshall extended Story's "supreme doctrine"
        in the Fairfax cases to cover all instances where a "necessary and
        proper" exercise of federal power was found.** (See Part One,
        Chapter VI.)

1820   *March 10. Loughborough* v. *Blake* confirmed Congress' power to
        levy taxes in District of Columbia, conformably with uniformity
        requirements for direct taxes in states.

        March 16. In case of land contract effected by Virginia legislation
        in 1788, Court held that contract clause of Constitution did not
        apply since Constitution did not go into effect until following year
        (*Owings* v. *Speed*).

1821   *February 12.* The doctrine in *Crowninshield* was extended, in
        Farmers & Mechanics Bank v. *Smith,* to a Pennsylvania law dis-
        charging insolvent debtors as impairment of contract.

        March 3. Extension of supremacy principle in *Cohens* v. *Virginia,*
        where Marshall limited state claims to immunity under Eleventh
        Amendment to immunity in suits by private parties. The Court
        ruled that it had jurisdiction in cases of conflict between federal
        and state law in criminal cases, although it then held that Congress
        had not intended District of Columbia lottery law to authorize
        ticket sales in areas outside District where forbidden.

        March 4. James Monroe inaugurated for second term.

1823   *February 28.* In *Johnson* v. *McIntosh,* Court denied validity of
        titles issued by Indians to individual landholders, holding it was
        exclusive prerogative of sovereign powers to acquire Indian lands.

        December 19. Death of Justice Livingston created first vacancy on
        Court in twelve years. Smith Thompson of New York succeeded
        him.

1824   *March 2.* **In the so-called "steamboat case" of *Gibbons* v. *Ogden,***

Marshall delivered sweeping definition of federal power under commerce clause of Constitution. (See Part One, Chapter VII.)

March 10. The Eleventh Amendment, granting immunity to states from suit by individuals, was held not to extend to state-chartered banks (*United States Bank* v. *Planters Bank*).

March 19. Court extended authority of McCulloch case by ruling in *Osborn* v. *Bank of United States* that Ohio official could not rely on Eleventh Amendment state immunity for personal immunity for acting under unconstitutional state law.

1825 *March 4.* John Quincy Adams became President after resolving of electoral tie in House of Representatives.

1826 *May 9.* Robert Trimble of Kentucky succeeded to seat of Justice Todd.

March 12. Court pronounced "unbroken package" doctrine to immunize interstate shipments from state taxation (*Brown* v. *Maryland*).

March 13. Marshall dissented from majority opinion in *Ogden* v. *Saunders,* which qualified Crowninshield rule on contractual aspects of bankruptcy relief.

1827 *March 10.* In a divided Court (4-to-3) with Chief Justice Marshall dissenting, it was held (*Ogden* v. *Saunders*) that New York insolvency law involved in *Crowninshield* case did not raise contract clause question where citizens of another state did not subject themselves to New York law.

March 12. A Maryland license on importers of foreign goods was held to violate the Constitution's provisions on commerce with foreign nations (*Brown* v. *Maryland*).

1829 *February 12.* Upon death of Justice Trimble, outgoing Adams administration nominated John Crittenden of Kentucky. Senate postponed action to permit incoming Jackson administration to choose new Justice.

March 4. Andrew Jackson inaugurated as President.

March 7. John McLean of Ohio was confirmed for Trimble's seat.

March 18. South Carolina tax on federal securities was held unconstitutional burden on federal powers under Bank doctrine (*Weston* v. *Charleston*).

March 20. A state law authorizing drainage of lands on small navigable streams was held not to violate commerce clause where Congress had not indicated intention to enter the field (*Willson* v. *Black Bird Creek Marsh Co.*).

1830 *January 6.* Justice Washington having died previous November, Henry Baldwin of Pennsylvania was confirmed as successor.

March 12. In *Craig* v. *Missouri* the Court held (4-to-3) that bills of credit issued by state violated Article I, Section X of Constitution.

March 18. The Court in *Cherokee Nation* v. *Georgia* evaded issue of Georgia's unconstitutional expropriation of Indian rights, holding that Cherokee had no standing to bring suit in Supreme Court.

March 22. Court ruled that where a charter fails to stipulate tax exempt status, no exemption is implied (*Providence Bank* v. *Billings*).

1831 *February 9.* In *Fisher's Lessor* v. *Cockerel* the Court denied jurisdiction to review appeal from state court where record failed to show federal question.

1832 *March 3.* In related case, *Worcester* v. *Georgia,* the Court held unconstitutional a Georgia law forbidding settlers sympathetic to Indians to settle on Indian lands.

1833 *March 4.* Jackson inaugurated for second Presidential term.

March 18. In *Barron* v. *Baltimore,* Marshall rejected argument that Bill of Rights was extended to states by Constitution.

1835 *January 9.* Congressman James M. Wayne of Georgia succeeded to Court following death of Justice Johnson.

March 3. Following resignation of Justice Duvall, Jackson nominated Roger B. Taney, former Attorney General and later Secretary of the Treasury, to succeed him. Senate postponed action, resentful of Taney's role in Jackson's fight on Bank of United States.

July 6. Chief Justice Marshall died in Philadelphia.

1836 *March 15.* Taney, whose name had been resubmitted by Jackson, this time to succeed Marshall, was confirmed. At the same time Duvall's seat, vacant for eleven months, was filled by Congressman Philip Pendleton Barbour of Virginia.

III

Marshall's Constitutional Opinions: A Voting Record

In the three decades from 1803 to 1833, Chief Justice John Marshall wrote, or signed his name as head of the Supreme Court, on thirty-four constitutional opinions. In thirty-two, these were majority opinions; in two, he was in dissent. Because of its constitutional significance, a thirty-fifth case—*Martin* v. *Hunter's Lessee*—is included; in this case it will be noted that Marshall took no part in the decision because he had had an interest in the subject matter in earlier years. An asterisk indicates a major case.

	Marshall	Cushing	Paterson	Washington	Chase	Moore	Johnson	Livingston	Todd	Duval	Story	Thompson	Trimble	McLean	Baldwin	Vote
1803																
Marbury v. *Madison*	O	o	o	o	o	o										6-0
1805																
United States v. *Fisher*	O	o	o	D	a		o									4-1
Hepburn v. *Ellzey*	O	o	o	o	o		a									5-0
1807																
Ex parte Bollman, Swartwout	O	a		o	o		o	a								4-0
1809																
Bank v. *Deveaux*	O	o		o	o		o	a								5-0
United States v. *Peters*	O	o		o	o		o	o								6-0
Hope Ins. Co. v. *Borden*	O	o		o	o		o	o								6-0
1810																
Fletcher v. *Peck*	O	a		o	a		D	o	o							4-1
1812																
U.S. v. *Hudson & Goodwin*	d			o			O	o	o	o	o					6-1
New Jersey v. *Wilson*	O			o			o	o	o	o	o					7-0
1816																
New Orleans v. *Winter*	O			o			o	o	o	o	o					7-0
Martin v. *Hunter's Lessee*	a			o			C	o	o	o	O					6-0

O = opinion of the Court. o = joining in opinion of the Court. C = concurring opionion. c = joining in concurring opionion. D = dissenting opinion. d = joining in dissent, or dissenting without opinion. a = absent or abstaining from participation in case, or in some instances an unfilled vacancy.

121

	Marshall	Cushing	Paterson	Washington	Chase	Moore	Johnson	Livingston	Todd	Duval	Story	Thompson	Trimble	McLean	Baldwin	Vote
1818																
United States v. *Bevans*	O			o			o	o	o	o	o					7-0
1819																
*Sturges v. *Crowninshield*	O			o			o	o	a	o	o					6-0
*McCulloch v. *Maryland*	O			o			o	o	a	o	o					6-0
**Dartmouth Coll.* v. *Woodward*	O			C			C	o	a	d	C					5-1
1820																
Loughborough v. *Blake*	O			o			o	o	o	o	o					7-0
Owings v. *Speed*	O			o			o	o	o	o	o					7-0
1821																
Bank v. *Smith*	O			o			o	o	o	o	o					7-0
*Cohens v. *Virginia*	O			o			o	o	o	o	o					7-0
1823																
Johnson v. *McIntosh*	O			o			o	o	o	o	o					7-0
1824																
*Gibbons v. *Ogden*	O			o			C		o	o	o	a				6-0
*Osborn v. *Bank*	O			o			D		o	o	o	o				6-1
U.S. Bank v. *Planters' Bank*	O			o			D		o	o	o	o				6-1
1827																
*Ogden v. *Saunders*	D			O			C			d	d	C	C			4-3
*Brown v. *Maryland*	O			o			o			o	o	D	o			6-1
1828																
Am. Ins. Co. v. *Canter*	O			o			o			o	o	o	o			7-0
1829																
*Willson v. *Black Bird Cr. Marsh Co.*	O			o			o			o	o	o		a		6-0
Weston v. *Charleston*	O			o			o			o	o	D		a		5-1
1830																
*Craig v. *Missouri*	O						D			o	o	D		D	o	4-3
*Providence Bank v. *Billings*	O						o			o	o	o		o	o	6-0
1831																
*Cherokee Nation v. *Georgia*	O						C			o	d	D		o	C	5-2
Fisher's Lessee v. *Cockrell*	O						o			o	o	o		o	D	6-1
1832																
*Worcester v. *Georgia*	O						a			o	o	o		c	d	5-1
1833																
*Barron v. *Baltimore*	O						o			o	o	o		o	a	6-0

PART THREE

OPINIONS
IN THE MAJOR CASES
AND
RELATED DOCUMENTS

I

Marbury *v.* Madison

EDITOR'S NOTE: In order to facilitate reference to the documents, clauses or sections directly relevant to the case are indicated in boldface type. To the same purpose, subheads have been inserted throughout the text of the opinions.

1. *Judiciary Act of September 24, 1789* (Section 13)

1 Stat., Ch. 20, pp. 80–81

SEC. 13. *And be it further enacted,* That the Supreme Court shall have exclusive jurisdiction of all controversies of a civil nature, where a state is a party, except between a state and its citizens; and except also between a state and citizens of other states, or aliens, in which case it shall have original but not exclusive jurisdiction. And shall have exclusively all such jurisdiction of suits or proceedings against ambassadors, or other public ministers, or their domestics, or domestic servants, as a court of law can have or exercise consistently with the law of nations; and original, but not exclusive jurisdiction of all suits brought by ambassadors, or other public ministers, or in which a consul, or vice consul, shall be a party. And the trial of issues in fact in the Supreme Court, in all actions at law against citizens of the United States, shall be by jury. **The Supreme Court** shall also have appellate jurisdiction from the circuit courts and courts of the several states, in the cases hereinafter especially provided for; and **shall have power to issue** writs of prohibition to the district courts, when proceeding as courts of admiralty and maritime jurisdiction, and **writs of mandamus in cases warranted by the principles and usages of law, to any courts appointed, or persons holding office, under the authority of the United States.**

2. *District of Columbia Act of February 27, 1801 (excerpt)*

2 Stat., Ch. 86, p. 107

SEC. 11. *Be it further enacted,* **That there shall be appointed in and for each of the said counties, such number of discreet persons to be justices of the peace, as the President of the United States shall from time to time think ex-**

pedient, to continue in office five years; and such justices, having taken an oath for the faithful and impartial discharge of the duties of the office, shall, in all matters, civil and criminal, and in whatever relates to the conservation of the peace, have all the powers vested in, and shall perform all the duties required of, justices of the peace, as individual magistrates, by the laws herein-before continued in force in those parts of said district, for which they shall have been respectively appointed; and they shall have cognizance in personal demands to the value of twenty dollars, exclusive of costs; which sum they shall not exceed, any law to the contrary notwithstanding; and they shall be entitled to receive for their services the fees allowed for like services by the laws hereinbefore adopted and continued, in the eastern part of said district.

3. *Opinion of the Supreme Court*

1 Cranch 137; opinion delivered February 24, 1803

At the last term, on the affidavits then read and filed with the clerk, a rule was granted in this case, requiring the secretary of state to show cause why a *mandamus* should not issue, directing him to deliver to William Marbury his commission as a justice of the peace for the county of Washington, in the district of Columbia.

No cause has been shown, and the present motion is for a *mandamus*. The peculiar delicacy of this case, the novelty of some of its circumstances, and the real difficulty attending the points which occur in it, require a complete exposition of the principles on which the opinion to be given by the court is founded. These principles have been, on the side of the applicant, very ably argued at the bar. In rendering the opinion of the court, there will be some departure in form, though not in substance, from the points stated in that argument.

In the order in which the court has viewed this subject, the following questions have been considered and decided: 1st. Has the applicant a right to the commission he demands? 2d. If he has a right, and that right has been violated, do the laws of his country afford him a remedy? 3d. If they do afford him a remedy, is it a *mandamus* issuing from this court?

Validity of Marbury's Claim

The first object of inquiry is—Has the applicant a right to the commission he demands? His right originates in an act of congress passed in February 1801, concerning the district of Columbia. After dividing the district into two counties, the 11th section of this law enacts, "that there shall be appointed in and for each of the said counties, such number of discreet persons to be justices of the peace, as the president of the United States shall, from time to time, think expedient, to continue in office for five years."

It appears, from the affidavits, that, in compliance with this law, a commission for William Marbury, as a justice of peace for the county of Washington, was signed by John Adams, then President of the United States; after which, the seal of the United States was affixed to it; but the commission has never reached the person for whom it was made out. In order to determine whether he is entitled to this commission, it becomes necessary to inquire, whether he has been appointed to the office. For if he has been appointed, the law continues him in office for five years, and he is entitled to the possession of those evidences of office, which, being completed, became his property.

Constitutional Provisions

The 2d section of the 2d article of the constitution declares, that "the president shall nominate, and by and with the advice and consent of the senate, shall appoint ambassadors, other public ministers and consuls, and all other officers of the United States, whose appointments are not otherwise provided for." The 3d section declares, that "he shall commission all the officers of the United States."

Legislative Provisions

An act of congress directs the secretary of state to keep the seal of the United States, "to make out and record, and affix the said seal to all civil commissions to officers of the United States, to be appointed by the president, by and with the consent of the senate, or by the president alone, provided, that the said seal shall not be affixed to any commission, before the same shall have been signed by the president of the United States.

These are the clauses of the constitution and laws of the United States, which affect this part of the case. They seem to contemplate three distinct operations: 1st. The nomination: this is the sole act of the president, and is completely voluntary. 2d. The appointment: this is also the act of the president, and is also a voluntary act, though it can only be performed by and with the advice and consent of the senate. 3d. The commission: to grant a commission to a person appointed, might, perhaps, be deemed a duty enjoined by the constitution. "He shall," says that instrument, "commission all the officers of the United States."

Commission as Evidence of Appointment

1. The acts of appointing to office, and commissioning the person appointed, can scarcely be considered as one and the same; since the power to perform them is given in two separate and distinct sections of the constitution. The distinction between the appointment and the commission, will be rendered more apparent, by adverting to that provision in the second section of the second article of the constitution, which authorizes congress "to vest, by law, the appointment of such inferior officers, as they think proper, in the president alone, in the courts of law, or in the heads of departments;" thus contemplating cases where the law may direct the president to commission an officer appointed by the courts, or by the heads of departments. In such a case, to issue a commission would be apparently a duty distinct from the appointment, the performance of which, perhaps, could not legally be refused.

Although that clause of the constitution which requires the president to commission all the officers of the United States, may never have been applied to officers appointed otherwise than by himself, yet it would be difficult to deny the legislative power to apply it to such cases. Of consequence, the constitutional distinction between the appointment to an office and the commission of an officer who has been appointed, remains the same, as if, in practice, the president had commissioned officers appointed by an authority other than his own. It follows, too, from the existence of this distinction, that if an appointment was to be evidenced by any public act, other than the commission, the performance of such public act would create the officer; and if he was not removable at the will of the president, would either give him a right to his commission, or enable him to perform the duties without it.

These observations are premised, solely for the purpose of rendering more intelligible those [which] apply more directly to the particular case under consideration.

This is an appointment made by the president, by and with the advice and consent of the senate, and is evidenced by no act but the commission itself. In such a case, therefore, the commission and the appointment seem inseparable; it being almost impossible to show an appointment, otherwise than by providing the existence of a commission; still the commission is not necessarily the appointment, though conclusive evidence of it.

But at what stage, does it amount to this conclusive evidence? The answer to this question seems an obvious one. The appointment being the sole act of the president, must be completely evidenced, when it is shown that he has done everything to be performed by him. Should the commission, instead of being evidence of an appointment, even be considered as constituting the appointment itself; still, it would be made, when the last act to be done by the president was performed, or, at farthest, when the commission was complete.

Signing of Commission

The last act to be done by the president is the signature of the commission: he has then acted on the advice and consent of the senate to his own nomination. The time for deliberation has then passed: he has decided. His judgment, on the advice and consent of the senate, concurring with his nomination, has been made, and the officer is appointed. This appointment is evidenced by an open unequivocal act; and being the last act required from the person making it, necessarily excludes the idea of its being, so far as respects the appointment, an inchoate and incomplete transaction.

Some point of time must be taken, when the power of the executive over an officer, not removable at his will, must cease. That point of time must be, when the constitutional power of appointment has been exercised. And this power has been exercised, when the last act, required from the person possessing the power, has been performed: this last act is the signature of the commission. This idea seems to have prevailed with the legislature, when the act passed converting the department of foreign affairs into the department of state. By that act, it is enacted, that the secretary of state shall keep the seal of the United States, "and shall make out and record, and shall affix the said seal to all civil commissions to officers of the United States, to be appointed by the president;" "provided, that the said seal shall not be affixed to any commission, before the same shall have been signed by the President of the United States; nor to any other instrument or act, without the special warrant of the president therefor."

Sealing of Commission

The signature is a warrant for affixing the great seal to the commission; and the great seal is only to be affixed to an instrument which is complete. It attests, by an act, supposed to be of public notoriety, the verity of the presidential signature. It is never to be affixed, until the commission is signed, because the signature, which gives force and effect to the commission, is conclusive evidence that the appointment is made.

The commission being signed, the subsequent duty of the secretary of state is prescribed by law, and not to be guided by the will of the president. He is to affix the seal of the United States to the commission, and is to record it. This is not a proceeding which may be varied, if the judgment of the executive shall suggest one more eligible; but is a precise course accurately marked out by law, and is to be strictly pursued. It is the duty of the secretary of state, to conform to the law, and in this he is an officer of the United States, bound to obey the laws. He acts, in this respect, as has been very properly stated at the bar, under the authority of law, and not by the instructions of the president. It is a ministerial act, which the law enjoins on a particular officer for a particular purpose.

If it should be supposed, that the solemnity of affixing the seal is necessary, not only to the validity of the commission, but even to the completion of an appointment, still, when the seal is affixed, the appointment is made, and the commission is valid. No other solemnity is required by law; no other act is to be performed on the part of the government. All that the executive can do, to invest the person with his office, is done; and unless the appointment be then made, the executive cannot make one without the co-operation of others.

After searching anxiously for the principles on which a contrary opinion may be supported, none have been found, which appear of sufficient force to maintain the opposite doctrine. Such as the imagination of the court could suggest, have been very deliberately examined, and after allowing them all the weight which it appears possible to give them, they do not shake the opinion which has been formed. In considering this question, it has been conjectured, that the commission may have been assimilated to a deed, to the validity of which delivery is essential. This idea is founded on the supposition, that the commission is not merely evidence of an appointment, but is itself the actual appointment; a supposition by no means unquestionable. But for the purpose of examining this objection fairly, let it be conceded, that the principle claimed for its support is established.

Delivery of Commission

The appointment being, under the constitution, to be made by the president personally, the delivery of the deed of appointment, if necessary to its completion, must be made by the president also. It is not necessary, that the delivery should be made personally to the grantee of the office: it never is so made. The law would seem to contemplate, that it should be made to the secretary of state, since it directs the secretary to affix the seal to the commission, after it shall have been signed by the president. If, then, the act of delivery be necessary to give validity to the commission, it has been delivered, when executed and given to the secretary, for the purpose of being sealed, recorded and transmitted to the party.

But in all cases of letters-patent, certain solemnities are required by law, which solemnities are the evidences of the validity of the instrument: a formal delivery to the person is not among them. In cases of commissions, the sign manual of the president, and the seal of the United States are those solemnities. This objection, therefore, does not touch the case.

Delivery Not a Legal Essential

It has also occurred as possible, and barely possible, that the transmission of the commission, and the acceptance thereof, might be deemed necessary to complete the right of the plaintiff. The transmission of the commission is a practice, directed by convenience, but not by law. It cannot, therefore, be necessary to constitute the appointment, which must precede it, and which is the mere act of the president. If the executive required that every person appointed to an office should himself take means to procure his commission, the appointment would not be the less valid on that account. The appointment is the sole act of the president; the transmission of the commission is the sole act of the officer to whom that duty is assigned, and may be accelerated or retarded by circumstances which can have no influence on the appointment. A commission is transmitted to a person already appointed; not to a person to be appointed or not, as the letter inclosing the commission should happen to get into the post-office and reach him in safety, or to miscarry.

It may have some tendency to elucidate this point, to inquire, whether the possession of the original commission be indispensably necessary to authorize a person, appointed to any office, to perform the duties of that office. If it was necessary, then a loss of the commission would lose the office. Not only negligence, but accident or fraud, fire or theft, might deprive an individual of his office. In such a case, I presume, it could not be doubted, but that a copy from the record of the office of the secretary of state would be, to every intent and purpose, equal to the original: the act of congress has expressly made it so. To give that copy validity, it would not be necessary to prove that the original had been transmitted and afterwards lost. The copy would be complete evidence that the original had existed, and that the appointment had been made, but not that the original had been transmitted. If, indeed, it should appear, that the original had been mislaid in the office of state, that circumstance will not affect the operation of the copy. When all the requisites have been performed, which authorize a recording officer to record any instrument whatever, and the order for that purpose has been given, the instrument is, in law, considered as recorded, although the manual labor of inserting it in a book kept for that purpose may not have been performed. In the case of commissions, the law orders the secretary of state to record them. When, therefore, they are signed and sealed, the order for their being recorded is given; and whether inserted in the book or not, they are in law recorded.

A copy of this record is declared equal to the original, and the fees to be paid by a person requiring a copy are ascertained by law. Can a keeper of a public record erase therefrom a commission which has been recorded? Or can he refuse a copy thereof to a person demanding it on the terms prescribed by law? Such a copy would, equally with the original, authorize the justice of peace to proceed in the performance of his duty, because it would, equally with the original, attest his appointment.

If the transmission of a commission be not considered as necessary to give validity to an appointment, still less is its acceptance. The appointment is the sole act of the president; the acceptance is the sole act of the officer, and is, in plain common sense, posterior to the appointment. As he may resign, so may he refuse to accept: but neither the one nor the other is capable of rendering the appointment a nonentity.

That this is the understanding of the government, is apparent from the whole tenor of its conduct. A commission bears date, and the salary of the officer commences, from his appointment; not from the transmission or acceptance of his commission. When a person appointed to any office refuses to accept that office, the successor is nominated in the place of the person who has declined to accept, and not in the place of the person who had been previously in office, and had created the original vacancy.

Opinion on Validity of Claim

It is, therefore, decidedly the opinion of the court, that when a commission has been signed by the president, the appointment is made; and that the commission is complete, when the seal of the United States has been affixed to it by the secretary of state.

Where an officer is removable at the will of the executive, the circumstance which completes his appointment is of no concern; because the act is at any time revocable; and the commission may be arrested, if still in the office. But when the officer is not removable at the will of the executive, the appointment is not revocable, and cannot be annulled: it has conferred legal rights which cannot be resumed. The discretion of the executive is to be exercised, until the appointment has been made. But having once made the appointment, his power over the office is terminated, in all cases where, by law, the officer is not removable by him. The right to the office is then in the person appointed, and he has the absolute unconditional power of accepting or rejecting it.

Mr. Marbury, then, since his commission was signed by the president, and sealed by the secretary of state, was appointed; and as the law creating the office, gave the officer a right to hold for five years, independent of the executive, the appointment was not revocable, but vested in the officer legal rights, which are protected by the laws of his country. To withhold his commission, therefore, is an act deemed by the court not warranted by law, but violative of a vested legal right.

Question of Remedy Under Law

2. This brings us to the second inquiry; which is: If he has a right, and that right has been violated, do the laws of his country afford him a remedy?

The very essence of civil liberty certainly consists in the right of every individual to claim the protection of the laws, whenever he receives an injury. One of the first duties of government is to afford that protection. In Great Britain, the king himself is sued in the respectful form of a petition, and he never fails to comply with the judgment of his court.

In the 3d vol. of his Commentaries (p. 23), Blackstone states two cases in which a remedy is afforded by mere operation of law. "In all other cases," he says, "it is a general and indisputable rule, that where there is a legal right, there is also a legal remedy by suit, or action at law, whenever that right is invaded." And afterwards (p. 109, of the same vol.), he says, "I am next to consider such injuries as are cognisable by the courts of the common law. And herein I shall, for the present, only remark, that all possible injuries whatsoever, that did not fall within the exclusive cognisance of either the ecclesiastical, military or maritime tribunals, are, for that very reason, within the cognisance of the common-law courts of justice; for it is a settled and invariable principle in the laws of England, that every right, when withheld, must have a remedy, and every injury its proper redress."

The government of the United States has been emphatically termed a government of laws, and not of men. It will certainly cease to deserve this high appellation, if the laws furnish no remedy for the violation of a vested legal right. If this obloquy is to be cast on the jurisprudence of our country, it must arise from the peculiar character of the case.

It behooves us, then, to inquire whether there be in its composition any ingredient which shall exempt it from legal investigation, or exclude the injured party from legal redress. In pursuing this inquiry, the first question which presents itself is, whether this can be arranged with that class of cases which come under the description of *damnum absque injuriâ;* a loss without an injury. This description of cases never has been considered, and it is believed, never can be considered, as comprehending offices of trust, of honor or of profit. The office of justice of peace in the district of Columbia is such an office; it is, therefore, worthy of the attention and guardianship of the laws. It has received that attention and guardianship: it has been created by a special act of congress, and has been secured, so far as the laws can give security, to the person appointed to fill it, for five years. It is not, then, on account of the worthlessness of the thing pursued, that the injured party can be alleged to be without remedy.

Discretion in General

Is it in the nature of the transaction? Is the act of delivering or withholding a commission to be considered as a mere political act, belonging to the executive department alone, for the performance of which entire confidence is placed by our constitution in the supreme executive; and for any misconduct respecting which, the injured individual has no remedy? That there may be such cases is not to be questioned; but that every act of duty, to be performed in any of the great departments of government, constitutes such a case, is not to be admitted.

By the act concerning invalids, passed in June 1794 (1 U.S. Stat. 392), the secretary of war is ordered to place on the pension list, all persons whose names are contained in a report previously made by him to congress. If he should refuse to do so, would the wounded veteran be without remedy? Is it to be contended, that where the law, in precise terms, directs the performance of an act, in which an individual is interested, the law is incapable of securing obedience to its mandate? Is it on account of the character of the person against whom the complaint is made? Is it to be contended that the heads of departments are not amenable to the laws of their country?

Whatever the practice on particular occasions may be, the theory of this principle will certainly never be maintained. No act of the legislature confers so extraordinary a privilege, nor can it derive countenance from the doctrines of the common law. After stating that personal injury from the king to a subject is presumed to be impossible, Blackstone (vol. 3, p. 255), says, "but injuries to the rights of property can scarcely be committed by the crown, without the intervention of its officers; for whom the law, in matters of right, entertains no respect or delicacy; but furnishes various methods of detecting the errors and misconduct of those agents, by whom the king has been deceived and induced to do a temporary injustice."

By the act passed in 1796, authorizing the sale of the lands above the mouth of Kentucky river (1 U.S. Stat. 464), the purchaser, on paying his purchase-money, becomes completely entitled to the property purchased; and on producing to the secretary of state the receipt of the treasurer, upon a certificate required by the law, the president of the United States is authorized to grant him a patent. It is further enacted, that all patents shall be countersigned by the secretary of state, and recorded in his office. If the secretary of state should choose to withhold this patent; or, the patent being lost, should refuse a copy of it; can it be imagined, that the law furnishes to the injured person no remedy? It is not believed, that any person whatever would attempt to maintain such a proposition.

It follows, then, that the question, whether the legality of an act of the head of a department be examinable in a court of justice or not, must always depend on the nature of that act. If some acts be examinable, and others not, there must be some rule of law to guide the court in the exercise of its jurisdiction. In some instances, there may be difficulty in applying the rule to particular cases; but there cannot, it is believed, be much difficulty in laying down the rule.

Executive Discretion

By the constitution of the United States, the president is invested with certain important political powers, in the exercise of which he is to use his own discretion, and is accountable only to his country in his political character, and to his own conscience. To aid him in the performance of these duties, he is authorized to appoint certain officers, who act by his authority, and in conformity with his orders. In such cases, their acts are his acts; and whatever opinion may be entertained of the manner in which executive discretion may be used, still there exists, and can exist, no power to control that discretion. The subjects are political: they respect the nation, not individual rights, and being entrusted to the executive, the decision of the executive is conclusive.

The application of this remark will be perceived, by adverting to the act of congress for establishing the department of foreign affairs. This officer, as his duties were prescribed by that act, is to conform precisely to the will of the president: he is the mere organ by whom that will is communicated. The acts of such an officer, as an officer, can never be examinable by the courts. But when the legislature proceeds to impose on that officer other duties; when he is directed peremptorily to perform certain acts; when the rights of individuals are dependent on the performance of those acts; he is so far the officer of the law; is amenable to the laws for his conduct; and cannot, at his discretion, sport away the vested rights of others.

The conclusion from this reasoning is, that where the heads of departments are the political or confidential agents of the executive, merely to execute the will of the president, or rather to act in cases in which the executive possesses a constitutional or legal discretion, nothing can be more perfectly clear, than that their acts are only politically examinable. But where a specific duty is assigned by law, and individual rights depend upon the performance of that duty, it seems equally clear, that the individual who considers himself injured, has a right to resort to the laws of his country for a remedy.

Executive Discretion Inapplicable

If this be the rule, let us inquire, how it applies to the case under the consideration of the court. The power of nominating to the senate, and the power of appointing the person nominated, are political powers, to be exercised by the president, according to his own discretion. When he has made an appointment, he has exercised his whole power, and his discretion has been completely applied to the case. If, by law, the officer be removable at the will of the president, then a new appointment may be immediately made, and the rights of the officer are terminated. But as a fact which has existed, cannot be made never to have existed, the appointment cannot be annihilated; and consequently, if the officer is by law not removable at the will of the president, the rights he has acquired are protected by the law, and are not resumable by the president. They cannot be extinguished by executive authority, and he has the privilege of asserting them in like manner, as if they had been derived from any other source.

The question whether a right has vested or not, is, in its nature, judicial, and must be tried by the judicial authority. If, for example, Mr. Marbury had taken the oaths of a magistrate, and proceeded to act as one; in consequence of which, a suit has been instituted against him, in which his defence had depended on his being a magistrate, the validity of his appointment must have been determined by judicial authority. So, if he conceives that, by virtue of his appointment, he has a legal right either to the commission which has been made out for him, or to a copy of that commission, it is equally a question examinable in a court, and the decision of the court upon it must depend on the opinion entertained of his appointment. That question has been discussed, and the opinion is, that the latest point of time which can be taken as that at which the appointment was complete, and evidenced, was when, after the signature of the president, the seal of the United States was affixed to the commission.

Opinion on Remedy

It is, then, the opinion of the Court: 1st. That by signing the commission of Mr. Marbury, the President of the United States appointed him a justice of peace for the county of Washington, in the district of Columbia; and that the seal of the United States, affixed thereto by the secretary of state, is conclusive testimony of the verity of the signature, and of the completion of the appointment; and that the appointment conferred on him a legal right to the office for the space of five years. 2d. That, having this legal title to the office, he has a consequent right to the commission; a refusal to deliver which is a plain violation of that right, for which the laws of his country afford him a remedy.

Appropriate Remedy: Nature of Writ

3. It remains to be inquired whether he is entitled to the remedy for which he applies? This depends on—1st. The nature of the writ applied for; and 2d. The power of this court.

1st. The nature of the writ. Blackstone, in the 3d volume of his Commentaries, page 110, defines a *mandamus* to be "a command issuing in the king's name, from the court of king's bench, and directed to any person, corporation or inferior court of judicature, within the king's dominions, requiring them to do some particular thing therein specified, which appertains to their office and duty, and which the court of king's bench has previously determined, or at least supposes, to be consonant to right and justice."

Lord MANSFIELD, in 3 Burr. 1267, in the case of *The King* v. *Baker et ai.,* states, with much precision and explicitness, the cases in which this writ may be used. "Whenever," says that very able judge, "there is a right to execute an office, perform a service, or exercise a franchise (more especially if it be in a matter of public concern, or attended with profit), and a person is kept out of possession, or dispossessed of such right, and has no other specific legal remedy, this court ought to assist by *mandamus,* upon reasons of justice, as the writ expresses, and upon reasons of public policy, to preserve peace, order and good government." In the same case, he says, "this writ ought to be used upon all occasions where the law has established no specific remedy, and where in justice and good government there ought to be one." In addition to the authorities now particularly cited, many others were relied on at the bar, which show how far the practice has conformed to the general doctrines that have been just quoted.

This writ, if awarded, would be directed to an officer of government, and its mandate to him would be, to use the words of Blackstone, "to do a particular thing therein specified, which appertains to his office and duty, and which the court has previously determined, or at least supposes, to be consonant to right and justice." Or, in the words of Lord MANSFIELD, the applicant, in this case, has a right to execute an office of public concern, and is kept out of possession of that right. These circumstances certainly concur in this case.

Still, to render the *mandamus* a proper remedy, the officer to whom it is to be directed, must be one to whom, on legal principles, such writ may be directed; and the person applying for it must be without any other specific and legal remedy.

Officials Liable to Writ

1. With respect to the officer to whom it would be directed. The intimate political relation subsisting between the president of the United States and the heads of departments, necessarily renders any legal investigation of the acts of one of those high officers peculiarly irksome, as well as delicate; and excites some hesitation with respect to the propriety of entering into such investigation. Impressions are often received, without much reflection or examination, and it is not wonderful, that in such a case as this, the assertion, by an individual, of his legal claims in a court of justice, to which claims it is the duty of that court to attend, should at first view be considered by some, as an attempt to intrude into the cabinet, and to intermeddle with the prerogatives of the executive.

It is scarcely necessary for the court to disclaim all pretensions to such a jurisdiction. An extravagance, so absurd and excessive, could not have been entertained for a moment. The province of the court is, solely, to decide on the rights of individuals, not to inquire how the executive, or executive officers, perform duties in which they have a discretion. Questions in their nature political, or which are, by the constitution and laws, submitted to the executive, can never be made in this court.

But, if this be not such a question; if, so far from being an intrusion into the secrets of the cabinet, it respects a paper which, according to law, is upon record, and to a copy of which the law gives a right, on the payment of ten cents; if it be no intermeddling with a subject over which the executive can be considered as having exercised any control; what is there, in the exalted station of the officer, which shall bar a citizen from asserting, in a court of justice, his legal rights, or shall forbid a court to listen to the claim, or to issue a *mandamus*, directing the performance of a duty, not depending on executive discretion, but on particular acts of congress, and the general principles of law?

If one of the heads of departments commits any illegal act, under color of his office, by which an individual sustains an injury, it cannot be pretended, that his office alone exempts him from being sued in the ordinary mode of proceeding, and being compelled to obey the judgment of the law. How then, can his office exempt him from this particular mode of deciding on the legality of his conduct, if the case be such a case as would, were any other individual the party complained of, authorize the process?

It is not by the office of the person to whom the writ is directed, but the nature of the thing to be done, that the propriety or impropriety of issuing a *mandamus* is to be determined. Where the head of a department acts in a case, in which executive discretion is to be exercised; in which he is the mere organ of executive will; it is again repeated, that any application to a court to control, in any respect, his conduct would be rejected without hesitation. But where he is directed by law to do a certain act, affecting the absolute rights of individuals, in the performance of which he is not placed under the particular direction of the president, and the performance of which the president cannot lawfully forbid, and therefore, is never presumed to have forbidden; as, for example, to record a commission or a patent for land, which has received all the legal solemnities; or to give a copy of such record; in such cases, it is not perceived, on what ground the courts of the country are further excused from the duty of giving judgment that right be done to an injured individual, than if the same services were to be performed by a person not the head of a department.

Constitutional Precedents

This opinion seems not now, for the first time, to be taken up in this country. It must be well recollected, that in 1792, an act passed, directing the secretary of war to place on the pension list such disabled officers and soldiers as should be reported to him, by the circuit courts, which act, so far as the duty was imposed on the courts, was deemed unconstitutional; but some of the judges, thinking that the law might be executed by them in the character of commissioners, proceeded to act, and to report in that character. This law being deemed unconstitutional, at the circuits, was repealed, and a different system was established; but the question whether those persons who had been reported by the judges, as commissioners, were entitled, in consequence of that report, to be placed on the pension list, was a legal question, properly determinable in the courts, although the act of placing such persons on the list was to be performed by the head of a department.

That this question might be properly settled, congress passed an act, in February 1793, making it the duty of the secretary of war, in conjunction with the attorney-general, to take such measures as might be necessary to obtain an adjudication of the supreme court of the United States on the validity of any such rights, claimed under the act aforesaid. After the passage of this act, a *mandamus* was moved for, to be directed to the secretary of war, commanding him to place on the pension list, a person stating himself to be on the report of the judges.

There is, therefore, much reason to believe, that this mode of trying the legal right of the complainant was deemed, by the head of a department, and by the highest law-officer of the United States, the most proper which could be selected for the purpose. When the subject was brought before the court, the decision was, not that a *mandamus* would not lie to the head of a department, directing him to perform an act, enjoined by law, in the performance of which an individual had a vested interest; but that a *mandamus* ought not to issue in that case; the decision necessarily to be made, if the report of the commissioners did not confer on the applicant a legal right. The judgment, in that case, is understood to have decided the merits of all claims of that description; and the persons, on the report of the commissioners, found it necessary to pursue the mode prescribed by the law, subsequent to that which had been deemed unconstitutional, in order to place themselves on the pension list. The doctrine, therefore, now advanced, is by no means a novel one.

Alternative Actions

It is true, that the *mandamus*, now moved for, is not for the performance of an act expressly enjoined by statute. It is to deliver a commission; on which subject, the acts of congress are silent. This difference is not considered as affecting the case. It has already been stated, that the applicant has, to that commission, a vested legal right, of which the executive cannot deprive him. He has been appointed to an office, from which he is not removable at the will of the executive; and being so appointed, he has a right to the commission which the secretary has received from the president for his use. The act of congress does not indeed order the secretary of state to send it to him, but it is placed in his hands for the person entitled to it; and cannot be more lawfully withheld by him, than by any other person.

It was at first doubted, whether the action of *detinue* was not a specific legal remedy for the commission which had been withheld from Mr. Marbury; in which case, a *mandamus* would be improper. But this doubt has yielded to the consideration, that the judgment in *detinue* is for the thing itself, *or* its value. The value of a public office, not to be sold, is incapable of being ascertained; and the applicant has a right to the office itself, or to nothing. He will obtain the office by obtaining the commission, or a copy of it, from the record.

Mandamus Held Proper Writ

This, then, is a plain case for a *mandamus,* either to deliver the commission, or a copy of it from the record; and it only remains to be inquired, whether it can issue from this court?

Appropriate Forum: Constitution

The act to establish the judicial courts of the United States authorizes the supreme court, "to issue writs of *mandamus,* in cases warranted by the principles and usages of law, to any courts appointed or persons holding office, under the authority of the United States." The secretary of state, being a person holding an office under the authority of the United States, is precisely within the letter of this description; and if this court is not authorized to issue a writ of *mandamus* to such an officer, it must be because the law is unconstitutional, and therefore, absolutely incapable of conferring the authority, and assigning the duties which its words purport to confer and assign.

The constitution vests the whole judicial power of the United States in one supreme court, and such inferior courts as congress shall, from time to time, ordain and establish. This power is expressly extended to all cases arising under the laws of the United States; and consequently, in some form, may be exercised over the present case; because the right claimed is given by a law of the United States.

Original Jurisdiction

In the distribution of this power, it is declared, that "the supreme court shall have original jurisdiction, in all cases affecting ambassadors, other public ministers and consuls, and those in which a state shall be a party. In all other cases, the supreme court shall have appellate jurisdiction." It has been insisted, at the bar, that as the original grant of jurisdiction to the supreme and inferior courts, is general, and the clause, assigning original jurisdiction to the supreme court, contains no negative or restrictive words, the power remains to the legislature, to assign original jurisdiction to that court, in other cases than those specified in the article which has been recited; provided those cases belong to the judicial power of the United States.

If it had been intended to leave it in the discretion of the legislature, to apportion the judicial power between the supreme and inferior courts, according to the will of that body, it would certainly have been useless to have proceeded further than to have defined the judicial power, and the tribunals in which it should be vested. The subsequent part of the section is mere surplusage—is entirely without meaning, if such is to be the construction. If congress remains at liberty to give this court appellate jurisdiction, where the constitution has declared their jurisdiction shall be original; and original jurisdiction where the constitution has declared it shall be appellate; the distribution of jurisdiction, made in the constitution, is form without substance. Affirmative words are often, in their operation, negative of other objects than those affirmed; and in this case, a negative or exclusive sense must be given to them, or they have no operation at all.

It cannot be presumed, that any clause in the constitution is intended to be without effect; and therefore, such a construction is inadmissible, unless the words require it. If the solicitude of the convention, respecting our peace with foreign powers, induced a provision that the supreme court should take original jurisdiction in cases which might be supposed to affect them; yet the clause would have proceeded no further than to provide for such cases, if no further restriction on the powers of congress had been intended. That they should have appellate jurisdiction in all other cases, with such exceptions as congress might make, is no restriction; unless the words be deemed exclusive of original jurisdiction.

When an instrument organizing, fundamentally, a judicial system, divides it into one supreme, and so many inferior courts as the legislature may ordain and establish; then enumerates its powers, and proceeds so far to distribute them, as to define the jurisdiction of the supreme court, by declaring the cases in which it shall take original jurisdiction, and that in others it shall take appellate jurisdiction, the plain import of the words seems to be, that in one class of cases, its jurisdiction is original, and not appellate; in the other, it is appellate, and not original. If any other construction would render the clause inoperative, that is an additional reason for rejecting such other construction, and for adhering to their obvious meaning. To enable this court, then, to issue a *mandamus*, it must be shown to be an exercise of appellate jurisdiction, or to be necessary to enable them to exercise appellate jurisdiction.

Appellate Jurisdiction

It has been stated at the bar, that the appellate jurisdiction may be exercised in a variety of forms, and that if it be the will of the legislature that a *mandamus* should be used for that purpose, that will must be obeyed. This is true, yet the jurisdiction must be appellate, not original. It is the essential criterion of appellate jurisdiction, that it revises and corrects the proceedings in a cause already instituted, and does not create that cause. Although, therefore, a *mandamus* may be directed to courts, yet to issue such a writ to an officer, for the delivery of a paper, is, in effect, the same as to sustain an original action for that paper, and therefore, seems not to belong to appellate, but to original jurisdiction. Neither is it necessary in such a case as this, to enable the court to exercise its appellate jurisdiction. The authority, therefore, given to the supreme court by the act establishing the judicial courts of the United States, to issue writs of *mandamus* to public officers, appears not to be warranted by the constitution; and it becomes necessary to inquire, whether a jurisdiction so conferred can be exercised.

The question, whether an act, repugnant to the constitution, can become the law of the land, is a question deeply interesting to the United States; but, happily, not of an intricacy proportioned to its interest. It seems only necessary to recognise certain principles, supposed to have been long and well established, to decide it. That the people have an original right to establish, for their future government, such principles as, in their opinion, shall most conduce to their own happiness, is the basis on which the whole American fabric has been erected. The exercise of this original right is a very great exertion; nor can it, nor ought it, to be frequently repeated. The principles, therefore, so established, are deemed fundamental: and as the authority from which they proceed is supreme, and can seldom act, they are designed to be permanent.

This original and supreme will organizes the government, and assigns to different departments their respective powers. It may either stop here, or establish certain limits not to be transcended by those departments. The government of the United States is of the latter description. The powers of the legislature are defined and limited; and that those limits may not be mistaken or forgotten, the constitution is written. To what purpose are powers limited, and to what purpose is that limitation committed to writing, if these limits may, at any time, be passed by those intended to be restrained? The distinction between a government with limited and unlimited powers is abolished, if those limits do not confine the persons on whom they are imposed, and if acts prohibited and acts allowed, are of equal obligation. It is a proposition too plain to be contested, that the constitution controls any legislative act repugnant to it; or that the legislature may alter the constitution by an ordinary act.

Between these alternatives, there is no middle ground. The constitution is either a superior paramount law, unchangeable by ordinary means, or it is on a level with ordinary legislative acts, and, like other acts, is alterable when the legislature shall please to alter it. If the former part of the alternative be true, then a legislative act, contrary to the constitution, is not law: if the latter part

That it thus reduces to nothing, what we have deemed the greatest improve-be true, then written constitutions are absurd attempts, on the part of the people, to limit a power, in its own nature, illimitable.

Legislation and Constitution

Certainly, all those who have framed written constitutions contemplate them as forming the fundamental and paramount law of the nation, and consequently, the theory of every such government must be, that an act of the legislature, repugnant to the constitution, is void. This theory is essentially attached to a written constitution, and is, consequently, to be considered, by this court, as one of the fundamental principles of our society. It is not, therefore, to be lost sight of, in the further consideration of this subject.

If an act of the legislature, repugnant to the constitution, is void, does it, notwithstanding its invalidity, bind the courts, and oblige them to give it effect? Or, in other words, though it be not law, does it constitute a rule as operative as if it was a law? This would be to overthrow, in fact, what was established in theory; and would seem, at first view, an absurdity too gross to be insisted on. It shall, however, receive a more attentive consideration.

Function of Judiciary

It is, emphatically, the province and duty of the judicial department, to say what the law is. Those who apply the rule to particular cases, must of necessity expound and interpret that rule. If two laws conflict with each other, the courts must decide on the operation of each. So, if a law be in opposition to the constitution; if both the law and the constitution apply to a particular case, so that the court must either decide that case, conformable to the law, disregarding the constitution; or conformable to the constitution, disregarding the law; the court must determine which of these conflicting rules governs the case: this is of the very essence of judicial duty. If then, the courts are to regard the constitution, and the constitution is superior to any ordinary act of the legislature, the constitution, and not such ordinary act, must govern the case to which they both apply.

Those, then, who controvert the principle, that the constitution is to be considered, in court, as a paramount law, are reduced to the necessity of maintaining that courts must close their eyes on the constitution, and see only the law. This doctrine would subvert the very foundation of all written constitutions. It would declare that an act which, according to the principles and theory of our government, is entirely void, is yet, in practice, completely obligatory. It would declare, that if the legislature shall do what is expressly forbidden, such act, notwithstanding the express prohibition, is in reality effectual. It would be giving to the legislature a practical and real omnipotence, with the same breath which professes to restrict their powers within narrow limits. It is prescribing limits, and declaring that those limits may be passed at pleasure.

ment on political institutions, a written constitution, would, of itself, be sufficient, in America, where written constitutions have been viewed with so much reverence, for rejecting the construction. But the peculiar expressions of the constitution of the United States furnish additional arguments in favor of its rejection. The judicial power of the United States is extended to all cases arising under the constitution. Could it be the intention of those who gave this power, to say, that in using it, the constitution should not be looked into? That a case arising under the constitution should be decided, without examining the instrument under which it arises? This is too extravagant to be maintained. In some cases, then, the constitution must be looked into by the judges. And if they can open it at all, what part of it are they forbidden to read or to obey?

Supremacy of Constitution

There are many other parts of the constitution which serve to illustrate this subject. It is declared, that "no tax or duty shall be laid on articles exported from any state." Suppose, a duty on the export of cotton, of tobacco or of flour; and a suit instituted to recover it. Ought judgment to be rendered in such a case? Ought the judges to close their eyes on the constitution, and only see the law?

The constitution declares "that no bill of attainder or *ex post facto* law shall be passed." If, however, such a bill should be passed, and a person should be prosecuted under it; must the court condemn to death those victims whom the constitution endeavors to preserve?

"No person," says the constitution, "shall be convicted of treason, unless on the testimony of two witnesses to the same *overt* act, or on confession in open court." Here, the language of the constitution is addressed especially to the courts. It prescribes, directly for them, a rule of evidence not to be departed from. If the legislature should change that rule, and declare one witness, or a confession out of court, sufficient for conviction, must the constitutional principle yield to the legislative act?

From these, and many other selections which might be made, it is apparent, that the framers of the constitution contemplated that instrument as a rule for the government of courts, as well as of the legislature. Why otherwise does it direct the judges to take an oath to support it? This oath certainly applies in an especial manner, to their conduct in their official character. How immoral to impose it on them, if they were to be used as the instruments, and the knowing instruments, for violating what they swear to support!

The oath of office, too, imposed by the legislature, is completely demonstrative of the legislative opinion on this subject. It is in these words: "I do solemnly swear, that I will administer justice, without respect to persons, and do equal right to the poor and to the rich; and that I will faithfully and impartially discharge all the duties incumbent on me as ———, according to the best of my abilities and understanding, agreeably to the constitution and laws of the United States." Why does a judge swear to discharge his duties agreeably to the constitution of the United States, if that constitution forms no rule for his government? If it is closed upon him, and cannot be inspected by him? If such be the real state of things, this is worse than solemn mockery. To prescribe, or to take this oath, becomes equally a crime.

It is also not entirely unworthy of observation, that in declaring what shall be the supreme law of the land, the constitution itself is first mentioned; and not the laws of the United States, generally, but those only which shall be made in pursuance of the constitution, have that rank.

Unconstitutionality

Thus, the particular phraseology of the constitution of the United States confirms and strengthens the principle, supposed to be essential to all written constitutions, that a law repugnant to the constitution is void; and that courts, as well as other departments, are bound by that instrument.

The rule must be discharged.

II

United States *v.* Burr

25 Fed. Cas. 1-209; various opinions rendered April 1-October 20, 1807

EDITOR'S NOTE: Burr's case actually consists of a series of rulings by Marshall as Circuit Justice, sometimes alone and sometimes sitting with District Judge Cyrus Griffin, on a succession of points raised in the course of a complicated prosecution. Only the most important opinions have been reproduced here.

1. *Jefferson's Proclamation of November 27, 1806*

James D. Richardson, *Messages and Papers of the Presidents* (Washington, D.C.: Government Printing Office, 1896), I, 404

Whereas information has been received that sundry persons, citizens of the United States or residents within the same, are conspiring and confederating together to begin and set on foot, provide, and prepare the means for a military expedition or enterprise against the dominions of Spain; that for this purpose they are fitting out and arming vessels in the western waters of the United States, collecting provisions, arms, military stores, and means; are deceiving and seducing honest and well-meaning citizens, under various pretenses, to engage in their criminal enterprises; are organizing, officering, and arming themselves for the same, contrary to the laws in such cases made and provided:

I have therefore thought proper to issue this my proclamation, warning and enjoining all faithful citizens who have been led without due knowledge or consideration to participate in the said unlawful enterprises to withdraw from the same without delay, and commanding all persons whatsoever engaged or concerned in the same to cease all further proceedings therein, as they will answer the contrary at their peril and incur prosecution with all the rigors of the law. And I hereby enjoin and require all officers, civil and military, of the United States, or of any of the States or Territories, and especially all governors and other executive authorities, all judges, justices, and other officers of the peace, all military officers of the Army or Navy of the United States, or officers of the militia, to be vigilant, each within his respective department and according to his functions, in searching out and bringing to condign punishment all persons engaged or concerned in such enterprise, in seizing and detaining, subject to the disposition of the law, all vessels, arms, military stores, or other means provided or providing for the same, and, in general, in preventing the carrying on such expedition or enterprise by all lawful means within their power; and I require all good and faithful citizens and others within the United States to be aiding and assisting herein, and especially in the discovery, apprehension, and bringing to justice of all such offenders, in preventing the execution of their unlawful designs, and in giving information against them to the proper authorities.

In testimony whereof I have caused the seal of the United States to be affixed to these presents, and have signed the same with my hand.

Given at the city of Washington on the 27th day of November, 1806, and in the year of the Sovereignty of the United States the thirty-first.

TH. JEFFERSON.

By the President:

JAMES MADISON,
Secretary of State.

2. *Jefferson's Special Message to Congress, January 22, 1807*

James D. Richardson, *Messages and Papers of the Presidents* (Washington, D.C.: Government Printing Office, 1896), I, 412

January 22, 1807.

To the Senate and House of Representatives of the United States:

Agreeably to the request of the House of Representatives communicated in their resolution of the 16th instant, I proceed to state, under the reserve therein expressed, information received touching an illegal combination of private individuals against the peace and safety of the Union, and a military expedition planned by them against the territories of a power in amity with the United States, with the measures I have pursued for suppressing the same.

I had for some time been in the constant expectation of receiving such further information as would have enabled me to lay before the Legislature the termination as well as the beginning and progress of this scene of depravity so far as it has been acted on the Ohio and its waters. From this the state of safety of the lower country might have been estimated on probable grounds, and the delay was indulged the rather because no circumstance had yet made it necessary to call in the aid of the legislative functions. Information now recently communicated has brought us nearly to the period contemplated. The mass of what I have received in the course of these transactions is voluminous, but little has been given under the sanction of an oath so as to constitute formal and legal evidence. It is chiefly in the form of letters, often containing such a mixture of rumors, conjectures, and suspicions as renders it difficult to sift out the real facts and unadvisable to hazard more than general outlines, strengthened by concurrent information or the particular credibility of the relator. In this state of the evidence, delivered sometimes, too, under the restriction of private confidence, neither safety nor justice will permit the exposing names, except that of the principal actor, whose guilt is placed beyond question.

Some time in the latter part of September I received intimations that designs were in agitation in the Western country unlawful and unfriendly to the peace of the Union, and that the prime mover in these was Aaron Burr, heretofore distinguished by the favor of his country. The grounds of these intimations being inconclusive, the objects uncertain, and the fidelity of that country known to be firm, the only measure taken was to urge the informants to use their best endeavors to get further insight into the designs and proceedings of the suspected persons and to communicate them to me.

It was not till the latter part of October that the objects of the conspiracy began to be perceived, but still so blended and involved in mystery that nothing distinct could be singled out for pursuit. In this state of uncertainty as to the crime contemplated, the acts done, and the legal course to be pursued, I thought it best to send to the scene where these things were principally in transaction a person in whose integrity, understanding, and discretion entire confidence could be reposed, with instructions to investigate the plots going on, to enter into conference (for which he had sufficient credentials) with the governors and all other officers, civil and military, and with their aid to do on the spot whatever should be necessary to discover the designs of the conspirators, arrest their means, bring their persons to punishment, and to call out the force of the country to suppress any unlawful enterprise in which it should be found they were engaged.

By this time it was known that many boats were under preparation, stores of provisions collecting, and an unusual number of suspicious characters in motion on the Ohio and its waters. Besides dispatching the confidential agent to that quarter, orders were at the same time sent to the governors of the Orleans and Mississippi Territories and to the commanders of the land and naval forces there to be on their guard against surprise and in constant readiness to resist any enterprise which might be attempted on the vessels, posts, or other objects under their care; and on the 8th of November instructions were forwarded to General Wilkinson to hasten an accommodation with the Spanish commandant on the Sabine, and as soon as that was effected to fall back with his principal force to the hither bank of the Mississippi for the defense of the interesting points on that river. By a letter received from that officer on the 25th of November, but dated October 21, we learnt that a confidential agent of Aaron Burr had been deputed to him with communications, partly written in cipher and partly oral, explaining his designs, exaggerating his resources, and making such offers of emolument and command to engage him and the army in his unlawful enterprise as he had flattered himself would be successful. The General, with the honor of a soldier and fidelity of a good citizen, immediately dispatched a trusty officer to me with information of what had passed, proceeding to establish such an understanding with the Spanish commandant on the Sabine as permitted him to withdraw his force across the Mississippi and to enter on measures for opposing the projected enterprise.

The General's letter, which came to hand on the 25th of November, as has been mentioned, and some other information received a few days earlier, when brought together developed Burr's general designs, different parts of which only had been revealed to different informants. It appeared that he contemplated two distinct objects, which might be carried on either jointly or separately, and either the one or the other first, as circumstances should direct. One of these was the severance of the Union of these States by the Alleghany Mountains; the other an attack on Mexico. A third object was provided, merely ostensible, to wit, the settlement of a pretended purchase of a tract of country on the Washita claimed by a Baron Bastrop. This was to serve as the pretext for all his preparations, an allurement for such followers as really wished to acquire settlements in that country and a cover under which to retreat in the event of a final discomfiture of both branches of his real design.

He found at once that the attachment of the Western country to the present Union was not to be shaken; that its dissolution could not be effected with the consent of its inhabitants, and that his resources were inadequate as yet to effect it by force. He took his course then at once, determined to seize on New Orleans, plunder the bank there, possess himself of the military and naval stores, and proceed on his expedition to Mexico, and to this object all his means and preparations were now directed. He collected from all the quarters where himself or his agents possessed influence all the ardent, restless, desperate, and disaffected persons who were ready for any enterprise analogous to their characters. He seduced good and well-meaning citizens, some by assurances that he possessed the confidence of the Government and was acting under its secret patronage, a pretense which procured some credit from the state of our differences with Spain, and others by offers of land in Bastrop's claim on the Washita.

This was the state of my information of his proceedings about the last of November, at which time, therefore, it was first possible to take specific measures to meet them. The proclamation of November 27, two days after the receipt of General Wilkinson's information, was now issued. Orders were dispatched to every interesting point on the Ohio and Mississippi from Pittsburg to New Orleans for the employment of such force either of the regulars or of the militia and of such proceedings also of the civil authorities as might enable them to seize on all the boats and stores provided for the enterprise, to arrest the persons concerned, and to suppress effectually the further progress of the enterprise. A little before the receipt of these orders in the State of Ohio our confidential agent, who had been diligently employed in investigating the conspiracy, had acquired sufficient information to open himself to the governor of that State and apply for the immediate exertion of the authority and power of the State to crush the combination. Governor Tiffin and the legislature, with a promptitude, an energy, and patriotic zeal which entitle them to a distinguished place in the affection of their sister States, effected the seizure of all the boats, provisions, and other preparations within their reach, and thus gave a first blow, materially disabling the enterprise in its outset.

In Kentucky a premature attempt to bring Burr to justice without sufficient evidence for his conviction had produced a popular impression in his favor and a general disbelief of his guilt. This gave him an unfortunate opportunity of hastening his equipments. The arrival of the proclamation and orders of the application and information of our confidential agent at length awakened the authorities of that State to the truth, and then produced the same promptitude and energy of which the neighboring State had set the example. Under an act of their legislature of December 23 militia was instantly ordered to different important points, and measures taken for doing whatever could yet be done. Some boats (accounts vary from five to double or treble that number) and persons (differently estimated from 100 to 300) had in the meantime passed the Falls of Ohio to rendezvous at the mouth of Cumberland with others expected down that river.

Not apprised till very late that any boats were building on Cumberland, the effect of the proclamation had been trusted to for some time in the State of Tennessee; but on the 19th of December similar communications and instructions with those to the neighboring States were dispatched by express to the governor and a general officer of the western division of the State, and on the 23d of December our confidential agent left Frankfort for Nashville to put into activity the means of that State also. But by information received yesterday I learn that on the 22d of December Mr. Burr descended the Cumberland with two boats merely of accommodation, carrying with him from that State no quota toward his unlawful enterprise. Whether after the arrival of the proclamation, of the orders, or of our agent any exertion which could be made by that State or the orders of the governor of Kentucky for calling out the militia at the mouth of Cumberland would be in time to arrest these boats and those from the Falls of Ohio is still doubtful.

On the whole, the fugitives from the Ohio, with their associates from Cumberland or any other place in that quarter, can not threaten serious danger to the city of New Orleans.

By the same express of December 19 orders were sent to the governors of Orleans and Mississippi, supplementary to those which had been given on the 25th of November, to hold the militia of their Territories in readiness to cooperate for their defense with the regular troops and armed vessels then under command of General Wilkinson. Great alarm, indeed, was excited at New Orleans by the exaggerated accounts of Mr. Burr, disseminated through his emissaries, of the armies and navies he was to assemble there. General Wilkinson had arrived there himself on the 24th of November, and had immediately put into activity the resources of the place for the purpose of its defense, and on the 10th of December he was joined by his troops from the Sabine. Great zeal was shewn by the inhabitants generally, the merchants of the place readily agreeing to the most laudable exertions and sacrifices for manning the armed vessels with their seamen, and the other citizens manifesting unequivocal fidelity to the Union and a spirit of determined resistance to their expected assailants.

Surmises have been hazarded that this enterprise is to receive aid from certain foreign powers; but these surmises are without proof or probability. The wisdom of the measures sanctioned by Congress at its last session has placed us in the paths of peace and justice with the only powers with whom we had any differences, and nothing has happened since which makes it either their interest or ours to pursue another course. No change of measures has taken place on our part; none ought to take place at this time. With the one, friendly arrangement was then proposed, and the law deemed necessary on the failure of that was suspended to give time for a fair trial of the issue.

With the same power friendly arrangement is now proceeding under good expectations, and the same law deemed necessary on failure of that is still suspended, to give time for a fair trial of the issue. With the other, negotiation was in like manner then preferred, and provisional measures only taken to meet the event of rupture. With the same power negotiation is still preferred, and provisional measures only are necessary to meet the event of rupture. While, therefore, we do not deflect in the slightest degree from the course we then assumed and are still pursuing with mutual consent to restore a good understanding, we are not to impute to them practices as irreconcilable to interest as to good faith, and changing necessarily the relations of peace and justice between us to those of war. These surmises are therefore to be imputed to the vauntings of the author of this enterprise to multiply his partisans by magnifying the belief of his prospects and support.

By letters from General Wilkinson of the 14th and 18th of December, which came to hand two days after the date of the resolution of the House of Representatives—that is to say, on the morning of the 18th instant—I received the important affidavit a copy of which I now communicate, with extracts of so much of the letters as comes within the scope of the resolution. By these it will be seen that of three of the principal emissaries of Mr. Burr whom the General had caused to be apprehended, one had been liberated by habeas corpus, and two others, being those particularly employed in the endeavor to corrupt the general and army of the United States, have been embarked by him for ports in the Atlantic States, probably on the consideration that an impartial trial could not be expected during the present agitations of New Orleans, and that that city was not as yet a safe place of confinement. As soon as these persons shall arrive they will be delivered to the custody of the law and left to such course of trial, both as to place and process, as its functionaries may direct. The presence of the highest judicial authorities, to be assembled at this place within a few days, the means of pursuing a sounder course of proceedings here than elsewhere, and the aid of the Executive means, should the judges have occasion to use them, render it equally desirable for the criminals as for the public that, being already removed from the place where they were first apprehended, the first regular arrest should take place here, and the course of proceedings receive here its proper direction.

TH: JEFFERSON.

3. *Affidavits of James Wilkinson et al.*

4 Cranch, App. at 456

Wilkinson's First Affidavit

"I, JAMES WILKINSON, Brigadier-General and Commander in Chief of the army of the United States, to warrant the arrest of Doctor Erick Bollman, on a charge of treason, misprision of treason, or such other offense against the government and laws of the United States as the following facts may legally charge him with, on my honor as a soldier; and on the Holy Evangelists of Almighty God, do declare and swear, that on the sixth day of November last, when in command at Natchitoches, I received by the hands of a Frenchman, a stranger to me, a letter from Doctor Erick Bollman, of which the following is a correct copy:

New Orleans, September 27, 1806.

"SIR: I have the honor to forward to your excellency the enclosed letters, which I was charged to deliver to you by our mutual friend: I shall remain for some time at this place, and should be glad to learn where and when I may have the pleasure of an interview with you. Have the goodness to inform me of it, and please to direct your letter to me care of   . or enclose it under cover to them.

    "I have the honor to be,

      "With great respect, Sir,

    "Your excellency's most obedient servant,

       (Signed).   "ERICK BOLLMAN.

    "Gen. Wilkinson."

Covering a communication in cipher from Colonel Aaron Burr, of which the following is substantially as fair an interpretation as I have heretofore been able to make, the original of which I hold in my possession; "I (Aaron Burr) have obtained funds, and have actually commenced the enterprise. Detachments from different points, and under different pretences, will rendezvous on the Ohio, 1st November. Everything internal and external favors views; protection of England is secured.

"T. is gone to Jamaica to arrange with the admiral of that station, and will meet at the Mississippi————England————navy of the United States are ready to join, and final orders are given to my friends and followers; it will be a host of choice spirits. Wilkinson shall be second to Burr only; Wilkinson shall dictate the rank and promotion of his officers. Burr will proceed westward 1st August, never to return: with him go his daughter; the husband will follow in October with a corps of worthies: send forthwith an intelligent and confidential friend, with whom Burr may confer; he shall return immediately with further interesting details; this is essential to concert and harmony of movement; send a list of all persons known to Wilkinson west of the mountains, who could be useful, with a note delineating their characters.

"By your messenger send me four or five of the commissions of your officers, which you can borrow under any pretence you please; they shall be returned faithfully; already are orders to the contractor given to forward six months' provisions to points Wilkinson may name; this shall not be used until the last moment, and then under proper injunctions; the project is brought to the point so long desired: Burr guarantees the result with his life and honor, the lives, the honor and fortunes of hundreds, the best blood of our country; Burr's plan of operations is to move down rapidly from the falls on the fifteenth of November, with the first five hundred or one thousand men, in light boats, now constructing for that purpose; to be at Natchez between the fifth and fifteenth of December, then to meet Wilkinson; then to determine whether it will be expedient, in the first instance, to seize on, or pass by, Baton Rouge; on receipt of this send Burr an answer; draw on Burr for all expenses, &c.

"The people of the country to which we are going are prepared to receive us; their agents now with Burr say that if we will protect their religion, and will not subject them to a foreign power, that in three weeks all will be settled. The Gods invite to glory and fortune; it remains to be seen whether we deserve the boon: the bearer of this goes express to you; he will hand a formal letter of introduction to you from Burr, a copy of which is hereunto subjoined: he is a man of inviolable honor and perfect discretion; formed to execute rather than to project; capable of relating facts with fidelity, and incapable of relating them otherwise; he is thoroughly informed of the plans and intentions of   , and will disclose to you as far as you inquire, and no further; he has imbibed a reverence for your character, and may be embarrassed in your presence; put him at ease and he will satisfy you; Doctor Bollman, equally confidential, better informed on the subject, and more intelligent, will hand this duplicate.

"29th July."

The day after my arrival at this city, the 26th of November last, I received another letter from the doctor, of which the following is a correct copy:

New Orleans, November 25th, 1806.

"SIR: "Your letter of the 16th inst. has been duly received; supposing that you will be much engaged this morning, I defer waiting on your excellency till you will be pleased to inform me of the time when it will be convenient for you to see me. I remain with great respect,

"Your Excellency's most obedient servant,

"ERICK BOLLMAN.

"His Excellency Gen. Wilkinson, Fauxbourg."

Marigny, the house between Madam Trevigne and M. Macarty.

On the 30th of the same month I waited in person on Doctor E. Bollman, when he informed me that he had not heard from Colonel Burr since his arrival here. That he (the said Doctor E. Bollman) had sent despatches to Colonel Burr by a Lieutenant Spence, of the navy, and that he had been advised of Spence's arrival at Nashville, in the state of Tennessee, and observed that Colonel Burr had proceeded too far to retreat; that he (Colonel Burr) had numerous and powerful friends in the United States, who stood pledged to support him with their fortunes, and that he must succeed. That he (the said Doctor E. Bollman) had written to Colonel Burr on the subject of provisions, and that he expected a supply would be sent from New York, and also from Norfolk, where Colonel Burr had strong connections. I did not see or hear from the doctor again until the 5th inst., when I called on him the second time. The mail having arrived the day before, I asked him whether he had received any intelligence from Colonel Burr; he informed me that he had seen a letter from Colonel Burr of the 30th October, in which he (Colonel Burr) gave assurances that he should be at Natchez with 2,000 men on the 20th December, inst. where he should wait until he heard from this place; that he would be followed by 4,000 men more, and that he, (Colonel Burr) if he had chosen, could have raised or got 12,000 as easily as 6,000, but that he did not think that number necessary. Confiding fully in this information, I became indifferent about further disguise. I then told the doctor that I should most certainly oppose Colonel Burr if he came this way. He replied that they must come here for equipments and shipping, and observed that he did not know what had passed between Colonel Burr and myself, obliqued at a sham defence, and waived the subject.

From the documents in my possession, and the several communications, verbal as well as written, from the said Doctor Erick Bollman, on this subject, I feel no hesitation in declaring under the solemn obligation of an oath, that he has committed misprision of treason against the government of the United States.

(Signed)   JAMES WILKINSON.

Signed and sworn to this 14th day of December, 1806, before me, one of the justices of the peace of this country.

(Signed)   J. CARRICK.

"Philadelphia, July 25, 1806.

"DEAR SIR:

"Mr. Swartwout, the brother of Colonel S. of New York, being on his way down the Mississippi, and presuming that he may pass you at some post on the river, has requested of me a letter of introduction, which I give with pleasure, as he is a most amiable young man, and highly respectable from his character and connections. I pray you to afford him any friendly offices which his situation may require, and beg you to pardon the trouble which this may give you.

"With entire respect,

"Your friend and obedient servant,

"A. BURR.

"His Excellency Gen. Wilkinson."

Message from the President of the United States to the Senate and House of Representatives:

I received from Gen. Wilkinson, on the 23d inst., his affidavit, charging Samuel Swartwout, Peter V. Ogden, and James Alexander, with the crimes described in the affidavit, a copy of which is now communicated to both houses of Congress.

It was announced to me at the same time, that Swartwout and Bollman, two of the persons apprehended by him, were arrived in this city in custody each of a military officer. I immediately delivered to the attorney of the United States, in this district, the evidence received against them, with instructions to lay the same before the judges, and apply for their process to bring the accused to justice, and I put into his hands orders to the officers having them in custody, to deliver them to the marshal on his application.   TH. JEFFERSON.

January 26, 1807.

Wilkinson's Second Affidavit

I, JAMES WILKINSON, Brigadier General and commander in chief of the army of the United States, to warrant the arrest of Samuel Swartwout, James Alexander, Esq., and Peter V. Ogden, on a charge of treason, misprision of treason or such other offence against the government and laws of the United States, as the following facts may legally charge them with, on the honor of a soldier, and on the Holy Evangelists of Almighty God, do declare and swear, that in the beginning of the month of October last, when in command at Natchitoches, a stranger was introduced to me by Colonel Cushing, by the name of Swartwout, who a few minutes after the colonel retired from the room, slipped into my hand a letter of formal introduction from Colonel Burr, of which the following is a correct copy:

"Philadelphia, 25th July, 1806.

"DEAR SIR:

"Mr. Swartwout, the brother of Colonel S., of New York, being on his way down the Mississippi, and presuming that he may pass you at some post on the river, has requested of me a letter of introduction, which I give with pleasure, as he is a most amiable young man, and highly respected from his character and connections. I pray you to afford him any friendly offices which his situation may require, and beg you to pardon the trouble which this may give you.

"With entire respect,

"Your friend and obedient servant.

(Signed) "A. BURR.

"His Excellency General Wilkinson."

Together with a packet, which, he informed me, he was charged by the same person to deliver me in private; this packet contained a letter in cipher from Colonel Burr, on which the following is substantially as fair an interpretation as I have heretofore been able to make, the original of which I hold in my possession:

"I, Aaron Burr, have obtained funds and have actually commenced the enterprise. Detachments from different points and under different pretences, will rendezvous on the Ohio, 1st November. Everything internal and external favors views; protection of England is secured; T———— is going to Jamaica, to arrange with the admiral on that station; it will meet on the Mississippi———— England————Navy of the United States are ready to join, and final orders are given to my friends and followers; it will be a host of choice spirits. Wilkinson shall be second to Burr only; Wilkinson shall dictate the rank and promotion of his officers. Burr will proceed westward 1st August, never to return; with him go his daughter; the husband will follow in October, with a corps of worthies.

"Send forwith an intelligent and confidential friend with whom Burr may confer; he shall return immediately with further interesting details; this is essential to concert and harmony of movement; send a list of all persons known to

Wilkinson, west of the mountains, who may be useful, with a note delineating their characters. By your messenger send me four or five of the commissions of your officers, which you can borrow under any pretence you please; they shall be returned faithfully. Already are orders to the contractor given to forward six months' provisions to points Wilkinson may name; this shall not be used until the last moment, and then under proper injunctions; the project is brought to the point so long desired; Burr guarantees the result with his life and honor; with the lives, the honor and fortunes of hundreds, the best blood of our country.

"Burr's plan of operations is to move down rapidly from the falls on the 15th November, with the first 500 or 1,000 men, in light boats now constructing for that purpose, to be at Natchez between the 5th and 15th of December; there to meet Wilkinson; there to determine whether it will be expedient, in the first instance, to seize on, or pass by, Baton Rouge; on receipt of this, send an answer; draw on Burr for all expenses, &c. The people of the country to which we are going are prepared to receive us; their agents now with Burr say, that if we will protect their religion, and will not subject them to a foreign power, that in three weeks all will be settled. The Gods invite to glory and fortune; it remains to be seen whether we deserve the boon; the bearer of this goes express to you; he will hand a formal letter of introduction to you from Burr; he is a man of inviolable honor and perfect discretion; formed to execute rather than to project; capable of relating facts with fidelity, and incapable of relating them otherwise; he is thoroughly informed of the plans and intentions of   , and will disclose to you as far as you inquire, and no further; he has imbibed a reverence for your character, and may be embarrassed in your presence; put him at ease and he will satisfy you.

"29th July."

I instantly resolved to avail myself of the reference made to the bearer, and in the course of some days drew from him (the said Swartwout) the following disclosure: "That he had been dispatched by Colonel Burr from Philadelphia, had passed through the states of Ohio and Kentucky, and proceeded from Louisville for St. Louis, where he expected to find me, but discovering at Kaskaskias that I had descended the river, he procured a skiff, hired hands, and followed me down the Mississippi to Fort Adams, and from thence set out for Natchitoches, in company with Captain Sparks and Hooke, under the pretense of a disposition to take part in the campaign against the Spaniards, then depending. That Colonel Burr with the support of a powerful association, extending from New York to New Orleans, was levying an armed body of 7,000 men from the state of New York and the western states and territories, with a view to carry an expedition against the Mexican provinces, and that 500 men under Colonel Swartwout and a Colonel or Major Tyler, were to descend the Alleghany, for whose accommodation light boats had been built, and were ready."

I inquired what would be their course; he said, "This territory would be revolutionized, where the people were ready to join them, and that there would be some seizing, he supposed, at New Orleans; that they expected to be ready to embark about the first of February, and intended to land at Vera Cruz, and to march from thence to Mexico." I observed that there were several millions of dollars in the bank of this place; to which he replied, "We know it full well;" and on remarking that they certainly did not mean to violate private property, he said they "merely meant to borrow, and would return it; that they must equip themselves in New Orleans; that they expected naval protection from Great Britain; that the Capt. ———, and the officers of our navy, were so disgusted with the government that they were ready to join; that similar disgusts prevailed throughout the western country, where the people were zealous in favor of the enterprise, and that pilot boat built schooners were contracted for along our southern coast for their service; that he had been accompanied from the falls of Ohio to Kaskaskias, and from thence to Fort Adams, by a Mr. Ogden, who had proceeded on to New Orleans with letters from Colonel Burr to his friends there." Swartwout asked me whether I had heard from Doctor Bollman; and on my answering in the negative, he expressed great surprise, and observed, "That the doctor and a Mr. Alexander had left Philadelphia before him, with despatches for me, and that they were to proceed by sea to New Orleans, where he said they must have arrived."

Though determined to deceive him if possible, I could not refrain telling Mr. Swartwout it was impossible that I could ever dishonor my commission; and I believe I duped him by my admiration of the plan, and by observing, "That although I could not join in the expedition, the engagements which the Spaniards had prepared for me in my front, might prevent my opposing it;" yet I did, the moment I had deciphered the letter, put it into the hands of Colonel Cushing, my adjutant and inspector, making the declaration that I should oppose the lawless enterprise with my utmost force. Mr. Swartwout informed me he was under engagements to meet Colonel Burr at Nashville the 20th of November, and requested of me to write him, which I declined; and on his leaving Natchitoches, about the 18th of October, I immediately employed Lieutenant T. A. Smith to convey the information, in substance, to the President, without the commitment of names; for, from the extraordinary nature of the project, and the more extraordinary appeal to me, I could not but doubt its reality, notwithstanding the testimony before me, and I did not attach solid belief to Mr. Swartwout's reports respecting their intentions on this territory and city, until I received confirmatory advice from St. Louis.

After my return from the Sabine, I crossed the country to Natchez, and on my descent of the Mississippi from that place, I found Swartwout and Peter V. Ogden at Fort Adams; with the latter I held no communication, but was informed by Swartwout, that he (Ogden) had returned so far from New Orleans, on his route to Tennessee, but had been so much alarmed by certain reports in circulation that he was afraid to proceed. I inquired whether he bore letters with him from New Orleans, and was informed by Swartwout that he did not, but that a Mr. Spence had been sent from New Orleans through the country to Nashville, with letters for Colonel Burr.

I reached this city the 25th ultimo, and on the next morning James Alexander, Esq., visited me; he inquired of me aside whether I had seen Doctor Bollman, and on my answering in the negative, he asked me whether I would suffer him to conduct Bollman to me, which I refused. He appeared desirous to communicate something, but I felt no inclination to inculpate this young man, and he left me. A few days after he paid me a second visit, and seemed desirous to communicate, which I avoided until he had risen to take leave; I then raised my finger, and observed, "Take care, you are playing a dangerous game." He answered, "It will succeed." I again observed, "Take care;" and he replied with a strong affirmation, "Burr will be here by the beginning of next month." In addition to these corroborating circumstances against Alexander, I beg leave to refer to the accompanying documents, A. B. From all which I feel no hesitation in declaring, under the solemn obligation of an oath, that I do believe the said Swartwout, Alexander, and Ogden, have been parties to, and have been concerned in, the insurrection formed, or forming, in the states and territories on the Ohio and Mississippi rivers, against the laws and constitution of the United States.

(Signed)   JAMES WILKINSON.

Sworn to, and subscribed before me, this 26th day of December, in the year of our Lord, 1806.

(Signed)   GEORGE POLLOCK.

Justice of the Peace, for the county of Orleans.

The following are the depositions made in open court and alluded to in the foregoing statement:

The Deposition of William Eaton, Esq.

Early last winter Col. Aaron Burr, late Vice-President of the United States, signified to me, at this place, that, under the authority of the general government, he was organizing a secret expedition against the Spanish provinces on our south-western borders, which expedition he was to lead, and in which he was authorized to invite me to take command of a division. I had never before been made personally acquainted with Col. Burr, and, having for many years been employed in foreign service, I knew but little about the estimation this gentleman now held in the opinion of his countrymen and his government; the rank and confidence by which he had so lately been distinguished, left me no right to suspect his patriotism. I knew him a soldier. In case of a war with the Spanish nation, which, from the tenor of the President's message to both houses of Congress, seemed probable, I should have thought it my duty to obey so honorable a call of my country; and, under that impression, I did engage to embark in the expedition. I had frequent interviews with Col. Burr in this city, and, for a considerable time, his object seemed to be to instruct me by maps, and other information, the feasibility of penetrating to Mexico; always carrying forward the idea that the measure was authorized by government.

At length, some time in February, he began by degrees to unveil himself. He reproached the government with want of character, want of gratitude, and want of justice. He seemed desirous of irritating resentment in my breast by dilating on certain injuries he felt I had suffered from reflections made on the floor of the house of representatives concerning my operations in Barbary, and from the delays of government in adjusting my claims for disbursements on that coast during my consular agency at Tunis; and he said he would point me to an honorable mode of indemnity.

I now began to entertain a suspicion that Mr. Burr was projecting an unauthorized military expedition, which, to me, was enveloped in mystery; and, desirous to draw an explanation from him, I suffered him to suppose me resigned to his counsel. He now laid open his project of revolutionizing the western country; separating it from the union; establishing a monarchy there, of which he was to be the sovereign, and New Orleans to be his capital; organizing a force on the waters of the Mississippi, and extending conquest to Mexico. I suggested a number of impediments to his scheme; such as the republican habits of the citizens of that country, and their affection towards our present administration of government; the want of funds; the resistance he would meet from the regular army of the United States on those frontiers; and the opposition of Miranda, in case he should succeed to republicanize the Mexicans.

Mr. Burr found no difficulty in removing these obstacles; he said he had, the preceding season, made a tour through that country, and had secured the attachment of the principal citizens of Kentucky, Tennessee and Louisiana, to his person and his measures; declared he had inexhaustible resources to funds; assured me the regular army would act with him, and would be re-inforced by ten or twelve thousand men from the above-mentioned states and territory, and from other parts of the union; said he had powerful agents in the Spanish territory; and, as for Miranda, said Mr. Burr, we must hang Miranda. He now proposed to give me the second command in his army. I asked him who should have the chief command? He said, General Wilkinson. I observed it was singular that he should count on General Wilkinson; the elevated rank and high trust he now held as commander in chief of our army and governor of a province, he would hardly put at hazard for any precarious prospects of aggrandizement. Mr. Burr said, General Wilkinson, balanced in the confidence of government, was doubtful of retaining much longer the consideration he now enjoyed, and was, consequently, prepared to secure to himself a permanency. I asked Mr. Burr if he knew General Wilkinson? He answered yes, and echoed the question. I said I knew him well. "What do you know of him?" said Mr. Burr. I know, I replied, that General Wilkinson will act as lieutenant to no man in existence. "You are in error," said Mr. Burr; "Wilkinson will act as lieutenant to me."

From the tenor of repeated conversations with Mr. Burr, I was induced to believe the plan of separating the union, which he had contemplated, had been communicated to, and approved of by, General Wilkinson; (though I now suspect it an artful argument of seduction;) and he often expressed a full confidence that the general's influence, the offer of double pay and double rations, the prospect of plunder, and the ambition of achievement, would draw the army into his measures. Mr. Burr talked of the establishment of an independent government west of the Alleghany as a matter of inherent constitutional right of the people, a change which would eventually take place, and for the operation of which the present crisis was peculiarly favorable. There was, said he, no energy in the government to be dreaded, and the divisions of political opinions throughout the union was a circumstance of which we should profit. There were very many enterprising men among us, who aspired to something beyond the dull pursuits of civil life, and who would volunteer in this enterprise, and the vast territory belonging to the United States, which offered to adventurers, and the mines of Mexico, and would bring strength to his standard from all quarters.

I listened to the exposition of Colonel Burr's view with seeming acquiescence. Every interview convinced me more and more that he had organized a deep-laid plot of treason in the west, in the accomplishment of which he felt fully confident. Till, at length, I discovered that his ambition was not bounded by the waters of the Mississippi and Mexico, but that he meditated overthrowing the present government of our country. He said, if he could gain over the marine corps, and secure the naval commanders, Truxton, Preble, Decatur, and others, he would turn Congress neck and heels out of doors, assassinate the President, seize on the treasury and the navy, and declare himself the protector of an energetic government. The honorable trust of corrupting the marine corps, and of sounding Commodore Preble and Captain Decatur, Colonel Burr proposed confiding to me. Shocked at this proposition, I dropped the mask, and exclaimed against his views.

He talked of the degraded situation of our country, and the necessity of a blow by which its energy and its dignity should be restored; said, if that blow could be struck here at this time, he was confident of the support of the best blood of America. I told Colonel Burr he deceived himself in presuming that he, or any other man, could excite a party in this country who would countenance him in such a plot of desperation, murder and treason. He replied, that he, perhaps, knew better the dispositions of the influential citizens of this country than I did. I told him one solitary word would destroy him. He asked what word? I answered, Usurper! He smiled at my hesitation, and quoted some great examples in his favor. I observed to him, that I had lately traveled from one extreme of the union to the other; and though I found a diversity of political opinion among the people, they appeared united at the most distant aspect of national danger. That, for the section of the union to which I belonged, I would vouch, that should he succeed in the first instance here, he would within six weeks afterwards have his throat cut by Yankee militia.

Though wild and extravagant Mr. Burr's last project, and though fraught with premeditated slaughter, I felt very easy on the subject, because its defeat he had deposited in my own hands. I did not feel so secure concerning that of disjointing the union. But the very interesting and embarrassing situation in which his communications placed me, left me, I confess, at a stand to know how to conduct myself with propriety. He had committed no overt act of aggression against law. I could draw nothing from him in writing, nor could I learn that he had exposed his plans to any person near me, by whom my testimony could be supported. He had mentioned to me no persons who were principally and decidedly engaged with him, except General Wilkinson, a Mr. Alston, who I found was his son-in-law, and a Mr. Ephraim Kibby, late a captain of rangers in General Wayne's army.

Satisfied that Mr. Burr was resolute in pushing his project of rebellion in the west of the Alleghany, and apprehensive that it was too well and too extensively organized to be easily suppressed, though I dreaded the weight of his character when laid in the balance against my solitary assertion, I brought myself to the resolution to endeavor to defeat it by getting him removed from among us, or to expose myself to all consequences by a disclosure of his intentions. Accordingly, I waited on the President of the United States, and after some desultory conversation, in which I aimed to draw his view to the westward, I used the freedom to say to the President I thought Mr. Burr should be sent out of this country, and gave for reason that I believed him dangerous in it. The President asked where he should be sent? I mentioned London and Cadiz. The President thought the trust too important, and seemed to entertain a doubt of Mr. Burr's integrity. I intimated that no one, perhaps, had stronger grounds to mistrust Mr.Burr's moral integrity than myself; yet, I believed ambition so much predominated over him, that when placed on an eminence, and put on his honor, respect to himself would insure his fidelity: his talents were unquestionable. I perceived the subject was disagreeable to the President; and to give it the shortest course to the point, declared my concern that if Mr. Burr were not in some way disposed of, we should, within eighteen months, have an insurrection, if not a revolution, on the waters of the Mississippi. The President answered, that he had too much confidence in the information, the integrity, and the attachment to the union, of the citizens of that country, to admit an apprehension of the kind. I am happy that events prove this confidence well placed.

As no interrogatories followed my expression of alarm, I thought silence on the subject, at that time and place, became me. But I detailed, about the same time, the whole projects of Mr. Burr to certain members of Congress. They believed Colonel Burr capable of anything, and agreed that the fellow ought to be hanged; but thought his projects too chimerical, and his circumstances too desperate, to give the subject the merit of serious consideration. The total security of feeling in those to whom I had rung the tocsin, induced me to suspect my own apprehensions unseasonable, or at least too deeply admitted; and, of course, I grew indifferent about the subject.

Mr. Burr's visits to me became less frequent, and his conversation less familiar. He appeared to have abandoned the idea of a general revolution, but seemed determined on that of the Mississippi; and, although I could perceive symptoms of distrust in him towards me, he manifested great solicitude to engage me with him in the enterprise. Weary of his importunity, and at once to convince him of my serious attachments, I gave the following toast to the public: The United States—Palsy to the brain that should plot to dismember, and leprosy to the hand that will not draw to defend, our union!

I doubt whether the sentiment was better understood by any of my acquaintances than Colonel Burr. Our intercourse ended here; we met but seldom afterwards. I returned to my farm in Massachusetts, and thought no more of Mr. Burr, nor his empire, till some time late in September or beginning of October, when a letter from Maurice Belknap, of Marietta, to Timothy E. Danielson, fell into my hands at Brimfield, which satisfied me that Mr. Burr had actually commenced his preparatory operations on the Ohio. I now spoke publicly of the fact; transmitted a copy of the letter from Belknap to the department of state, and about the same time forwarded, through the hands of the Postmaster-General, to the President of the United States, a statement in substance of what is here above detailed concerning the Mississippi conspiracy of the said Colonel Aaron Burr, which is said to have been the first formal intelligence received by the executive on the subject of the conspirator being in motion.

I know not whether my country will allow me the merit of correctness of conduct in this affair. The novelty of the duty might, perhaps, have embarrassed stronger minds than mine. The uprightness of my intentions, I hope will not be questioned.

The interviews between Colonel Burr and myself, from which the foregoing statement has resulted, were chiefly in this city, in the months of February and March, last year.

WILLIAM EATON.

Washington City, Jan. 26, 1807.
Sworn to in open court this 26th day of January, 1807.

WILLIAM BRENT, Clerk.

Deposition of James L. Donaldson

In open court personally appears James Lowry Donaldson, who, being duly sworn, deposeth and saith, that he was in the city of New Orleans, in the Orleans territory, and the environs of said city, from the 15th day of October to the 10th day of December, 1806; that during the latter part of this time he was frequently in the company of General James Wilkinson, and visited the general the day after his arrival at New Orleans. On this occasion, this deponent received in confidence from General Wilkinson information to the following purport: that the general had undoubted and indisputable evidence of a treasonable design formed by Aaron Burr and others to dismember the union, by a separation of the western states and territories from the Atlantic states; that New Orleans was in immediate danger, and that he had concluded a hasty compromise with the Spaniards, so as to be able to withdraw his troops instantly to this the immediate object of attack and great vulnerable point; that he had received a letter from Burr holding forth great inducements to him to become a party, of which he showed me the original in cipher, and another written paper purporting to be a deciphered copy of the letter.

He expressed great indignation at the plot, and surprise that one so well acquainted with him as Burr should dare to make to him so degrading a proposal, and declared his determination of defeating the enterprise, or perishing in the attempt. He observed, in addition, that there were many agents of Mr. Burr then in the town, who had already been assiduous in their visits, and towards whom he was determined to act with cautious ambiguity, so as at the same time to become possessed of the whole extent of the plan, the persons engaged, and the time of its execution, and also to prevent any attempt on his person, of which he declared he had serious apprehensions. Of the number of these agents he was not aware, but mentioned the names of two of whom he was certain, Messrs. Bollman and Alexander. From time to time, as this deponent had interviews with General Wilkinson, he informed this deponent that he had received additional information respecting the movements and designs of Burr by means of these agents, of whom he considered Bollman as the principal.

In the course of these transactions, this deponent was employed by General Wilkinson in the copying of certain papers and documents, and preparing certain despatches for the general government, which the general intended to forward by the brig Thetis. While thus employed at the general's lodgings, this deponent has remarked, upon two different occasions, a person knock for admittance at a door with a window in it opposite the table where this deponent was sitting, who, this deponent was informed by General Wilkinson, was Doctor Bollman. Upon these occasions the general has suddenly risen from his seat, and accompanied this person in a number of turns up and down a balcony in the front of the house, apparently engaged in deep conversation. Upon the latter of these occasions the general, on his return into the chamber, said to this deponent, "That is Doctor Bollman; his infatuation is truly extraordinary; he persists in his belief that I am with Burr, and has this moment shown me a letter from the latter, in which he says that he is to be at Natchez on the 20th December with 2,000 men, that 4,000 will follow in the course of a few days, and that he could, with the same ease, have procured double that number." General Wilkinson then observed that he had obtained all the information he wanted, and that the affair would not be kept much longer a secret from the public.

When this deponent left the city of New Orleans, the inhabitants of that city were in a state of great alarm, and apprehended a serious attack from Mr. Burr and his confederates; this deponent understood that mercantile business was much embarrassed, and great fears were entertained of considerable commercial failures in consequence of the embargo which had been imposed; that General Wilkinson was taking strong measures of defense, and that 400 persons were then actually engaged in the fortifications of the city.

And further this deponent saith not.

JAMES L. DONALDSON.

Sworn to in open court.

WILLIAM BRENT, Clerk.

January 26 1807.

Deposition of Lieutenant W. Wilson

I left New Orleans on my way to this city on the 15th of December last; at that time and for some time preceding, the strongest apprehensions and belief universally prevailed among the inhabitants of that city, that Aaron Burr and his confederates had prepared an armed force, and were advancing to attack and plunder the city; in consequence of which the greatest alarms prevailed, a general stagnation of business ensued, and the danger was credited there as a matter of public notoriety; that Brigadier-General Wilkinson, with the army of the United States, was at New Orleans, occupied in the most active military preparations for the defense of the place; repairing the forts, mounting cannon, collecting ammunition, &c. All under the firm persuasion and belief that such an attack was meditated, and about very speedily to take place, by the said Burr; this deponent knows that the general was decidedly of opinion, from the most satisfactory information, that the said Burr and his confederates were advancing with an armed force against this place.

And further this deponent saith not.

(Signed)

WILLIAM WILSON.

Sworn to in open court this 27th day of January, 1807.

WILLIAM BRENT, Clerk.

The deposition of Ensign W. C. Mead is precisely similar to that of Lieut. Wilson except that the former states that he left New Orleans on the 19th of December.

4. *Ex parte Bollman and ex parte Swartwout*

4 Cranch 75; opinion delivered February 21, 1807

MARSHALL, CH. J. The prisoners have been brought before this court on a writ of *habeas corpus,* and the testimony on which they were committed having been fully examined and attentively considered, the court is now to declare the law upon their case.

This being a mere inquiry, which, without deciding upon guilt, precedes the institution of a prosecution, the question to be determined is, whether the accused shall be discharged or held to trial; and if the latter, in what place they are to be tried, and whether they shall be confined or admitted to bail. "If," says a very learned and accurate commentator, "upon this inquiry, it manifestly appears that no such crime has been committed, or that the suspicion entertained of the prisoner was wholly groundless, in such cases only, is it lawful totally to discharge him. Otherwise, he must either be committed to prison or give bail."

The specific charge brought against the prisoners is treason, in levying war against the United States. As there is no crime which can more excite and agitate the passions of men than treason, no charge demands more from the tribunal before which it is made, a deliberate and temperate inquiry. Whether this inquiry be directed to the fact or to the law, none can be more solemn, none more important to the citizen or to the government; none can more affect the safety of both.

To prevent the possibility of those calamities which result from the extension of treason to offences of minor importance, that great fundamental law which defines and limits the various departments of our government, has given a rule on the subject both to the legislature and the courts of America, which neither can be permitted to transcend. "Treason against the United States shall consist only in levying war against them, or in adhering to their enemies, giving them aid and comfort."

To constitute that specific crime for which the prisoners now before the court have been committed, war must be actually levied against the United States. However flagitious may be the crime of conspiring to subvert by force the government of our country, such conspiracy is not treason. To conspire to levy war, and actually to levy war, are distinct offences. The first must be brought into open action, by the assemblage of men for a purpose treasonable in itself, or the fact of levying war cannot have been committed. So far has this principle been carried, that, in a case reported by Ventris, and mentioned in some modern treatises on criminal law, it has been determined, that the actual enlistment of men, to serve against the government, does not amount to levying war. It is true, that in that case, the soldiers enlisted were to serve without the realm, but they were enlisted within it, and if the enlistment for a treasonable purpose could amount to levying war, then war had been actually levied.

Constructive Treason

It is not the intention of the court to say, that no individual can be guilty of this crime, who has not appeared in arms against his country. On the contrary, if war be actually levied, that is, if a body of men be actually assembled, for the purpose of effecting by force a treasonable purpose, all those who perform any part, however minute, or however remote from the scene of action, and who are actually leagued in the general conspiracy, are to be considered as traitors. But there must be an actual assembling of men, for the treasonable purpose, to constitute a levying of war.

Crimes so atrocious as those which have for their object the subversion by violence of those laws and those institutions which have been ordained in order to secure the peace and happiness of society, are not to escape punishment, because they have not ripened into treason. The wisdom of the legislature is competent to provide for the case; and the framers of our constitution, who not only defined and limited the crime, but with jealous circumspection attempted to protect their limitation, by providing that no person should be convicted of it, unless on the testimony of two witnesses to the same *overt* act, or on confession in open court, must have conceived it more safe, that punishment, in such cases, should be ordained by general laws, formed upon deliberation, under the influence of no resentments, and without knowing on whom they were to operate, than that it should be inflicted under the influence of those passions which the occasion seldom fails to excite, and which a flexible definition of the crime, or a construction which would render it flexible, might bring into operation. It is, therefore, more safe, as well as more consonant to the principles of our constitution, that the crime of treason should not be extended by construction to doubtful cases; and that crimes not clearly within the constitutional definition, should receive such punishment as the legislature in its wisdom may provide.

Levying War Defined

To complete the crime of levying war against the United States, there must be an actual assemblage of men for the purpose of executing a treasonable design. In the case now before the court, a design to overturn the government of the United States, in New Orleans, by force, would have been unquestionably a design which, if carried into execution, would have been treason, and the asemblage of a body of men for the purpose of carrying it into execution, would amount to levying of war against the United States; but no conspiracy for this object, no enlisting of men to effect it, would be an actual levying of war.

In conformity with the principles now laid down, have been the decisions heretofore made by the judges of the United States. The opinions given by Judge PATERSON and Judge IREDELL, in cases before them, imply an actual assembling of men, though they rather designed to remark on the purpose to which the force was to be applied than on the nature of the force itself. Their opinions, however, contemplate the actual employment of force. Judge CHASE, in the trial of *Fries,* was more explicit. He stated the opinion of the court to be, "that if a body of people conspire and meditate an insurrection to resist or oppose the execution of any statute of the United States, by force, they are only guilty of a high misdemeanor; but if they proceed to carry such intention into execution, by force, that they are guilty of the treason of levying war; and the *quantum* of the force employed neither lessens nor increases the crime: whether by one hundred, or one thousand persons, is wholly immaterial." "The court are of opinion," continued Judge CHASE, on that occasion, "that a combination or conspiracy to levy war against the United States is not treason, unless combined with an attempt to carry such combination or conspiracy into execution; some actual force or violence must be used, in pursuance of such design to levy war; but it is altogether immaterial, whether the force used is sufficient to effectuate the object; any force connected with the intention will constitute the crime of levying war." *

Relevance of Testimony

The application of these general principles to the particular case before the court, will depend on the testimony which has been exhibited against the accused. The first deposition to be considered is that of General Eaton. This gentleman connects in one statement the purport of numerous conversations held with Col. Burr, throughout the last winter. In the course of these conversations, were communicated various criminal projects, which seem to have been revolving in the mind of the projector. An expedition against Mexico seems to have been the first and most matured part of his plan, if indeed it did not constitute a distinct and separate plan, upon the success of which, other schemes, still more culpable, but not yet well digested, might depend. Maps and other information preparatory to its execution, and which would rather indicate that it was the immediate object, had been procured, and for a considerable time, in

* The Whisky Rebellion in western Pennsylvania at the close of the eighteenth century precipitated armed resistance to federal revenue agents and resulted in several treason trials, e.g., *Case of Fries,* 9 Fed. Cas. 826, No. 5126 (1799); *United States* v. *Mitchell,* 26 Fed. Cas. 1277, No. 15,788 (1795); and *United States* v. *Vigol,* 28 Fed. Cas. 376, No. 16,621 (1795), heard by various Circuit Justices, e.g., Samuel Chase, James Iredell and William Paterson.

repeated conversations, the whole efforts of Col. Burr were directed to prove to the witness, who was to have held a high command under him, the practicability of the enterprise, and in explaining to him the means by which it was to be effected.

This deposition exhibits the various schemes of Col. Burr, and its materiality depends on connecting the prisoners at the bar in such of those schemes as were treasonable. For this purpose, the affidavit of General Wilkinson, comprehending in its body the substance of a letter from Col. Burr, has been offered, and was received by the circuit court. To the admission of this testimony, great and serious objections have been made. It has been urged, that it is a voluntary or rather an extra-judicial affidavit, made before a person not appearing to be a magistrate, and contains the substance only of a letter, of which the original is retained by the person who made the affidavit.

The objection that the affidavit is extra-judicial, resolves itself into the question, whether one magistrate may commit on an affidavit taken before another magistrate. For if he may, an affidavit made as the foundation of a commitment, ceases to be extra-judicial, and the person who makes it would be as liable to a prosecution for perjury as if the warrant of commitment had been issued by the magistrate before whom the affidavit was made. To decide that an affidavit made before one magistrate, would not justify a commitment by another, might in many cases be productive of great inconvenience, and does not appear susceptible of abuse, if the verity of the certificate be established. Such an affidavit seems admissible, on the principle that before the accused is put upon his trial, all the proceedings are *ex parte*. The court, therefore, overrule this objection.

That which questions the character of the person who has, on this occasion, administered the oath, is next to be considered. The certificate from the office of the department of state has been deemed insufficient by the counsel for the prisoners, because the law does not require the appointment of magistrates for the territory of New Orleans to be certified to that office; because the certificate is in itself informal, and because it does not appear that the magistrates had taken the oath required by the act of congress. The first of these objections is not supported by the law of the case, and the second may be so readily corrected, that the court has proceeded to consider the subject, as if it were corrected, retaining, however, any final decision, if against the prisoners, until the correction shall be made. With regard to the third, the magistrate must be presumed to have taken the requisite oaths, since he is found acting as a magistrate.

Letter to Wilkinson

On the admissibility of that part of the affidavit which purports to be as near the substance of the letter from Col. Burr to General Wilkinson, as the latter could interpret it, a division of opinion has taken place in the court. Two judges are of opinion, that as such testimony delivered in the presence of the prisoner on his trial, would be totally inadmissible, neither can it be considered as a foundation for a commitment. Although, in making a commitment, the magistrate does not decide on the guilt of the prisoner, yet he does decide on the probable cause, and a long and painful imprisonment may be the consequence of his decision. This probable cause, therefore, ought to be proved by testimony, in itself legal, and which, though from the nature of the case it must be *ex parte,* ought in most other respects, to be such as a court and jury might hear. Two judges are of opinion, that in this incipient stage of the prosecution, an affidavit stating the general purport of a letter may be read, particularly, where the person in possession of it is at too great a distance to admit of its being obtained, and that a commitment may be founded on it.

Under this embarrassment, it was deemed necessary to look into the affidavit, for the purpose of discovering whether, if admitted, it contains matter which would justify the commitment of the prisoners at the bar on the charge of treason. That the letter from Col. Burr to General Wilkinson relates to a military enterprise meditated by the former, has not been questioned. If this enterprise was against Mexico, it would amount to a high misdemeanor; if against any of the territories of the United States, or if, in its progress, the subversion of the government of the United States, in any of their territories, was a mean, clearly and necessarily, to be employed, if such mean formed a substantive part of the plan, the assemblage of a body of men to effect it, would be levying war against the United States.

The letter is in language which furnishes no distinct view of the design of the writer. The co-operation, however, which is stated to have been secured, points strongly to some expedition against the territories of Spain. After making these general statements, the writer becomes rather more explicit, and says, "Burr's plan of operations is to move down rapidly from the falls, on the 15th of November, with the first 500 or 1000 men, in light boats now constructing for that purpose, to be at Natchez, between the 5th and 15th of December, there to meet Wilkinson; then to determine whether it will be expedient, in the first instance, to seize on, or to pass by, Baton Rouge. The people of the country to which we are going are prepared to receive us. Their agents, now with Burr, say, that if we will protect their religion, and will not subject them to a foreign power, in three weeks, all will be settled."

There is no expression in these sentences, which would justify a suspicion, that any territory of the United States was the object of the expedition. For what purpose, seize on Baton Rouge? Why engage Spain against this enterprise, if it was designed against the United States? "The people of the country to which we are going are prepared to receive us." This language is peculiarly appropriate to a foreign country. It will not be contended, that the terms would be inapplicable to a territory of the United States, but other terms would more aptly convey the idea, and Burr seems to consider himself as giving information of which Wilkinson was not possessed. When it is recollected, that he was the governor of a territory adjoining that which must have been threatened, if a territory of the United States was threatened, and that he commanded the army, a part of which was stationed in that territory, the probability that the information communicated related to a foreign country, it must be admitted, gains strength.

"Their agents, now with Burr, say, that if we will protect their religion, and will not subject them to a foreign power, in three weeks, all will be settled."

This is apparently the language of a people who, from the contemplated change in their political situation, feared for their religion, and feared that they would be made the subjects of a foreign power. That the Mexicans should entertain these apprehensions was natural, and would readily be believed. They were, if the representation made of their dispositions be correct, about to place themselves much in the power of men who professed a different faith from theirs, and who, by making them dependent on England or the United States, would subject them to a foreign power. That the people of New Orleans, as a people, if really engaged in the conspiracy, should feel the same apprehensions, and require assurances on the same points, is by no means so obvious.

Failure of Proof of Treason

There certainly is not in the letter delivered to General Wilkinson, so far as the letter is laid before the court, one syllable which has a necessary or a natural reference to an enterprise against any territory of the United States. That the bearer of this letter must be considered as acquainted with its contents, is not to be controverted. The letter and his own declarations evince the fact. After stating himself to have passed through New York, and the western states and territories, without insinuating that he had performed on his route any act whatever which was connected with the enterprise, he states their object to be, "to carry an expedition to the Mexican provinces." This statement may be considered as explanatory of the letter of Col. Burr, if the expressions of that letter could be thought ambiguous.

But there are other declarations made by Mr. Swartwout, which constitute the difficulty of this case. On an inquiry from General Wilkinson, he said, "this territory would be revolutionized, where the people were ready to join them, and that there would be some seizing, he supposed, at New Orleans." If these words import that the government established by the United States in any of its territories, was to be revolutionized by force, although merely as a step to, or a mean of executing some greater projects, the design was unquestionably treasonable, and any assemblage of men for that purpose would amount to a levying of war. But on the import of the words, a difference of opinion exists. Some of the judges suppose, they refer to the territory against which the expedition was intended; others to that in which the conversation was held. Some consider the words, if even applicable to a territory of the United States, as alluding to a revolution to be effected by the people, rather than by the party conducted by Col. Burr.

Overt Act Required

But whether this treasonable intention be really imputable to the plan or not, it is admitted, that it must have been carried into execution by an open assemblage of men for that purpose, previous to the arrest of the prisoner, in order to consummate the crime as to him; and a majority of the court is of opinion, that the conversation of Mr. Swartwout affords no sufficient proof of such assembling. The prisoner stated, that "Col. Burr, with the support of a powerful association, extending from New York to New Orleans, was levying an armed body of 7000 men from the state of New York and the western states and territories, with a view to carry an expedition to the Mexican territories." That the association, whatever may be its purpose, is not treason, has been already stated. That levying an army may or may not be treason, and that this depends on the intention with which it is levied, and on the point to which the parties have advanced, has been also stated. The mere enlisting of men, without assembling them, is not levying war. The question, then, is, whether this evidence proves Col. Burr to have advanced so far in levying an army, as actually to have assembled them.

It is argued, that since it cannot be necessary that the whole 7000 men should have assembled, their commencing their march, by detachments, to the place of rendezvous, must be sufficient to constitute the crime. This position is correct, with some qualification. It cannot be necessary, that the whole army should assemble, and that the various parts which are to compose it should have combined. But it is necessary, that there should be an actual assemblage, and therefore, the evidence should make the fact unequivocal. The travelling of individuals to the place of rendezvous would, perhaps, not be sufficient. This would be an equivocal act, and has no warlike appearance. The meeting of particular bodies of men, and their marching from places of partial to a place of general rendezvous, would be such an assemblage.

The particular words used by Mr. Swartwout are, that Col. Burr "was levying an armed body of 7000 men." If the term levying, in this place, imports that they were assembled, then such fact would amount, if the intention be against the United States, to levying war. If it barely imports that he was enlisting or engaging them in his service, the fact would not amount to levying war. It is thought sufficiently apparent, that the latter is the sense in which the term was used. The fact alluded to, if taken in the proper sense, is of a nature so to force itself upon the public view, that if the army had actually assembled, either together or in detachments, some evidence of such assembling would have been laid before the court.

The words used by the prisoner, in reference to seizing at New Orleans, and borrowing, perhaps by force, from the bank, though indicating a design to rob, and consequently, importing a high offence, do not designate the specific crime of levying war against the United States.

Evidence Insufficient to Commit

It is, therefore, the opinion of a majority of the court, that in the case of Samuel Swartwout there is not sufficient evidence of his levying war against the United States to justify his commitment on the charge of treason.

Against Erick Bollman, there is still less testimony. Nothing has been said by him, to support the charge that the enterprise in which he was engaged had any other object than was stated in the letter of Col. Burr. Against him, therefore, there is no evidence to support a charge of treason.

That both of the prisoners were engaged in a most culpable enterprise against the dominions of a power at peace with the United States, those who admit the affidavit of General Wilkinson cannot doubt. But that no part of this crime was committed in the district of Columbia, is apparent. It is, therefore, the unanimous opinion of the court that they cannot be tried in this district.

The law read on the part of the prosecution is understood to apply only to offences committed on the high seas, or in any river, haven, basin or bay, not within the jurisdiction of any particular state. In those cases, there is no court which has particular cognisance of the crime, and therefore, the place in which the criminal shall be apprehended, or, if he be apprehended, where no court has exclusive jurisdiction, that to which he shall be first brought, is substituted for the place in which the offence was committed.

But in this case, a tribunal for the trial of the offence, wherever it may have been committed, had been provided by congress; and at the place where the prisoners were seized by the authority of the commander-in-chief, there existed such a tribunal. It would, too, be extremely dangerous to say, that because the prisoners were apprehended, not by a civil magistrate, but by the military power, there could be given by law a right to try the persons so seized, in any place which the general might select, and to which he might direct them to be carried.

The act of congress which the prisoners are supposed to have violated, describes as offenders those who begin or set on foot, or provide, or prepare, the means for any military expedition or enterprise to be carried on from thence against the dominions of a foreign prince or state with whom the United States are at peace. There is a want of precision in the description of the offence which might produce some difficulty in deciding what cases would come within it.

But several other questions arise, which a court consisting of four judges finds itself unable to decide, and therefore, as the crime with which the prisoners stand charged has not been committed, the court can only direct them to be discharged. This is done, with the less reluctance, because the discharge does not acquit them from the offence which there is probable cause for supposing they have committed, and if those whose duty it is to protect the nation, by prosecuting offenders against the laws, shall suppose those who have been charged with treason to be proper objects for punishment, they will, when possessed of less exceptionable testimony, and when able to say at what place the offence has been committed, institute fresh proceedings against them.

5. *Opinion on Question of Bailable Offense*

25 Fed. Cas. No. 14,692a; opinion rendered April 1, 1807

MARSHALL, Chief Justice. I am required on the part of the attorney for the United States to commit the accused on two charges: (1) For setting on foot and providing the means for an expedition against the territories of a nation at peace with the United States. (2) For committing high treason against the United States.

On an application of this kind I certainly should not require that proof which would be necessary to convict the person to be committed, on a trial in chief; nor should I even require that which should absolutely convince my own mind of the guilt of the accused: but I ought to require, and I should require, that probable cause be shown; and I understand probable cause to be a case made out by proof furnishing good reason to believe that the crime alleged has been committed by the person charged with having committed it.

I think this opinion entirely reconcilable with that quoted from Judge Blackstone. When that learned and accurate commentator says, that "if upon an inquiry it manifestly appears that no such crime has been committed, or that the suspicion entertained of the prisoner was wholly groundless, in such cases only it is lawful totally to discharge him, otherwise he must be committed to prison or give bail," I do not understand him as meaning to say that the hand of malignity may grasp any individual against whom its hate may be directed, or whom it may capriciously seize, charge him with some secret crime, and put him on the proof of his innocence.

But I understand that the foundation of the proceeding must be a probable cause to believe there is guilt; which probable cause is only to be done away in the manner stated by Blackstone. The total failure of proof on the part of the accuser would be considered by that writer as being in itself a legal manifestation of the innocence of the accused. In inquiring, therefore, into the charges exhibited against Aaron Burr, I hold myself bound to consider how far those charges are supported by probable cause.

Eaton–Wilkinson Testimony

The first charge stands upon the testimony of General Eaton and General Wilkinson. The witness first named proves that among other projects which were more criminal, Colonel Burr meditated an expedition against the Mexican dominions of Spain. This deposition may be considered as introductory to the affidavit of General Wilkinson, and as explanatory of the objects of any military preparations which may have been made. I proceed, then, to that affidavit. To make the testimony of General Wilkinson bear on Colonel Burr, it is necessary to consider as genuine the letter stated by the former to be, as nearly as he can make it, an interpretation of one received in cypher from the latter.

Exclude this letter, and nothing remains in the testimony which can in the most remote degree affect Colonel Burr. That there are to the admissibility of this part of the affidavit great and obvious objections need not be stated to those who know with how much caution proceedings in criminal cases ought to be instituted, and who know that the highest tribunal of the United States has been divided on them. When this question came before the supreme court, I felt the full force of these objections, although I did not yield to them. On weighing in my own mind the reasons for and against acting, in this stage of the business, on that part of the affidavit, those in favor of doing so appeared to me to preponderate, and, as this opinion was not overruled, I hold myself still at liberty to conform to it. That the original letter, or a true copy of it accompanied by the cypher, would have been much more satisfactory, is not to be denied; but I thought, and I still think, that, upon a mere question whether the accused shall be brought to trial or not, upon an inquiry not into guilt but into probable cause, the omission of a circumstance which is indeed important, but which does not disprove the positive allegations of an affidavit, ought not to induce its rejection or its absolute disbelief, when the maker of the affidavit is at too great a distance to repair the fault.

I could not in this stage of the prosecution absolutely discredit the affidavit, because the material facts alleged may very well be within the knowledge of the witness, although he has failed to state explicitly all the means by which this knowledge is obtained. Thus, General Wilkinson states that this letter was received from Colonel Burr, but does not say that it was in his hand-writing, nor does he state the evidence which supports this affirmation. But, in addition to the circumstance that the positive assertion of the fact ought not perhaps, in this stage of the inquiry, to be disregarded, the nature of the case furnishes that evidence. The letter was in cypher. General Wilkinson, it is true, does not say that a cypher had been previously settled between Colonel Burr and himself, in which they might correspond on subjects which, though innocent, neither of them might wish to subject to the casualties of a transportation from the Atlantic to the Mississippi; but when we perceive that Colonel Burr has written in cypher, and that General Wilkinson is able to decypher the letter, we must either presume that the bearer of the letter was also the bearer of its key, or that the key was previously in possession of the person to whom the letter was addressed.

In stating particularly the circumstances attending the delivery of this letter, General Wilkinson does not say that it was accompanied by the key, or that he felt any surprise at its being in cypher. For this reason, as well as because there is not much more security in sending a letter in cypher, accompanied by its key, than there is in sending a letter not in cypher, I think it more reasonable to suppose that the key was previously in possession of Wilkinson. If this was the fact, the letter being written in a cypher previously settled between himself and Colonel Burr, is, in this stage of the inquiry at least, a circumstance which sufficiently supports the assertion that the letter was written by Colonel Burr. The enterprise described in this letter is obviously a military enterprise, and must have been intended either against the United States, or against the territories of some other power on the continent, with all of whom the United States were at peace.

The expressions of this letter must be admitted to furnish at least probable cause for believing that the means for the expedition were provided. In every part of it we find declarations indicating that he was providing the means for the expedition; and as these means might be provided in secret, I do not think that further testimony ought to be required to satisfy me that there is probable cause for committing the prisoner on this charge. Since it will be entirely in the power of the attorney general to prefer an indictment against the prisoner, for any other offence which he shall think himself possessed of testimony to support, it is, in fact, immaterial whether the second charge be expressed in the warrant of commitment or not; but as I hold it to be my duty to insert every charge alleged on the part of the United States, in support of which probable cause is shown, and to insert none in support of which probable cause is not shown, I am bound to proceed in the inquiry.

Charge of Treason

The second charge exhibited against the prisoner is high treason against the United States in levying war against them. As this is the most atrocious offence which can be committed against the political body, so is it the charge which is most capable of being employed as the instrument of those malignant and vin-dictive passions which may rage in the bosoms of contending parties struggling for power. It is that of which the people of America have been most jealous, and therefore, while other crimes are unnoticed, they have refused to trust the national legislature with the definition of this, but have themselves declared in their constitution that "it shall consist only in levying war against the United States, or in adhering to their enemies, giving them aid and comfort."

This high crime consists of overt acts, which must be proved by two wit-nesses, or by the confession of the party in open court. Under the control of this constitutional regulation, I am to inquire whether the testimony laid before me furnishes probable cause in support of this charge. The charge is, that the fact itself has been committed, and the testimony to support it must furnish probable cause for believing that it has been actually committed, or it is insuffi-cient for the purpose for which it is adduced. Upon this point, too, the testi-mony of General Eaton is first to be considered. That part of his deposition which bears upon this charge is the plan disclosed by the prisoner for seizing upon New Orleans, and revolutionizing the Western states. That this plan, if consummated by overt acts, would amount to treason, no man will controvert.

But it is equally clear that an intention to commit treason is an offence en-tirely distinct from the actual commission of that crime. War can only be levied by the employment of actual force. Troops must be embodied, men must be assembled, in order to levy war. If Colonel Burr had been apprehended on making these communications to General Eaton, could it have been alleged that he had gone further than to meditate the crime? Could it have been said that he had actually collected forces and had actually levied war? Most certainly it could not. The crime really complete was a conspiracy to commit treason, not an actual commission of treason.

If these communications were not treason at the instant they were made, no lapse of time can make them so. They are not in themselves acts. They may serve to explain the intention with which acts were committed, but they cannot supply those acts if they be not proved. The next testimony is the deposition of General Wilkinson, which consists of the letter already noticed, and of the communications made by the bearer of that letter. This letter has already been considered by the supreme court of the United States, and has been declared to import, taken by itself or in connection with Eaton's deposition, rather an expe-dition against Mexico than the territories of the United States. By that decision I am bound, whether I concurred in it or not. But I did concur in it.

On this point the court was unanimous. It is, however, urged that the decla-rations of Swartwout may be connected with the letter and used against Colonel Burr. Although the confession of one man cannot criminate another, yet I am inclined to think that, on a mere inquiry into probable cause, the declaration of Swartwout made on this particular occasion may be used against Colonel Burr. My reason for thinking so is, that Colonel Burr's letter authorizes Mr. Swartwout to speak in his name. He empowers Mr. Swartwout to make to Gen-eral Wilkinson verbal communications explanatory of the plans and designs of Burr, which Burr adopts as his own explanations.

However inadmissible, therefore, this testimony may be on a trial in chief, I am inclined to admit it on this inquiry. If it be admitted, what is its amount? Upon this point, too, it appears that the supreme court was divided. I therefore hold myself at liberty to pursue my own opinion, which was, that the words, "this territory must be revolutionized," did not so clearly apply to a foreign territory as to reject that sense which would make them applicable to a territory of the United States, at least so far as to admit of further inquiry into their meaning. And if a territory of the United States was to be revolutionized, though only as a means for an expedition against a foreign power, the act would be treason. This reasoning leads to the conclusion that there is probable cause for the allegation that treasonable designs were entertained by the prisoner so late as July last, when this letter was written.

Previous Treason Definition Distinguished

It remains to inquire whether there is also probable cause to believe that these designs have been ripened into the crime itself, by actually levying war against the United States. It has been already observed that, to constitute this crime, troops must be embodied, men must be actually assembled; and these are facts which cannot remain invisible. Treason may be machinated in secret, but it can be perpetrated only in open day, and in the eye of the world. Testimony of a fact which in its own nature is so notorious ought to be unequivocal. The testimony now offered has been laid before the supreme court of the United States and has been determined in the Cases of Bollman and Swartwout, [4 Cranch (8 U.S.) 75], not to furnish probable cause for the opinion that war had been actually levied.

Whatever might have been the inclination of my own mind in that case, I should feel much difficulty in departing from the decision then made, unless this case could be clearly distinguished from it. I will, however, briefly review the arguments which have been urged, and the facts now before me, in order to show more clearly the particular operation they have on my own judgment. The fact to be established is, that in pursuance of these designs, previously entertained, men have been actually assembled for the purpose of making war against the United States; and on the showing of probable cause that this fact has been committed, depends the issue of the present inquiry.

The first piece of testimony relied on to render this fact probable is the declaration of Mr. Swartwout, that "Colonel Burr was levying an armed body of 7,000 men from the state of New York, and the Western states and territories, with a view to carry an expedition against the Mexican provinces." The term "levying" has been said, according to the explanation of the lexicons, to mean the embodying of troops, and therefore to prove what is required. Although I do not suppose that Mr. Swartwout had consulted a dictionary, I have looked into Johnson for the term, and find its first significance to be "to raise;" its second, "to bring together." In common parlance, it may signify the one or the other. But its sense is certainly decided by the fact. If when Mr. Swartwout left Colonel Burr, which must be supposed to have been in July, he was actually embodying men from New York to the Western states, what could veil his troops from human sight? An invisible army is not the instrument of war, and had these troops been visible, some testimony relative to them could have been adduced.

I take the real sense, then, in which this term was used to be, that Colonel Burr was raising, or in other words engaging or enlisting, men through the country described, for the enterprise he meditated. The utmost point to which this testimony can be extended is, that it denotes a future embodying of men, which is more particularly mentioned in the letter itself, and that it affords probable cause to believe that the troops did actually embody at the period designated for their assembling, which is sufficient to induce the justice to whom the application is made to commit for trial. I shall readily avow my opinion, that the strength of the presumption arising from this testimony ought to depend greatly on the time at which the application is made. If soon after the period at which the troops were to assemble, when full time had not elapsed to ascertain the fact, these circumstances had been urged as the ground for a commitment on the charge of treason, I should have thought them entitled to great consideration.

I will not deny that, in the Cases of Bollman and Swartwout, I was not perfectly satisfied that they did not warrant an inquiry into the fact. But I think every person must admit that the weight of these circumstances daily diminishes. Suspicion may deserve great attention when the means of ascertaining its real grounds are not yet possessed; but when those means are, or may have been acquired, if facts to support suspicion, be not shown, every person, I think, must admit that the ministers of justice at least ought not officially to entertain it. This, I think, must be conceded by all; but whether it be conceded by others or not, it is the dictate of my own judgment, and in the performance of my duty I can know no other guide.

Inadequacy of U.S. Evidence

The fact to be proved in this case is an act of public notoriety. It must exist in the view of the world, or it cannot exist at all. The assembling of forces to levy war is a visible transaction, and numbers must witness it. It is therefore capable of proof; and when time to collect this proof has been given, it ought to be adduced, or suspicion becomes ground too weak to stand upon. Several months have elapsed since this fact did occur, if it ever occurred. More than five weeks have elapsed since the opinion of the supreme court has declared the necessity of proving the fact, if it exists. Why is it not proved?

To the executive government is intrusted the important power of prosecuting those whose crimes may disturb the public repose or endanger its safety. It would be easy, in much less time than has intervened since Colonel Burr has been alleged to have assembled his troops, to procure affidavits establishing the fact. If, in November or December last, a body of troops had been assembled on the Ohio, it is impossible to suppose that affidavits establishing the fact could not have been obtained by the last of March. I ought not to believe that there has been any remissness on the part of those who prosecute on this important and interesting subject; and consequently, when at this late period no evidence that troops have been actually embodied is given. I must say that the suspicion which in the first instance might have been created ought not to be continued, unless this want of proof can be in some manner accounted for.

It is stated by the attorney for the United States that, as affidavits can only be voluntary, the difficulty of obtaining them accounts for the absence of proof. I cannot admit this position. On the evidence furnished by this very transaction of the attachment felt by our western for their eastern brethren, we justly felicitate ourselves.

How inconsistent with this fact is the idea that no man could be found who would voluntarily depose that a body of troops had actually assembled, whose object must be understood to be hostile to the Union, and whose object was detested and defeated by the very people who could give the requisite information! I cannot doubt that means to obtain information have been taken on the part of the prosecution; if it existed, I cannot doubt the practicability of obtaining it; and its non-production at this late hour does not, in my opinion, leave me at liberty to give to those suspicions which grow out of other circumstances that weight to which at an earlier day they might have been entitled. I shall not therefore insert in the commitment the charge of high treason. I repeat, that this is the less important, because it detracts nothing from the right of the attorney to prefer an indictment for high treason, should he be furnished with the necessary testimony.

Admission to Bail

The CHIEF JUSTICE having delivered his opinion, observed, that as Colonel Burr would be put on his trial for carrying on a military expedition against a nation with whom the United States were at peace, his case was of course bailable. Some discussion then arose as to the amount of bail to be required. The sum was finally fixed at ten thousand dollars; and after a brief adjournment, Colonel Burr, with five sureties entered into a recognizance in that sum, for his appearance at the next circuit court for the district of Virginia, to commence on the 22d day of May following.

6. *Opinion on Subpoena to Jefferson*

25 Fed. Cas. No. 14,692d; opinion rendered June 10, 1807

MARSHALL, Chief Justice [with GRIFFIN, District Judge]. The object of the motion now to be decided is to obtain copies of certain orders, understood to have been issued to the land and naval officers of the United States for the apprehension of the accused, and an original letter from General Wilkinson to the president in relation to the accused, with the answer of the president to that letter, which papers are supposed to be material to the defence. As the legal mode of effecting this object, a motion is made for a subpœna duces tecum, to be directed to the president of the United States. In opposition to this motion, a preliminary point has been made by the counsel for the prosecution. It has been insisted by them that, until the grand jury shall have found a true bill, the party accused is not entitled to subpœnas nor to the aid of the court to obtain his testimony.

It will not be said that this opinion is now, for the first time, advanced in the United States; but certainly it is now, for the first time, advanced in Virginia. So far back as any knowledge of our jurisprudence is possessed, the uniform practice of this country has been, to permit any individual, who was charged with any crime, to prepare for his defence, and to obtain the process of the court, for the purpose of enabling him so to do. This practice is as convenient and as consonant to justice as it is to humanity. It prevents, in a great measure, those delays which are never desirable, which frequently occasion the loss of testimony, and which are often oppressive. That would be the inevitable consequence of withholding from a prisoner the process of the court, until the indictment against him was found by the grand jury.

The right of an accused person to the process of the court to compel the attendance of witnesses seems to follow, necessarily, from the right to examine those witnesses; and, wherever the right exists, it would be reasonable that it should be accompanied with the means of rendering it effectual. It is not doubted that a person who appears before a court under a recognizance, must expect that a bill will be preferred against him, or that a question concerning the continuance of the recognizance will be brought before the court.

In the first event, he has the right, and it is perhaps his duty, to prepare for his defence at the trial. In the second event, it will not be denied that he possesses the right to examine witnesses on the question of continuing his recognizance. In either case it would seem reasonable that he should be entitled to the process of the court to procure the attendance of his witnesses. The genius and character of our laws and usages are friendly, not to condemnation at all events, but to a fair and impartial trial; and they consequently allow to the accused the right of preparing the means to secure such a trial. The objection that the attorney may refuse to proceed at this time, and that no day is fixed for the trial, if he should proceed, presents no real difficulty. It would be a very insufficient excuse to a prisoner, who had failed to prepare for his trial, to say that he was not certain the attorney would proceed against him.

Had the indictment been found at the first term, it would have been in some measure uncertain whether there would have been a trial at this, and still more uncertain on what day that trial would take place; yet subpœnas would have issued returnable to the first day of the term; and if after its commencement other subpœnas had been required, they would have issued, returnable as the court might direct. In fact, all process to which the law has affixed no certain return day is made returnable at the discretion of the court. General principles, then, and general practice are in favor of the right of every accused person, so soon as his case is in court, to prepare for his defence, and to receive the aid of the process of the court to compel the attendance of his witnesses.

Constitutional Rights

The constitution and laws of the United States will now be considered for the purpose of ascertaining how they bear upon the question. The sixth amendment to the constitution gives to the accused, "in all criminal prosecutions, a right to a speedy and public trial, and to compulsory process for obtaining witnesses in his favor." The right given by this article must be deemed sacred by the courts, and the article should be so construed as to be something more than a dead letter. What can more effectually elude the right to a speedy trial than the declaration that the accused shall be disabled from preparing for it until an indictment shall be found against him?

It is certainly much more in the true spirit of the provision which secures to the accused a speedy trial, that he should have the benefit of the provision which entitles him to compulsory process as soon as he is brought into court. This observation derives additional force from a consideration of the manner in which this subject has been contemplated by congress. It is obviously the intention of the national legislature, that in all capital cases the accused shall be entitled to process before indictment found. The words of the law are, "and every such person or persons accused or indicted of the crimes aforesaid (that is, of treason or any other capital offence), shall be allowed and admitted in his said defence to make any proof that he or they can produce by lawful witness or witnesses, and shall have the like process of the court where he or they shall be tried, to compel his or their witnesses to appear at his or their trial as is usually granted to compel witnesses to appear on the prosecution against them." This provision is made for persons accused or indicted.

From the imperfection of human language, it frequently happens that sentences which ought to be the most explicit are of doubtful construction; and in this case the words "accused or indicted" may be construed to be synonymous, to describe a person in the same situation, or to apply to different stages of the prosecution. The word "or" may be taken in a conjunctive or a disjunctive sense. A reason for understanding them in the latter sense is furnished by the section itself. It commences with declaring that any person who shall be accused and indicted of treason shall have a copy of the indictment, and at least three days before his trial. This right is obviously to be enjoyed after an indictment, and therefore the words are, "accused and indicted."

So with respect to the subsequent clause, which authorizes a party to make his defence, and directs the court, on his application, to assign him counsel. The words relate to any person accused and indicted. But, when the section proceeds to authorize the compulsory process for witnesses, the phraseology is changed. The words are, "and every such person or persons accused or indicted," &c., thereby adapting the expression to the situation of an accused person both before and after indictment. It is to be remarked, too, that the person so accused or indicted is to have "the like process to compel his or their witnesses to appear at his or their trial, as is usually granted to compel witnesses to appear on the prosecution against him."

The fair construction of this clause would seem to be, that with respect to the means of compelling the attendance of witnesses to be furnished by the court, the prosecution and defence are placed by the law on equal ground. The right of the prosecutor to take out subpoenas, or to avail himself of the aid of the court, in any stage of the proceedings previous to the indictment. is not controverted. This act of congress, it is true, applies only to capital cases; but persons charged with offences not capital have a constitutional and a legal right to examine their testimony; and this act ought to be considered as declaratory of the common law in cases where this constitutional right exists.

Rights Essential to Defense

Upon immemorial usage, then, and upon what is deemed a sound construction of the constitution and law of the land, the court is of opinion that any person charged with a crime in the courts of the United States has a right, before as well as after indictment, to the process of the court to compel the attendance of his witnesses. Much delay and much inconvenience may be avoided by this construction; no mischief, which is perceived, can be produced by it. The process would only issue when, according to the ordinary course of proceeding, the indictment would be tried at the term to which the subpœna is made returnable; so that it becomes incumbent on the accused to be ready for his trial at that term.

This point being disposed of, it remains to inquire whether a subpœna duces tecum can be directed to the president of the United States, and whether it ought to be directed in this case? This question originally consisted of two parts. It was at first doubted whether a subpœna could issue, in any case, to the chief magistrate of the nation; and if it could, whether that subpœna could do more than direct his personal attendance; whether it could direct him to bring with him a paper which was to constitute the gist of his testimony.

While the argument was opening, the attorney for the United States avowed his opinion that a general subpœna might issue to the president; but not a subpœna duces tecum. This terminated the argument on that part of the question. The court, however, has thought it necessary to state briefly the foundation of its opinion, that such a subpœna may issue. In the provisions of the constitution, and of the statute, which gives to the accused a right to the compulsory process of the court, there is no exception whatever. The obligation, therefore, of those provisions is general; and it would seem that no person could claim an exemption from them, but one who would not be a witness. At any rate, if an exception to the general principle exist, it must be looked for in the law of evidence.

The exceptions furnished by the law of evidence (with one only reservation), so far as they are personal, are of those only whose testimony could not be received. The single reservation alluded to is the case of the king. Although he may, perhaps, give testimony, it is said to be incompatible with his dignity to appear under the process of the court. Of the many points of difference which exist between the first magistrate in England and the first magistrate of the United States, in respect to the personal dignity conferred on them by the constitutions of their respective nations, the court will only select and mention two.

It is a principle of the English constitution that the king can do no wrong, that no blame can be imputed to him, that he cannot be named in debate. By the constitution of the United States, the president, as well as any other officer of the government, may be impeached, and may be removed from office on high crimes and misdemeanors. By the constitution of Great Britain, the crown is hereditary, and the monarch can never be a subject. By that of the United States, the president is elected from the mass of the people, and, on the expiration of the time for which he is elected, returns to the mass of the people again. How essentially this difference of circumstances must vary the policy of the laws of the two countries, in reference to the personal dignity of the executive chief, will be perceived by every person.

In this respect the first magistrate of the Union may more properly be likened to the first magistrate of a state; at any rate, under the former Confederation; and it is not known ever to have been doubted, but that the chief magistrate of a state might be served with a subpœna ad testificandum. If, in any court of the United States, it has ever been decided that a subpœna cannot issue to the president, that decision is unknown to this court.

Duties of President

If, upon any principle, the president could be construed to stand exempt from the general provisions of the constitution, it would be, because his duties as chief magistrate demand his whole time for national objects. But it is apparent that this demand is not unremitting; and, if it should exist at the time when his attendance on a court is required, it would be shown on the return of the subpœna, and would rather constitute a reason for not obeying the process of the court than a reason against its being issued.

In point of fact it cannot be doubted that the people of England have the same interest in the service of the executive government, that is, of the cabinet counsel, that the American people have in the service of the executive of the United States, and that their duties are as arduous and as unremitting. Yet it has never been alleged, that a subpœna might not be directed to them. It cannot be denied that to issue a subpœna to a person filling the exalted position of the chief magistrate is a duty which would be dispensed with more cheerfully than it would be performed; but, if it be a duty, the court can have no choice in the case.

If, then, as is admitted by the counsel for the United States a subpœna may issue to the president, the accused is entitled to it of course; and whatever difference may exist with respect to the power to compel the same obedience to the process, as if it had been directed to a private citizen, there exists no difference with respect to the right to obtain it. The guard, furnished to this high officer, to protect him from being harassed by vexatious and unnecessary subpœnas, is to be looked for in the conduct of a court after those subpœnas have issued; not in any circumstance which is to precede their being issued.

If, in being summoned to give his personal attendance to testify, the law does not discriminate between the president and a private citizen, what foundation is there for the opinion that this difference is created by the circumstance that his testimony depends on a paper in his possession, not on facts which have come to his knowledge otherwise than by writing? The court can perceive no foundation for such an opinion. The propriety of introducing any paper into a case, as testimony, must depend on the character of the paper, not on the character of the person who holds it.

A subpœna duces tecum, then, may issue to any person to whom an ordinary subpœna may issue, directing him to bring any paper of which the party praying it has a right to avail himself as testimony; if, indeed, that be the necessary process for obtaining the view of such a paper. When this subject was suddenly introduced, the court felt some doubt concerning the propriety of directing a subpœna to the chief magistrate, and some doubt also concerning the propriety of directing any paper in his possession, not public in its nature, to be exhibited in court. The impression that the questions which might arise in consequence of such process, were more proper for discussion on the return of the process than on its issuing, was then strong on the mind of the judges; but the circumspection with which they would take any step which would in any manner relate to that high personage, prevented their yielding readily to those impressions, and induced the request that those points, if not admitted, might be argued. The result of that argument is a confirmation of the impression originally entertained.

Universal Subpoena Power

The court can perceive no legal objection to issuing a subpœna duces tecum to any person whatever, provided the case be such as to justify the process. This is said to be a motion to the discretion of the court. This is true. But a motion to its discretion is a motion, not to its inclination, but to its judgment; and its judgment is to be guided by sound legal principles. A subpœna duces tecum varies from an ordinary subpœna only in this; that a witness is summoned for the purpose of bringing with him a paper in his custody. In some of our sister states whose system of jurisprudence is erected on the same foundation with our own, this process, we learn, issues of course. In this state it issues, not absolutely of course, but with leave of the court.

No case, however, exists as is believed, in which the motion has been founded on an affidavit, in which it has been denied, or in which it has been opposed. It has been truly observed that the opposite party can, regularly, take no more interest in the awarding a subpœna duces tecum than in awarding an ordinary subpœna. In either case he may object to any delay, the grant of which may be implied in granting the subpœna; but he can no more object regularly to the legal means of obtaining testimony, which exists in the papers, than in the mind of the person who may be summoned. If no inconvenience can be sustained by the opposite party, he can only oppose the motion in the character of an amicus curiæ, to prevent the court from making an improper order, or from burthening some officer by compelling an unnecessary attendance.

This court would certainly be very unwilling to say that upon fair construction the constitutional and legal right to obtain its process, to compel the attendance of witnesses, does not extend to their bringing with them such papers as may be material in the defence. The literal distinction which exists between the cases is too much attenuated to be countenanced in the tribunals of a just and humane nation. If, then, the subpœna be issued without inquiry into the manner of its application, it would seem to trench on the privileges which the constitution extends to the accused; it would seem to reduce his means of defence within narrower limits than is designed by the fundamental law of our country, if an overstrained rigor should be used with respect to his right to apply for papers deemed by himself to be material.

In the one case the accused is made the absolute judge of the testimony to be summoned; if, in the other, he is not a judge, absolutely for himself, his judgment ought to be controlled only so far as it is apparent that he means to exercise his privileges not really in his own defence, but for purposes which the court ought to discountenance. The court would not lend its aid to motions obviously designed to manifest disrespect to the government; but the court has no right to refuse its aid to motions for papers to which the accused may be entitled, and which may be material in his defence.

These observations are made to show the nature of the discretion which may be exercised. If it be apparent that the papers are irrelative to the case, or that for state reasons they cannot be introduced into the defence, the subpœna duces tecum would be useless. But, if this be not apparent, if they may be important in the defence, if they may be safely read at the trial, would it not be a blot in the page which records the judicial proceedings of this country, if, in a case of such serious import as this, the accused should be denied the use of them? . . .

Necessity of Subpoena

"In compliance with the intimation from the bench yesterday, the defendant has disclosed by the affidavit which I have just read, the points to which he expects the witnesses who have been summoned will testify. If the court cannot or will not issue compulsory process to bring in the witnesses who are the objects of this application, then the cause will not be postponed.

"Or, if it appears to the court, that the matter disclosed by the affidavit might not be given in evidence, if the witness were now here, then we cannot expect that our motion will be successful. For it would be absurd to suppose that the court will postpone the trial on account of the absence of witnesses whom they cannot compel to appear, and of whose voluntary attendance there is too much reason to despair; or, on account of the absence of witnesses who, if they were before the court, could not be heard on the trial." See the trials of Smith and Ogden [supra].* This argument states, unequivocally, the purpose for which a special affidavit was required.

The counsel for the United States considered the subject in the same light. After exhibiting an affidavit for the purpose of showing that the witnesses could not probably possess any material information, Mr. Standford said: "It was decided by the court yesterday that it was incumbent on the defendant, in order to entitle himself to a postponement of the trial on account of the absence of these witnesses, to show in what respect they are material for his defence. It was the opinion of the court that the general affidavit, in common form, would not be sufficient for this purpose, but that the particular facts expected from the witnesses must be disclosed in order that the court might, upon those facts, judge of the propriety of granting the postponement."

The court frequently treated the subject so as to show the opinion that the

---

* *United States* v. *Smith and Ogden* was another treason trial in 1795, together with those cited above at page 164.

special affidavit was required only on account of the continuance; but what is conclusive on this point is, that after deciding the testimony of the witnesses to be such as could not be offered to the jury, Judge Paterson was of opinion that a rule, to show cause why an attachment should not issue, ought to be granted. He could not have required the materiality of the witness to be shown on a motion, the success of which did not, in his opinion, in any degree depend on that materiality; and which he granted after deciding the testimony to be such as the jury ought not to hear. It is, then, most apparent that the opinion of Judge Paterson has been misunderstood, and that no inference can possibly be drawn from it, opposed to the principle which has been laid down by the court. That principle will therefore be applied to the present motion.

Letter from Wilkinson

The first paper required is the letter of General Wilkinson, which was referred to in the message of the president to congress. The application of that letter to the case is shown by the terms in which the communication was made. It is a statement of the conduct of the accused made by the person who is declared to be the essential witness against him. The order for producing this letter is opposed:

First, because it is not material to the defense. It is a principle, universally acknowledged, that a party has a right to oppose to the testimony of any witness against him, the declarations which that witness has made at other times on the same subject. If he possesses this right, he must bring forward proof of those declarations. This proof must be obtained before he knows positively what the witness will say; for if he waits until the witness has been heard at the trial, it is too late to meet him with his former declarations.

Those former declarations, therefore, constitute a mass of testimony, which a party has a right to obtain by way of precaution, and the positive necessity of which can only be decided at the trial. It is with some surprise an argument was heard from the bar, insinuating that the award of a subpœna on this ground gave the countenance of the court to suspicions affecting the veracity of a witness who is to appear on the part of the United States. This observation could not have been considered.

In contests of this description, the court takes no part; the court has no right to take a part. Every person may give in evidence, testimony such as is stated in this case. What would be the feelings of the prosecutor if, in this case, the accused should produce a witness completely exculpating himself, and the attorney for the United States should be arrested in his attempt to prove what the same witness had said upon a former occasion, by a declaration from the bench that such an attempt could not be permitted, because it would imply a suspicion in the court that the witness had not spoken the truth? Respecting so unjustifiable an interposition but one opinion would be formed.

Confidentiality of Letter

The second objection is, that the letter contains matter which ought not to be disclosed. That there may be matter, the production of which the court would not require, is certain; but, in a capital case, that the accused ought, in some form, to have the benefit of it, if it were really essential to his defence, is a position which the court would very reluctantly deny. It ought not to be believed that the department which superintends prosecutions in criminal cases, would be inclined to withhold it.

What ought to be done under such circumstances presents a delicate question, the discussion of which, it is hoped, will never be rendered necessary in this country. At present it need only be said that the question does not occur at this time. There is certainly nothing before the court which shows that the letter in question contains any matter the disclosure of which would endanger the public safety. If it does contain such matter, the fact may appear before the disclosure is made. If it does contain any matter which it would be imprudent to disclose, which it is not the wish of the executive to disclose, such matter, if it be not immediately and essentially applicable to the point, will, of course, be suppressed.

It is not easy to conceive that so much of the letter as relates to the conduct of the accused can be a subject of delicacy with the president. Everything of this kind, however, will have its due consideration on the return of the subpœna.

Copy Held Unacceptable

Thirdly, it has been alleged that a copy may be received instead of the original, and the act of congress has been cited in support of this proposition. This argument presupposes that the letter required is a document filed in the department of state, the reverse of which may be and most probably is the fact. Letters addressed to the president are most usually retained by himself. They do not belong to any of the departments. But, were the facts otherwise, a copy might not answer the purpose. The copy would not be superior to the original, and the original itself would not be admitted, if denied, without proof that it was in the handwriting of the witness.

Suppose the case put at the bar of an indictment on this letter for a libel, and on its production it should appear not to be in the handwriting of the person indicted. Would its being deposited in the department of state make it his writing, or subject him to the consequence of having written it? Certainly not. For the purpose, then, of showing the letter to have been written by a particular person, the original must be produced, and a copy could not be admitted.

On the confidential nature of this letter much has been said at the bar, and authorities have been produced which appear to be conclusive. Had its contents been orally communicated, the person to whom the communications were made could not have excused himself from detailing them, so far as they might be deemed essential in the defence. Their being in writing gives no additional sanctity; the only difference produced by the circumstance is, that the contents of the paper must be proved by the paper itself, not by the recollection of the witness.

Much has been said about the disrespect to the chief magistrate, which is implied by this motion, and by such a decision of it as the law is believed to require. These observations will be very truly answered by the declaration that this court feels many, perhaps, peculiar motives for manifesting as guarded a respect for the chief magistrate of the Union as is compatible with its official duties.

To go beyond these would exhibit a conduct which would deserve some other appellation than the term respect. It is not for the court to anticipate the event of the present prosecution. Should it terminate as is expected on the part of the United States, all those who are concerned in it should certainly regret that a paper which the accused believed to be essential to his defence, which may, for aught that now appears, be essential, had been withheld from him.

I will not say, that this circumstance would, in any degree, tarnish the reputation of the government; but I will say, that it would justly tarnish the reputation of the court which had given its sanction to its being withheld. Might I be permitted to utter one sentiment, with respect to myself, it would be to deplore, most earnestly, the occasion which should compel me to look back on any part of my official conduct with so much self-reproach as I should feel, could I declare, on the information now possessed, that the accused is not entitled to the letter in question, if it should be really important to him.

Reply to Letter

The propriety of requiring the answer to this letter is more questionable. It is alleged that it most probably communicates orders showing the situation of this country with Spain, which will be important on the misdemeanor. If it contain matter not essential to the defence, and the disclosure be unpleasant to the executive, it certainly ought not to be disclosed. This is a point which will appear on the return. The demand of the orders which have been issued, and which have been, as is alleged, published in the Natchez Gazette, is by no means unusual. Such documents have often been produced in the courts of the United States and the courts of England.

If they contain matter interesting to the nation, the concealment of which is required by the public safety, that matter will appear upon the return. If they do not, and are material, they may be exhibited. It is said they cannot be material, because they cannot justify any unlawful resistance which may have been employed or meditated by the accused. Were this admitted, and were it also admitted that such resistance would amount to treason, the orders might still be material; because they might tend to weaken the endeavor to connect such overt act with any overt act of which this court may take cognizance.

The court, however, is rather inclined to the opinion that the subpœna in such case ought to be directed to the head of the department in whose custody the orders are. The court must suppose that the letter of the secretary of the navy, which has been stated by the attorney for the United States, to refer the counsel for the prisoner to his legal remedy for the copies he desired, alluded to such a motion as is now made.

The affidavit on which the motion is grounded has not been noticed. It is believed that such a subpœna, as is asked, ought to issue, if there exist any reason for supposing that the testimony may be material, and ought to be admitted. It is only because the subpœna is to those who administer the government of this country, that such an affidavit was required as would furnish probable cause to believe that the testimony was desired for the real purposes of defence, and not for such as this court will forever discountenance.

7. *Jefferson's Reply to Subpoena*
25 Fed. Cases No. 14,693

Washington, June 17, 1807.

Sir:* In answering your letter of the 9th, which desired a communication of one to me from General Wilkinson, specified by its date, I informed you in mine of the 12th that I had delivered it, with all other papers respecting the charges against Aaron Burr, to the attorney general when he went to Richmond; that I had supposed he had left them in your possession, but would immediately write to him, if he had not, to forward that particular letter without delay. I wrote to him accordingly on the same day, but having no answer I know not whether he has forwarded the letter. I stated in the same letter that I had desired the secretary of war to examine his office in order to comply with your further request to furnish copies of the orders which had been given respecting Aaron Burr and his property; and, in a subsequent letter of the same day, I forwarded you copies of two letters from the secretary at war, which appeared to be within the description expressed in your letter. The order from the secretary of the navy you said you were in possession of.

The receipt of these papers has, I presume, so far anticipated, and others this day forwarded, will have substantially fulfilled the object of a subpœna from the district court of Richmond, requiring that those officers and myself should attend the court in Richmond, with the letter of General Wilkinson, the answer to that letter, and the orders of the department of war and the navy therein generally described. No answer to General Wilkinson's letter, other than a mere acknowledgement of its receipt in a letter written for a different purpose, was ever written by myself or any other.

To these communications of papers I will add, that if the defendant suppose there are any facts within the knowledge of the heads of departments or of myself, which can be useful for his defence, from a desire of doing anything our situation will permit in furtherance of justice, we shall be ready to give him the benefit of it, by way of deposition through any persons whom the court shall authorize to take our testimony at this place. I know indeed that this cannot be done but by consent of parties, and I therefore authorize you to give consent on the part of the United States. Mr. Burr's consent will be given of course, if he suppose the testimony useful.

As to our personal attendance at Richmond, I am persuaded the court is sensible that paramount duties to the nation at large control the obligation of compliance with its summons in this case, as it would should we receive a similar one to attend the trials of Blennerhassett and others in the Mississippi territory, those instituted at St. Louis and other places on the western waters, or at

* The addressee is United States Attorney George Hay.

any place other than the seat of government. To comply with such calls would leave the nation without an executive branch, whose agency nevertheless is understood to be so constantly necessary that it is the sole branch which the constitution requires to be always in function. It could not, then, intend that it should be withdrawn from its station by any co-ordinate authority.

With respect to papers, there is certainly a public and private side to our offices. To the former belong grants of land, patents for inventions, certain commissions, proclamations, and other papers patent in their nature. To the other belong mere executive proceedings. All nations have found it necessary that, for the advantageous conduct of their affairs, some of these proceedings, at least, should remain known to their executive functionary only. He, of course, from the nature of the case, must be the sole judge of which of them the public interest will permit publication.

Hence, under our constitution, in requests of papers from the legislative to the executive branch, an exception is carefully expressed, 'as to those which he may deem the public welfare may require not to be disclosed,' as you will see in the inclosed resolution of the house of representatives, which produced the message of January 22d, respecting this case. The respect mutually due between the constituted authorities in their official intercourse, as well as sincere dispositions do for every one what is just, will always insure from the executive, in exercising the duty of discrimination confided to him, the same candor and integrity to which the nation has, in like manner, trusted in the disposal of its judiciary authorities. Considering you as the organ for communicating these sentiments to the court, I address them to you for that purpose, and salute you with esteem and respect.   Thos. Jefferson.

8. *Opinion on Definition of Treason*

25 Fed. Cas. No. 14,693; opinion rendered August 31, 1807

MARSHALL, Chief Justice, delivered the opinion of the court as follows:

The question now to be decided has been argued in a manner worthy of its importance, and with an earnestness evincing the strong conviction felt by the counsel on each side that the law is with them. A degree of eloquence seldom displayed on any occasion has embellished a solidity of argument and a depth of research by which the court has been greatly aided in forming the opinion it is about to deliver. The testimony adduced on the part of the United States to prove the overt act laid in the indictment having shown, and the attorney for the United States having admitted, that the prisoner was not present when that act, whatever may be its character, was committed, and there being no reason to doubt but that he was at a great distance, and in a different state, it is objected to the testimony offered on the part of the United States to connect him with those who committed the overt act, that such testimony is totally irrelevant, and must, therefore, be rejected. The arguments in support of this motion respect in part the merits of the case as it may be supposed to stand independent of the pleadings, and in part as exhibited by the pleadings.

Constitutional Provisions

On the first division of the subject two points are made: 1st. That, conformably to the constitution of the United States, no man can be convicted of treason who was not present when the war was levied. 2d. That if this construction be erroneous, no testimony can be received to charge one man with the overt acts of others until those overt acts as laid in the indictment be proved to the satisfaction of the court. The question which arises on the construction of the constitution, in every point of view in which it can be contemplated, is of infinite moment to the people of this country and to their government, and requires the most temperate and the most deliberate consideration. "Treason against the United States shall consist only in levying war against them."

Levying War

What is the natural import of the words "levying war?" And who may be said to levy it? Had their first application to treason been made by our constitution they would certainly have admitted of some latitude of construction. Taken most literally, they are, perhaps, of the same import with the words "raising or creating war"; but as those who join after the commencement are equally the objects of punishment, there would probably be a general admission that the term also comprehended making war or carrying on war. In the construction which courts would be required to give these words, it is not improbable that those who should raise, create, make, or carry on war, might be comprehended.

The various acts which would be considered as coming within the term would be settled by a course of decisions; and it would be affirming boldly to say that those only who actually constituted a portion of the military force appearing in arms could be considered as levying war. There is no difficulty in affirming that there must be a war or the crime of levying it cannot exist; but there would often be considerable difficulty in affirming that a particular act did or did not involve the person committing it in the guilt and in the fact of levying war.

If, for example, an army should be actually raised for the avowed purpose of carrying on open war against the United States and subverting their government, the point must be weighed very deliberately, before a judge would venture to decide that an overt act of levying war had not been committed by a commissary of purchases, who never saw the army, but who, knowing its object, and leaguing himself with the rebels, supplied that army with provisions, or, by a recruiting officer holding a commission in the rebel service, who, though never in camp, executed the particular duty assigned to him.

But the term is not for the first time applied to treason by the constitution of the United States. It is a technical term. It is used in a very old statute of that country whose language is our language, and whose laws form the substratum of our laws. It is scarcely conceivable that the term was not employed by the framers of our constitution in the sense which had been affixed to it by those from whom we borrowed it. So far as the meaning of any terms, particularly terms of art, is completely ascertained, those by whom they are employed must

be considered as employing them in that ascertained meaning, unless the contrary be proved by the context. . . .

Although we find among the commentators upon treason enough to satisfy
the inquiry, what is a state of internal war? yet no precise information can be
acquired from them which would enable us to decide with clearness whether
persons not in arms, but taking part in a rebellion, could be said to levy war,
independently of that doctrine which attaches to the accessory the guilt of his
principal. If in adjudged cases this question have been taken up and directly
decided, the court has not seen those cases. The argument which may be drawn
from the form of the indictment, though strong, is not conclusive. In the precedent found in Tremaine, Mary Speake, who was indicted for furnishing provisions to the party of the Duke of Monmouth, is indicted for furnishing
provisions to those who were levying war, not for levying war herself.*

It may correctly be argued that, had this act amounted to levying war, she
would have been indicted for levying war; and the furnishing of provisions
would have been laid as the overt act. The court felt this when the precedent
was produced. But the argument, though strong, is not conclusive, because, in
England, the inquiry, whether she had become a traitor by levying war, or by
giving aid and comfort to those who were levying war, was unimportant; and
because, too, it does not appear from the indictment that she was actually concerned in the rebellion—that she belonged to the rebel party, or was guilty of
anything further than a criminal speculation in selling them provisions.

Constitutional Limitation

It is not deemed necessary to trace the doctrine, that in treason all are principals, to its source. Its origin is most probably stated correctly by Judge
Tucker in a work, the merit of which is with pleasure acknowledged. † But if a
spurious doctrine have been introduced into the common law, and have for
centuries been admitted as genuine, it would require great hardihood in a judge
to reject it. Accordingly, we find those of the English jurists who seem to disapprove the principle declaring that it is now too firmly settled to be shaken.

It is unnecessary to trace this doctrine to its source for another reason: the
terms of the constitution comprise no question respecting principal and accessory, so far as either may be truly and in fact said to levy war. Whether in England a person would be indicted in express terms for levying war or for assisting
others in levying war, yet if in correct and legal language he can be said to have
levied war, and if it have never been decided that the act would not amount to
levying war, his case may, without violent construction, be brought within the
letter and the plain meaning of the constitution.

In examining these words, the argument which may be drawn from felonies,
as, for example, from murder, is not more conclusive. Murder is the single act

* Sir John Tremaine, *Placita Coronae, or, Pleas of the Crown* (London, 1723).
† *Blackstone's Commentaries, with Notes of Reference to the Constitution and
Laws of the United States*, edited by St. George Tucker (Philadelphia, 5 vol., 1803).
The best recent work is J. W. Hurst, *The Law of Treason in the United States* (West-
port, Conn., 1971).

of killing with malice aforethought. But war is a complex operation, composed of many parts, co-operating with each other. No one man or body of men can perform them all if the war be of any continuance. Although, then, in correct and in law language, he alone is said to have murdered another who has perpetrated the fact of killing, or has been present aiding that fact, it does not follow that he alone can have levied war who has borne arms.

All those who perform the various and essential military parts of prosecuting the war, which must be assigned to different persons, may with correctness and accuracy be said to levy war. Taking this view of the subject, it appears to the court that those who perform a part in the prosecution of the war may correctly be said to levy war and to commit treason under the constitution. It will be observed that this opinion does not extend to the case of a person who performs no act in the prosecution of the war—who counsels and advises it—or who, being engaged in the conspiracy, fails to perform his part.

Whether such persons may be implicated by the doctrine that whatever would make a man an accessory in felony makes him a principal in treason, or are excluded because that doctrine is inapplicable to the United States, the constitution having declared that treason shall consist only in levying war, and having made the proof of overt acts necessary to conviction, is a question of vast importance, which it would be proper for the supreme court to take a fit occasion to decide, but which an inferior tribunal would not willingly determine unless the case before them should require it.

Bollman–Swartwout Rule

It may now be proper to notice the opinion of the supreme court in the case of the United States against Bollman and Swartwout. It is said that this opinion, in declaring that those who do not bear arms may yet be guilty of treason, is contrary to law, and is not obligatory because it is extra-judicial and was delivered on a point not argued. This court is therefore required to depart from the principle there laid down. It is true that, in that case, after forming the opinion that no treason could be committed because no treasonable assemblage had taken place, the court might have dispensed with proceeding further in the doctrines of treason.

But it is to be remembered that the judges might act separately, and perhaps at the same time on the various prosecutions which might be instituted, and that no appeal lay from their decisions. Opposite judgments on the point would have presented a state of things infinitely to be deplored by all. It was not surprising, then, that they should have made some attempt to settle principles which would probably occur, and which were in some degree connected with the point before them. The court had employed some reasoning to show that without the actual embodying of men war could not be levied.

It might have been inferred from this that those only who were so embodied could be guilty of treason. Not only to exclude this inference, but also to affirm the contrary, the court proceeded to observe: "It is not the intention of the court to say that no individual can be guilty of this crime who has not appeared in arms against his country. On the contrary, if war be actually levied, that is, if a body of men be actually assembled for the purpose of effecting by force a treasonable object, all those who perform any part, however minute, or however remote from the scene of action, and who are actually leagued in the general conspiracy, are to be considered as traitors."

This court is told that if this opinion be incorrect it ought not to be obeyed, because it was extra-judicial. For myself, I can say that I could not lightly be prevailed on to disobey it, were I even convinced that it was erroneous; but I would certainly use any means which the law placed in my power to carry the question again before the supreme court for reconsideration, in a case in which it would directly occur and be fully argued.

The court which gave this opinion was composed of four judges. At the time I thought them unanimous, but I have since had reason to suspect that one of them, whose opinion is entitled to great respect, and whose indisposition prevented his entering into the discussions, on some of those points which were not essential to the decision of the very case under consideration, did not concur in this particular point with his brethren. Had the opinion been unanimous, it would have been given by a majority of the judges. But should the three who were absent concur with that judge who was present, and who perhaps dissents from what was then the opinion of the court, a majority of the judges may over-rule this decision. I should, therefore, feel no objection, although I then thought and still think the opinion perfectly correct, to carry the point, if possible, again before the supreme court, if the case should depend upon it. In saying that I still think the opinion perfectly correct, I do not consider myself as going further than the preceding reasoning goes. Some gentlemen have argued as if the supreme court had adopted the whole doctrine of the English books on the subject of accessories to treason.

But certainly such is not the fact. Those only who perform a part, and who are leagued in the conspiracy, are declared to be traitors. To complete the definition both circumstances must concur. They must "perform a part," which will furnish the overt act; and they must be "leagued in conspiracy." The person who comes within this description in the opinion of the court levies war. The present motion, however, does not rest upon this point; for if under this indictment the United States might be let in to prove the part performed by the prisoner, if he did perform any part, the court could not stop the testimony, in its present stage.

Nature of Overt Act

2d. The second point involves the character of the overt act which has been given in evidence, and calls upon the court to declare whether that act can amount to levying war. Although the court ought now to avoid any analysis of the testimony which has been offered in this case, provided the decision of the motion should not rest upon it, yet many reasons concur in giving peculiar propriety to a delivery, in the course of these trials, of a detailed opinion on the question, what is levying war? As this question has been argued at great length, it may probably save much trouble to the counsel now to give that opinion.

In opening the case, it was contended by the attorney for the United States, and has since been maintained on the part of the prosecution, that neither arms nor the application of force or violence are indispensably necessary to constitute the fact of levying war. To illustrate these positions, several cases have been stated, many of which would clearly amount to treason. In all of them, except that which was probably intended to be this case, and on which no observation will be made, the object of the assemblage was clearly treasonable. Its character was unequivocal, and was demonstrated by evidence furnished by the assemblage itself. There was no necessity to rely upon information drawn from extrinsic sources, or, in order to understand the fact, to pursue a course of intricate reasoning, and to conjecture motives.

A force is supposed to be collected for an avowed treasonable object, in a condition to attempt that object, and to have commenced the attempt by moving towards it. I state these particulars, because although the cases put may establish the doctrine they are intended to support—may prove that the absence of arms, or the failure to apply force to sensible objects by the actual commission of violence on those objects, may be supplied by other circumstances— yet they also serve to show that the mind requires those circumstances to be satisfied that war is levied. Their construction of the opinion of the supreme court is, I think, thus far correct.

It is certainly the opinion which was at the time entertained by myself; and which is still entertained. If a rebel army, avowing its hostility to the sovereign power, should front that of the government, should march and countermarch before it, should manœuvre in its face, and should then disperse from any cause whatever without firing a gun—I confess I could not, without some surprise, hear gentlemen seriously contend that this could not amount to an act of levying war. A case equally strong may be put with respect to the absence of military weapons. If the party be in a condition to execute the purposed treason without the usual implements of war, I can perceive no reason for requiring those implements in order to constitute the crime.

American Cases

Several judges of the United States have given opinions at their circuits on the subject, all of which deserve, and will receive the particular attention of this court.

In his charge to the grand jury, when John Fries was indicted in consequence of a forcible opposition to the direct tax, Judge Iredell is understood to have said: "I think I am warranted in saying that if, in the case of the insurgents who may come under your consideration, the intention was to prevent by force of arms the execution of an act of the congress of the United States altogether, any forcible opposition, calculated to carry that intention into effect, was a levying of war against the United States, and, of course, an act of treason." To levy war, then, according to this opinion of Judge Iredell, required the actual exertion of force.

Judge Patterson, in his opinions delivered in two different cases, seems not to differ from Judge Iredell. He does not, indeed, precisely state the employment of force as necessary to constitute a levying war, but in giving his opinion, in cases in which force was actually employed, he considers the crime in one case as dependent on the intention; and in the other case he says: "Combining these facts and this design," (that is, combining actual force with a treasonable design,) "the crime is high treason." Judge Peters has also indicated the opinion that force was necessary to constitute the crime of levying war.

Judge Chase has been particularly clear and explicit. In an opinion which he appears to have prepared on great consideration, he says: "The court are of opinion that if a body of people conspire and meditate an insurrection to resist or oppose the execution of a statute of the United States by force, they are only guilty of a high misdemeanor; but if they proceed to carry such intention into execution by force, that they are guilty of the treason of levying war; and the quantum of the force employed neither increases nor diminishes the crime; whether by one hundred or one thousand persons is wholly immaterial.*

"The court are of opinion that a combination or conspiracy to levy war against the United States is not treason unless combined with an attempt to carry such combination or conspiracy into execution; some actual force or violence must be used in pursuance of such design to levy war; but that it is altogether immaterial whether the force used be sufficient to effectuate the object. Any force connected with the intention will constitute the crime of levying of war." In various parts of the opinion delivered by Judge Chase, in the case of Fries, the same sentiments are to be found. It is to be observed that these judges are not content that troops should be assembled in a condition to employ force. According to them some degree of force must have been actually employed.

The judges of the United States, then, so far as their opinions have been quoted, seem to have required still more to constitute the fact of levying war than has been required by the English books. Our judges seem to have required the actual exercise of force, the actual employment of some degree of violence. This, however, may be, and probably is, because, in the cases in which their opinions were given, the design not having been to overturn the government, but to resist the execution of a law, such an assemblage as would be sufficient for the purpose would require the actual employment of force to render the object unequivocal.

Bollman–Swartwout Case

But it is said all these authorities have been overruled by the decision of the supreme court in the case of U.S. v. Swartwout [4 Cranch (8 U.S.) 75]. If the supreme court have indeed extended the doctrine of treason further than it has heretofore been carried by the judges of England or of this country, their decision would be submitted to. At least this court could go no further than to endeavor again to bring the point directly before them.

It would, however, be expected that an opinion which is to overrule all former precedents, and to establish a principle never before recognized, should be expressed in plain and explicit terms. A mere implication ought not to prostrate a principle which seems to have been so well established. Had the intention

* Cf. the Whisky Rebellion cases cited above at pages 164, 181.

been entertained to make so material a change in this respect, the court ought to have expressly declared that any assemblage of men whatever, who had formed a treasonable design, whether in force or not, whether in a condition to attempt the design or not, whether attended with warlike appearances or not, constitutes the fact of levying war.

Yet no declaration to this amount is made. Not an expression of the kind is to be found in the opinion of the supreme court. The foundation on which this argument rests is the omission of the court to state that the assemblage which constitutes the fact of levying war ought to be in force, and some passages which show that the question respecting the nature of the assemblage was not in the mind of the court when the opinion was drawn; which passages are mingled with others which at least show that there was no intention to depart from the course of the precedents in cases of treason by levying war.

Every opinion, to be correctly understood, ought to be considered with a view to the case in which it was delivered. In the case of the United States against Bollman and Swartwout, there was no evidence that even two men had ever met for the purpose of executing the plan in which those persons were charged with having participated.

It was, therefore, sufficient for the court to say that unless men were assembled, war could not be levied. That case was decided by this declaration. The court might indeed have defined the species of assemblage which would amount to levying of war; but, as this opinion was not a treatise on treason, but a decision of a particular case, expressions of doubtful import should be construed in reference to the case itself, and the mere omission to state that a particular circumstance was necessary to the consummation of the crime ought not to be construed into a declaration that the circumstance was unimportant. General expressions ought not to be considered as overruling settled principles, without a direct declaration to that effect. After these preliminary observations, the court will proceed to examine the opinion which has occasioned them.

Restatement of Definition

The first expression in it bearing on the present question is, "To constitute that specific crime for which the prisoner now before the court has been committed, war must be actually levied against the United States. However flagitious may be the crime of conspiracy to subvert by force the government of our country, such conspiracy is not treason. To conspire to levy war and actually to levy war are distinct offences. The first must be brought into operation by the assemblage of men for a purpose treasonable in itself, or the fact of levying war cannot have been committed."

Although it is not expressly stated that the assemblage of men for the purpose of carrying into operation the treasonable intent which will amount to levying war must be an assemblage in force, yet it is fairly to be inferred from the context; and nothing like dispensing with force appears in this paragraph. The expressions are, "to constitute the crime, war must be actually levied." A conspiracy to levy war is spoken of as "a conspiracy to subvert by force the government of our country."

Speaking in general terms of an assemblage of men for this or for any other purpose, a person would naturally be understood as speaking of an assemblage in some degree adapted to the purpose. An assemblage to subvert by force the government of our country, and amounting to a levying of war, should be an assemblage in force. In a subsequent paragraph the court says: "It is not the intention of the court to say that no individual can be guilty of this crime who has not appeared in arms against his country. On the contrary, if war be actually levied, that is, if a body of men be actually assembled in order to effect by force a treasonable purpose, all those who perform any part, however minute, &c., and who are actually leagued in the general conspiracy, are traitors.

"But there must be an actual assembling of men for the treasonable purpose to constitute a levying of war." The observations made on the preceding paragraph apply to this. "A body of men actually assembled, in order to effect by force a treasonable purpose," must be a body assembled with such appearance of force as would warrant the opinion that they were assembled for the particular purpose. An assemblage to constitute an actual levying of war should be an assemblage with such appearance of force as would justify the opinion that they met for the purpose. This explanation, which is believed to be the natural, certainly not a strained explanation of the words, derives some additional aid from the terms in which the paragraph last quoted commences: "It is not the intention of the court to say that no individual can be guilty of treason who has not appeared in arms against his country."

These words seem intended to obviate an inference which might otherwise have been drawn from the preceding paragraph. They indicate that in the mind of the court the assemblage stated in that paragraph was an assemblage in arms; that the individuals who composed it had appeared in arms against their country; that is, in other words, that the assemblage was a military, a warlike assemblage. The succeeding paragraph in the opinion relates to a conspiracy, and serves to show that force and violence were in the mind of the court, and that there was no idea of extending the crime of treason by construction beyond the constitutional definition which had been given of it.

Overt Act Still Required

Returning to the case actually before the court, it is said: "A design to overturn the government of the United States in New Orleans by force would have been unquestionably a design which if carried into execution would have been treason; and the assemblage of a body of men for the purpose of carrying it into execution would amount to levying of war against the United States." Now what could reasonably be said to be an assemblage of a body of men for the purpose of overturning the government of the United States in New Orleans by force? Certainly an assemblage in force; an assemblage prepared, and intending to act with force; a military assemblage.

The decisions theretofore made by the judges of the United States are, then, declared to be in conformity with the principles laid down by the supreme court. Is this declaration compatible with the idea of departing from those opinions on a point within the contemplation of the court? The opinions of Judge Patterson and Judge Iredell are said "to imply an actual assembling of men, though they rather designed to remark on the purpose to which the force was to be applied than on the nature of the force itself." This observation certainly indicates that the necessity of an assemblage of men was the particular point the court meant to establish, and that the idea of force was never separated from this assemblage.

The opinion of Judge Chase is next quoted with approbation. This opinion in terms requires the employment of force. After stating the verbal communication said to have been made by Mr. Swartwout to General Wilkinson, the court says, "If these words import that the government of New Orleans was to be revolutionized by force, although merely as a step to, or a means of, executing some greater projects, the design was unquestionably treasonable; and any assemblage of men for that purpose would amount to a levying of war."

The words "any assemblage of men," if construed to affirm that any two or three of the conspirators who might be found together after this plan had been formed would be the act of levying war, would certainly be misconstrued. The sense of the expression, "any assemblage of men," is restricted by the words "for this purpose." Now, could it be in the contemplation of the court that a body of men would assemble for the purpose of revolutionizing New Orleans by force, who should not themselves be in force?

After noticing some difference of opinion among the judges respecting the import of the words said to have been used by Mr. Swartwout, the court proceeds to observe: "But whether this treasonable intention be really imputable to the plan or not, it is admitted that it must have been carried into execution by an open assemblage for that purpose, previous to the arrest of the prisoner, in order to consummate the crime as to him." Could the court have conceived "an open assemblage" "for the purpose of overturning the government of New Orleans by force," to be only equivalent to a secret, furtive assemblage without the appearance of force?

After quoting the words of Mr. Swartwout, from the affidavit, in which it was stated that Mr. Burr was levying an army of 7,000 men, and observing that the treason to be inferred from these words would depend on the intention with which it was levied, and on the progress which had been made in levying it, the court says: "The question, then, is whether this evidence prove Colonel Burr to have advanced so far in levying an army as actually to have assembled them." Actually to assemble an army of 7,000 men is unquestionably to place those who are so assembled in a state of open force. But as the mode of expression used in this passage might be misconstrued so far as to countenance the opinion that it would be necessary to assemble the whole army in order to constitute the fact of levying war, the court proceeds to say: "It is argued that since it cannot be necessary that the whole 7,000 men should be assembled, their commencing their march by detachments to the place of rendezvous must be sufficient to constitute the crime.

"This position is correct with some qualification. It cannot be necessary that the whole army should assemble, and that the various parts which are to compose it should have combined. But it is necessary there should be an actual assemblage; and therefore this evidence should make the fact unequivocal. The travelling of individuals to the place of rendezvous would, perhaps, not be sufficient. This would be an equivocal act, and has no warlike appearance. The meeting of particular bodies of men, and their march from places of partial to a place of general rendezvous, would be such an assemblage."

The position here stated by the counsel for the prosecution is that the army "commencing its march by detachments to the place of rendezvous (that is, of the army) must be sufficient to constitute the crime." This position is not admitted by the court to be universally correct. It is said to be "correct with some qualification." What is that qualification? "The travelling of individuals to the place of rendezvous (and by this term is not to be understood one individual by himself, but several individuals, either separately or together, but not in military form) would perhaps not be sufficient." Why not sufficient? Because, says the court, "this would be an equivocal act and has no warlike appearance."

The act, then, should be unequivocal and should have a warlike appearance. It must exhibit, in the words of Sir Matthew Hale, *speciem belli,* the appearance of war. This construction is rendered in some measure necessary when we observe that the court is qualifying the position, "that the army commencing their march by detachments to the place of rendezvous must be sufficient to constitute the crime." In qualifying this position they say, "the travelling of individuals would perhaps not be sufficient."

Now, a solitary individual travelling to any point, with any intent, could not, without a total disregard of language, be termed a marching detachment. The court, therefore, must have contemplated several individuals travelling together, and the words being used in reference to the position they intended to qualify, would seem to indicate the distinction between the appearances attending the usual movement of a company of men for civil purposes, and that military movement which might, in correct language, be denominated "marching by detachments." The court then proceeded to say: "The meeting of particular bodies of men, and their marching from places of partial to a place of general rendezvous, would be such an assemblage."

Practical Effect of Acts

It is obvious from the context that the court must have intended to state a case which would in itself be unequivocal, because it would have a warlike appearance. The case stated is that of distinct bodies of men assembling at different places, and marching from these places of partial to a place of general rendezvous. When this has been done an assemblage is produced which would in itself be unequivocal. But when is it done? What is the assemblage here described? The assemblage formed of the different bodies of partial at a place of general rendezvous.

In describing the mode of coming to this assemblage the civil term "travelling" is dropped, and the military term "marching" is employed. If this were intended as a definition of an assemblage which would amount to levying war, the definition requires an assemblage at a place of general rendezvous, composed of bodies of men who had previously assembled at places of partial rendezvous.

But this is not intended as a definition; for clearly if there should be no places of partial rendezvous, if troops should embody in the first instance in great force for the purpose of subverting the government by violence, the act would be unequivocal; it would have a warlike appearance; and it would, according to the opinion of the supreme court, properly construed, and according to English authorities, amount to levying war. But this, though not a definition, is put as an example, and surely it may be safely taken as an example. If different bodies of men, in pursuance of a treasonable design, plainly proved, should assemble in warlike appearance at places of partial rendezvous, and should march from those places to a place of general rendezvous, it is difficult to conceive how such a transaction could take place without exhibiting the appearance of war, without an obvious display of force.

At any rate, a court in stating generally such a military assemblage as would amount to levying war, and having a case before it in which there was no asesmblage whatever, cannot reasonably be understood, in putting such an example, to dispense with those appearances of war which seem to be required by the general current of authorities. Certainly it ought not to be so understood when it says in express terms that "it is more safe as well as more consonant to the principles of our constitution that the crime of treason should not be extended by construction to doubtful cases; and that crimes not clearly within the constitutional definition should receive such punishment as the legislature in its wisdom may provide."

Use of Actual Force

After this analysis of the opinion of the supreme court, it will be observed that the direct question, whether an assemblage of men which might be construed to amount to a levying of war must appear in force or in military form, was not in argument or in fact before the court, and does not appear to have been in terms decided. The opinion seems to have been drawn without particularly adverting to this question; and, therefore, upon a transient view of particular expressions, might inspire the idea that a display of force, that appearances of war, were not necessary ingredients to constitute the fact of levying war.

But upon a more intent and more accurate investigation of this opinion, although the terms force and violence are not employed as descriptive of the assemblage, such requisites are declared to be indispensable as can scarcely exist without the appearance of war and the existence of real force. It is said that war must be levied in fact; that the object must be one which is to be effected by force; that the assemblage must be such as to prove that this is its object; that it must not be an equivocal act, without a warlike appearance; that it must be an open assemblage for the purpose of force. In the course of this opinion, decisions are quoted and approved which require the employment of force to constitute the crime.

It seems extremely difficult, if not impossible, to reconcile these various declarations with the idea that the supreme court considered a secret, unarmed meeting, although that meeting be of conspirators, and although it met with a treasonable intent, as an actual levying of war. Without saying that the assemblage must be in force or in warlike form, it expresses itself so as to show that this idea was never discarded; and it uses terms which cannot be otherwise satisfied.

The opinion of a single judge certainly weighs as nothing if opposed to that of the supreme court; but if he were one of the judges who assisted in framing that opinion, if while the impression under which it was framed was yet fresh upon his mind he delivered an opinion on the same testimony, not contradictory to that which had been given by all the judges together, but showing the sense in which he understood terms that might be differently expounded, it may fairly be said to be in some measure explanatory of the opinion itself.

To the judge before whom the charge against the prisoner at the bar was first brought the same testimony was offered with that which had been exhibited before the supreme court; and he was required to give an opinion in almost the same case. Upon this occasion he said "war can only be levied by the employment of actual force. Troops must be embodied, men must be assembled, in order to levy war." Again he observed: "The fact to be proved in this case is an act of public notoriety. It must exist in the view of the world, or it cannot exist at all.

"The assembling of forces to levy war is a visible transaction; and numbers must witness it." It is not easy to doubt what kind of assemblage was in the mind of the judge who used these expressions; and it is to be recollected that he had just returned from the supreme court, and was speaking on the very facts on which the opinion of that court was delivered. The same judge, in his charge to the grand jury who found this bill, observed: "To constitute the fact of levying war it is not necessary that hostilities shall have actually commenced by engaging the military force of the United States, or that measures of violence against the government shall have been carried into execution.

"But levying war is a fact, in the constitution of which force is an indispensable ingredient. Any combination to subvert by force the government of the United States, violently to dismember the Union, to compel a change in the administration, to coerce the repeal or adoption of a general law, is a conspiracy to levy war; and if the conspiracy be carried into effect by the actual employment of force, by the embodying and assembling of men for the purpose of executing the treasonable design which was previously conceived, it amounts to levying of war. It has been held that arms are not essential to levying war, provided the force assembled be sufficient to attain, or, perhaps, to justify attempting the object without them." This paragraph is immediately followed by a reference to the opinion of the supreme court.*

It requires no commentary upon these words to show that, in the opinion of the judge who uttered them, an assemblage of men which should constitute the fact of levying war must be an assemblage in force, and that he so understood the opinion of the supreme court. If in that opinion there may be found in some passages a want of precision, and an indefiniteness of expression, which

* Marshall is referring to his opinion of April 1; cf. Document No. 5.

has occasioned it to be differently understood by different persons, that may well be accounted for when it is recollected that in the particular case there was no assemblage whatever. In expounding that opinion the whole should be taken together, and in reference to the particular case in which it was delivered.

It is, however, not improbable that the misunderstanding has arisen from this circumstance: The court unquestionably did not consider arms as an indispensable requisite to levying war. An assemblage adapted to the object might be in a condition to effect or to attempt it without them. Nor did the court consider the actual application of the force to the object as at all times an indispensable requisite; for an assemblage might be in a condition to apply force, might be in a state adapted to real war, without having made the actual application of that force. From these positions, which are to be found in the opinion, it may have been inferred, it is thought too hastily, that the nature of the assemblage was unimportant, and that war might be considered as actually levied by any meeting of men, if a criminal intention can be imputed to them by testimony of any kind whatever.

Test Applied to Burr Actions

It has been thought proper to discuss this question at large, and to review the opinion of the supreme court, although this court would be more disposed to leave the question of fact, whether an overt act of levying war were committed on Blennerhassett's Island to the jury, under this explanation of the law, and to instruct them that unless the assemblage on Blennerhassett's Island was an assemblage in force, was a military assemblage in a condition to make war, it was not a levying of war, and that they could not construe it into an act of war, than to arrest the further testimony which might be offered to connect the prisoner with that assemblage, or to prove the intention of those who assembled together at that place. This point, however, is not to be understood as decided. It will, perhaps, constitute an essential inquiry in another case.

Before leaving the opinion of the supreme court entirely, on the question of the nature of the assemblage which will constitute an act of levying war, this court cannot forbear to ask, why is an assemblage absolutely required? Is it not to judge in some measure of the end by the proportion which the means bear to the end? Why is it that a single armed individual entering a boat, and sailing down the Ohio for the avowed purpose of attacking New Orleans, could not be said to levy war? Is it not that he is apparently not in a condition to levy war? If this be so, ought not the assemblage to furnish some evidence of its intention and capacity to levy war before it can amount to levying war? And ought not the supreme court, when speaking of an assemblage for the purpose of effecting a treasonable object by force, be understood to indicate an assemblage exhibiting the appearance of force? The definition of the attorney for the United States deserves notice in this respect. It is, "When there is an assemblage of men, convened for the purpose of effecting by force a treasonable object, which force is meant to be employed before the assemblage disperses, this is treason."

To read this definition without adverting to the argument, we should infer that the assemblage was itself to effect by force the treasonable object, not to join itself to some other bodies of men and then to effect the object by their combined force. Under this construction, it would be expected the appearance of the assemblage would bear some proportion to the object, and would indicate the intention; at any rate, that it would be an assemblage in force. This construction is most certainly not that which was intended; but it serves to show that general phrases must always be understood in reference to the subject-matter and to the general principles of law.

Counts in Indictment

On that division of the subject which respects the merits of the case connected with the pleadings, two points are also made: 1st. That this indictment, having charged the prisoner with levying war on Blennerhassett's Island, and containing no other overt act, cannot be supported by proof that war was levied at that place by other persons in the absence of the prisoner, even admitting those persons to be connected with him in one common treasonable conspiracy. 2dly. That admitting such an indictment could be supported by such evidence, the previous conviction of some person, who committed the act which is said to amount to levying war, is indispensable to the conviction of a person who advised or procured that act.

As to the first point, the indictment contains two counts, one of which charges that the prisoner, with a number of persons unknown, levied war on Blennerhassett's Island, in the county of Wood, in the district of Virginia; and the other adds the circumstance of their proceeding from that island down the river for the purpose of seizing New Orleans by force. In point of fact, the prisoner was not on Blennerhassett's Island, nor in the county of Wood, nor in the district of Virginia.

In considering this point, the court is led first to inquire whether an indictment for levying war must specify an overt act, or would be sufficient if it merely charged the prisoner in general terms with having levied war, omitting the expression of place or circumstance. The place in which a crime was committed is essential to an indictment, were it only to show the jurisdiction of the court. It is, also, essential for the purpose of enabling the prisoner to make his defence.

That at common law an indictment would have been defective which did not mention the place in which the crime was committed can scarcely be doubted. This necessity is rendered the stronger by the constitutional provision that the offender "shall be tried in the state and district wherein the crime shall have been committed," and by the act of congress which requires that twelve petit jurors at least shall be summoned from the county where the offence was committed.

A description of the particular manner in which the war was levied seems, also, essential to enable the accused to make his defence. The law does not expect a man to be prepared to defend every act of his life which may be suddenly and without notice alleged against him. In common justice, the particular fact with which he is charged ought to be stated, and stated in such a manner as to afford a reasonable certainty of the nature of the accusation and the circumstances which will be adduced against him. . . .

Liability of Burr

The whole treason laid in this indictment is the levying of war in Blennerhassett's Island; and the whole question to which the inquiry of the court is now directed is whether the prisoner was legally present at that fact. I say this is the whole question; because the prisoner can only be convicted on the overt act laid in the indictment. With respect to this prosecution, it is as if no other overt act existed. If other overt acts can be inquired into, it is for the sole purpose of proving the particular fact charged. It is an evidence of the crime consisting of this particular fact, not as establishing the general crime by a distinct fact.

The counsel for the prosecution have charged those engaged in the defence with considering the overt act as treason, whereas it ought to be considered solely as the evidence of the treason; but the counsel for the prosecution seem themselves not to have sufficiently adverted to this clear principle; that though the overt act may not be itself the treason, it is the sole act of that treason which can produce conviction. It is the sole point in issue between the parties. And the only division of that point, if the expression be allowed, which the court is now examining, is the constructive presence of the prisoner at the fact charged.

To return, then, to the application of the cases. Had the prisoner set out with the party from Beaver for Blennerhassett's Island, or perhaps had he set out for that place, though not from Beaver, and had arrived in the island, he would have been present at the fact. Had he not arrived in the island, but had taken a position near enough to co-operate with those on the island, to assist them in any act of hostility, or to aid them if attacked, the question whether he was constructively present would be a question compounded of law and fact, which would be decided by the jury, with the aid of the court, so far as respected the law.

In this case the accused would have been of the particular party assembled on the island, and would have been associated with them in the particular act of levying war said to have been committed on the island. But if he was not with the party at any time before they reached the island; if he did not join them there, or intend to join them there; if his personal co-operation in the general plan was to be afforded elsewhere, at a great distance, in a different state; if the overt acts of treason to be performed by him were to be distinct overt acts—then he was not of the particular party assembled at Blennerhassett's Island, and was not constructively present, aiding and assisting in the particular act which was there committed.

The testimony on this point, so far as it has been delivered, is not equivocal. There is not only no evidence that the accused was of the particular party which assembled on Blennerhassett's Island, but the whole evidence shows he was not of that party. In felony, then, admitting the crime to have been completed on the island, and to have been advised, procured, or commanded by the accused, he would have been incontestably an accessory and not a principal. But in treason, it is said, the law is otherwise, because the theatre of action is more extensive. The reasoning applies in England as strongly as in the United States. While in '15 and '45 the family of Stuart sought to regain the crown they had forfeited, the struggle was for the whole kingdom, yet no man was ever considered as legally present at one place, when actually at another; or as aiding in one transaction while actually employed in another.

With the perfect knowledge that the whole nation may be the theatre of action, the English books unite in declaring that he who counsels, procures, or aids in treason, is guilty accessorially, and solely in virtue of the common law principle that what will make a man an accessory in felony makes him a principal in treason. So far from considering a man as constructively present at every overt act of the general treason in which he may have been concerned, the whole doctrine of the books limits the proof against him to those particular overt acts of levying war with which he is charged.

What would be the effect of a different doctrine? Clearly that which has been stated. If a person levying war in Kentucky may be said to be constructively present and assembled with a party carrying on war in Virginia at a great distance from him, then he is present at every overt act performed anywhere. He may be tried in any state on the continent, where any overt act has been committed. He may be proved to be guilty of an overt act laid in the indictment in which he had no personal participation, by proving that he advised it, or that he committed other acts. This is, perhaps, too extravagant to be in terms maintained. Certainly it cannot be supported by the doctrines of the English law.

American Precedents

The opinion of Judge Paterson in Mitchell's Case has been cited on this point, 2 Dall. [2 U.S.] 348. The indictment is not specially stated, but from the case as reported, it must have been either general for levying war in the county of Allegany, and the overt act must have been the assemblage of men and levying of war in that county, or it must have given a particular detail of the treasonable transactions in that county.

The first supposition is the most probable, but let the indictment be in the one form or the other, and the result is the same. The facts of the case are that a large body of men, of whom Mitchell was one, assembled at Braddock's field, in the county of Alleghany, for the purpose of committing acts of violence at Pittsburg; that there was also an assemblage at a different time at Couch's fort, at which the prisoner also attended.

The general and avowed object of that meeting was to concert measures for resisting the execution of a public law. At Couch's fort the resolution was taken to attack the house of the inspector, and the body there assembled marched to that house and attacked it. It was proved by the competent number of witnesses that he was at Couch's fort armed; that he offered to reconnoitre the house to be attacked; that he marched with the insurgents towards the house; that he was with them after the action attending the body of one of his comrades who was killed in it. One witness swore positively that he was present at the burning of the house; and a second witness said that "it run in his head that he had seen him there." That a doubt should exist in such a case as this is strong evidence of the necessity that the overt act should be unequivocally proved by two witnesses.

But what was the opinion of the judge in this case? Couch's fort and Neville's house being in the same county, the assemblage having been at Couch's fort, and the resolution to attack the house having been there taken, the body having for the avowed purpose moved in execution of that resolution towards the house to be attacked, he inclined to think that the act of marching was in itself levying war. If it was, then the overt act laid in the indictment was consummated by the assemblage at Couch's and the marching from thence; and Mitchell was proved to be guilty by more than two positive witnesses.

But without deciding this to be the law, he proceeded to consider the meeting at Couch's, the immediate marching to Neville's house, and the attack and burning of the house, as one transaction. Mitchell was proved by more than two positive witnesses to have been in that transaction, to have taken an active part in it; and the judge declared it to be unnecessary that all should have seen him at the same time and place. But suppose not a single witness had proved Mitchell to have been at Couch's, on on the march, or at Neville's.

Suppose he had been at the time notoriously absent in a different state. Can it be believed by any person who observes the caution with which Judge Paterson required the constitutional proof of two witnesses to the same overt act, that he would have said Mitchell was constructively present, and might, on that straining of a legal fiction, be found guilty of treason? Had he delivered such an opinion, what would have been the language of this country respecting it? Had he given this opinion, it would have required all the correctness of his life to strike his name from that bloody list in which the name of Jeffreys is enrolled.

But to estimate the opinion in Mitchell's Case, let its circumstances be transferred to Burr's Case. Suppose the body of men assembled in Blennerhassett's Island had previously met at some other place in the same county; that Burr had been proved to be with them by four witnesses; that the resolution to march to Blennerhassett's Island for a treasonable purpose had been there taken; that he had been seen on the march with them; that one witness had seen him on the island; that another thought he had seen him there; that he had been seen with the party directly after leaving the island; that this indictment had charged the levying of war in Wood county generally—the cases would, then, have been precisely parallel; and the decision would have been the same. In conformity with principle and with authority, then, the prisoner at the bar was neither legally nor actually present at Blennerhassett's Island; and the court is strongly inclined to the opinion that without proving an actual or legal presence by two witnesses, the overt act laid in this indictment cannot be proved.

Actual Presence of Burr

But this opinion is controverted on two grounds: The first is, that the indictment does not charge the prisoner to have been present. The second, that although he was absent, yet if he caused the assemblage, he may be indicted as being present, and convicted on evidence that he caused the treasonable act. The first position is to be decided by the indictment itself. The court understands the allegation differently from the attorney for the United States.

The court understands it to be directly charged that the prisoner did assemble with the multitude, and did march with them. Nothing will more clearly test this construction than putting the case into a shape which it may possibly take. Suppose the law be that the indictment would be defective unless it alleged the presence of the person indicted at the act of treason.

If, upon a special verdict, facts should be found which amounted to a levying of war by the accused, and his counsel should insist that he could not be condemned because the indictment was defective in not charging that he was himself one of the assemblage which constituted the treason, or because it alleged the procurement defectively, would the attorney admit this construction of his indictment to be correct? I am persuaded he would not, and that he ought not to make such a concession.

If, after a verdict, the indictment ought to be construed to allege that the prisoner was one of the assemblage at Blennerhassett's Island, it ought to be so construed now. But this is unimportant; for if the indictment alleges that the prisoner procured the assemblage, that procurement becomes part of the overt act, and must be proved, as will be shown hereafter. . . .

Constructive Presence

But suppose the law to be as is contended by the counsel for the United States. Suppose an indictment charging an individual with personally assembling among others, and thus levying war, may be satisfied with the proof that he caused the assemblage. What effect will this law have upon this case? The guilt of the accused, if there be any guilt, does not consist in the assemblage, for he was not a member of it.

The simple fact of assemblage no more affects one absent man than another. His guilt, then, consists in procuring the assemblage, and upon this fact depends his criminality. The proof relative to the character of an assemblage must be the same whether a man be present or absent. In the general, to charge any individual with the guilt of an assemblage, the fact of his presence must be proved; it constitutes an essential part of the overt act.

If, then, the procurement be substituted in the place of presence, does it not also constitute an essential part of the overt act? Must it not also be proved? Must it not be proved in the same manner that presence must be proved? If in one case the presence of the individual make the guilt of the assemblage his guilt, and in the other case the procurement by the individual make the guilt of the assemblage his guilt, then presence and procurement are equally component parts of the overt act, and equally require two witnesses.

Collateral points may, say the books, be proved according to the course of the common law; but is this a collateral point? Is the fact, without which the accused does not participate in the guilt of the assemblage if it was guilty, a collateral point? This cannot be.

The presence of the party, where presence is necessary, being a part of the overt act, must be positively proved by two witnesses. No presumptive evidence, no facts from which presence may be conjectured or inferred, will satisfy the constitution and the law. If procurement take the place of presence and become part of the overt act, then no presumptive evidence, no facts from which the procurement may be conjectured or inferred, can satisfy the constitution and the law.

The mind is not to be led to the conclusion that the individual was present by a train of conjectures, of inferences, or of reasoning; the fact must be proved by two witnesses. Neither, where procurement supplies the want of presence, is the mind to be conducted to the conclusion that the accused procured the assembly by a train of conjectures or inferences, or of reasoning; the fact itself must be proved by two witnesses, and must have been committed within the district.

If it be said that the advising or procurement of treason is a secret transaction, which can scarcely ever be proved in the manner required by this opinion, the answer which will readily suggest itself is, that the difficulty of proving a fact will not justify conviction without proof. Certainly it will not justify conviction without a direct and positive witness in a case where the constitution requires two. The more correct inference from this circumstance would seem to be, that the advising of the fact is not within the constitutional definition of the crime.

To advise or procure a treason is in the nature of conspiring or plotting treason, which is not treason in itself. If, then, the doctrines of Keyling, Hale, and East,* be understood in the sense in which they are pressed by the counsel for the prosecution, and are applicable in the United States, the fact that the accused procured the assemblage on Blennerhassett's Island must be proved, not circumstantially, but positively, by two witnesses, to charge him with that assemblage. But there are still other most important considerations which must be well weighed before this doctrine can be applied to the United States.

Sixth Amendment

The [6th] amendment to the constitution has been pressed with great force, and it is impossible not to feel its application to this point. The accused cannot be said to be "informed of the nature and cause of the accusation" unless the indictment give him that notice which may reasonably suggest to him the point on which the accusation turns, so that he may know the course to be pursued in his defence.

It is also well worthy of consideration, that this doctrine, so far as it respects treason, is entirely supported by the operation of the common law, which is said to convert the accessory before the fact into the principal, and to make the act of the principal his act. The accessory before the fact is not said to have levied war. He is not said to be guilty under the statute, but the common law

---

* Sir Edward East, *Treatise on the Pleas of the Crown, etc.* (London, 2 vol., 1803; Philadelphia, 1806); Matthew Hale, *History of the Pleas of the Crown* (London, 2 vol., 1736–39); John Keyling, *A Report of Divers Cases in Pleas of the Crown, etc.* (London, 1708).

attaches to him the guilt of that fact which he has advised or procured; and, as contended, makes it his act.

This is the operation of the common law, not the operation of the statute. It is an operation, then, which can only be performed where the common law exists to perform it. It is the creature of the common law, and the creature presupposes its creator. To decide, then, that this doctrine is applicable to the United States would seem to imply the decision that the United States, as a nation, have a common law which creates and defines the punishment of crimes accessorial in their nature.

It would imply the further decision that these accessorial crimes are not, in the case of treason, excluded by the definition of treason given in the constitution. I will not pretend that I have not individually an opinion on these points; but it is one which I should give only in a case which absolutely required it, unless I could confer respecting it with the judges of the supreme court.*

I have said that this doctrine cannot apply to the United States without implying those decisions respecting the common law which I have stated; because, should it be true, as is contended, that the constitutional definition of treason comprehends him who advises or procures an assemblage that levies war, it would not follow that such adviser or procurer might be charged as having been present at the assemblage.

If the adviser or procurer be within the definition of levying war, and, independent of the agency of the common law, do actually levy war, then the advisement or procurement is an overt act of levying war. If it be the overt act on which he is to be convicted, then it must be charged in the indictment; for he can only be convicted on proof of the overt acts which are charged.

To render this distinction more intelligible, let it be recollected that, although it should be conceded that since the statute of William and Mary he who advises or procures a treason may, in England, be charged as having committed that treason, by virtue of the common law operation, which is said, so far as respects the indictment, to unite the accessorial to the principal offence and permit them to be charged as one, yet it can never be conceded that he who commits one overt act under the statute of Edward can be charged and convicted on proof of another overt act. If, then, procurement be an overt act of treason under the constitution, no man can be convicted for the procurement under an indictment charging him with actually assembling, whatever may be the doctrine of the common law in the case of an accessorial offender.†

* Cf. the 1812 opinion on federal criminal jurisdiction, in *United States* v. *Hudson & Goodwin*, 11 U.S. 32.

† 25 Edw. III, Stat. 5, Ch. 2 (1350) asserted the Crown's prerogative in defining the act of treason. It was mitigated in 1695 by the Treason Act, which, despite its merging of accessory and principal, provided essentially the same definition of treason, and established the same requirements of proof, as the Constitution. Early American state laws "received" the common law as of 1606, thus carrying into their own rules of decision the 1305 statute but not the statute of 1695. The Federal Constitution thus became the authority for mitigating the medieval statute.

Mere Assembly Not Overt Act

It may not be improper in this place again to advert to the opinion of the supreme court, and to show that it contains nothing contrary to the doctrine now laid down. That opinion is, that an individual may be guilty of treason "who has not appeared in arms against his country; that if war be actually levied, that is, if a body of men be actually assembled for the purpose of effecting by force a treasonable object, all those who perform any part, however minute, or however remote from the scene of action, and who are actually leagued in the general conspiracy, are to be considered as traitors."

This opinion does not touch the case of a person who advises or procures an assemblage, and does nothing further. The advising, certainly, and perhaps the procuring, is more in the nature of a conspiracy to levy war than of the actual levying of war. According to the opinion, it is not enough to be leagued in the conspiracy, and that war be levied, but it is also necessary to perform a part: that part is the act of levying war.

That part, it is true, may be minute, it may not be the actual appearance in arms, and it may be remote from the scene of action, that is, from the place where the army is assembled; but it must be a part, and that part must be performed by a person who is leagued in the conspiracy. This part, however minute or remote, constitutes the overt act of which alone the person who performs it can be convicted.

The opinion does not declare that the person who has performed this remote and minute part may be indicted for a part which was, in truth, performed by others, and convicted on their overt acts. It amounts to this and nothing more, that when war is actually levied, not only those who bear arms, but those also who are leagued in the conspiracy, and who perform the various distinct parts which are necessary for the prosecution of war, do, in the sense of the constitution, levy war. It may possibly be the opinion of the supreme court that those who procure a treason and do nothing further are guilty under the constitution. I only say that opinion has not yet been given, still less has it been indicated that he who advises shall be indicted as having performed the fact.

Opinion of Applicable Law

It is, then, the opinion of the court that this indictment can be supported only by testimony which proves the accused to have been actually or constructively present when the assemblage took place on Blennerhassett's Island; or by the admission of the doctrine that he who procures an act may be indicted as having performed that act.

It is further the opinion of the court that there is no testimony whatever which tends to prove that the accused was actually or constructively present when that assemblage did take place; indeed, the contrary is most apparent. With respect to admitting proof of procurement to establish a charge of actual presence, the court is of opinion that if this be admissible in England on an indictment for levying war, which is far from being conceded, it is admissible only by virtue of the operation of the common law upon the statute, and therefore is not admissible in this country unless by virtue of a similar operation—a point far from being established, but on which, for the present, no opinion is given. If, however, this point be established, still the procurement must be proved in the same manner and by the same kind of testimony which would be required to prove actual presence.

Conviction of Another Party

The second point in this division of the subject is the necessity of adducing the record of the previous conviction of some one person who committed the fact alleged to be treasonable. This point presupposes the treason of the accused, if any have been committed, to be accessorial in its nature. Its being of this description, according to the British authorities, depends on the presence or absence of the accused at the time the fact was committed.

The doctrine on this subject is well understood, has been most copiously explained, and need not be repeated. That there is no evidence of his actual or legal presence is a point already discussed and decided. It is, then, apparent that but for the exception to the general principle which is made in cases of treason, those who assembled at Blennerhassett's Island, if that assemblage were such as to constitute the crime, would be principals, and those who might really have caused that assemblage, although in truth the chief traitors, would in law be accessories.

It is a settled principle in the law that the accessory cannot be guilty of a greater offence than his principal. The maxim is "Accessorius sequitur naturam sui principalis"—"The accessory follows the nature of his principal." Hence results the necessity of establishing the guilt of the principal before the accessory can be tried; for the degree of guilt which is incurred by counselling or commanding the commission of a crime depends upon the actual commission of that crime.

No man is an accessory to murder unless the fact has been committed. The fact can only be established in a prosecution against the person by whom a crime has been perpetrated. The law supposes a man more capable of defending his own conduct than any other person, and will not tolerate that the guilt of A shall be established in a prosecution against B. Consequently, if the guilt of B depends on the guilt of A, A must be convicted before B can be tried. It would exhibit a monstrous deformity indeed in our system, if B might be executed for being accessory to a murder committed by A, and A should afterwards, upon a full trial, be acquitted of the fact.

For this obvious reason, although the punishment of a principal and accessory was originally the same, and although in many instances it is still the same, the accessory could in no case be tried before the conviction of his principal, nor can he yet be tried previous to such conviction, unless he require it, or unless a special provision to that effect be made by statute. If, then, this were a felony, the prisoner at the bar could not be tried until the crime were established by the conviction of the person by whom it was actually perpetrated.

Is the law otherwise in this case, because in treason all are principals? Let this question be answered by reason and by authority. Why is it that in felonies, however atrocious, the trial of the accessory can never precede the conviction of the principal? Not because the one is denominated the principal and the other the accessory; for that would be ground on which a great law principle could never stand. Not because there was, in fact, a difference in the degree of moral guilt; for in the case of murder committed by a hardy villain for a bribe, the person plotting the murder and giving the bribe is, perhaps, of the two, the blacker criminal; and were it otherwise, this would furnish no argument for precedence in trial.

What, then, is the reason? It has been already given. The legal guilt of the accessory depends on the guilt of the principal; and the guilt of the principal can only be established in a prosecution against himself. Does not this reason apply in full force to a case of treason? The legal guilt of the person who planned the assemblage on Blennerhassett's Island depends not simply on the criminality of the previous conspiracy, but on the criminality of that asemblage. If those who perpetrated the fact be not traitors, he who advised the fact cannot be a traitor. His guilt, then, in contemplation of law, depends on theirs; and their guilt can only be established in a prosecution against themselves.

Whether the adviser of this assemblage be punishable with death as a principal or as an accessory, his liability to punishment depends on the degree of guilt attached to an act which has been perpetrated by others; and which, if it be a criminal act, renders them guilty also. His guilt, therefore, depends on theirs; and their guilt cannot be legally established in a prosecution against him.

Principal and Accessory

The whole reason of the law, then, relative to the principal and accessory, so far as respects the order of trial, seems to apply in full force to a case of treason committed by one body of men in conspiracy with others who are absent. If from reason we pass to authority, we find it laid down by Hale, Foster, and East, in the most explicit terms, that the conviction of some one who has committed the treason must precede the trial of him who has advised or procured it. . . .

These authorities have been read and commented on at such length that it cannot be necessary for the court to bring them again into view. It is the less necessary because it is not understood that the law is controverted by the counsel for the United States. It is, however, contended that the prisoner has waived his right to demand the conviction of some one person who was present at the fact, by pleading to his indictment.

Had this indictment even charged the prisoner according to the truth of the case, the court would feel some difficulty in deciding that he had, by implication, waived his right to demand a species of testimony essential to his conviction. The court is not prepared to say that the act which is to operate against his rights did not require that it should be performed with a full knowledge of its operation. It would seem consonant to the usual course of proceeding in other respects in criminal cases, that the prisoner should be informed that he had a right to refuse to be tried until some person who committed the act should be convicted; and that he ought not to be considered as waiving the right to demand the record of conviction, unless with the full knowledge of that right he consented to be tried.

The court, however, does not decide what the law would be in such a case. It is unnecessary to decide it; because pleading to an indictment, in which a man is charged as having committed an act, cannot be construed to waive a right which he would have possessed had he been charged with having advised the act. No person indicted as a principal can be expected to say, "I am not a principal. I am an accessory. I did not commit, I only advised the act."

The authority of the English cases on this subject depends, in a great measure, on the adoption of the common law doctrine of accessorial treasons. If that doctrine be excluded, this branch of it may not be directly applicable to treasons committed within the United States. If the crime of advising or procuring a levying of war be within the constitutional definition of treason, then he who advises or procures it must be indicted on the very fact; and the question whether the treasonableness of the act may be decided in the first instance in the trial of him who procured it, or must be decided in the trial of one who committed it, will depend upon the reason, as it respects the law of evidence, which produced the British decisions with regard to the trial of principal and accessory, rather than on the positive authority of those decisions. This question is not essential in the present case; because if the crime be within the constitutional definition, it is an overt act of levying war, and, to produce a conviction, ought to have been charged in the indictment.

Appropriate Tribunal

The law of the case being thus far settled, what ought to be the decision of the court on the present motion? Ought the court to sit and hear testimony which cannot affect the prisoner, or ought the court to arrest that testimony? On this question much has been said—much that may perhaps be ascribed to a misconception of the point really under consideration. The motion has been treated as a motion confessedly made to stop irrelevant testimony; and, in the course of the argument, it has been repeatedly stated, by those who oppose the motion, that irrevelant testimony may and ought to be stopped.

That this statement is perfectly correct is one of those fundamental principles in judicial proceedings which is acknowledged by all, and is founded in the absolute necessity of the thing. No person will contend that, in a civil or criminal case, either party is at liberty to introduce what testimony he pleases, legal or illegal, and to consume the whole term in details of facts unconnected with the particular case. Some tribunal, then, must decide on the admissibility of testimony. The parties cannot constitute this tribunal; for they do not agree. The jury cannot constitute it; for the question is whether they shall hear the testimony or not.

Who, then, but the court can constitute it? It is of necessity the peculiar province of the court to judge of the admissibility of testimony. If the court admit improper or reject proper testimony, it is an error of judgment; but it is an error committed in the direct exercise of their judicial functions. The present indictment charges the prisoner with levying war against the United States, and alleges an overt act of levying war. That overt act must be proved, according to the mandates of the constitution and of the act of congress, by two witnesses. It is not proved by a single witness.

The presence of the accused has been stated to be an essential component part of the overt act in this indictment, unless the common law principle respecting accessories should render it unnecessary; and there is not only no witness who has proved his actual or legal presence, but the fact of his absence is not controverted. The counsel for the prosecution offer to give in evidence subsequent transactions at a different place and in a different state, in order to prove—what? The overt act laid in the indictment? That the prisoner was one of those who assembled at Blennerhassett's Island? No: that is not alleged.

It is well known that such testimony is not competent to establish such a fact. The constitution and law require that the fact should be established by two witnesses; not by the establishment of other facts from which the jury might reason to this fact. The testimony, then, is not relevant. If it can be introduced, it is only in the character of corroborative or confirmatory testimony, after the overt act has been proved by two witnesses in such manner that the question of fact ought to be left with the jury.

The conclusion that in this state of things no testimony can be admissible is so inevitable that the counsel for the United States could not resist it. I do not understand them to deny that, if the overt act be not proved by two witnesses so as to be submitted to the jury, all other testimony must be irrelevant; because no other testimony can prove the act. Now, an assemblage on Blennerhassett's Island is proved by the requisite number of witnesses; and the court might submit it to the jury whether that assemblage amounted to a levying of war; but the presence of the accused at that assemblage being nowhere alleged except in the indictment, the overt act is not proved by a single witness; and, of consequence, all other testimony must be irrelevant.

The only difference between this motion as made, and the motion in the form which the counsel for the United States would admit to be regular, is this: It is now general for the rejection of all testimony. It might be particular with respect to each witness as adduced. But can this be wished, or can it be deemed necessary? If enough be proved to show that the indictment cannot be supported, and that no testimony, unless it be of that description which the attorney for the United States declares himself not to possess, can be relevant, why should a question be taken on each witness?

The opinion of this court on the order of testimony has frequently been adverted to as deciding this question against the motion. If a contradiction between the two opinions exist, the court cannot perceive it. It was said that levying war is an act compounded of law and fact, of which the jury, aided by the court, must judge. To that declaration the court still adheres. It was said that if the overt act were not proved by two witnesses, no testimony in its nature corroborative or confirmatory was admissible, or could be relevant.

From that declaration there is certainly no departure. It has been asked, in allusion to the present case, if a general commanding an army should detach troops for a distant service, would the men composing that detachment be traitors, and would the commander-in-chief escape punishment? Let the opinion which has been given answer this question. Appearing at the head of an army would, according to this opinion, be an overt act of levying war. Detaching a military corps from it for military purposes might, also, be an overt act of levying war. It is not pretended that he would not be punishable for these acts. It is only said that he may be tried and convicted on his own acts in the state where those acts were committed, not on the acts of others in the state where those others acted.

Notice of Popular Excitement

Much has been said in the course of the argument on points on which the court feels no inclination to comment particularly; but which may, perhaps not improperly, receive some notice. That this court dares not usurp power is most true. That this court dares not shrink from its duty is not less true. No man is desirous of placing himself in a disagreeable situation. No man is desirous of becoming the peculiar subject of calumny. No man, might he let the bitter cup pass from him without self-reproach, would drain it to the bottom. But if he have no choice in the case, if there be no alternative presented to him but a dereliction of duty or the opprobrium of those who are denominated the world, he merits the contempt as well as the indignation of his country who can hesitate which to embrace.

That gentlemen, in a case the most interesting, in the zeal with which they advocate particular opinions, and under the conviction in some measure produced by that zeal, should, on each side, press their arguments too far, should be impatient at any deliberation in the court, and should suspect or fear the operation of motives to which alone they can ascribe that deliberation, is, perhaps, a frailty incident to human nature; but if any conduct on the part of the court could warrant a sentiment that it would deviate to the one side or the other from the line prescribed by duty and by law, that conduct would be viewed by the judges themselves with an eye of extreme severity, and would long be recollected with deep and serious regret.

The arguments on both sides have been intently and deliberately considered. Those which could not be noticed, since to notice every argument and authority would swell this opinion to a volume, have not been disregarded. The result of the whole is a conviction, as complete as the mind of the court is capable of receiving on a complex subject, that the motion must prevail. No testimony relative to the conduct or declarations of the prisoner elsewhere, and subsequent to the transaction on Blennerhassett's Island, can be admitted; because such testimony, being in its nature merely corroborative and incompetent to prove the overt act in itself, is irrelevant until there be proof of the overt act by two witnesses. This opinion does not comprehend the proof by two witnesses that the meeting on Blennerhassett's Island was procured by the prisoner. On that point the court for the present withholds its opinion for reasons which have been already assigned; and as it is understood from the statements made on the part of the prosecution that no such testimony exists, if there be such let it be offered, and the court will decide upon it.

The jury have now heard the opinion of the court on the law of the case. They will apply that law to the facts, and will find a verdict of guilty or not guilty as their own consciences may direct.

III

Trustees of Dartmouth College
v. Woodward

1. *Judiciary Act of September 24, 1789* (Section 25)
   1 Stat., Ch. 20, pp. 85–87.

SEC. 25. And be it further enacted, **That a final judgment or decree in any suit, in the highest court of law or equity of a State in which a decision in the suit could be had,** where is drawn in question the validity of a treaty or statute of, or an authority exercised under the United States, and the decision is against their validity; or **where is drawn in question the validity of a statute of, or an authority exercised under any State, on the ground of their being repugnant to the constitution,** treaties or laws **of the United States, and the decision is in favour of such their validity,** or where is drawn in question the construction of any clause of the constitution, or of a treaty, or statute of, or commission held under the United States, and the decision is against the title, right, privilege or exemption specially set up or claimed by either party, under such clause of the said Constitution, treaty, statute or commission, **may be re-examined and reversed or affirmed in the Supreme Court of the United States upon a writ of error,** the citation being signed by the chief justice, or judge or chancellor of the court rendering or passing the judgment or decree complained of, or by a justice of the Supreme Court of the United States, in the same manner and under the same regulations, and the writ shall have the same effect, as if the judgment or decree complained of had been rendered or passed in a circuit court, and the proceeding upon the reversal shall also be the same, except that the Supreme Court, instead of remanding the cause for a final decision as before provided, may at their discretion, if the cause shall have been once remanded before, proceed to a final decision of the same, and award execution. But no other error shall be assigned or regarded as a ground of reversal in any such case as aforesaid, than such as appears on the face of the record, and immediately respects the before mentioned questions of validity or construction of the said constitution, treaties, statutes, commissions, or authorities in dispute.

2. *Fletcher* v. *Peck*

7 Cranch 126 (1810)

MARSHALL, CH. J.—The pleadings being now amended, this cause comes on again to be heard on sundry demurrers, and on a special verdict.

The suit was instituted on several covenants contained in a deed made by John Peck, the defendant in error, conveying to Robert Fletcher, the plaintiff in error, certain lands which were part of a large purchase made by James Gunn and others, in the year 1795, from the state of Georgia, the contract for which was made in the form of a bill passed by the legislature of that state.

The first count in the declaration set forth a breach in the second covenant contained in the deed. The covenant is, "that the legislature of the state of Georgia, at the time of passing the act of sale aforesaid, had good right to sell and dispose of the same, in manner pointed out by the said act." The breach assigned is, that the legislature had no power to sell. The plea in bar sets forth the constitution of the state of Georgia, and avers that the lands sold by the defendant to the plaintiff, were within that state. It then sets forth the granting act, and avers the power of the legislature to sell and dispose of the premises as pointed out by the act. To this plea, the plaintiff below demurred, and the defendant joined in demurrer.

That the legislature of Georgia, unless restrained by its own constitution, possesses the power of disposing of the unappropriated lands within its own limits, in such manner as its own judgment shall dictate, is a proposition not to be controverted. The only question, then, presented by this demurrer, for the consideration of the court, is this, did the then constitution of the state of Georgia prohibit the legislature to dispose of the lands, which were the subject of this contract, in the manner stipulated by the contract?

The question, whether a law be void for its repugnancy to the constitution, is, at all times, a question of much delicacy, which ought seldom, if ever, to be decided in the affirmative, in a doubtful case. The court, when impelled by duty to render such a judgment, would be unworthy of its station, could it be unmindful of the solemn obligations which that station imposes. But it is not on slight implication and vague conjecture, that the legislature is to be pronounced to have transcended its powers, and its acts to be considered as void. The opposition between the constitution and the law should be such that the judge feels a clear and strong conviction of their incompatibility with each other. In this case, the court can perceive no such opposition. In the constitution of Georgia, adopted in the year 1789, the court can perceive no restriction on the legislative power, which inhibits the passage of the act of 1795. The court cannot say that, in passing that act, the legislature has transcended its powers, and violated the constitution. In overruling the demurrer, therefore, to the first plea, the circuit court committed no error.

The 3d covenant is, that all the title which the state of Georgia ever had in the premises had been legally conveyed to John Peck, the grantor. The 2d count assigns, in substance, as a breach of this covenant, that the original grantees from the state of Georgia promised and assured divers members of the legislature, then sitting in general assembly, that if the said members would assent to, and vote for, the passing of the act, and if the said bill should pass, such members should have a share of, and be interested in, all the lands purchased from the said state by virtue of such law. And that divers of the said members, to whom the said promises were made, were unduly influenced thereby, and under such influence, did vote for the passing of the said bill; by reason whereof, the said law was a nullity, &c., and so the title of the state of Georgia did not pass to the said Peck, &c. The plea to this count, after protesting that the promises it alleges were not made, avers, that until after the purchase made from the original grantees by James Greenleaf, under whom the said Peck claims, neither the said James Greenleaf, nor the said Peck, nor any of the mesne vendors between the said Greenleaf and Peck, had any notice or knowledge that any such promises or assurances were made by the said original grantees, or either of them, to any members of the legislature of the state of Georgia. To this plea, the plaintiff demurred generally, and the defendant joined in the demurrer.

Corruption in Legislature

That corruption should find its way into the governments of our infant republics, and contaminate the very source of legislation, or that impure motives should contribute to the passage of a law, or the formation of a legislative contract, are circumstances most deeply to be deplored. How far a court of justice would, in any case, be competent, on proceedings instituted by the state itself, to vacate a contract thus formed, and to annul rights acquired, under that contract, by third persons having no notice of the improper means by which it was obtained, is a question which the court would approach with much circumspection. It may well be doubted, how far the validity of a law depends upon the motives of its framers, and how far the particular inducements, operating on members of the supreme sovereign power of a state, to the formation of a contract by that power, are examinable in a court of justice. If the principle be conceded, that an act of the supreme sovereign power might be declared null by a court, in consequence of the means which procured it, still would there be much difficulty in saying to what extent those means must be applied to produce this effect. Must it be direct corruption? or would interest or undue influence of any kind be sufficient? Must the vitiating cause operate on a majority? or on what number of the members? Would the act be null, whatever might be the wish of the nation? or would its obligation or nullity depend upon the public sentiment? If the majority of the legislature be corrupted, it may well be doubted, whether it be within the province of the judiciary to control their conduct, and, if less than a majority act from impure motives, the principle by which judicial interference would be regulated, is not clearly discerned. Whatever difficulties this subject might present, when viewed under aspects of which it may be susceptible, this court can perceive none in the particular pleadings now under consideration.

This is not a bill brought by the state of Georgia, to annul the contract, nor does it appear to the court, by this count, that the state of Georgia is dissatisfied with the sale that has been made. The case, as made out in the pleadings, is simply this: One individual who holds lands in the state of Georgia, under a deed covenanting that the title of Georgia was in the grantor, brings an action of covenant upon this deed, and assigns, as a breach, that some of the members of the legislature were induced to vote in favor of the law, which constituted the contract, by being promised an interest in it, and that, therefore, the act is a mere nullity. This solemn question cannot be brought thus collaterally and inci- dentally before the court. It would be indecent, in the extreme, upon a private contract, between two individuals, to enter into an inquiry respecting the cor- ruption of the sovereign power of a state. If the title be plainly deduced from a legislative act, which the legislature might constitutionally pass, if the act be clothed with all the requisite forms of a law, a court, sitting as a court of law, cannot sustain a suit brought by one individual against another, founded on the allegation that the act is a nullity, in consequence of the impure motives which influenced certain members of the legislature which passed the law. The circuit court, therefore, did right in overruling this demurrer.

The 4th covenant in the deed is, that the title to the premises has been, in no way, constitutionally or legally impaired, by virtue of any subsequent act of any subsequent legislature of the state of Georgia. The third count recites the undue means practised on certain members of the legislature, as stated in the second count, and then alleges that, in consequence of these practices, and of other causes, a subsequent legislature passed an act annulling and rescinding the law under which the conveyance to the original grantees was made, declaring that conveyance void, and asserting the title of the state to the lands it con- tained. The count proceeds to recite at large, this rescinding act, and concludes with averring that, by reason of this act, the title of the said Peck in the premises was constitutionally and legally impaired, and rendered null and void. After protesting, as before, that no such promises were made as stated in this count, the defendant again pleads that himself and the first purchaser under the origi- nal grantees, and all intermediate holders of the property, were purchasers with- out notice. To this plea, there is a demurrer and joinder.

The importance and the difficulty of the questions, presented by these plead- ings, are deeply felt by the court. The lands in controversy vested absolutely in James Gunn and others, the original grantees, by the conveyance of the gover- nor, made in pursuance of an act of assembly, to which the legislature was fully competent. Being thus in full possession of the legal estate, they, for a valuable consideration, conveyed portions of the land to those who were willing to pur- chase. If the original transaction was infected with fraud, these purchasers did not participate in it, and had no notice of it. They were innocent. Yet the legis- lature of Georgia has involved them in the fate of the first parties to the trans- action, and, if the act be valid, has annihilated their rights also. The legislature of Georgia was a party to this transaction; and for a party to pronounce its own deed invalid, whatever cause may be assigned for its invalidity, must be con- sidered as a mere act of power, which must find its vindication in a train of reasoning not often heard in courts of justice.

Plea in Mitigation

But the real party, it is said, are the people, and when their agents are un- faithful, the acts of those agents cease to be obligatory. It is, however, to be recollected, that the people can act only by these agents, and that, while within the powers conferred on them, their acts must be considered as the acts of the people. If the agents be corrupt, others may be chosen, and, if their contracts be examinable, the common sentiment, as well as common usage of mankind, points out a mode by which this examination may be made, and their validity determined.

If the legislature of Georgia was not bound to submit its pretensions to those tribunals which are established for the security of property, and to decide on human rights, if it might claim to itself the power of judging in its own case, yet there are certain great principles of justice, whose authority is universally acknowledged, that ought not to be entirely disregarded. If the legislature be its own judge in its own case, it would seem equitable, that its decision should be regulated by those rules which would have regulated the decision of a judicial tribunal. The question was, in its nature, a question of title, and the tribunal which decided it was either acting in the character of a court of justice, and performing a duty usually assigned to a court, or it was exerting a mere act of power in which it was controlled only by its own will.

If a suit be brought to set aside a conveyance obtained by fraud, and the fraud be clearly proved, the conveyance will be set aside, as between the parties; but the rights of third persons, who are purchasers without notice, for a valuable consideration, cannot be disregarded. Titles which, according to every legal test, are perfect, are acquired with that confidence which is inspired by the opinion that the purchaser is safe. If there be any concealed defect, arising from the conduct of those who had held the property long before he acquired it, of which he had no notice, that concealed defect cannot be set up against him. He has paid his money for a title good at law, he is innocent, whatever may be the guilt of others, and equity will not subject him to the penalties attached to that guilt. All titles would be insecure, and the intercourse between man and man would be very seriously obstructed, if this principle be overturned. A court of chancery, therefore, had a bill been brought to set aside the conveyance made to James Gunn and others, as being obtained by improper practices with the legislature, whatever might have been its decision as respected the original grantees, would have been bound, by its own rules, and by the clearest principles of equity, to leave unmolested those who were purchasers, without notice, for a valuable consideration.

If the legislature felt itself absolved from those rules of property which are common to all the citizens of the United States, and from those principles of equity which are acknowledged in all our courts, its act is to be supported by its power alone, and the same power may divest any other individual of his lands, if it shall be the will of the legislature so to exert it.

Offsetting Considerations

It is not intended to speak with disrespect of the legislature of Georgia, or of its acts. Far from it. The question is a general question, and is treated as one. For although such powerful objections to a legislative grant, as are alleged against this, may not again exist, yet the principle, on which alone this rescinding act is to be supported, may be applied to every case to which it shall be the will of any legislature to apply it. The principle is this: that a legislature may, by its own act, divest the vested estate of any man whatever, for reasons which shall, by itself, be deemed sufficient.

In this case, the legislature may have had ample proof that the original grant was obtained by practices which can never be too much reprobated, and which would have justified its abrogation, so far as respected those to whom crime was imputable. But the grant, when issued, conveyed an estate in fee-simple to the grantee, clothed with all the solemnities which law can bestow. This estate was transferrable; and those who purchased parts of it were not stained by that guilt which infected the original transaction. Their case is not distinguishable from the ordinary case of purchasers of a legal estate, without knowledge of any secret fraud which might have led to the emanation of the original grant. According to the well-known course of equity, their rights could not be affected by such fraud. Their situation was the same, their title was the same, with that of every other member of the community who holds land by regular conveyances from the original patentee.

Is the power of the legislature competent to the annihilation of such title, and to a resumption of the property thus held? The principle asserted is, that one legislature is competent to repeal any act which a former legislature was competent to pass; and that one legislature cannot abridge the powers of a succeeding legislature. The correctness of this principle, so far as respects general legislation, can never be controverted. But, if an act be done under a law, a succeeding legislature cannot undo it. The past cannot be recalled by the most absolute power. Conveyances have been made, those conveyances have vested legal estates, and, if those estates may be seized by the sovereign authority, still, that they originally vested is a fact, and cannot cease to be a fact. When, then, a law is in its nature a contract, when absolute rights have vested under that contract, a repeal of the law cannot divest those rights; and the act of annulling them, if legitimate, is rendered so by a power applicable to the case of every individual in the community.

It may well be doubted, whether the nature of society and of government does not prescribe some limits to the legislative power; and if any be prescribed, where are they to be found, if the property of an individual, fairly and honestly acquired, may be seized without compensation? To the legislature, all legislative power is granted; but the question, whether the act of transferring the property of an individual to the public, be in the nature of the legislative power, is well worthy of serious reflection. It is the peculiar province of the legislature, to prescribe general rules for the government of society; the application of those rules to individuals in society would seem to be the duty of other departments. How far the power of giving the law may involve every other power, in cases where the constitution is silent, never has been, and perhaps never can be, definitely stated.

Restraints of Constitution

The validity of this rescinding act, then, might well be doubted, were Georgia a single sovereign power. But Georgia cannot be viewed as a single, unconnected, sovereign power, on whose legislature no other restrictions are imposed than may be found in its own constitution. She is a part of a large empire; she is a member of the American union; and that union has a constitution, the supremacy of which all acknowledge, and which imposes limits to the legislatures of the several states, which none claim a right to pass. The constitution of the United States declares that no state shall pass any bill of attainder, *ex post facto* law, or law impairing the obligation of contracts.

Does the case now under consideration come within this prohibitory section of the constitution? In considering this very interesting question, we immediately ask ourselves, what is a contract? Is a grant a contract? A contract is a compact between two or more parties, and is either executory or executed. An executory contract is one in which a party binds himself to do, or not to do, a particular thing; such was the law under which the conveyance was made by the governor. A contract executed is one in which the object of contract is performed; and this, says Blackstone, differs in nothing from a grant. The contract between Georgia and the purchasers was executed by the grant. A contract executed, as well as one which is executory, contains obligations binding on the parties. A grant, in its own nature, amounts to an extinguishment of the right of the grantor, and implies a contract not to re-assert that right. A party is, therefore, always estopped by his own grant.

Since, then, in fact, a grant is a contract executed, the obligation of which still continues, and since the constitution uses the general term contract, without distinguishing between those which are executory and those which are executed, it must be construed to comprehend the latter as well as the former. A law annulling conveyances between individuals, and declaring that the grantors should stand seised of their former estates, notwithstanding those grants, would be as repugnant to the constitution, as a law discharging the vendors of property from the obligation of executing their contracts by conveyances. It would be strange, if a contract to convey was secured by the constitution, while an absolute conveyance remained unprotected.

If, under a fair construction of the constitution, grants are comprehended under the term contracts, is a grant from the state excluded from the operation of the provision? Is the clause to be considered as inhibiting the state from impairing the obligation of contracts between two individuals, but as excluding from that inhibition contracts made with itself? The words themselves contain no such distinction. They are general, and are applicable to contracts of every description. If contracts made with the state are to be exempted from their operation, the exception must arise from the character of the contracting party, not from the words which are employed.

Obligations of Federalism

Whatever respect might have been felt for the state sovereignties, it is not to be disguised, that the framers of the constitution viewed, with some apprehension, the violent acts which might grow out of the feelings of the moment; and that the people of the United States, in adopting that instrument, have manifested a determination to shield themselves and their property from the effects of those sudden and strong passions to which men are exposed. The restrictions on the legislative power of the states are obviously founded in this sentiment; and the constitution of the United States contains what may be deemed a bill of rights for the people of each state.

No state shall pass any bill of attainder, *ex post facto* law, or law impairing the obligation of contracts. A bill of attainder may affect the life of an individual, or may confiscate his property, or may do both. In this form, the power of the legislature over the lives and fortunes of individuals is expressly restrained. What motive, then, for implying, in words which import a general prohibition to impair the obligation of contracts, an exception in favor of the right to impair the obligation of those contracts into which the state may enter?

The state legislatures can pass no *ex post facto* law. An *ex post facto* law is one which renders an act punishable in a manner in which it was not punishable when it was committed. Such a law may inflict penalties on the person, or may inflict pecuniary penalties which swell the public treasury. The legislature is then prohibited from passing a law by which a man's estate, or any part of it, shall be seized for a crime which was not declared, by some previous law, to render him liable to that punishment. Why, then, should violence be done to the natural meaning of words for the purpose of leaving to the legislature the power of seizing, for public use, the estate of an individual, in the form of a law annulling the title by which he holds that estate? The court can perceive no sufficient grounds for making this distinction. This rescinding act would have the effect of an *ex post facto* law. It forfeits the estate of Fletcher for a crime not committed by himself, but by those from whom he purchased. This cannot be effected in the form of an *ex post facto* law, or bill of attainder; why then, is it allowable in the form of a law annulling the original grant?

The argument in favor of presuming an intention to except a case, not excepted by the words of the constitution, is susceptible of some illustration from a principle originally ingrafted in that instrument, though no longer a part of it. The constitution, as passed, gave the courts of the United States jurisdiction in suits brought against individual states. A state, then, which violated its own contract was suable in the courts of the United States for that violation. Would it have been a defence in such a suit to say, that the state had passed a law absolving itself from the contract? It is scarcely to be conceived, that such a defence could be set up. And yet, if a state is neither restrained by the general principles of our political institutions, nor by the words of the constitution, from impairing the obligation of its own contracts, such a defence would be a valid one. This feature is no longer found in the constitution; but it aids in the construction of those clauses with which it was originally associated.*

Holding on the Question

It is, then, the unanimous opinion of the court, that, in this case, the estate having passed into the hands of a purchaser for a valuable consideration, without notice, the state of Georgia was restrained, either by general principles which are common to our free institutions, or by the particular provisions of the constitution of the United States, from passing a law whereby the estate of the plaintiff in the premises so purchased could be constitutionally and legally

* Cf. Eleventh Amendment, and commentary thereon, page 113.

impaired and rendered null and void. In overruling the demurrer to the 3d plea, therefore, there is no error.

The first covenant in the deed is, that the state of Georgia, at the time of the act of the legislature thereof, entitled as aforesaid, was legally seised in fee of the soil thereof, subject only to the extinguishment of part of the Indian title thereon. The 4th count assigns, as a breach of this covenant, that the right to the soil was in the United States, and not in Georgia. To this count, the defendant pleads, that the state of Georgia was seised; and tenders an issue on the fact in which the plaintiff joins. On this issue, a special verdict is found.

The jury finds the grant of Carolina by Charles II. to the Earl of Clarendon and others, comprehending the whole country from 36 deg. 30 min. north lat. to 29 deg. north lat., and from the Atlantic to the South Sea. They find that the northern part of this territory was afterwards erected into a separate colony, and that the most northern part of the 35 deg. of north lat. was the boundary line between North and South Carolina. That seven of the eight proprietors of the Carolinas surrendered to George II. the year 1729, who appointed a governor of South Carolina. That in 1732, George II. granted to the Lord Viscount Percival and others, seven-eighths of the territory between the Savannah and the Alatamaha, and extending west to the South Sea, and that the remaining eighth part, which was still the property of the heir of Lord Carteret, one of the original grantees of Carolina, was afterwards conveyed to them. This territory was constituted a colony and called Georgia. That the governor of South Carolina continued to exercise jurisdiction south of Georgia. That in 1752, the grantees surrendered to the crown. That in 1754, a governor was appointed by the crown, with a commission describing the boundaries of the colony. That a treaty of peace was concluded between Great Britain and Spain, in 1763, in which the latter ceded to the former Florida, with Fort St. Augustin and the bay of Pensacola.

That in October 1763, the King of Great Britain issued a proclamation, creating four new colonies, Quebec, East Florida, West Florida and Grenada; and prescribing the bounds of each, and further declaring that all the lands between the Alatamaha and St. Mary's should be annexed to Georgia. The same proclamation contained a clause reserving, under the dominion and protection of the crown, for the use of the Indians, all the lands on the western waters, and forbidding a settlement on them, or a purchase of them from the Indians. The lands conveyed to the plaintiff lie on the western waters. That in November 1763, a commission was issued to the governor of Georgia, in which the boundaries of that province are described, as extending westward to the Mississippi. A commission, describing boundaries of the same extent, was afterwards granted in 1764.*

That a war broke out between Great Britain and her colonies, which terminated in a treaty of peace acknowledging them as sovereign and independent states. That in April 1787, a convention was entered into between the states of South Carolina and Georgia, settling the boundary line between them. The jury

* Cf. generally Swindler, ed., *Sources and Documents of United States Constitutions* (Dobbs Ferry, N.Y. 1973, 1976) vols. II and VII, on Georgia and North Carolina.

afterwards describe the situation of the lands mentioned in the plaintiff's declaration, in such manner that their lying within the limits of Georgia, as defined in the proclamation of 1763, in the treaty of peace, and in the convention between that state and South Carolina, has not been questioned.

The counsel for the plaintiff rest their argument on a single proposition. They contend, that the reservation for the use of the Indians, contained in the proclamation of 1763, excepts the lands on the western waters from the colonies within whose bounds they would otherwise have been, and that they were acquired by the revolutionary war. All acquisitions during the war, it is contended, were made by the joint arms, for the joint benefit of the United States, and not for the benefit of any particular state. The court does not understand the proclamation as it is understood by the counsel for the plaintiff. The reservation for the use of the Indians appears to be a temporary arrangement, suspending, for a time, the settlement of the country reserved, and the powers of the royal governor within the territory reserved, but is not conceived to amount to an alteration of the boundaries of the colony. If the language of the proclamation be, in itself, doubtful, the commissions subsequent thereto, which were given to the governors of Georgia, entirely remove the doubt.

The question, whether the vacant lands within the United States became a joint property, or belonged to the separate states, was a momentous question which, at one time, threatened to shake the American confederacy to its foundation. This important and dangerous contest has been compromised, and the compromise is not now to be disturbed.

It is the opinion of the court, that the particular land stated in the declaration appears, from this special verdict, to lie within the state of Georgia, and that the state of Georgia had power to grant it.

Some difficulty was produced by the language of the covenant, and of the pleadings. It was doubted, whether a state can be seised in fee of lands, subject to the Indian title, and whether a decision that they were seised in fee, might not be construed to amount to a decision that their grantee might maintain an ejectment for them, notwithstanding that title. The majority of the court is of opinion, that the nature of the Indian title, which is certainly to be respected by all courts, until it be legitimately extinguished, is not such as to be absolutely repugnant to seisin in fee on the part of the state.*

Dissent by Justice Johnson

JOHNSON, J.—In this case, I entertain, on two points, an opinion different from that which has been delivered by the court.

I do not hesitate to declare, that a state does not possess the power of revoking its own grants. But I do it, on a general principle, on the reason and nature of things; a principle which will impose laws even on the Deity. A contrary opinion can only be maintained upon the ground, that no existing legislature can abridge the powers of those which will succeed it. To a certain extent, this is certainly correct; but the distinction lies between power and interest, the right of jurisdiction and the right of soil.

* Cf. subsequent case, *Johnson* v. *McIntosh,* in 1823, page 122.

The right of jurisdiction is essentially connected to, or rather identified with, the national sovereignty. To part with it, is to commit a species of political suicide. In fact, a power to produce its own annihilation, is an absurdity in terms. It is a power as utterly incommunicable to a political as to a natural person. But it is not so with the interests or property of a nation. Its possessions nationally are in no wise necessary to its political existence; they are entirely accidental, and may be parted with, in every respect, similarly to those of the individuals who compose the community. When the legislature have once conveyed their interest or property in any subject to the individual, they have lost all control over it; have nothing to act upon; it has passed from them; is vested in the individual; becomes intimately blended with his existence, as essentially so as the blood that circulates through his system. The government may indeed demand of him the one or the other, not because they are not his, but because whatever is his, is his country's.

As to the idea, that the grants of a legislature may be void, because the legislature are corrupt, it appears to me to be subject to insuperable difficulties. The acts of the supreme power of a country must be considered pure, for the same reason that all sovereign acts must be considered just; because there is no power that can declare them otherwise. The absurdity in this case would have been strikingly perceived, could the party who passed the act of cession have got again into power, and declared themselves pure, and the intermediate legislature corrupt. The security of a people against the misconduct of their rulers, must lie in the frequent recurrence to first principles, and the imposition of adequate constitutional restrictions. Nor would it be difficult, with the same view, for laws to be framed which would bring the conduct of individuals under the review of adequate tribunals, and make them suffer under the consequences of their own immoral conduct.

I have thrown out these ideas, that I may have it distinctly understood, that my opinion on this point is not founded on the provision in the constitution of the United States, relative to laws impairing the obligation of contracts. It is much to be regretted, that words of less equivocal signification had not been adopted in that article of the constitution. There is reason to believe, from the letters of Publius,* which are well known to be entitled to the highest respect, that the object of the convention was to afford a general protection to individual rights against the acts of the state legislatures. Whether the words, "acts impairing the obligation of contracts," can be construed to have the same force as must have been given to the words "obligation and *effect* of contracts," is the difficulty in my mind.

There can be no solid objection to adopting the technical definition of the word "contract," given by Blackstone. The etymology, the classical signification, and the civil law idea of the word, will all support it. But the difficulty arises on the word "obligation," which certainly imports an existing moral or physical necessity. Now, a grant or conveyance by no means necessarily implies the continuance of an obligation, beyond the moment of executing it. It is most generally but the consummation of a contract, is *functus officio*, the moment it

---

* *The Federalist* papers were signed in the pen name Publius; cf. No. 44 (Middletown, Conn., Joseph Cooke, ed., 1961).

is executed, and continues afterwards to be nothing more than the evidence that a certain act was done.

Contract Obligations

I enter with great hesitation upon this question, because it involves a subject of the greatest delicacy and much difficulty. The states and the United States are continually legislating on the subject of contracts, prescribing the mode of authentication, the time within which suits shall be prosecuted for them, in many cases, affecting existing contracts by the laws which they pass, and declaring them to cease or lose their effect for want of compliance, in the parties, with such statutory provisions. All these acts appear to be within the most correct limits of legislative powers, and most beneficially exercised, and certainly could not have been intended to be affected by this constitutional provision; yet where to draw the line, or how to define or limit the words, "obligation of contracts," will be found a subject of extreme difficulty.

To give it the general effect of a restriction of the state powers in favor of private rights, is certainly going very far beyond the obvious and necessary import of the words, and would operate to restrict the states in the exercise of that right which every community must exercise, of possessing itself of the property of the individual, when necessary for public uses; a right which a magnanimous and just government will never exercise without amply indemnifying the individual, and which perhaps amounts to nothing more than a power to oblige him to sell and convey, when the public necessities require it.

The other point on which I dissent from the opinion of the court, is relative to the judgment which ought to be given on the first count. Upon that count, we are called upon substantially to decide, "that the state of Georgia, at the time of passing the act of cession, was legally seised in fee of the soil (then ceded), subject only to the extinguishment of part of the Indian title." That is, that the state of Georgia was seised of an estate in fee-simple in the lands in question, subject to another estate, we know not what, nor whether it may not swallow up the whole estate decided to exist in Georgia. It would seem, that the mere vagueness and uncertainty of this covenant would be a sufficient objection to deciding in favor of it, but to me it appears, that the facts in the case are sufficient to support the opinion that the state of Georgia had not a fee-simple in the land in question.

This is a question of much delicacy, and more fitted for a diplomatic or legislative than a judicial inquiry. But I am called upon to make a decision, and I must make it upon technical principles. The question is, whether it can be correctly predicated of the interest or estate which the state of Georgia had in these lands, "that the state was seised thereof, in fee-simple." To me it appears, that the interest of Georgia in that land amounted to nothing more than a mere possibility, and that her conveyance thereof could operate legally only as a covenant to convey or to stand seised to a use.

Indian Rights Affected

The correctness of this opinion will depend upon a just view of the state of the Indian nations. This will be found to be various. Some have totally extinguished their national fire, and submitted themselves to the laws of the states; others have, by treaty, acknowledged that they hold their national existence at the will of the state within which they reside; others retain a limited sovereignty, and the absolute proprietorship of their soil: the latter in the case of the tribes to the west of Georgia. We legislate upon the conduct of strangers or citizens within their limits, but innumerable treaties formed with them acknowledge them to be an independent people, and the uniform practice of acknowledging their right of soil, by purchasing from them, and restraining all persons from encroaching upon their territory, makes it unnecessary to insist upon their right of soil. Can, then, one nation be said to be seised of a fee-simple in lands, the right of soil of which is in another nation? It is awkward, to apply the technical idea of a fee-simple to the interests of a nation, but I must consider an absolute right of soil as an estate to them and their heirs.

A fee-simple interest may be held in reversion, but our law will not admit the idea of its being limited after a fee-simple. In fact, if the Indian nations be the absolute proprietors of their soil, no other nation can be said to have the same interest in it. What, then, practically, is the interest of the states in the soil of the Indians within their boundaries? Unaffected by particular treaties, it is nothing more than what was assumed at the first settlement of the country, to wit, a right of conquest, or of purchase, exclusively of all competitors, within certain defined limits. All the restrictions upon the right of soil in the Indians, amount only to an exclusion of all competitors from their markets; and the limitation upon their sovereignty amounts to the right of governing every person within their limits, except themselves. If the interest in Georgia was nothing more than a pre-emptive right, how could that be called a fee-simple, which was nothing more than a power to acquire a fee-simple by purchase, when the proprietors should be pleased to sell? And if this ever was anything more than a mere possibility, it certainly was reduced to that state, when the state of Georgia ceded to the United States, by the constitution, both the power of pre-emption and of conquest, retaining for itself only a resulting right dependent on a purchase or conquest to be made by the United States.

I have been very unwilling to proceed to the decision of this cause at all. It appears to me to bear strong evidence, upon the face of it, of being a mere feigned case. It is our duty to decide on the rights, but not on the speculations of parties. My confidence, however, in the respectable gentlemen who have been engaged for the parties, has induced me to abandon my scruples, in the belief that they would never consent to impose a mere feigned case upon this court.

3. *Charter of Dartmouth College*

George the Third, by the grace of God, of Great Britain, France and Ireland, King, Defender of the Faith, and so forth, To all to whom these presents shall come, Greeting:

Whereas, it hath been represented to our trusty and well-beloved John Wentworth, Esq., governor and commander-in-chief, in and over our province of New Hampshire, in New England, in America, that the Reverend Eleazar Wheelock, of Lebanon, in the colony of Connecticut, in New England, aforesaid, now doctor in divinity, did, on or about the year of our Lord 1754, at his own expense, on his own estate and plantation, set on foot an Indian charity school, and for several years, through the assistance of well-disposed persons in America, clothed, maintained and educated a number of the children of the Indian natives, with a view to their carrying the Gospel, in their own language, and spreading the knowledge of the great Redeemer, among their savage tribes, and hath actually employed a number of them as missionaries and school-masters in the wilderness, for that purpose: and by the blessing of God upon the endeavors of said Wheelock, the design became reputable among the Indians, insomuch that a large number desired the education of their children in said school, and were also disposed to receive missionaries and school-masters, in the wilderness, more than could be supported by the charitable contributions in these American colonies. Whereupon, the said Eleazar Wheelock thought it expedient, that endeavors should be used to raise contributions from well-disposed persons in England, for the carrying on and extending said undertaking; and for that purpose the said Eleazar Wheelock requested the Rev. Nathaniel Whitaker, now doctor in divinity to go over to England for that purpose, and sent over with him the Rev. Samson Occom, an Indian minister, who had been educated by the said Wheelock. And to enable the said Whitaker to the more successful performance of said work, on which he was sent, said Wheelock gave him a full power of attorney, by which said Whitaker solicited those worthy and generous contributors to the charity, viz., The Right Honorable William, Earl of Dartmouth, the Honorable Sir Sidney Stafford Smythe, Knight, one of the barons of his Majesty's court of exchequer, John Thornton, of Clapham, in the county of Surrey, Esquire, Samuel Roffey, of Lincoln's Inn Fields, in the county of Middlesex, Esquire, Charles Hardy, of the parish of Saint Mary-le-bonne, in said county, Esquire, Daniel West, of Christ's church, Spitalfields, in the county aforesaid, Esquire, Samuel Savage, of the same place, gentleman, Josiah Roberts, of the parish of St. Edmund the King, Lombard Street, London, gentleman, and Robert Keen, of the parish of Saint Botolph, Aldgate, London, gentleman, to receive the several sums of money, which should be contributed, and to be trustees for the contributors to such charity, which they cheerfully agreed to. Whereupon, the said Whitaker did, by virtue of said power of attorney, constitute and appoint the said Earl of Dartmouth, Sir Sidney Stafford Smythe, John Thornton, Samuel Roffey, Charles Hardy and Daniel West, Esquires, and Samuel Savage, Josiah Roberts and Robert Keen, gentlemen, to be trustees of the money which had then been contributed, and which should, by his means, be contributed for said purpose; which trust they have accepted, as by their engrossed declaration of the same, under their hands and seals, well executed, fully appears, and the same has also been ratified, by a deed of trust, well executed by the said Wheelock.

And the said Wheelock further represents, that he has, by power of attorney, for many weighty reasons, given full power to the said trustees, to fix upon and determine the place for said school, most subservient to the great end in view; and to enable them understandingly, to give the preference, the said Wheelock has laid before the said trustees, the several offers which have been generously made in the several governments in America, to encourage and invite the settlement of said school among them, for their own private emolument, and the increase of learning in their respective places, as well as for the furtherance of the general design in view. And whereas, a large number of the proprietors of lands in the western part of this our province of New Hampshire, animated and excited thereto, by the generous example of his excellency, their governor, and by the liberal contributions of many noblemen and gentlemen in England, and especially by the consideration, that such a situation would be as convenient as any for carrying on the great design among the Indians; and also, considering, that without the least impediment to the said design, the same school may be enlarged and improved to promote learning among the English, and be a means to supply a great number of churches and congregations, which are likely soon to be formed in that new country, with a learned and orthodox ministry; they, the said proprietors, have promised large tracts of land, for the uses aforesaid, provided the school shall be settled in the western part of our said province. And they, the said right honorable, honorable and worthy trustees, before mentioned, having maturely considered the reasons and arguments, in favor of the several places proposed, have given the preference to the western part of our said province, lying on Connecticut river, as a situation most convenient for said school.

And the said Wheelock has further represented a necessity of a legal incorporation, in order to the safety and well-being of said seminary, and its being capable of the tenure and disposal of lands and bequests for the use of the same. And the said Wheelock has also represented, that for many weighty reasons, it will be expedient, at least, in the infancy of said institution, or till it can be accommodated in that new country, and he and his friends be able to remove and settle, by and round about it, that the gentlemen, whom he has already nominated in his last will (which he has transmitted to the aforesaid gentlemen of the trust in England), to be trustees in America, should be of the corporation now proposed. And also, as there are already large collections for said school, in the hands of the aforesaid gentlemen of the trust, in England, and all reasons to believe, from their singular wisdom, piety and zeal to promote the Redeemer's cause (which has already procured for them the utmost confidence of the kingdom), we may expect they will appoint successors in time to come, who will be men of the same spirit, whereby great good may and will accrue many ways to the institution, and much be done, by their example and influence, to encourage and facilitate the whole design in view; for which reason, said Wheelock desires, that the trustees aforesaid may be vested with all that power therein, which can consist with their distance from the same.

Grant of Charter

KNOW YE, THEREFORE, that We, considering the premises, and being willing to encourage the laudable and charitable design of spreading Christian knowledge among the savages of our American wilderness, and also that the best means of education be established in our province of New Hampshire, for the benefit of said province, do, of our special grace, certain knowledge and mere motion, by and with the advice of our counsel for said province, by these presents, will, ordain, grant and constitute, that there be a college erected in our said province of New Hampshire, by the name of Dartmouth College, for the education and instruction of youth of the Indian tribes in this land, in reading, writing and all parts of learning, which shall appear necessary and expedient, for civilizing and christianizing children of pagans, as well as in all liberal arts and sciences, and also of English youth and any others. And the trustees of said college may and shall be one body corporate and politic, in deed, action and name, and shall be called, named and distinguished by the name of the Trustees of Dartmouth College.

And further, we have willed, given, granted, constituted and ordained, and by this our present charter, of our special grace, certain knowledge and mere motion, with the advice aforesaid, do, for us, our heirs and successors for ever, will, give, grant, constitute and ordain, that there shall be in the said Dartmouth College, from henceforth and for ever, a body politic, consisting of trustees of said Dartmouth College. And for the more full and perfect erection of said corporation and body politic, consisting of trustees of Dartmouth College, we, of our special grace, certain knowledge and mere motion, do, by these presents, for us, our heirs and successors, make, ordain, constitute and appoint our trusty and well-beloved John Wentworth, Esq., governor of our said province of New Hampshire for the time being, and our trusty and well-beloved Theodore Atkinson, Esq., now president of our council of our said province, George Jaffrey and Daniel Peirce, Esq'rs, both of our said council, and Peter Gilman, Esq., now speaker of our house of representatives in said province, and William Pitkin, Esq., one of the assistants of our colony of Connecticut, and our said trusty and well-beloved Eleazar Wheelock, of Lebanon, doctor in divinity, Benjamin Pomroy, of Hebron, James Lockwood, of Weathersfield, Timothy Pitkin and John Smalley, of Farmington, and William Patten, of Hartford, all of our said colony of Connecticut, ministers of the gospel (the whole number of said trustees consisting, and hereafter for ever to consist, of twelve and no more) to be trustees of said Dartmouth College, in this our province of New Hampshire.

Trustees' Powers

And we do further, of our special grace, certain knowledge and mere motion, for us, our heirs and successors, will, give, grant and appoint, that the said trustees and their successors shall for ever hereafter be, in deed, act and name, a body corporate and politic, and that they, the said body corporate and politic, shall be known and distinguished, in all deeds, grants, bargains, sales, writings, evidences or otherwise howsoever, and in all courts for ever hereafter, plea and be impleaded by the name of the Trustees of Dartmouth College; and that the said corporation, by the name aforesaid, shall be able, and in law capable, for the use of said Dartmouth College, to have, get, acquire, purchase, receive, hold, possess and enjoy, tenements, hereditaments, jurisdictions and franchises, for themselves and their successors, in fee-simple, or otherwise howsoever, and to purchase, receive or build any house or houses, or any other buildings, as they shall think needful and convenient, for the use of said Dartmouth College, and in such town in the western part of our said province of New Hampshire, as shall, by said trustees, or the major part of them, be agreed on; their said agreement to be evidenced by an instrument in writing, under their hands, ascertaining the same: And also to receive and dispose of any lands, goods, chattels and other things, of what nature soever, for the use aforesaid: And also to have, accept and receive any rents, profits, annuities, gifts, legacies, donations or bequests of any kind whatsoever, for the use aforesaid; so, nevertheless, that the yearly value of the premises do not exceed the sum of 6000*l.* sterling; and therewith, or otherwise, to support and pay, as the said trustees, or the major part of such of them as are regularly convened for the purpose, shall agree, the president, tutors and other officers and ministers of said Dartmouth College; and also to pay all such missionaries and school-masters as shall be authorized, appointed and employed by them, for civilizing and christianizing, and instructing the Indian natives of this land, their several allowances; and also their respective annual salaries or allowances, and all such necessary and contingent charges, as from time to time shall arise and accrue, relating to the said Dartmouth College: And also, to bargain, sell, let or assign, lands, tenements or hereditaments, goods or chattels, and all other things whatsoever, by the name aforesaid in as full and ample a manner, to all intents and purposes, as a natural person, or other body politic or corporate, is able to do, by the laws of our realm of Great Britain, or of said province of New Hampshire.

And further, of our special grace, certain knowledge and mere motion, to the intent that our said corporation and body politic may answer the end of their erection and constitution, and may have perpetual succession and continuance for ever, we do, for us, our heirs and successors, will, give and grant unto the Trustees of Dartmouth College, and to their successors for ever, that there shall be, once a year, and every year, a meeting of said trustees, held at said Dartmouth College, at such time as by said trustees, or the major part of them, at any legal meeting of said trustees, shall be agreed on; the first meeting to be called by the said Eleazar Wheelock, as soon as conveniently may be, within one year next after the enrolment of these our letters-patent, at such time and place as he shall judge proper. And the said trustees, or the major part of any seven or more of them, shall then determine on the time for holding the annual meeting aforesaid, which may be altered as they shall hereafter find most convenient. And we further order and direct, that the said Eleazar Wheelock shall notify the time for holding said first meeting, to be called as aforesaid, by sending a letter to each of said trustees, and causing an advertisement thereof to be printed in the New Hampshire Gazette, and in some public newspaper printed in the colony of Connecticut. But in case of the death or incapacity of the said Wheelock, then such meeting to be notified in manner aforesaid, by the governor or commander-in-chief of our said province for the time being. And we do also, for us, our heirs and successors, hereby will, give and grant unto the said Trustees of Dartmouth College, aforesaid, and to their successors for ever, that when any seven or more of the said trustees, or their successors, are convened and met together, for the service of said Dartmouth College, at any time or times, such seven or more shall be capable to act as fully and amply, to all intents and purposes, as if all the trustees of said college were personally present —and all affairs and actions whatsoever, under the care of said trustees, shall be determined by the majority or greater number of those seven or more trustees so convened and met together.

And we do further will, ordain and direct, that the president, trustees, professors, tutors and all such officers as shall be appointed for the public instruction and government of said college, shall, before they undertake the execution of their offices or trusts, or within one year after, take the oaths and subscribe the declaration provided by an act of parliament made in the first year of King George the First, entitled "an act for the further security of his majesty's person and government, and the succession of the crown in the heirs of the late Princess Sophia, being Protestants, and for the extinguishing the hopes of the pretended Prince of Wales, and his open and secret abettors;" that is to say, the president, before the governor of our said province for the time being, or by one by him empowered to that service, or by the president of our said council, and the trustees, professors, tutors and other officers, before the president of said college for the time being, who is hereby empowered to administer the same; an entry of all which shall be made in the records of said college.

Governance of College

And we do, for us, our heirs, and successors, hereby will, give and grant full power and authority to the president hereafter by us named, and to his successors, or, in case of his failure, to any three or more of the said trustees, to appoint other occasional meetings, from time to time, of the said seven trustees, or any greater number of them, to transact any matter or thing necessary to be done before the next annual meeting, and to order notice to the said seven, or any greater number of them, of the times and places of meeting for the service aforesaid, by a letter under his or their hands, of the same, one month before said meeting: provided always, that no standing rule or order be made or altered, for the regulation of said college, nor any president or professor be chosen or displaced, nor any other matter or thing transacted or done, which shall continue in force after the then next annual meeting of the said trustees, as aforesaid.

And further, we do, by these presents, for us, our heirs and successors, create, make, constitute, nominate and appoint our trusty and well-beloved Eleazar Wheelock, doctor in divinity, the founder of said college, to be president of said Dartmouth College, and to have the immediate care of the education and government of such students as shall be admitted into said Dartmouth College for instruction and education; and do will, give and grant to him, in said office, full power, authority and right, to nominate, appoint, constitute and ordain, by his last will, such suitable and meet person or persons as he shall choose to succeed him in the presidency of said Dartmouth College; and the person so appointed, by his last will, to continue in office, vested with all the powers, privileges, jurisdiction and authority of a president of said Dartmouth

College; that is to say, so long and until such appointment by said last will shall be disapproved by the trustees of said Dartmouth College.

And we do also, for us, our heirs and successors, will, give and grant to the said trustees of said Dartmouth College, and to their successors for ever, or any seven or more of them, convened as aforesaid, that in the case of the ceasing or failure of a president, by any means whatsoever, that the said trustees do elect, nominate and appoint such qualified person as they, or the major part of any seven or more of them, convened for that purpose as above directed, shall think fit, to be president of said Dartmouth College, and to have the care of the education and government of the students as aforesaid; and in case of the ceasing of a president as aforesaid, the senior professor or tutor, being one of the trustees, shall exercise the office of a president, until the trustees shall make choice of and appoint, a president as aforesaid; and such professor or tutor, or any three or more of the trustees, shall immediately appoint a meeting of the body of the trustees for the purpose aforesaid. And also we do will, give and grant to the said trustees, convened as aforesaid, that they elect, nominate and appoint so many tutors and professors to assist the president in the education and government of the students belonging thereto, as they the said trustees shall, from time to time, think needful and serviceable to the interests of said Dartmouth College. And also, that the said trustees or their successors, or the major part of any seven or more of them, convened for that purpose as above directed, shall, at any time, displace and discharge from the service of said Dartmouth College, any or all such officers, and elect others in their room and stead, as before directed. And also, that the said trustees, or their successors, or the major part of any seven of them which shall convene for that purpose, as above directed, do, from time to time, as occasion shall require, elect, constitute and appoint a treasurer, a clerk, an usher and a steward for the said Dartmouth College, and appoint to them, and each of them, their respective businesses and trust; and displace and discharge from the service of said college, such treasurer, clerk, usher or steward, and to elect others in their room and stead; which officers so elected, as before directed, we do for us, our heirs and successors, by these presents, constitute and establish in their respective offices, and do give to each and every of them full power and authority to exercise the same in said Dartmouth College, according to the directions, and during the pleasure of said trustees, as fully and freely as any like officers in any of our universities, colleges or seminaries of learning in our realm of Great Britain, lawfully may or ought to do.

Succession of Trustees

And also, that the said trustees and their successors, or the major part of any seven or more of them, which shall convene for that purpose, as is above directed, as often as one or more of said trustees shall die, or by removal or otherwise shall, according to their judgment, become unfit or incapable to serve the interests of said college, do, as soon as may be after the death, removal or such unfitness or incapacity of such trustee or trustees, elect and appoint such trustee or trustees as shall supply the place of him or them so dying, or becoming incapable to serve the interests of said college; and every trustee so elected and appointed shall, by virtue of these presents, and such election and appointment, be vested with all the powers and privileges which any of the other trustees of said college are hereby vested with. And we do further will, ordain and direct, that from and after the expiration of two years from the enrolment of these presents, such vacancy or vacancies as may or shall happen, by death or otherwise, in the aforesaid number of trustees, shall be filled up by election as aforesaid, so that when such vacancies shall be filled up unto the complete number of twelve trustees, eight of the aforesaid whole number of the body of trustees shall be resident, and respectable freeholders of our said province of New Hampshire, and seven of said whole number shall be laymen.

And we do further, of our special grace, certain knowledge and mere motion, will, give and grant unto the said trustees of Dartmouth College, that they, and their successors, or the major part of any seven of them, which shall convene for that purpose, as is above directed, may make, and they are hereby fully empowered, from time to time, fully and lawfully to make and establish such ordinances, orders and laws, as may tend to the good and wholesome government of the said college, and all the students and the several officers and ministers thereof, and to the public benefit of the same, not repugnant to the laws and statutes of our realm of Great Britain, or of this our province of New Hampshire, and not excluding any person of any religious denomination whatsoever, from free and equal liberty and advantage of education, or from any of the liberties and privileges or immunities of the said college, on account of his or their speculative sentiments in religion, and of his or their being of a religious profession different from the said trustees of the said Dartmouth College. And such ordinances, orders and laws, which shall as aforesaid be made, we do, for us, our heirs and successors, by these presents, ratify, allow of, and confirm, as good and effectual to oblige and bind all the students, and the several officers and ministers of the said college. And we do hereby authorize and empower the said trustees of Dartmouth College, and the president, tutors and professors by them elected and appointed as aforesaid, to put such ordinances, orders and laws in execution, to all proper intents and purposes.

And we do further, of our special grace, certain knowledge and mere motion, will, give, and grant unto the said trustees of said Dartmouth College, for the encouragement of learning, and animating the students of said college to diligence and industry, and a laudable progress in literature, that they, and their successors, or the major part of any seven or more of them, convened for that purpose, as above directed, do, by the president of said college, for the time being, or any other deputed by them, give and grant any such degree or degrees to any of the students of the said college, or any others by them thought worthy thereof, as are usually granted in either of the universities, or any other college in our realm of Great Britain; and that they sign and seal diplomas or certificates of such graduations, to be kept by the graduates as perpetual memorials and testimonials thereof.

And we do further, of our special grace, certain knowledge and mere motion, by these presents, for us, our heirs and successors, give and grant unto the trustees of said Dartmouth College, and to their successors, that they and their successors shall have a common seal, under which they may pass all diplomas or certificates of degrees, and all other affairs and business of, and concerning the said college; which shall be engraven in such a form and with such an inscription as shall be devised by the said trustees, for the time being, or by the major part of any seven or more of them, convened for the service of the said college, as is above directed.

And we do further, for us, our heirs and successors, give and grant unto the said trustees of the said Dartmouth College, and their successors, or to the major part of any seven or more of them, convened for the service of the said college, full power and authority, from time to time, to nominate and appoint all other officers and ministers, which they shall think convenient and necessary for the service of the said college, not herein particularly named or mentioned; which officers and ministers we do hereby empower to execute their offices and trusts, as fully and freely as any of the officers and ministers in our universities or colleges in our realm of Great Britain lawfully may or ought to do.

And further, that the generous contributors to the support of this design of spreading the knowledge of the only true God and Saviour among the American savages, may, from time to time, be satisfied that their liberalities are faithfully disposed of, in the best manner, for that purpose, and that others may, in future time, be encouraged in the exercise of the like liberality, for promoting the same pious design, it shall be the duty of the president of said Dartmouth College, and of his successors, annually, or as often as he shall be thereunto desired or required, to transmit the right honorable, honorable, and worthy gentlemen of the trust, in England, before mentioned, a faithful account of the improvements and disbursements of the several sums he shall receive from the donations and bequests made in England, through the hands of said trustees, and also advise them of the general plans laid, and prospects exhibited, as well as a faithful account of all remarkable occurrences, in order, if they shall think expedient, that they may be published. And this to continue so long as they shall perpetuate their board of trust, and there shall be any of the Indian natives remaining to be proper objects of that charity. And lastly, our express will and pleasure is, and we do, by these presents, for us, our heirs and successors, give and grant unto the said trustees of Dartmouth College, and to their successors for ever, that these our letters-patent, on the enrolment thereof in the secretary's office of our province of New Hampshire aforesaid, shall be good and effectual in the law, to all intents and purposes, against us, our heirs and successors, without any other license, grant or confirmation from us, our heirs and successors, hereafter by the said trustees to be had and obtained, notwithstanding the not writing or misrecital, not naming or misnaming the aforesaid offices, franchises, privileges, immunities or other the premises, or any of them, and notwithstanding a writ of *ad quod damnum* hath not issued forth to inquire of the premises, or any of them, before the ensealing hereof, any statute, act, ordinance, or provision, or any other matter or thing to the contrary notwithstanding. To have and to hold, all and singular the privileges, advantages, liberties, immunities, and all other the premises herein and hereby granted, or which are meant, mentioned or intended to be herein and hereby given and granted, unto them, the said trustees of Dartmouth College, and to their successors for ever. In testimony whereof, we have caused these our letters to be made patent, and the public seal of our said province of New Hampshire to be hereunto affixed. Witness our trusty and well-beloved John Wentworth, Esquire, governor and commander-in-chief in and over our said province, &c., this thirteenth day of December, in the tenth year of our reign, and in the year of our Lord 1769.

4. New Hampshire Statutes

Act of June 27, 1816

An act to amend the charter, and enlarge and improve the corporation of Dartmouth College.

Whereas, knowledge and learning generally diffused through a community, are essential to the preservation of a free government, and extending the opportunities and advantages of education is highly conducive to promote this end, and by the constitution it is made the duty of the legislators and magistrates, to cherish the interests of literature, and the sciences, and all seminaries established for their advancement; and as the college of the state may, in the opinion of the legislature, be rendered more extensively useful: therefore—

§ 1. Be it enacted, &c., that the corporation, heretofore called and known by the name of the Trustees of Dartmouth College, shall ever hereafter be called and known by the name of the Trustees of Dartmouth University; and the whole number of said trustees shall be twenty-one, a majority of whom shall form a *quorum* for the transaction of business; and they and their successors in that capacity, as hereby constituted, shall respectively for ever have, hold, use, exercise and enjoy all the powers, authorities, rights, property, liberties, privileges and immunities which have hitherto been possessed, enjoyed and used by the Trustees of Dartmouth College, except so far as the same may be varied or limited by the provisions of this act. And they shall have power to determine the times and places of their meetings, and manner of notifying the same; to organize colleges in the university; to establish an institute, and elect fellows and members thereof: to appoint such officers as they may deem proper, and determine their duties and compensation, and also to displace them; to delegate the power of supplying vacancies in any of the offices of the university, for any term of time not extending beyond their next meeting: to pass ordinances for the government of the students, with reasonable penalties, not inconsistent with the constitution and laws of this state; to prescribe the course of education, and confer degrees; and to arrange, invest and employ the funds of the university.

§ 2. And be it further enacted, that there shall be a board of overseers, who shall have perpetual succession, and whose number shall be twenty-five, fifteen of whom shall constitute a *quorum* for the transaction of business. The president of the senate, and the speaker of the house of representatives of New Hampshire, the governor and lieutenant-governor of Vermont, for the time being, shall be members of said board, *ex officio*. The board of overseers shall have power to determine the times and places of their meetings, and manner of notifying the same; to inspect and confirm, or disapprove and negative, such votes and proceedings of the board of trustees as shall relate to the appointment and removal of president, professors and other permanent officers of the university, and determine their salaries; to the establishment of colleges and professorships, and the erection of new college buildings: provided always, that the said negative shall be expressed within sixty days from the time of said overseers being furnished with copies of such acts: provided also, that all votes and proceedings of the board of trustees shall be valid and effectual, to all intents and purposes, until such negative of the board of overseers be expressed, according to the provisions of this act.

§ 3. Be it further enacted, that there shall be a treasurer of said corporation, who shall be duly sworn, and who, before he enters upon the duties of his office, shall give bonds, with sureties, to the satisfaction of the corporation, for the faithful performance thereof; and also a secretary to each of the boards of trustees and overseers, to be elected by the said boards, respectively, who shall keep a just and true record of the proceedings of the board for which he was chosen. And it shall furthermore be the duty of the secretary of the board of trustees to furnish, as soon as may be, to the said board of overseers, copies of the records of such votes and proceedings, as by the provisions of this act are made subject to their revision and control.

§ 4. Be it further enacted, that the president of Dartmouth University, and his successors in office, shall have the superintendence of the government and instruction of the students, and may preside at all meetings of the trustees, and do and execute all the duties devolving by usage on the president of a university. He shall render annually to the governor of this state an account of the number of students, and of the state of the funds of the university; and likewise copies of all important votes and proceedings of the corporation and overseers, which shall be made out by the secretaries of the respective boards.

§ 5. Be it further enacted, that the president and professors of the university shall be nominated by the trustees, and approved by the overseers: and shall be liable to be suspended or removed from office in manner as before provided. And each of the two boards of trustees and overseers shall have power to suspend and remove any member of their respective boards.

§ 6. Be it further enacted, that the governor and counsel are hereby authorized to fill all vacancies in the board of overseers, whether the same be original vacancies, or are occasioned by the death, resignation or removal of any member. And the governor and counsel in like manner shall, by appointments, as soon as may be, complete the present board of trustees to the number of twenty-one, as provided for by this act, and shall have power also to fill all vacancies that may occur previous to, or during the first meeting of the said board of trustees. But the president of said university for the time being, shall, nevertheless, be a member of said board of trustees, *ex officio*. And the governor and council shall have power to inspect the doings and proceedings of the corporation, and of all the officers of the university, whenever they deem it expedient; and they are hereby required to make such inspection, and report the same to the legislature of this state, as often as once in every five years. And the governor is hereby authorized and requested to summon the first meeting of the said trustees and overseers, to be held at Hanover, on the 26th day of August next.

§ 7. Be it further enacted, that the president and professors of the university, before entering upon the duties of their offices, shall take the oath to support the constitution of the United States and of this state; certificates of which shall be in the office of the secretary of this state, within sixty days from their entering on their offices respectively.

§ 8. Be it further enacted, that perfect freedom of religious opinion shall be enjoyed by all the officers and students of the university; and no officer or student shall be deprived of any honors, privileges or benefits of the institution, on account of his religious creed or belief. The theological colleges which may be established in the university shall be founded on the same principles of religious freedom; and any man, or body of men, shall have a right to endow colleges or professorships of any sect of the Protestant Christian religion: and the trustees shall be held and obliged to appoint professors of learning and piety of such sects, according to the will of the donors.

Approved, June 27th, 1816.

Act of December 16, 1816

An act in addition to, and in amendment of, an act, entitled, "an act to amend the charter, and enlarge and improve the Corporation of Dartmouth College."

Whereas, the meetings of the trustees and overseers of Dartmouth University, which were summoned agreeably to the provisions of said act, failed of being duly holden, in consequence of a *quorum* of neither said trustees nor overseers attending at the time and place appointed, whereby the proceedings of said corporation have hitherto been, and still are delayed:

§ 1. Be it enacted, &c., that the governor be, and he is hereby authorized and requested to summon a meeting of the trustees of Dartmouth University, at such time and place as he may deem expedient. And the said trustees, at such meeting, may do and transact any matter or thing, within the limits of their jurisdiction and power, as such trustees, to every intent and purpose, and as fully and completely as if the same were transacted at any annual or other meeting. And the governor, with advice of council, is authorized to fill all vacancies that have happened, or may happen in the board of said trustees, previous to their next annual meeting. And the governor is hereby authorized to summon a meeting of the overseers of said university, at such time and place as he may consider proper. And provided, a less number than a *quorum* of said board of overseers convene at the time and place appointed for such meeting of their board, they shall have power to adjourn, from time to time, until a *quorum* shall have convened.

§ 2. And be it further enacted, that so much of the act, to which this is an addition, as makes necessary any particular number of trustees or overseers of said university, to constitute a *quorum* for the transaction of business, be, and the same hereby is repealed; and that hereafter, nine of said trustees, convened agreeably to the provisions of this act, or to those of that to which this is an addition, shall be a *quorum* for transacting business; and that in the board of trustees, six votes at least shall be necessary for the passage of any act or resolution. And provided also, that any smaller number than nine of said trustees, convened at the time and place appointed for any meeting of their board, according to the provisions of this act, or that to which this is an addition, shall have power to adjourn from time to time, until a *quorum* shall have convened.

§ 3. And be it further enacted, that each member of said board of trustees, already appointed or chosen, or hereafter to be appointed or chosen, shall, before entering on the duties of his office, make and subscribe an oath for the faithful discharge of the duties aforesaid; which oath shall be returned to, and filed in the office of the secretary of state, previous to the next regular meeting of said board, after said member enters on the duties of his office, as aforesaid.

Approved, December 18th, 1816.

Act of December 26, 1816

An act in addition to an act, entitled, "an act in addition to, and in amendment of, an act, entitled, an act to amend the charter and enlarge and improve the corporation of Dartmouth College."

Be it enacted &c., that if any person or persons shall assume the office of president, trustee, professor, secretary, treasurer, librarian or other officer of Dartmouth University; or by any name, or under any pretext, shall, directly or indirectly, take upon himself or themselves the discharge of any of the duties of either of those offices, except it be pursuant to, and in conformity with, the provisions of an act, entitled, "an act to amend the charter and enlarge and improve the corporation of Dartmouth College," or, of the "act, in addition to and in amendment of an act, entitled, an act to amend the charter and enlarge and improve the corporation of Dartmouth College," or shall in any way, directly or indirectly, wilfully impede or hinder any such officer or officers already existing, or hereafter to be appointed agreeably to the provisions of the acts aforesaid, in the free and entire discharge of the duties of their respective offices, conformably to the provisions of said acts, the person or persons so offending shall, for each offence, forfeit and pay the sum of five hundred dollars, to be recovered by any person who shall sue therefor, one-half thereof to the use of the prosecutor, and the other half to the use of said university.

And be it further enacted, that the person or persons who sustained the offices of secretary and treasurer of the trustees of Dartmouth College, next before the passage of the act, entitled, "an act to amend the charter and enlarge and improve the corporation of Dartmouth College," shall continue to hold and discharge the duties of those offices, as secretary and treasurer of the trustees of Dartmouth University, until another person or persons be appointed, in his or their stead, by the trustees of said university. And that the treasurer of said university, so existing, shall, in his office, have the care, management, direction and superintendence of the property of said corporation, whether real or personal, until a *quorum* of said trustees shall have convened in a regular meeting.

Approved, December 26th, 1816.

5. *Trustees of Dartmouth College* v. *Woodward*
1 N. H. 111 (1817)

RICHARDSON, C. J. This cause which is trover * for sundry articles alleged to be the property of the plaintiffs, comes before the court upon a statement of facts, in which it is agreed by the parties that the trustees of *Dartmouth College* were a body corporate duly organized under a charter bearing date December 13, 1769; that the several articles mentioned in the writ, were the property of that body corporate, and that before the commencement of this action, the said articles being in the possession of the defendant, he refused, although duly requested, to deliver them to the plaintiffs. Upon these facts it is clear, that judgment must be rendered for the plaintiffs, unless the facts upon which the defendant relies, constitute a legal defence.

By an act of this state passed June 27, 1816, entitled "An act to amend the charter and enlarge and improve the corporation of *Dartmouth College*," it is among other things enacted "that the corporation heretofore called and known by the name of the *Trustees of Dartmouth College,* shall ever hereafter be called and known by the name of the *Trustees of Dartmouth University,* and the whole number of said trustees shall be twenty-one, a majority of whom shall form a quorum for the transaction of business, and they and their successors in that capacity as hereby constituted, shall respectively forever have, hold, use, exercise and enjoy all the powers, authorities, rights, property, liberties, privileges and immunities which have hitherto been possessed, enjoyed and used by the trustees of *Dartmouth College*."—"And the governor and council shall by appointment as soon as may be, complete the present board of trustees to the number of twenty-one as provided for by this act, and shall have power also to fill all vacancies that may occur previous to, or during the first meeting of said board of trustees." By an act of this state passed December 18, 1816, entitled "An act in addition to and in amendment of an act entitled an act to amend the charter," &c. it is declared "that the governor with advice of council is authorized to fill all vacancies that have happened, or may happen in the board of said trustees previous to their next annual meeting."

It is agreed by the parties, that in pursuance of the provisions of these acts, the governor and council "completed the said board of trustees to the number of twenty-one," by appointing nine new trustees who accepted the trust; and that previous to the commencement of this action, at a meeting of the trustees of *Dartmouth University* held as the law requires, and composed of two of the former trustees of *Dartmouth College* and the nine new trustees appointed

---

* Trover was originally an action against one who found (Fr. *trouver*) another's property and converted it to his own use.

as aforesaid, being a sufficient number to constitute a quorum of the whole board of twenty-one, the defendant was duly appointed treasurer and secretary of the trustees of *Dartmouth University;* and the articles mentioned in the plaintiffs' writ duly committed to his custody as the property of the *University.*

Contention of Old Trustees

It is also agreed, that nine of the old trustees of *Dartmouth College* have individually and as far as by law they could, as a corporation, refused to accept the provisions of the acts of June 27, and December 18, 1816, and still claim to be a corporation as constituted by the charter of 1769, and to have the same control over the property which belonged to the *College,* as they had before those acts were passed. And this action is brought to enforce that claim. If those parts of the acts above mentioned, which authorize the appointment of new trustees, are valid and binding upon the trustees of *Dartmouth College* without their consent, this action cannot be maintained: because in that case the corporation must now be considered as composed of twenty-one members, and any claim of a minority of the corporation to control the affairs of the institution in opposition to the majority is clearly without any legal foundation.

But if on the other hand those acts are to be considered in that respect as unconstitutional and void, then the appointment and all the doings of the new trustees are invalid; the corporation remains as constituted by the charter of 1769; and the plaintiffs must prevail in this action. The decision of the cause must therefore depend upon the question, Whether the legislature had a constitutional right to authorize the appointment of new trustees without the consent of the corporation?

This cause has been argued on both sides with uncommon learning and ability, and we have witnessed with pleasure and with pride a display of talents and eloquence upon this occasion in the highest degree honourable to the profession of the law in this state. If the counsel of the plaintiffs have failed to convince us that the action can be maintained, it has not been owing to any want of diligence in research, or ingenuity in reasoning, but to a want of solid and substantial grounds on which to rest their arguments.

A complaint that private rights protected by the constitution have been invaded, will at all times deserve and receive the most deliberate consideration of this court. The cause of an individual whose rights have been infringed by the legislature in violation of the constitution, becomes at once the cause of all. For if a private right be thus infringed to-day, and that infringement be sanctioned by a judicial decision to-morrow, there will be next day a precedent for the violation of the rights of every man in the community; and so long as that precedent is followed, the constitution will be in fact to a certain extent repealed.

An unconstitutional act must always be presumed to have been passed inadvertently or through misapprehension; and it is equally to be presumed that every honest legislature will rejoice when such an act is declared void, and the supremacy of the constitution maintained. But we must not for a moment forget, that the question submitted to our decision in such cases, is always one of mere constitutional right;—sitting here as judges, we have nothing to do with the policy or expediency of the acts of the legislature. The legislative power of this state extends to every proper object of legislation, and is limited only by our constitutions and by the fundamental principles of all government and the unalienable rights of mankind.

In giving a construction however to a doubtful clause in the constitution, we might with propriety weigh the conveniences and inconveniences which would result from a particular construction, because in such a case arguments drawn from those sources might have a tendency to shew the probable intention of the makers of the constitution. But when the constitutional right to pass a law is clear, the question of expediency belongs exclusively to the legislature. Nor is an act in any case to be presumed to be contrary to the constitution. The opposition between that instrument and the act should be such as to produce upon our minds a clear and strong conviction of their incompatibility with each other before we pronounce the act void.

A decent respect for the other branches of the government, ought to induce us to weigh well the reasons upon which we found our opinions upon questions of this kind, and not to refuse to execute a law, till we are able to vindicate our judgment by sound and unanswerable arguments. For if we refuse to execute an act warranted by the constitution, our decision in effect alters that instrument, and imposes new restraints upon the legislative power, which the people never intended. On the other hand, if clearly convinced that an act of the legislature is unconstitutional, we should be unworthy of the station in which we are placed if we shrunk from the duties which that station imposes.

Nature of Corporations

In order to determine the question submitted to us, it seems necessary in the first place to ascertain the nature of corporations.—A corporation aggregate is a collection of many individuals united into one body under a special name, having perpetual succession under an artificial form, and vested by the policy of the law with the capacity of acting in several respects as an individual, and having collectively certain faculties which the individuals have not.

A corporation considered as a faculty, is an artificial, invisible body, existing only in contemplation of law: and can neither employ its franchises nor hold its property, for its own benefit. In another view, a corporation may be considered as a body of individuals having collectively particular faculties and capacities, which they can employ for their own benefit, or for the benefit of others, according to the purposes for which their particular faculties and capacities were bestowed. In either view it is apparent, that all beneficial interests both in the franchises and the property of corporations, must be considered as vested in natural persons, either in the people at large, or in individuals; and that with respect to this interest, corporations may be divided into *public* and *private*.

Private corporations are those which are created for the immediate benefit and advantage of individuals, and their franchises may be considered as privileges conferred on a number of individuals to be exercised and enjoyed by them in the form of a corporation. These privileges may be given to the corporators for their own benefit, or for the benefit of other individuals.

In either case the corporation must be viewed in relation to the franchises as a trustee, and each of those, who are beneficially interested in them, as a *cestui que trust.* The property of this kind of corporations and the profits arising from the employment of their property and the exercise of their franchises, in fact belongs to individuals. To this class belong all the companies incorporated in this state, for the purpose of making canals, turnpike roads and bridges; also banking, insurance and manufacturing companies, and many others. Both the franchises and the property of these corporations exist collectively in all the individuals of whom they are composed; not however as natural persons, but as a body politic, while the beneficial interest in both is vested severally in the several members, according to their respective shares.

This interest of each individual is a part of his property. It may be sold and transferred, may, in many cases be seized and sold upon a *fieri facias,** and is assets in the hands of his administrator. This is by no means a new view of this subject. . . .

Public Corporations

Public corporations are those which are created for public purposes, and whose property is devoted to the objects for which they are created. The corporators have no private beneficial interest, either in their franchises or their property. The only private right which individuals can have in them, is the right of being, and of acting as members, Every other right and interest attached to them can only be enjoyed by individuals like the common privileges of free citizens, and the common interest which all have in the property belonging to the state. Counties, towns, parishes, &c. considered as corporations, clearly fall within this description.

A corporation, all of whose franchises are exercised for public purposes, is a public corporation. Thus if the legislature should incorporate a number of individuals, for the purpose of making a canal, and should reserve all the profits arising from it to the state, though all the funds might be given to the corporation by individuals, it would in fact be a public corporation. So if the state should purchase all the shares in one of our banking companies, it would immediately become a public corporation. Because in both cases all the property and franchises of the corporations would in fact be public property.

A gift to a corporation created for public purposes is in reality a gift to the public. On the other hand, if the legislature should incorporate a banking company for the benefit of the corporators, and should give the corporation all the necessary funds, it would be a private corporation. Because a gift to such a corporation would be only a gift to the corporators. So should the state purchase a part of the shares in one of our banks, it would still remain a private corporation so far as individuals retained a private interest in it. Thus it seems, that whether a corporation is to be considered as public or private, depends upon the objects for which its franchises are to be exercised; and that as a corporation possesses franchises and property only to enable it to answer the

* *Fieri facias* (or *fi. fa.*) was a writ ordering the sheriff or other appropriate official to levy a sufficient amount on the goods of a debtor to satisfy the judgment against him.

purposes of its creation—a gift to a corporation is in truth a gift, to those who are interested in those purposes.

Whether an incorporated college, founded and endowed by an individual, who had reserved to himself a control over its affairs as a private visitor, must be viewed as a public or as a private corporation, it is not necessary now to decide, because it does not appear that *Dartmouth College* was subject to any private visitation whatever.

Dartmouth Charter

Upon looking into the charter of *Dartmouth College* we find that the king, "being willing to encourage the laudable and charitable design of spreading christian knowledge among the savages of our *American* wilderness, and also that the best means of education be established in the province of *New-Hampshire*, for the benefit of said province," ordained that there should be a *College* created in said province by the name of *Dartmouth College*, "for the education and instruction of youth of the indian tribes, in this land, in reading, writing and all parts of learning, which should appear necessary and expedient for civilizing and christianizing children of pagans, as well as in all liberal arts and sciences, and also of *English* youth and any others;" and that there should be in the said *Dartmouth College* from thenceforth and forever a body politic, consisting of trustees of *Dartmouth College*. He then "made, ordained, constituted and appointed" twelve individuals to be trustees of the *College,* and declared that they and their successors, should forever thereafter be a body corporate, by the name of the *Trustees of Dartmouth College;* and that said corporation should be "able, and in law capable for the use of said *College,* to have, get, acquire, purchase, receive, hold, possess and enjoy tenements, hereditaments, jurisdictions and franchises, for themselves and their successors, in fee simple or otherwise;"—and "to receive and dispose of any lands, goods, chattels and other things of what nature soever, for the use aforesaid; and also to have, accept and receive any rents, profits, annuities, gifts, legacies, donations or bequests, of any kind whatsoever, for the use aforesaid."

Such are the objects, and such the nature of this corporation, appearing upon the face of the charter. It was created for the purpose of holding and managing property for the use of the *College;* and the *College* was founded for the purpose of "spreading the knowledge of the great Redeemer" among the savages and of furnishing "the best means of education" to the province of *New-Hampshire*. These great purposes are surely, if any thing can be, matters of public concern. Who has any private interest either in the objects or the property of this institution? The trustees themselves have no greater interest in the spreading of Christian knowledge among the Indians, and in providing the best means of education, than any other individuals in the community. Nor have they any private interest in the property of this institution,—nothing that can be sold or transferred, that can descend to their heirs, or can be assets in the hands of their administrators.

If all the property of the institution were destroyed, the loss would be exclusively public, and no private loss to them. So entirely free are they from any private interest in this respect, that they are competent witnesses in causes where the corporation is a party, and the property of the corporation in contest. . . .

The office of trustee of *Dartmouth College* is, in fact, a public trust, as much so as the office of governor, or of judge of this court; and for any breach of trust, the state has an unquestionable right, through its courts of justice, to call them to an account. The trustees have the same interest in the corporate property, which the governor has in the property of the state, and which we have in the fines we impose upon the criminals convicted before this court. Nor is it any private concern of theirs, whether their powers, as corporators, shall be extended or lessened, any more than it is our private concern whether the jurisdiction of this court shall be enlarged or diminished. They have no private right in the institution, except the right of office,—the right of being trustees, and of acting as such. It therefore seems to us, that if such a corporation is not to be considered as a public corporation, it would be difficult to find one that could be so considered.

Powers of Legislature

It becomes then, unnecessary to decide in this case, how far the legislature possesses a constitutional right to interfere in the concerns of private corporations. It may not, however, be improper to remark, that it would be difficult to find a satisfactory reason why the property and immunities of such corporations should not stand, in this respect, on the same ground with the property and immunities of individuals.

In deciding a case like this, where the complaint is that corporate rights have been unconstitutionally infringed, it is the duty of the court to strip off the forms and fictions with which the policy of the law has clothed those rights, and look beyond that intangible creature of the law, the corporation, which *in form* possesses them, to the individuals and to the public, to whom, in *reality,* they belong, and who alone can be injured by a violation of them. This action, therefore, though *in form* the complaint of the corporation, must be considered as *in substance* the complaint of the trustees themselves.

The acts in question can only effect *public* or *private* rights and interests. With regard to the rights and interests which the public may have in the institution—no provision in the constitution of this state, nor of the *United States,* is recollected, which can protect them from legislative interference. We have been referred to no such provision in the argument. The clauses in those constitutions, upon which the plaintiffs' counsel have relied, were most manifestly, intended to protect private rights only.

All public interests are proper objects of legislation; and it is peculiarly the province of the legislature, to determine by what laws those interests shall be regulated. Nor is the expediency, or the policy of such laws, a subject for judicial decision. The constitution has given to the general court full power and authority to make and ordain all such laws "as they may judge for the benefit and welfare of this state." Should we assume the power of declaring statutes valid or invalid, according to our opinion of their expediency, it would not be endured for a moment, but would be justly viewed by all, as a wanton usurpation, altogether repugnant to the principles of our government. Nor are these plaintiffs competent to call in question the validity of these laws in a court of justice, on the ground that they are injurious to the public interests.

A law is only the public will duly expressed. These trustees are the servants of the public, and the servant is not to resist the will of his master, in a matter that concerns that master alone. If these acts be injurious to the public interests, the remedy is to be sought in their repeal, not in courts of law. But if these acts infringe *private* rights, protected by the constitution, whether the trustees themselves, or of others, whose rights they, from their situation, are competent to vindicate, then the plaintiffs have proper grounds, upon which to submit their validity to our decision.

All private rights in this institution must belong, either to those who founded, or whose bounty has endowed it; to the officers and students of the college; or to the trustees.

Corporate Interests Affected

As to those who founded or who have endowed it; no person of this description, who claims any private right, has been pointed out or is known to us. It is not understood that any person claims to be a visitor of this college. An absolute donation of land or money to an institution of this kind, creates no private right in it. Besides, if the private rights of founders or donors have been infringed by these acts, it is their business to vindicate their own rights. It is no concern of these plaintiffs. When founders and donors complain, it will be our duty to hear and decide; but we cannot adjudicate upon their rights, till they come judicially before us. It has been strenuously urged to us, in the argument, that these acts will tend to discourage donations, and are therefore impolitic. Be it so. That was a consideration very proper to be weighed by those who made the acts, but is entitled to no weight in this decision.

The officers and students of the college have, without doubt, private rights in the institution—rights which courts of justice are bound to notice—rights, which, if unjustly infringed, even by the trustees themselves, this court, upon a proper application, would feel itself bound to protect. But for any injury done to their rights, they have their own remedy. It would be unjust to prejudge their case on this occasion. They are not parties to this record, and cannot be legally heard in the discussion of this cause. If no form of action given them by law can be conceived, it is because these acts do no injury to their rights. . . .

But it seems to us impossible to suppose, that the legislature intended by these acts, to dissolve the old corporation or to create a new one, nor do we conceive that the addition of new members, can in any case be considered as a dissolution of a corporation. The legislature of this state have not unfrequently annexed tracts of inhabited territory to towns, and thereby added new members to the corporation. Yet who ever supposed that this was a dissolution of the old, and the creation of a new corporation. Our statute of December 11, 1812, *N. H. Laws* 184. makes the shares and interest of any person, in any incorporated company, liable to be seized and sold upon execution, and gives to the purchaser all the privileges appertaining thereto; and of course makes him a member of the corporation. But the thought probably never occurred to any man, that when a new member is added, by virtue of that act, the corporation is thereby dissolved, and a new one created. Yet that act has at least, as much dissolving, and as much creating force, as the acts now under consideration.

Differentiated Interests

The plaintiffs, in taking this ground, seem not to have adverted to a material distinction, which certainly exists between the rights and faculties relating to corporations, which can exist only in the corporators, as natural persons, and the corporate rights and faculties, which can exist only in the corporation. The right to the beneficial interest in the corporate property, can only exist in natural persons. But the legal title and ownership in corporate property, can in no case be considered as vested in the several corporators, as natural persons, either jointly or severally, but collectively in all, as one body politic, made capable by the policy of the law, of holding property as an individual. This artificial individual, which is said to be immortal, holds in all cases the legal title.

Hence a corporation may maintain trespass against any of its members who intermeddle with its property, without its consent. Hence too, the legal title of a corporation in lands, will not pass by the deed of all its members. This faculty of holding property as an individual, which the policy of the law vests in a body of natural persons, that can be perpetuated by known rules of law, is one of the great ends and uses of an incorporation. But the natural persons who compose this artificial, immortal individual, in which the property is vested, must, in the nature of things, be continually fluctuating and changing; and yet the artificial individual remains in contemplation of law the same.

It is therefore clear, that the legal identity of a corporation does not depend upon its being composed of the same natural persons, and that an addition of new members to a corporation, cannot in itself, make it a new and different corporation. The immortality of a corporation depends upon a continued accession of new members. The mode in which this accession is affected, is immaterial. A few of our corporations are perpetuated by a power of electing new members, placed in the corporations themselves. But most of our public, and all of our private corporations, are perpetuated by mere operation of law, without any corporate act whatever. Nor, by the addition of new members, is any part of the legal title to the corporate property, transferred from the old to the new members. That title remains unaltered in the corporation. The old members had not personally any such title that could be taken from them; and the new members had personally acquired none.

The error of the plaintiffs on this subject, probably originated in their supposing that the legal title to corporate property is vested in the corporators, in the same manner that the title to partnership property is vested in co-partners. Indeed their counsel endeavoured to illustrate this point, by comparing corporate to partnership property. And if the comparison had been just, the inferences which the counsel made, would also have been just. But the comparison does not hold, unless we are entirely mistaken as to the manner in which the legal title to corporate property is vested. The addition of new members by a legislative act, even to a private corporation does not necessarily divest the old corporators of any private beneficial interest, which they may individually have in the corporate property.

Suppose the legislature should enact, that the governor should be ex-officio a member of all the banking corporations in the state. This might give him a personal influence in the management of their concerns, but would give him no beneficial interest whatever in the corporate property. The interest of the stockholders would remain the same. In the case of corporations, where all the benefit derived from them consists in the privileges incident to membership, as in incorporated library companies, it may be otherwise. But in the property of public corporations, there is no private beneficial interest that can be divested. We are therefore of opinion, that these acts, if valid, do not dissolve the old corporation, nor create a new one; nor do they operate in such manner as to change or transfer any legal title, or beneficial interest, in the corporate property, but the legal title remains in the corporation, and the beneficial interest in the public, unaffected.

Contracts and Charters

It has also been contended, that it depends altogether upon contract, whether the old trustees shall become members of the corporation as now organized; that there can be no contract without consent, and that therefore, these acts cannot bind the old trustees without their consent, and must, in the nature of things, be invalid. The whole amount of this argument is this: a statute, which attempts to compel the members of a corporation to become members of that corporation, differently organized, without their consent, is invalid; and as these acts make such an attempt, they are therefore invalid.

To this there are two decisive answers. 1. Neither of the propositions upon which the conclusion rests is true. 2. Admitting the premises to be correct, the legitimate conclusion to be drawn from them, is wholly irrelevant to the question in this case. In the first place, the proposition that it depends altogether upon contract, whether individuals shall become members of particular corporations, is not universally true; and so far as respects public corporations, it is never true. The legislature has a most unquestionable right to compel individuals to become members of public corporations. Thus when a town is incorporated, all the inhabitants become members of the corporation, and continue members so long as they reside within its limits, whether they consent or not.

Nor is there any good reason to doubt that the legislature possess the right to compel individuals to accept the office of trustees of *Dartmouth College,* however the corporation may be organized, any more than there is to doubt the right of the legislature to compel individuals to serve as town officers, as is done by our statute of February 8, 1791, *Laws,* 241. or to be enrolled in the militia, and hazard their lives in defence of the state.

It is a fundamental principle of all governments, recognized in the twelfth article of our bill of rights, that a state has a right to the personal service of its citizens, whenever the public necessity requires it,—and the government has a right to judge of that necessity. . . .

Nor is the proposition, that these acts attempt to compel the old trustees to become members of this corporation as now organized, without their consent, true. They are left perfectly at liberty to continue members of the corporation or not according to their own pleasure. It is enacted, that the board shall hereafter consist of twenty-one members; but it is not enacted that they shall continue members of it against their consent. They had, before these acts were passed, a perfect right to resign when they pleased; and that right is not impaired by these acts.

Consent of Old Trustees

But, in the second place, admitting the premises to be true, the legitimate conclusion does not bear upon the question in this case. The fair conclusion to be drawn from the premises, is, that these acts, so far as they attempt to compel the old members to become members of the corporation as now organized, are invalid. But the question here is not, whether the legislature can compel the old trustees to become members of the newly organized corporation, but whether it has a constitutional right to make a new organization of the corporation, by adding new members? And it is very apparent, that although the legislature may not possess the power to do the one, yet still it may have a constitutional right to do the other.

There is a clear distinction between laws binding corporate bodies, and laws attempting to bind individuals to continue members of corporate bodies. Thus the legislature has an undoubted right, at all times, to pass laws binding the whole body politic of the state; but it is by no means clear, that the legislature has at all times a right to compel individuals to remain in the state, and be subject to those laws. So the legislature has a right to incorporate towns; but can it compel the inhabitants to remain in them, and continue members of such corporations?

But what is such a new organization of a corporation as cannot be made without the consent of the corporators? If new members cannot be added, can any new duty be imposed upon a corporation; or can the corporate powers and faculties be in any way limited, without such consent? Our statute of June 21, 1814, *Laws* 284. makes it the duty of the several incorporated banks, to make a return of the state of their several banks, to the governor and council annually, in June, under a penalty of one thousand dollars. If the doctrine of these plaintiffs be true, may not the stockholders say that they cannot be compelled to be members of corporations, subject to new and different duties, without their consent, and that therefore this act is void? And may not the same argument be used in regard to the acts of June 11, 1803, and June 17, 1807, which prohibit banks from issuing bills of a certain description? In fact, does not this doctrine amount to a denial of the right to legislate at all, on the subject of corporations, without their consent?

Limits to Corporate Actions

But, although an artificial individual, capable of holding the legal title to property, may be created by the policy of the law, and a kind of artificial will and judgment as to the management of its concerns, given to it by making the consent of a number of natural persons necessary in all its acts; yet still this artificial will and judgment is, after all, only the private will and judgment of natural persons, in some respects limited and restricted.

In this point of view, a corporation may be considered as a body of natural persons, having power and authority vested in them, to manage the corporate concerns in such a manner as a majority of a competent number of them may judge and determine to be best calculated to answer the ends of the incorporation. And it has been truly said, by the counsel of the plaintiffs, that by the charter of 1769 exclusive power and authority was given to the twelve trustees, to manage the affairs of this corporation in such manner as a majority of any seven or more of them, duly convened for the purpose, might judge most expedient to answer the purposes of the institution; and that the right of the twelve, to exercise that exclusive power and authority is taken away by these acts, and others admitted to share that power and authority with them.

Such is, without doubt, the operation of these acts; and it seems to us that this is the whole ground of complaint, which the plaintiffs can have. These acts compel the old trustees to sacrifice no private interest whatever, but merely to admit others to aid them, in the management of the concerns of a public institution; and if they have no private views to answer, nor private wishes to gratify, in the management of these concerns, (and it would be very uncharitable to suppose they can have, for it is extremely dishonorable to prostitute public interest to private purposes) it is not very easy to see how this can furnish any very solid ground of complaint. Had the affairs and concerns of *Dartmouth College* been their own private affairs and concerns, such an interference would have had a very different complexion.

Constitutional Issue

But the plaintiffs contend that these acts impair their right to manage the affairs of this institution, in violation of that clause of the fifteenth article in our bill of rights, which declares that "no subject shall be arrested, imprisoned, despoiled or deprived of his property, immunities or privileges, put out of the protection of the law, exiled or deprived of his life, liberty or estate, but by the judgment of his peers or the law of the land."

That the right to manage the affairs of this college, is a privilege within the meaning of this clause of the bill of rights, is not to be doubted. But how a privilege can be protected from the operation of a law of the land, by a clause in the constitution declaring that it shall not be taken away, but by the law of the land, is not very easily understood. This clause in our bill of rights, seems to have been taken from the 29th chapter of Magna Charta. "No freeman shall be taken or imprisoned, or be disseized of his freehold, or liberties, or free customs, or be out-lawed or exiled, or any otherwise destroyed, nor will we pass upon him nor condemn him, but by lawful judgment of his peers, or by the law of the land." . . .

Due Process Question

We have public statutes, authorizing the selectmen of towns to take the lands of individuals for highways, and empowering fire-wards "to pull down, blow up or remove any house or buildings," when necessary to stop the progress of fire. We have private acts, giving to turnpike corporations authority to take the land of individuals for their roads. Under all these statutes, the property of individuals is often taken without their consent; and yet it seems never to have been doubted that those statutes were "the law of the land," within the meaning of the constitution. By the statute of December 24, 1805, entitled, "an act respecting idle persons," judges of probate are authorized, in certain cases, to appoint guardians of idle persons, and thereby take from them all controul over both their real and personal estate. This act has been in our statute book nearly twelve years, as a part of "the law of the land," and no one has ever called its validity in question. . . .

No one of the acts just mentioned, seems to afford to the individuals, whose property and privileges may be affected by them, a less solid ground of complaint than the acts in question do to the plaintiffs. If the latter be repugnant to this clause in the constitution, so must be the former. There seems to be no substantial difference in the cases, on which a solid distinction can be founded. If we decide that these acts are not "the law of the land," because they interfere with private rights, all other acts, interfering with private rights, may, for aught we see, fall within the same principle; and what statute does not either directly or indirectly interfere with private rights? The principle would probably make our whole statute book a dead letter. We cannot adopt it; but are clearly of opinion that these acts, if not repugnant to any other constitutional provision, are "the law of the land," within the true sense of the constitution.

U.S. Constitution

But it is said, that the charter of 1769 is a contract, the validity of which is impaired by these acts, in violation of that clause in the tenth section of the first article of the constitution of the *United States*, which declares that "No state shall pass any law, impairing the obligations of contracts." It has probably never yet been decided, that a charter of this kind is a contract, within the meaning of the constitution of the *United States*. None of the cases cited were like the present. . . .

This clause in the constitution of the *United States*, was obviously intended to protect private rights of property, and embraces all contracts relating to private property, whether executed or executory, and whether between individuals, between states, or between states and individuals. The word "contracts" must however be taken, in its common and ordinary acceptation, as an actual agreement between parties, by which something is granted or stipulated, immediately for the benefit of the actual parties.

But this clause was not intended to limit the power of the states, in relation to their own public officers and servants, or to their own civil institutions, and must not be construed to embrace contracts, which are in their nature, mere matters of civil institution; nor grants of power and authority, by a state to individuals, to be exercised for purposes merely public. Thus marriage is a contract; but being a mere matter of civil institution, is not within the meaning of this clause. A law, therefore, authorizing divorces, though it impairs the validity of marriage contracts, is not a violation of the constitution of the *United States*. Thus, too, many of our penal statutes give a part of the penalties and forfeitures incurred under them, to particular individuals, and whenever a penalty or forfeiture is incurred, such individuals have a vested right to sue for and recover such forfeitures and penalties. But a repeal of those acts, at any time before an actual recovery, has always been held to divest this right. . . .

Yet this right seems never to have been called in question, on the ground that their charters were contracts, within the meaning of this clause. All our judges, justices of the peace, sheriffs, &c. hold their offices under grants from the governor and council, in pursuance of statutes. But who ever supposed that these grants were contracts within the meaning of this clause of the constitution of the *United States*. The distinction we have here endeavored to lay down, between the contracts which are, and which are not intended by that instrument, seems to us to be clear and obvious. If the charter of a public institution, like that of *Dartmouth College*, is to be construed as a contract, within the intent of the constitution of the *United States*, it will, in our opinion, be difficult to say what powers, in relation to their public institutions, if any, are left to the states. It is a construction, in our view, repugnant to the very principles of all government, because it places all the public institutions of all the states beyond legislative control. For it is clear that congress possesses no powers on the subject. We are therefore clearly of opinion, that the charter of *Dartmouth College* is not a contract, within the meaning of this clause in the constitution of the *United States*.

Contract Limitations

But admitting that charter to have been such a contract, what was the contract? Can it be construed to be a contract on the part of the king with the corporators, whom he appointed, and their successors, that they should forever have the control of the affairs of this institution, and be forever free from all legislative interference, and that their number should be augmented or diminished, however strongly the public interest might require it? Such a contract, in relation to a public institution, would, as we conceive, be absurd and repugnant to the principles of all government.

The king had no power to make such a contract, and thus bind the sovereign authority on a subject of mere public concern. Nor does our legislature possess the power to make such a contract. Had it been provided in the act of June 1816, that the twenty-one trustees should forever have the exclusive control of this institution, and that no future legislature should add to their number, does any one suppose such a provision would have been binding upon a future legislature? Or suppose the legislature should enact that the number of judges of this court should never be augmented; is it possible to suppose that such an act could abridge the power of a succeeding legislature on the subject? We think not.

A distinction is to be taken between particular grants, by the legislature, of property or privileges to individuals, for their own benefit, and grants of power and authority to be exercised for public purposes. The former is in its nature, special legislation, in relation to private rights; the latter is general legislation, in relation to the common interests of all. Chief justice *Marshall,* in the case of *Fletcher* vs. *Peck*, 6 Cranch 135, adverts to this distinction, where he says "the correctness of this principle, that one legislature cannot abridge the powers of a succeeding legislature so far as respects general legislation, can never be controverted. But if an act be done under a law, a succeeding legislature cannot undo it. The past cannot be recalled by the most absolute power. Conveyances have been made; those conveyances have vested legal estates, and if those estates may be seized by the sovereign authority, still that they originally vested, is a fact and cannot cease to be a fact." We are therefore of opinion, that if this charter can be construed to be a contract within the meaning of the constitution of the *United States:* yet still it contains no contract binding on the legislature, that the number of trustees shall not be augmented, and that the validity of the contract is not impaired by these acts.

Public Policy Issue

I have looked into this case with all the attention of which I am capable, and with a most painful anxiety to discover the true principles upon which it ought to be decided. No man prizes more highly than I do, the literary institutions of our country, or would go farther to maintain their just rights and privileges. But I cannot bring myself to believe, that it would be consistent with sound policy, or ultimately with the true interests of literature itself, to place the great public institutions, in which all the young men, destined for the liberal professions, are to be educated, within the absolute control of a few individuals, and out of the control of the sovereign power—not consistent with sound policy, because it is a matter of too great moment, too intimately connected with the public welfare and prosperity, to be thus entrusted in the hands of a few.

The education of the rising generation is a matter of the highest public concern, and is worthy of the best attention of every legislature. The immediate care of these institutions must be committed to individuals, and the trust will be faithfully executed so long as it is recollected to be a mere public trust, and that there is a superintending power, that can and will correct every abuse of it. But make the trustees independent, and they will ultimately forget that their office is a public trust—will at length consider these institutions as their own—will overlook the great purposes for which their powers were originally given, and will exercise them only to gratify their own private views and wishes, or to promote the narrow purposes of a sect or a party.

It is idle to suppose that courts of law can correct every abuse of such a trust. Courts of law cannot legislate. There may be many abuses which can be corrected by the sovereign power alone. Nor would such exemption from legislative control be consistent with the true interests of literature itself, because these institutions must stand in constant need of the aid and patronage of the legislature and the public; and without such aid and patronage, they can never flourish. Their prosperity depends entirely upon the public estimation in which they are held. It is of the highest importance that they should be fondly cherished by the best affections of the people, that every citizen should feel that he has an interest in them, and that they constitute a part of that inestimable inheritance which he is to transmit to his posterity in the institutions of his country.

But these institutions, if placed in a situation to dispute the public will, would eventually fall into the hands of men, who would be disposed to dispute it; and contests would inevitably arise, in which the great interests of literature would be forgotten. Those who resisted that will, would become at once the object of popular jealousy and distrust: their motives, however pure, would be called in question, and their resistance would be believed to have originated in private and interested views, and not in a regard to the public welfare. It would avail these institutions nothing that the public will was wrong, and that their right could be maintained in opposition to it, in a court of law. A triumph there might be infinitely more ruinous than defeat. Whoever knows the nature of a popular government, knows that such a contest could not be thus settled by one engagement. Such a triumph would only protract the destructive contest. The last misfortune which can befall one of these institutions, is to become the subject of popular contention.

Legislative Supremacy

I am aware that this power in the hands of the legislature may, like every other power, at times be unwisely exercised; but where can it be more securely lodged? If those whom the people annually elect to manage their public affairs, cannot be trusted, who can? The people have most emphatically enjoined it in the constitution, as a duty upon "the legislators and magistrates, in all future periods of the government, to cherish the interests of literature and the sciences and all seminaries and public schools." And those interests will be cherished, both by the legislature and the people, so long as there is virtue enough left to maintain the rest of our institutions.

Whenever the people and their rulers shall become corrupt enough to wage war with the sciences and liberal arts, we may be assured that the time will have arrived, when all our institutions, our laws, our liberties must pass away,—when all that can be dear to freemen, or that can make their country dear to them, must be lost, and when a government and institutions must be established, of a very different character from those under which it is our pride and our happiness to live.

In forming my opinion in this case, however, I have given no weight to any considerations of expediency. I think the legislature had a clear constitutional right to pass the laws in question. My opinion may be incorrect, and our judgment erroneous; but it is the best opinion which, upon the most mature consideration, I have been able to form. It is, certainly, to me a subject of much consolation, to know that if we have erred, our mistakes can be corrected, and be prevented from working any ultimate injustice. If the plaintiffs think themselves aggrieved by our decision, they can carry the cause to another tribunal where it can be re-examined, and our judgment be reversed or affirmed, as the law of the case may seem to that tribunal to require.

                                        Judgment for the defendant.

6. *Opinion of the Supreme Court*

4 Wheaton 624 (1819)

February 2d, 1819. The opinion of the court was delivered by MARSHALL, Ch. J.—This is an action of trover, brought by the Trustees of Dartmouth College against William H. Woodward, in the state court of New Hampshire, for the book of records, corporate seal, and other corporate property, to which the plaintiffs allege themselves to be entitled. A special verdict, after setting out the rights of the parties, finds for the defendant, if certain acts of the legislature of New Hampshire, passed on the 27th of June, and on the 18th of December 1816, be valid, and binding on the trustees, without their assent, and not repugnant to the constitution of the United States; otherwise, it finds for the plaintiffs. The superior court of judicature of New Hampshire rendered a judgment upon this verdict for the defendant, which judgment has been brought before this court by writ of error. The single question now to be considered is, do the acts to which the verdict refers violate the constitution of the United States?

This court can be insensible neither to the magnitude nor delicacy of this question. The validity of a legislative act is to be examined; and the opinion of the highest law tribunal of a state is to be revised—an opinion which carries with it intrinsic evidence of the diligence, of the ability, and the integrity with which it was formed. On more than one occasion, this court has expressed the cautious circumspection with which it approaches the consideration of such questions; and has declared, that in no doubtful case, would it pronounce a legislative act to be contrary to the constitution. But the American people have said, in the constitution of the United States, that "no state shall pass any bill of attainder, *ex post facto* law, or law impairing the obligation of contracts." In the same instrument, they have also said, "that the judicial power shall extend to all cases in law and equity arising under the constitution." On the judges of this court, then, is imposed the high and solemn duty of protecting, from even legislative violation, those contracts which the constitution of our country has placed beyond legislative control; and, however irksome the task may be, this is a duty from which we dare not shrink.

The title of the plaintiffs originates in a charter dated the 13th day of December, in the year 1769, incorporating twelve persons therein mentioned, by the name of "The Trustees of Dartmouth College," granting to them and their successors the usual corporate privileges and powers, and authorizing the trustees, who are to govern the college, to fill up all vacancies which may be created in their own body.

The defendant claims under three acts of the legislature of New Hampshire, the most material of which was passed on the 27th of June 1816, and is entitled, "an act to amend the charter, and enlarge and improve the corporation of Dartmouth College." Among other alterations in the charter, this act increases the number of trustees to twenty-one, gives the appointment of the additional members to the executive of the state, and creates a board of overseers, with power to inspect and control the most important acts of the trustees. This board consists of twenty-five persons. The president of the senate, the speaker of the house of representatives, of New Hampshire, and the governor and lieutenant-governer of Vermont, for the time being, are to be members *ex officio*. The board is to be completed by the governor and council of New Hampshire, who are also empowered to fill all vacancies which may occur. The acts of the 18th and 26th of December are supplemental to that of the 27th of June, and are principally intended to carry that act into effect. The majority of the trustees of the college have refused to accept this amended charter, and have brought this suit for the corporate property, which is in possession of a person holding by virtue of the acts which have been stated.

Charter as a Contract

It can require no argument to prove, that the circumstances of this case constitute a contract. An application is made to the crown for a charter to incorporate a religious and literary institution. In the application, it is stated, that large contributions have been made for the object, which will be conferred on the corporation, as soon as it shall be created. The charter is granted, and on its faith the property is conveyed. Surely, in this transaction every ingredient of a complete and legitimate contract is to be found. The points for consideration are, 1. Is this contract protected by the constitution of the United States? 2. Is it impaired by the acts under which the defendant holds?

1. On the first point, it has been argued, that the word "contract," in its broadest sense, would comprehend the political relations between the government and its citizens, would extend to offices held within a state, for state purposes, and to many of those laws concerning civil institutions, which must change with circumstances, and be modified by ordinary legislation; which deeply concern the public, and which, to preserve good government, the public judgment must control. That even marriage is a contract, and its obligations are affected by the laws respecting divorces. That the clause in the constitution, if construed in its greatest latitude, would prohibit these laws. Taken in its broad, unlimited sense, the clause would be an unprofitable and vexatious interference with the internal concerns of a state, would unnecessarily and unwisely embarrass its legislation, and render immutable those civil institutions, which are established for purposes of internal government, and which, to subserve those purposes, ought to vary with varying circumstances. That as the framers of the constitution could never have intended to insert in that instrument, a provision so unnecessary, so mischievous, and so repugnant to its general spirit, the term "contract" must be understood in a more limited sense.

That it must be understood as intended to guard against a power, of at least doubtful utility, the abuse of which had been extensively felt; and to restrain the legislature in future from violating the right to property. That, anterior to the formation of the constitution, a course of legislation had prevailed in many, if not in all, of the states, which weakened the confidence of man in man, and embarrassed all transactions between individuals, by dispensing with a faithful performance of engagements. To correct this mischief, by restraining the power which produced it, the state legislatures were forbidden "to pass any law impairing the obligation of contracts," that is, of contracts respecting property, under which some individual could claim a right to something beneficial to himself; and that, since the clause in the constitution must in construction receive some limitation, it may be confined, and ought to be confined, to cases of this description; to cases within the mischief it was intended to remedy.*

State Powers Generally

The general correctness of these observations cannot be controverted. That the framers of the constitution did not intend to restrain the states in the regulation of their civil institutions, adopted for internal government, and that the instrument they have given us, is not to be so construed, may be admitted. The provision of the constitution never has been understood to embrace other contracts, than those which respect property, or some object of value, and confer rights which may be asserted in a court of justice. It never has been understood to restrict the general right of the legislature to legislate on the subject of divorces. Those acts enable some tribunals, not to impair a marriage contract, but to liberate one of the parties, because it has been broken by the other. When any state legislature shall pass an act annulling all marriage contracts, or allowing either party to annul it, without the consent of the other, it will be time enough to inquire, whether such an act be constitutional.

The parties in this case differ less on general principles, less on the true construction of the constitution in the abstract, than on the application of those principles to this case, and on the true construction of the charter of 1769. This is the point on which the cause essentially depends. If the act of incorporation be a grant of political power, if it create a civil institution, to be employed in the administration of the government, or if the funds of the college be public property, or if the state of New Hampshire, as a government, be alone interested in its transactions, the subject is one in which the legislature of the state may act according to its own judgment, unrestrained by any limitation of its power imposed by the constitution of the United States.

But if this be a private eleemosynary institution, endowed with a capacity to take property, for objects unconnected with government, whose funds are bestowed by individuals, on the faith of the charter; if the donors have stipulated for the future disposition and management of those funds, in the manner prescribed by themselves; there may be more difficulty in the case, although neither the persons who have made these stipulations, nor those for whose benefit they were made, should be parties to the cause. Those who are no longer interested in the property, may yet retain such an interest in the preservation of their own arrangements, as to have a right to insist, that those arrangements shall be held sacred. Or, if they have themselves disappeared, it becomes a subject of serious and anxious inquiry, whether those whom they have legally empowered to represent them for ever, may not assert all the rights which they possessed, while in being; whether, if they be without per-

---

* On the tendency of state laws to impair contracts, prior to the adoption of the Federal Constitution, cf. *The Federalist*, No. 44.

sonal representatives, who may feel injured by a violation of the compact, the trustees be not so completely their representatives, in the eye of the law, as to stand in their place, not only as respects the government of the college, but also as respects the maintenance of the college charter. It becomes then the duty of the court, most seriously to examine this charter, and to ascertain its true character.

Charter Provisions

From the instrument itself, it appears, that about the year 1754, the Rev. Eleazer Wheelock established, at his own expense, and on his own estate, a charity school for the instruction of Indians in the Christian religion. The success of this institution inspired him with the design of soliciting contributions in England, for carrying on and extending his undertaking. In this pious work, he employed the Rev. Nathaniel Whitaker, who, by virtue of a power of attorney from Dr. Wheelock, appointed the Earl of Dartmouth and others, trustees of the money, which had been, and should be, contributed; which appointment Dr. Wheelock confirmed by a deed of trust, authorizing the trustees to fix on a site for the college. They determined to establish the school on Connecticut river, in the western part of New Hampshire; that situation being supposed favorable for carrying on the original design among the Indians, and also for promoting learning among the English; and the proprietors in the neighborhood having made large offers of land, on condition that the college should there be placed. Dr. Wheelock then applied to the crown for an act of incorporation; and represented the expediency of appointing those whom he had, by his last will, named as trustees in America, to be members of the proposed corporation. "In consideration of the premises," "for the education and instruction of the youth of the Indian tribes," &c., "and also of English youth, and any others," the charter was granted, and the trustees of Dartmouth College were, by that name, created a body corporate, with power, for the use of the said college, to acquire real and personal property, and to pay the president, tutors and other officers of the college, such salaries as they shall allow.

The charter proceeds to appoint Eleazer Wheelock, "the founder of said college," president thereof, with power, by his last will, to appoint a successor, who is to continue in office, until disapproved by the trustees. In case of vacancy, the trustees may appoint a president, and in case of the ceasing of a president, the senior professor or tutor, being one of the trustees, shall exercise the office, until an appointment shall be made. The trustees have power to appoint and displace professors, tutors and other officers, and to supply any vacancies which may be created in their own body, by death, resignation, removal or disability; and also to make orders, ordinances and laws for the government of the college, the same not being repugnant to the laws of Great Britain, or of New Hampshire, and not excluding any person on account of his speculative sentiments in religion, or his being of a religious profession different from that of the trustees. This charter was accepted, and the property, both real and personal, which had been contributed for the benefit of the college, was conveyed to, and vested in, the corporate body.

From this brief review of the most essential parts of the charter, it is apparent, that the funds of the college consisted entirely of private donations. It is, perhaps, not very important, who were the donors. The probability is, that the Earl of Dartmouth, and the other trustees in England, were, in fact, the largest contributors. Yet the legal conclusion, from the facts recited in the charter, would probably be, that Dr. Wheelock was the founder of the college. The origin of the institution was, undoubtedly, the Indian charity school, established by Dr. Wheelock, at his own expense. It was at his instance, and to enlarge this school, that contributions were solicited in England. The person soliciting these contributions was his agent; and the trustees, who received the money, were appointed by, and act under, his authority. It is not too much to say, that the funds were obtained by him, in trust, to be applied by him to the purposes of his enlarged school. The charter of incorporation was granted at his instance. The persons named by him, in his last will, as the trustees of his charity-school, compose a part of the corporation, and he is declared to be the founder of the college, and its president for life. Were the inquiry material, we should feel some hesitation in saying, that Dr. Wheelock was not, in law, to be considered as the founder (1 Bl. Com. 481) of this institution, and as possessing all the rights appertaining to that character. But be this as it may, Dartmouth College is really endowed by private individuals, who have bestowed their funds for the propagation of the Christian religion among the Indians, and for the promotion of piety and learning generally. From these funds, the salaries of the tutors are drawn; and these salaries lessen the expense of education to the students. It is then an eleemosynary (1 Bl. Com. 471), and so far as respects its funds, a private corporation.*

Private Character of College

Do its objects stamp on it a different character? Are the trustees and professors public officers, invested with any portion of political power, partaking in any degree in the administration of civil government, and performing duties which flow from the sovereign authority? That education is an object of national concern, and a proper subject of legislation, all admit. That there may be an institution, founded by government, and placed entirely under its immediate control, the officers of which would be public officers, amenable exclusively to government, none will deny. But is Dartmouth College such an institution? Is education altogether in the hands of government? Does every teacher of youth become a public officer, and do donations for the purpose of education necessarily become public property, so far that the will of the legislature, not the will of the donor, becomes the law of the donation? These questions are of serious moment to society, and deserve to be well considered.

Doctor Wheelock, as the keeper of his charity-school, instructing the Indians in the art of reading, and in our holy religion; sustaining them at his own expense, and on the voluntary contributions of the charitable, could scarcely be considered as a public officer, exercising any portion of those du-

* The two citations of Blackstone's *Commentaries* relate to the English law of corporations, particularly as it was defined at the time of the 1769 charter.

ties which belong to government; nor could the legislature have supposed, that his private funds, or those given by others, were subject to legislative management, because they were applied to the purposes of education. When, afterwards, his school was enlarged, and the liberal contributions made in England, and in America, enabled him to extend his care to the education of the youth of his own country, no change was wrought in his own character, or in the nature of his duties. Had he employed assistant-tutors with the funds contributed by others, or had the trustees in England established a school, with Dr. Wheelock at its head, and paid salaries to him and his assistants, they would still have been private tutors; and the fact, that they were employed in the education of youth, could not have converted them into public officers, concerned in the administration of public duties, or have given the legislature a right to interfere in the management of the fund. The trustees, in whose care that fund was placed by the contributors, would have been permitted to execute their trust, uncontrolled by legislative authority.

Whence, then, can be derived the idea, that Dartmouth College has become a public institution, and its trustees public officers, exercising powers conferred by the public for public objects? Not from the source whence its funds were drawn; for its foundation is purely private and eleemosynary—not from the application of those funds; for money may be given for education, and the persons receiving it do not, by being employed in the education of youth, become members of the civil government. Is it from the act of incorporation? Let this subject be considered.

Nature of Corporation

A corporation is an artificial being, invisible, intangible, and existing only in contemplation of law. Being the mere creature of law, it possesses only those properties which the charter of its creation confers upon it, either expressly, or as incidental to its very existence. These are such as are supposed best calculated to effect the object for which it was created. Among the most important are immortality, and, if the expression may be allowed, individuality; properties, by which a perpetual succession of many persons are considered as the same, and may act as a single individual. They enable a corporation to manage its own affairs, and to hold property, without the perplexing intricacies, the hazardous and endless necessity, of perpetual conveyances for the purpose of transmitting it from hand to hand. It is chiefly for the purpose of clothing bodies of men, in succession, with these qualities and capacities, that corporations were invented, and are in use. By these means, a perpetual succession of individuals are capable of acting for the promotion of the particular object, like one immortal being. But this being does not share in the civil government of the country, unless that be the purpose for which it was created. Its immortality no more confers on it political power, or a political character, than immortality would confer such power or character on a natural person. It is no more a state instrument, than a natural person exercising the same powers would be. If, then, a natural person, employed by individuals in the education of youth, or for the government of a seminary in which youth is educated, would not become a public officer, or be considered as a member of the civil government, how is it, that this artificial being, created by law, for the purpose of being employed by the same individuals, for the same purposes, should become a part of the civil government of the country? Is it because its existence, its capacities, its powers, are given by law? Because the government has given it the power to take and to hold property, in a particular form, and for particular purposes, has the government a consequent right substantially to change that form, or to vary the purposes to which the property is to be applied? This principle has never been asserted or recognised, and is supported by no authority. Can it derive aid from reason?

The objects for which a corporation is created are universally such as the government wishes to promote. They are deemed beneficial to the country; and this benefit constitutes the consideration, and in most cases, the sole consideration of the grant. In most eleemosynary institutions, the object would be difficult, perhaps unattainable, without the aid of a charter of incorporation. Charitable or public-spirited individuals, desirous of making permanent appropriations for charitable or other useful purposes, find it impossible to effect their design securely and certainly, without an incorporating act. They apply to the government, state their beneficent object, and offer to advance the money necessary for its accomplishment, provided the government will confer on the instrument which is to execute their designs the capacity to execute them. The proposition is considered and approved. The benefit to the public is considered as an ample compensation for the faculty it confers, and the corporation is created. If the advantages to the public constitute a full compensation for the faculty it gives, there can be no reason for exacting a further compensation, by claiming a right to exercise over this artificial being, a power which changes its nature, and touches the fund, for the security and application of which it was created. There can be no reason for implying in a charter, given for a valuable consideration, a power which is not only not expressed, but is in direct contradiction to its express stipulations.

From the fact, then, that a charter of incorporation has been granted, nothing can be inferred, which changes the character of the institution, or transfers to the government any new power over it. The character of civil institutions does not grow out of their incorporation, but out of the manner in which they are formed, and the objects for which they are created. The right to change them is not founded on their being incorporated, but on their being the instruments of government, created for its purposes. The same institutions, created for the same objects, though not incorporated, would be public institutions, and, of course, be controllable by the legislature. The incorporating act neither gives nor prevents this control. Neither, in reason, can the incorporating act change the character of a private eleemosynary institution.

Beneficial Interests

We are next led to the inquiry, for whose benefit the property given to Dartmouth College was secured? The counsel for the defendant have insisted, that the beneficial interest is in the people of New Hampshire. The charter, after reciting the preliminary measures which had been taken, and the application for an act of incorporation, proceeds thus: "Know ye, therefore, that we, considering the premises, and being willing to encourage the laudable and charitable design of spreading Christian knowledge among the savages of our American wilderness, and also that the best means of education be established in our province of New Hampshire, for the benefit of said province, do, of our special grace," &c.

Do these expressions bestow on New Hampshire any exclusive right to the property of the college, any exclusive interest in the labors of the professors? Or do they merely indicate a willingness that New Hampshire should enjoy those advantages which result to all from the establishment of a seminary of learning in the neighborhood? On this point, we think it impossible to entertain a serious doubt. The words themselves, unexplained by the context, indicate, that the "benefit intended for the province" is that which is derived from "establishing the best means of education therein;" that is, from establishing in the province, Dartmouth College, as constituted by the charter. But, if these words, considered alone, could admit of doubt, that doubt is completely removed, by an inspection of the entire instrument.

The particular interests of New Hampshire never entered into the mind of the donors, never constituted a motive for their donation. The propagation of the Christian religion among the savages, and the dissemination of useful knowledge among the youth of the country, were the avowed and the sole objects of their contributions. In these, New Hampshire would participate; but nothing particular or exclusive was intended for her. Even the site of the college was selected, not for the sake of New Hampshire, but because it was "most subservient to the great ends in view," and because liberal donations of land were offered by the proprietors, on condition that the institution should be there established. The real advantages from the location of the college, are, perhaps, not less considerable to those on the west, than to those on the east side of Connecticut river. The clause which constitutes the incorporation, and expresses the objects for which it was made, declares those objects to be the instruction of the Indians, "and also of English youth, and any others." So that the objects of the contributors, and the incorporating act, were the same; the promotion of Christianity, and of education generally, not the interests of New Hampshire particularly.

From this review of the charter, it appears, that Dartmouth College is an eleemosynary institution, incorporated for the purpose of perpetuating the application of the bounty of the donors, to the specified objects of that bounty; that its trustees or governors were originally named by the founder, and invested with the power of perpetuating themselves; that they are not public officers, nor is it a civil institution, participating in the administration of government; but a charity-school, or a seminary of education, incorporated for the preservation of its property, and the perpetual application of that property to the objects of its creation.

Source of Funds

Yet a question remains to be considered, of more real difficulty, on which more doubt has been entertained, than on all that have been discussed. The founders of the college, at least, those whose contributions were in money, have parted with the property bestowed upon it, and their representatives have no interest in that property. The donors of land are equally without interest, so long as the corporation shall exist. Could they be found, they are unaffected by any alteration in its constitution, and probably regardless of its form, or even of its existence. The students are fluctuating, and no individual among our youth has a vested interest in the institution, which can be asserted in a court of justice. Neither the founders of the college, nor the youth for whose benefit it was founded, complain of the alteration made in its charter, or think themselves injured by it. The trustees alone complain, and the trustees have no beneficial interest to be protected. Can this be such a contract, as the constitution intended to withdraw from the power of state legislation? Contracts, the parties to which have a vested beneficial interest, and those only, it has been said, are the objects about which the constitution is solicitous, and to which its protection is extended.

The court has bestowed on this argument the most deliberate consideration, and the result will be stated. Dr. Wheelock, acting for himself, and for those who, at his solicitation, had made contributions to his school, applied for this charter, as the instrument which should enable him, and them, to perpetuate their beneficent intention. It was granted. An artificial, immortal being, was created by the crown, capable of receiving and distributing for ever, according to the will of the donors, the donations which should be made to it. On this being, the contributions which had been collected were immediately bestowed. These gifts were made, not indeed to make a profit for the donors, or their posterity, but for something, in their opinion, of inestimable value; for something which they deemed a full equivalent for the money with which it was purchased. The consideration for which they stipulated, is the perpetual application of the fund to its object, in the mode prescribed by themselves. Their descendants may take no interest in the preservation of this consideration. But in this respect their descendants are not their representatives; they are represented by the corporation. The corporation is the assignee of their rights, stands in their place, and distributes their bounty, as they would themselves have distributed it, had they been immortal. So, with respect to the students who are to derive learning from this source; the corporation is a trustee for them also. Their potential rights, which, taken distributively, are imperceptible, amount collectively to a most important interest. These are, in the aggregate, to be exercised, asserted and protected, by the corporation. They were as completely out of the donors, at the instant of their being vested in the corporation, and as incapable of being asserted by the students, as at present.

Legislative Powers

According to the theory of the British constitution, their parliament is omnipotent. To annul corporate rights might give a shock to public opinion, which that government has chosen to avoid; but its power is not questioned. Had parliament, immediately after the emanation of this charter, and the execution of those conveyances which followed it, annulled the instrument, so that the living donors would have witnessed the disappointment of their hopes, the perfidy of the transaction would have been universally acknowledged. Yet, then, as now, the donors would have no interest in the property; then, as now, those who might be students would have had no rights to be violated; then, as now, it might be said, that the trustees, in whom the rights of all were combined, possessed no private, individual, beneficial interests in the property confided to their protection. Yet the contract would, at that time, have been deemed sacred by all. What has since occurred, to strip it of its inviolability? Circumstances have not changed it. In reason, in justice, and in law, it is now, what it was in 1769.

This is plainly a contract to which the donors, the trustees and the crown (to whose rights and obligations New Hampshire succeeds) were the original parties. It is a contract made on a valuable consideration. It is a contract for the security and disposition of property. It is a contract, on the faith of which, real and personal estate has been conveyed to the corporation. It is, then, a contract within the letter of the constitution, and within its spirit also, unless the fact, that the property is invested by the donors in trustees, for the promotion of religion and education, for the benefit of persons who are perpetually changing, though the objects remain the same, shall create a particular exception, taking this case out of the prohibition contained in the constitution.

It is more than possible, that the preservation of rights of this description was not particularly in the view of the framers of the constitution, when the clause under consideration was introduced into that instrument. It is probable, that interferences of more frequent occurrence, to which the temptation was stronger, and of which the mischief was more extensive, constituted the great motive for imposing this restriction on the state legislatures. But although a particular and a rare case may not, in itself, be of sufficient magnitude to induce a rule, yet it must be governed by the rule, when established, unless some plain and strong reason for excluding it can be given. It is not enough to say, that this particular case was not in the mind of the convention, when the article was framed, nor of the American people, when it was adopted. It is necessary to go further, and to say that, had this particular case been suggested, the language would have been so varied, as to exclude it, or it would have been made a special exception. The case being within the words of the rule, must be within its operation likewise, unless there be something in the literal construction, so obviously absurd or mischievous, or repugnant to the general spirit of the instrument, as to justify those who expound the constitution in making it an exception.

Constitutional Restraint

On what safe and intelligible ground, can this exception stand? There is no expression in the constitution, no sentiment delivered by its contemporaneous expounders, which would justify us in making it. In the absence of all authority of this kind, is there, in the nature and reason of the case itself, that which would sustain a construction of the constitution, not warranted by its words? Are contracts of this description of a character to excite so little interest, that we must exclude them from the provisions of the constitution, as being unworthy of the attention of those who framed the instrument? Or does public policy so imperiously demand their remaining exposed to legislative alteration, as to compel us, or rather permit us, to say, that these words, which were introduced to give stability to contracts, and which in their plain import comprehend this contract, must yet be so construed as to exclude it?

Almost all eleemosynary corporations, those which are created for the promotion of religion, of charity or of education, are of the same character. The law of this case is the law of all. In every literary or charitable institution, unless the objects of the bounty be themselves incorporated, the whole legal interest is in trustees, and can be asserted only by them. The donors, or claimants of the bounty, if they can appear in court at all, can appear only to complain of the trustees. In all other situations, they are identified with, and personated by, the trustees; and their rights are to be defended and maintained by them. Religion, charity and education are, in the law of England, legatees or donees, capable of receiving bequests or donations in this form. They appear in court, and claim or defend by the corporation. Are they of so little estimation in the United States, that contracts for their benefit must be excluded from the protection of words, which in their natural import include them? Or do such contracts so necessarily require new modelling by the authority of the legislature, that the ordinary rules of construction must be disregarded, in order to leave them exposed to legislative alteration?

All feel, that these objects are not deemed unimportant in the United States. The interest which this case has excited, proves that they are not. The framers of the constitution did not deem them unworthy of its care and protection. They have, though in a different mode, manifested their respect for science, by reserving to the government of the Union the power "to promote the progress of science and useful arts, by securing for limited times, to authors and inventors, the exclusive right to their respective writings and discoveries." They have, so far, withdrawn science, and the useful arts, from the action of the state governments. Why then should they be supposed so regardless of contracts made for the advancement of literature, as to intend to exclude them from provisions, made for the security of ordinary contracts between man and man? No reason for making this supposition is perceived.

Theory of College Founding

If the insignificance of the object does not require that we should exclude contracts respecting it from the protection of the constitution; neither, as we conceive, is the policy of leaving them subject to legislative alteration so apparent, as to require a forced construction of that instrument, in order to effect it. These eleemosynary institutions do not fill the place, which would otherwise be occupied by government, but that which would otherwise remain vacant. They are complete acquisitions to literature. They are donations to education; donations, which any government must be disposed rather to encourage than to discountenance. It requires no very critical examination of the human mind, to enable us to determine, that one great inducement to these gifts is the conviction felt by the giver, that the disposition he makes of them is immutable. It is probable, that no man ever was, and that no man ever will be, the founder of a college, believing at the time, that an act of incorporation constitutes no security for the institution; believing, that it is immediately to be deemed a public institution, whose funds are to be governed and applied, not by the will of the donor, but by the will of the legislature. All such gifts are made in the pleasing, perhaps, delusive hope, that the charity will flow for ever in the channel which the givers have marked out for it. If every man finds in his own bosom strong evidence of the universality of this sentiment, there can be but little reason to imagine, that the framers of our constitution were strangers to it, and that, feeling the necessity and policy of giving permanence and security to contracts, of withdrawing them from the influence of legislative bodies, whose fluctuating policy, and repeated interferences, produced the most perplexing and injurious embarrassments, they still deemed it necessary to leave these contracts subject to those interferences. The motives for such an exception must be very powerful, to justify the construction which makes it.

Theory of Charter Power

The motives suggested at the bar grow out of the original appointment of the trustees, which is supposed to have been in a spirit hostile to the genius of our government, and the presumption, that if allowed to continue themselves, they now are, and must remain for ever, what they originally were. Hence is inferred the necessity of applying to this corporation, and to other similar corporations, the correcting and improving hand of the legislature. It has been urged repeatedly, and certainly with a degree of earnestness which attracted attention, that the trustees, deriving their power from a regal source, must, necessarily, partake of the spirit of their origin; and that their first principles, unimproved by that resplendent light which has been shed around them, must continue to govern the college, and to guide the students.

Before we inquire into the influence which this argument ought to have on the constitutional question, it may not be amiss to examine the fact on which it rests. The first trustees were undoubtedly named in the charter, by the crown; but at whose suggestion were they named? By whom were they selected? The charter informs us. Dr. Wheelock had represented, "that for many weighty reasons, it would be expedient, that the gentlemen whom he had already nominated, in his last will, to be trustees in America, should be of the corporation now proposed." When, afterwards, the trustees are named in the charter, can it be doubted, that the persons mentioned by Dr. Wheelock in his will were appointed? Some were probably added by the crown, with the approbation of Dr. Wheelock. Among these, is the doctor himself. If any others were appointed, at the instance of the crown, they are the governor, three members of the council, and the speaker of the house of representatives of the colony of New Hampshire. The stations filled by these persons ought to rescue them from any other imputation than too great a dependence on the crown. If, in the revolution that followed, they acted under the influence of this sentiment, they must have ceased to be trustees; if they took part with their countrymen, the imputation, which suspicion might excite, would no longer attach to them. The original trustees, then, or most of them, were named by Dr. Wheelock, and those who were added to his nomination, most probably, with his approbation, were among the most eminent and respectable individuals in New Hampshire.

The only evidence which we possess of the character of Dr. Wheelock is furnished by this charter. The judicious means employed for the accomplishment of his object, and the success which attended his endeavors, would lead to the opinion, that he united a sound understanding to that humanity and benevolence which suggested his undertaking. It surely cannot be assumed, that his trustees were selected without judgment. With as little probability can it be assumed, that while the light of science, and of liberal principles, pervades the whole community, these originally benighted trustees remain in utter darkness, incapable of participating in the general improvement; that while the human race is rapidly advancing, they are stationary. Reasoning *à priori,* we should believe, that learned and intelligent men, selected by its patrons for the government of a literary institution, would select learned and intelligent men for their successors; men as well fitted for the government of a college as those who might be chosen by other means. Should this reasoning ever prove erroneous, in a particular case, public opinion, as has been stated at the bar, would correct the institution. The mere possibility of the contrary would not justify a construction of the constitution, which should exclude these contracts from the protection of a provision whose terms comprehend them.

The opinion of the court, after mature deliberation, is, that this is a contract, the obligation of which cannot be impaired, without violating the constitution of the United States. This opinion appears to us to be equally supported by reason, and by the former decisions of this court.

Evidence of Impairment

2. We next proceed to the inquiry, whether its obligation has been impaired by those acts of the legislature of New Hampshire, to which the special verdict refers?

From the review of this charter, which has been taken, it appears that the whole power of governing the college, of appointing and removing tutors, of fixing their salaries, of directing the course of study to be pursued by the students, and of filling up vacancies created in their own body, was vested in the trustees. On the part of the crown, it was expressly stipulated, that this corporation, thus constituted, should continue for ever; and that the number of trustees should for ever consist of twelve, and no more. By this contract, the crown was bound, and could have made no violent alteration in its essential terms, without impairing its obligation.

By the revolution, the duties, as well as the powers, of government devolved on the people of New Hampshire. It is admitted, that among the latter was comprehended the transcendent power of parliament, as well as that of the executive department. It is too clear, to require the support of argument, that all contracts and rights respecting property, remained unchanged by the revolution. The obligations, then, which were created by the charter to Dartmouth College, were the same in the new, that they had been in the old government. The power of the government was also the same. A repeal of this charter, at any time prior to the adoption of the present constitution of the United States, would have been an extraordinary and unprecedented act of power, but one which could have been contested only by the restrictions upon the legislature, to be found in the constitution of the state. But the constitution of the United States has imposed this additional limitation, that the legislature of a state shall pass no act "impairing the obligation of contracts."

It has been already stated, that the act "to amend the charter, and enlarge and improve the corporation of Dartmouth College," increases the number of trustees to twenty-one, gives the appointment of the additional members to the executive of the state, and creates a board of overseers, to consist of twenty-five persons, of whom twenty-one are also appointed by the executive of New Hampshire, who have power to inspect and control the most important acts of the trustees.

On the effect of this law, two opinions cannot be entertained. Between acting directly, and acting through the agency of trustees and overseers, no essential difference is perceived. The whole power of governing the college is transferred from trustees, appointed according to the will of the founder, expressed in the charter, to the executive of New Hampshire. The management and application of the funds of this eleemosynary institution, which are placed by the donors in the hands of trustees named in the charter, and empowered to perpetuate themselves, are placed by this act under the control of the government of the state. The will of the state is substituted for the will of the donors, in every essential operation of the college. This is not an immaterial change.

The founders of the college contracted, not merely for the perpetual application of the funds which they gave, to the objects for which those funds were given; they contracted also, to secure that application by the constitution of the corporation. They contracted for a system, which should, so far as human foresight can provide, retain for ever the government of the literary institution they had formed, in the hands of persons approved by themselves. This system is totally changed. The charter of 1769 exists no longer. It is re-organized; and re-organized in such a manner, as to convert a literary institution, moulded according to the will of its founders, and placed under the control of private literary men, into a machine entirely subservient to the will of government. This may be for the advantage of this college in particular, and may be for the advantage of literature in general; but it is not according to the will of the donors, and is subversive of that contract, on the faith of which their property was given.

In the view which has been taken of this interesting case, the court has confined itself to the rights possessed by the trustees, as the assignees and representatives of the donors and founders, for the benefit of religion and literature. Yet, it is not clear, that the trustees ought to be considered as destitute of such beneficial interest in themselves, as the law may respect. In addition to their being the legal owners of the property, and to their having a freehold right in the powers confided to them, the charter itself countenances the idea, that trustees may also be tutors, with salaries. The first president was one of the original trustees; and the charter provides, that in case of vacancy in that office, "the senior professor or tutor, being one of the trustees, shall exercise the office of president, until the trustees shall make choice of, and appoint a president."

According to the tenor of the charter, then, the trustees might, without impropriety, appoint a president and other professors from their own body. This is a power not entirely unconnected with an interest. Even if the proposition of the counsel for the defendant were sustained; if it were admitted, that those contracts only are protected by the constitution, a beneficial interest in which is vested in the party, who appears in court to assert that interest; yet it is by no means clear, that the trustees of Dartmouth College have no beneficial interest in themselves. But the court has deemed it unnecessary to investigate this particular point, being of opinion, on general principles, that in these private eleemosynary institutions, the body corporate, as possessing the whole legal and equitable interest, and completely representing the donors, for the purpose of executing the trust, has rights which are protected by the constitution.

Marshall's Holding

It results from this opinion, that the acts of the legislature of New Hampshire, which are stated in the special verdict found in this cause, are repugnant to the constitution of the United States; and that the judgment on this special verdict ought to have been for the plaintiffs. The judgment of the state court must, therefore, be reversed.

Washington's Concurrence

WASHINGTON, Justice.—This cause turns upon the validity of certain laws of the state of New Hampshire, which have been stated in the case, and which, it is contended by the counsel for the plaintiffs in error, are void, being repugnant to the constitution of that state, and also to the constitution of the United States. Whether the first objection to these laws be well founded or not, is a question with which this court, in this case, has nothing to do: because it has no jurisdiction, as an appellate court, over the decisions of a state court, except in cases where is drawn in question the validity of a treaty, or statute of, or an authority exercised under, the United States, and the decision is against their validity; or where is drawn in question the validity of a statute of, or an authority exercised under, any state, on the ground of their being repugnant to the constitution, treaties or laws of the United States, and the decision is in favor of their validity; or where is drawn in question the construction of any clause of the constitution, or of a treaty, or statute of, or commission held under, the United States, and the decision is against the title, right, privilege or exemption specially set up or claimed by either party, under such clause of the said constitution, treaty, statute or commission.

The clause in the constitution of the United States which was drawn in question in the court from whence this transcript has been sent, is that part of the tenth section of the first article, which declares, that "no state shall pass any bill of attainder, *ex post facto* law, or any law impairing the obligation of contracts." The decision of the state court is against the title specially claimed by the plaintiffs in error, under the above clause, because they contend, that the laws of New Hampshire, above referred to, impair the obligation of a contract, and are, consequently, repugnant to the above clause of the constitution of the United States, and void. There are, then, two questions for this court to decide: 1st. Is the charter granted to Dartmouth College on the 13th of December 1769, to be considered as a contract? If it be, then, 2d. Do the laws in question impair its obligation?

Nature of a Contract

1. What is a contract? It may be defined to be a transaction between two or more persons, in which each party comes under an obligation to the other, and each reciprocally acquires a right to whatever is promised by the other. Powell on Cont. 6. Under this definition, says Mr. Powell, it is obvious, that every feoffment, gift, grant, agreement, promise, &c., may be included, because in all there is a mutual consent of the minds of the parties concerned in them, upon an agreement between them respecting some property or right that is the object of the stipulation. He adds, that the ingredients requisite to form a contract, are, parties, consent, and an obligation to be created or dissolved: these must all concur, because the regular effect of all contracts is, on one side, to acquire, and on the other, to part with, some property or rights; or to abridge, or to restrain natural liberty, by binding the parties to do, or restraining them from doing, something which before they might have done, or omitted. If a doubt could exist that a grant is a contract, the point was decided in the case of *Fletcher* v. *Peck,* 6 Cranch 87, in which it was laid down, that a contract is either executory or executed; by the former, a party binds himself to do, or not to do, a particular thing; the latter is one in which the object of the contract is performed, and this differs in nothing from a grant; but whether executed or executory, they both contain obligations binding on the parties, and both are equally within the provisions of the constitution of the United States, which forbids the state governments to pass laws impairing the obligation of contracts.

If, then, a grant be a contract, within the meaning of the constitution of the United States, the next inquiry is, whether the creation of a corporation by charter, be such a grant, as includes an obligation of the nature of a contract, which no state legislature can pass laws to impair? A corporation is defined by Mr. Justice Blackstone to be a franchise. It is, says he, "a franchise for a number of persons, to be incorporated and exist as a body politic, with a power to maintain perpetual succession, and to do corporate acts, and each individual of such corporation is also said to have a franchise or freedom."

This franchise, like other franchises, is an incorporeal hereditament, issuing out of something real or personal, or concerning or annexed to, and exercisable within a thing corporate. To this grant, or this franchise, the parties are the king and the persons for whose benefit it is created, or trustees for them. The assent of both is necessary. The subjects of the grant are not only privileges and immunities, but property, or, which is the same thing, a capacity to acquire and to hold property in perpetuity.

Certain obligations are created, binding both on the grantor and the grantees. On the part of the former, it amounts to an extinguishment of the king's prerogative to bestow the same identical franchise on another corporate body, because it would prejudice his prior grant. It implies, therefore, a contract not to re-assert the right to grant the franchise to another, or to impair it. There is also an implied contract, that the founder of a private charity, or his heirs, or other persons appointed by him for that purpose, shall have the right to visit, and to govern the corporation, of which he is the acknowledged founder and patron, and also, that in case of its dissolution, the reversionary right of the founder to the property, with which he had endowed it, should be preserved inviolate. . . .

New Hampshire Legislation

2. The next question is, do the acts of the legislature of New Hampshire of the 27th of June, and 18th and 26th of December 1816, impair this contract, within the true intent and meaning of the constitution of the United States? Previous to the examination of this question, it will be proper clearly to mark the distinction between the different kinds of lay aggregate corporations, in order to prevent any implied decision by this court of any other case, than the one immediately before it.

We are informed, . . . that there are two kinds of corporations aggregate, viz., such as are for public government, and such as are for private charity. The first are those for the government of a town, city or the like; and being for public advantage, are to be governed according to the law of the land. The validity and justice of their private laws and constitutions are examinable in the king's courts. Of these, there are no particular founders, and consequently, no particular visitor; there are no patrons of these corporations. But private and particular corporations for charity, founded and endowed by private persons, are subject to the private government of those who erect them, and are to be visited by them or their heirs, or such other persons as they may appoint. The only rules for the government of these private corporations are the laws and constitutions assigned by the founder. This right of government and visitation arises from the property which the founder had in the lands assigned to support the charity; and as he is the author of the charity, the law invests him with the necessary power of inspecting and regulating it. The authorities are full, to prove, that a college is a private charity, as well as an hospital, and that there is, in reality, no difference between them, except in degree; but they are within the same reason, and both eleemosynary.

These corporations, civil and eleemosynary, which differ from each other so especially in their nature and constitution, may very well differ in matters which concern their rights and privileges, and their existence and subjection to public control. The one is the mere creature of public institution, created exclusively for the public advantage, without other endowments than such as the king, or government, may bestow upon it, and having no other founder or visitor than the king or government, the *fundator incipiens*. The validity and justice of its laws and constitution are examinable by the courts having jurisdiction over them; and they are subject to the general law of the land. It would seem reasonable, that such a corporation may be controlled, and its constitution altered and amended by the government, in such manner as the public interest may require. Such legislative interferences cannot be said to impair the contract by which the corporation was formed, because there is, in reality, but one party to it, the trustees or governors of the corporation being merely the trustees for the public, the *cestui que trust* of the foundation. These trustees or governors have no interest, no privileges or immunities, which are violated by such interference, and can have no more right to complain of them, than an ordinary trustee, who is called upon in a court of equity to execute the trust. They accepted the charter, for the public benefit alone, and there would seem to be no reason, why the government, under proper limitations, should not alter or modify such a grant, at pleasure. But the case of a private corporation is entirely different. That is the creature of private benefaction, for a charity or private purpose. It is endowed and founded by private persons, and subject to their control, laws and visitation, and not to the general control of the government; and all these powers, rights and privileges flow from the property of the founder in the funds assigned for the support of the charity. Although the king, by the grant of the charter, is, in some sense, the founder of all eleemosynary corporations, because, without his grant, they cannot exist; yet the patron or endower is the perficient founder, to whom belongs, as of right, all the powers and privileges, which have been described. With such a corporation, it is not competent for the legislature to interfere. It is a franchise, or incorporeal hereditament, founded upon private property, devoted by its patron to a private charity, of a peculiar kind, the offspring of his own will and pleasure, to be managed and visited by persons of his own appointment, according to such laws and regulations as he, or the persons so selected, may ordain.

Parties to Contract

It has been shown, that the charter is a contract on the part of the government, that the property with which the charity is endowed, shall be for ever vested in a certain number of persons, and their successors, to subserve the particular purposes designated by the founder, and to be managed in a particular way. If a law increases or diminishes the number of the trustees, they are not the persons which the grantor agreed should be the managers of the fund. If it appropriate the fund intended for the support of a particular charity, to that of some other charity, or to an entirely different charity, the grant is in effect set aside, and a new contract substituted in its place; thus disappointing completely the intentions of the founder, by changing the objects of his bounty. And can it be seriously contended, that a law, which changes so materially the terms of a contract, does not impair it? In short, does not every alteration of a contract, however unimportant, even though it be manifestly for the interest of the party objecting to it, impair its obligation? If the assent of all the parties to be bound by a contract, be of its essence, how is it possible, that a new contract, substituted for, or engrafted on another, without such assent, should not violate the old charter? . . .

Contract Impairment

If these principles, before laid down, be correct, it cannot be denied, that the obligations of the charter to Dartmouth College are impaired by the laws under consideration. The name of the corporation, its constitution and government, and the objects of the founder, and of the grantor of the charter, are totally changed. By the charter, the property of this founder was vested in twelve trustees, and no more, to be disposed of by them, or a majority, for the support of a college, for the education and instruction of the Indians, and also of English youth, and others. Under the late acts, the trustees and visitors are different; and the property and franchises of the college are transferred to different and new uses, not contemplated by the founder. In short, it is most obvious, that the effect of these laws is to abolish the old corporation, and to create a new one in its stead. The laws of Virginia, referred to in the case of *Terrett* v. *Taylor,* authorized the overseers of the poor to sell the glebes belonging to the Protestant Episcopal Church, and to appropriate the proceeds to other uses. The laws in question divest the trustees of Dartmouth College of the property vested in them by the founder, and vest it in other trustees, for the support of a different institution, called Dartmouth University. In what respects do they differ? Would the difference have been greater in principle, if the law had appropriated the funds of the college to the making of turnpike roads, or to any other purpose of a public nature? In all respects, in which the contract has been altered, without the assent of the corporation, its obligations have been impaired; and the degree can make no difference in the construction of the above provision of the constitution.

It has been insisted, in the argument at the bar, that Dartmouth College was a mere civil corporation, created for a public purpose, the public being deeply interested in the education of its youth; and that, consequently, the charter was as much under the control of the government of New Hampshire, as if the corporation had concerned the government of a town or city. But it has been shown, that the authorities are all the other way. There is not a case to be found which contradicts the doctrine . . . that a college, founded by an individual, or individuals, is a private charity, subject to the government and visitation of the founder, and not to the unlimited control of the government.

It is objected, in this case, that Dr. Wheelock is not the founder of Dartmouth College. Admit, he is not. How would this alter the case? Neither the king, nor the province of New Hampshire was the founder; and if the contributions made by the governor of New Hampshire, by those persons who granted lands for the college, in order to induce its location in a particular part of the state, by the other liberal contributors in England and America, bestow upon them claims equal with Dr. Wheelock, still it would not alter the nature of the corporation, and convert it into one for public government. It would still be a private eleemosynary corporation, a private charity, endowed by a number of persons, instead of a single individual. But the fact is, that whoever may mediately have contributed to swell the funds of this charity, they were bestowed at the solicitation of Dr. Wheelock, and vested in persons appointed by him, for the use of a charity, of which he was the immediate founder, and is so styled in the charter.

Upon the whole, I am of opinion, that the above acts of New Hampshire, not having received the assent of the corporate body of Dartmouth College, are not binding on them, and, consequently, that the judgment of the state court ought to be reversed.

JOHNSON, Justice, concurred, for the reasons stated by the Chief Justice.

LIVINGSTON, Justice, concurred, for the reasons stated by the Chief Justice, and Justices WASHINGTON and STORY.

Story's Concurrence

STORY, Justice.—This is a cause of great importance, and as the very learned discussions, as well here, as in the state court, show, of no inconsiderable difficulty. There are two questions, to which the appellate jurisdiction of this court properly applies. 1. Whether the original charter of Dartmouth College is a contract, within the prohibitory clause of the constitution of the United States, which declares, that no state shall pass any "law impairing the obligation of contracts"? 2. If so, whether the legislative acts of New Hampshire of the 27th of June, and of the 18th and 27th of December 1816, or any of them, impair the obligations of that charter?

It will be necessary, however, before we proceed to discuss these questions, to institute an inquiry into the nature, rights and duties of aggregate corporations, at common law; that we may apply the principles, drawn from this source, to the exposition of this charter, which was granted emphatically with reference to that law.

Corporations Generally

An aggregate corporation, at common law, is a collection of individuals, united into one collective body, under a special name, and possessing certain immunities, privileges and capacities, in its collective character, which do not belong to the natural persons composing it. Among other things, it possesses the capacity of perpetual succession, and of acting by the collected vote or will of its component members, and of suing and being sued in all things touching its corporate rights and duties. It is, in short, an artificial person, existing in contemplation of law, and endowed with certain powers and franchises which, though they must be exercised through the medium of its natural members, are yet considered as subsisting in the corporation itself, as distinctly as if it were a real personage. Hence, such a corporation may sue and be sued by its own members, and may contract with them in the same manner, as with any strangers. . . . A great variety of these corporations exist, in every country governed by the common law; in some of which, the corporate existence is perpetuated by new elections, made from time to time; and in others, by a continual accession of new members, without any corporate act. Some of these corporations are, from the particular purposes to which they are devoted, denominated spiritual, and some lay; and the latter are again divided into civil and eleemosynary corporations. It is unnecessary, in this place, to enter into any examination of civil corporations. Eleemosynary corporations are such as are constituted for the perpetual distribution of the free-alms and bounty of the founder, in such manner as he has directed; and in this class, are ranked hospitals for the relief of poor and impotent persons, and colleges for the promotion of learning and piety, and the support of persons engaged in literary pursuits. . . .

Another division of corporations is into public and private. Public corporations are generally esteemed such as exist for public political purposes only, such as towns, cities, parishes and counties; and in many respects, they are so, although they involve some private interests; but strictly speaking, public corporations are such only as are founded by the government, for public purposes, where the whole interests belong also to the government. If, therefore, the foundation be private, though under the charter of the government, the corporation is private, however extensive the uses may be to which it is devoted, either by the bounty of the founder, or the nature and objects of the institution.

For instance, a bank created by the government for its own uses, whose stock is exclusively owned by the government, is, in the strictest sense, a public corporation. So, an hospital created and endowed by the government for general charity. But a bank, whose stock is owned by private persons, is a private corporation, although it is erected by the government, and its objects and operations partake of a public nature. The same doctrine may be affirmed of insurance, canal, bridge and turnpike companies. In all these cases, the uses may, in a certain sense, be called public, but the corporations are private; as much so, indeed, as if the franchises were vested in a single person.

This reasoning applies in its full force to eleemosynary corporations. An hospital, founded by a private benefactor, is, in point of law, a private corporation, although dedicated by its charter to general charity. So, a college, founded and endowed in the same manner, although, being for the promotion of learning and piety, it may extend its charity to scholars from every class in the community, and thus acquire the character of a public institution. This is the unequivocal doctrine of the authorities; and cannot be shaken but by undermining the most solid foundations of the common law. . . .

"A devise to the poor of the parish is a public charity. Where testators leave it to the discretion of a trustee to choose out the objects, though each particular object may be said to be private, yet in the extensiveness of the benefit accruing from them, they may properly be called public charities. A sum to be disposed of by A. B., and his executors, at their discretion, among poor house-keepers, is of this kind." The charity, then, may, in this sense, be public, although it may be administered by private trustees; and for the same reason, it may thus be public, though administered by a private corporation. The fact, then, that the charity is public, affords no proof that the corporation is also public; and consequently, the argument, so far as it is built on this foundation, falls to the ground. If, indeed, the argument were correct, it would follow, that almost every hospital and college would be a public corporation; a doctrine utterly irreconcilable with the whole current of decisions since the time of Lord COKE.

Public Corporations

When, then, the argument assumes, that because the charity is public, the corporation is public, it manifestly confounds the popular, with the strictly legal, sense of the terms. And if it stopped here, it would not be very material to correct the error. But it is on this foundation, that a superstructure is erected, which is to compel a surrender of the cause. When the corporation is said, at the bar, to be public, it is not merely meant, that the whole community may be the proper objects of the bounty, but that the government have the sole right, as trustees of the public interests, to regulate, control and direct the corporation, and its funds and its franchises, at its own good will and pleasure. Now, such an authority does not exist in the government, except where the corporation, is in the strictest sense, public; that is, where its whole interests and franchises are the exclusive property and domain of the government itself. If it had been otherwise, courts of law would have been spared many laborious adjudications in respect to eleemosynary corporations, and the visitatorial powers over them, from the time of Lord HOLT down to the present day. . . .

Nay, more, private trustees for charitable purposes would have been liable to have the property confided to their care taken away from them, without any assent or default on their part, and the administration submitted, not to the control of law and equity, but to the arbitrary discretion of the government. Yet, who ever thought before, that the munificent gifts of private donors for general charity became instantaneously the property of the government; and that the trustees appointed by the donors, whether corporate or unincorporated, might be compelled to yield up their rights to whomsoever the government might appoint to administer them? If we were to establish such a principle, it would extinguish all future eleemosynary endowments; and we should find as little of public policy, as we now find of law to sustain it.

An eleemosynary corporation, then, upon a private foundation, being a private corporation, it is next to be considered, what is deemed a foundation, and who is the founder. This cannot be stated with more brevity and exactness, than in the language of the elegant commentator upon the laws of England: "The founder of all corporations (says Sir William Blackstone), in the strictest and original sense, is the king alone, for he only can incorporate a society; and in civil corporations, such as mayor, commonalty, &c., where there are no possessions or endowments given to the body, there is no other founder but the king; but in eleemosynary foundations, such as colleges and hospitals, where there is an endowment of lands, the law distinguishes and makes two species of foundation, the one *fundatio incipiens,* or the incorporation, in which sense the king is the general founder of all colleges and hospitals; the other *fundatio perficiens,* or the dotation of it, in which sense, the first gift of the revenues is the foundation, and he who gives them is, in the law, the founder; and it is in this last sense, we generally call a man the founder of a college or hospital." . . .*

Nature of Trusteeship

To all eleemosynary corporations, a visitatorial power attaches, as a necessary incident; for these corporations being composed of individuals, subject to human infirmities, are liable, as well as private persons, to deviate from the end of their institution. The law, therefore, has provided, that there shall somewhere exist a power to visit, inquire into, and correct all irregularities and abuses in such corporations, and to compel the original purposes of the charity to be faithfully fulfilled. . . . The nature and extent of this visitatorial power has been expounded with admirable fulness and accuracy by Lord HOLT in one of his most celebrated judgments. . . . And of common right, by the dotation, the founder and his heirs are the legal visitors, unless the founder has appointed and assigned another person to be visitor. For the founder may, if he please, at the time of the endowment, part with his visitatorial power, and the person to whom it is assigned will, in that case, possess it in exclusion of the founder's heirs. . . .

This visitatorial power is, therefore, an hereditament founded in property, and valuable, in intendment of law; and stands upon the maxim, that he who gives his property, has a right to regulate it in future. It includes also the legal right of patronage, for as Lord HOLT justly observes, "patronage and visitation are necessary consequents one upon another." No technical terms are necessary to assign or vest the visitatorial power; it is sufficient if, from the nature of the duties to be performed by particular persons, under the charter, it can be inferred, that the founder meant to part with it in their favor; and he may divide it among various persons, or subject it to any modifications or control, by the fundamental statutes of the corporation. But where the appointment is given in general terms, the whole power vests in the appointee. . . . In the construction of charters, too, it is a general rule, that if the objects of the charity are incorporated, as for instance, the master and fellows of a college, or the master and poor of a hospital, the visitatorial power, in the absence of any special appointment, silently vests in the founder and his heirs. But where trustees or governors are incorporated to manage the charity, the visitatorial power is deemed to belong to them in their corporate character. . . .

When a private eleemosynary corporation is thus created, by the charter

* Story's opinion is based on principles of equity, as establishing the moral rightness of the contract clause. Several of his technical terms warrant explanation: *dotation* is a civil law (French) term for the endowment of a charitable institution by its founder; *amotion* is the illegal removal of a corporation officer; *cestui que use* or *cestui que trust* is law French for the beneficiary of a trust agreement.

of the crown, it is subject to no other control on the part of the crown, than what is expressly or implicitly reserved by the charter itself. Unless a power be reserved for this purpose, the crown cannot, in virtue of its prerogative, without the consent of the corporation, alter or amend the charter, or divest the corporation of any of its franchises, or add to them, or add to, or diminish, the number of the trustees, or remove any of the members, or change or control the administration of the charity, or compel the corporation to receive a new charter. This is the uniform language of the authorities, and forms one of the most stubborn, and well settled doctrines of the common law.

Controlling Laws

But an eleemosynary, like every other corporation, is subject to the general law of the land. It may forfeit corporate franchises, by *misuser* or *non-user* of them. It is subject to the controlling authority of its legal visitor, who, unless restrained by the terms of the charter, may amend and repeal its statutes, remove its officers, correct abuses, and generally superintend the management of the trusts. Where, indeed, the visitatorial power is vested in the trustees of the charity, in virtue of their incorporation, there can be no amotion of them from their corporate capacity. But they are not, therefore, placed beyond the reach of the law. As managers of the revenues of the corporation, they are subject to the general superintending power of the court of chancery, not as itself possessing a visitatorial power, or a right to control the charity, but as possessing a general jurisdiction, in all cases of an abuse of trust, to redress grievances and suppress frauds. . . . And where a corporation is a mere trustee of a charity, a court of equity will go yet further; and though it cannot appoint or remove a corporator, it will, yet, in a case of gross fraud, or abuse of trust, take away the trust from the corporation, and vest it in other hands. . . .

Thus much it has been thought proper to premise respecting the nature, rights, and duties of eleemosynary corporations, growing out of the common law. We may now proceed to an examination of the original charter of Dartmouth College.

Analysis of Charter

It begins, by a recital, among other things, that the Rev. Eleazer Wheelock, of Lebanon, in Connecticut, about the year 1754, at his own expense, on his own estate, set on foot an Indian charity-school; and by the assistance of other persons, educated a number of the children of the Indians, and employed them as missionaries and school-masters among the savage tribes; that the design became reputable among the Indians, so that more desired the education of their children at the school, than the contributions in the American colonies would support; that the said Wheelock thought it expedient to endeavor to procure contributions in England, and requested the Rev. Nathaniel Whitaker to go to England, as his attorney, to solicit contribution, and also solicited the Earl of Dartmouth and others, to receive the contributions and become trustees thereof, which they cheerfully agreed to, and he constituted them trustees accordingly, by a power of attorney, and they testified their acceptance by a sealed instrument; that the said Wheelock also authorized the trustees to fix and determine upon the place for the said school; and to enable them understandingly to give the preference, laid before them, the several offers of the governments in America, inviting the settlement of the school among them; that a large number of the proprietors of lands, in the western parts of New Hampshire, to aid the design, and considering that the same school might be enlarged and improved to promote learning among the English, and to supply the churches there with an orthodox ministry, promised large tracts of land for the uses aforesaid, provided the school should be settled in the western part of said province; that the trustees, thereupon, gave a preference to the western part of said province, lying on Connecticut river, as a situation most convenient for said school.

That the said Wheelock further represented the necessity for a legal incorporation, in order to the safety and well-being of said seminary, and its being capable of the tenure and disposal of lands and bequests for the use of the same; that in the infancy of said institution, certain gentlemen whom he had already nominated in his last will (which he had transmitted to the trustees in England), to be trustees in America, should be the corporation now proposed; and lastly, that there were already large contributions for said school in the hands of the trustees in England, and further success might be expected; for which reason, the said Wheelock desired they might be invested with all that power therein, which could consist with their distance from the same. The charter, after these recitals, declares, that the king, considering the premises, and being willing to encourage the charitable design, and that the best means of education might be established in New Hampshire for the benefit thereof, does, of his special grace, certain knowledge and mere motion, ordain and grant, that there be a college erected in New Hampshire, by the name of Dartmouth College, for the education and instruction of youth of the Indian tribes, and also of English youth and others; that the trustees of said college shall be a corporation for ever, by the name of the Trustees of Dartmouth College: that the then governor of New Hampshire, the said Wheelock, and ten other persons, specially named in the charter, shall be trustees of the said college, and that the whole number of trustees shall for ever thereafter consist of twelve, and no more; that the said corporation shall have power to sue and to be sued by their corporate name, and to acquire and hold for the use of the said Dartmouth College, lands, tenements, hereditaments and franchises; to receive, purchase and build any houses for the use of said college, in such town in the western part of New Hampshire, as the trustees, or a major part of them, shall, by a written instrument, agree on; and to receive, accept and dispose of any lands, goods, chattels, rents, gifts, legacies, &c., not exceeding the yearly value of 6000*l.*

It further declares, that the trustees, or a major part of them, regularly convened (for which purpose seven shall form a quorum), shall have authority to appoint and remove the professors, tutors and other officers of the college, and to pay them, and also such missionaries and school-masters as shall be employed by the trustees for instructing the Indians, salaries and allowances, as well as other corporate expenses, out of the corporate funds. It further declares, that, the said trustees, as often as one or more of the trustees shall die, or, by removal or otherwise, shall, according to their judgment, become unfit or incapable to serve the interests of the college, shall have power to elect and appoint other trustees in their stead, so that when the whole number shall be complete of twelve trustees, eight shall be resident freeholders of New Hampshire, and seven of the whole number, laymen.

It further declares, that the trustees shall have power, from time to time, to make and establish rules, ordinances and laws, for the government of the college, not repugnant to the laws of the land, and to confer collegiate degrees. It further appoints the said Wheelock, whom it denominates "the *founder* of the college," to be president of the college, with authority to appoint his successor, who shall be president, until disapproved of by the trustees. It then concludes with a direction, that it shall be the duty of the president to transmit to the trustees in England, so long as they should perpetuate their board, and as there should be Indian natives remaining to be proper objects of the bounty, an annual account of all the disbursements from the donations in England, and of the general plans and prosperity of the institution.

Private Nature of Charter

Such are the most material clauses of the charter. It is observable, in the first place, that no endowment whatever is given by the crown; and no power is reserved to the crown or government in any manner to alter, amend or control the charter. It is also apparent, from the very terms of the charter, that Dr. Wheelock is recognised as the founder of the college, and that the charter is granted upon his application, and that the trustees were in fact nominated by him. In the next place, it is apparent, that the objects of the institution are purely charitable, for the distribution of the private contributions of private benefactors. The charity was, in the sense already explained, a public charity, that is, for the general promotion of learning and piety; but in this respect, it was just as much public before, as after the incorporation. The only effect of the charter was to give permanency to the design, by enlarging the sphere of its action, and granting a perpetuity of corporate powers and franchises, the better to secure the administration of the benevolent donations. As founder, too, Dr. Wheelock and his heirs would have been completely clothed with the visitatorial power; but the whole government and control, as well of the officers as of the revenues of the college, being with his consent assigned to the trustees in their corporate character, the visitatorial power, which is included in this authority, rightfully devolved on the trustees. As managers of the property and revenues of the corporation, they were amenable to the jurisdiction of the judicial tribunals of the state; but as visitors, their discretion was limited only by the charter, and liable to no supervision or control, at least, unless it was fraudulently misapplied.

From this summary examination it follows, that Dartmouth College was, under its original charter, a private eleemosynary corporation, endowed with the usual privileges and franchises of such corporations, and among others, with a legal perpetuity, and was exclusively under the government and control of twelve trustees, who were to be elected and appointed, from time to time, by the existing board, as vacancies or removals should occur.

Charter as Contract

We are now led to the consideration of the first question in the cause, whether this charter is a contract, within the clause of the constitution prohibiting the states from passing any law impairing the obligation of contracts. In the case of *Fletcher* v. *Peck,* 6 Cranch 87, 136, this court laid down its exposition of the word "contract" in this clause, in the following manner: "A contract is a compact between two or more persons, and is either executory or executed. An executory contract is one, in which a party binds himself to do, or not to do, a particular thing. A contract executed is one in which the object of the contract is performed; and this, says Blackstone, differs in nothing from a grant. A contract executed, as well as one that is executory, contains obligations binding on the parties. A grant, in its own nature, amounts to an extinguishment of the right of the grantor, and implies a contract not to re-assert that right. A party is always estopped by his own grant." This language is perfectly unambiguous, and was used in reference to a grant of land by the governor of a state, under a legislative act. It determines, in the most unequivocal manner, that the grant of a state is a contract, within the clause of the constitution now in question, and that it implies a contract not to re-assume the rights granted; *à fortiori,* the doctrine applies to a charter or grant from the king.

But it is objected, that the charter of Dartmouth College is not a contract contemplated by the constitution, because no valuable consideration passed to the king, as an equivalent for the grant, it purporting to be granted *ex mero motû,* and further, that no contracts, merely voluntary, are within the prohibitory clause. It must be admitted, that mere executory contracts cannot be enforced at law, unless there be a valuable consideration to sustain them; and the constitution certainly did not mean to create any new obligations, or give any new efficacy to nude pacts. But it must, on the other hand, be also admitted, that the constitution did intend to preserve all the obligatory force of contracts, which they have by the general principles of law. Now, when a contract has once passed, *bonâ fide,* into grant, neither the king, nor any private person, who may be the grantor, can recall the grant of the property, although the conveyance may have been purely voluntary. A gift, completely executed, is irrevocable. The property conveyed by it becomes, as against the donor, the absolute property of the donee; and no subsequent change of intention of the donor can change the rights of the donee. . . . And a gift by the crown of incorporeal hereditaments, such as corporate franchises, when executed, comes completely within the principle, and is, in the strictest sense of the terms, a grant. . . . Was it ever imagined, that land, voluntarily granted to any person by a state, was liable to be resumed, at its own good pleasure? Such a pretension would, under any circumstances, be truly alarming; but in a country like ours, where thousands of land-titles had their origin in gratuitous grants of the states, it would go far to shake the foundations of the best settled estates. And a grant of franchises is not, in point of principle, distinguishable from a grant of any other property. If, therefore, this charter were a pure donation, when the grant was complete, and accepted by the grantees, it involved a contract, that the grantees should hold, and the grantor should not re-assume the grant, as much as if it had been founded on the most valuable consideration.

But it is not admitted, that this charter was not granted for what the law deems a valuable consideration. For this purpose, it matters not how trifling the consideration may be; a pepper-corn is as good as a thousand dollars. Nor is it necessary, that the consideration should be a benefit to the grantor. It is sufficient, if it import damage or loss, or forbearance of benefit, or any act done or to be done, on the part of the grantee. It is unnecessary to state cases; they are familiar to the mind of every lawyer. . . .

Implied Undertakings

With these principles in view, let us now examine the terms of this charter. It purports, indeed, on its face, to be granted "of the special grace, certain knowledge and *mere motion*" of the king; but these words were introduced for a very different purpose from that now contended for. It is a general rule of the common law (the reverse of that applied in ordinary cases), that a grant of the king, at the suit of the grantee, is to be construed most beneficially for the king, and most strictly against the grantee. Wherefore, it is usual to insert in the king's grants, a clause, that they are made, not at the suit of the grantee, but of the special grace, certain knowledge and mere motion of the king; and then they receive a more liberal construction. This is the true object of the clause in question, as we are informed by the most accurate authorities. . . . But the charter also, on its face, purports to be granted, in consideration of the premises in the introductory recitals.

Now, among these recitals, it appears, that Dr. Wheelock had founded a charity-school at his own expense, on his own estate; that divers contributions had been made in the colonies, by others, for its support; that new contributions had been made, and were making, in England, for this purpose, and were in the hands of trustees appointed by Dr. Wheelock to act in his behalf; that Dr. Wheelock had consented to have the school established at such other place as the trustees should select; that offers had been made by several of the governments in America, inviting the establishment of the school among them; that offers of land had also been made by divers proprietors of lands in the western parts of New Hampshire, if the school should be established there; that the trustees had finally consented to establish it in New Hampshire; and that Dr. Wheelock represented that, to effectuate the purposes of all parties, an incorporation was necessary.

Can it be truly said, that these recitals contain no legal consideration of benefit to the crown, or of forbearance of benefit on the other side? Is there not an implied contract by Dr. Wheelock, if a charter is granted, that the school shall be removed from his estate to New Hampshire? and that he will relinquish all his control over the funds collected, and to be collected, in England, under his auspices, and subject to his authority? that he will yield up the management of his charity-school to the trustees of the college? that he will relinquish all the offers made by other American governments, and devote his patronage to this institution? It will scarcely be denied, that he gave up the right any longer to maintain the charity-school already established on his own estate; and that the funds collected for its use, and subject to his management, were yielded up by him, as an endowment of the college. The very language of the charter supposes him to be the legal owner of the funds of the charity-school, and in virtue of this endowment, declares him the founder of the college. It matters not, whether the funds were great or small; Dr. Wheelock had procured them, by his own influence, and they were under his control, to be applied to the support of his charity-school; and when he relinquished this control, he relinquished a right founded in property acquired by his labors. Besides, Dr. Wheelock impliedly agreed to devote his future services to the college, when erected, by becoming president thereof, at a period when sacrifices must necessarily be made to accomplish the great design in view.

If, indeed, a pepper-corn be, in the eye of the law, of sufficient value to found a contract, as upon a valuable consideration, are these implied agreements, and these relinquishments of right and benefit, to be deemed wholly worthless? It has never been doubted, that an agreement not to exercise a trade in a particular place was a sufficient consideration to sustain a contract for the payment of money; *à fortiori,* the relinquishment of property which a person holds, or controls the use of, as a trust, is a sufficient consideration; for it is parting with a legal right. Even a right of patronage (*jus patronatus*) is of great value in intendment of law. Nobody doubts, that an advowson is a valuable hereditament; and yet, in fact, it is but a mere trust, or right of nomination to a benefice, which cannot be legally sold to the intended incumbent. . . . In respect to Dr. Wheelock, then, if a consideration be necessary to support the charter as a contract, it is to be found in the implied stipulations on his part in the charter itself. He relinquished valuable rights, and undertook a laborious office, in consideration of the grant of the incorporation.

Implied Acceptances

This is not all. A charter may be granted upon an executory, as well as an executed or present consideration. When it is granted to persons who have not made application for it, until their acceptance thereof, the grant is yet *in fieri.* Upon the acceptance, there is an implied contract on the part of the grantees, in consideration of the charter, that they will perform the duties, and exercise the authorities conferred by it. . . .

There is yet another view of this part of the case, which deserves the most weighty consideration. The corporation was expressly created for the purpose of distributing in perpetuity the charitable donations of private benefactors. By the terms of the charter, the trustees, and their successors, in their corporate capacity, were to receive, hold and exclusively manage all the funds so contributed. The crown, then, upon the face of the charter, pledged its faith that the donations of private benefactors should be perpetually devoted to their original purposes, without any interference on its own part, and should be for ever administered by the trustees of the corporation, unless its corporate franchises should be taken away by due process of law. From the very nature of the case, therefore, there was an implied contract on the part of the crown, with every benefactor, that if he would give his money, it should be deemed a charity protected by the charter, and be administered by the corporation, according to the general law of the land. As, soon, then, as a donation was made to the corporation, there was an implied contract, springing up, and founded on a valuable consideration, that the crown would not revoke or alter the charter, or change its administration, without the consent of the corporation. There was also an implied contract between the corporation itself, and every benefactor, upon a like consideration, that it would administer his bounty according to the terms, and for the objects stipulated in the charter.

In every view of the case, if a consideration was necessary (which I utterly deny) to make the charter a valid contract, a valuable consideration did exist, as to the founder, the trustees, and the benefactors. And upon the soundest legal principles, the charter may be properly deemed, according to the various aspects in which it is viewed, as a several contract with each of these parties, in virtue of the foundation, or the endowment of the college, or the acceptance of the charter, or the donations to the charity.

Time of Performance

And here we might pause: but there is yet remaining another view of the subject, which cannot consistently be passed over without notice. It seems to be assumed by the argument of the defendant's counsel, that there is no contract whatsoever, in virtue of the charter, between the crown and the corporation itself. But it deserves consideration, whether this assumpton can be sustained upon a solid foundation.

If this had been a new charter, granted to an existing corporation, or a grant of lands to an existing corporation, there could not have been a doubt, that the grant would have been an executed contract with the corporation; as much so, as if it had been to any private person. But it is supposed, that as this corporation was not then in existence, but was created and its franchises bestowed, *uno flatû,* the charter cannot be construed a contract, because there was no person *in rerum naturæ,* with whom it might be made. Is this, however, a just and legal view of the subject? If the corporation had no existence, so as to become a contracting party, neither had it, for the purpose of receiving a grant of the franchises. The truth is, that there may be a priority of operation of things in the same grant; and the law distinguishes and gives such priority, wherever it is necessary to effectuate the objects of the grant. . . . From the nature of things, the artificial person called a corporation, must be created, before it can be capable of taking anything. When, therefore, a charter is granted, and it brings the corporation into existence, without any act of natural persons who compose it, and gives such corporation any privileges, franchises or property, the law deems the corporation to be first brought into existence, and then clothes it with the granted liberties and property. When, on the other hand, the corporation is to be brought into existence, by some future acts of the corporators, the franchises remain in abeyance, until such acts are done, and when the corporation is brought into life, the franchises instantaneously attach to it. There may be, in intendment of law, a priority of time, even in an instant, for this purpose. . . . And if the corporation have an existence, before the grant of its other franchises attaches, what more difficulty is there in deeming the grant of these franchises a contract with it, than if granted by another instrument, at a subsequent period?

Schedule of Performance

It behooves those also, who hold, that a grant to a corporation, not then in existence, is incapable of being deemed a contract, on that account, to consider, whether they do not, at the same time, establish, that the grant itself is a nullity, for precisely the same reason. Yet such a doctrine would strike us all, as pregnant with absurdity, since it would prove that an act of incorporation could never confer any authorities, or rights or property on the corporation it created. It may be admitted, that two parties are necessary to form a perfect contract; but it is denied, that it is necessary, that the assent of both parties must be at the same time. If the legislature were voluntarily to grant land in fee, to the first child of A., to be hereafter born; as soon as such child should be born, the estate would vest in it. Would it be contended, that such grant, when it took effect, was revocable, and not an executed contract, upon the acceptance of the estate? The same question might be asked, in a case of a gratuitous grant by the king, or the legislature, to A. for life, and afterwards, to the heirs of B., who is then living. Take the case of a bank, incorporated for a limited period, upon the express condition that it shall pay out of its corporate funds, a certain sum, as the consideration for the charter, and after the corporation is organized, a payment duly made of the sum, out of the corporate funds; will it be contended, that there is not a subsisting contract between the government and the corporation, by the matters thus arising *ex post facto,* that the charter shall not be revoked, during the stipulated period? Suppose, an act declaring that all persons, who should thereafter pay into the public treasury a stipulated sum, should be tenants in common of certain lands belonging to the state, in certain proportions; if a person, afterwards born, pays the stipulated sum into the treasury, is it less a contract with him, than it would be with a person *in esse* at the time the act passed? We must admit, that there may be future springing contracts, in respect to persons not now *in esse,* or we shall involve ourselves in inextricable difficulties. And if there may be, in respect to natural persons, why not also in respect to artificial persons, created by the law, for the very purpose of being clothed with corporate powers? I am unable to distinguish between the case of a grant of land or of franchises to an existing corporation, and a like grant to a corporation brought into life for the very purpose of receiving the grant. As soon as it is *in esse,* and the franchises and property become vested and executed in it, the grant is just as much an executed contract, as if its prior existence had been established for a century.

Supposing, however, that in either of the views which have been suggested, the charter of Dartmouth College is to be deemed a contract, we are yet met with several objections of another nature. It is, in the first place, contended, that it is not a contract, within the prohibitory clause of the constitution, because that clause was never intended to apply to mere contracts of civil institution, such as the contract of marriage, or to grants of power to state officers, or to contracts relative to their offices, or to grants of trust to be exercised for purposes merely public, where the grantees take no beneficial interest.

Binding of Parties

It is admitted, that the state legislatures have power to enlarge, repeal and limit the authorities of public officers, in their official capacities, in all cases, where the constitutions of the states respectively do not prohibit them; and this, among others, for the very reason, that there is no express or implied contract, that they shall always, during their continuance in office, exercise such authorities; they are to exercise them only during the good pleasure of the legislature. But when the legislature makes a contract with a public officer, as in the case of a stipulated salary for his services, during a limited period, this, during the limited period, is just as much a contract, within the purview of the constitutional prohibition, as a like contract would be between two private citizens. Will it be contended, that the legislature of a state can diminish the salary of a judge, holding his office during good behavior? Such an authority has never yet been asserted, to our knowledge. It may also be admitted, that corporations for mere public government, such as towns, cities and counties, may in many respects be subject to legislative control. But it will hardly be contended, that even in respect to such corporations, the legislative power is so transcendent, that it may at its will take away the private property of the corporation, or change the uses of its private funds, acquired under the public faith. Can the legislature confiscate to its own use the private funds which a municipal corporation holds under its charter, without any default or consent of the corporators? If a municipal corporation be capable of holding devises and legacies to charitable uses (as many municipal corporations are), does the legislature, under our forms of limited government, possess the authority to seize upon those funds, and appropriate them to other uses, at its own arbitrary pleasure, against the will of the donors and donees? From the very nature of our governments, the public faith is pledged the other way; and that pledge constitutes a valid compact; and that compact is subject only to judicial inquiry, construction and abrogation. This court have already had occasion, in other causes, to express their opinion on this subject; and there is not the slightest inclination to retract it.

As to the case of the contract of marriage, which the argument supposes not to be within the reach of the prohibitory clause, because it is a matter of civil institution, I profess not to feel the weight of the reason assigned for the exception. In a legal sense, all contracts, recognised as valid in any country, may be properly said to be matters of civil institution, since they obtain their obligation and construction *jure loci contractûs*. Titles to land, constituting part of the public domain, acquired by grants under the provisions of existing laws by private persons, are certainly contracts of civil institution. Yet no one ever supposed, that when acquired *bonâ fide,* they were not beyond the reach of legislative revocation. And so, certainly, is the established doctrine of this court. A general rule, regulating divorces from the contract of marriage, like a law regulating remedies in other cases of breaches of contracts, is not necessarily a law impairing the obligation of such a contract. It may be the only effectual mode of enforcing the obligations of the contract on both sides. A law punishing a breach of a contract, by imposing a forfeiture of the rights acquired under it, or dissolving it, because the mutual obligations were no longer observed, is, in no correct sense, a law impairing the obligations of the contract.

Could a law, compelling a specific performance, by giving a new remedy, be justly deemed an excess of legislative power? Thus far the contract of marriage has been considered with reference to general laws regulating divorces upon breaches of that contract. But if the argument means to assert, that the legislative power to dissolve such a contract, without such a breach on either side, against the wishes of the parties, and without any judicial inquiry to ascertain a breach, I certainly am not prepared to admit such a power, or that its exercise would not entrench upon the prohibition of the constitution. If, under the faith of existing laws, a contract of marriage be duly solemnized, or a marriage settlement be made (and marriage is always in law a valuable consideration for a contract), it is not easy to perceive, why a dissolution of its obligations, without any default or assent of the parties, may not as well fall within the prohibition, as any other contract for a valuable consideration. A man has just as good a right to his wife, as to the property acquired under a marriage contract. He has a legal right to her society and her fortune; and to divest such right, without his default, and against his will, would be as flagrant a violation of the principles of justice, as the confiscation of his own estate. I leave this case, however, to be settled, when it shall arise. I have gone into it, because it was urged with great earnestness upon us, and required a reply. It is sufficient now to say, that as at present advised, the argument derived from this source, does not press my mind with any new and insurmountable difficulty.

Beneficial Interests

In respect also to grants and contracts, it would be far too narrow a construction of the constitution, to limit the prohibitory clause to such only where the parties take for their own private benefit. A grant to a private trustee, for the benefit of a particular *cestui que trust,* or for any special, private or public charity, cannot be the less a contract, because the trustee takes nothing for his own benefit. A grant of the next presentation to a church is still a contract, although it limit the grantee to a mere right of nomination or patronage. . . . The fallacy of the argument consists, in assuming the very ground in controversy. It is not admitted, that a contract with a trustee is, in its own nature, revocable, whether it be for special or general purposes, for public charity or particular beneficence.

A private donation, vested in a trustee, for objects of a general nature, does not thereby become a public trust, which the government may, at its pleasure, take from the trustee, and administer in its own way. The truth is, that the government has no power to revoke a grant, even of its own funds, when given to a private person, or a corporation, for special uses. It cannot recall its own endowments, granted to any hospital or college, or city or town, for the use of such corporations. The only authority remaining to the government is judicial, to ascertain the validity of the grant, to enforce its proper uses, to suppress frauds, and, if the uses are charitable, to secure their regular administration, through the means of equitable tribunals, in cases where there would otherwise be a failure of justice.

Another objection growing out of, and connected with that which we have been considering, is, that no grants are within the constitutional prohibition, except such as respect property in the strict sense of the term; that is to say, beneficial interests in lands, tenements and hereditaments, &c., which may be sold by the grantees, for their own benefit: and that grants of franchises, immunities and authorities not valuable to the parties, as property, are excluded from its purview. No authority has been cited to sustain this distinction, and no reason is perceived to justify its adoption. There are many rights, franchises and authorities, which are valuable in contemplation of law, where no beneficial interest can accrue to the possessor. A grant of the next presentation to a church, limited to the grantee alone, has been already mentioned.

A power of appointment, reserved in a marriage settlement, either to a party or a stranger, to appoint uses in favor of third persons, without compensation, is another instance. A grant of lands to a trustee, to raise portions or pay debts, is, in law, a valuable grant, and conveys a legal estate. Even a power, given by will, to executors, to sell an estate for payment of debts is, by the better opinions and authority, coupled with a trust, and capable of survivorship. . . . Many dignities and offices, existing at common law, are merely honorary, and without profit, and sometimes are onerous. Yet a grant of them has never been supposed the less a contract on that account. In respect to franchises, whether corporate or not, which include a pernancy of profits, such as a right of fishery, or to hold a ferry, a market or a fair, or to erect a turnpike, bank or bridge, there is no pretence to say, that grants of them are not within the constitution. Yet they may, in point of fact, be of no exchangeable value to the owners. They may be worthless in the market. The truth, however, is, that all incorporeal hereditaments, whether they be immunities, dignities, offices or franchises, or other rights, are deemed valuable in law. The owners have a legal estate and property in them, and legal remedies to support and recover them, in case of any injury, obstruction or disseisin of them. Whenever they are the subjects of a contract or grant, they are just as much within the reach of the constitution as any other grant.

Nor is there any solid reason why a contract for the exercise of a mere authority should not be just as much guarded, as a contract for the use and dominion of property. Mere naked powers, which are to be exercised for the exclusive benefit of the grantor, are revocable by him, for that very reason. But it is otherwise, where a power is to be exercised in aid of a right vested in the grantee. . . .

Corporate Rights

In respect to corporate franchises, they are, properly speaking, legal estates, vested in the corporation itself, as soon as it is *in esse*. They are not mere naked powers, granted to the corporation; but powers coupled with an interest.

The property of the corporation rests upon the possession of its franchises; and whatever may be thought, as to the corporators, it cannot be denied, that the corporation itself has a legal interest in them. It may sue and be sued for them. Nay, more, this very right is one of its ordinary franchises. "It is likewise a franchise," says Mr. Justice Blackstone, "for a number of persons to be incorporated and subsist as a body politic, with power to maintain perpetual succession, and do other corporate acts; and each individual member of such corporation is also said to have a franchise or freedom." . . . In order to get rid of the legal difficulty of these franchises being considered as valuable hereditaments or property, the counsel for the defendant are driven to contend, that the corporators or trustees are mere agents of the corporation, in whom no beneficial interest subsists; and so nothing but a naked power is touched, by removing them from the trust; and then to hold the corporation itself a mere ideal being, capable indeed of holding property or franchises, but having no interest in them which can be the subject of contract.

Neither of these positions is admissible. The former has been already sufficiently considered, and the latter may be disposed of in a few words. The corporators are not mere agents, but have vested rights in their character, as corporators. The right to be a freeman of a corporation, is a valuable temporal right. It is a right of voting and acting in the corporate concerns, which the law recognises and enforces, and for a violation of which it provides a remedy. It is founded on the same basis as the right of voting in public elections; it is as sacred a right; and whatever might have been the prevalence of former doubts, since the time of Lord HOLT, such a right has always been deemed a valuable franchise or privilege. . . .

This reasoning, which has been thus far urged, applies with full force to the case of Dartmouth College. The franchises granted by the charter were vested in the trustees, in their corporate character. The lands and other property, subsequently acquired, were held by them in the same manner. They were the private demesnes of the corporation, held by it, not, as the argument supposes, for the use and benefit of the people of New Hampshire, but, as the charter itself declares, "for the use of Dartmouth College." There were not, and in the nature of things, could not be, any other *cestui que use,* entitled to claim those funds. They were, indeed, to be devoted to the promotion of piety and learning, not at large, but in that college and the establishments connected with it: and the mode in which the charity was to be applied, and the objects of it, were left solely to the trustees, who were the legal governors and administrators of it. No particular person in New Hampshire possessed a vested right in the bounty; nor could he force himself upon the trustees as a proper object. The legislature itself could not deprive the trustees of the corporate funds, nor annul their discretion in the application of them, nor distribute them among its own favorites.

Could the legislature of New Hampshire have seized the land given by the state of Vermont to the corporation, and appropriated it to uses distinct from those intended by the charity, against the will of the trustees? This question cannot be answered in the affirmative, until it is established that the legislature may lawfully take the property of A. and give it to B.; and if it could not take away or restrain the corporate funds, upon what pretence can it take away or restrain the corporate franchises? Without the franchises, the funds could not be used for corporate purposes; but without the funds, the possession of the franchises might still be of inestimable value to the college, and to the cause of religion and learning.

Trustees' Interests

Thus far, the rights of the corporation itself, in respect to its property and franchises, have been more immediately considered. But there are other rights and privileges, belonging to the trustees, collectively and severally, which are deserving of notice. They are intrusted with the exclusive power to manage the funds, to choose the officers, and to regulate the corporate concerns, according to their own discretion. The *jus patronatûs* is vested in them. The visitatorial power, in its most enlarged extent, also belongs to them. When this power devolves upon the founder of a charity, it is an hereditament, descendible in perpetuity to his heirs, and in default of heirs, it escheats to the government. . . . It is a valuable right, founded in property, as much so as the right of patronage in any other case. It is a right which partakes of a judicial nature.

May not the founder as justly contract for the possession of this right, in return for his endowment, as for any other equivalent? And if, instead of holding it as an hereditament, he assigns it in perpetuity to the trustees of the corporation, is it less a valuable hereditament in their hands? The right is not merely a collective right in all the trustees; each of them also has a franchise in it. Lord HOLT says, "it is agreeable to reason, and the rules of law, that a franchise should be vested in the corporation aggregate, and yet the benefit redound to the particular members, and be enjoyed by them in their private capacities. Where the privilege of election is used by particular persons, it is a particular right vested in each particular man." . . . Each of the trustees had a right to vote in all elections. If obstructed in the exercise of it, the law furnished him with an adequate recompense in damages. If ousted unlawfully from his office, the law would, by a *mandamus,* compel a restoration.

It is attempted, however, to establish that the trustees have no interest in the corporate franchises, because it is said, that they may be witnesses, in a suit brought against the corporation. The case cited at the bar certainly goes the length of asserting, that in a suit brought against a charitable corporation, for a recompense for services performed for the corporation, the governors, constituting the corporation (but whether intrusted with its funds or not by the act of incorporation does not appear), are competent witnesses against the plaintiff. . . . But assuming this case to have been rightly decided (as to which, upon the authorities, there may be room to doubt), the corporators being technically parties to the record . . . , it does not establish, that in a suit for the corporate property vested in the trustees in their corporate capacity, the trustees are competent witnesses. At all events, it does not establish, that in a suit for the corporate franchises to be exercised by the trustees, or to enforce their visitatorial power, the trustees would be competent witnesses. On a *mandamus* to restore a trustee to his corporate or visitatorial power, it will not be contended, that the trustee is himself a competent witness, to establish his own rights, or the corporate rights. Yet, why not, if the law deems that a trustee has no interest in the franchise? The test of interest assumed in the argument proves nothing in this case. It is not enough, to establish, that the trustees are sometimes competent witnesses; it is necessary to show, that they are always so, in respect to the corporate franchises, and their own. It will not be pretended, that in a suit for damages for obstruction in the exercise of his official powers, a trustee is a disinterested witness. Such an obstruction is not a *damnum absque injuriâ*. Each trustee has a vested right, and legal interest, in his office, and it cannot be divested but by due course of law. The illustration, therefore, lends no new force to the argument, for it does not establish, that when their own rights are in controversy, the trustees have no legal interest in their offices.

The principal objections having been thus answered, satisfactorily, at least, to my own mind, it remains only to declare, that my opinion, after the most mature deliberation is, that the charter of Dartmouth College, granted in 1769, is a contract within the purview of the constitutional prohibition.

I might now proceed to the discussion of the second question; but it is necessary previously to dispose of a doctrine which has been very seriously urged at the bar, viz., that the charter of Dartmouth College was dissolved at the revolution, and is, therefore, a mere nullity. . . .

Vested Rights of College

The remaining inquiry is, whether the acts of the legislature of New Hampshire, now in question, or any of them, impair the obligations of the charter of Dartmouth College. The attempt certainly is to force upon the corporation a new charter, against the will of the corporators. Nothing seems better settled, at the common law, than the doctrine, that the crown cannot force upon a private corporation a new charter, or compel the old members to give up their own franchises, or to admit new members into the corporation. . . . Neither can the crown compel a man to become a member of such corporation, against his will. . . . As little has it been supposed, that under our limited governments, the legislature possessed such transcendent authority. On one occasion, a very able court held, that the state legislature had no authority to compel a person to become a member of a mere private corporation, created for the promotion of a private enterprise, because every man had a right to refuse a grant. . . . On another occasion, the same learned court declared, that they were all satisfied, that the rights legally vested in a corporation cannot be controlled or destroyed by any subsequent statute, unless a power for that purpose be reserved to the legislature in the act of incorporation. . . . The principles are so consonant with justice, sound policy and legal reasoning, that it is difficult to resist the impression of their perfect correctness. The application of them, however, does not, from our limited authority, properly belong to the appellate jurisdiction of this court in this case.

A very summary examination of the acts of New Hampshire will abundantly show, that in many material respects they change the charter of Dartmouth College. The act of the 27th of June 1816, declares that the corporation known by the name of the Trustees of Dartmouth College shall be called the

Trustees of Dartmouth University. That the whole number of trustees shall be twenty-one, a majority of whom shall form a *quorum;* that they and their successors shall hold, use, and enjoy for ever, all the powers, authorities, rights, property, liberties, privileges and immunities, heretofore held, &c., by the trustees of Dartmouth College, except where the act otherwise provides; that they shall also have power to determine the times and places of their meetings, and manner of notifying the same; to organize colleges in the university; to establish an institute, and elect fellows and members thereof; to appoint and displace officers, and determine their duties and compensation; to delegate the power of supplying vacancies in any of the offices of the university for a limited term; to pass ordinances for the government of the students; to prescribe the course of education; and to arrange, invest and employ the funds of the university. The act then provides for the appointment of a board of twenty-five overseers, fifteen of whom shall form a *quorum,* of whom five are to be such *ex officio,* and the residue of the overseers, as well as the new trustees, are to be appointed by the governor and council. The board of overseers are, among other things, to have power, "to inspect and confirm, or disapprove and negative, such votes and proceedings of the board of trustees as shall relate to the appointment and removal of president, professors, and other permanent officers of the university, and determine their salaries; to the establishment of colleges and professorships, and the erection of new college buildings." The act then provides, that the president and professors shall be nominated by the trustees, and appointed by the overseers, and shall be liable to be suspended and removed in the same manner; and that each of the two boards of trustees and overseers shall have power to suspend and remove any member of their respective boards. The supplementary act of the 18th of December 1816, declares, that nine trustees shall form a *quorum,* and that six votes at least shall be necessary for the passage of any act or resolution. The act of the 26th of December 1816, contains other provisions, not very material to the question before us.

Facts of Impairment

From this short analysis, it is apparent, that, in substance, a new corporation is created, including the old corporators, with new powers, and subject to a new control; or that the old corporation is newly organized and enlarged, and placed under an authority hitherto unknown to it. The board of trustees are increased from twelve to twenty-one. The college becomes a university. The property vested in the old trustees is transferred to the new board of trustees, in their corporate capacities. The *quorum* is no longer seven, but nine. The old trustees have no longer the sole right to perpetuate their sucession, by electing other trustees, but the nine new trustees are, in the first instance, to be appointed by the governor and council, and the new board are then to elect other trustees, from time to time, as vacancies occur. The new board, too, have the power to suspend or remove any member, so that a minority of the old board, co-operating with the new trustees, possess the unlimited power to remove the majority of the old board. The powers, too, of the corporation are varied. It has authority to organize new colleges in "the university, and to establish an institute, and elect fellows and members thereof." A board of overseers is created (a board utterly unknown to the old charter), and is invested with a general supervision and negative upon all the most important acts and proceedings of the trustees. And to give complete effect to this new authority, instead of the right to appoint, the trustees are in future only to nominate, and the overseers are to approve, the president and professors of the university.

If these are not essential changes, impairing the rights and authorities of the trustees, and vitally affecting the interests and organization of Dartmouth College, under its old charter, it is difficult to conceive what acts, short of an unconditional repeal of the charter, could have that effect. If a grant of land or franchises be made to A., in trust for special purposes, can the grant be revoked, and a new grant thereof be made to A., B. and C., in trust for the same purposes, without violating the obligation of the first grant? If property be vested by grant in A. and B., for the use of a college, or an hospital, of private foundation, is not the obligation of that grant impaired, when the estate is taken from their exclusive management, and vested in them in common with ten other persons? If a power of appointment be given to A. and B., is it no violation of their right, to annul the appointment, unless it be assented to by five other persons, and then confirmed by a distinct body? If a bank or insurance company, by the terms of its charter, be under the management of directors, elected by the stockholders, would not the rights acquired by the charter be impaired, if the legislature should take the right of election from the stockholders, and appoint directors unconnected with the corporation? These questions carry their own answers along with them. The common sense of mankind will teach us, that all these cases would be direct infringements of the legal obligations of the grants to which they refer; and yet they are, with no essential distinction, the same as the case now at the bar.

Unconstitutionality

In my judgment, it is perfectly clear, that any act of a legislature which takes away any powers or franchises vested by its charter in a private corporation, or its corporate officers, or which restrains or controls the legitimate exercise of them, or transfers them to other persons, without its assent, is a violation of the obligations of that charter. If the legislature mean to claim such an authority, it must be reserved in the grant. The charter of Dartmouth College contains no such reservation; and I am, therefore, bound to declare, that the acts of the legislature of New Hampshire, now in question, do impair the obligations of that charter, and are, consequently, unconstitutional and void.

In pronouncing this judgment, it has not for one moment escaped me, how delicate, difficult and ungracious is the task devolved upon us. The predicament in which this court stands in relation to the nation at large, is full of perplexities and embarrassments. It is called to decide on causes between citizens of different states, between a state and its citizens, and between different states. It stands, therefore in the midst of jealousies and rivalries of conflicting parties, with the most momentous interests confided to its care. Under such circumstances, it never can have a motive to do more than its duty; and I trust, it will always be found to possess firmness enough to do that.

Under these impressions, I have pondered on the case before us with the most anxious deliberation. I entertain great respect for the legislature, whose acts are in question. I entertain no less respect for the enlightened tribunal whose decision we are called upon to review. In the examination, I have endeavored to keep my steps *super antiquas vias* of the law, under the guidance of authority and principle. It is not for judges to listen to the voice of persuasive eloquence, or popular appeal. We have nothing to do, but to pronounce the law as we find it; and having done this, our justification must be left to the impartial judgment of our country.

DUVALL, Justice, dissented.

Upon the suggestion of the plaintiff's counsel, that the defendant had died since the last term, the court ordered the judgment to be entered *nunc pro tunc* as of that term, as follows: —

Judgment

This cause came on to be heard, on the transcript of the record, and was argued by counsel: And thereupon, all and singular the premises being seen, and by the court now here fully understood, and mature deliberation being thereupon had, it appears to this court, that the said acts of the legislature of New Hampshire, of the 27th of June and of the 18th and 26th of December, Anno Domini 1816, in the record mentioned, are repugnant to the constitution of the United States, and so not valid; and therefore, that the said superior court of judicature of the state of New Hampshire erred, in rendering judgment on the said special verdict in favor of the said plaintiffs; and that the said court ought to have rendered judgment thereon, that the said trustees recover against the said Woodward, the amount of damages found and assessed, in and by the verdict aforesaid, viz., the sum of $20,000: Whereupon, it is considered, ordered and adjudged by this court, now here, that the aforesaid judgment of the said superior court of judicature of the state of New Hampshire be, and the same hereby is, reversed and annulled: And this court, proceeding to render such judgment in the premises as the said superior court of judicature ought to have rendered, it is further considered by this court, now here, that the said trustees of Dartmouth College do recover against the said William Woodward the aforesaid sum of $20,000, with costs of suit; and it is by this court, now here, further ordered, that a special mandate do go from this court to the said superior court of judicature, to carry this judgment into execution.

IV

McCulloch *v.* Maryland

1. *Martin* v. *Hunter's Lessee* (excerpts)
   14 U.S. (1 Wheaton), 323 (1816)

STORY, J., delivered the opinion of the court.

This is a writ of error from the court of appeals of Virginia, founded upon the refusal of that court to obey the mandate of this court, requiring the judgment rendered in this very cause, at February term, 1813, to be carried into due execution. The following is the judgment of the court of appeals rendered on the mandate: "The court is unanimously of opinion, that the appellate power of the supreme court of the United States does not extend to this court, under a sound construction of the constitution of the United States; that so much of the 25th section of the act of congress to establish the judicial courts of the United States, as extends the appellate jurisdiction of the supreme court to this court, is not in pursuance of the constitution of the United States; that the writ of error, in this cause, was improvidently allowed under the authority of that act; that the proceedings thereon in the supreme court were, *coram non judice,** in relation to this court, and that obedience to its mandate be declined by the court."

The questions involved in this judgment are of great importance and delicacy. Perhaps it is not too much to affirm, that, upon their right decision, rest some of the most solid principles which have hitherto been supposed to sustain and protect the constitution itself. The great respectability, too, of the court whose decisions we are called upon to review, and the entire deference which we entertain for the learning and ability of that court, add much to the difficulty of the task which has so unwelcomely fallen upon us. It is, however, a source of consolation, that we have had the assistance of most able and learned arguments to aid our inquiries; and that the opinion which is now to be pronounced has been weighed with every solicitude to come to a correct result, and matured after solemn deliberation.

---

* "Not before a [proper] court"—in this case, a claim that the Supreme Court lacked jurisdiction in *Fairfax's Devisee* v. *Hunter's Lessee* in 1813.

Before proceeding to the principal questions, it may not be unfit to dispose of some preliminary considerations which have grown out of the arguments at the bar.

The constitution of the United States was ordained and established, not by the states in their sovereign capacities, but emphatically, as the preamble of the constitution declares, by "the people of the United States." There can be no doubt that it was competent to the people to invest the general government with all the powers which they might deem proper and necessary; to extend or restrain these powers according to their own good pleasure, and to give them a paramount and supreme authority. As little doubt can there be, that the people had a right to prohibit to the states the exercise of any powers which were, in their judgment, incompatible with the objects of the general compact; to make the powers of the state governments, in given cases, subordinate to those of the nation, or to reserve to themselves those sovereign authorities which they might not choose to delegate to either. The constitution was not, therefore, necessarily carved out of existing state sovereignties, nor a surrender of powers already existing in state institutions, for the powers of the states depend upon their own constitutions; and the people of every state had the right to modify and restrain them, according to their own views of policy or principle. On the other hand, it is perfectly clear that the sovereign powers vested in the state governments, by their respective constitutions, remained unaltered and unimpaired, except so far as they were granted to the government of the United States.

These deductions do not rest upon general reasoning, plain and obvious as they seem to be. They have been positively recognised by one of the articles in amendment of the constitution, which declares, that "the powers not delegated to the United States by the constitution, nor prohibited by it to the states, are reserved to the *states* respectively, or *to the people*."

The government, then, of the United States, can claim no powers which are not granted to it by the constitution, and the powers actually granted, must be such as are expressly given, or given by necessary implication. On the other hand, this instrument, like every other grant, is to have a reasonable construction, according to the import of its terms; and where a power is expressly given in general terms, it is not to be restrained to particular cases, unless that construction grow out of the context expressly, or by necessary implication. The words are to be taken in their natural and obvious sense, and not in a sense unreasonably restricted or enlarged.

The constitution unavoidably deals in general language. It did not suit the purposes of the people, in framing this great charter of our liberties, to provide for minute specifications of its powers, or to declare the means by which those powers should be carried into execution. It was foreseen that this would be a perilous and difficult, if not an impracticable, task. The instrument was not intended to provide merely for the exigencies of a few years, but was to endure through a long lapse of ages, the events of which were locked up in the inscrutable purposes of Providence. It could not be foreseen what new changes and modifications of power might be indispensable to effectuate the general objects of the charter; and restrictions and specifications, which, at the present, might seem salutary, might, in the end, prove the overthrow of the system itself. Hence its powers are expressed in general terms, leaving to the legislature, from time to time, to adopt its own means to effectuate legitimate objects, and to mould and model the exercise of its powers, as its own wisdom, and the public interests, should require. . . .

But, even admitting that the language of the constitution is not mandatory, and that congress may constitutionally omit to vest the judicial power in courts of the United States, it cannot be denied that when it is vested, it may be exercised to the utmost constitutional extent.

This leads us to the consideration of the great question as to the nature and extent of the appellate jurisdiction of the United States. We have already seen that appellate jurisdiction is given by the constitution to the supreme court in all cases where it has not original jurisdiction; subject, however, to such exceptions and regulations as congress may prescribe. It is, therefore, capable of embracing every case enumerated in the constitution, which is not exclusively to be decided by way of original jurisdiction. But the exercise of appellate jurisdiction is far from being limited by the terms of the constitution to the supreme court. There can be no doubt that congress may create a succession of inferior tribunals, in each of which it may vest appellate as well as original jurisdiction. The judicial power is delegated by the constitution in the most general terms, and may, therefore, be exercised by congress under every variety of form, of appellate or original jurisdiction. And as there is nothing in the constitution which restrains or limits this power, it must, therefore, in all other cases, subsist in the utmost latitude of which, in its own nature, it is susceptible.

As, then, by the terms of the constitution, the appellate jurisdiction is not limited as to the supreme court, and as to this court it may be exercised in all other cases than those of which it has original cognizance, what is there to restrain its exercise over state tribunals in the enumerated cases? The appellate power is not limited by the terms of the third article to any particular courts. The words are, "the judicial power (which includes appellate power) shall extend to *all cases,*" &c., and "in all other cases before mentioned the supreme court shall have appellate jurisdiction." It is the *case,* then, and not *the court,* that gives the jurisdiction. If the judicial power extends to the case, it will be in vain to search in the letter of the constitution for any qualification as to the tribunal where it depends. It is incumbent, then, upon those who assert such a qualification to show its existence by necessary implication. If the text be clear and distinct, no restriction upon its plain and obvious import ought to be admitted, unless the inference be irresistible.

If the constitution meant to limit the appellate jurisdiction to cases pending in the courts of the United States, it would necessarily follow that the jurisdiction of these courts would, in all the cases enumerated in the constitution, be exclusive of state tribunals. How otherwise could the jurisdiction extend to *all* cases arising under the constitution, laws, and treaties of the United States, or *to all cases* of admiralty and maritime jurisdiction? If some

of these cases might be entertained by state tribunals, and no appellate jurisdiction as to them should exist, then the appellate power would not extend
to *all*, but to *some*, cases. If state tribunals might exercise concurrent jurisdiction over all or some of the other classes of cases in the constitution without
control, then the appellate jurisdiction of the United States might, as to such
cases, have no real existence, contrary to the manifest intent of the constitution. Under such circumstances, to give effect to the judicial power, it must
be construed to be exclusive; and this not only when the *casus fœderis* should
arise directly, but when it should arise, incidentally, in cases pending in state
courts. This construction would abridge the jurisdiction of such court far more
than has been ever contemplated in any act of congress.

On the other hand, if, as has been contended, a discretion be vested in
congress to establish, or not to establish, inferior courts at their own pleasure, and congress should not establish such courts, the appellate jurisdiction
of the supreme court would have nothing to act upon, unless it could act
upon cases pending in the state courts. Under such circumstances it must be
held that the appellate power would extend to state courts; for the constitution is peremptory that it shall extend to certain enumerated cases, which
cases could exist in no other courts. Any other construction, upon this supposition, would involve this strange contradiction, that a discretionary power
vested in congress, and which they might rightfully omit to exercise, would
defeat the absolute injunctions of the constitution in relation to the whole
appellate power.

But it is plain that the framers of the constitution did contemplate that
cases within the judicial cognizance of the United States not only might but
would arise in the state courts, in the exercise of their ordinary jurisdiction.
With this view the sixth article declares, that "this constitution, and the laws
of the United States which shall be made in pursuance thereof, and all treaties made, or which shall be made, under the authority of the United States,
shall be the supreme law of the land, and the judges in every state shall be
bound thereby, any thing in the constitution or laws of any state to the contrary notwithstanding." It is obvious that this obligation is imperative upon
the state judges in their official, and not merely in their private, capacities.
From the very nature of their judicial duties they would be called upon to
pronounce the law applicable to the case in judgment. They were not to decide merely according to the laws or constitution of the state, but according
to the constitution, laws and treaties of the United States—"the supreme law
of the land."

A moment's consideration will show us the necessity and propriety of
this provision in cases where the jurisdiction of the state courts is unquestionable. Suppose a contract for the payment of money is made between citizens of the same state, and performance thereof is sought in the courts of
that state; no person can doubt that the jurisdiction completely and exclusively
attaches, in the first instance, to such courts. Suppose at the trial the defendant sets up in his defence a tender under a state law, making paper money
a good tender, or a state law, impairing the obligation of such contract, which
law, if binding, would defeat the suit. The constitution of the United States

has declared that no state shall make any thing but gold or silver coin a tender in payment of debts, or pass a law impairing the obligation of contracts. If congress shall not have passed a law providing for the removal of such a suit to the courts of the United States, must not the state court proceed to hear and determine it? Can a mere plea in defence be of itself a bar to further proceedings, so as to prohibit an inquiry into its truth or legal propriety, when no other tribunal exists to whom judicial cognizance of such cases is confided? Suppose an indictment for a crime in a state court, and the defendant should allege in his defence that the crime was created by an *ex post facto* act of the state, must not the state court, in the exercise of a jurisdiction which has already rightfully attached, have a right to pronounce on the validity and sufficiency of the defence? It would be extremely difficult, upon any legal principles, to give a negative answer to these inquiries. Innumerable instances of the same sort might be stated, in illustration of the position; and unless the state courts could sustain jurisdiction in such cases, this clause of the sixth article would be without meaning or effect, and public mischiefs, of a most enormous magnitude, would inevitably ensue.

It must, therefore, be conceded that the constitution not only contemplated, but meant to provide for cases within the scope of the judicial power of the United States, which might yet depend before state tribunals. It was foreseen that in the exercise of their ordinary jurisdiction, state courts would incidentally take cognizance of cases arising under the constitution, the laws, and treaties of the United States. Yet to all these cases the judicial power, by the very terms of the constitution, is to extend. It cannot extend by original jurisdiction if that was already rightfully and exclusively attached in the state courts, which (as has been already shown) may occur; it must, therefore, extend by appellate jurisdiction, or not at all. It would seem to follow that the appellate power of the United States must, in such cases, extend to state tribunals; and if in such cases, there is no reason why it should not equally attach upon all others within the purview of the constitution. . . .

2. Charter of Second Bank of the United States

3 Stat. 266, ch. 44; Act of April 10, 1816

Be it enacted by the Senate and House of Representatives of the United States of America, in Congress assembled, That a bank of the United States of America shall be established, with a capital of thirty-five millions of dollars, divided into three hundred and fifty thousand shares, of one hundred dollars each share. Seventy thousand shares, amounting to the sum of seven millions of dollars, part of the capital of the said bank, shall be subscribed and paid for by the United States, in the manner hereinafter specified; and two hundred and eighty thousand shares, amounting to the sum of twenty-eight millions of dollars, shall be subscribed and paid for by individuals, companies, or corporations, in the manner hereinafter specified.

SEC. 2. *And be it further enacted,* That subscriptions for the sum of twenty-eight millions of dollars, towards constituting the capital of the said bank, shall be opened on the first Monday in July next, at the following places:

that is to say, at Portland, in the District of Maine; at Portsmouth, in the state of New Hampshire; at Boston, in the state of Massachusetts; at Providence, in the state of Rhode Island; at Middletown, in the state of Connecticut; at Burlington, in the state of Vermont; at New York, in the state of New York; at New Brunswick, in the state of New Jersey; at Philadelphia, in the state of Pennsylvania; at Wilmington, in the state of Delaware; at Baltimore, in the state of Maryland; at Richmond, in the state of Virginia; at Lexington, in the state of Kentucky; at Cincinnati, in the state of Ohio; at Raleigh, in the state of North Carolina; at Nashville, in the state of Tennessee; at Charleston, in the state of South Carolina; at Augusta, in the state of Georgia; at New Orleans, in the state of Louisiana; and at Washington, in the district of Columbia. . . .

SEC. 5. *And be it further enacted,* That it shall be lawful for the United States to pay and redeem the funded debt subscribed to the capital of the said bank at the rates aforesaid, in such sums, and at such times, as shall be deemed expedient, any thing in any act or acts of Congress to the contrary thereof notwithstanding. And it shall also be lawful for the president, directors, and company, of the said bank, to sell and transfer for gold and silver coin, or bullion, the funded debt subscribed to the capital of the said bank as aforesaid: *Provided always,* That they shall not sell more thereof than the sum of two millions of dollars in any one year; nor sell any part thereof at any time within the United States, without previously giving notice of their intention to the Secretary of the Treasury, and offering the same to the United States for the period of fifteen days, at least, at the current price, not exceeding the rates aforesaid. . . .

SEC. 10. *And be it further enacted,* That the directors, for the time being shall have power to appoint such officers, clerks, and servants, under them as shall be necessary for executing the business of the said corporation, and to allow them such compensation for their services, respectively, as shall be reasonable; and shall be capable of exercising such other powers and authorities for the well governing and ordering of the officers of the said corporation, as shall be prescribed, fixed, and determined, by the laws, regulations, and ordinances, of the same.

SEC. 11. *And be it further enacted,* That the following rules, restrictions, limitations, and provisions, shall form and be fundamental articles of the constitution of the said corporation, to wit: . . .

Ninth. The said corporation shall not, directly or indirectly, deal or trade in any thing except bills of exchange, gold or silver bullion, or in the sale of goods really and truly pledged for money lent and not redeemed in due time, or goods which shall be the proceeds of its lands. It shall not be at liberty to purchase any public debt whatsoever, nor shall it take more than at the rate of six per centum per annum for or upon its loans or discounts. . . .

SEC. 14. *And be it further enacted,* That the bills or notes of the said corporation originally made payable, or which shall have become payable on demand, shall be receivable in all payments to the United States, unless otherwise directed by act of Congress.

SEC. 15. *And be it further enacted,* That during the continuance of this act, and whenever required by the Secretary of the Treasury, the said corporation shall give the necessary facilities for transferring the public funds from place to place, within the United States, or the territories thereof, and for distributing the same in payment of the public creditors, without charging commissions or claiming allowance on account of difference of exchange, and shall also do and perform the several and respective duties of the commissioners of loans for the several states, or of any one or more of them, whenever required by law.

SEC. 16. *And be it further enacted,* That the deposits of the money of the United States, in places in which the said bank and branches thereof may be established, shall be made in said bank or branches thereof, unless the Secretary of the Treasury shall at any time otherwise order and direct; in which case the Secretary of the Treasury shall immediately lay before Congress, if in session, and if not, immediately after the commencement of the next session, the reasons of such order or direction.

3. *Rules and Regulations for the Government of the Offices of Discount and Deposit Established by the Bank of the United States*

From a Publication of the Bank (Philadelphia, 1817)

WHEREAS, by the act incorporating the subscribers to the Bank of the United States, the directors are authorized and empowered to establish Offices of Discount and Deposit within the United States, or the Territories thereof, subject to such regulations as they shall deem proper, not being contrary to law, or the constitution of the Bank; therefore, We, the Directors, by virtue of the power and authority vested in us, do resolve, that the following rules and regulations be established, for the government of the Offices of Discount and Deposit of the Bank of the United States:

Article I.

The Directors of the Bank of the United States shall annually appoint not less than nine Directors for each Office, a majority of whom shall constitute a Board. . . .

Article IV.

The Directors of the Bank of the United States shall appoint the Cashiers of the Offices of Discount and Deposit.

Article V.

It shall be the duty of the Cashier, carefully to observe the conduct of all persons employed under him, and report to the Board such instances of neglect, incapacity or bad conduct as he may discover in any of them; daily to examine the settlement of the cash account of the office; take charge of the cash, and whenever the actual amount disagrees with the balance of the cash account, report the same to the President and Directors without delay; to attend all meetings of the Board; keep a fair and regular record of its proceedings; give such information to the Board as may be required; consult with committees when requested, on subjects referred by the Board; and also to perform such other services as may be required of him by the Board.

4. *Maryland Statute Taxing Foreign Banks*

Maryland Acts 1818

An Act to impose a Tax on all Banks or Branches thereof in the State of Maryland, not chartered by the Legislature.

Be it enacted by the General Assembly of Maryland, That if any Bank has established, or shall without authority from the State first had and obtained, establish any branch, office of discount and deposit, or office of pay and receipt, in any part of this State, it shall not be lawful for the said branch, office of discount and deposit, or office of pay and receipt, to issue notes in any manner, of any other denomination than five, ten, twenty, fifty, one hundred, five hundred and one thousand dollars, and no note shall be issued except upon stamped paper of the following denominations; that is to say, every five dollar note shall be upon a stamp of ten cents; every ten dollar note upon a stamp of twenty cents; every twenty dollar note, upon a stamp of thirty cents; every fifty dollar note, upon a stamp of fifty cents; every one hundred dollar note, upon a stamp of one dollar; every five hundred dollar note, upon a stamp of ten dollars; and every thousand dollar note, upon a stamp of twenty dollars; which paper shall be furnished by the Treasurer of the Western Shore, under the direction of the Governor and Council, to be paid for upon delivery; *Provided always,* That any institution of the above description may relieve itself from the operation of the provisions aforesaid, by paying annually, in advance, to the Treasurer of the Western Shore, for the use of the State, the sum of fifteen thousand dollars.

And be it enacted, That the President, Cashier, each of the Directors and Officers of every institution established, or to be established as aforesaid, offending against the provisions aforesaid, shall forfeit a sum of five hundred dollars for each and every offence, and every person having any agency in circulating any note aforesaid, not stamped as aforesaid directed, shall forfeit a sum not exceeding one hundred dollars; every penalty aforesaid to be recovered by indictment, or action of debt, in the County Court of the county where the offence shall be committed, one half to the informer, and the other half to the use of the State.

And be it enacted, That this act shall be in full force and effect from and after the first day of May next.

5. *McCulloch v. Maryland*

From MS Volume TH#18, Judgments of the Maryland Court of Appeals, June Term 1818, pages 146-154.

It is admitted by the parties in this case by their counsel that there was passed on the tenth day of April, eighteen hundred and sixteen, by the Congress of the United States an act entitled, "an act to incorporate the subscribers to the Bank of the United States," and that there was passed, on the eleventh day of February eighteen hundred and eighteen, by the General Assembly of Maryland, an act entitled, "an act to impose a tax on all Banks or Branches thereof in the State of Maryland not chartered by the Legislature," which said acts are made part of this statement and it is agreed may be read from the statute books in which they are respectively printed. It is further admitted that the President, Directors and Company of the Bank of the United States incorporated by the act of Congress aforesaid did organize themselves and go into full operation in the City of Philadelphia in the State of Pennsylvania in pursuance of the said act and that they did on the [first] day of [October]* eighteen hundred and seventeen establish a branch of the said Bank or an office of Discount and Deposit in the City of Baltimore in the State of Maryland which has from that time until the first day of May eighteen hundred and eighteen and ever since transacted and carried on business as a bank or office of Discount and Deposit, and as a Branch of the said Bank of the United States by issuing Bank notes and discounting promissory notes and performing the operations usual and customary for Banks to do and perform under the authority and by the direction of the said President, Directors and Company of the Bank of the United States established at Philadelphia as aforesaid.

It is further admitted that the said President, Directors and Company of the said Bank had no authority to establish the said Branch or office of Discount and Deposit at the City of Baltimore from the State of Maryland otherwise than the said State's having adopted the Constitution of the United States, and composing one of the States of the Union. It is further admitted that James William McCulloch, being the Cashier of the said Branch or office of Discount and Deposit, did on the several days set forth in the declaration in this cause, issue the said respective Bank notes therein described from the said Branch or office to a certain George Williams in the city of Baltimore in part payment of a promissory note of the said Williams discounted by the said Branch or office, which said respective bank notes were not nor was either of them so issued on stamp paper in the manner proscribed by the act of assembly aforesaid.

It is further admitted that the said President, Directors and Company of the Bank of the United States and the said Branch or office of Discount and Deposit have not, nor has either of them, paid in advance or otherwise the sum of fifteen thousand dollars to the Treasurer of the Western Shore for the use of the State of Maryland before the issuing of the said notes or any of them, nor since those periods. And it is further admitted that the Treasurer of the Western Shore of Maryland under the direction of the Governor and Council of the said State was ready and offered to deliver to the said President, Directors and Company of the said Bank and to the said Branch or office of Discount and deposit, stamp paper of the kind and denomination required and described in the said act of assembly.

* Date of first branches reported by Bank of the United States.

Question Before Trial Court

The question submitted to the Court for their decision in this case is as to the validity of the said act of the General Assembly of Maryland on the grounds of its being repugnant to the Constitution of the United States, and the act of Congress aforesaid or to one of them. Upon the foregoing statement of facts and the pleadings in this cause (all errors in which are hereby agreed to be mutually released) if the Court should be of opinion that the plaintiffs are entitled to recover, then judgment, it is agreed, shall be entered for the plaintiffs for twenty five hundred dollars and costs of suit. But if the Court should be of opinion that the plaintiffs are not entitled to recover upon the statement and pleadings aforesaid then judgment of *non pros* shall be entered with costs to the Defendant. It is agreed that either party may appeal from the decision of the County Court to the Court of Appeals and from the decision of the Court of Appeals to the Supreme Court of the United States according to the modes and usages of law and have the same benefit of this statement of facts in the same manner as could be had if a Jury had been sworn and empannelled in this cause and a special verdict had been found, or these facts had appeared and been stated in an exception taken to the opinion of the Court and the Court's direction to the Jury thereon.

Baltimore 18th May 1818

Samuel Livermore of counsel for Plffs.
Nathl Williams of counsel for Deft.

Whereupon all and singular the premises being [in] the county court here seen, heard and fully understood, and mature deliberation thereupon had, for that it appears to the county court here that the said State of Maryland and John James, who sues as aforesaid, are entitled to recover against the said James W. McCulloch upon the statement and pleadings aforesaid of the said sum of two thousand five hundred dollars current money in manner and form as the said State of Maryland and John James who sues as aforesaid have above demanded against him.

Verdict of Trial Court

Therefore it is considered by the county court here that the said State of Maryland and the said John James who sues as aforesaid recover against the said James W. McCulloch the said sum of two thousand five hundred dollars current money, the debt aforesaid which the said James W. McCulloch by force of the act of assembly aforesaid hath forfeited and owes to the said State of Maryland and the said John James, whereof the said State of Maryland may have the sum of one thousand two hundred and fifty dollars current money for the said State's moiety; and the said John James who sues as aforesaid may have the other sum of one thousand two hundred and fifty dollars current money for his moiety according to the form of the act of assembly aforesaid. . . .

And thereupon the said James W. McCulloch by his attorney aforesaid prays an appeal from the judgment aforesaid, so as aforesaid rendered to the

Court of Appeals for the Western Shore of the State of Maryland and to him it is granted.

It is therefore ordered by the Court here that the Record and proceedings aforesaid in the plea aforesaid with all things thereunto relating be transmitted to the said Court of appeals and they are transmitted accordingly.

Test. Wm. Gibson, clk.

In testimony that the foregoing is a true copy from the record of proceedings of Baltimore County Court in the above mentioned cause I have hereunto set my hand and affixed the seal of my office this fourth day of June in the year of our Lord one thousand eight hundred and eighteen.

Wm. Gibson, clk.

Review in Court of Appeals

And now come into the Court of Appeals here as well the said James W. McCulloch by Nathaniel Williams and William H. Winder his attorneys as the said State of Maryland and John James who sues as aforesaid by Luther Martin their attorney; and thereupon on motion of the said State of Maryland and John James who sues as aforesaid by their attorney aforesaid, it is ruled by the court here that the said James W. McCulloch assign the errors in the record of proceedings aforesaid or in giving the judgment aforesaid, so as aforesaid brought before the Court of Appeals here for correcting the errors supposed to be therein, or judgment by the Court of Appeals here will be entered against him in default thereof. And the said James W. McCulloch by his attorney aforesaid says, that in the record of proceedings aforesaid and also in the giving of judgment aforesaid there is manifest error in this, to wit, that by the record aforesaid it appears that the judgment aforesaid, in the plea aforesaid given was given for the said State of Maryland and John James who sues as aforesaid against the said James W. McCulloch, when by the law of the land that judgment ought to have been given for the said James W. McCulloch against the said State of Maryland and John James who sues as aforesaid; therefore, in that there is manifest error, and he prays that the judgment aforesaid for that error, and others being in the record of proceedings aforesaid, may be reversed, annulled, and held entirely as void, and that he the said James W. McCulloch may be restored to all things which he hath lost by occasion of the said judgment, and that the said State of Maryland and John James who sues as aforesaid may rejoin to the errors aforesaid, and so forth.

And thereupon it is ruled by the Court of appeals here that the said State of Maryland and John James who sues as aforesaid join in the errors by the said James W. McCulloch above assigned in the record of proceedings aforesaid, or judgment by the Court of Appeals here will be rendered against them in default thereof. And the said State of Maryland and John James who sues as aforesaid by their attorney aforesaid say there is no error in the record of proceedings aforesaid nor in the giving of the judgment aforesaid, and they pray that the Court of Appeals here will proceed to the examination as well of the record of proceedings aforesaid as of the matters aforesaid by the said James W. Mc-Culloch above for error assigned, and that the said Judgment may be in all things affirmed, and so forth. Whereupon as well the record and proceedings aforesaid and the judgment given in form aforesaid as the matters aforesaid by the said James W. McCulloch above for error assigned being seen and by the Court of Appeals here that there is no error in the record of proceedings aforesaid, nor in the giving of the judgment aforesaid.

Court of Appeals Affirms

Therefore it is considered by the Court of Appeals here that the judgment aforesaid, given in form aforesaid, be in all things affirmed and stand in full force and effect, the said causes for error above assigned and alleged in any wise notwithstanding. And it is further considered by the Court of Appeals here that the said State of Maryland and John James who sues as aforesaid have execution against the said James W. McCulloch as well for the debt, damages, costs, and charges aforesaid adjudged unto them in the said County Court of Baltimore, as also the sum of twelve dollars adjudged unto the said John James, who sues as aforesaid by the Court of Appeals here on his assent, for his costs and charges which he hath sustained by occasion of the delay of the execution of judgment aforesaid, by pretext of the prosecution of the said appeal by the said James W. McCulloch of and upon the premises as aforesaid prosecuted

Test.   Th. Harris, clk.

Writ of Error to Supreme Court

Afterwards, to wit, on the eleventh day of September in the year of our Lord one thousand eight hundred and eighteen, the aforesaid James W. McCulloch by his attorneys aforesaid produced to the Court of appeals here the writ of the United States for the correcting of errors of and upon the premises, commanding the record and proceedings of the judgment last aforesaid so as aforesaid rendered, with all things concerning the same, to be transmitted to the Supreme Court of the United States, which said writ of error followed in these words to wit.

Order of Record for Review

UNITED STATES S. CT.

The President of the United States to the Judges of the Court of Appeals of the State of Maryland being the highest Court of law and equity in the said State. Because in the record and proceedings as also in the rendition of the judgment of a plea which is in the said court of appeals held for the Western Shore of the said State, before you or some of you on an appeal from Baltimore County Court, wherein James W. McCulloch was appellant and the State of Maryland and John James who sued in that behalf as well for the said State as for himself were appellees, a manifest error hath happened to the great damage of the said James W. McCulloch, as by his complaint appears; we being willing that error, if any hath been, should be duly corrected and full and speedy justice done to the parties aforesaid in this behalf, do command you, if judgment be therein given, that then under your seal distinctly and openly you send the record and proceedings aforesaid with all things concerning the same to the Supreme Court of the United States, together with this writ so that you have the same at Washington on the first Monday of February next, in the said Supreme Court to be then and there held, that the record and proceedings aforesaid being inspected the said Supreme Court may cause further to be done therein to correct that error, what of right and according to the law and custom of the United States should be done.

Witness the Honorable John Marshall, Chief Justice of the said Supreme Court, this first Monday of August in the year of our Lord one thousand eight hundred and eighteen and of the Independence of the United States the forty-third.

Allowed.

E.B. Caldwell, clk, Sup Ct U.S.
G. Duval, associate J.S.C.U.S. and
presiding J. 4 Circuit

August 28, 1818

In pursuance whereof and according to the form and effect of the act of the Congress of the United States in such case made and provided a transcript of the record and proceedings of the Judgment last aforesaid so as aforesaid rendered with all things concerning the same together with the said writ of error were transmitted to the said Supreme Court of the United States accordingly

Test.   Th. Harris, clk.

6. *Opinion of the Supreme Court*

4 Wheaton 197; opinion rendered March 7, 1819

MARSHALL, Ch. J., delivered the opinion of the court.—In the case now to be determined, the defendant, a sovereign state, denies the obligation of a law enacted by the legislature of the Union, and the plaintiff, on his part, contests the validity of an act which has been passed by the legislature of that state. The constitution of our country, in its most interesting and vital parts, is to be considered; the conflicting powers of the government of the Union and of its members, as marked in that constitution, are to be discussed; and an opinion given, which may essentially influence the great operations of the government. No tribunal can approach such a question without a deep sense of its importance, and of the awful responsibility involved in its decision. But it must be decided peacefully, or remain a source of hostile legislation, perhaps, of hostility of a still more serious nature; and if it is to be so decided, by this tribunal alone can the decision be made. On the supreme court of the United States has the constitution of our country devolved this important duty.

Power to Charter Bank

The first question made in the cause is—has congress power to incorporate a bank? It has been truly said, that this can scarcely be considered as an open question, entirely unprejudiced by the former proceedings of the nation respecting it. The principle now contested was introduced at a very early period of our history, has been recognised by many successive legislatures, and has been acted upon by the judicial department, in cases of peculiar delicacy, as a law of undoubted obligation.

It will not be denied, that a bold and daring usurpation might be resisted, after an acquiescence still longer and more complete than this. But it is conceived, that a doubtful question, one on which human reason may pause, and the human judgment be suspended, in the decision of which the great principles of liberty are not concerned, but the respective powers of those who are equally the representatives of the people, are to be adjusted; if not put at rest by the practice of the government, ought to receive a considerable impression from that practice. An exposition of the constitution, deliberately established by legislative acts, on the faith of which an immense property has been advanced, ought not to be lightly disregarded.

The power now contested was exercised by the first congress elected under the present constitution. The bill for incorporating the Bank of the United States did not steal upon an unsuspecting legislature, and pass unobserved. Its principle was completely understood, and was opposed with equal zeal and ability. After being resisted, first, in the fair and open field of debate, and afterwards, in the executive cabinet, with as much persevering talent as any measure has ever experienced, and being supported by arguments which convinced minds as pure and as intelligent as this country can boast, it became a law. The original act was permitted to expire; but a short experience of the embarrassments to which the refusal to revive it exposed the government, convinced those who were most prejudiced against the measure of its necessity, and induced the passage of the present law. It would require no ordinary share of intrepidity, to assert that a measure adopted under these circumstances, was a bold and plain usurpation, to which the constitution gave no countenance. These observations belong to the cause; but they are not made under the impression, that, were the question entirely new, the law would be found irreconcilable with the constitution.

In discussing this question, the counsel for the state of Maryland have deemed it of some importance, in the construction of the constitution, to consider that instrument, not as emanating from the people, but as the act of sovereign and independent states. The powers of the general government, it has been said, are delegated by the states, who alone are truly sovereign; and must be exercised in subordination to the states, who alone possess supreme dominion. It would be difficult to sustain this proposition. The convention which framed the constitution was indeed elected by the state legislatures. But the instrument, when it came from their hands, was a mere proposal, without obligation, or pretensions to it. It was reported to the then existing congress of the United States, with a request that it might "be submitted to a convention of delegates, chosen in each state by the people thereof, under the recommendation of its legislature, for their assent and ratification."

This mode of proceeding was adopted; and by the convention, by congress, and by the state legislatures, the instrument was submitted to the *people*. They acted upon it in the only manner in which they can act safely, effectively and wisely, on such a subject, by assembling in convention. It is true, they assembled in their several states—and where else should they have assembled? No political dreamer was ever wild enough to think of breaking down the lines which separate the states, and of compounding the American people into one common mass. Of consequence, when they act, they act in their states. But the measures they adopt do not, on that account, cease to be the measures of the people themselves, or become the measures of the state governments.

Source of Constitution

From these conventions, the constitution derives its whole authority. The government proceeds directly from the people; is "ordained and established," in the name of the people; and is declared to be ordained, "in order to form a more perfect union, establish justice, insure domestic tranquillity, and secure the blessings of liberty to themselves and to their posterity." The assent of the states, in their sovereign capacity, is implied, in calling a convention, and thus submitting that instrument to the people. But the people were at perfect liberty to accept or reject it; and their act was final. It required not the affirmance, and could not be negatived, by the state governments. The constitution, when thus adopted, was of complete obligation, and bound the state sovereignties.

It has been said, that the people had already surrendered all their powers to the state sovereignties, and had nothing more to give. But, surely, the question whether they may resume and modify the powers granted to government, does not remain to be settled in this country. Much more might the legitimacy of the general government be doubted, had it been created by the states. The powers delegated to the state sovereignties were to be exercised by themselves, not by a distinct and independent sovereignty, created by themselves.

To the formation of a league, such as was the confederation, the state sovereignties were certainly competent. But when, "in order to form a more perfect union," it was deemed necessary to change this alliance into an effective government, possessing great and sovereign powers, and acting directly on the people, the necessity of referring it to the people, and of deriving its powers directly from them, was felt and acknowledged by all. The government of the Union, then (whatever may be the influence of this fact on the case), is, emphatically and truly, a government of the people. In form, and in substance, it emanates from them. Its powers are granted by them, and are to be exercised directly on them, and for their benefit.

This government is acknowledged by all, to be one of enumerated powers. The principle, that it can exercise only the powers granted to it, would seem too apparent, to have required to be enforced by all those arguments, which its enlightened friends, while it was depending before the people, found it necessary to urge; that principle is now universally admitted. But the question respecting the extent of the powers actually granted, is perpetually arising, and will probably continue to arise, so long as our system shall exist. In discussing these questions, the conflicting powers of the general and state governments must be brought into view, and the supremacy of their respective laws, when they are in opposition, must be settled.

Supremacy of Constitution

If any one proposition could command the universal assent of mankind, we might expect it would be this—that the government of the Union, though limited in its powers, is supreme within its sphere of action. This would seem to result, necessarily, from its nature. It is the government of all; its powers are delegated by all; it represents all, and acts for all. Though any one state may be willing to control its operations, no state is willing to allow others to control them. The nation, on those subjects on which it can act, must necessarily bind its component parts.

But this question is not left to mere reason: the people have, in express terms, decided it, by saying, "this constitution, and the laws of the United States, which shall be made in pursuance thereof," "shall be the supreme law of the land," and by requiring that the members of the state legislatures, and the officers of the executive and judicial departments of the states, shall take the oath of fidelity to it. The government of the United States, then, though limited in its powers, is supreme; and its laws, when made in pursuance of the constitution, form the supreme law of the land, "anything in the constitution or laws of any state to the contrary notwithstanding."

Among the enumerated powers, we do not find that of establishing a bank or creating a corporation. But there is no phrase in the instrument which, like the articles of confederation, excludes incidental or implied powers; and which requires that everything granted shall be expressly and minutely described. Even the 10th amendment, which was framed for the purpose of quieting the excessive jealousies which had been excited, omits the word "expressly," and declares only, that the powers "not delegated to the United States, nor prohibited to the states, are reserved to the states or to the people;" thus leaving the question, whether the particular power which may become the subject of contest, has been delegated to the one government, or prohibited to the other, to depend on a fair construction of the whole instrument. The men who drew and adopted this amendment had experienced the embarrassments resulting from the insertion of this word in the articles of confederation, and probably omitted it, to avoid those embarrassments.

A constitution, to contain an accurate detail of all the subdivisions of which its great powers will admit, and of all the means by which they may be carried into execution, would partake of the prolixity of a legal code, and could scarcely be embraced by the human mind. It would, probably, never be understood by the public. Its nature, therefore, requires, that only its great outlines should be marked, its important objects designated, and the minor ingredients which compose those objects, be deduced from the nature of the objects themselves. That this idea was entertained by the framers of the American constitution, is not only to be inferred from the nature of the instrument, but from the language. Why else were some of the limitations, found in the 9th section of the 1st article, introduced? It is also, in some degree, warranted, by their having omitted to use any restrictive term which might prevent its receiving a fair and just interpretation. In considering this question, then, we must never forget that it is a *constitution* we are expounding.

Doctrine of Implied Powers

Although, among the enumerated powers of government, we do not find the word "bank" or "incorporation," we find the great powers, to lay and collect taxes; to borrow money; to regulate commerce; to declare and conduct a war; and to raise and support armies and navies. The sword and the purse, all the external relations, and no inconsiderable portion of the industry of the nation, are intrusted to its government. It can never be pretended, that these vast powers draw after them others of inferior importance, merely because they are inferior. Such an idea can never be advanced. But it may with great reason be contended, that a government, intrusted with such ample powers, on the due execution of which the happiness and prosperity of the nation so vitally depends, must also be intrusted with ample means for their execution.

The power being given, it is the interest of the nation to facilitate its execution. It can never be their interest, and cannot be presumed to have been their intention, to clog and embarrass its execution, by withholding the most appropriate means. Throughout this vast republic, from the St. Croix to the Gulf of Mexico, from the Atlantic to the Pacific, revenue is to be collected and expended, armies are to be marched and supported. The exigencies of the nation may require, that the treasure raised in the north should be transported to the south, that raised in the east, conveyed to the west, or that this order should be reversed. Is that construction of the constitution to be preferred, which would render these operations difficult, hazardous and expensive? Can we adopt that construction (unless the words imperiously require it), which would impute to the framers of that instrument, when granting these powers for the public good, the intention of impeding their exercise, by withholding a choice of means?

If, indeed, such be the mandate of the constitution, we have only to obey; but that instrument does not profess to enumerate the means by which the powers it confers may be executed; nor does it prohibit the creation of a corporation, if the existence of such a being be essential, to the beneficial exercise of those powers. It is, then, the subject of fair inquiry, how far such means may be employed.

Necessary and Proper Powers

It is not denied, that the powers given to the government imply the ordinary means of execution. That, for example, of raising revenue, and applying it to national purposes, is admitted to imply the power of conveying money from place to place, as the exigencies of the nation may require, and of employing the usual means of conveyance. But it is denied, that the government has its choice of means; or, that it may employ the most convenient means, if, to employ them, it be necessary to erect a corporation. On what foundation does this argument rest? On this alone: the power of creating a corporation, is one appertaining to sovereignty, and is not expressly conferred on congress.

This is true. But all legislative powers appertain to sovereignty. The original power of giving the law on any subject whatever, is a sovereign power; and if the government of the Union is restrained from creating a corporation, as a means for performing its functions, on the single reason that the creation of a corporation is an act of sovereignty; if the sufficiency of this reason be acknowledged, there would be some difficulty in sustaining the authority of congress to pass other laws for the accomplishment of the same objects. The government which has a right to do an act, and has imposed on it, the duty of performing that act, must, according to the dictates of reason, be allowed to select the means; and those who contend that it may not select any appropriate means, that one particular mode of effecting the object is excepted, take upon themselves the burden of establishing that exception.

The creation of a corporation, it is said, appertains to sovereignty. This is admitted. But to what portion of sovereignty does it appertain? Does it belong to one more than to another? In America, the powers of sovereignty are divided between the government of the Union, and those of the states. They are each sovereign, with respect to the objects committed to it, and neither sovereign, with respect to the objects committed to the other. We cannot comprehend that train of reasoning, which would maintain, that the extent of power granted by the people is to be ascertained, not by the nature and terms of the grant, but by its date.

Some state constitutions were formed before, some since that of the United States. We cannot believe, that their relation to each other is in any degree dependent upon this circumstance. Their respective powers must, we think, be precisely the same, as if they had been formed at the same time. Had they been formed at the same time, and had the people conferred on the general government the power contained in the constitution, and on the states the whole residuum of power, would it have been asserted, that the government of the Union was not sovereign, with respect to those objects which were intrusted to it, in relation to which its laws were declared to be supreme? If this could not have been asserted, we cannot well comprehend the process of reasoning which maintains, that a power appertaining to sovereignty cannot be connected with that vast portion of it which is granted to the general government, so far as it is calculated to subserve the legitimate objects of that government. The power of creating a corporation, though appertaining to sovereignty, is not, like the power of making war, or levying taxes, or of regulating commerce, a great substantive and independent power, which cannot be implied as incidental to other powers, or used as a means of executing them. It is never the end for which other powers are exercised, but a means by which other objects are accomplished. No contributions are made to charity, for the sake of an incorporation, but a corporation is created to administer the charity; no seminary of learning is instituted, in order to be incorporated, but the corporate character is conferred to subserve the purposes of education. No city was ever built, with the sole object of being incorporated, but is incorporated as affording the best means of being well governed. The power of creating a corporation is never used for its own sake, but for the purpose of effecting something else. No sufficient reason is, therefore, perceived, why it may not pass as incidental to those powers which are expressly given, if it be a direct mode of executing them.

Construction of Clause

But the constitution of the United States has not left the right of congress to employ the necessary means, for the execution of the powers conferred on the government, to general reasoning. To its enumeration of powers is added, that of making "all laws which shall be necessary and proper, for carrying into execution the foregoing powers, and all other powers vested by this constitution, in the government of the United States, or in any department thereof." The counsel for the state of Maryland have urged various arguments, to prove that this clause, though, in terms, a grant of power, is not so, in effect; but is really restrictive of the general right, which might otherwise be implied, of selecting means for executing the enumerated powers. In support of this proposition, they have found it necessary to contend, that this clause was inserted for the purpose of conferring on congress the power of making laws. That, without it, doubts might be entertained, whether congress could exercise its powers in the form of legislation.

But could this be the object for which it was inserted? A government is created by the people, having legislative, executive and judicial powers. Its legislative powers are vested in a congress, which is to consist of a senate and house of representatives. Each house may determine the rule of its proceedings; and it is declared, that every bill which shall have passed both houses, shall, before it becomes a law, be presented to the president of the United States. The 7th section describes the course of proceedings, by which a bill shall become a law; and, then, the 8th section enumerates the powers of congress. Could it be necessary to say, that a legislature should exercise legislative powers, in the shape of legislation? After allowing each house to prescribe its own course of proceeding, after describing the manner in which a bill should become a law, would it have entered into the mind of a single member of the convention, that an express power to make laws was necessary, to enable the legislature to make them? That a legislature, endowed with legislative powers, can legislate, is a proposition too self-evident to have been questioned.

But the argument on which most reliance is placed, is drawn from that peculiar language of this clause. Congress is not empowered by it to make all laws, which may have relation to the powers conferred on the government, but such only as may be *"necessary and proper"* for carrying them into execution. The word *"necessary"* is considered as controlling the whole sentence, and as limiting the right to pass laws for the execution of the granted powers, to such as are indispensable, and without which the power would be nugatory. That it excludes the choice of means, and leaves to congress, in each case, that only which is most direct and simple.

Is it true, that this is the sense in which the word "necessary" is always used? Does it always import an absolute physical necessity, so strong, that one thing to which another may be termed necessary, cannot exist without that other? We think it does not. If reference be had to its use, in the common affairs of the world, or in approved authors, we find that it frequently imports no more than that one thing is convenient, or useful, or essential to another. To employ the means necessary to an end, is generally understood as employing any means calculated to produce the end, and not as being confined to those single means, without which the end would be entirely unattainable. Such is the character of human language, that no word conveys to the mind, in all situations, one single definite idea; and nothing is more common than to use words in a figurative sense.

Almost all compositions contain words, which, taken in their rigorous sense, would convey a meaning different from that which is obviously intended. It is essential to just construction, that many words which import something excessive, should be understood in a more mitigated sense—in that sense which common usage justifies. The word "necessary" is of this description. It has not a fixed character, peculiar to itself. It admits of all degrees of comparison; and is often connected with other words, which increase or diminish the impression the mind receives of the urgency it imports. A thing may be necessary, very necessary, absolutely or indispensably necessary. To no mind would the same idea be conveyed by these several phrases. The comment on the word is well illustrated by the passage cited at the bar, from the 10th section of the 1st article of the constitution. It is, we think, impossible to compare the sentence which prohibits a state from laying "imposts, or duties on imports or exports, except what may be *absolutely* necessary for executing its inspection laws," with that which authorizes congress "to make all laws which shall be necessary and proper for carrying into execution" the powers of the general government, without feeling a conviction, that the convention understood itself to change materially the meaning of the word "necessary," by prefixing the word "absolutely." This word, then, like others, is used in various senses; and, in its construction, the subject, the context, the intention of the person using them, are all to be taken into view.

"Constitution . . . for Ages to Come"

Let this be done in the case under consideration. The subject is the execution of those great powers on which the welfare of a nation essentially depends. It must have been the intention of those who gave these powers, to insure, so far as human prudence could insure, their beneficial execution. This could not be done, by confiding the choice of means to such narrow limits as not to leave it in the power of congress to adopt any which might be appropriate, and which were conducive to the end. This provision is made in a constitution, intended to endure for ages to come, and consequently, to be adapted to the various *crises* of human affairs. To have prescribed the means by which government should, in all future time, execute its powers, would have been to change, entirely, the character of the instrument, and give it the properties of a legal code. It would have been an unwise attempt to provide, by immutable rules, for exigencies which, if foreseen at all, must have been seen dimly, and which can be best provided for as they occur. To have declared, that the best means shall not be used, but those alone, without which the power given would be nugatory, would have been to deprive the legislature of the capacity to avail itself of experience, to exercise its reason, and to accommodate its legislation to circumstances.

If we apply this principle of construction to any of the powers of the government, we shall find it so pernicious in its operation that we shall be compelled to discard it. The powers vested in congress may certainly be carried into execution, without prescribing an oath of office. The power to exact this security for the faithful performance of duty, is not given, nor is it indispensably necessary. The different departments may be established; taxes may be imposed and collected; armies and navies may be raised and maintained; and money may be borrowed, without requiring an oath of office. It might be argued, with as much plausibility as other incidental powers have been assailed, that the convention was not unmindful of this subject. The oath which might be exacted—that of fidelity to the constitution—is prescribed, and no other can be required. Yet, he would be charged with insanity, who should contend, that the legislature might not superadd, to the oath directed by the constitution, such other oath of office as its wisdom might suggest.

So, with respect to the whole penal code of the United States: whence arises the power to punish, in cases not prescribed by the constitution? All admit, that the government may, legitimately, punish any violation of its laws; and yet, this is not among the enumerated powers of congress. The right to enforce the observance of law, by punishing its infraction, might be denied, with the more plausibility, because it is expressly given in some cases. Congress is empowered "to provide for the punishment of counterfeiting the securities and current coin of the United States," and "to define and punish piracies and felonies committed on the high seas, and offences against the law of nations." The several powers of congress may exist, in a very imperfect state, to be sure, but they may exist and be carried into execution, although no punishment should be inflicted, in cases where the right to punish is not expressly given.

Take, for example, the power "to establish post-offices and post-roads." This power is executed, by the single act of making the establishment. But, from this has been inferred the power and duty of carrying the mail along the post-road, from one post-office to another. And from this implied power, has again been inferred the right to punish those who steal letters from the post-office, or rob the mail. It may be said, with some plausibility, that the right to carry the mail, and to punish those who rob it, is not indispensably necessary to the establishment of a post-office and post-road. This right is indeed essential to the beneficial exercise of the power, but not indispensably necessary to its existence. So, of the punishment of the crimes of stealing or falsifying a record or process of a court of the United States, or of perjury in such court. To punish these offences, is certainly conducive to the due administration of justice. But courts may exist, and may decide the causes brought before them, though such crimes escape punishment.

Case for Broad Construction

The baneful influence of this narrow construction on all the operations of the government, and the absolute impracticability of maintaining it, without rendering the government incompetent to its great objects, might be illustrated by numerous examples drawn from the constitution, and from our laws. The good sense of the public has pronounced, without hesitation, that the power of punishment appertains to sovereignty, and may be exercised, whenever the sovereign has a right to act, as incidental to his constitutional powers It is a means for carrying into execution all sovereign powers, and may be used, although not indispensably necessary. It is a right incidental to the power, and conducive to its beneficial exercise.

If this limited construction of the word "necessary" must be abandoned, in order to punish, whence is derived the rule which would reinstate it, when the government would carry its powers into execution, by means not vindictive in their nature? If the word "necessary" means "needful," "requisite," "essential," "conducive to," in order to let in the power of punishment for the infraction of law; why is it not equally comprehensive, when required to authorize the use of means which facilitate the execution of the powers of government, without the infliction of punishment?

In ascertaining the sense in which the word "necessary" is used in this clause of the constitution, we may derive some aid from that with which it is associated. Congress shall have power "to make all laws which shall be necessary and proper to carry into execution" the powers of the government. If the word "necessary" was used in that strict and rigorous sense for which the counsel for the state of Maryland contend, it would be an extraordinary departure from the usual course of the human mind, as exhibited in composition, to add a word, the only possible effect of which is, to qualify that strict and rigorous meaning; to present to the mind the idea of some choice means of legislation, not strained and compressed within the narrow limits for which gentlemen contend.

But the argument which most conclusively demonstrates the error of the construction contended for by the counsel for the state of Maryland, is founded on the intention of the convention, as manifested in the whole clause. To waste time and argument in proving that, without it, congress might carry its powers into execution, would be not much less idle, than to hold a lighted taper to the sun. As little can it be required to prove, that in the absence of this clause, congress would have some choice of means. That it might employ those which, in its judgment, would most advantageously effect the object to be accomplished. That any means adapted to the end, any means which tended directly to the execution of the constitutional powers of the government, were in themselves constitutional. This clause, as construed by the state of Maryland, would abridge, and almost annihilate, this useful and necessary right of the legislature to select its means. That this could not be intended, is, we should think, had it not been already controverted, too apparent for controversy.

Place in Constitution

We think so for the following reasons: 1st. The clause is placed among the powers of congress, not among the limitations on those powers. 2d. Its terms purport to enlarge, not to diminish the powers vested in the government. It purports to be an additional power, not a restriction on those already granted. No reason has been, or can be assigned, for thus concealing an intention to narrow the discretion of the national legislature, under words which purport to enlarge it. The framers of the constitution wished its adoption, and well knew that it would be endangered by its strength, not by its weakness. Had they been capable of using language which would convey to the eye one idea, and, after deep reflection, impress on the mind, another, they would rather have disguised the grant of power, than its limitation. If, then, their intention had been, by this clause, to restrain the free use of means which might otherwise have been implied, that intention would have been inserted in another place, and would have been expressed in terms resembling these. "In carrying into execution the foregoing powers, and all others," &c., "no laws shall be passed but such as are necessary and proper." Had the intention been to make this clause restrictive, it would unquestionably have been so in form as well as in effect.

The result of the most careful and attentive consideration bestowed upon this clause is, that if it does not enlarge, it cannot be construed to restrain the powers of congress, or to impair the right of the legislature to exercise its best judgment in the selection of measures to carry into execution the constitutional powers of the government. If no other motive for its insertion can be suggested, a sufficient one is found in the desire to remove all doubts respecting the right to legislate on that vast mass of incidental powers which must be involved in the constitution, if that instrument be not a splendid bauble.

Vested Power Is Plenary

We admit, as all must admit, that the powers of the government are limited, and that its limits are not to be transcended. But we think the sound construction of the constitution must allow to the national legislature that discretion, with respect to the means by which the powers it confers are to be carried into execution, which will enable that body to perform the high duties assigned to it, in the manner most beneficial to the people. Let the end be legitimate, let it be within the scope of the constitution, and all means which are appropriate, which are plainly adapted to that end, which are not prohibited, but consist with the letter and spirit of the constitution, are constitutional.

That a corporation must be considered as a means not less usual, not of higher dignity, not more requiring a particular specification than other means, has been sufficiently proved. If we look to the origin of corporations, to the manner in which they have been framed in that government from which we have derived most of our legal principles and ideas, or to the uses to which they have been applied, we find no reason to suppose, that a constitution, omitting, and wisely omitting, to enumerate all the means for carrying into execution the great powers vested in government, ought to have specified this. Had it been intended to grant this power, as one which should be distinct and independent, to be exercised in any case whatever, it would have found a place among the enumerated powers of the government. But being considered merely as a means, to be employed only for the purpose of carrying into execution the given powers, there could be no motive for particularly mentioning it.

The propriety of this remark would seem to be generally acknowledged, by the universal acquiescence in the construction which has been uniformly put on the 3d section of the 4th article of the constitution. The power to "make all needful rules and regulations respecting the territory or other property belonging to the United States," is not more comprehensive, than the power "to make all laws which shall be necessary and proper for carrying into execution" the powers of the government. Yet all admit the constitutionality of a territorial government, which is a corporate body.

If a corporation may be employed, indiscriminately with other means, to carry into execution the powers of the government, no particular reason can be assigned for excluding the use of a bank, if required for its fiscal operations. To use one, must be within the discretion of congress, if it be an appropriate mode of executing the powers of government. That it is a convenient, a useful, and essential instrument in the prosecution of its fiscal operations, is not now a subject of controversy. All those who have been concerned in the administration of our finances, have concurred in representing its importance and necessity; and so strongly have they been felt, that statesmen of the first class, whose previous opinions against it had been confirmed by every circumstance which can fix the human judgment, have yielded those opinions to the exigencies of the nation. Under the confederation, congress, justifying the measure by its necessity, transcended, perhaps, its powers, to obtain the advantage of a bank; and our own legislation attests the universal conviction of the utility of this measure. The time has passed away, when it can be necessary to enter into any discussion, in order to prove the importance of this instrument, as a means to effect the legitimate objects of the government.

But were its necessity less apparent, none can deny its being an appropriate measure; and if it is, the decree of its necessity, as has been very justly observed, is to be discussed in another place. Should congress, in the execution of its powers, adopt measures which are prohibited by the constitution; or should congress, under the pretext of executing its powers, pass laws for the accomplishment of objects not intrusted to the government; it would become the painful duty of this tribunal, should a case requiring such a decision come before it, to say, that such an act was not the law of the land. But where the law is not prohibited, and is really calculated to effect any of the objects intrusted to the government, to undertake here to inquire into the decree of its necessity, would be to pass the line which circumscribes the judicial department, and to tread on legislative ground. This court disclaims all pretensions to such a power.

State Powers in Same Area

After this declaration, it can scarcely be necessary to say, that the existence of state banks can have no possible influence on the question. No trace is to be found in the constitution, of an intention to create a dependence of the government of the Union on those of the states, for the execution of the great powers assigned to it. Its means are adequate to its ends; and on those means alone was it expected to rely for the accomplishment of its ends. To impose on it the necessity of resorting to means which it cannot control, which another government may furnish or withhold, would render its course precarious, the result of its measures uncertain, and create a dependence on other governments, which might disappoint its most important designs, and is incompatible with the language of the constitution. But were it otherwise, the choice of means implies a right to choose a national bank in preference to state banks, and congress alone can make the election.

Constitutionality of Bank

After the most deliberate consideration, it is the unanimous and decided opinion of this court, that the act to incorporate the Bank of the United States is a law made in pursuance of the constitution, and is a part of the supreme law of the land.

The branches, proceeding from the same stock, and being conducive to the complete accomplishment of the object, are equally constitutional. It would have been unwise, to locate them in the charter, and it would be unnecessarily inconvenient, to employ the legislative power in making those subordinate arrangements. The great duties of the bank are prescribed; those duties require branches; and the bank itself may, we think, be safely trusted with the selection of places where those branches shall be fixed; reserving always to the government the right to require that a branch shall be located where it may be deemed necessary.

It being the opinion of the court, that the act incorporating the bank is constitutional; and that the power of establishing a branch in the state of Maryland might be properly exercised by the bank itself, we proceed to inquire—

Conflicting State Laws

2. Whether the state of Maryland may, without violating the constitution, tax that branch? That the power of taxation is one of vital importance; that it is retained by the states; that it is not abridged by the grant of a similar power to the government of the Union; that it is to be concurrently exercised by the two governments—are truths which have never been denied. But such is the paramount character of the constitution, that its capacity to withdraw any subject from the action of even this power, is admitted. The states are expressly forbidden to lay any duties on imports or exports, except what may be absolutely necessary for executing their inspection laws. If the obligation of this prohibition must be conceded—if it may restrain a state from the exercise of its taxing power on imports and exports—the same paramount character would seem to restrain, as it certainly may restrain, a state from such other exercise of this power, as is in its nature incompatible with, and repugnant to, the constitutional laws of the Union. A law, absolutely repugnant to another, as entirely repeals that other as if express terms of repeal were used.

On this ground, the counsel for the bank place its claim to be exempted from the power of a state to tax its operations. There is no express provision for the case, but the claim has been sustained on a principle which so entirely pervades the constitution, is so intermixed with the materials which compose it, so interwoven with its web, so blended with its texture, as to be incapable of being separated from it, without rending it into shreds. This great principle is, that the constitution and the laws made in pursuance thereof are supreme; that they control the constitution and laws of the respective states, and cannot be controlled by them. From this, which may be almost termed an axiom, other propositions are deduced as corollaries, on the truth or error of which, and on their application to this case, the cause has been supposed to depend. These are, 1st. That a power to create implies a power to preserve: 2d. That a power to destroy, if wielded by a different hand, is hostile to, and incompatible with these powers to create and to preserve: 3d. That where this repugnancy exists, that authority which is supreme must control, not yield to that over which it is supreme.

These propositions, as abstract truths, would, perhaps, never be controverted. Their application to this case, however, has been denied; and both in maintaining the affirmative and the negative, a splendor of eloquence, and strength of argument, seldom, if ever, surpassed, have been displayed.

Burden of State Tax

The power of congress to create, and of course, to continue, the bank, was the subject of the preceding part of this opinion; and is no longer to be considered as questionable. That the power of taxing it by the states may be exercised so as to destroy it, is too obvious to be denied. But taxation is said to be an absolute power, which acknowledges no other limits than those expressly prescribed in the constitution, and like sovereign power of every other description, is intrusted to the discretion of those who use it. But the very terms of this argument admit, that the sovereignty of the state, in the article of taxation itself, is subordinate to, and may be controlled by the constitution of the United States. How far it has been controlled by that instrument, must be a question of construction. In making this construction, no principle, not declared, can be admissible, which would defeat the legitimate operations of a supreme government. It is of the very essence of supremacy, to remove all obstacles to its action within its own sphere, and so to modify every power vested in subordinate governments, as to exempt its own operations from their own influence. This effect need not be stated in terms. It is so involved in the declaration of supremacy, so necessarily implied in it, that the expression of it could not make it more certain. We must, therefore, keep it in view, while construing the constitution.

The argument on the part of the state of Maryland, is, not that the states may directly resist a law of congress, but that they may exercise their acknowledged powers upon it, and that the constitution leaves them this right, in the confidence that they will not abuse it. Before we proceed to examine this argument, and to subject it to test of the constitution, we must be permitted to bestow a few considerations on the nature and extent of this original right of taxation, which is acknowledged to remain with the states. It is admitted, that the power of taxing the people and their property, is essential to the very existence of government, and may be legitimately exercised on the objects to which it is applicable, to the utmost extent to which the government may choose to carry it. The only security against the abuse of this power, is found in the structure of the government itself. In imposing a tax, the legislature acts upon its constituents. This is, in general, a sufficient security against erroneous and oppressive taxation.

The people of a state, therefore, give to their government a right of taxing themselves and their property, and as the exigencies of government cannot be limited, they prescribe no limits to the exercise of this right, resting confidently on the interest of the legislator, and on the influence of the constituent over their representative, to guard them against its abuse. But the means employed by the government of the Union have no such security, nor is the right of a state to tax them sustained by the same theory. Those means are not given by the people of a particular state, not given by the constituents of the legislature, which claim the right to tax them, but by the people of all the states. They are given by all, for the benefit of all—and upon theory, should be subjected to that government only which belongs to all.

It may be objected to this definition, that the power of taxation is not confined to the people and property of a state. It may be exercised upon every object brought within its jurisdiction. This is true. But to what source do we trace this right? It is obvious, that it is an incident of sovereignty, and is co-extensive with that to which it is an incident. All subjects over which the sovereign power of a state extends, are objects of taxation; but those over which it does not extend, are, upon the soundest principles, exempt from taxation. This proposition may almost be pronounced self-evident.

Paramount Federal Power

The sovereignty of a state extends to everything which exists by its own authority, or is introduced by its permission; but does it extend to those means which are employed by congress to carry into execution powers conferred on that body by the people of the United States? We think it demonstrable, that it does not. Those powers are not given by the people of a single state. They are given by the people of the United States, to a government whose laws, made in pursuance of the constitution, are declared to be supreme. Consequently, the people of a single state cannot confer a sovereignty which will extend over them.

If we measure the power of taxation residing in a state, by the extent of sovereignty which the people of a single state possess, and can confer on its government, we have an intelligible standard, applicable to every case to which the power may be applied. We have a principle which leaves the power of taxing the people and property of a state unimpaired; which leaves to a state the command of all its resources, and which places beyond its reach, all those powers which are conferred by the people of the United States on the government of the Union, and all those means which are given for the purpose of carrying those powers into execution. We have a principle which is safe for the states, and safe for the Union. We are relieved, as we ought to be, from clashing sovereignty; from interfering powers; from a repugnancy between a right in one government to pull down, what there is an acknowledged right in another to build up; from the incompatibility of a right in one government to destroy, what there is a right in another to preserve. We are not driven to the perplexing inquiry, so unfit for the judicial department, what degree of taxation is the legitimate use, and what degree may amount to the abuse of the power. The attempt to use it on the means employed by the government of the Union, in pursuance of the constitution, is itself an abuse, because it is the usurpation of a power which the people of a single state cannot give. We find, then, on just theory, a total failure of this original right to tax the means employed by the government of the Union, for the execution of its powers. The right never existed, and the question whether it has been surrendered, cannot arise.

But, waiving this theory for the present, let us resume the inquiry, whether this power can be exercised by the respective states, consistently with a fair construction of the constitution? That the power to tax involves the power to destroy; that the power to destroy may defeat and render useless the power to create; that there is a plain repugnance in conferring on one government a power to control the constitutional measures of another, which other, with respect to those very measures, is declared to be supreme over that which exerts the control, are propositions not to be denied. But all inconsistencies are to be reconciled by the magic of the word *confidence*. Taxation, it is said, does not necessarily and unavoidably destroy. To carry it to the excess of destruction, would be an abuse, to presume which, would banish that confidence which is essential to all government. But is this a case of confidence? Would the people of any one state trust those of another with a power to control the most insignificant operations of their state government? We know they would not. Why, then, should we suppose, that the people of any one state should be willing to trust those of another with a power to control the operations of a government to which they have confided their most important and most valuable interests? In the legislature of the Union alone, are all represented. The legislature of the Union alone, therefore, can be trusted by the people with the power of controlling measures which concern all, in the confidence that it will not be abused. This, then, is not a case of confidence, and we must consider it is as it really is.

Limits to State Powers

If we apply the principle for which the state of Maryland contends, to the constitution, generally, we shall find it capable of changing totally the character of that instrument. We shall find it capable of arresting all the measures of the government, and of prostrating it at the foot of the states. The American people have declared their constitution and the laws made in pursuance thereof, to be supreme; but this principle would transfer the supremacy, in fact, to the states. If the states may tax one instrument, employed by the government in the execution of its powers, they may tax any and every other instrument. They may tax the mail; they may tax the mint; they may tax patent-rights; they may tax the papers of the custom-house; they may tax judicial process; they may tax all the means employed by the government, to an excess which would defeat all the ends of government. This was not intended by the American people. They did not design to make their government dependent on the states.

Gentlemen say, they do not claim the right to extend state taxation to these objects. They limit their pretensions to property. But on what principle, is this distinction made? Those who make it have furnished no reason for it, and the principle for which they contend denies it. They contend, that the power of taxation has no other limit than is found in the 10th section of the 1st article of the constitution; that, with respect to everything else, the power of the states is supreme, and admits of no control. If this be true, the distinction between property and other subjects to which the power of taxation is applicable, is merely arbitrary, and can never be sustained. This is not all. If the controlling power of the states be established; if their supremacy as to taxation be acknowledged; what is to restrain their exercising control in any shape they may please to give it? Their sovereignty is not confined to taxation; that is not the only mode in which it might be displayed. The question is, in truth, a question of supremacy; and if the right of the states to tax the means employed by the general government be conceded, the declaration that the constitution, and the laws made in pursuance thereof, shall be the supreme law of the land, is empty and unmeaning declamation.

In the course of the argument, the Federalist has been quoted; and the opinions expressed by the authors of that work have been justly supposed to be entitled to great respect in expounding the constitution. No tribute can be paid to them which exceeds their merit; but in applying their opinions to the cases which may arise in the progress of our government, a right to judge of their correctness must be retained; and to understand the argument, we must examine the proposition it maintains, and the objections against which it is directed. The subject of those numbers, from which passages have been cited, is the unlimited power of taxation which is vested in the general government. The objection to this unlimited power, which the argument seeks to remove, is stated with fulness and clearness. It is, "that an indefinite power of taxation in the latter (the government of the Union) might, and probably would, in time, deprive the former (the government of the states) of the means of providing for their own necessities; and would subject them entirely to the mercy of the national legislature. As the laws of the Union are to become the supreme law of the land; as it is to have power to pass all laws that may be necessary for carrying into execution the authorities with which it is proposed to vest it; the national government might, at any time, abolish the taxes imposed for state objects, upon the pretence of an interference with its own. It might allege a necessity for doing this, in order to give efficacy to the national revenues; and thus, all the resources of taxation might, by degrees, become the subjects of federal monopoly, to the entire exclusion and destruction of the state governments."

The objections to the constitution which are noticed in these numbers, were to the undefined power of the government to tax, not to the incidental privilege of exempting its own measures from state taxation. The consequences apprehended from this undefined power were, that it would absorb all the objects of taxation, "to the exclusion and destruction of the state governments." The arguments of the Federalist are intended to prove the fallacy of these apprehensions; not to prove that the government was incapable of executing any of its powers, without exposing the means it employed to the embarrassments of state taxation. Arguments urged against these objections, and these apprehensions, are to be understood as relating to the points they mean to prove. Had the authors of those excellent essays been asked, whether they contended for that construction of the constitution, which would place within the reach of the states those measures which the government might adopt for the execution of its powers; no man, who has read their instructive pages, will hesitate to admit, that their answer must have been in the negative.

Concurrent Powers

It has also been insisted, that, as the power of taxation in the general and state governments is acknowledged to be concurrent, every argument which would sustain the right of the general government to tax banks chartered by the states, will equally sustain the right of the states to tax banks chartered by the general government. But the two cases are not on the same reason. The people of all the states have created the general government, and have conferred upon it the general power of taxation. The people of all the states, and the states themselves, are represented in congress, and, by their representatives, exercise this power. When they tax the chartered institutions of the states, they tax their constituents; and these taxes must be uniform. But when a state taxes the operations of the government of the United States, it acts upon institutions created, not by their own constituents, but by people over whom they claim no control. It acts upon the measures of a government created by others as well as themselves, for the benefit of others in common with themselves. The difference is that which always exists, and always must exist, between the action of the whole on a part, and the action of a part on the whole—between the laws of a government declared to be supreme, and those of a government which, when in opposition to those laws, is not supreme.

But if the full application of this argument could be admitted, it might bring into question the right of congress to tax the state banks, and could not prove the rights of the states to tax the Bank of the United States.

The court has bestowed on this subject its most deliberate consideration. The result is a conviction that the states have no power, by taxation or otherwise, to retard, impede, burden, or in any manner control, the operations of the constitutional laws enacted by congress to carry into execution the powers vested in the general government. This is, we think, the unavoidable consequence of that supremacy which the constitution has declared. We are unanimously of opinion, that the law passed by the legislature of Maryland, imposing a tax on the Bank of the United States, is unconstitutional and void.

This opinion does not deprive the states of any resources which they originally possessed. It does not extend to a tax paid by the real property of the bank, in common with the other real property within the state, nor to a tax imposed on the interest which the citizens of Maryland may hold in this institution, in common with other property of the same description throughout the state. But this is a tax on the operations of the bank, and is, consequently, a tax on the operation of an instrument employed by the government of the Union to carry its powers into execution. Such a tax must be unconstitutional.

Judgment

This cause came on to be heard, on the transcript of the record of the court of appeals of the state of Maryland, and was argued by counsel: on consideration whereof, it is the opinion of this court, that the act of the legislature of Maryland is contrary to the constitution of the United States, and void; and therefore, that the said court of appeals of the state of Maryland erred, in affirming the judgment of the Baltimore county court, in which judgment was rendered against James W. McCulloch; but that the said court of appeals of Maryland ought to have reversed the said judgment of the said Baltimore county court, and ought to have given judgment for the said appellant, McCulloch: It is, therefore, adjudged and ordered, that the said judgment of the said court of appeals of the state of Maryland in this case, be, and the same hereby is, reversed and annulled. And this court, proceeding to render such judgment as the said court of appeals should have rendered; it is further adjudged and ordered, that the judgment of the said Baltimore county court be reversed and annulled, and that judgment be entered in the said Baltimore county court for the said James W. McCulloch.

7. *Cohens* v. *Virginia*

19 U.S. (6 Wheaton), 378ff.

1. The first question to be considered is, whether the jurisdiction of this court is excluded by the character of the parties, one of them being a state, and the other a citizen of that state. The second section of the third article of the constitution defines the extent of the judicial power of the United States. Jurisdiction is given to the courts of the Union, in two classes of cases. In the first, their jurisdiction depends on the character of the cause, whoever may be the parties. This class comprehends "all cases in law and equity arising under this constitution, the laws of the United States, and treaties made, or which shall be made, under their authority." This clause extends the jurisdiction of the court to all the cases described, without making in its terms any exception whatever, and without any regard to the condition of the party. If there be any exception, it is to be implied, against the express words of the article. In the second class, the jurisdiction depends entirely on the character of the parties. In this are comprehended "controversies between two or more states, between a state and citizens of another state," and "between a state and foreign states, citizens or subjects." If these be the parties, it is

entirely unimportant, what may be the subject of controversy. Be it what it may, these parties have a constitutional right to come into the courts of the Union.

The counsel for the defendant in error have stated, that the cases which arise under the constitution must grow out of those provisions which are capable of self-execution; examples of which are to be found in the 2d section of the 4th article, and in the 10th section of the 1st article. A case which arises under a law of the United States must, we are likewise told, be a right given by some act which becomes necessary to execute the powers given in the constitution, of which the law of naturalization is mentioned as an example.

The use intended to be made of this exposition of the first part of the section, defining the extent of the judicial power, is not clearly understood. If the intention be merely to distinguish cases arising under the constitution, from those arising under a law, for the sake of precision in the application of this argument, these propositions will not be controverted. If it be, to maintain that a case arising under the constitution, or a law, must be one in which a party comes into court to demand something conferred on him by the constitution or a law, we think, the construction too narrow. A case in law or equity consists of the right of the one party, as well as of the other, and may truly be said to arise under the constitution or a law of the United States, whenever its correct decision depends on the construction of either. Congress seems to have intended to give its own construction of this part of the constitution in the 25th section of the judiciary act; and we perceive no reason to depart from that construction.

Eleventh Amendment

The jurisdiction of the court, then, being extended by the letter of the constitution to all cases arising under it, or under the laws of the United States, it follows, that those who would withdraw any case of this description from that jurisdiction, must sustain the exemption they claim, on the spirit and true meaning of the constitution, which spirit and true meaning must be so apparent as to overrule the words which its framers have employed. The counsel for the defendant in error have undertaken to do this; and have laid down the general proposition, that a sovereign independent state is not suable, except by its own consent.

This general proposition will not be controverted. But its consent is not requisite in each particular case. It may be given in a general law. And if a state has surrendered any portion of its sovereignty, the question, whether a liability to suit be a part of this portion, depends on the instrument by which the surrender is made. If, upon a just construction of that instrument, it shall appear, that the state has submitted to be sued, then it has parted with this sovereign right of judging, in every case, on the justice of its own pretensions, and has intrusted that power to a tribunal in whose impartiality it confides.

The American states, as well as the American people, have believed a close and firm union to be essential to their liberty and to their happiness. They have been taught by experience, that this union cannot exist, without a government for the whole; and they have been taught by the same experience, that this government would be a mere shadow, that must disappoint all their hopes, unless invested with large portions of that sovereignty which belongs to independent states. Under the influence of this opinion, and thus instructed by experience, the American people, in the conventions of their respective states, adopted the present constitution.

If it could be doubted, whether, from its nature, it were not supreme, in all cases where it is empowered to act, that doubt would be removed by the declaration, that "this constitution, and the laws of the United States which shall be made in pursuance thereof, and all treaties made, or which shall be made, under the authority of the United States, shall be the supreme law of the land; and the judges in every state shall be bound thereby; anything in the constitution or laws of any state to the contrary notwithstanding." This is the authoritative language of the American people; and, if gentlemen please, of the American states. It marks, with lines too strong to be mistaken, the characteristic distinction between the government of the Union, and those of the states. The general government, though limited as to its objects, is supreme with respect to those objects. This principle is a part of the constitution; and if there be any who deny its necessity, none can deny its authority. . . .

Appellate Jurisdiction

It has been also contended, that this jurisdiction, if given, is original, and cannot be exercised in the appellate form. The words of the constitution are, "in all cases affecting ambassadors, other public ministers and consuls, and those in which a state shall be a party, the supreme court shall have original jurisdiction. In all the other cases before mentioned, the supreme court shall have appellate jurisdiction." This distinction between original and appellate jurisdiction, excludes, we are told, in all cases, the exercise of the one where the other is given.

The constitution gives the supreme court original jurisdiction, in certain enumerated cases, and gives it appellate jurisdiction in all others. Among those in which jurisdiction must be exercised, in the appellate form, are cases arising under the constitution and laws of the United States. These provisions of the constitution are equally obligatory, and are to be equally respected. If a state be a party, the jurisdiction of this court is original; if the case arise under a constitution or a law, the jurisdiction is appellate. But a case to which a state is a party may arise under the constitution or a law of the United States. What rule is applicable to such a case? What then, becomes the duty of the court? Certainly, we think, so to construe the constitution, as to give effect to both provisions, so far as it is possible to reconcile them, and not to permit their seeming repugnancy to destroy each other. We must endeavor so to construe them, as to preserve the true intent and meaning of the instrument.

In one description of cases, the jurisdiction of the court is founded entirely on the character of the parties; and the nature of the controversy is not contemplated by the constitution—the character of the parties is everything, the nature of the case nothing. In the other description of cases, the jurisdiction is founded entirely on the character of the case, and the parties are not contemplated by the constitution—in these, the nature of the case is everything, the character of the parties nothing. When, then, the constitution declares the jurisdiction, in cases where a state shall be a party, to be original, and in all cases arising under the constitution or a law, to be appellate, the conclusion seems irresistible, that its framers designed to include in the first class, those cases in which jurisdiction is given, because a state is a party; and to include in the second, those in which jurisdiction is given, because the case arises under the constitution or a law.

This reasonable construction is rendered necessary by other considerations. That the constitution or a law of the United States is involved in a case, and makes a part of it, may appear in the progress of a cause, in which the courts of the Union, but for that circumstance, would have no jurisdiction, and which, of consequence, could not originate in the supreme court; in such a case, the jurisdiction can be exercised only in its appellate form. To deny its exercise in this form, is to deny its existence, and would be to construe a clause, dividing the power of the supreme court, in such a manner, as in a considerable degree to defeat the power itself. All must perceive, that this construction can be justified only where it is absolutely necessary. We do not think the article under consideration presents that necessity.

It is observable, that in this distributive clause, no negative words are introduced. This observation is not made, for the purpose of contending, that the legislature may "apportion the judicial power between the supreme and inferior courts, according to its will." That would be, as was said by this court in the case of *Marbury* v. *Madison,* to render the distributive clause "mere surplusage," to make it "form without substance." This cannot, therefore, be the true construction of the article. But although the absence of negative words will not authorize the legislature to disregard the distribution of the power previously granted, their absence will justify a sound construction of the whole article, so as to give every part its intended effect. It is admitted, that "affirmative words are often, in their operation, negative of other objects than those affirmed;" and that where "a negative or exclusive sense must be given to them, or they have no operation at all," they must receive that negative or exclusive sense. But where they have full operation without it; where it would destroy some of the most important objects for which the power was created; then, we think, affirmative words ought not to be construed negatively.

Case Determines Jurisdiction

The constitution declares, that in cases where a state is a party, the supreme court shall have original jurisdiction; but does not say, that its appellate jurisdiction shall not be exercised in cases where, from their nature, appellate jurisdiction is given, whether a state be or be not a party. It may be conceded, that where the case is of such a nature, as to admit of its originating in the supreme court, it ought to originate there; but where, from its nature, it cannot originate in that court, these words ought not to be so construed as to require it. There are many cases in which it would be found extremely difficult, and subversive of the spirit of the constitution, to maintain the construction, that appellate jurisdiction cannot be exercised, where one of the parties might sue or be sued in this court.

The constitution defines the jurisdiction of the supreme court, but does not define that of the inferior courts. Can it be affirmed, that a state might not sue the citizen of another state in a circuit court? Should the circuit court decide for or against its jurisdiction, should it dismiss the suit, or give judgment against the state, might not its decision be revised in the supreme court? The argument is, that it could not; and the very clause which is urged to prove, that the circuit court could give no judgment in the case, is also urged to prove, that its judgment is irreversible. A supervising court, whose peculiar province it is to correct the errors of an inferior court, has no power to correct a judgment given without jurisdiction, because, in the same case, that supervising court has original jurisdiction. Had negative words been employed, it would be difficult to give them this construction, if they would admit of any other. But without negative words, this irrational construction can never be maintained.

So, too, in the same clause, the jurisdiction of the court is declared to be original, "in cases affecting ambassadors, other public ministers and consuls." There is, perhaps, no part of the article under consideration so much required by national policy as this; unless it be that part which extends the judicial power "to all cases arising under the constitution, laws and treaties of the United States." It has been generally held, that the state courts have a concurrent jurisdiction with the federal courts, in cases to which the judicial power is extended, unless the jurisdiction of the federal courts be rendered exclusive by the words of the third article. If the words, "to all cases," give exclusive jurisdiction in cases affecting foreign ministers, they may also give exclusive jurisdiction, if such be the will of congress, in cases arising under the constitution, laws and treaties of the United States. Now, suppose an individual were to sue a foreign minister in a state court, and that court were to maintain its jurisdiction, and render judgment against the minister, could it be contended, that this court would be incapable of revising such judgment, because the constitution had given it original jurisdiction in the case? If this could be maintained, then a clause inserted for the purpose of excluding the jurisdiction of all other courts than this, in a particular case, would have the effect of excluding the jurisdiction of this court, in that very case, if the suit were to be brought in another court, and that court were to assert jurisdiction. This tribunal, according to the argument which has been urged, could neither revise the judgment of such other court, nor suspend its proceedings: for a writ of prohibition, or any other similar writ, is in the nature of appellate process. . . .

Reviewable State Judgments

2. The second objection to the jurisdiction of the court is, that its appellate power cannot be exercised, in any case, over the judgment of a state court. This objection is sustained chiefly by arguments drawn from the sup-

posed total separation of the judiciary of a state from that of the Union, and their entire independence of each other. The argument considers the federal judiciary as completely foreign to that of a state; and as being no more connected with it, in any respect whatever, than the court of a foreign state. If this hypothesis be just, the argument founded on it, is equally so; but if the hypothesis be not supported by the constitution, the argument fails with it. This hypothesis is not founded on any words in the constitution, which might seem to countenance it, but on the unreasonableness of giving a contrary construction to words which seem to require it; and on the incompatibility of the application of the appellate jurisdiction to the judgments of state courts, with that constitutional relation which subsists between the government of the Union and the governments of those states which compose it.

Let this unreasonableness, this total incompatibility, be examined. That the United States form, for many, and for most important purposes, a single nation, has not yet been denied. In war, we are one people. In making peace, we are one people. In all commercial regulations, we are one and the same people. In many other respects, the American people are one; and the government which is alone capable of controlling and managing their interests in all these respects, is the government of the Union. It is their government, and in that character, they have no other. America has chosen to be, in many respects, and to many purposes, a nation; and for all these purposes, her government is complete; to all these objects, it is competent. The people have declared, that in the exercise of all powers given for these objects, it is supreme. It can, then, in effecting these objects, legitimately control all individuals or governments within the American territory. The constitution and laws of a state, so far as they are repugnant to the constitution and laws of the United States, are absolutely void. These states are constituent parts of the United States; they are members of one great empire—for some purposes sovereign, for some purposes subordinate.

In a government so constituted, is it unreasonable, that the judicial power should be competent to give efficacy to the constitutional laws of the legislature? That department can decide on the validity of the constitution or law of a state, if it be repugnant to the constitution or to a law of the United States. Is it unreasonable, that it should also be empowered to decide on the judgment of a state tribunal enforcing such unconstitutional law? Is it so very unreasonable, as to furnish a justification for controlling the words of the constitution? We think it is not. We think, that in a government, acknowledgedly supreme, with respect to objects of vital interest to the nation, there is nothing inconsistent with sound reason, nothing incompatible with the nature of government, in making all its departments supreme, so far as respects those objects, and so far as is necessary to their attainment. The exercise of the appellate power over those judgments of the state tribunals which may contravene the constitution or laws of the United States, is, we believe, essential to the attainment of those objects.

The propriety of intrusting the construction of the constitution, and laws made in pursuance thereof, to the judiciary of the Union, has not, we believe, as yet, been drawn into question. It seems to be a corollary from this political axiom, that the federal courts should either possess exclusive jurisdiction in such cases, or a power to revise the judgment rendered in them, by the state tribunals. If the federal and state courts have concurrent jurisdiction in all cases arising under the constitution, laws and treaties of the United States; and if a case of this description brought in a state court cannot be removed before judgment, nor revised after judgment, then the construction of the constitution, laws and treaties of the United States, is not confided particularly to their judicial department, but is confided equally to that department and to the state courts, however they may be constituted. "Thirteen independent courts," says a very celebrated statesman (and we have now more than twenty such courts) "of final jurisdiction over the same causes, arising upon the same laws, is a hydra in government, from which nothing but contradiction and confusion can proceed." Dismissing the unpleasant suggestion, that any motives which may not be fairly avowed, or which ought not to exist, can ever influence a state or its courts, the necessity of uniformity, as well as correctness in expounding the constitution and laws of the United States, would itself suggest the propriety of vesting in some single tribunal, the power of deciding, in the last resort, all cases in which they are involved. . . .

V

Gibbons *v.* Ogden

1. *An Act for Enrolling and Licensing Ships . . . in the Coasting Trade and Fisheries*

1 Stat. 305, Ch. VIII; February 18, 1793

SECTION 1. *Be it enacted by the Senate and House of Representatives of the United States of America in Congress assembled,* That ships or vessels, enrolled by virtue of "An act for registering and clearing vessels, regulating the coasting trade, and for other purposes," and those of twenty tons and upwards, which shall be enrolled after the last day of May next, in pursuance of this act, and having a license in force, or if less than twenty tons, not being enrolled shall have a license in force, as is herein after required, and no others, shall be deemed ships or vessels of the United States, entitled to the privileges of ships or vessels employed in the coasting trade or fisheries. . . .

SEC. 20. *And be it further enacted,* That when any ship or vessel of the United States, registered according to law, shall be employed in going from any one district in the United States, to any other district, such ship or vessel, and the master or commander thereof, with the goods she may have on board, previous to her departure from the district, where she may be, and also, upon her arrival in any other district, shall be subject (except as to the payment of fees) to the same regulations, provisions, penalties and forfeitures, and the like duties as are imposed on like officers, as is provided by the sixteenth and seventeenth sections of this act, for ships or vessels licensed for carrying on the coasting trade: *Provided however,* that nothing herein contained, shall be construed to extend to registered ships or vessels of the United States, having on board goods, wares and merchandise of foreign growth or manufacture, brought into the United States in such ship or vessel from a foreign port, and on which the duties have not been paid or secured, according to law. . . .

SEC. 22. *And be it further enacted,* That the master or commander of every ship or vessel, employed in the transportation of goods from district to district, that shall put into a port, other than the one to which she was bound, shall, within twenty-four hours of his arrival, if there be an officer residing at such port, and she continue there so long, make report of his arrival, to such officer, with the name of the place he came from, and to which he is bound, with an account of his lading; and if the master of such ship or vessel shall neglect or refuse to do the same, he shall forfeit twenty dollars. . . .

SEC. 31. *And be it further enacted,* That if any person or persons shall assault, resist, obstruct, or hinder any officer in the execution of this act, or of any other act or law of the United States, herein mentioned, or of any of the powers or authorities vested in him by this act, or any other act or law, as aforesaid, all and every person and persons so offending, shall, for every such offence, for which no other penalty is particularly provided, forfeit five hundred dollars. . . .

SEC. 33. *Provided nevertheless, and be it further enacted,* That in all cases where the whole or any part of the lading, or cargo, on board any ship or vessel, shall belong bona fide to any person or persons other than the master, owner, or mariners of such ship or vessel, and upon which the duties shall have been previously paid or secured, according to law, shall be exempted from any forfeiture under this act, any thing therein contained to the contrary notwithstanding.

2. New York Monopoly Statute
Act of April 9, 1811

I. *Be it enacted by the People of the State of New-York, represented in Senate and Assembly,* **That the several forfeitures mentioned in the act, entitled "an act for the further encouragement of steam-boats on the waters of this state, and for other purposes," passed the eleventh day of April, one thousand eight hundred and eight, shall be deemed to accrue on the day on which any boat or boats moved by steam or fire, not navigating under the licence of Robert R. Livingston and Robert Fulton, their associates or assigns, shall navigate any of the waters of this state, or those within its jurisdiction, in contravention of the said act; and that Robert R. Livingston and Robert Fulton, their associates and assigns, shall and may be entitled to the same remedy, both in law and equity, for the recovery of the said boat and engine or boats and engines, tackle and apparel, as if the same had been tortiously and wrongfully taken out of their possession.**

II. *And be it further enacted,* That when any writ, suit or action is brought for the recovery of such forfeitures, the defendant or defendants to such writ, suit or action, the captain, mariners and others employed in so navigating in contravention of the said law, shall be prohibited by writ of injunction from navigating with or employing the said boat or boats, engine or engines, or from removing the same or any part thereof out of the jurisdiction of the court, or to any other place than that which shall be directed for their safe keeping by the court during the pendancy of such suit or suits, action or actions, or after judgment shall be obtained, if such judgment shall be against the defendants, or the matter or thing forfeited.

3. *Livingston* v. *Van Ingen* (*New York*)

1 Johns. Rep. 557; opinion rendered March 8, 1812

Yates's Opinion

YATES, J. This is an appeal from an order of the Court of Chancery, refusing to grant an injunction.

The appellants claim an exclusive right to navigate the waters of this state, by steam, for a limited time, grounded upon several statutes of this state, by which this right is granted, and intended to be protected and secured to them.

The respondents contend that the laws are void, as repugnant to the constitution and laws of the *United States,* and, therefore, give no right to the appellants upon which the relief, or injunction sought by their bill, could be founded. Two questions, consequently, arise.

1. As to the constitutionality of the laws:

2. Admitting their validity, whether the appellants are entitled to enjoin the respondents, according to the prayer of their bill, or to any other remedy than that prescribed by the legislature.

The importance of this decision must be evident to every one that hears me; no question has, perhaps, ever presented itself to this court of greater magnitude, involving principles so highly interesting to the community. In making up my opinion, therefore, I have endeavored to bestow the strictest attention, in order to bring my mind to a satisfactory and correct conclusion on the subject.

Legislative History

The first law, passed in *March,* 1798, recited, that whereas it had been suggested to the people of this state, represented in senate and assembly, that *Robert R. Livingston was the possessor of a mode of applying the steam engine, to propel a boat on new and advantageous principles,* but that he was deterred from carrying the same into effect, by the existence of a law granting and securing to *John Fitch* the sole right of making and employing the steam-boat by him invented; that Fitch was either dead, or had withdrawn himself from the state, without having made any attempt, in the space of more than ten years, to execute the plan for which he obtained the exclusive privilege, whereby the same was justly forfeited. By this act privileges similar to those before granted to *Fitch* were granted to Mr. *Livingston,* for twenty years, on his satisfying the governor, lieutenant-governor and the surveyor-general of this state, of his having built a boat, of at least twenty tons' capacity, which should be propelled by steam, and the mean of whose progress through the water, with and against the ordinary current of *Hudson* river, taken together, should not be less than four miles an hour; and that he should, at no time, omit, for the space of one year, to have a boat of such construction plying between the cities of *New-York* and *Albany.*

The same privilege was granted, in *April,* 1803, to Messrs. *Livingston* and

Fulton, the present appellants. In 1807, the act was extended for two years, within which time it was not contended but that the provisions in the first act were complied with, the boat being built, and the experiment proving successful. In *April,* 1808, an act passed for the further encouragement of steam-boats in the waters of this state, and for other purposes. This law enacted, that whenever *Robert R. Livingston* and *Robert Fulton,* and such persons as they might associate with them, should establish one or more steam-boats, or vessels other than that already established, they should, for each and every such additional boat, be entitled to five years prolongation of their grant or contract with this state; provided, nevertheless, that the whole term of their exclusive privileges should not exceed thirty years after the passing of that act; that no person or persons, without the license of the persons entitled to the exclusive right to navigate the waters of this state by boats moved by steam or fire, or those holding the major part of the interest of such privilege, should set in motion, or navigate upon the waters of this state, or within the jurisdiction thereof, any boat or vessel moved by steam or fire; and the person or persons, so navigating with boats or vessels moved by steam or fire, in contravention of the exclusive right of the appellants, and their associates and legal representatives, should forfeit *such boat or boats and vessels, together with the engines, tackle and apparel thereof, to the appellants and their associates.*

Authority to Issue Grant

After the most minute examination of those statutes, I cannot find that Mr. *Livingston,* originally, nor Mr. *Fulton,* subsequently, pretended to be the inventors of their steam-boats; on the contrary, by the recital in the law of 1798, *Livingston* represents himself to be the possessor of a mode of applying the steam engine to propel a boat on new and advantageous principles.

This power of granting exclusive privileges, must necessarily exist somewhere, as the legitimate source from whence the encouragement and extension of useful improvements is derived; and from its nature, it is generally exercised by the sovereign authority of every civilized country; and in no government can it be placed in safer hands to ensure those important advantages than in our own, where the sovereignty is in the representatives of the people. Before the adoption of the constitution of the *United States,* every state in the union, unquestionably, possessed the uncontrolled exercise of this power within its own territory, and most of them exercised it, as will appear on an examination of the laws passed by the legislatures of some of the states, several of which have been stated to this court. This, however, is so plain and evident a proposition, that a recurrence to those laws cannot be necessary to establish it.

Constitutionality of Grant

The laws granting and securing this exclusive right, it is contended, are unconstitutional:

1. Because they interfere with the powers of congress to regulate patents.
2. Because they interfere with the regulation of commerce.

I do not think it necessary, on this occasion, to enter generally into the discussion of the powers granted to congress, and which are to be considered as exclusive, or which ought to be deemed concurrent. It cannot now be questioned, particularly since the amendments to the constitution of the *United States* were adopted, that according to the tenth article of those amendments, "the powers not delegated to the *United States* by the constitution, nor prohibited by it to the states, are reserved to the states respectively, or to the people." By the eighth section of the constitution, among the powers granted to congress, it is stated, that they shall have power "to promote the progress of science and useful arts, by securing, for limited times, to authors and inventors, the exclusive right to their respective writings and discoveries."

Thus it appears, in the exercise of this power, they are limited to authors and inventors only; this clause, therefore, never can admit of so extensive a construction, as to prohibit the respective states from exercising the power of securing to persons introducing useful inventions (without being the authors or inventors) the exclusive benefit of such inventions, for a limited time; a power no less instrumental in promoting the progress of science and the useful arts, and, consequently, equally essential to the prosperity of the country. The beneficial effects experienced by other countries, particularly *England,* sufficiently show the policy and propriety of passing laws for the encouragement of imported inventions. This power, then, evidently necessary and useful, is not granted to congress by the clause as to authors and inventors, and as it is not taken away by any other part of the constitution, it must, of course, be retained by the respective states, to be exercised by them, until it interferes with the laws of the *United States,* passed to secure the author or inventor. It is not probable that such collision will take place. Whenever it does occur, it remains exclusively with the courts of the *United States* to interpose; and no doubt can be entertained, but that the person claiming a right by patent, as inventor, would prevail, and the state law would give way to the superior power of congress.

Monopoly and Commerce

The laws granting this exclusive privilege to the appellants cannot interfere with the regulation of commerce. It never could have been intended that the navigable waters within the territory of the respective states, should not be subject to their municipal regulations. Such a construction might, with equal propriety, be applied to turnpike roads, ferries, bridges and various other local objects, and thus, in the vortex of this construction, almost all subjects of legislation would be swallowed up, and it might, eventually, lead to the total prostration of internal improvements.

To all municipal regulations, therefore, in relation to the navigable waters of the state, according to the true construction of the constitution, to which the citizens of this state are subject, the citizens of other states, when within the state territory, are equally subjected; and until a discrimination is made, no constitutional barrier does exist. The constitution of the *United States* intends that the same immunities and privileges shall be extended to all the citizens equally, for the wise purpose of preventing local jealousies, which discriminations (always deemed odious) might otherwise produce. As this constitution, then, according to my view, does not prevent the operation of those laws granting this exclusive privilege to the appellants, they are entitled to the full benefit of them.

By the law of 1808, the boats, together with the engine, tackle and apparel thereof, are forfeited to the appellants; and a question is raised here, whether they are entitled to any other remedy than that prescribed by the legislature.

This right being claimed under an express grant by the statute, creating the forfeiture, and no doubt remaining of the existence of the boats, the presumption was irresistible that they navigated contrary to the statute, and that the property was in the appellants. The injunction, therefore, on those grounds, might well have been ordered. I cannot discover what injury could arise, by preventing such acts as might create the forfeiture afterwards; it could only operate as a prohibition to navigating contrary to the statute. . . .

Injunction to Issue

From these and numerous other cases, no doubt can exist that the injunction, in this instance, ought to have issued. My opinion, therefore, is, that the order of his honor the chancellor ought to be reversed, and that the cause should be sent back with directions to enjoin the respondents.

VAN NESS, J. was of the same opinion, and gave his reasons.

SPENCER, J. being related to some of the parties concerned, declined giving any opinion.

Thompson's Opinion

THOMPSON, J. In examining the questions which have been presented in this case, I shall pursue the order adopted on the argument; by first inquiring into the right claimed by the appellants; and secondly, whether, if the right be established in them, they are entitled to an injunction to restrain the respondents from an infringement of that right.

In considering the first branch of this subject, I deem it unnecessary to go into a particular inquiry as to the constitutional power and authority of the legislature to grant exclusive privileges upon the *navigable waters* within this state. All objections heretofore raised against the laws in question on this ground, have been, in a great measure, abandoned by the respondents' counsel. I would observe, however, generally, that viewing this state as an independent sovereignty, not having surrendered any of its constitutional powers to the government of the *United States,* I am at a loss to discover any reasons why this power should be denied to the legislature. There is certainly no express prohibition in our constitution, nor do I see any reasons, growing out of the nature and principles of our government, for denying to it this act of sovereignty. It appears to me a necessary and indispensable power, which, under a wise and discreet exercise of it, will be productive of very beneficial effects. The power of granting exclusive privileges upon land, has not been, in the least degree, questioned; and the same reasons, both of principle and policy, will allow to the government the exercise of analogous powers upon the waters within the jurisdiction of the state. No distinction appears to have been recognised in the practice of our government. Grants of land under the water, the exclusive right of ferriage, and the regulation of the fisheries in the *Hudson* river, as well as canals, turnpike roads, and exclusive privileges of running stage-wagons, have all been occasionally subjects of legislative bounty and provision.

All the arguments which have been urged against the policy or expediency of granting exclusive privileges in general, or the particular privilege which forms the present subject of inquiry, have been addressed to the wrong forum. They are arguments for legislative, not for judicial consideration. We are called upon to pronounce what the law is, not what it ought to be. In a legislative capacity, considerations of policy and expediency are entitled to their due weight, to convince the judgment or guide the discretion. But in a judicial capacity, no such latitudinary power is given; we are under the solemnity of an oath to decide the rights and claims of parties, according to existing law. Unless, therefore, we are prepared to pronounce the appellants' claim, as set up, to be absolutely void, their right must be considered fixed and established.

Constitutional Question

I shall not stop to examine whether it be competent for the courts of justice in this state, to disregard acts of the legislature, and declare them unconstitutional and void. The counsel for the appellants have not put their cause upon that ground. But admitting such a power in the judiciary, it ought to be exercised with great caution and circumspection, and in extreme cases only. It certainly affords a strong and powerful argument in favor of the constitutionality of a law, that it has passed not only that branch of the legislature which constitutes the greater portion of our court of *dernier resort,* but also the Council of Revision, which is composed of the governor and the two highest judicial tribunals of the state, (next to this court,) and whose peculiar province it is to examine and make all constitutional objections to bills, before they become laws. If this affords grounds of argument in favor of a single law, which might have passed hastily and without due consideration, how strong and cogent is it in favor of a series of laws, on the same subject, from time to time, enlarging and strengthening the same right or claim; and more especially, as one of those laws has been passed since the present controversy has arisen, and after the attention of the several branches of the legislature must have been called to the objections now raised against them. With such a weight of *prima facie* evidence in favor of the constitutionality of these laws, I should not have boldness enough to pronounce them void, without the most clear, satisfactory and unanswerable reasons. I shall proceed, however, to examine the force of the objections which have been raised against the constitutionality of the laws, giving to the appellants the exclusive right to navigate the waters of the state by steam, uninfluenced by any presumption in favor of their validity.

These objections grow out of that part of the constitution of the *United States* which gives to Congress, 1st. The power to promote the progress of science and useful arts, by securing, for limited times, to authors and *inventors,* the exclusive right to their respective writings and discoveries; and, 2dly. The power to regulate commerce with foreign nations, and among the several states, and with the *Indian* tribes. (Art. 1. s. 8.) It is an undeniable rule of construction, applicable to the constitution of the *United States,* that all powers and rights of sovereignty, possessed and enjoyed by the several states, as independent governments, before the adoption of the constitution, and which are not either expressly, or by necessary implication, delegated to the general government, are retained by the states. This has been the uniform understanding of the ablest jurists, ever since the formation of that government; and it is a rule indispensably necessary, in order to preserve harmony in the administration of the different governments, and prevent that collision which a partial consolidation is peculiarly calculated to produce.

This was the object contemplated and intended to be secured by the tenth article of the amendments of the constitution, which declares, that the powers not delegated to the *United States* by the constitution, nor prohibited by it, to the states, are reserved to the states respectively, or to the people. If, then, the grant of the right or privilege claimed by the appellants, would, before the adoption of the constitution, have been a legitimate exercise of state sovereignty, it would, I think, under the rule of construction which I have suggested, be a strained interpretation of that instrument, to say such sovereignty has been thereby surrendered by the state. This power is certainly not denied to the states, nor exclusively granted to the union, by *express terms:* and those powers which are exclusive, by necessary implication, must be such as are created by the constitution, and which did not antecedently form a part of state sovereignty, or the objects of which, from their nature, are beyond the reach and control of the state governments.

An express prohibition to the states, against the exercise of powers of that description, would have been useless and absurd. I might go through the various powers given to congress, and illustrate the truth of the position I have laid down, but shall refer only to one or two. Congress have power to *borrow money on the credit of the United States.* This is an exclusive power by necessary implication. It is a power created by the constitution. No prohibition to the states was necessary, and indeed would have been absurd; because this never was, before the adoption of the constitution, within the scope of state power: no state being able to pledge the credit of the *United States* for the repayment of the money borrowed. The power to constitute tribunals, inferior to the Supreme Court, falls under the same class.

State Jurisdiction

But it is obvious that the mere grant of a power to congress does not necessarily vest it exclusively in that body. Congress has power to lay and collect taxes. But this does not preclude the states from the exercise of a like power, except so far as they are expressly restrained, in relation to duties on imports and exports. Thus we see that there are subjects upon which the *United States* and the individual states must, of necessity, have *concurrent* jurisdiction; and all the fears and apprehensions of collision in the exercise of these powers, which have been urged in argument, are unfounded. The constitution has guarded against such an event, by providing that the laws of the *United States* shall be the supreme law of the land, any thing in the constitution of any state to the contrary notwithstanding. In case of collision, therefore, the state laws must yield to the superior authority of the *United States.*

The power given to congress to promote the progress of science and useful arts is restricted to the rights of *authors* and *inventors,* and their rights are only to be secured for a limited time. Whatever power the states had over these subjects prior to the adoption of the constitution, and which have not been granted to the general government, and which are not within the scope and purview of its authority, must, beyond all possible doubt, be retained by the states. The appellants do not, in the case before us, claim as *inventors,* but only as *possessors* of a mode of applying the steam-engine to propel boats on new and advantageous principles. The right, therefore, claimed by them, as granted by the laws of this state, was beyond the reach of congressional authority; and the idea ought not for a moment to be indulged that, even admitting this to be a foreign and imported improvement, it is not worthy of legislative patronage and protection.

The power given to congress on this subject was intended for the benefit of authors and inventors, and to secure their rights throughout the *United States.* The state government could only give this security within its own jurisdiction. It was, therefore, a wise and useful provision in the constitution, calculated to encourage the arts and sciences, which ought to be a favorite object with every enlightened government. But because the states have delegated to congress this power, in a limited degree, shall it be denied to them to lend their aid in protecting and patronising useful improvements in any way they may think proper, not repugnant to the right secured under the authority of congress? Such a doctrine appears to me degrading to state sovereignty, and unnecessarily relinquishing a power not contemplated by the constitution. For the purpose of the present suit, the appellants are to be considered as the *possessors* only of the invention, and in that point of view I cannot discover the remotest doubt as to the constitutionality of the laws, the subject matter of them not being within the purview of any power given to congress.

But if the appellants are considered the *inventors,* and entitled to a patent, or as having actually obtained one, it cannot operate as an exclusion of all legislative authority and interference, to aid and protect the rights thus obtained under the general government. If the subject matter be within the scope of state jurisdiction, and the power is exercised in harmony with, and in subordination to, the superior power of congress, it is, beyond all doubt, legitimately exercised. If any person should appear claiming under a patent, in hostility to the privilege granted by this state, that would be a paramount right, and must prevail, if set up in a court having jurisdiction of the question; though it may well be doubted, whether even a patent could be set up, in the courts of this state, against these laws, as that might involve questions arising under the laws of the *United States,* which belong exclusively to the courts of the *United States.* . . .

Scope of State Power

It was admitted by the respondents' counsel, that, had not congress begun to exercise the power given by this clause in the constitution, the subject matter would have been within the scope of state jurisdiction. Why this should make any difference, I am unable to conceive, as long as the power exercised by the state is not repugnant to, or incompatible with, that exercised by congress. That the mere grant of a power to congress does not necessarily imply an exclusion of state jurisdiction, has been the practical construction of the constitution in a variety of cases. As, for instance, congress have the power to provide for the punishment of counterfeiting the current coin of the *United States;* yet the legislature of this state has provided for the punishment of the same offence; and numerous other instances might be mentioned, if necessary. The only restriction upon the state government, in the exercise of all concurrent powers is, that the state must act in subordination to the general government.

It is not a sufficient reason for denying to the states the exercise of a power, that it *may* possibly interfere with the acts of the general government. It will be time enough to surrender the power when such interference shall arise. The framers of the constitution foresaw the possibility of such a state of things, and wisely provided the remedy, by making the laws of the *United States* the supreme law of the land. Thus guarded, there can be no possible inconvenience result from the two governments exercising legislative authority over the same subject. But for the purpose of deciding the present question, it is unnecessary to go thus far, because the laws in question extend protection to the appellants as *possessors* only of the improvement, and this not being a subject within the authority of congress, there cannot arise any interference or collision of power.

The objection to the laws under consideration, on the ground that they interfere with the power given to congress, "to regulate commerce with foreign nations, and among the several states, and with the *Indian* tribes," is less colorable than the former; for admitting the power here granted to belong exclusively to the general government, it does not, in any manner whatever, interfere with these laws, or extend to the rights and privileges which they are intended to secure. They neither concern foreign commerce, nor commerce among the several states, nor with the *Indian* tribes, but only give to the appellants the exclusive privilege of navigating all waters, *within* the jurisdiction of this state, by every species of boat or water-craft, which might be impelled by force of fire or steam.

If this can, in any sense, be considered a regulation of commerce, it is the internal commerce of the state, over which congress has no power; and if the right to regulate internal commerce, or the intercourse between different parts of the state, ever belonged to the state government, it is still retained; for it never has been, either expressly or impliedly, yielded to the general government. To deny to the legislature this right, would be at once striking from our statute-book grants, almost innumerable, of a similar nature; all our turnpike roads, toll-bridges, canals, ferries, and the like, more or less concern commerce, or the intercourse between different parts of the state, and must depend on the same principles with the privileges granted to the appellants.

The truth, however, is, that none of them relate to commerce within the sense and meaning of the term as used in the constitution; they are mere municipal regulations, with which congress have no concern. It can answer no valuable end, to enter into any speculative inquiry as to what would be the effect upon the appellants' rights under these laws, should congress, in regulating commerce, interfere with them. No such interference has as yet arisen, and it will be time enough to consider that question when it does arise. The general and conclusive answer, however, to all such supposed collisions of power, is what has already been mentioned, that the laws of congress are paramount, and must prevail.

I have thus noticed the principal arguments which have been urged against the constitutionality of the laws under which the appellants set up their claim, and I am satisfied that the objections are untenable; and unless these laws are absolutely void, the right of the appellants is clearly established.

Right to Injunction

The only remaining inquiry, is, whether they are entitled to an injunction, to restrain the respondents from an infringement of that right; and this, it appears to me, must follow as a matter of course. It has been contended that an injunction ought not to issue until the appellants' right has been first settled at law. This is, by no means, the universal, or even the common rule of practice on the subject. Where the right is doubtful, and that doubt can only be removed by a trial at law, there is some plausibility in requiring a party to establish his right before an injunction is granted. But this is not always the course, even in doubtful cases. There are many instances in the books, where the courts have said that possession, under color of title, is enough to enjoin and continue the injunction, until it is proved, at law, that it is only color, and not real title. . . .

I think it unnecessary to pursue the question as to the remedy any farther, or to notice all the cases cited on the argument. I have looked into most of them, and am fully satisfied that if the appellants have the right claimed, the remedy cannot be denied to them. I the more readily abstain from taking up any more time in this examination, because I understood the respondents' counsel as, in a great measure, abandoning all opposition to an injunction, if the right was determined against them. Upon the whole, from a very attentive examination of the case, I entertain a clear and decided opinion in favor of the validity of the appellants' right, as granted by the acts of the legislature, and that they are entitled to the remedy asked for to protect and secure them in the enjoyment of it.

I am accordingly of opinion, that the decree of the Court of Chancery ought to be reversed.

Kent's Opinion

KENT, Ch. J. The great point in this cause is, whether the several acts of the legislature which have been passed in favor of the appellants, are to be regarded as constitutional and binding.

This house, sitting in its judicial capacity as a court, has nothing to do with the policy of expediency of these laws. The only question here is, whether the legislature had authority to pass them. If we can satisfy ourselves upon this point, or, rather, unless we are fully persuaded that they are void, we are bound to obey them, and give them the requisite effect.

In the first place, the presumption must be admitted to be extremely strong in favor of their validity. There is no very obvious constitutional objection, or it would not so repeatedly have escaped the notice of the several branches of the government, when these acts were under consideration. There are, in the whole, five different statutes, passed in the years 1798, 1803, 1807, 1808 and 1811, all relating to one subject, and all granting or confirming to the appellants, or one of them, the exclusive privilege of using steam-boats upon the navigable waters of this state. The last act was passed after the right of the appellants was drawn into question, and made known to the legislature, and that act was, therefore, equivalent to a declaratory opinion of high authority, that the former laws were valid and constitutional.

The act in the year 1798 was peculiarly calculated to awaken attention, as it was the first act that was passed upon the subject, after the adoption of the federal constitution, and it would naturally lead to a consideration of the power of the state to make such a grant. That act was, therefore, a legislative exposition given to the powers of the state governments, and there were circumstances existing at the time, which gave that exposition singular weight and importance. It was a new and original grant to one of the appellants, encouraging him, by the pledge of an exclusive privilege for twenty years, to engage, according to the language of the preamble to the statute, in the "uncertainty and hazard of a very expensive experiment."

The legislature must have been clearly satisfied of their competency to make this pledge, or they acted with deception and injustice towards the individual on whose account it was made. There were members in that legislature, as well as in all the other departments of the government, who had been deeply concerned in the study of the constitution of the *United States,* and who were masters of all the critical discussions which had attended the interesting progress of its adoption. Several of them had been members of the state convention, and this was particularly the case with the exalted character, who at that time was chief magistrate of this state, (Mr. *Jay,*) and who was distinguished, as well in the *council of revision,* as elsewhere, for the scrupulous care and profound attention with which he examined every question of a constitutional nature.

After such a series of statutes, for the last fourteen years, and passed under such circumstances, it ought not to be any light or trivial difficulty that should induce us to set them aside. Unless the court should be able to vindicate itself by the soundest and most demonstrable argument, a decree prostrating all these laws would weaken, as I should apprehend, the authority and sanction of law in general, and impair, in some degree, the public confidence, either in the intelligence or integrity of the government.

But we are not to rest upon presumption alone; we must bring these laws to the test of a severer scrutiny.

State's Reserved Power

If they are void, it must be because the people of this state have alienated to the government of the *United States* their whole original power over the subject matter of the grant. No one can entertain a doubt of a competent power existing in the legislature, prior to the adoption of the federal constitution. The capacity to grant separate and exclusive privileges appertains to every sovereign authority. It is a necessary attribute of every independent government. All our bank charters, turnpike, canal and bridge companies, ferries, markets, &c. are grants of exclusive privileges for beneficial public purposes. These grants may possibly be inexpedient or unwise, but that has nothing to do with the question of constitutional right.

The legislative power, in a single, independent government, extends to every proper object of power, and is limited only by its own constitutional provisions, or by the fundamental principles of all government, and the unalienable rights of mankind. In the present case, the grant to the appellants took away no vested right. It interfered with no man's property. It left every citizen to enjoy all the rights of navigation, and all the use of the waters of this state which he before enjoyed. There was, then, no injustice, no violation of first principles, in a grant to the appellants, for a limited time, of the exclusive benefit of their own hazardous and expensive experiments. The first impression upon every unprejudiced mind would be, that there was justice and policy in the grant. Clearly, then, it is valid, unless the power to make it be taken away by the constitution of the *United States*.

We are not called upon to say affirmatively what powers have been granted to the general government, or to what extent. Those powers, whether express or implied, may be plenary and sovereign, in reference to the specified objects of them. They may even be liberally construed in furtherance of the great and essential ends of the government. To this doctrine I willingly accede. But the question here is, not what powers are granted to that government, but what powers are retained by this, and, particularly, whether the states have absolutely parted with their original power of granting such an exclusive privilege, as the one now before us. It does not follow, that because a given power is granted to congress, the states cannot exercise a similar power. We ought to bear in mind certain great rules or principles of construction peculiar to the case of a confederated government, and by attending to them in the examination of the subject, all our seeming difficulties will vanish.

Theory of Federalism

When the people create a single, entire government, they grant at once all the rights of sovereignty. The powers granted are indefinite, and incapable of enumeration. Every thing is granted that is not expressly reserved in the constitutional charter, or necessarily retained as inherent in the people. But when a federal government is erected with only a portion of the sovereign power, the rule of construction is directly the reverse, and every power is reserved to the member that is not, either in express terms, or by necessary implication, taken away from them, and vested exclusively in the federal head.

This rule has not only been acknowledged by the most intelligent friends to the constitution, but is plainly declared by the instrument itself. Congress have power to lay and collect taxes, duties and excises, but as these powers are not given exclusively, the states have a concurrent jurisdiction, and retain the same absolute powers of taxation which they possessed before the adoption of the constitution, except the power of laying an impost, which is expressly taken away. This very exception proves that, without it, the states would have retained the power of laying an impost; and it further implies, that in cases not excepted, the authority of the states remains unimpaired.

This principle might be illustrated by other instances of grants of power to congress with a prohibition to the states from exercising the like powers; but it becomes unnecessary to enlarge upon so plain a proposition, as it is removed beyond all doubt by the tenth article of the amendments to the constitution. That article declares that "the powers not delegated to the *United States* by the constitution, nor prohibited by it to the states, are reserved to the states respectively, or to the people." The ratification of the constitution by the convention of this state, was made with the explanation and understanding, that "every power, jurisdiction and right, which was not *clearly* delegated to the general government, remained to the people of the several states, or to their respective state governments."

There was a similar provision in the articles of confederation, and the principle results from the very nature of the federal government, which consists only of a defined portion of the undefined mass of sovereign power originally vested in the several members of the union. There may be inconveniences, but generally there will be no serious difficulty, and there cannot well be any interruption of the public peace, in the concurrent exercise of those powers. The powers of the two governments are each supreme within their respective constitutional spheres. They may each operate with full effect upon different subjects, or they may, as in the case of taxation, operate upon different parts of the same object. The powers of the two governments cannot indeed be supreme over each other, for that would involve a contradiction. When those powers, therefore, come directly in contact, as when they are aimed at each other, or at one indivisible object, the power of the state is subordinate, and must yield. The legitimate exercise of the constitutional powers of the general government becomes the supreme law of the land, and the national judiciary is specially charged with the maintenance of that law, and this is the true and efficient power to preserve order, dependence and harmony in our complicated system of government.

Constitutional Construction

We have, then, nothing to do in the ordinary course of legislation, with the possible contingency of a collision, nor are we to embarrass ourselves in the anticipation of theoretical difficulties, than which nothing could, in general, be more fallacious. Such a doctrine would be constantly taxing our sagacity, to see whether the law might not contravene some future regulation of commerce, or some moneyed or some military operation of the *United States*. Our most simple municipal provisions would be enacted with diffidence, for fear we might involve ourselves, our citizens and our consciences in some case of usurpation. Fortunately, for the peace and happiness of this country, we have a plainer path to follow. We do not handle a work of such hazardous consequence. . . .

Our safe rule of construction and of action is this, that if any given power was originally vested in this state, if it has not been exclusively ceded to congress, or if the exercise of it has not been prohibited to the states, we may then go on in the exercise of the power until it comes practically in collision with the actual exercise of some congressional power. When that happens to be the case, the state authority will so far be controlled, but it will still be good in all those respects in which it does not absolutely contravene the provision of the paramount law.

This construction of the powers of the federal compact has the authority of Mr. *Hamilton.* In the thirty-second number of the *Federalist,* he admits that all the authorities of which the states are not explicitly devested, remain with them in full vigor, and that in all cases in which it was deemed improper that a like authority with that granted to the union should reside in the states, there was the most pointed care in the constitution to insert negative clauses. He further states that there are only three cases of the alienation of the state sovereignty; 1. Where the grant to the general government is, in express terms, exclusive; 2. Where a like power is expressly prohibited to the states; and, 3. Where an authority in the states would be absolutely and totally contradictory and repugnant to one granted to the union; and it must be, he says, an immediate constitutional repugnancy that can, by implication, alienate and extinguish a pre-existing right of sovereignty. The same view of the powers of the federal and state governments, and the same rules of interpretation, were given by him, in the discussions which the constitution underwent in our state convention, and they seem generally, if not unanimously, to have been acquiesced in by the members of that very respectable assembly. . . .

These opinions may be regarded as the best evidence of the sense of the authors of that instrument, the best test of its principles, and the most accurate contemporary exposition to which we can recur. For every one acquainted with the history of those times, well knows that the principles of the constitution, in the progress of its adoption through the *United States,* were discussed in the several conventions, and before the public, by men of the most powerful talents, and with the most animated zeal for the public welfare. There were many distinguished individuals, and none more so than the one to whom I have referred, who had bestowed intense thought, not only upon the science of civil government at large, but who had specially and deeply studied the history and nature, the tendency and genius of the federal system of government, of which the *European* confederacies had given us imperfect examples, and to which system, as improved by more skilful artists, the destinies of this country were to be confided. Principles of construction solemnly sanctioned at that day, and flowing from such sources, [are] to be regarded by us, and by posterity, as coming in the language of truth, and with the force of authority.

Commerce Clause

I now proceed to apply these general rules to those parts of the constitution which are supposed to have an influence on the present question.

The provision that the citizens of each state shall be entitled to all privileges and immunities of citizens in the several states, has nothing to do with this case. It means only that citizens of other states shall have equal rights with our own citizens, and not that they shall have different or greater rights. Their persons and property must, in all respects, be equally subject to our law. This is a very clear proposition, and the provision itself was taken from the articles of the confederation. The two paragraphs of the constitution by which it is contended that the original power in the state governments to make the grant has been withdrawn, and vested exclusively in the union, are, 1. The power to regulate commerce with foreign nations, and among the several states; and, 2. The power to secure to authors and inventors the exclusive right to their writings and discoveries.

1. *As to the power to regulate commerce.*

This power is not, in express terms, exclusive, and the only prohibition upon the states is, that they shall not enter into any treaty or compact with each other, or with a foreign power, nor lay any duty on tonnage, or on imports or exports, except what may be necessary for executing their inspection laws. Upon the principles above laid down, the states are under no other constitutional restriction, and are, consequently, left in possession of a vast field of commercial regulation; all the internal commerce of the state by land and water remains entirely, and I may say exclusively, within the scope of its original sovereignty.

The congressional power relates to external not internal commerce, and it is confined to the *regulation* of that commerce. To what extent these regulations may be carried, it is not our present duty to inquire. The limits of this power seem not to be susceptible of precise definition. It may be difficult to draw an exact line between those regulations which relate to external and those which relate to internal commerce, for every regulation of the one will, directly or indirectly, affect the other. To avoid doubts, embarrassment and contention on this complicated question, the general rule of interpretation which has been mentioned, is extremely salutary. It removes all difficulty, by its simplicity and certainty.

The states are under no other restrictions than those expressly specified in the constitution, and such regulations as the national government may, by treaty, and by laws, from time to time, prescribe. Subject to these restrictions, I contend, that the states are at liberty to make their own commercial regulations. There can be no other safe or practicable rule of conduct, and this, as I have already shown, is the true constitutional rule arising from the nature of our federal system. This does away all color for the suggestion that the steamboat grant is illegal and void under this clause in the constitution. It comes not within any prohibition upon the states, and it interferes with no existing regulation.

Federal Question

Whenever the case shall arise of an exercise of power by congress which shall be directly repugnant and destructive to the use and enjoyment of the appellants' grant, it would fall under the cognizance of the federal courts, and they would, of course, take care that the laws of the union are duly supported. I must confess, however, that I can hardly conceive of such a case, because I do not, at present, perceive any power which congress can lawfully carry to that extent. But when there is no existing regulation which interferes with the grant, nor any pretence of a constitutional interdict, it would be most extraordinary for us to adjudge it void, on the mere contingency of a collision with some future exercise of congressional power. Such a doctrine is a monstrous heresy. It would go, in a great degree, to annihilate the legislative power of the states. May not the legislature declare that no bank paper shall circulate, or be given or received in payment, but what originates from some incorporated bank of our own, or that none shall circulate under the nominal value of one dollar?

But suppose congress should institute a national bank, with authority to issue and circulate throughout the union, bank notes, as well below as above that nominal value: this would so far control the state law, but it would remain valid and binding, except as to the paper of the national bank. The state law would be absolute, until the appearance of the national bank, and then it would have a qualified effect, and be good *pro tanto*. So, again, the legislature may declare that it shall be unlawful to vend lottery tickets, unless they be tickets of lotteries authorized by a law of this state, and who will question the validity of the provision? But suppose congress should deem it expedient to establish a national lottery, and should authorize persons in each state to vend the tickets, this would so far control the state prohibition, and leave it in full force as to all other lotteries.*

The possibility that a national bank, or a national lottery, might be instituted, would be a very strange reason for holding the state laws to be absolutely null and void. It strikes me to be an equally inadmissible proposition, that the state is devested of a capacity to grant an exclusive privilege of navigating a steam-boat, within its own waters, merely because we can imagine that congress, in the plenary exercise of its power to regulate commerce, may make some regulation inconsistent with the exercise of this privilege. When such a case arises, it will provide for itself; and there is, fortunately, a paramount power in the Supreme Court of the *United States* to guard against the mischiefs of collision.

Future Federal Law

The grant to the appellants may, then, be considered as taken subject to such future commercial regulations as congress may lawfully prescribe. Congress, indeed, has not any direct jurisdiction over our interior commerce or waters. *Hudson* river is the property of the people of this state, and the legislature have the same jurisdiction over it that they have over the land, or over

---

* Just as *Livingston* v. *Van Ingen* anticipated the issue eventually litigated in *Gibbons* v. *Ogden* a decade later, Judge (later Justice) Thompson also takes this opportunity to denigrate the constitutionality of the First Bank of the United States, which was to expire in the same year of this opinion (1812) and was to present, in the Second Bank of the United States, the constitutional question in 1819 in *McCulloch* v. *Maryland*. The recurrent constitutional issue of a national lottery came indirectly before the Supreme Court in 1821 in *Cohens* v. *Virginia*.

any of our public highways, or over the waters of any of our rivers or lakes. They may, in their sound discretion, regulate and control, enlarge or abridge the use of its waters, and they are in the habitual exercise of that sovereign right. If the constitution had given to congress exclusive jurisdiction over our navigable waters, then the argument of the respondents would have applied; but the people never did, nor ever intended, to grant such a power; and congress have concurrent jurisdiction over the navigable waters no further than may be incidental and requisite to the due regulation of commerce between the states, and with foreign nations.

What has been the uniform, practical construction of this power? Let us examine the code of our statute laws. Our turnpike roads, our toll-bridges, the exclusive grant to run stage-wagons, our laws relating to paupers from other states, our *Sunday* laws, our rights of ferriage over navigable rivers and lakes, our auction licenses, our licenses to retail spirituous liquors, the laws to restrain hawkers and pedlars; what are all these provisions but regulations of internal commerce, affecting as well the intercourse between the citizens of this and other states, as between our own citizens? So we also exercise, to a considerable degree, a concurrent power with congress in the regulation of external commerce.

What are our inspection laws relative to the staple commodities of this state, which prohibit the exportation, except upon certain conditions, of flour, of salt provisions, of certain articles of lumber, and of pot and pearl ashes, but regulations of external commerce? Our health and quarantine laws, and the laws prohibiting the importation of slaves, are striking examples of the same kind. So the act relative to the poor, which requires all masters of vessels coming from abroad to report and give security to the mayor of *New-York*, that the passengers, being aliens, shall not become chargeable as paupers, and in case of default, making even the ship or vessel from which the alien shall be landed liable to seizure, is another and very important regulation affecting foreign commerce.

Are we prepared to say, in the face of all these regulations, which form such a mass of evidence of the uniform construction of our powers, that a special privilege for the exclusive navigation by a steam-boat upon our waters, is void, because it may, by possibility, and in the course of events, interfere with the power granted to congress to regulate commerce? Nothing, in my opinion, would be more preposterous and extravagant. Which of our existing regulations may not equally interfere with the power of congress?

It is said that a steam-boat may become the vehicle of foreign commerce; and, it is asked, can then the entry of them into this state, or the use of them within it, be prohibited? I answer yes, equally as we may prohibit the entry or use of slaves, or of pernicious animals, or an obscene book, or infectious goods, or any thing else that the legislature shall deem noxious or inconvenient. Our quarantine laws amount to an occlusion of the port of *New-York* from a portion of foreign commerce, for several months in the year; and the mayor is even authorized under those laws to stop all commercial intercourse with the ports of any neighboring state. No doubt these powers may be abused, or exercised in bad faith, or with such jealousy and hostility towards our neighbors, as to call for some explicit and paramount regulation of congress on the subject of foreign commerce, and of commerce between the states. Such cases may easily be supposed, but it is not logical to reason from the abuse against the lawful existence of a power; and until such congressional regulations appear, the legislative will of this state, exercised on a subject within its original jurisdiction, and not expressly prohibited to it by the constitution of the *United States,* must be taken to be of valid and irresistible authority.

Federal Patent Power

2. If the grant is not inconsistent with the power of congress to regulate commerce, there is as little pretence to hold it repugnant to the power to grant patents. That power only secures, for a limited time, to authors and inventors the exclusive privilege to their writings and discoveries; and as it is not granted, by exclusive words, to the *United States,* nor prohibited to the individual states, it is a concurrent power which may be exercised by the states, in a variety of cases, without any infringement of the congressional power. A state cannot take away from an individual his patent right, and render it common to all the citizens. This would contravene the act of congress, and would be, therefore, unlawful. But if an author or inventor, instead of resorting to the act of congress, should apply to the legislature of this state for an exclusive right to his production, I see nothing to hinder the state from granting it, and the operation of the grant would, of course, be confined to the limits of this state. Within our own jurisdiction, it would be complete and perfect. So a patentee under the act of congress may have the time of his monopoly extended by the legislature of any state, beyond the term of fourteen or twenty-eight years allowed by that law.*

Congress may secure, for a limited time, an exclusive right throughout the union; but there is nothing in the constitution to take away from the states the power to enlarge the privilege within their respective jurisdictions. The states are not entirely devested of their original sovereignty over the subject matter; and whatever power has not been clearly granted to the union, remains with them. Again, the power granted to congress goes no further than to secure to the author or inventor a right of property, which, like every other species of property, must be used and enjoyed within each state, according to the laws of such state. The power of congress is only to ascertain and define the right of property; it does not extend to regulating the use of it. That must be exclusively of local cognisance. If the author's book or print contains matter injurious to the public morals or peace, or if the inventor's machine or other production will have a pernicious effect upon the public health or safety, no doubt a competent authority remains with the states to restrain the use of the patent right. That species of property must likewise be subject to taxation, and to the pay-

---

* Thompson's theory of state and federal powers in the field of patent law was not addressed (and qualified) by the Supreme Court until well into the twentieth century; cf. *Free* v. *Bland*, 369 U.S. 663 (1962) and *Sears, Roebuck & Co.* v. *Stiffet Co.*, 376 U.S. 225 (1964).

ment of debts, as other personal property. The national power will be fully satisfied, if the property created by patent be, for the given time, enjoyed and used exclusively, *so far* as under the policy of the several states the property shall be deemed fit for toleration and use. There is no need of giving this power any broader construction in order to attain the end for which it was granted, which was to reward the beneficent efforts of genius, and to encourage the useful arts.

Validity of Patent

If, then, the respondents were in possession of a patent for their steam-boat, as original inventors, our statute prohibition, not being made against the use of steam-boats, as *per se* injurious, would possibly, before a competent tribunal, be obliged to yield to the patent right, as being founded on the paramount law. But even this plea would not answer in this case; for if the respondents were in possession of such a patent, the state courts could not take notice of it. They cannot enforce a patent right, nor can they declare the patent void, if obtained by fraud or imposition. The acts of congress have vested the federal courts with the exclusive cognisance of all infringements of patent rights; and such was the opinion and decision of the Supreme Court of this state in a late case. . . . None of our courts could receive a plea of a patent right, in justification of a breach of the statutes: we should be obliged to send the party to the courts of the *United States,* in order to test the validity of his patent, and to seek the competent redress.

But the respondents show no patent, and the appellants have not obtained their grant, as *inventors* of the steam-boat, and, therefore, the privilege is totally unconnected with the patent power. It seems to be admitted that congress are authorized to grant patents only to the *inventor* of the useful art. The act of congress of 25th *February,* 1793, . . . applies only to the inventor, and the applicant for the patent must make oath that he believes he is the true inventor or discoverer of the art or improvement. The act of 22d *April,* 1800, . . . extends the benefit of the former law to aliens, after two years' residence, on their making oath that such invention, art or discovery, hath not, to their belief, been known or used either in this or any foreign country.

There cannot, then, be any aid or encouragement, by means of an exclusive right under the law of the *United States,* to importers from abroad of any useful invention or improvement. Such persons must resort to the patronage of the state governments, in which the power to reward their expensive and hazardous exertions was originally vested, and in which it still remains. The grant of 1798, was made to Chancellor *Livingston,* as "the *possessor* of a mode of applying the steam engine to propel a boat on new and advantageous principles." This power to encourage the importation of improvements, by the grant of an exclusive enjoyment, for a limited period, is extremely useful, and the *English* nation have long perceived and felt its beneficial effects. This will appear by a cursory view of the law of that country. . . .

. . . And can we for a moment suppose that such a power does not exist in the several states? We have seen that it does not belong to congress, and if it does not reside in the states, it resides nowhere, and is wholly extinguished. This would be leaving the states in a condition of singular and contemptible imbecility. The power is important in itself, and may be most beneficially exercised for the encouragement of the arts; and if well and judiciously exercised, it may ameliorate the condition of society, by enriching and adorning the country with useful and elegant improvements.

This ground is clear of any constitutional difficulty, and renders the argument in favor of the validity of the statutes perfectly conclusive. And permit me here to add, that I think the power has been wisely applied, in the instance before us, to the creation of the privilege now in controversy. Under its auspices the experiment of navigating boats by steam has been made, and crowned with triumphant success. Every lover of the arts, every patron of useful improvement, every friend to his country's honor, has beheld this success with pleasure and admiration. From this single source the improvement is progressively extending to all the navigable waters of the *United States,* and it promises to become a great public blessing, by giving astonishing facility, despatch and safety, not only to travelling, but to the internal commerce of this country. It is difficult to consider even the known results of the undertaking, without feeling a sentiment of good will and gratitude towards the individuals by whom they have been procured, and who have carried on their experiment with patient industry, at great expense, under repeated disappointments, and while constantly exposed to be held up, as dreaming projectors, to the *whips and scorns of time.* So far from charging the authors of the grant with being rash and inconsiderate, or from wishing to curtail the appellants of their liberal recompense, I think the prize has been dearly earned and fairly won, and that the statutes bear the stamp of an enlightened and munificent spirit.

If the legal right be in favor of the appellants, the remedy prayed for by their bill is a matter of course. One of the learned counsel for the respondents, with his usual frankness, seemed, in a great degree, to concede this point. . . .

Effect of Injunction

It would only be productive of litigation and mischief, to allow the respondents to continue the use of their boats, if the right be against them. Their counsel admit that they must not only forfeit the boats, but must answer in damages for all the intermediate profits. If the legal right be with the appellants, this is the proper court, and this is the proper time to declare it. This court, from its peculiar constitutional structure, unites with it the highest court of common law, and nothing would be more useless than to withhold an injunction until the chancellor had sent the question to be tried at law, when the judges before whom it is to be tried, are members of this court, and have already declared their opinion. The legal question can never be tried by a jury. It is not a question of fact. The single point is the constitutionality of the statutes. That point never can be more fully and more ably argued than it has been before this court, and if we are of opinion that the acts are constitutional, they *must* be obeyed. We are bound to cause them to be obeyed. There is no escape from this duty.

If we refuse the injunction, it ought to be for some substantial reason. We must not put it upon the mere *hoc volo, sic jubeo, sit pro ratione voluntas.* There must be some solid principle, that will correspond with the character, as well as satisfy the conscience of this court. If the laws are valid, it would be of pernicious consequence not to arrest the further progress of their violation. It is impossible for any act to be committed which attracts more universal notice, and if wrong and illegal, none which has a more fatal influence upon the general habits of respect and reverence for the legislative authority. The boats cannot run but in the face of day, and in the presence, as it were, of the whole people, whose laws are set at defiance, nor without seducing thousands, by the contagion of example, into an approbation and support of the trespass.

I am sensible that the case is calculated to excite sympathy. I feel it with others, and I sincerely wish that the respondents had brought the laws to a test, at less risk and expense; for every one who had eyes to read, or ears to hear the contents of our statute book, must have been astonished at the boldness and rashness of the experiment. But in proportion to the respectability and strength of the combination, should be the vigor of our purpose to maintain the law. If we were to suffer the plighted faith of this state to be broken, upon a mere pretext, we should become a reproach and a by-word throughout the union. It was a saying of *Euripedes,* and often repeated by *Cæsar,* that if right was ever to be violated, it was for the sake of power. We follow a purer and nobler system of morals, and one which teaches us that right is never to be violated. This principle ought to be kept steadfast in every man's breast; and above all, it ought to find an asylum in the sanctuary of justice.

I am accordingly of opinion, that the order of the Court of Chancery be reversed, and that an injunction be awarded.

LEWIS, Senator, and TOWNSEND, Senator, being related to some of the parties, declined giving any opinions.

The other senators declared their concurrence in the opinions delivered by the judges. The following order was, thereupon, unanimously adopted and directed to be entered:

Injunction Ordered

"Whereupon, after hearing counsel, as well for the appellants as for the respondents, upon the order of the Court of Chancery, complained of by the appellants, and considering and hereby declaring the exclusive privilege granted by the legislature of this state, to the appellants, as mentioned in their bill of complaint, valid, and that the same ought to be enjoyed by them according to law;

"It is, therefore, ORDERED, ADJUDGED and DECREED, and this court doth, accordingly, ORDER, ADJUDGE and DECREE, that the order of the Court of Chancery complained of be *reversed*. And this court doth further ORDER, ADJUDGE and DECREE, that a writ of injunction issue, restraining and prohibiting the respondents from using and employing the boat or vessel, called the *Hope,* in the bill mentioned, on any of the waters of this state, in contravention of the legislative grant and privilege made to, and vested in, the appellants, as in their bill set forth; and that such injunction be continued until the final hearing of the cause in the Court of Chancery; and that the injunction ought then to be made perpetual, so long as the exclusive right and privilege of the appellants shall continue under the acts of the legislature of this state, in the bill set forth; unless, on the final hearing of the cause, the equity contained in the appellants' bill shall be destroyed, by the new matter to be set forth and established by the respondents.

"And it is further ORDERED, ADJUDGED and DECREED, that the record be remitted to the Court of Chancery, to the end, that the order, judgment and decree, of this court, may be forthwith executed, by awarding such injunction."

Judgment of Reversal.

4. *Gibbons* v. *Ogden* (*New York*)

17 Johnson (New York) 488; January 1820

PLATT, J. This is an appeal from an order of the Court of Chancery, denying a motion for dissolving an injunction, whereby the steam-boat of the appellant was restrained from running between *Elizabeth-town Point* in *New-Jersey* and the city of *New-York*.

The great question which arose in the case of *Livingston and Fulton* v. *Van Ingen and others,* (9 *Johns. Rep.* 507.) whether this state had the power to grant an exclusive right of navigating its waters with steam-boats, is again raised in this cause. That question was then elaborately and profoundly discussed on appeal in this court: and after mature consideration, this court, by a unanimous decree, decided, that the statutes of this state for granting and securing to *Livingston* and *Fulton,* and their assigns, that exclusive privilege, were constitutional and valid.

Immediately after that decision, many persons who had resisted the claim to such exclusive privilege, yielding obedience to that decree, as settling the question by the highest judicial tribunal of the state, became purchasers of that privilege under *Livingston* and *Fulton.* The respondent, *Aaron Ogden,* stands before this court as an assignee under them, and claims the benefit of his purchase. His right is denied by the appellant; 1st. On the old ground, that the state had no power to grant such exclusive privilege in any case; and, 2dly, That he (the appellant) derives authority to navigate his steam-boats under the act of Congress of the 18th of *February,* 1793, for enrolling and licensing coasting vessels, &c.

As to the first general question, I consider it as no longer open for discussion here. It would be trifling with the rights of individuals, and highly derogatory to the character of the court, if it were now to depart from its former deliberate decision on the very same point.

As to the second ground relied on by the appellant, to wit, the *coasting license,* I am unable to discern how that can vary the merits of the question, as presented in the case of *Livingston* v. *Van Ingen.*

U.S. Coasting License

The act of Congress for enrolling and licensing coasting ships, or vessels, &c. enacts, that "no ships or vessels, except such as shall be so enrolled and licensed, shall be deemed ships or vessels of the *United States,* entitled to the privileges of ships or vessels employed in the coasting trade or fisheries." (sect. 1.) And the same act also declares, that every ship or vessel engaged in the coasting trade, &c., and not being so enrolled and licensed, "shall pay the same fees and tonnage in every port of the *United States* at which she may arrive, as ships or vessels not belonging to a citizen or citizens of the *United States;* and if she have on board any articles of foreign growth or manufacture, or distilled spirits other than sea-stores, the ship or vessel, with her tackle and lading, shall be forfeited." (sect. 6.)

From these provisions, and an examination of the various regulations of that statute, and from all the laws of the *United States* on that subject, it appears, that the only design of the federal government, in regard to the enrolling and licensing of vessels, was to establish a criterion of *national character,* with a view to enforce the laws which impose *discriminating duties* on *American* vessels, and those of foreign countries.

The term *"license"* seems not to be used in the sense imputed to it by the counsel for the appellant: that is, a *permit to trade;* or as giving *a right of transit.* Because it is perfectly clear, that such a vessel, coasting from one state to another, would have exactly the same right to trade, and the same right of transit, whether she had the coasting license or not. She does not, therefore, derive her right from the *license;* the only effect of which is, to determine her national character, and the rate of duties which she is to pay.

Avoidance of Conflict

Whatever may be the abstract right of Congress, to pass laws for regulating trade, which might come in collision, and conflict with the exclusive privilege granted by this state, it is sufficient, now, for the protection of the respondent, that the statute of the *United States* relied on by the appellant, is not of that character.

Whether Congress have the power to authorize the coasting trade to be carried on, in vessels propelled by steam, so as to give a *paramount right,* in opposition to the special license given by this state, is a question not yet presented to us. No such act of Congress yet exists, and it will be time enough to discuss that question when it arises.

I am decidedly of opinion, therefore, that the *coasting license* affords no aid or support to the title of the appellant, to run a steam-boat on our waters, in opposition to the laws of this state.

The real merits of this case fall precisely within the decision of this court, in the case of *Livingston, &c.* v. *Van Ingen.* As a *senator,* I was a party to that decision; and concurred in it, for the reasons which were then assigned by the learned judges who delivered the opinion of the court. Those reasons are before the public: and I have not the vanity to believe, that I could add any thing to their force or perspicuity. I, therefore, deem it my only remaining duty to say, that in my judgment, the decree of his honor the chancellor, in this case, ought to be *affirmed.*

This being the unanimous opinion of the court, it was thereupon ORDERED,

ADJUDGED and DECREED, that the decretal order of the Court of Chancery made in this cause, on the 6th of *October,* 1819, and from which order the appellant in this cause has appealed to this court, be, and the same is hereby, in all things, affirmed, with costs to be taxed and paid by the appellant to the respondent; and that the record be remitted, &c.

Decree of affirmance.

5. *Elkison* v. *Deliesseline* (*South Carolina*)

8 Fed. Cas. p. 493 (No. 4, 366); August 1823

JOHNSON, Circuit Justice. The motion submitted by Mr. King in behalf of the prisoner is for the writ of habeas corpus ad subjiciendum; and if he should fail in this motion then for the writ de homine replegiando; the one regarding the prisoner in a criminal, the other in a civil aspect; the first motion having for its object his discharge from confinement absolutely, the other his discharge on bail, with a view to try the question of the validity of the law under which he is held in confinement. A document in nature of a return, under the hand and seal of the sheriff, has been laid on my table by the gentlemen who conduct the opposition, from which it appears that the prisoner is in the sheriff's custody under an act of this state, passed in December last: and, indeed, the whole cause has been argued under the admission that he is in confinement under the third section of that act, as he states in his petition.

The act is entitled "An act for the better regulation of free negroes and persons of color, and for other purposes." And the third section is in these words: "That if any vessel shall come into any port or harbor of this state, from any other state or foreign port, having on board any free negroes or persons of color, as cooks, stewards, or mariners, or in any other employment on board said vessel, such free negroes or persons of color shall be seized and confined in gaol until such vessel shall clear out and depart from this state; and that when said vessel is ready to sail the captain of said vessel shall be bound to carry away the said free negro, or free person of color, and to pay the expenses of his detention; and, in case of his neglect or refusal so to do, he shall be liable to be indicted, and on conviction thereof shall be fined in a sum not less than one thousand dollars, and imprisoned not less than two months; and such free negroes, or persons of color, shall be deemed and taken as absolute slaves, and sold in conformity to the provisions of the act passed on the 20th December, 1820, aforesaid."

As to the description or character of this individual, it was admitted that he was taken by the sheriff under this act out of the ship Homer, a British ship trading from Liverpool to this place. From the shipping articles it appears that he was shipped in Liverpool; from the captain's affidavit that he had known him several years in Liverpool as a British subject; and from his own affidavit that he is a native subject of Great Britain, born in Jamaica. . . .

Right of Secession

Two questions have now been made in argument; the first on the law of the case, the second on the remedy. On the unconstitutionality of the law under which this man is confined, it is not too much to say, that it will not bear argument; and I feel myself sanctioned in using this strong language, from considering the course of reasoning by which it has been defended. Neither of the gentlemen has attempted to prove that the power therein assumed by the state can be exercised without clashing with the general powers of the United States to regulate commerce; but they have both strenuously contended, that ex necessitate it was a power which the state must and would exercise, and, indeed, Mr. Holmes concluded his argument with the declaration, that, if a dissolution of the Union must be the alternative, he was ready to meet it.

Nor did the argument of Col. Hunt deviate at all from the same course. Giving it in the language of his own summary, it was this: South Carolina was a sovereign state when she adopted the constitution; a sovereign state cannot surrender a right of vital importance; South Carolina, therefore, either did not surrender this right, or still possesses the power to resume it, and whether it is necessary, or when it is necessary, to resume it, she is herself the sovereign judge. But it was not necessary to give this candid expose of the grounds which this law assumes; for it is a subject of positive proof, that it is altogether irreconcilable with the powers of the general government; that it necessarily compromits the public peace, and tends to embroil us with, if not separate us from, our sister states; in short, that it leads to a dissolution of the Union, and implies a direct attack upon the sovereignty of the United States. . . .

And here it is proper to notice that part of the argument against the motion, in which it was insisted on that this law was passed by the state in exercise of a concurrent right. "Concurrent" does not mean "paramount," and yet, in order to divest a right conferred by the general government, it is very clear that the state right must be more than concurrent. But the right of the general government to regulate commerce with the sister states and foreign nations is a paramount and exclusive right; and this conclusion we arrive at, whether we examine it with reference to the words of the constitution, or the nature of the grant. That this has been the received and universal construction from the first day of the organization of the general government is unquestionable; and the right admits not of a question any more than the fact.

Plenary Commerce Power

In the constitution of the United States, the most wonderful instrument ever drawn by the hand of man, there is a comprehension and precision that is unparalleled; and I can truly say, that after spending my life in studying it, I still daily find in it some new excellence. It is true that it contains no prohibition on the states to regulate foreign commerce. Nor was such a prohibition necessary, for the words of the grant sweep away the whole subject, and leave nothing for the states to act upon. Wherever this is the case, there is no prohibitory clause interposed in the constitution. Thus, the states are not prohibited from regulating the value of foreign coins or fixing a standard of weights and measures, for the very words imply a total, unlimited grant.

The words in the present case are, "to regulate commerce with foreign nations, and among the several states, and with the Indian tribes." If congress can regulate commerce, what commerce can it not regulate? And the navigation of ships has always been held, by all nations, to appertain to commercial regulations.

But the case does not rest here. In order to sustain this law, the state must also possess a power paramount to the treaty-making power of the United States, expressly declared to be a part of the supreme legislative power of the land; for the seizure of this man, on board a British ship, is an express violation of the commercial convention with Great Britain of 1815. Our commerce with that nation does not depend upon the mere negative sanction of not being prohibited. A reciprocal liberty of commerce is expressly stipulated for and conceded by that treaty; to this the right of navigating their ships in their own way, and particularly by their own subjects, is necessarily incident. If policy requires any restriction of this right, with regard to a particular class of subjects of either contracting party, it must be introduced by treaty. The opposite party cannot introduce it by a legislative act of his own. Such a law as this could not be passed even by the general government, without furnishing a just cause of war. . . .

Upon the whole I am led to the conclusion that the third clause of the act under consideration is unconstitutional and void, and the party petitioner, as well as the shipmaster, is entitled to actions as in ordinary cases. That I possess no power to issue the writ of habeas corpus; but for that remedy he must have recourse to the state authorities. That as to the writ de homine replegiando I have no right to refuse it; but although it will unquestionably lie to a vendee under the sheriff, I doubt whether it can avail the party against the sheriff himself. The counsel will then consider whether he will sue it out.

6. *Opinion of the Supreme Court*

9 Wheaton 1; opinion rendered March 2, 1824

March 2d, 1824. MARSHALL, Ch. J., delivered the opinion of the court, and, after stating the case, proceeded as follows:—The appellant contends, that this decree is erroneous, because the laws which purport to give the exclusive privilege it sustains, are repugnant to the constitution and laws of the United States. They are said to be repugnant—1st. To that clause in the constitution which authorizes congress to regulate commerce. 2d. To that which authorizes congress to promote the progress of science and useful arts.

The state of New York maintains the constitutionality of these laws; and their legislature, their council of revision, and their judges, have repeatedly concurred in this opinion. It is supported by great names—by names which have all the titles to consideration that virtue, intelligence and office can bestow. No tribunal can approach the decision of this question, without feeling a just and real respect for that opinion which is sustained by such authority; but it is the province of this court, while it respects, not to bow to it implicitly; and the judges must exercise, in the examination of the subject, to its formation. It has been said, that they were sovereign, were completely that understanding which Providence has bestowed upon them, with that independence which the people of the United States expect from this department of the government.

As preliminary to the very able discussions of the constitution, which we have heard from the bar, and as having some influence on its construction, reference has been made to the political situation of these states, anterior independent, and were connected with each other only by a league. This is true. But when these allied sovereigns converted their league into a government, when they converted their congress of ambassadors, deputed to deliberate on their common concerns, and to recommend measures of general utility, into a legislature, empowered to enact laws on the most interesting subjects, the whole character in which the states appear, underwent a change, the extent of which must be determined by a fair consideration of the instrument by which that change was effected.

Construing Constitution

This instrument contains an enumeration of powers expressly granted by the people to their government. It has been said, that these powers ought to be construed strictly. But why ought they to be so construed? Is there one sentence in the constitution which gives countenance to this rule? In the last of the enumerated powers, that which grants, expressly, the means for carrying all others into execution, congress is authorized "to make all laws which shall be necessary and proper" for the purpose. But this limitation on the means which may be used, is not extended to the powers which are conferred; nor is there one sentence in the constitution, which has been pointed out by the gentlemen of the bar, or which we have been able to discern, that prescribes this rule. We do not, therefore, think ourselves justified in adopting it. What do gentlemen mean, by a strict construction? If they contend only against that enlarged construction, which would extend words beyond their natural and obvious import, we might question the application of the term, but should not controvert the principle. If they contend for that narrow construction which, in support of some theory not to be found in the constitution, would deny to the government those powers which the words of the grant, as usually understood, import, and which are consistent with the general views and objects of the instrument—for that narrow construction, which would cripple the government, and render it unequal to the objects for which it is declared to be instituted, and to which the powers given, as fairly understood, render it competent—then we cannot perceive the propriety of this strict construction, nor adopt it as the rule by which the constitution is to be expounded. As men, whose intentions require no concealment, generally employ the words which most directly and aptly express the ideas they intend to convey, the enlightened patriots who framed our constitution, and the people who adopted it, must be understood to have employed words in their natural sense, and to have intended what they have said.

If, from the imperfection of human language, there should be serious doubts respecting the extent of any given power, it is a well-settled rule, that the objects for which it was given, especially, when those objects are expressed in the instrument itself, should have great influence in the construction. We know of no reason for excluding this rule from the present case. The grant does not convey power which might be beneficial to the grantor, if retained by himself, or which can inure solely to the benefit of the grantee; but is an investment of power for the general advantage, in the hands of agents selected for that purpose; which power can never be exercised by the people themselves, but must be placed in the hands of agents, or lie dormant. We know of no rule for construing the extent of such powers, other than is given by the language of the instrument which confers them, taken in connection with the purposes for which they were conferred.

Commerce Clause

The words are, "congress shall have power to regulate commerce with foreign nations, and among the several states, and with the Indian tribes." The subject to be regulated is commerce; and our constitution being, as was aptly said at the bar, one of enumeration, and not of definition, to ascertain the extent of the power, it becomes necessary to settle the meaning of the word. The counsel for the appellee would limit it to traffic, to buying and selling, or the interchange of commodities, and do not admit that it comprehends navigation. This would restrict a general term, applicable to many objects, to one of its significations. Commerce, undoubtedly, is traffic, but it is something more—it is intercourse. It describes the commercial intercourse between nations, and parts of nations, in all its branches, and is regulated by prescribing rules for carrying on that intercourse.

The mind can scarcely conceive a system for regulating commerce between nations, which shall exclude all laws concerning navigation, which shall be silent on the admission of the vessels of the one nation into the ports of the other, and be confined to prescribing rules for the conduct of individuals, in the actual employment of buying and selling, or of barter. If commerce does not include navigation, the government of the Union has no direct power over that subject, and can make no law prescribing what shall constitute American vessels, or requiring that they shall be navigated by American seamen. Yet this power has been exercised from the commencement of the government, has been exercised with the consent of all, and has been understood by all to be a commercial regulation. All America understands, and has uniformly understood, the word "commerce," to comprehend navigation. It was so understood, and must have been so understood, when the constitution was framed. The power over commerce, including navigation, was one of the primary objects for which the people of America adopted their government, and must have been contemplated in forming it. The convention must have used the word in that sense, because all have understood it in that sense; and the attempt to restrict it comes too late.

If the opinion that "commerce," as the word is used in the constitution, comprehends navigation also, requires any additional confirmation, that additional confirmation is, we think, furnished by the words of the instrument itself. It is a rule of construction, acknowledged by all, that the exceptions from a power mark its extent; for it would be absurd, as well as useless, to except from a granted power, that which was not granted—that which the words of the grant could not comprehend. If, then, there are in the constitution plain exceptions from the power over navigation, plain inhibitions to the exercise of that power in a particular way, it is a proof that those who made these exceptions, and prescribed these inhibitions, understood the power to which they applied as being granted. The 9th section of the last article declares, that "no preference shall be given, by any regulation of commerce or revenue, to the ports of one state over those of another." This clause cannot be understood as applicable to those laws only which are passed for the purposes of revenue, because it is expressly applied to commercial regulations; and the most obvious preference which can be given to one port over another, in regulating commerce, relates to navigation. But the subsequent part of the sentence is still more explicit. It is, "nor shall vessels bound to or from one state, be obliged to enter, clear or pay duties in another." These words have a direct reference to navigation.

Power of Government

The universally acknowledged power of the government to impose embargoes, must also be considered as showing, that all America is united in that construction which comprehends navigation in the word commerce. Gentlemen have said, in argument, that this is a branch of the war-making power, and that an embargo is an instrument of war, not a regulation of trade. That it may be, and often is, used as an instrument of war, cannot be denied. An embargo may be imposed, for the purpose of facilitating the equipment or manning of a fleet, or for the purpose of concealing the progress of an expedition preparing to sail from a particular port. In these, and in similar cases, it is a military instrument, and partakes of the nature of war. But all embargoes are not of this description. They are sometimes resorted to, without a view to war, and with a single view to commerce. In such case, an embargo is no more a war measure, than a merchantman is a ship of war, because both are vessels which navigate the ocean with sails and seamen. When congress imposed that embargo which, for a time, engaged the attention of every man in the United States, the avowed object of the law was, the protection of commerce, and the avoiding of war. By its friends and its enemies, it was treated as a commercial, not as a war measure.

The persevering earnestness and zeal with which it was opposed, in a part of our country which supposed its interests to be vitally affected by the act, cannot be forgotten. A want of acuteness in discovering objections to a measure to which they felt the most deep-rooted hostility, will not be imputed to those who were arrayed in opposition to this. Yet they never suspected that navigation was no branch of trade, and was, therefore, not comprehended in the power to regulate commerce. They did, indeed, contest the constitutionality of the act, but, on a principle which admits the construction for which the appellant contends. They denied that the particular law in question was made in pursuance of the constitution, not because the power could not act directly on vessels, but because a perpetual embargo was the annihilation, and not the regulation of commerce. In terms, they admitted the applicability of the words used in the constitution to vessels; and that, in a case which produced a degree and an extent of excitement, calculated to draw forth every principle on which legitimate resistance could be sustained. No example could more strongly illustrate the universal understanding of the American people on this subject.*

Definition of Powers

The word used in the constitution, then, comprehends, and has been always understood to comprehend, navigation within its meaning; and a power to regulate navigation, is as expressly granted, as if that term had been added to the word "commerce." To what commerce does this power extend? The constitution informs us, to commerce "with foreign nations, and among the several states, and with the Indian tribes." It has, we believe, been universally admitted, that these words comprehend every species of commercial intercourse between the United States and foreign nations. No sort of trade can be carried on between this country and any other, to which this power does not extend. It has been truly said, that commerce, as the word is used in the constitution, is a unit, every part of which is indicated by the term.

If this be the admitted meaning of the word, in its application to foreign nations, it must carry the same meaning throughout the sentence, and remain a unit, unless there be some plain intelligible cause which alters it. The subject to which the power is next applied, is to commerce, "among the several states." The word "among" means intermingled with. A thing which is among others, is intermingled with them. Commerce among the states, cannot stop at the external boundary line of each state, but may be introduced into the interior. It is not intended to say, that these words comprehend that commerce, which is completely internal, which is carried on between man and man in a state, or between different parts of the same state, and which does not extend to or affect other states. Such a power would be inconvenient, and is certainly unnecessary.

Comprehensive as the word "among" is, it may very properly be restricted to that commerce which concerns more states than one. The phrase is not one which would probably have been selected to indicate the completely interior traffic of a state, because it is not an apt phrase for that purpose; and the enumeration of the particular classes of commerce to which the power was to be extended, would not have been made, had the intention been to

* In a series of unilateral attempts to compel England and France to relax their hostile maritime policies as these affected American trade, the Jefferson and Madison administrations tried several legislative quarantines. The Non-Importation Act (April 1806), the Embargo Act (December 1807) and the Non-Intercourse Act (March 1809) all failed to affect English or French policies, but virtually ruined American commerce and shipping. The attempts were abandoned in 1810.

extend the power to every description. The enumeration presupposes something not enumerated; and that something, if we regard the language or the subject of the sentence, must be the exclusively internal commerce of a state. The genius and character of the whole government seem to be, that its action is to be applied to all the external concerns of the nation, and to those internal concerns which affect the states generally; but not to those which are completely within a particular state, which do not affect other states, and with which it is not necessary to interfere, for the purpose of executing some of the general powers of the government. The completely internal commerce of a state, then, may be considered as reserved for the state itself.

But in regulating commerce with foreign nations, the power of congress does not stop at the jurisdictional lines of the several states. It would be a very useless power, if it could not pass those lines. The commerce of the United States with foreign nations, is that of the whole United States; every district has a right to participate in it. The deep streams which penetrate our country in every direction, pass through the interior of almost every state in the Union, and furnish the means of exercising this right. If congress has the power to regulate it, that power must be exercised whenever the subject exists. If it exists within the states, if a foreign voyage may commence or terminate at a port within a state, then the power of congress may be exercised within a state.

Commerce Among States

This principle is, if possible, still more clear, when applied to commerce "among the several states." They either join each other, in which case they are separated by a mathematical line, or they are remote from each other, in which case other states lie between them. What is commerce "among" them; and how is it to be conducted? Can a trading expedition between two adjoining states, commence and terminate outside of each? And if the trading intercourse be between two states remote from each other, must it not commence in one, terminate in the other, and probably pass through a third? Commerce among the states must, of necessity, be commerce with the states. In the regulation of trade with the Indian tribes, the action of the law, especially, when the constitution was made, was chiefly within a state. The power of congress, then, whatever it may be, must be exercised within the territorial jurisdiction of the several states. The sense of the nation on this subject, is unequivocally manifested by the provisions made in the laws for transporting goods, by land, between Baltimore and Providence, between New York and Philadelphia, and between Philadelphia and Baltimore.

Commerce Power

We are now arrived at the inquiry—what is this power? It is the power to regulate; that is, to prescribe the rule by which commerce is to be governed. This power, like all others vested in congress, is complete in itself, may be exercised to its utmost extent, and acknowledges no limitations, other than are prescribed in the constitution. These are expressed in plain terms, and do not affect the questions which arise in this case, or which have been discussed at the bar. If, as has always been understood, the sovereignty of congress, though limited to specified objects, is plenary as to those objects, the power over commerce with foreign nations, and among the several states, is vested in congress as absolutely as it would be in a single government, having in its constitution the same restrictions on the exercise of the power as are found in the constitution of the United States. The wisdom and the discretion of congress, their identity with the people, and the influence which their constituents possess at elections, are, in this, as in many other instances, as that, for example, of declaring war, the sole restraints on which they have relied, to secure them from its abuse. They are the restraints on which the people must often rely solely, in all representative governments. The power of congress, then, comprehends navigation, within the limits of every state in the Union; so far as that navigation may be, in any manner, connected with "commerce with foreign nations, or among the several states, or with the Indian tribes." It may, of consequence, pass the jurisdictional line of New York, and act upon the very waters to which the prohibition now under consideration applies.

But it has been urged, with great earnestness, that although the power of congress to regulate commerce with foreign nations, and among the several states, be co-extensive with the subject itself, and have no other limits than are prescribed in the constitution, yet the states may severally exercise the same power, within their respective jurisdictions. In support of this argument, it is said, that they possessed it as an inseparable attribute of sovereignty, before the formation of the constitution, and still retain it, except so far as they have surrendered it by that instrument; that this principle results from the nature of the government, and is secured by the tenth amendment; that an affirmative grant of power is not exclusive, unless in its own nature it be such that the continued exercise of it by the former possessor is inconsistent with the grant, and that this is not of that description. The appellant, conceding these postulates, except the last, contends, that full power to regulate a particular subject, implies the whole power, and leaves no residuum; that a grant of the whole is incompatible with the existence of a right in another to any part of it. Both parties have appealed to the constitution, to legislative acts, and judicial decisions; and have drawn arguments from all these sources, to support and illustrate the propositions they respectively maintain.

General or Broad Terms

The grant of the power to lay and collect taxes is, like the power to regulate commerce, made in general terms, and has never been understood to interfere with the exercise of the same power by the states; and hence has been drawn an argument which has been applied to the question under consideration. But the two grants are not, it is conceived, similar in their terms or their nature. Although many of the powers formerly exercised by the states, are transferred to the government of the Union, yet the state governments remain, and constitute a most important part of our system. The power of taxation is indispensable to their existence, and is a power which, in its own nature, is capable of residing in, and being exercised by, different authorities, at the same time. We are accustomed to see it placed, for different purposes, in different hands. Taxation is the simple operation of taking small portions from a perpetually accumulating mass, susceptible of almost infinite division; and a power in one to take what is necessary for certain purposes, is not, in its nature, incompatible with a power in another to take what is necessary for other purposes. Congress is authorized to lay and collect taxes, &c., to pay the debts, and provide for the common defence and general welfare of the United States.

This does not interfere with the power of the states to tax for the support of their own governments; nor is the exercise of that power by the states, an exercise of any portion of the power that is granted to the United States. In imposing taxes for state purposes, they are not doing what congress is empowered to do. Congress is not empowered to tax for those purposes which are within the exclusive province of the states. When, then, each government exercises the power of taxation, neither is exercising the power of the other. But when a state proceeds to regulate commerce with foreign nations, or among the several states, it is exercising the very power that is granted to congress, and is doing the very thing which congress is authorized to do. There is no analogy, then, between the power of taxation and the power of regulating commerce.

Locus of Power

In discussing the question, whether this power is still in the states, in the case under consideration, we may dismiss from it the inquiry, whether it is surrendered by the mere grant to congress, or is retained until congress shall exercise the power. We may dismiss that inquiry, because it has been exercised, and the regulations which congress deemed it proper to make, are now in full operation. The sole question is, can a state regulate commerce with foreign nations and among the states, while congress is regulating it?

The counsel for the respondent answer this question in the affirmative, and rely very much on the restrictions in the 10th section, as supporting their opinion. They say, very truly, that limitations of a power furnish a strong argument in favor of the existence of that power, and that the section which prohibits the states from laying duties on imports or exports, proves that this power might have been exercised, had it not been expressly forbidden; and, consequently, that any other commercial regulation, not expressly forbidden, to which the original power of the state was competent, may still be made. That this restriction shows the opinion of the convention, that a state might impose duties on exports and imports, if not expressly forbidden, will be conceded; but that it follows, as a consequence, from this concession, that a state may regulate commerce with foreign nations and among the states, cannot be admitted.

We must first determine, whether the act of laying "duties or imposts on imports or exports," is considered, in the constitution, as a branch of the taxing power, or of the power to regulate commerce. We think it very clear, that it is considered as a branch of the taxing power. It is so treated in the first clause of the 8th section: "Congress shall have power to lay and collect taxes, duties, imposts and excises;" and before commerce is mentioned, the rule by which the exercise of this power must be governed, is declared. It is, that all duties, imposts and excises shall be uniform. In a separate clause of the enumeration, the power to regulate commerce is given, as being entirely distinct from the right to levy taxes and imposts, and as being a new power, not before conferred.

The constitution, then, considers these powers as substantive, and distinct from each other; and so places them in the enumeration it contains. The power of imposing duties on imports is classed with the power to levy taxes, and that seems to be its natural place. But the power to levy taxes could never be considered as abridging the right of the states on that subject; and they might, consequently, have exercised it, by levying duties on imports or exports, had the constitution contained no prohibition on this subject. This prohibition, then, is an exception from the acknowledged power of the states to levy taxes, not from the questionable power to regulate commerce.

"A duty of tonnage" is as much a tax, as a duty on imports or exports; and the reason which induced the prohibition of those taxes, extends to this also. This tax may be imposed by a state, with the consent of congress; and it may be admitted, that congress cannot give a right to a state, in virtue of its own powers. But a duty of tonnage, being part of the power of imposing taxes, its prohibition may certainly be made to depend on congress, without affording any implication respecting a power to regulate commerce. It is true, that duties may often be, and in fact often are, imposed on tonnage, with a view to the regulation of commerce; but they may be also imposed, with a view to revenue; and it was, therefore, a prudent precaution, to prohibit the states from exercising this power.

The idea that the same measure might, according to circumstances, be arranged with different classes of power, was no novelty to the framers of our constitution. Those illustrious statesmen and patriots had been, many of them, deeply engaged in the discussions which preceded the war of our revolution, and all of them were well read in those discussions. The right to regulate commerce, even by the imposition of duties, was not controverted; but the right to impose a duty for the purpose of revenue, produced a war as important, perhaps, in its consequences to the human race, as any the world has ever witnessed. These restrictions, then, are on the taxing power, not on that to regulate commerce; and presuppose the existence of that which they restrain, not of that which they do not purport to restrain.

But the inspection laws are said to be regulations of commerce, and are certainly recognised in the constitution, as being passed in the exercise of a power remaining with the states. That inspection laws may have a remote and considerable influence on commerce, will not be denied; but that a power to regulate commerce is the source from which the right to pass them is derived, cannot be admitted. The object of inspection laws, is to improve the quality of articles produced by the labor of a country; to fit them for exportation; or, it may be, for domestic use. They act upon the subject, before it becomes an article of foreign commerce, or of commerce among the states, and prepare it for that purpose. They form a portion of that immense mass of legislation, which embraces everything within the territory of a state, not surrendered to the general government; all which can be most advantageously exercised by the states themselves. Inspection laws, quarantine laws, health laws of every description, as well as laws for regulating the internal commerce of a state, and those which respect turnpike-roads, ferries, &c., are component parts of this mass.

Power of States

No direct general power over these objects is granted to congress; and, consequently, they remain subject to state legislation. If the legislative power of the Union can reach them, it must be for national purposes; it must be, where the power is expressly given for a special purpose, or is clearly incidental to some power which is expressly given. It is obvious, that the government of the Union, in the exercise of its express powers, that, for example, of regulating commerce with foreign nations and among the states, may use means that may also be employed by a state, in the exercise of its acknowledged powers; that, for example, of regulating commerce within the state. If congress license vessels to sail from one port to another, in the same state, the act is supposed to be, necessarily, incidental to the power expressly granted to congress, and implies no claim of a direct power to regulate the purely internal commerce of a state, or to act directly on its system of police. So, if a state, in passing laws on subjects acknowledged to be within its control, and with a view to those subjects, shall adopt a measure of the same character with one which congress may adopt, it does not derive its authority from the particular power which has been granted, but from some other, which remains with the state, and may be executed by the same means.

All experience shows, that the same measures, or measures scarcely distinguishable from each other, may flow from distinct powers; but this does not prove that the powers themselves are identical. Although the means used in their execution may sometimes approach each other so nearly as to be confounded, there are other situations in which they are sufficiently distinct, to establish their individuality.

In our complex system, presenting the rare and difficult scheme of one general government, whose action extends over the whole, but which possesses only certain enumerated powers; and of numerous state governments, which retain and exercise all powers not delegated to the Union, contests respecting power must arise. Were it even otherwise, the measures taken by the respective governments to execute their acknowledged powers, would often be of the same description, and might, sometimes, interfere. This, however, does not prove that the one is exercising, or has a right to exercise, the powers of the other.

Acts of Congress

The acts of congress, passed in 1796 and 1799, . . . empowering and directing the officers of the general government to conform to, and assist in the execution of the quarantine and health laws of a state, proceed, it is said, upon the idea that these laws are constitutional. It is undoubtedly true, that they do proceed upon that idea; and the constitutionality of such laws has never, so far we are informed, been denied. But they do not imply an acknowledgment that a state may rightfully regulate commerce with foreign nations, or among the states; for they do not imply that such laws are an exercise of that power, or enacted with a view to it. On the contrary, they are treated as quarantine and health laws, are so denominated in the acts of congress, and are considered as flowing from the acknowledged power of a state, to provide for the health of its citizens.

But as it was apparent, that some of the provisions made for this purpose, and in virtue of this power, might interfere with, and be affected by the laws of the United States, made for the regulation of commerce, congress, in that spirit of harmony and conciliation which ought always to characterize the conduct of governments standing in the relation which that of the Union and those of the states bear to each other, has directed its officers to aid in the execution of these laws; and has, in some measure, adapted its own legislation to this object, by making provisions in aid of those of the states. But in making these provisions, the opinion is unequivocally manifested, that congress may control the state laws, so far as it may be necessary to control them, for the regulation of commerce.

The act passed in 1803 . . . prohibiting the importation of slaves into any state which shall itself prohibit their importation, implies, it is said, an admission that the states possessed the power to exclude or admit them; from which it is inferred, that they possess the same power with respect to other articles. If this inference were correct, if this power was exercised, not under any particular clause in the constitution, but in virtue of a general right over the subject of commerce, to exist as long as the constitution itself, it might now be exercised. Any state might now import African slaves into its own territory. But it is obvious, that the power of the states over this subject, previous to the year 1808, constitutes an exception to the power of congress to regulate commerce, and the exception is expressed in such words, as to manifest clearly the intention to continue the pre-existing right of the states to admit or exclude, for a limited period. The words are, "the migration or importation of such persons as any of the states, now existing, shall think proper to admit, shall not be prohibited by the congress, prior to the year 1808." The whole object of the exception is, to preserve the power to those states which might be disposed to exercise it; and its language seems to the court to convey this idea unequivocally. The possession of this particular power, then, during the time limited in the constitution, cannot be admitted to prove the possession of any other similar power.

It has been said, that the act of August 7th, 1789, acknowledges a concurrent power in the states to regulate the conduct of pilots, and hence is inferred an admission of their concurrent right with congress to regulate commerce with foreign nations, and amongst the states. But this inference is not, we think, justified by the fact. Although congress cannot enable a state to legislate, congress may adopt the provisions of a state on any subject. When the government of the Union was brought into existence, it found a system for the regulation of its pilots in full force in every state. The act which has been mentioned, adopts this system, and gives it the same validity as if its provisions had been specially made by congress.

But the act, it may be said, is prospective also, and the adoption of laws to be made in future, presupposes the right in the maker to legislate on the subject. The act unquestionably manifests an intention to leave this subject entirely to the states, until congress should think proper to interpose; but the very enactment of such a law indicates an opinion that it was necessary; that the existing system would not be applicable to the new state of things, unless expressly applied to it by congress. But this section is confined to pilots within the "bays, inlets, rivers, harbors and ports of the United States," which are, of course, in whole or in part, also within the limits of some particular state. The acknowledged power of a state to regulate its police, its domestic trade, and to govern its own citizens, may enable it to legislate on this subject, to a considerable extent; and the adoption of its system by congress, and the application of it to the whole subject of commerce, does not seem to the court to imply a right in the states so to apply it of their own authority. But the adoption of the state system being temporary, being only "until further legislative provision shall be made by congress," shows, conclusively, an opinion, that congress could control the whole subject, and might adopt the system of the states, or provide one of its own.

Limits to State Power

A state, it is said, or even a private citizen, may construct light-houses. But gentlemen must be aware, that if this proves a power in a state to regulate commerce, it proves that the same power is in the citizen. States, or individuals who own lands, may, if not forbidden by law, erect on those lands what buildings they please; but this power is entirely distinct from that of regulating commerce, and may, we presume, be restrained, if exercised so as to produce a public mischief.

These acts were cited at the bar for the purpose of showing an opinion in congress, that the states possess, concurrently with the legislature of the Union, the power to regulate commerce with foreign nations and among the states. Upon reviewing them, we think, they do not establish the proposition they were intended to prove. They show the opinion, that the states retain powers enabling them to pass the laws to which allusion has been made, not that those laws proceed from the particular power which has been delegated to congress.

It has been contended by the counsel for the appellant, that, as the word "to regulate" implies in its nature, full power over the thing to be regulated, it excludes, necessarily, the action of all others that would perform the same operation on the same thing. That regulation is designed for the entire result, applying to those parts which remain as they were, as well as to those which are altered. It produces a uniform whole, which is as much disturbed and deranged by changing what the regulating power designs to leave untouched, as that on which it has operated. There is great force in this argument, and the court is not satisfied that it has been refuted.

Conflict with Federal Powers

Since, however, in exercising the power of regulating their own purely internal affairs, whether of trading or police, the states may sometimes enact laws, the validity of which depends on their interfering with, and being contrary to, an act of congress passed in pursuance of the constitution, the court will enter upon the inquiry, whether the laws of New York, as expounded by the highest tribunal of that state, have, in their application to this case, come into collision with an act of congress, and deprived a citizen of a right to which that act entitles him. Should this collision exist, it will be immaterial, whether those laws were passed in virtue of a concurrent power "to regulate commerce with foreign nations and among the several states," or, in virtue of a power to regulate their domestic trade and police. In one case and the other, the acts of New York must yield to the law of congress; and the decision sustaining the privilege they confer, against a right given by a law of the Union, must be erroneous. This opinion has been frequently expressed in this court, and is founded, as well on the nature of the government, as on the words of the constitution.

In argument, however, it has been contended, that if a law passed by a state, in the exercise of its acknowledged sovereignty, comes into conflict with a law passed by congress in pursuance of the constitution, they affect the subject, and each other, like equal opposing powers. But the framers of our constitution foresaw this state of things, and provided for it, by declaring the supremacy not only of itself, but of the laws made in pursuance of it. The nullity of any act, inconsistent with the constitution, is produced by the declaration, that the constitution is the supreme law. The appropriate application of that part of the clause which confers the same supremacy on laws and treaties, is to such acts of the state legislatures as do not transcend their powers, but though enacted in the execution of acknowledged state powers, interfere with, or are contrary to, the laws of congress, made in pursuance of the constitution, or some treaty made under the authority of the United States. In every such case, the act of congress, or the treaty, is supreme; and the law of the state, though enacted in the exercise of powers not controverted, must yield to it.

In pursuing this inquiry at the bar, it has been said, that the constitution does not confer the right of intercourse between state and state. That right derives its source from those laws whose authority is acknowledged by civilized man throughout the world. This is true. The constitution found it an existing right, and gave to congress the power to regulate it. In the exercise of this power, congress has passed "an act for enrolling or licensing ships or vessels to be employed in the coasting trade and fisheries, and for regulating the same." The counsel for the respondent contend, that this act does not give the right to sail from port to port, but confines itself to regulating a pre-existing right, so far only as to confer certain privileges on enrolled and licensed vessels in its exercise.

Supremacy of Federal Power

It will at once occur, that, when a legislature attaches certain privileges and exemptions to the exercise of a right over which its control is absolute, the law must imply a power to exercise the right. The privileges are gone, if the right itself be annihilated. It would be contrary to all reason, and to the course of human affairs, to say that a state is unable to strip a vessel of the particular privileges attendant on the exercise of a right, and yet may annul the right itself; that the state of New York cannot prevent an enrolled and licensed vessel, proceeding from Elizabethtown, in New Jersey, to New York, from enjoying, in her course, and on her entrance into port, all the privileges conferred by the act of congress; but can shut her up in her own port, and prohibit altogether her entering the waters and ports of another state. To the court, it seems very clear, that the whole act on the subject of the coasting trade, according to those principles which govern the construction of statutes, implies, unequivocally, an authority to license vessels to carry on the coasting trade.

But we will proceed briefly to notice those sections which bear more directly on the subject. The first section declares, that vessels enrolled by virtue of a previous law, and certain other vessels, enrolled as described in that act, and having a license in force, as is by the act required, "and no others, shall be deemed ships or vessels of the United States, entitled to the privileges of ships or vessels employed in the coasting trade." This section seems to the court to contain a positive enactment, that the vessels it describes shall be entitled to the privileges of ships or vessels employed in the coasting trade. These privileges cannot be separated from the trade, and cannot be enjoyed, unless the trade may be prosecuted. The grant of the privilege is an idle, empty form, conveying nothing, unless it convey the right to which the privilege is attached, and in the exercise of which its whole value consists. To construe these words otherwise than as entitling the ships or vessels described, to carry on the coasting trade, would be, we think, to disregard the apparent intent of the act.

The fourth section directs the proper officer to grant to a vessel qualified to receive it, "a license for carrying on the coasting trade," and prescribes its form. After reciting the compliance of the applicant with the previous requisites of the law, the operative words of the instrument are, "license is hereby granted for the said steam-boat Bellona, to be employed in carrying on the coasting trade for one year from the date hereof, and no longer." These are not the words of the officer; they are the words of the legislature; and convey as explicitly the authority the act intended to give, and operate as effectually, as if they had been inserted in any other part of the act, than in the license itself. The word "license," means permission or authority; and a license to do any particular thing, is a permission or authority to do that thing; and, if granted by a person having power to grant it, transfers to the grantee the right to do whatever it purports to authorize. It certainly transfers to him all the right which the grantor can transfer, to do what is within the terms of the license. Would the validity or effect of such an instrument be questioned by the respondent, if executed by persons claiming regularly under the laws of New York? The license must be understood to be what it purports to be, a legislative authority to the steam-boat Bellona, "to be employed in carrying on the coasting trade, for one year from this date."

Nature of License

It has been denied, that these words authorize a voyage from New Jersey to New York. It is true, that no ports are specified; but it is equally true, that the words used are perfectly intelligible, and do confer such authority as unquestionably, as if the ports had been mentioned. The coasting trade is a term well understood. The law has defined it; and all know its meaning perfectly. The act describes, with great minuteness, the various operations of a vessel engaged in it; and it cannot, we think, be doubted, that a voyage from New Jersey to New York, is one of those operations.

Notwithstanding the decided language of the license, it has also been maintained, that it gives no right to trade; and that its sole purpose is to confer the American character. The answer given to this argument, that the American character is conferred by the enrolment, and not by the license, is, we think, founded too clearly in the words of the law, to require the support of any additional observations. The enrolment of vessels designed for the coasting trade, corresponds precisely with the registration of vessels designed for the foreign trade, and requires every circumstance which can constitute the American character. The license can be granted only to vessels already enrolled, if they be of the burden of twenty tons and upwards; and requires no circumstance essential to the American character. The object of the license, then, cannot be to ascertain the character of the vessel, but to do what it professes to do—that is, to give permission to a vessel already proved by her enrolment to be American, to carry on the coasting trade.

But if the license be a permit to carry on the coasting trade, the respondent denies that these boats were engaged in that trade, or that the decree under consideration has restrained them from prosecuting it. The boats of the appellant were, we are told, employed in the transportation of passengers; and this is no part of that commerce which congress may regulate. If, as our whole course of legislation on this subject shows, the power of congress has been universally understood in America, to comprehend navigation, it is a very persuasive, if not a conclusive, argument, to prove that the construction is correct; and, if it be correct, no clear distinction is perceived between the power to regulate vessels employed in transporting men for hire, and property for hire. The subject is transferred to congress, and no exception to the grant can be admitted, which is not proved by the words, or the nature of the thing. A coasting vessel employed in the transportation of passengers, is as much a portion of the American marine, as one employed in the transportation of a cargo; and no reason is perceived, why such vessel should be withdrawn from the regulating power of that government, which has been thought best fitted for the purpose generally. The provisions of the law respecting native seamen, and respecting ownership, are as applicable to vessels carrying men, as to vessels carrying manufactures; and no reason is perceived, why the power over the subject should not be placed in the same hands.

The argument urged at the bar, rests on the foundation, that the power of congress does not extend to navigation, as a branch of commerce, and can only be applied to that subject, incidentally and occasionally. But if that foundation be removed, we must show some plain, intelligible distinction, supported by the constitution, or by reason, for discriminating between the power of congress over vessels employed in navigating the same seas. We can perceive no such distinction. If we refer to the constitution, the inference to be drawn from it is rather against the distinction. The section which restrains congress from prohibiting the migration or importation of such persons as any of the states may think proper to admit, until the year 1808, has always been considered as an exception from the power to regulate commerce, and certainly seems to class migration with importation. Migration applies as appropriately to voluntary, as importation does to involuntary, arrivals; and so far as an exception from a power proves its existence, this section proves that the power to regulate commerce applies equally to the regulations of vessels employed in transporting men, who pass from place to place voluntarily, and to those who pass involuntarily.

Elements of Commerce Power

If the power reside in congress, as a portion of the general grant to regulate commerce, then, acts applying that power to vessels generally, must be construed as comprehending all vessels. If none appear to be excluded by the language of the act, none can be excluded by construction. Vessels have always been employed to a greater or less extent in the transportation of passengers, and have never been supposed to be, on that account, withdrawn from the control or protection of congress. Packets which ply along the coast, as well as those which make voyages between Europe and America, consider the transportation of passengers as an important part of their business.

Yet it has never been suspected, that the general laws of navigation did not apply to them. The duty act, §§ 23 and 46, contains provisions respecting passengers, and shows, that vessels which transport them, have the same rights, and must perform the same duties, with other vessels. They are governed by the general laws of navigation. In the progress of things, this seems to have grown into a particular employment, and to have attracted the particular attention of government. Congress was no longer satisfied with comprehending vessels engaged specially in this business, within those provisions which were intended for vessels generally; and on the 2d of March 1819, passed "an act regulating passenger ships and vessels." This wise and humane law provides for the safety and comfort of passengers, and for the communication of everything concerning them which may interest the government, to the department of state, but makes no provision concerning the entry of the vessel, or her conduct in the waters of the United States. This, we think, shows conclusively the sense of congress (if, indeed, any evidence to that point could be required), that the pre-existing regulations comprehended passenger ships among others; and in prescribing the same duties, the legislature must have considered them as possessing the same rights.

If, then, it were even true, that the Bellona and the Stoudinger were employed exclusively in the conveyance of passengers between New York and New Jersey, it would not follow, that this occupation did not constitute a part of the coasting trade of the United States, and was not protected by the license annexed to the answer. But we cannot perceive how the occupation of these vessels can be drawn into question, in the case before the court. The laws of New York, which grant the exclusive privilege set up by the respondent, take no notice of the employment of vessels, and relate only to the principle by which they are propelled. Those laws do not inquire whether vessels are engaged in transporting men or merchandise, but whether they are moved by steam or wind. If by the former, the waters of New York are closed against them, though their cargoes be dutiable goods, which the laws of the United States permit them to enter and deliver in New York. If by the latter, those waters are free to them, though they should carry passengers only.

In conformity with the law, is the bill of the plaintiff in the state court. The bill does not complain that the Bellona and the Stoudinger carry passengers, but that they are moved by steam. This is the injury of which he complains, and is the sole injury against the continuance of which he asks relief. The bill does not even allege, specially, that those vessels were employed in the transportation of passengers, but says, generally, that they were employed "in the transportation of passengers, or otherwise." The answer avers only, that they were employed in the coasting trade, and insists on the right to carry on any trade authorized by the license. No testimony is taken, and the writ of injunction and decree restrain these licensed vessels, not from carrying passengers, but from being moved through the waters of New York by steam, for any purpose whatever. The questions, then, whether the conveyance of passengers be a part of the coasting trade, and whether a vessel can be protected in that occupation by a coasting license, are not, and cannot be, raised in this case. The real and sole question seems to be, whether a steam-machine, in actual use, deprives a vessel of the privileges conferred by a license.

Nature of Subject of Law

In considering this question, the first idea which presents itself is, that the laws of congress for the regulation of commerce, do not look to the principle by which vessels are moved. That subject is left entirely to individual discretion; and in that vast and complex system of legislative enactment concerning it, which embraces everything that the legislature thought it necessary to notice, there is not, we believe, one word respecting the peculiar principle by which vessels are propelled through the water, except what may be found in a single act, granting a particular privilege to steam-boats. With this exception, every act, either prescribing duties, or granting privileges, applies to every vessel, whether navigated by the instrumentality of wind or fire, of sails or machinery. The whole weight of proof, then, is thrown upon him who would introduce a distinction to which the words of the law give no countenance. If a real difference could be admitted to exist between vessels carrying passengers and others, it has already been observed, that there is no fact in this case which can bring up that question. And if the occupation of steam-boats be a matter of such general notoriety, that the court may be presumed to know it, although not specially informed by the record, then we deny that the transportation of passengers is their exclusive occupation. It is a matter of general history, that, in our western waters, their principal employment is the transportation of merchandise; and all know, that in the waters of the Atlantic, they are frequently so employed.

But all inquiry into this subject seems to the court to be put completely at rest, by the act already mentioned, entitled, "an act for the enrolling and licensing of steam-boats." This act authorizes a steam-boat employed, or intended to be employed, only in a river or bay of the United States, owned wholly or in part by an alien, resident within the United States, to be enrolled and licensed as if the same belonged to a citizen of the United States. This act demonstrates the opinion of congress, that steam-boats may be enrolled and licensed, in common with vessels using sails. They are, of course, entitled to the same privileges, and can no more be restrained from navigating waters, and entering ports which are free to such vessels, than if they were wafted on their voyage by the winds, instead of being propelled by the agency of fire. The one element may be as legitimately used as the other, for every commercial purpose authorized by the laws of the Union; and the act of a state inhibiting the use of either, to any vessels having a license under the act of congress, comes, we think, in direct collision with that act.

"Necessary and Proper" Power

As this decides the cause, it is unnecessary to enter in an examination of that part of the constitution which empowers congress to promote the progress of science and the useful arts.

The court is aware that, in stating the train of reasoning by which we have been conducted to this result, much time has been consumed in the attempt to demonstrate propositions which may have been thought axioms. It is felt, that the tediousness inseparable from the endeavor to prove that which is already clear, is imputable to a considerable part of this opinion. But it was unavoidable. The conclusion to which we have come, depends on a chain of principles which it was necessary to preserve unbroken; and although some of them were thought nearly self-evident, the magnitude of the question, the weight of character belonging to those from whose judgment we dissent, and the argument at the bar, demanded that we should assume nothing.

Powerful and ingenious minds, taking, as postulates, that the powers expressly granted to the government of the Union, are to be contracted, by construction, into the narrowest possible compass, and that the original powers of the states are retained, if any possible construction will retain them, may, by a course of well-digested, but refined and metaphysical reasoning, founded on these premises, explain away the constitution of our country, and leave it, a magnificent structure, indeed, to look at, but totally unfit for use. They may so entangle and perplex the understanding, as to obscure principles, which were before thought quite plain, and induce doubts where, if the mind were to pursue its own course, none would be perceived. In such a case, it is peculiarly necessary to recur to safe and fundamental principles, to sustain those principles, and, when sustained, to make them the tests of the arguments to be examined.

Johnson's Concurrence

JOHNSON, Justice.—The judgment entered by the court in this cause, has my entire approbation; but having adopted my conclusions on views of the subject materially different from those of my brethren, I feel it incumbent on me to exhibit those views. I have also another inducement: in questions of great importance and great delicacy, I feel my duty to the public best discharged, by an effort to maintain my opinions in my own way.

In attempts to construe the constitution, I have never found much benefit resulting from the inquiry, whether the whole, or any part of it, is to be construed strictly or liberally. The simple, classical, precise, yet comprehensive language in which it is couched, leaves, at most, but very little latitude for construction; and when its intent and meaning are discovered, nothing remains but to execute the will of those who made it, in the best manner to effect the purposes intended. The great and paramount purpose was, to unite this mass of wealth and power, for the protection of the humblest individual; his rights, civil and political, his interests and prosperity, are the sole end; the rest are nothing but the means. But the principal of those means, one so essential as to approach nearer the characteristics of an end, was the independence and harmony of the states, that they may the better subserve the purposes of cherishing and protecting the respective families of this great republic.

Nature of Federal Power

The strong sympathies, rather than the feeble government, which bound the states together during a common war, dissolved on the return of peace; and the very principles which gave rise to the war of the revolution, began to threaten the confederacy with anarchy and ruin. The states had resisted a tax imposed by the parent state, and now reluctantly submitted to, or altogether rejected, the moderate demands of the confederation. Every one recollects the painful and threatening discussions, which arose on the subject of the five per cent. duty. Some states rejected it altogether; others insisted on collecting it themselves; scarcely any acquiesced without reservations which deprived it altogether of the character of a national measure; and at length, some repealed the laws by which they had signified their acquiescence.

For a century, the states had submitted, with murmurs, to the commercial restrictions imposed by the parent state; and now, finding themselves in the unlimited possession of those powers over their own commerce, which they had so long been deprived of, and so earnestly coveted, that selfish principle which, well controlled, is so salutary, and which, unrestricted, is so unjust and tyrannical, guided by inexperience and jealousy, began to show itself in iniquitous laws and impolitic measures, from which grew up a conflict of commercial regulations, destructive to the harmony of the states, and fatal to their commercial interest abroad. This was the immediate cause that led to the forming of a convention.

As early as 1778, the subject had been pressed upon the attention of congress, by a memorial from the state of New Jersey; and in 1781, we find a resolution presented to that body, by one of the most enlightened men of his day (Dr. Witherspoon), affirming, that "it is indispensably necessary, that the United States, in congress assembled, should be vested with a right of superintending the commercial regulations of every state, that none may take place that shall be partial or contrary to the common interests." The resolution of Virginia (January 21st, 1786), appointing her commissioners, to meet commissioners from other states, expresses their purpose to be, "to take into consideration the trade of the United States, to consider how far an uniform system in their commercial regulations may be necessary to their common interests and their permanent harmony." And Mr. Madison's resolution, which led to that measure, is introduced by a preamble entirely explicit to this point: "Whereas, the relative situation of the United States has been found, on trial, to require uniformity in their commercial regulations, as the only effectual policy for obtaining, in the ports of foreign nations, a stipulation of privileges reciprocal to those enjoyed by the subjects of such nations in the ports of the United States, for preventing animosities, which cannot fail to arise among the several states, from the interference of partial and separate regulations," &c., "therefore, resolved," &c.

Purpose of Commerce Clause

The history of the times will, therefore, sustain the opinion, that the grant of power over commerce, if intended to be commensurate with the evils existing, and the purpose of remedying those evils, could be only commensurate with the power of the states over the subject. And this opinion is supported by a very remarkable evidence of the general understanding of the whole American people, when the grant was made. There was not a state in the Union, in which there did not, at that time, exist a variety of commercial regulations; concerning which it is too much to suppose, that the whole ground covered by those regulations was immediately assumed by actual legislation, under the authority of the Union. But where was the existing statute on this subject, that a state attempted to execute? Or by what state was it ever thought necessary to repeal those statutes? By common consent, those laws dropped lifeless from their statute books, for want of the sustaining power that had been relinquished to congress.

And the plain and direct import of the words of the grant, is consistent with this general understanding. The words of the constitution are, "congress shall have power to regulate commerce with foreign nations, and among the several states, and with the Indian tribes." It is not material, in my view of the subject, to inquire whether the article *a* or *the* should be prefixed to the word "power." Either, or neither, will produce the same result: if either, it is clear, that the article *the* would be the proper one, since the next preceding grant of power is certainly exclusive, to wit, "to borrow money on the credit of the United States." But mere verbal criticism I reject. My opinion is founded on the application of the words of the grant to the subject of it.

Nature of Commerce Power

The "power to regulate commerce," here meant to be granted, was that power to regulate commerce which previously existed in the states. But what was that power? The states were, unquestionably, supreme; and each possessed that power over commerce, which is acknowledged to reside in every sovereign state. The definition and limits of that power are to be sought among the features of international law; and, as it was not only admitted, but insisted on by both parties, in argument, that, "unaffected by a state of war, by treaties, or by municipal regulations, all commerce among independent states was legitimate," there is no necessity to appeal to the oracles of the *jus commune* for the correctness of that doctrine. The law of nations, regarding man as a social animal, pronounces all commerce legitimate, in a state of peace, until prohibited by positive law. The power of a sovereign state over commerce, therefore, amounts to nothing more than a power to limit and restrain it at pleasure. And since the power to prescribe the limits to its freedom, necessarily implies the power to determine what shall remain unrestrained, it follows, that the power must be exclusive; it can reside but in one potentate; and hence, the grant of this power carries with it the whole subject, leaving nothing for the state to act upon.

And such has been the practical construction of the act. Were every law on the subject of commerce repealed to-morrow, all commerce would be lawful; and, in practice, merchants never inquire what is permitted, but what is forbidden commerce. Of all the endless variety of branches of foreign commerce, now carried on to every quarter of the world, I know of no one that is permitted by act of congress, any otherwise than by not being forbidden. No statute of the United States, that I know of, was ever passed, to permit a commerce, unless in consequence of its having been prohibited by some previous statute.

I speak not here of the treaty-making power, for that is not exercised under the grant now under consideration. I confine my observation to *laws* properly so called. And even where freedom of commercial intercourse is made a subject of stipulation in a treaty, it is generally with a view to the removal of some previous restriction; or the introduction of some new privilege—most frequently, is identified with the return to a state of peace. But another view of the subject leads directly to the same conclusion. Power to regulate foreign commerce, is given in the same words, and in the same breath, as it were, with that over the commerce of the states and with the Indian tribes. But the power to regulate foreign commerce is necessarily exclusive. The states are unknown to foreign nations; their sovereignty exists only with relation to each other and the general government. Whatever regulations foreign commerce should be subjected to in the ports of the Union, the general government would be held responsible for them; and all other regulations, but those which congress had imposed, would be regarded by foreign nations as trespasses and violations of national faith and comity.

Breadth of Commerce Power

But the language which grants the power as to one description of commerce, grants it as to all; and, in fact, if ever the exercise of a right, or acquiescence in a construction, could be inferred from contemporaneous and continued assent, it is that of the exclusive effect of this grant. A right over the subject has never been pretended to, in any instance, except as incidental to exercise of some other unquestionable power.

The present is an instance of the assertion of that kind, as incidental to a municipal power; that of superintending the internal concerns of a state, and particularly, of extending protection and patronage, in the shape of a monopoly, to genius and enterprise. The grant to Livingston and Fulton interferes with the freedom of intercourse among the states; and on this principle, its constitutionality is contested.

When speaking of the power of congress over navigation, I do not regard it as a power incidental to that of regulating commerce; I consider it as the thing itself; inseparable from it as vital motion is from vital existence. Commerce, in its simplest signification, means an exchange of goods; but in the advancement of society, labor, transportation, intelligence, care, and various mediums of exchange, become commodities, and enter into commerce; the subject, the vehicle, the agent, and their various operations, become the objects of commercial regulation. Ship-building, the carrying trade, and propagation of seamen, are such vital agents of commercial prosperity, that the nation which could not legislate over these subjects, would not possess power to regulate commerce.

That such was the understanding of the framers of the constitution, is conspicuous from provisions contained in that instrument. The first clause of the 9th section, not only considers the right of controlling personal ingress or migration, as implied in the powers previously vested in congress over commerce, but acknowledges it as a legitimate subject of revenue. And although the leading object of this section undoubtedly was, the importation of slaves, yet the words are obviously calculated to comprise persons of all descriptions, and to recognise in congress a power to prohibit, where the states permit, although they cannot permit, when the states prohibit. The treaty-making power undoubtedly goes further. So, the fifth clause of the same section furnishes an exposition of the sense of the convention as to the power of congress over navigation: "nor shall vessels bound to or from one state, be obliged to enter, clear or pay duties in another."

Power Over Navigation

But it is almost laboring to prove a self-evident proposition, since the sense of mankind, the practice of the world, the contemporaneous assumption, and continued exercise of the power, and universal acquiescence, have so clearly established the right of congress over navigation, and the transportation of both men and their goods, as not only incidental to, but actually of the essence of, the power to regulate commerce. As to the transportation of passengers, and passengers in a steam-boat, I consider it as having been solemnly recognised by the state of New York, as a subject both of commercial regulation and of revenue. She has imposed a transit duty upon steam-boat pass:ngers arriving at Albany, and unless this be done in the exercise of her control over personal intercourse, as incident to internal commerce, I know not on what principle the individual has been subjected to this tax. The subsequent imposition upon the steam-boat itself, appears to be but a commutation, and operates as an indirect, instead of a direct, tax upon the same subject. The passenger pays it at last.

It is impossible, with the views which I entertain of the principle on which the commercial privileges of the people of the United States, among themselves, rests, to concur in the view which this court takes of the effect of the coasting license in this cause. I do not regard it as the foundation of the right set up in behalf of the appellant. If there was any one object riding over every other in the adoption of the constitution, it was to keep the commercial intercourse among the states free from all invidious and partial restraints. And I cannot overcome the conviction, that if the licensing act was repealed to-morrow, the rights of the appellant to a reversal of the decision complained of, would be as strong as it is under this license. One-half the doubts in life arise from the defects of language, and if this instrument had been called an exemption, instead of a license, it would have given a better idea of its character. Licensing acts, in fact, in legislation, are universally restraining acts; as, for example, acts licensing gaming-houses, retailers of spiritous liquors, &c. The act, in this instance, is distinctly of that character, and forms part of an extensive system, the object of which is to encourage American shipping, and place them on an equal footing with the shipping of other nations.

Almost every commercial nation reserves to its own subjects a monopoly of its coasting trade; and a countervailing privilege in favor of American shipping is contemplated in the whole legislation of the United States on this subject. It is not to give the vessel an American character, that the license is granted; that effect has been correctly attributed to the act of her enrolment. But it is to confer on her American privileges, as contradistinguished from foreign; and to preserve the government from fraud by foreigners, in surreptitiously intruding themselves into the American commercial marine, as well as frauds upon the revenue, in the trade coastwise, that this whole system is projected. Many duties and formalities are necessarily imposed upon the American foreign commerce, which would be burdensome in the active coasting trade of the states, and can be dispensed with. A higher rate of tonnage also is imposed, and this license entitles the vessels that take it, to those exemptions, but to nothing more. A common register, equally entitles vessels to carry on the coasting trade, although it does not exempt them from the forms of foreign commerce, or from compliance with the 16th and 17th sections of the enrolling act. And even a foreign vessel may be employed coastwise, upon complying with the requisitions of the 24th section. I consider the license, therefore, as nothing more than what it purports to be, according to the 1st section of this act, conferring on the licensed vessel certain privileges in that trade, not conferred on other vessels; but the abstract right of commercial intercourse, stripped of those privileges, is common to all.

Proper State Powers

Yet there is one view, in which the license may be allowed considerable influence in sustaining the decision of this court. It has been contended, that the grants of power to the United States over any subject, do not, necessarily, paralyze the arm of the states, or deprive them of the capacity to act on the same subject. That this can be the effect only of prohibitory provisions in their own constitutions, or in that of the general government. The *vis vitæ* of power is still existing in the states, if not extinguished by the constitution of the United States. That, although, as to all those grants of power which may be called aboriginal, with relation to the government, brought into existence by the constitution, they, of course, are out of the reach of state power; yet, as to all concessions of powers which previously existed in the states, it was otherwise. The practice of our government certainly has been, on many subjects, to occupy so much only of the field open to them, as they think the public interests require. Witness the jurisdiction of the circuit courts, limited both as to cases and as to amount; and various other instances that might be cited. But the license furnishes a full answer to this objection; for although one grant of power over commerce, should not be deemed a total relinquishment of power over the subject, but amounting only to a power to assume, still the power of the states must be at an end, so far as the United States have, by their legislative act, taken the subject under their immediate superintendence. So far as relates to the commerce coastwise, the act under which this license is granted, contains a full expression of congress on this subject. Vessels, from five tons upwards, carrying on the coasting trade, are made the subject of regulation by that act. And this license proves, that this vessel has complied with that act, and been regularly ingrafted into one class of the commercial marine of the country.

It remains, to consider the objections to this opinion, as presented by the counsel for the appellee. On those which had relation to the particular character of this boat, whether as a steam-boat or a ferry-boat, I have only to remark, that in both those characters, she is expressly recognised as an object of the provisions which relate to licenses. The 12th section of the act of 1793, has these words, "that when the master of any ship or vessel, ferry-boats excepted, shall be changed," &c. And the act which exempts licensed steam-boats from the provisions against alien interests, shows such boats to be both objects of the licensing act, and objects of that act, when employed exclusively within our bays and rivers.

Limits to State Powers

But the principal objections to these opinions arise, 1st. From the unavoidable action of some of the municipal powers of the states, upon commercial subjects. 2d. From passages in the constitution, which are supposed to imply a concurrent power in the states in regulating commerce.

It is no objection to the existence of distinct, substantive powers, that, in their application, they bear upon the same subject. The same bale of goods, the same cask of provisions, or the same ship, that may be the subject of commercial regulation, may also be the vehicle of disease. And the health laws that require them to be stopped and ventilated, are no more intended as regulations on commerce, than the laws which permit their importation, are intended to innoculate the community with disease. Their different purposes mark the distinction between the powers brought into action; and while frankly exercised, they can produce no serious collision. As to laws affecting ferries, turnpike-roads, and other subjects of the same class, so far from meriting the epithet of commercial regulations, they are, in fact, commercial facilities, for which, by the consent of mankind, a compensation is paid, upon the same principle that the whole commercial world submit to pay light-money to the Danes.

Inspection laws are of a more equivocal nature, and it is obvious, that the constitution has viewed that subject with much solicitude. But so far from sustaining an inference in favor of the power of the states over commerce, I cannot but think, that the guarded provisions of the 10th section, on this subject, furnish a strong argument against that inference. It was obvious, that inspection laws must combine municipal with commercial regulations; and while the power over the subject is yielded to the states, for obvious reasons, an absolute control is given over state legislation on the subject, so far as that legislation may be exercised, so as to affect the commerce of the country. The inferences to be correctly drawn from this whole article, appear to me to be altogether in favor of the exclusive grant to congress of power over commerce, and the reverse of that which the appellee contends for.

This section contains the positive restrictions imposed by the constitution upon state power. The first clause of it, specifies those powers which the states are precluded from exercising, even though the congress were to permit them. The second, those which the states may exercise with the consent of congress. And here, the sedulous attention to the subject of state exclusion from commercial power, is strongly marked. Not satisfied with the express grant to the United States of the power over commerce, this clause negatives the exercise of that power to the states, as to the only two objects which would ever tempt them to assume the exercise of that power, to wit, the collection of a revenue from imposts and duties on imports and exports; or from a tonnage-duty. As to imposts on imports or exports, such a revenue might have been aimed at directly, by express legislation, or indirectly, in the form of inspection laws; and it became necessary to guard against both. Hence, first, the consent of congress to such imposts or duties, is made necessary; and as to inspection laws, it is limited to the minimum of expenses. Then, the money so raised shall be paid into the treasury of the United States, or may be sued for, since it is declared to be for their use.

And lastly, all such laws may be modified, or repealed, by an act of congress. It is impossible for a right to be more guarded. As to a tonnage-duty, that could be recovered in but one way; and a sum so raised, being obviously necessary for the execution of health-laws, and other unavoidable port expenses, it was intended that it should go into the state treasuries; and nothing more was required, therefore, than the consent of congress. But this whole clause, as to these two subjects, appears to have been introduced *ex abundanti cautelâ*, to remove every temptation to an attempt to interfere with the powers of congress over commerce, and to show how far congress might consent to permit the states to exercise that power. Beyond those limits, even by the consent of congress, they could not exercise it. And thus, we have the whole effect of the clause. The inference which counsel would deduce from it, is neither necessary nor consistent with the general purpose of the clause.

Related Powers

But instances have been insisted on, with much confidence, in argument, in which, by municipal laws, particular regulations respecting their cargoes have been imposed upon shipping in the ports of the United States; and one, in which forfeiture was made the penalty of disobedience. Until such laws have been tested by exceptions to their constitutionality, the argument certainly wants much of the force attributed to it; but admitting their constitutionality, they present only the familiar case of punishment inflicted by both governments upon the same individual. He who robs the mail, may also steal the horse that carries it, and would, unquestionably, be subject to punishment, at the same time, under the laws of the state in which the crime is committed, and under those of the United States. And these punishments may interfere, and one render it impossible to inflict the other, and yet the two governments would be acting under powers that have no claim to identity.

It would be in vain to deny the possibility of a clashing and collision between the measures of the two governments. The line cannot be drawn with sufficient distinctness between the municipal powers of the one, and the commercial powers of the other. In some points, they meet and blend, so as scarcely to admit of separation. Hitherto, the only remedy has been applied which the case admits of; that of a frank and candid co-operation for the general good. Witness the laws of congress requiring its officers to respect the inspection laws of the states, and to aid in enforcing their health laws; that which surrenders to the states the superintendence of pilotage, and the many laws passed to permit a tonnage-duty to be levied for the use of their ports. Other instances could be cited, abundantly to prove that collision must be sought to be produced; and when it does arise, the question must be decided, how far the powers of congress are adequate to put it down. Wherever the powers of the respective governments are frankly exercised, with a distinct view to the ends of such powers, they may act upon the same object, or use the same means, and yet the powers be kept perfectly distinct. A resort to the same means, therefore, is no argument to prove the identity of their respective powers.

I have not touched upon the right of the states to grant patents for inventions or improvements, generally, because it does not necessarily arise in this cause. It is enough for all the purposes of this decision, if they cannot exercise it so as to restrain a free intercourse among the states.

Order of Court

DECREE.—This cause came to be heard, on the transcript of the record of the court for the trial of impeachments and correction of errors of the state of

New York, and was argued by counsel: On consideration whereof, this court is of opinion, that the several licenses to the steam-boats, the Stoudinger and the Bellona, to carry on the coasting trade, which are set up by the appellant, Thomas Gibbons, in his answer to the bill of the respondent, Aaron Ogden, filed in the court of chancery for the state of New York, which were granted under an act of congress, passed in pursuance of the constitution of the United States, gave full authority to those vessels to navigate the waters of the United States, by steam or otherwise, for the purpose of carrying on the coasting trade, any law of the state of New York to the contrary notwithstanding; and that so much of the several laws of the state of New York, as prohibits vessels, licensed according to the laws of the United States, from navigating the waters of the state of New York, by means of fire or steam, is repugnant to the said constitution, and void.

This court is, therefore, of opinion, that the decree of the court of New York for the trial of impeachments and the correction of errors, affirming the decree of the chancellor of that state, which perpetually enjoins the said Thomas Gibbons, the appellant, from navigating the waters of the state of New York with the steam-boats, the Stoudinger and the Bellona, by steam or fire, is erroneous, and ought to be reversed, and the same is hereby reversed and annulled: And this court doth further direct, order and decree, that the bill of the said Aaron Ogden be dismissed, and the same is hereby dismissed accordingly.

Appendix

THE DOCTRINE OF JUDICIAL REVIEW

MR. MARSHALL, MR. JEFFERSON AND MR. MARBURY *

———

WARREN E. BURGER
Chief Justice of the United States

Lord Bryce once observed that

> No feature of the government of the United States has awakened so much curiosity in the European mind, caused so much discussion, received so much admiration, and been more frequently misunderstood, than the duties assigned to the Supreme Court and the functions which it discharges in guarding the Ark of the Constitution.[1]

I should add that in some quarters, the Supreme Court's guardianship of that Ark probably has received more guarded praise than in distant places where its impact is purely theoretical.

Lord Bryce, of course, had reference to the doctrine of judicial review, sometimes described as the doctrine of judicial supremacy, in the interpretation of constitutional terms and principles. The writings of Jeremy Bentham reveal little as to his views on this question other than fleeting and uncomplimentary references to the notion that mere judges should be able to declare null and void the acts of a legislative body,[2] and I gather that this view continues to have considerable acceptance in England.

---

* The annual Bentham Club Lecture was delivered at the University of London and originally published in the university's annual collection, *Current Legal Problems 1972* (London, 1972). This selection from the Chief Justice's lecture is reprinted by permission of the copyright owners.

[1] James Bryce, *The American Commonwealth*, Vol. I (New York, 1931), p. 242.

[2] "By this unincompetence, by this negation of all limits, this also is to be understood, namely, that let the legislature do what it will, nothing that it does is to be regarded as null and void: in other words, it belongs not to any judge so to pronounce concerning it: for, to give such powers to any judge would be to give to the judge . . . a power superior to that of the legislature itself." *9 The Works of Jeremy Bentham*, "The Constitutional Code," p. 121 (Bowring ed., 1843).

MARBURY v. MADISON: ACT I, THE SETTING

It is helpful to an understanding of this subject to examine it in the setting in which *Marbury* v. *Madison* was decided in 1803 with all its momentous consequences for our country and to suggest to you that this great case had its antecedents in our colonial experience, and its taproots in the declarations of fundamental rights of Englishmen back to Magna Carta.

Very early in the history of our country the colonial experience of living under a parliamentary system with no check on the legislative or executive branch, except that of popular will in a limited way, led our Founding Fathers to feel strongly the need for limitations on all branches of government. The intellectual spadework for the system ultimately adopted for our federal government had been done, of course, by such seventeenth- and eighteenth-century political theorists as Hobbes and Locke.[3] As we know, the great rationalist Montesquieu contributed the notion of a separation of powers within the government itself, in order that each branch might act as a sort of brake upon the others.[4] As the system works today, one of the checks exercised by the Supreme Court involves measuring executive or legislative action against the Constitution whenever a challenge to such action is first properly brought within the framework of a "case" or "controversy,"[5] and then properly brought within the "appellate jurisdiction"[6] of the Supreme Court.

It has been suggested from time to time that the subject of judicial review of Congressional Acts was not in the minds of the delegates to the Constitutional Convention in 1787. However, such an obviously important question could not have entirely eluded their attention. Some of the delegates, without doubt, looked to an independent judiciary with fixed tenure as a means of protecting the states against the powers of the new national government, whose scope was as yet unseen and unknown and therefore feared. Others, particularly the propertied classes, probably regarded a Supreme Court and an independent Federal Judiciary as a source of protection against the egalitarian popular government advocated by Jefferson. They could not fail to be aware that the exercise of such powers by the judiciary must in some way involve limitations on legislative and executive action.

Some residual controversy remains as to the exercise of judicial review today, but it is largely as to scope, not basic power. It is now accepted that the original assertion of the power was not judicial usurpation as Jefferson considered it.[7] Needless to say, the major challenges to the power have occurred during those periods when, for whatever reason, the Supreme Court

---

[3] Thomas Jefferson, in writing the Declaration of Independence, relied heavily upon Locke's *Second Treatise on Government*, almost to the point of plagiarism.

[4] Montesquieu's *L'Esprit des Lois* contains the clearest expression of the principle.

[5] "The judicial Power shall extend to . . . Cases . . . [and] Controversies. . . ." U.S. Const. Art. III, § 2, cl. 1.

[6] "[T]he supreme Court shall have appellate Jurisdiction both as to Law and Fact, with such Exceptions, and under such Regulations as the Congress shall make." U.S. Const. Art. III, § 2, cl. 2.

[7] Although most scholars agree that Article III (granting the judicial power and extending it to "Cases . . . arising under this Constitution, [and] the Laws of the

has been under attack for its role in contemporary affairs. As an example, many polemics as well as some of the most thoughtful and scholarly challenges were written during the 1930s when, to many of its critics, the Supreme Court represented the dead hand of the past impeding legitimate experimentation and innovation in trying to cope with a crisis. At present, it is fair to say that, absent some unforeseeable convulsion of great magnitude, the doctrine of judicial review, as announced by Marshall in 1803 in *Marbury* v. *Madison*,[8] is likely to remain part of the American system.

It is often assumed that the doctrine was the invention of Chief Justice John Marshall in that most famous of all his opinions. It is true, of course, that Chief Justice Marshall first announced this keystone doctrine of our constitutional law in the *Marbury* case; and it is also true that our written Constitution makes no reference to the theory in defining judicial power.[9] But Marshall was not and never claimed to be the originator of the doctrine since he was well aware of a growing acceptance of the idea that constitutional adjudication was inherent in the very nature of a written constitution. This is not to disparage Marshall, for he was the one who recognized the need to enunciate the doctrine as part of Federal jurisprudence and seized—some might say forced—the first opportunity to assert the power of the Court to measure an act of Congress by the yardstick of the Constitution.

But this takes me ahead of my story, and I must turn back to 1776, the very year of the Declaration of Independence. In that year the people of the town of Concord, Massachusetts, held a Town Meeting and adopted a resolution that "a Constitution alterable by the Supreme Legislative is no security at all to the subject, against encroachment of the Governing Part on any or on all their rights and privileges." Earlier, when the Colony of Massachusetts Bay was under British Colonial rule, the sturdy farm people of Berkshire County refused to let the Colonial courts sit from 1775 to 1780 until the people of Massachusetts adopted a Constitution with a Bill of Rights enforceable by judges.

United States . . .") coupled with the Supremacy Clause in Article VI, cl. 2, necessarily includes the power to disregard state or federal statutes found to be unconstitutional, several major efforts to lay a scholarly basis for the contrary conclusion have been made. See, *e.g.* Boudin, *Government by Judiciary* (1932), and Crosskey, *Politics and the Constitution in the History of the United States* (1953). However, the understanding of the Constitutional Convention seems to have been quite clearly in favour of such a power, see *e.g.* Farrand, *The Framing of the Constitution* (1913) and C. Warren, *The Making of the Constitution* (1937 ed.). See generally Hart and Wechsler, *The Federal Courts and the Federal System*, 7–37.

[8] 1 Cranch 137 (1803).

[9] The reasons for not writing it into the Constitution are speculative at best. Perhaps it would have been too controversial for some; it could have delayed the final draft; others may have thought it part of the warp and woof of a system of delegated and divided power. In any event, since our Constitution is a document to divide and assign powers and governing functions, the choice of the "one supreme Court" to construe and enforce "the supreme Law of the Land" seems simple, and the grant of power a necessary corollary of that choice. Thus the omission of any reference to the theory may have been due to an unwillingness to elucidate the obvious.

Notice the premise in these events, twenty-five years before *Marbury*, that a written constitution would govern the acts of a legislature and protect fundamental liberties. And notice also the tacit assumption that the judicial branch was the appropriate vehicle for providing that protection.

In 1793, ten years before Marshall's decision in *Marbury* v. *Madison*, Spencer Roane, a great judge of the Virginia Court and an intimate of Thomas Jefferson, said, in the case of *Kamper* v. *Hawkins*,

If the legislature may infringe this Constitution [of Virginia], it is no longer fixed; . . . and the liberties of the people are wholly at the mercy of the legislature.[10]

To be sure, Judge Roane was speaking to the power of the state courts to strike down legislative acts contrary to the Virginia Constitution, but conceptually the doctrine is indistinguishable from *Marbury*. In 1793 the Commonwealth of Virginia, of course, regarded itself as a sovereign at least equal to the new National Government. Some lawyers, including very good ones of that day, would later hesitate and ponder before taking the final step to make the doctrine equally applicable to a Federal Constitution and a Federal Legislature, but very quickly their strong sense of the rights of the states, that were widely viewed as sovereign in the eighteenth and early nineteenth centuries, would impel them to accept such a restraint on the federal legislative body. Their hesitation was no more than that of thoughtful men chary of granting open-ended power to anyone.

Although I attributed a certain uniqueness to the American doctrine of judicial review as formally articulated in *Marbury* v. *Madison*, it is quite clear that this, like almost all else in our law, has its roots in English legal thought.

Magna Carta, of course, was primarily intended by the Barons as a limitation on King John; but it has come to stand for a limitation on princes and parliaments alike. In one of the very early opinions of the Supreme Court of the United States,[11] one of many containing references to Magna Carta, it was said:

. . . after volumes spoken and written [about the guarantees of Magna Carta], the good sense of mankind has at length settled down to this: *that they were intended to secure the individual from the arbitrary exercise of the powers of government.* . . . (Emphasis supplied.)

[10] *Kamper* v. *Hawkins*, 1 Virginia Cases 20, 38 (1793). This is by no means the only state case in which state legislative acts were declared unconstitutional by state courts or in which the principle of judicial review was announced. In addition to Virginia, a number of states had each either announced the principle or strongly hinted at it. Among them were Maryland (*Whittington* v. *Polk*, 1 Harris & Johnson 236, 241 (1802)), South Carolina (*Lindsay* v. *Comm'rs.*, 2 Bay 38, 61–62 (1796); also *Bowman* v. *Middleton*, 1 Bay 252, 254 (1792), a conspicuous case in which the court declared an act void because it was against "common right" and "magna charta"), North Carolina (*State* v. ——, 1 Haywood 28, 29, 40 (1794), Kentucky (*Stidger* v. *Rogers*, 2 Kentucky 52 (1801)), New Jersey (*State* v. *Parkhurst*, 4 Halstead 427 (1802)), and Pennsylvania (*Austin* v. *Univ. of Pennsylvania*, 1 Yeates 260 (1793)). For further detail and a more complete list of early State cases, see McLaughlin, *A Constitutional History of the United States*, 312, n. 34.

[11] *Bank of Columbia* v. *Okely*, 4 Wheat. 235, 244 (1819).

Another thread of influence originates with the struggle between Lord Coke and the Stuart kings. Coke's writings and Reports were well known to the American colonists and, even though the dictum in *Dr. Bonham's Case* has never been very closely followed in England, it has been seminal in our law. In that case Coke asserted that:

. . . in many cases, the common law will controul Acts of Parliament, and sometimes adjudge them to be utterly void: for when an Act of Parliament is against common right and reason, or repugnant, or impossible to be performed, the common law will controul it, and adjudge such Act to be void.[12]

And even that super authoritarian, Cromwell, said, 150 years before *Marbury* v. *Madison*:

In every government, there must be something fundamental, somewhat like a Magna Carta which would be unalterable. . . .[13]

I doubt that the stern Mr. Cromwell intended to propound the idea that a judicial body like our Supreme Court, independent of both the executive and legislative branches, should be empowered to act as a sort of umpire, but obviously he was concerned about unbridled legislative power.

A very important point of departure from England's jurisprudence was the American insistence on written guarantees that would be definite and would narrow the area for interpretation. Each of the thirteen original states of the Union had a written constitution, giving tangible expression to what the farmers of Concord and Berkshire, Massachusetts, demanded as early as 1775. Having said that the idea of written guarantees in a constitution departed in a sense from England's precedents, I am bound to note that even this idea traces directly back to Magna Carta and to the written charters of the colonies.

An important function of a constitution is its organic allocation of powers of government and in this area alone the authority must reside somewhere for a binding pronouncement that, for example, treaty-making power is shared by the Executive and the Senate, that the veto power is exclusively for the Executive, the overriding power exclusively in the Congress. More than a decade before *Marbury*, Justices of the Supreme Court sitting on circuit held that state laws contrary to the Federal Constitution were invalid and this was confirmed in *Van Horne Lessee* v. *Dorrance*.[14] In his opinion in that case Justice Paterson, sitting on circuit, asserted flatly:

I take it to be a clear position; that if a legislative act oppugns a constitutional principle, the former must give way, and . . . it will be the duty of the Court to adhere to the Constitution, and to declare the act null and void.[15]

[12] (1610) 8 Co. 113b, 118a, 77 E.R. 646, 652. For a more complete discussion, see Haines, *The American Doctrine of Judicial Supremacy*, 29–43 (1959).

[13] Oliver Cromwell, *Letters and Speeches* (Carlyle), Part 7, Speech 3 (September 12, 1654).

[14] 2 Dallas 304 (1795). S. 25 of the Judiciary Act of 1789 in terms granted federal appellate jurisdiction to review judgments of state courts concerning the validity of a treaty or statute of the United States under the Federal Constitution. S. 1, Statutes at Large 85.

[15] *Ibid.* at 309.

We see, therefore, that long before *Marbury* American political leaders, including many of the most distinguished lawyers and judges in the Colonies and in the original thirteen states, accepted it as fundamental that a written Constitution was a restraint on every part of the federal government. It does not disparage John Marshall's greatness as a judge or a statesman to say that when he wrote the opinion in *Marbury* he was doing little more than declaring what was widely accepted by so many of the best legal minds of his day —at least when they could divorce politics from reason! If it had not come in *Marbury*, it would have come later but John Marshall was not a man to wait for perfect opportunities if a plausible one offered itself. It had to be said, and *Marbury* was the fortuitous circumstance that made it possible to establish this great principle early in our history.

The setting in which this great case developed is important. The incumbent President Adams was defeated by Thomas Jefferson in the election of November 1800. But between the time of the election and the following March when Jefferson actually took office, Adams remained in control of the government and in control of what we call a "lame duck" Congress.[16] One of the first things he did after his defeat was to encourage the ailing Chief Justice Ellsworth to resign. The Federalist Adams was, of course, deeply concerned about the future of the country, and undoubtedly about the future of the Supreme Court in the hands of Jefferson and his Republicans. Parenthetically, I should point out that political parties change their names in our country as well as in yours, for Jefferson's Republican Party became the present Democratic Party.

An interesting footnote to history, often overlooked in the appropriate recognition of John Marshall and the wisdom of John Adams in appointing him, emerges from the circumstance that Marshall was not Adams' first choice for Chief Justice after Ellsworth resigned. John Jay, who had served as the first Chief Justice of the United States by appointment of George Washington, resigned as Chief Justice in 1795 to become Governor of New York State. Adams wrote to Jay urging him to return to his old position as Chief Justice but he declined. Interestingly, Jay refused because, as he put it, "I left the [Supreme] Bench perfectly convinced that under a system so defective, it would not obtain the energy, weight and dignity which are essential to its affording due support to the National Government, nor acquire the public confidence and respect which, as the last resort of the justice of the nation, it should possess." [17] His decision not to return to the court in that frame of mind, thus opening the way for Marshall, was one of the most fortuitous events in the two centuries of our history.

---

[16] In Marshall's time, the old Congress met in December after the November elections, and the newly elected Members did not take their seats until the following March. Since some of the old Members had been voted out of office, the December to March came to be called a "lame duck Congress." The problem has been solved by the 20th Amendment which shortens the delay between the time a Member is elected and the time he takes his seat.

[17] C. Warren, 1 *The Supreme Court in United States History* 173.

Whatever Jay may have thought of the office, you may be sure that Jefferson was anything but overjoyed at the eleventh hour appointment of John Marshall, who was his distant kinsman but not a friend.

Jefferson's deep and bitter hostility toward Marshall is one of the unplumbed mysteries of this complex man. Some historians explain it in terms of his opposition to Marshall's judicial philosophy, but other explanations are also suggested.[18] Jefferson's choice for Chief Justice, had Marshall not been appointed, was Spencer Roane, an able Virginia judge. Yet Judge Roane, described by Professor Charles Warren [19] as "an ardent strict constructionist of the Constitution," showed his basic agreement with Marshall in an opinion for the Virginia court in 1793, stating:

> It is the province of the judiciary to expound the laws. . . . It may say too, that an act of assembly has not changed the Constitution [of Virginia], though its words are expressly to that effect. . . . [I]t is conceived, for the reasons above mentioned, that the legislature have not power to change the fundamental laws. . . . [W]ould you have them [judges] to shut their eyes against that law which is of the highest authority of any . . . ? [20]

From the day Jefferson took office as President on March 4, 1801, those who were even slightly aware of his hostility toward the Supreme Court, the Federal Judicial Branch as a whole, and John Marshall in particular, could sense that these events foreshadowed a collision of two strong men who had quite different views as to how the United States could best fulfil its destiny.

Underlying the impending conflict was a very fundamental difference between the Federalist belief that a strong national government was the key to the future of the new nation and the opposing belief of the Jeffersonian radical Republicans who feared all centralised power and wanted to keep the states the strong and indeed the dominant political power. When he took office Jefferson still looked with considerable favour on the French Revolution, notwithstanding its later excesses and horrors. Jefferson had been largely aloof from the hardships of our war of rebellion; he lacked the firsthand experience that Washington, Hamilton, and even Marshall, as a junior officer, shared in a war in which thirteen quarrelsome and dis-united colony-states, functioning through an impotent confederation and a parochial Congress, fumbled and almost failed in raising, equipping and maintaining armies. Jefferson's lifelong passion for minimal government had never been subjected to the acid test of trying to conduct a war with a truly "minimal" government.

Jefferson's remarkable political instincts enabled him to see, far ahead of his contemporaries, that the latent power of the National Judiciary, and especially the Supreme Court, could be a major obstacle to his dream of a

[18] S. E. Morison, *The Oxford History of the American People*, at p. 362, states: "Toward Marshall his kinsman Jefferson entertained an implacable hatred because he [Marshall] had shown him up and broken the sentimental . . . bubble in the XYZ affair."

[19] C. Warren, *Congress, The Constitution and the Supreme Court* (1935 ed.), 58–59.

[20] *Kamper* v. *Hawkins*, 1 Virginia Cases 20, 38 (1793), *supra*.

simple, loose-jointed, national confederation, linking but not binding the several states.[21] But Jefferson was at heart a majoritarian. What the People wanted, the People would have.

Whatever his earlier beliefs, by 1800 Jefferson's distrust of an opposition to the federal judiciary had hardened. From 1800 onward, Jefferson did not waver in this attitude, and in 1820 we find him declaring that:

> to consider the judges as the ultimate arbiters of all constitutional questions . . . would place us under the despotism of an oligarchy.[22]

Similarly, in a letter to a friend dated August 18, 1821, Jefferson wrote— some would say, prophetically—

> Is has long . . . been my opinion, and I have never shrunk from its expression . . . that the germ of dissolution of our federal government is in the Constitution of the federal judiciary; an irresponsible body (for impeachment is scarcely a scare-crow), working like gravity by night and by day, gaining a little today and a little tomorrow, and advancing its noiseless step like a thief, over the field of jurisdiction, until all shall be usurped from the States, and the government of all be consolidated into one. To this I am opposed; because when all government, domestic and foreign, in little as in great things, shall be drawn to Washington as the centre of all power, it will render powerless the checks provided of one government on another, and will become as venal and oppressive as the government from which we separated.[23]

From the time he was President to the end of his life, Jefferson did not alter his hostility either to strong central government or to the federal judiciary, and the Supreme Court, in particular, was the target of repeated bitter comments. Of course, in the United States we judges have had to learn to accept philosophically all manner of "slings and arrows," and by modern standards Jefferson's characterisation of Federal judges as "thieves" is a fairly moderate comment. If he ever recognised that the unsound pronouncements of the Supreme Court could be "reversed" through the constitutional amending process by the People he trusted so much, I have not discovered evidence of it. However, Jefferson would also well understand difficulties of the amending process.

MARBURY v. MADISON: THE SECOND ACT

So much for the setting. We now come to the final act.

As sometimes is true of great events in history, *Marbury* v. *Madison* was an accident. But it was an accident which the solid, steady and resourceful Marshall exploited to the fullest. The accident or fortuitous combination was

---

[21] Somewhere along the line in the development of his political philosophy, Jefferson had lost trust in the belief, expressed in a letter to a friend in 1798, that "the laws of the land, administered by upright judges, would protect you from any exercise of power unauthorized by the Constitution of the United States." Jefferson to Rowan, 9/26/1798: Ford ed., *Writings*, VIII, 448.

[22] Jefferson to Jarvis, 9/28/1820: Ford ed., *Writings*, XII, 162.

[23] H. A. Washington Ed., *The Writings of Thomas Jefferson*, VII, 216.

the coincidence of a need, an opportunity, and a man—a man with the fore-sight, the wit and the courage to make the most of his chance.

Adams, as I have noted, was a "lame duck" President after November 1800, with a "lame duck" Congress on hand for five months after the election. Naturally he made as many appointments as possible. Persuading Ellsworth to resign to make way for Marshall as Chief Justice was one step. The appointment of a goodly number of Federal judges was another. But the far lesser post of Justice of the Peace was the grist of Marbury's case. The story is too well known to be chronicled in detail. Marbury was one of those whose commission as a Justice of the Peace was signed by President Adams and sealed by Marshall (who was still acting as President Adams' Secretary of State even after being appointed Chief Justice and confirmed by the Senate). But Marbury's commission was not delivered. Legend, supported by letters, tells us this was because of Marshall's careless error as he hastened to complete his duties as Secretary of State and don his robe as Chief Justice before March 4, 1801.

The minor office of Justice of the Peace was hardly worth a law-suit, but Marbury was a spunky fellow and he sought a direct mandamus in the Supreme Court against Madison, Jefferson's Secretary of State, to compel what Marbury rightly claimed was the purely ministerial act of delivering the commissions that Madison's predecessor Marshall, as Secretary of State, had forgotten to mail out. In the Supreme Court it can be assumed that the first reaction was, "of course," since the Judiciary Act provided that precise remedy—mandamus by an original action in the Supreme Court.

Marshall saw it otherwise. If mandamus issued and Jefferson's Administration ignored it—as was likely—the first confrontation between court and Executive would be lost—and all of it over a Justice of the Peace commission! The court could stand hard blows, but not ridicule, and the ale houses would rock with hilarious laughter. If the court simply refused to issue mandamus in the face of the very explicit authority of the Federalist-drafted Judiciary Act of 1789, this, too, would be an ignominious retreat by the court —a court fearing to act because it would not be obeyed.

But if, as no one had even remotely suspected up to that time, Congress could not vest original jurisdiction in the Supreme Court in any cases except those specifically recited in Article III, then the court could say, "Yes, Marbury was duly confirmed"; and "Yes, the Commission was duly signed and sealed"; and "Yes, this court may examine into the manner in which the Executive conducts its own affairs"; and "Yes, delivery is a purely ministerial act," and "Yes, it is shameful that the new administration will not perform the simple, ministerial act of delivery"; but the court could also say, "However, this court has no power under the Constitution to entertain any original action except those specified in Article III, and hence section 13 of the Judiciary Act of 1789 [24] purporting to give the Supreme Court such authority

[24] s. 13 of the First Judiciary Act provided: "The Supreme Court . . . shall have power to issue writs of . . . mandamus . . . to any courts appointed, or persons holding office . . . of the United States." 1 Stat. 81.

is invalid and, sadly, this action to compel the Executive to do its duty cannot be entertained here as an original action."

And this is precisely what Marshall persuaded the court to do in a
straight-faced, long-winded opinion that exhaustively, and exhaustingly, ex-
plored every possible alternative. After doing so, he sadly concluded that the
Federalist Congress of 1789 had passed, and the Federalist President, George
Washington, had signed, an Act—drafted by no less than Ellsworth, Marshall's
distinguished predecessor—that everyone had thought excellent for thirteen
years, but section 13 of which was void because it conflicted with Article
III of the Constitution.

Jefferson's Secretary of State, Madison, had won the battle; Marbury, the
Federalist, had lost, and the real war, the great war over the supremacy of
the Supreme Court in constitutional adjudication, had been won by Marshall
—and by the United States.

Because it was a small case—almost a joke—few people cared. But Jefferson the lawyer and politician saw that he had been outmanoeuvred by the
holding of the court near the time of an election—1803—when it would be
very difficult to make an issue of a case decided in his favour and against
Marbury, his political opponent. Not even a Pyrrhic Victory! Small wonder
he likened the federal judiciary to thieves in the night!

For salt and vinegar in Jefferson's wounds, in the same Term the Supreme
Court announced in solemn tones with respect to another section of the same
Judiciary Act of 1789 (as to which its section 13 had now been declared
void) that:

practice and acquiescence under it [the Act of 1789] for a period of several
years [thirteen years!], commencing with the organization of the judicial system . . .
has . . . fixed the construction . . . [and] is too strong . . . to be shaken . . . is at
rest, and ought not now to be disturbed.

Marshall is spared the charge of judicial hypocrisy for, having sat as the trial
judge on circuit, he took no part in the case in which this was said, *Stuart* v.
Laird.[25]

Not for fifty-four years after *Marbury* did the court hold another Act of
Congress unconstitutional.[26] In another irony of history, the court decided in
1857 that Congress had no power to ban slavery in the Louisiana Territory
under an 1820 Act known as the Missouri Compromise. This case was the
infamous *Dred Scott* decision [27] that added fuel to the fires leading to our
Civil War.

Another interesting footnote to Mr. Marbury's case is that after 10,000
words, more or less, Marshall held that the court had no jurisdiction of the
case since the statute purporting to create jurisdiction was void. So we have,

[25] 1 Cranch 299, 309 (1803).
[26] However, in *Martin* v. *Hunter's Lessee*, 1 Wheaton 304 (1816), Justice Story
for the Court firmly asserted the power of the Supreme Court to invalidate a state
statute contrary to the Federal Constitution.
[27] *Scott* v. *Sandford*, 19 Howard 393 (1857).

perhaps, the most important single opinion of the court in nearly 200 years pronounced in the context of a holding that the court had no jurisdiction at all! From this, of course, we authoritatively conclude that the court always has jurisdiction to decide its own jurisdiction!

As with so many great conceptions, the idea of judicial review of legislation now seems simple and inevitable in the perspective of history. People, not governments, delegated certain powers to the national government and placed limits on those powers by specific and general reservations. The people having flatly stated certain guarantees relating to religious freedom, to speech, to searches, seizures and arrests, would it be reasonable to think that legislative action could alter those rights? The very explicit procedures for constitutional amendments, standing alone, negate the idea that a written constitution could be altered by legislative or executive action. The language of Article III vesting judicial power "in one Supreme Court" for "all Cases, in Law and Equity, arising under this Constitution, the Laws of the United States, and Treaties . . ." would be sterile indeed if the Supreme Court would not exercise that judicial power by deciding conflicts between the Constitution, federal laws and treaties on the one hand, and Acts of Congress, the Executive or States on the other.

EPILOGUE

To speak of the doctrine of judicial review and of *Marbury*, and fail to add at least a few more words on Marshall would be to serve a great claret without letting it breathe and in a thick porcelain mug.

When one speaks of the "Great Chief Justice" on our side of the Atlantic, every literate person knows the reference is to John Marshall. It does not disparage his unique qualities but rather emphasises his unparalleled gifts to note that he had no formal education and read law at William and Mary College for a mere few weeks before he was admitted to practice. This becomes more important when we remember that his contemporaries included Alexander Hamilton, Thomas Jefferson, James Madison and Aaron Burr who were all highly educated in the classics, all deeply read and trained in law.

There are several other factors, all relating to the political climate of the day, that may help to understand Marshall and his place in history. Going back to the appointment of the first court in 1790, we must recall that there were no political parties and it was then devoutly hoped that none would evolve. But men who risk all to conduct a revolution must be passionate believers, and our Founding Fathers were just that.

It is not at all surprising, therefore, that when the newly-created Supreme Judicial Court of the United States [28] met for the first time on February 1, 1790, it was composed of men who tended to reflect the views of George Washington and his administration. In short, they were all federalists —the word was not uniformly capitalised then—and they were firm believers in the need for a strong federal or national government as a condition of sur-

---

[28] The Journal of the Court used this title for the Court until the February 1791 Session.

vival. The Federalists remained in power until Jefferson defeated them in 1800—over twelve years. Quite naturally, then, when Marshall came to the Supreme Court every one of its members shared his political and judicial philosophy.

Since the court had delivered opinions in only a handful of cases when John Marshall was appointed, there could hardly be a more propitious moment for a judge of great intellectual capacity and remarkable qualities of statesmanship to ascend the highest court in the country. He had every advantage in his favour: he was very literally writing on a clean slate, with the support of five colleagues who shared his basic philosophy, and he had the wit and courage to make the most of his opportunity. As a soldier in the Continental Army, he had learned the need for a unified and strong national government to ensure the cohesiveness essential to survival of a new nation composed of three million highly individualistic and scattered people. As a political leader of Virginia, a member of its legislature, a member of the national Congress and a Secretary of State, he understood government. Moreover, as one of the leaders in the Virginia struggle to secure adoption of the new Constitution over the vigorous opposition of men of such stature as Thomas Jefferson and Patrick Henry, he knew how fragile were the ties that held the former colonies together.

Thus to the everlasting benefit of a country begotten in revolution and weaned in confusion and conflict, the United States of America was to be tutored in constitutional law for thirty-four formative years by a man who knew precisely what was needed to make a strong nation.

Small wonder, then, that John Adams in 1823, looking back, saw his appointment of Marshall to the court as one of his greatest contributions to his country. How indeed could there have been a greater one?

Notes

PART ONE

I. John Marshall, His Court and His Times

1. *Debates and Other Proceedings of the Convention of Virginia . . . the 2d of June, 1788* (Petersburg, Va. 1788), II, 28 ff.; reprinted in Herbert A. Johnson, Charles L. Cullen, and Nancy G. Harris, eds., *The Papers of John Marshall* (Chapel Hill: University of North Carolina Press, 1974), I, 256.
2. 5 U.S. (1 Cranch) 137 (1803).
3. *Bracken* v. *William and Mary College,* 1 Call (Va.) 139 (1797).
4. 17 U.S. (4 Wheaton) 518 (1819).
5. Cf. the extensive use of common law authorities in Marshall's argument in the William and Mary case, n. 3 above, and in the opinions in the Burr treason trial. (Part Three, Ch. II). See also W. F. Swindler, "John Marshall's Preparation for the Bar: Some Observations from his Law Notes," 11 *Am. Journ. Legal Hist.* 207 (1967).
6. Cf. Baker, Leonard, *John Marshall: A Life in Law* (New York: Macmillan, 1974), 86-89.
7. Kennedy, John P., *Memoirs of the Life of William Wirt* (Philadelphia, 1849), II, 46, quoted in Albert J. Beveridge, *Life of John Marshall* (Boston: Little, Brown & Co., 1919), III, 192-93.
8. *Ware* v. *Hylton,* 3 U.S. (Dallas) 199 (1796).
9. Beveridge, *Marshall,* III, 187.
10. King, Charles L., ed., *Life and Correspondence of Rufus King* (New York, 1894-1900), II, 234-35, quoted in Beveridge, *Marshall,* III, 192.
11. The reference is to an alleged bill of attainder enacted in the administration of Governor Patrick Henry; cf. Johnson et al., eds., *Marshall Papers,* I, 257nn. 2, 3.
12. *id.,* 259.
13. The commission originally was made up of Elbridge Gerry and others, sent by President Washington to Paris to attempt to arbitrate the French spoliation claims of the United States. Marshall and Coatesworth Pinckney joined Gerry under appointments from Adams. Beveridge, *Marshall,* III, chs. vi-ix is somewhat overenthusiastic about Marshall's accomplishments; compare with Baker, *Marshall,* Book III.
14. Cf. Beveridge, *Marshall,* III, 458-71; Baker, *Marshall,* 318-23.
15. *Annals of Congress* (6th Cong., 1st sess.), 596-619.
16. Adams to Benjamin Rush, March 4, 1809; *Old Family Letters* (Philadelphia, 1892), 219; quoted in Beveridge, *Marshall,* III, 486.

17. Marshall to Otis, August 5, 1800; Otis Mss., Massachusetts Historical Society; quoted in Beveridge, *Marshall*, III, 515.

18. Cf. Nathan Schachner, *Aaron Burr* (New York: Thomas Yoseloff, 1937), 200 ff.; 280 ff.

19. Beveridge, *Marshall*, III, p. 129n.

20. *id.*, pp. 119-20.

21. Of many comments on the appointment, cf. Beveridge, *Marshall*, III, ch. xii; Baker, *Marshall*, Bk. IV; cf. also Kathryn Turner, "Federalist Policy and the Judiciary Act of 1801," 22 *Wm. & Mary Q.* (3d ser.) 1 (1965).

22. Cf. Journals of the Supreme Court for the 1815 term, and the annual review of Supreme Court statistics in 90 *Harv. L. Rev.* 276 (1976).

23. *McCulloch* v. *Maryland*, 14 U.S. (1 Wheaton), 316, 421 (1819).

24. The basic biographical data for these and other members of the Court may be most readily found in Fred L. Israel and Leon Friedmann, eds., *Justices of the United States Supreme Court: Their Lives and Major Decisions* (New York: Bowker/Chelsea House, 1969), Volume I for the Marshall period.

25. An excellent study of Johnson is Donald A. Morgan's *Justice William Johnson, the First Dissenter* (Columbia: University of South Carolina Press, 1954); cf. esp. chs. x-xv.

26. Morgan, *Johnson*, ch. x.

27. Cf. article on Livingston by Gerald T. Dunne in Friedman and Israel, *Justices of the United States Supreme Court, etc.*, I, at 388.

28. Two recent biographies of Story are Gerald T. Dunne's *Justice Joseph Story and the Rise of the Supreme Court* (Boston: Little, Brown & Co., 1971), and James McClellan, *Joseph Story and the American Constitution* (Norman: University of Oklahoma Press, 1971).

29. Cf. Joseph C. Burke, "The Cherokee Cases: A Study in Law, Politics and Morality," 21 *Stanford L. Rev.* 500 (1969).

30. DeTocqueville, Alexis, *Democracy in America,* ed. Phillips Bradley (New York: Alfred A. Knopf, 1956), I, 100.

31. *id.*, 150-51.

II. The Supreme Court and Congress

1. Supreme Court Minute Book A, 114-17; cf. Irwin S. Rhodes, *Papers of John Marshall: A Descriptive Calendar* (Norman: University of Oklahoma Press, 1969), I, 459.

2. For the volume of business conducted by the Supreme Court during its first decade, cf. Julius Goebel, *Antecedents and Beginnings to 1800* (Volume I in the Oliver Wendell Holmes Devise History of the Supreme Court; New York: Macmillan, 1971), 802 ff.

3. Message of December 8, 1801. James B. Richardson, ed., *A Compilation of the Messages and Papers of the Presidents* (Washington: U.S. Government Printing Office, 1896), I, 331.

4. Cf. Charles Warren, "New Light on the History of the Federal Judiciary Act of 1789," 37 *Harv. L. Rev.* 49 (1923); and cf. Goebel, *Antecedents,* Ch. XI.

5. With the expansion of the circuits from three to six in 1801 and 1802, some relief was afforded by placing one, instead of two, Justices on each Circuit Court. 2 *Stat.* 89, 132, 156.

6. Annals of Congress (7th Cong., 1st Sess.), 26; quoted in Beveridge, *Marshall*, III, 59.

7. When the Commerce Court, established in 1909, was abolished four years later, its judges were distributed among the several circuits, thereby avoiding a constitutional question. 36 *Stat.* 1146; 38 *Stat.* 219.

8. The right of the President to remove appointed officials who had been confirmed by the Senate was upheld in 1926 (*Myers* v. *United States,* 272 U.S. 252), but denied in 1935 (*Humphrey's Executor* v. *United States,* 295 U.S. 602).

9. Cf. *Stuart* v. *Laird,* 5 U.S. (1 Cranch) 299 (1803). Justice Paterson, for the Court, observed that "the question is at rest, and ought not now to be disturbed."

10. This was done again by Congress in 1866 (14 *Stat.* 209) to deny President Andrew Johnson an opportunity to make appointments to the Court. Before the number of vacancies dropped to the seven positions provided by the legislation, Congress raised the number to nine, where it has remained, since 1869 (16 *Stat.* 44).

11. Cf. William F. Swindler, "The High Court of Congress: Impeachment Trials, 1796–1936," 60 *Am. Bar Assn. J.* 420 (1974).

12. Charles Warren, *The Supreme Court in United States History* (Boston: Little, Brown & Co., 1922), I, 236; Baker, *Marshall,* 397.

13. Cf. Rhodes, *Calendar,* I, 480-83.

14. Cf. generally James M. Smith, *Freedom's Fetters: The Alien and Sedition Acts and American Civil Liberties* (Ithaca, N.Y.: Cornell University Press, 1956).

15. Cf. Marquis James, *The Life of Andrew Jackson* (Indianapolis: Bobbs-Merrill Co., 1938), chs. xxxiii, xxxiv.

16. Cf. William Van Alstyne, "A Critical Guide to *Marbury* v. *Madison*," *Duke L. J.* (February 1969), 1.

17. As late as March 16, Marshall was still signing papers as Secretary of State. Rhodes, *Calendar,* I, 455.

18. Warren, *Supreme Court,* I, 236 f.

19. Cf. Baker, *Marshall,* 396-99.

20. Cf. Beveridge, *Marshall,* III, 125 ff.

21. 5 U.S. (1 Cranch) 308; Beveridge, *Marshall,* III, 130.

22. Cf. the discussion of this distinction in *Glidden Co.* v. *Zdanok,* 370 U.S. 530, 605 (1962).

23. Cf. especially the famous instructions set down by the Court for argument in the original school desegregation case, *Brown* v. *Board of Education,* 345 U.S. 972-73 (1953); and the invitation to argue a specific question in the original right-to-counsel case, *Gideon* v. *Wainwright (sub nom. Cochran),* 370 U.S. 908 (1962).

24. Cf. Van Alstyne, *loc. cit.,* p. 10.

III. The Supreme Court and the President

1. Cf. W. F. McCaleb, *The Aaron Burr Conspiracy* (Magnolia, Mass.: Peter Smith, 1936), ch. ii; T. P. Abernethy, *The Burr Conspiracy* (New York: Argosy, 1954), chs. i-iii.

2. Cf. T. P. Abernethy, *The South in the New Nation* (Baton Rouge: Louisiana State University Press, 1961), chs. v, vii.

3. Cf. Schachner, *Burr,* ch. xx; McCaleb, *Burr Conspiracy,* 132 ff.

4. Warren, *Supreme Court,* I, ch. vi.

5. Cf. article on Griffin in *Dictionary of American Biography* (New York: Charles Scribner's Sons, 1932, 1960), IV, 618 f.

6. 25 *Fed. Cases,* No. 14,692a. Cf. note 18 below.

7. 25 *Fed. Cases,* No. 14,692b, pp. 26-27.

8. Articles on most of the participants will be found under their names in the *Dictionary of American Biography.*

9. Cf. Dumas Malone, *Jefferson the President: Second Term, 1805–1809* (Volume V in the author's monumental biography; Boston: Little, Brown & Co., 1974), chs. xvii, xviii; Warren, *Supreme Court,* I, 306.

10. Beveridge, *Marshall,* III, chs. 6-9; Baker, *Marshall,* 445-518.

11. Cf. Goebel, *Antecedents,* ch. xii.

12. Beveridge, *Marshall,* III, 448.

13. *id.,* 451.

14. *id.,* 455.

15. *id.,* 523.

16. *id.,* 414.

17. Cf. Schachner, *Jefferson,* ch. 59; Malone, *Jefferson,* V, ch. xiii-xix; Beveridge, *Marshall,* III, ch. vi.

18. On the protracted procedural matters on the Burr trial, cf. 25 *Fed. Cases,* viz.: April 1, 1807, distinguishing between treason and high misdemeanor, No. 14,692a, at p. 2; May 26, motion to commit Burr, No. 14,692b, at p. 25; May 28, admissibility of certain affidavits, No. 14,692c, at p. 27; June 13, issuance of subpoena to Jefferson, No. 14,692d, at p. 30; June 18, refusal of witness to testify to Burr's authorship of cipher letter, No. 14,692e, at p. 38; June 28, settlement of Eaton's claims by government held not to be contempt of court, No. 14,692f, at p. 41; August 11, persons with fixed opinions as to Burr's guilt disqualified as jurors, No. 14,692g, at 49; August 18, order of proof held to be at option of government, No. 14,692h, at p. 52; August 31, instructions to jury in treason trial, No. 14,693, at p. 55; September 3, misdemeanor trial, No. 16,694, at p. 187; October 20, binding over to Ohio jurisdiction, No. 14,694a, at p. 201.

19. *Haupt* v. *United States,* 330 U.S. 631 (1947); *Kawakita* v. *United States,* 343 U.S. 717 (1952); and cf. *Cramer* v. *United States,* 325 U.S. 1 (1945).

20. 418 U.S. 683 (1974).

21. Cf. O. Hood Phillips, *Constitutional and Administrative Law* (London: Sweet & Maxwell, 5th ed., 1973), ch. 13.

22. 418 U.S., at 703.

23. Cf. *Environmental Protection Agency* v. *Mink,* 410 U.S. 73 (1973).

24. 418 U.S., at 705.

25. *Id.,* at 706.

IV. The Supreme Court and the Individual

1. Cf. the involvement of a later Supreme Court Justice in a duel, albeit before his judicial career; John P. Frank, *Justice Daniel Dissenting* (Cambridge, Mass.: Harvard University Press, 1964), 7-10, 158-59.

2. Malone, *Jefferson,* V, chs. i, vii-x.

3. Beveridge, *Marshall,* III, ch. viii; Baker, *Marshall,* IV, Ch. 4.

4. Cf. Baker, *Marshall,* 490 f.

5. 7 & 8 Will. III, c.3; 9 Stats. at L. 389. Cf. also J. Hurst, *The Law of Treason in the United States—Selected Essays* (Westport, Conn.: Greenwood Press, 1971).

6. Warren, *Supreme Court,* I, ch. vi.

7. 25 *Fed. Cases,* No. 14,693, pp. 92, 93.

8. *id.*, pp. 94, 95.
9. Beveridge, *Marshall,* III, 494.
10. *id.*, 496-502.
11. Cf. note 5, above.
12. Beveridge, *Marshall,* III, 513-14.
13. On the unused draft of the message, cf. Beveridge, *Marshall,* III, 530-31.
14. Richardson, *Messages,* I, 429 (italics supplied).
15. Malone, *Jefferson,* V, chs. xxii-xxviii.
16. Cf. Samuel Engle Burr, Jr., *Napoleon's Dossier on Aaron Burr* (San Antonio, Tex.: Naylor Co., 1969), Part II.
17. Cf. article on Burr in *Dictionary of American Biography,* II, 313-20.

V. The Supreme Court and the States

1. Holmes, Oliver Wendell, *Collected Legal Papers* (New York: Harcourt, Brace & Co., 1920), 295 f.
2. 14 U.S. (1 Wheaton) 304 (1816).
3. 17 U.S. (4 Wheaton) 316 (1819).
4. The case is listed, but not reported, in 9 *Fed. Cases,* No. 4,865, p. 272; papers are in the Federal Records Center in Waltham, Massachusetts.
5. Beveridge, *Marshall,* III, 585. Marshall was briefly promoted as a Federalist candidate to oppose Madison in 1812. *id.,* IV, 31-33.
6. 10 U.S. (6 Cranch) 87 (1810).
7. 11 U.S. (7 Cranch) 164 (1812).
8. 13 U.S. (9 Cranch) 43 (1815).
9. 11 U.S. (7 Cranch) 603 (1813).
10. 1 Munford (Va.) 223, 232 (1809).
11. 14 U.S. (1 Wheaton) 304 (1816).
12. 17 U.S. (4 Wheaton) 122 (1819).
13. 25 U.S. (12 Wheaton) 213 (1827).
14. Cf. Francis S. Stites, *Private Interest and Public Gain: The Dartmouth College Case, 1819* (Minneapolis: University of Minnesota Press, 1972), 29.
15. Dunne, *Joseph Story and the Rise of the Supreme Court,* 155.
16. Dunne, *op. cit.,* 155; cf. Shirley, John S., *The Dartmouth College Cases and the Supreme Court* (St. Louis, 1879), 280.
17. On "diversity jurisdiction" generally, cf. Marshall's opinion in *Bank* v. *Deveaux,* 9 U.S. (5 Cranch) 61, 87 (1809); and cf. the American Law Institute study, *Diversity Jurisdiction Between State and Federal Courts* (Philadelphia: American Law Institute, 1969), 99-110, 458-64.
18. Dunne, *Story,* 170-72.
19. 17 U.S. (4 Wheaton) 518, 651 (1819).
20. 29 U.S. (4 Peters) 514 (1830).
21. 36 U.S. (11 Peters) 420 (1837).
22. 25 U.S. (12 Wheaton) 213 (1827).
23. 27 U.S. (2 Peters) 244 (1829).
24. 36 U.S. (1 Peters) 102 (1837).
25. 46 U.S. (5 Howard) 504 (1847).

VI. The Supreme Law of the Land

1. Cf. J. T. Holdsworth and D. R. Dewey, *The First and Second Banks of the United States* (Washington, 1910; Sen. Doc. 571, 61st Cong., 2d Sess.,), 9 ff.
2. *id.,* 147 ff.
3. Warren, *Supreme Court,* I, ch. xii.
4. 6 U.S. (2 Cranch) 358 (1805).
5. Warren, *Supreme Court,* I, 506.
6. *id.,* 509
7. 17 U.S. (4 Wheaton) 421; cf. Felix Frankfurter, *The Commerce Clause Under Marshall, Taney and Waite* (Chapel Hill: University of North Carolina Press, 1937), 19.
8. 17 U.S., at 433.
9. Warren, *Supreme Court,* I, 504 f.
10. Beveridge, *Marshall,* IV, 309-12.
11. 14 U.S. (1 Wheaton) 304, 326 (1816); cf. 17 U.S., at 419.
12. *id.,* at 405.
13. Warren, *Supreme Court,* I, 546 f.
14. *id.,* 551.
15. Gunther, Gerald, *John Marshall's Defence of McCulloch* v. *Maryland* (Stanford: Stanford University Press, 1969), 13.
16. Cf. article on Roane in *Dictionary of American Biography,* VIII, 642-43.
17. Gunther, *Defense,* 14-15.
18. Compiled from issues of the *Richmond Enquirer* in the Virginia State Library, Richmond, Virginia; for reproduction of complete texts of articles, cf. Gunther, *Defense,* 155-214.

VII. The Implement of National Power

1. 1 Johns. Rep. 557 (1812).
2. 4 Johns. Ch. 48 (1819).
3. *id.,* 94.
4. *id.,* 57.
5. *id.,* 176.
6. *id.,* 570.
7. 5 Johns. Ch. 250 (1821).
8. 6 N. J. L. 236 (1822).
9. *id.,* 582; 8 N. J. L. 288 (1825).
10. *Gibbons* v. *Ogden,* 19 U.S. (6 Wheaton) 448 (1821).
11. *Gibbons* v. *Ogden,* 17 Johns. Rep. 488 (1820).
12. Beveridge, *Marshall,* IV, 403-8.
13. Richardson, *Messages,* II, 142.
14. Warren, *Supreme Court,* I, 596.
15. Cf. Frankfurter, *Commerce Clause,* 13-20.
16. Cf. article on Vesey in *Dictionary of American Biography,* X, 258.
17. Cf. generally *Edwards* v. *California,* 314 U.S. 160 (1941); Frankfurter, *Commerce Clause,* 17.
18. Warren, *Supreme Court,* I, 602n.

19. *id.,* 606.

20. *id.,* 603.

21. *id.,* 604.

22. 22 U.S., at 222.

23. *Brown* v. *Maryland,* 25 U.S. (12 Wheaton) 419 (1827).

24. *Willson* v. *Black Bird Creek Marsh Co.,* 27 U.S. (2 Peters) 244 (1829).

25. *New York* v. *Miln,* 36 U.S. (11 Peters) 102 (1837).

26. *Cooley* v. *Board of Wardens,* 53 U.S. (12 Howard) 290 (1851).

27. Cf. *Munn* v. *Illinois,* 94 U.S. 113 (1877).

28. *United States* v. *E. C. Knight Co.,* 156 U.S. 1 (1895).

29. *Northern Sec. Co.* v. *United States,* 193 U.S. 197 (1904).

30. *Loewe* v. *Lawlor,* 208 U.S. 274 (1908).

31. *Champion* v. *Ames,* 188 U.S. 321 (1903).

32. *Shreveport Rate Case,* 234 U.S. 342 (1914).

33. *Hammer* v. *Dagenhart,* 247 U.S. 251 (1918).

34. Cf. William F. Swindler, *Court and Constitution in the 20th Century: The Old Legality, 1889–1933* (New York: Bobbs-Merrill Co., 1969), chs. 13, 14.

35. Cf. William F. Swindler, *The New Legality, 1933–1958* (New York: Bobbs-Merrill Co., 1970), ch. 2.

36. *N. L. R. B.* v. *Jones & Laughlin Steel Corp.,* 301 U.S. 1 (1937).

37. *Heart of Atlanta Motel Co.* v. *United States,* 379 U.S. 241 (1964).

38. *id.,* at 257.

Selected Bibliography

The literature on John Marshall, the Supreme Court, and the Constitution is large and continually increasing. For the Chief Justice himself, a current and well-researched biography is Leonard Baker's *John Marshall: A Life in Law* (New York: Macmillan, 1974); Albert J. Beveridge's four-volume *Life of John Marshall* (Boston: Houghton, Mifflin, 1919) is also the product of exhaustive research but its eulogistic commentaries on most of Marshall's constitutional accomplishments are a bit much for the modern reader. There ought to be, but as yet is not, a comprehensive comparative study of Marshall and Jefferson, those star-crossed antagonists of the formative generation in national history. Julian P. Boyd prepared a thoughtful paper entitled, "The Chasm That Separated John Marshall and Thomas Jefferson," which appeared in *Essays on the American Constitution* (Englewood Cliffs, N.J.: Prentice-Hall, 1964), edited by Gottfried Dietze, while an older study of value is William E. Dodd's "Chief Justice Marshall and Virginia, 1813–1821," in the *American Historical Review* for July 1907. Dumas Malone's superlative multivolume biography of Jefferson discusses the President's position objectively in *Jefferson the President: Second Term, 1805–1809* (Boston: Little, Brown, 1974), while Nathan Schachner has an insightful discussion in *Thomas Jefferson: A Biography* (New York: Stokes, 1951).

A reference of particular usefulness, for the period up to the date of its own publication, is *A Bibliography of John Marshall* (Washington: Government Printing Office, 1956), edited by James A. Servies for the Marshall bicentennial.

As for the Court and the Constitution, Volume II of Charles Warren's *Supreme Court in United States History* (Boston: Little, Brown, 4 v., 1922–27) is still the best scholarly treatment of the period, at least until the long-pending volumes by Gerald Gunther and George Haskins are published in the comprehensive Oliver Wendell Holmes Devise History of the Supreme Court. John A. Garraty wrote a series of articles on great constitutional cases for *American Heritage* magazine which were subsequently published in book form under the title *Quarrels That Have Shaped the Constitution* (New York: Harper & Row, 1964). Alan F. Westin's *An Autobiography of the Supreme Court* (New York: Macmillan, 1963) is a compendium of behind-the-scenes descriptions by various Justices, while Paul A. Freund's *On Understanding the Supreme Court* (Boston: Little, Brown, 1949) is an excellent general introduction. As for histories of the Constitution, three of the best are Carl B. Swisher's *American Constitutional Development* (Boston: Houghton, Mifflin, 2d ed., 1954), Andrew C. McLaughlin's *Constitutional History of the United States* (New York: Appleton, Century, 1935), and Hampton Carson's monumental volume prepared for the New York State Bar Association and published as *The Supreme Court of the United States: Its History* (Philadelphia: Huber & Co., 1892).

A biographical dictionary of the Supreme Court was compiled by Fred L. Israel and Leon Friedman under the title *Justices of the United States Supreme Court, 1789–1966: Their Lives and Major Decisions* (New York: Bowker/ Chelsea House, 4 vol., 1969). The best single volume of judicial interpretation of the Constitution is the work periodically updated by the Congressional Research Service of the Library of Congress and simply titled *The Constitution of the United States, Annotated* (Washington: Government Printing Office, 1970 with 1977 supp.). A useful short introduction is Bernard Schwartz's *American Constitutional Law* (Cambridge: Cambridge University Press, 1955), written to familiarize British students with the subject. For the interested layman, the Supreme Court Historical Society publishes an annual *Yearbook* featuring historical events and personages in the Court's history, while the Federal Bar Association some years ago sponsored a highly readable and handsomely illustrated booklet under the title *Equal Justice Under Law* (Washington: Federal Bar Association, rev. ed., 1975).

John Marshall wrote very little about himself. The *Autobiographical Sketch* edited by John S. Adams in 1937 (New York: DaCapo, repr. 1974) is hardly more than a fragment, and one of the most charming personal insights is provided in his letters to his wife, edited by Frances Norton Mason under the title *My Dearest Polly* (Richmond: Garrett & Massie, 1961). A recent publication of interest is Andrew Oliver's *Portraits of John Marshall* (Charlottesville: University Press of Virginia, 1977). Two major projects on Marshall documents are Irwin S. Rhodes's *The Papers of John Marshall: A Descriptive Catalog* (Norman: University of Oklahoma Press, 2 vols., 1969), and *The Papers of John Marshall,* a multivolume collection sponsored jointly by the College of William and Mary and the Institute of Early American History and Culture. The first volume, edited by Herbert A. Johnson, appeared in 1974; following volumes, under the editorship of Charles Cullen, will begin appearing in 1978 under the imprint of the University of North Carolina Press for the Institute. Two efforts have been made to collect the Chief Justice's constitutional writings—Joseph P. Cotton's 1903 collection of *Constitutional Decisions of John Marshall* (New York: DaCapo repr., 1969); and John E. Oster's *Political and Economic Doctrines of John Marshall,* first published in 1906 (New York: DaCapo repr., 1967). A short collection, edited by Erwin C. Surrency, is *The Marshall Reader* (Dobbs Ferry, N.Y.: Oceana, 1955).

Biographical works, in addition to the definitive studies by Baker and Beveridge already mentioned, include Samuel J. Konefsky's *John Marshall and Alexander Hamilton* (New York: Macmillan, 1967), and David G. Loth's

Chief Justice: John Marshall and the Growth of the Republic (New York: Norton, 1949). At the time of the bicentennial of Marshall's birth, Melville M. Jones edited a symposium under the title *John Marshall: A Reappraisal* (New York: DaCapo repr., 1971). A good comparative study is Philip B. Kurland's *James Bradley Thayer, Oliver Wendell Holmes and Felix Frankfurter on John Marshall* (Chicago: University of Chicago Press, 1967), and an excellent analysis of the early Marshall years is Richard E. Ellis's *The Jeffersonian Crisis* (New York: Oxford University Press, 1971).

Among other studies of Marshall's works are Robert K. Faulkner's *Jurisprudence of John Marshall* (Princeton: Princeton University Press, 1968) and Edward S. Corwin's *John Marshall and the Constitution* (New Haven: Yale University Press, 1919). Two works which should be read in comparison with each other are Thomas S. Craigmyle's *John Marshall in Diplomacy and Law* (New York: Scribner's, 1933) and Benjamin M. Ziegler's *The International Law of John Marshall* (Chapel Hill: University of North Carolina Press, 1939).

Specific studies of the constitutional cases in the present volume include Professor Corwin's *The Doctrine of Judicial Review* (Princeton: Princeton University Press, 1914), and the unique analysis by Gerald Gunther in *John Marshall's Defense of McCulloch* v. *Maryland* (Stanford: Stanford University Press, 1969). William Van Alstyne's article, "The Background to *Marbury* v. *Madison*" in the *Duke Law Journal* for Spring 1971 is also instructive reading.

The criminal trial of Aaron Burr has excited attention over the years and will be revived when the Burr papers, now being edited by Princeton University Press, are eventually published. Gore Vidal's novel, *Burr* (New York: Random House, 1974) attested to the degree of public fascination with the subject by becoming a best seller. Other books on the man and his trials include Francis F. Beirne's *Shout Treason: The Trial of Aaron Burr* (New York: Hastings House, 1959), James Parton's old *Life and Times of Aaron Burr* (Boston: Mason Brown, 1872), Herbert S. Parmet and Marie B. Hecht's *Aaron Burr* (New York: Macmillan, 1967), and Nathan Schachner's *Aaron Burr: A Biography* (New York: Stokes, 1937). William S. Sufford edited *The Blennerhassett Papers* (Cincinnati: 1861) which, along with David Robertson's *Report of the Trials of Aaron Burr* (Philadelphia: 1808) is still the best documentary source. See also Samuel E. Burr, Jr., *Napoleon's Dossier on Aaron Burr* (San Antonio: Naylor, 1969).

Other Justices of the Marshall era have attracted varying amounts of biographical study. At one end of the spectrum is the two-volume transcript of the *Trial of Samuel Chase* (New York: DaCapo repr., 1970), while at the other end is Justice Baldwin's *A General View of the Origin and Nature of the Constitution and Government of the United States* (New York: DaCapo repr., 1970). An excellent biography by Donald G. Morgan is *Justice William Johnson: The First Dissenter* (Columbia: University of South Carolina Press, 1954).

Justice Story, of course, is the towering figure among Marshall's associates. Aside from his own monumental *Commentaries on the Constitution of the United States* (New York: DaCapo repr., 3 vol., 1970), and his son's valuable collection—William Wetmore Story, *The Miscellaneous Writings of Joseph*

Story (Boston: Little, Brown, 1852)—there are two current works: Gerald T. Dunne, *Joseph Story and the Rise of the Supreme Court* (Boston: Little, Brown, 1971), and James McClellan, *Joseph Story and the American Constitution* (Norman: University of Oklahoma Press, 1971). See also Charles Warren's "The Story–Marshall Correspondence, 1819–1831," in the *William and Mary Quarterly* (2d ser.) for January 1941.

A valuable perspective may be gained from works of Marshall's successor. See Walker Lewis's *Without Fear or Favor* (Boston: Houghton, Mifflin, 1965), Carl B. Swisher's *Roger B. Taney* (Hamden, Conn.: Archon Books repr. 1961), and Charles W. Smith, Jr.'s *Roger B. Taney, Jacksonian Jurist* (Chapel Hill: University of North Carolina Press, 1936).

Index

NOTE: Part One, *The Shaping of Judicial Federalism,* is thoroughly indexed. Parts Two, *John Marshall's Constitution,* and Three, *Opinions in the Major Cases and Related Documents,* are indexed by main subjects and their subheadings.